# STRENGTH in NUMBERS

## A LESBIAN, GAY and BISEXUAL RESOURCE

## ALSO FROM VISIBLE INK PRESS

### The Gay & Lesbian Literary Companion

"If the term 'belles-lettres' ever applied to a small press anthology, it surely applies to this magnificent collection of stories, poems and articles from no less than 45 writers." *Small Press Review*

In addition to presenting excerpts from fiction, poetry, plays, and essays, *The Gay & Lesbian Literary Companion* discusses the writers' lives and art and provides a complete list of their published writings. By Sharon Malinowski and Christa Brelin with consulting editor Malcolm Boyd, 7 1/4" x 9 1/4" Paperback, 585 pages, 75 photos, ISBN 0-7876-0033-4.

### Resourceful Woman

"Invaluable.... This book is a dream come true." *Ms.*

The ultimate handbook of options for women in all stages of life, *Resourceful Woman* helps you discover, explore, and evaluate alternatives through a lively mix of articles, creative writing, and valuable resource information. By Shawn Brennan and Julie Winklepleck, 7 1/4" x 9 1/4" Paperback, 833 pages, 76 photos, ISBN 0-8103-8594-5.

# STRENGTH in NUMBERS

## A LESBIAN, GAY and BISEXUAL RESOURCE

Edited by Christa Brelin

Foreword by Jenie Hall, Director of the Bridges Project of the American Friends Service Committee

Detroit • New York • Washington D.C. • Toronto

**Strength in Numbers: A Lesbian, Gay, and Bisexual Resource**



Published by Visible Ink Press™
a division of Gale Research
835 Penobscot Building
Detroit, MI 48226-4094

Visible Ink Press is a trademark of Gale Research Inc.

Cover photo © D. Young-Wolff, courtesy Photo Edit. Back cover photo ©Felicia Martinez, courtesy Photo Edit.

Most Visible Ink Press™ books are available at special quantity discounts when purchased in bulk by corporations, organizations, or groups. Customized printings, special imprints, messages, and excerpts can be produced to meet your needs. For more information, contact Special Markets Manager, Visible Ink Press, 835 Penobscot Bldg., Detroit, MI 48226. Or call 1-800-776-6265.

Art Director: Michelle DiMercurio

---

**Library of Congress Cataloging-in-Publication Data**

Strength in numbers: a lesbian, gay, and bisexual resource/ edited by Christa Brelin.

p. cm.
Includes index.
ISBN 0-7876-0881-5
1. Homosexuality—United States—Societies, etc.—Directories. 2. Gays—Services for—United States—Directories.
HQ76.3.U5S77 1996
306.76'6'02573—dc20 96-8233
CIP

---

Printed in the United States of America

10 9 8 7 6 5 4 3 2 1

# FOREWORD

Each week at the Bridges Project we receive phone calls and letters detailing incidents of discrimination, ridicule, or abuse that lesbian, gay, bisexual, and transgender (LGBT) individuals and those who love them face. The Bridges Project of the American Friends Service Committee acts as a national resource project focused on providing materials and referrals to counter the isolation that LGBT youth face. In the course of our work we have found that those who support LGBT youth also experience extreme isolation. The experiences reflect the statistics and reports of abuse and high-risk behaviors that lesbian, gay, bisexual, and transgender people of all ages encounter.

Beyond the horrible experiences that we respond to, Bridges also receives every week letters and phone calls from folks breaking down the isolation of themselves and others. These callers and letter writers exemplify what many reports and studies do not show: the tremendous determination that LGBT people display to overcome or prevent further isolation.

*Strength in Numbers: A Lesbian, Gay, and Bisexual Resource* is a vivid affirmation of unity and the will to create community. Every listing and entry in this book builds on the story of an individual or group of individuals who chose to reach out and risk rather than live alone in fear. The organizations and people highlighted here are a small sampling of the countless heroes and heroines who weave through our everyday lives. Each of them makes their impact felt when one organizes, comes "out," or simply reaches out to another who seems isolated.

In the late summer of 1991 I had the extraordinary opportunity to walk 300 miles in two weeks through rural Washington State. The purpose of the walk was to raise awareness and understanding of the extreme isolation that lesbian and gay rural youth experience. Overcast skies dominated much of our journey and on our first day, all I considered was whether we had gathered enough supplies. We walked through endless deserts that turned to wheat fields, then back to deserts, then became mountains, then suburban sprawl. There were four of us and one dog. More than once on a day's walk, no more than three or four vehicles passed us, and quite often we walked in silence out of exhaustion.

My most vivid memories of the journey are not of blisters or sore muscles but of the people's lives who touched us. Their experiences raised my awareness and understanding of others' fear and courage.

I recall the gay couple living in the town of 3,000 who took us in for the night even though they were afraid of how the town might respond. The white Camaro that tried to run me off the road while its driver contemptuously sipped a fast-food milkshake. The parents who talked of their sons and daughters as they fixed us beds to sleep in and prepared meals for us. The faces of children peering from behind curtains in the town where their parents had pulled them from school upon hearing of our trek. The roses from the mother who drove an hour to offer them to us. And countless others, like the watermelon man who visited us one lunch break because he thought we would appreciate some cooling down in the mid-day desert sun. I learned from all of these folks what it was to feel overwhelmed by hate and then surprised by unexpected allies.

If you are fortunate enough to live in a city or town that houses programs and groups such as those listed in this resource, reach out and get involved. Your participation will change both yours and someone else's lives. If you are unaware of groups or programs in your city or town, start meeting with friends in someone's living room or church. Call, write, or visit cities and towns near yours to find out what their programs offer and how they began. Finally, many of the chapters in this guide list additional ways to connect with folks through the Internet and electronic mail. If you have access, check these services out to find a way to make a contribution beyond where you live.

While coming out as LGBT people and allies, we must understand that our actions may make us targets of hate and bigotry. However, as my good friend PJ Walkling points out, we must also acknowledge that our visibility acts as an oasis of hope to others. *Strength in Numbers* is a tribute to those who dare to broaden the lines of loving.

Thank you to the editors and publisher for their vision in recognizing all of our strength in numbers, courage, and love. This resource serves as a reminder that each of us is an expression of centuries of survival. Our legacy will continue for centuries to come.

Jenie Hall
Director, Bridges Project
of the American Friends
Service Committee

Somehow we find each other. We find each other at school or work, sensing a kindred spirit and tentatively drawing near. We find each other in our bookstores or bars, in many cities our only public meeting places. We find each other from afar, as pen pals or online correspondents. We find each other at music festivals or softball diamonds or theater productions or art galleries or marching in Pride rallies. And we find each other through organizations like those listed in this book—social support groups, political action groups, professional associations, religious organizations, and others. Somehow we find each other, and when we do, we cherish the bonds we form.

People close to me have wondered, in all sincerity: Why do we gather? Why establish a gay Catholic organization? Why a lesbian film festival? Why a queer lawyers association? Why a women's music festival or a gay men's chorus? Why a whole organization for our families and friends? Why a whole high school for gay, lesbian, bisexual, and transgendered teens? And above all, why do we gather in *public?* What are those Pride rallies supposed to accomplish? Why parade like that?

Well.

First, we gather in public to draw attention to the fact that although lesbian, gay, bisexual, and transgendered people are called citizens, that citizenship is not fully recognized. As long as we can legally be fired from our jobs or removed from military service for being lesbian, gay, bisexual, or transgendered; as long as our children can legally be taken from us at the whim of a bigoted judge; as long as our high schools continue to ignore the open harassment and inner torment of their gay and lesbian students; as long as the violent crimes against us are still considered our fault; as long as influential politicians and religious leaders speak of us as enemies of our own nation; as long as people with AIDS are divided, officially by health care organizations and unofficially by judgmental individuals, into those who "deserve" it and those who don't; as long as our marriages are not granted the same legal and economic status as heterosexual marriages—as long as these conditions exist, we

*One million people parade up 17th Street during the 1993 March on Washington, DC. (Photo by Bruce Young; courtesy Reuters/Bettmann.)*

do not have full citizenship in our own country. And as long as these conditions exist, we will gather to parade that fact in front of our neighbors, our nation, and our world, demanding the recognition of full citizenship that is ours to claim.

Second, and equally important, we gather for friendship—because we like each other. We gather because it's fun. We gather to affirm to ourselves and prove to others how many of us exist. We gather to draw the support and affection we cannot find in the world at large from our own tremendous, flamboyant family reunion. We gather to gain strength in our number.

*Strength in Numbers: A Lesbian, Gay, and Bisexual Resource* will show you some of the ways we and our allies have gathered for fun, support, and action. The 10 chapters in this book, ranging from Arts to Youth, list organizations worldwide that support the community of lesbian, gay, bisexual, and transgendered people and our friends and families. Each chapter is arranged geographically by country, then state or province, to help you find the groups nearest you. At the end of each chapter you'll find a list of Internet Web sites and other online sources of information. The geographic index in the back of the book lists all the organizations—whether social, religious, youth-oriented, and so on—together by state, and the general index will help you find the specific organization you're seeking. In addition, throughout the book you'll find several "spotlight" features of notable individuals or groups.

Some of the organizations in *Strength in Numbers* are huge, with a national office and hundreds of local branches across the country, and powerful on a national and even international scale. Others are small, consisting of a few people staffing a hotline or meeting periodically in one another's homes, and important on a more personal, individual level. We've undoubtedly left many out, as new groups spring up and old groups merge, move, and change their names or telephone numbers. Please tell us, by returning the card enclosed at the back of the book, about the groups near you that we've left out, and we'll include them in the next edition of *Strength in Numbers.*

Christa Brelin
Editor

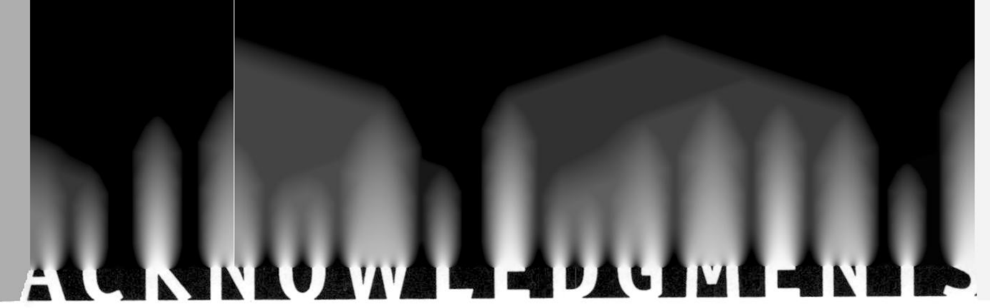

For putting us in touch with so many inspiring organizations, many thanks to Jenie Hall, Director, and Ken Carl, Volunteer Executive Assistant, at the Bridges Project of the American Friends Service Committee.

The online resources listed at the end of each chapter are reprinted with permission from *Online Access* magazine of Chicago, Illinois. Many thanks to Kathryn McCabe, Editor-in-Chief, and Denise Barr, Managing Editor, for supplying these listings.

For providing information, finding photos and resource material, making connections, and otherwise helping out, thanks to Affirmations Lesbian and Gay Community Center, Jan Stevenson at *Between the Lines* newspaper, Dignity/USA, *Feminist Bookstore News* (who supplied the bookstore listings), the Hetrick-Martin Institute, Wayne Snellen at the Leslie-Lohman Gay Art Foundation, Barbara Grier at Naiad Press, the NAMES Project, Jeffrey Garrett at PFLAG National, Louise Knapp at Word Is Out Women's Bookstore in Boulder, and the many other individuals and organizations who supplied, augmented, or verified the information listed in this book.

Thank you Kathy Dauphinais for speedy keying and thorough proofreading; thank you Theresa Rocklin and Carol Schwartz for lending your database expertise; thank you Pam Hayes and Kim Smilay for efficient photo processing; and thank you Marco Di Vita at the Graphix Group for excellent typesetting.

For a lovely design, kudos to Art Director Michelle DiMercurio.

Much appreciation also goes to the writers who contributed to *Strength in Numbers:* Lisa Breck, Michael Bronski, Dean Dauphinais, Eric Dobson, Lee Gasaway, Jim Kepner, Patricia Montemurri, Tim Retzloff, Devra Sladics, and Jane Slaughter.

For my Visible Ink Press colleagues—Dean Dauphinais, Judy (Kidu) Galens, Becky Nelson, and Leslie Norback—thanks for demonstrating strength in the number five.

Finally, for verifying information, supplying photos, and contributing to this book in ways impossible to measure, thank you Pam Mc Intosh and all the little helpers, Katie, Sadie, Sophie, and Tasha.

# LITERATURE

Michelangelo, Sappho, Keith Haring, Melissa Etheridge, and you—each of us continually finds a way to express creatively who we are and what is valuable to us. Whatever your method of expression—singing with a chorus or in a band or alone in the car, doodling privately or displaying your artwork, telling stories to friends or writing them down or acting on stage—you'll find in this chapter, dedicated to the creative arts and literature, some of the groups in North America and elsewhere who preserve and promote our creative expression.

Here you'll find information about the *Ladyslipper Catalog,* that outstanding source of women's music of all kinds (as well as some fine "Mehn's Music" too). You'll learn how to find gay and lesbian theaters and producers through the annual *Purple Circuit Directory,* published by the Glendale, California group Artists Confronting AIDS. Gay and lesbian bookstores—each of them a wellspring of literature, art, and community news—from throughout the United States and Canada are listed here, as well as the publishers of lesbian, gay, bisexual, and transgender literature.

As well, you'll meet Barbara Grier and Donna J. McBride, founders of Tallahassee, Florida's Naiad Press, the largest and oldest active lesbian publisher, and Boulder, Colorado's Word Is Out Bookstore—a small but growing community treasure that's representative of so many of our hometown bookstores. You'll also learn about SoHo's Leslie-Lohman Gay Art Foundation, whose dedication to preserving our artwork is a credit to our community, and Detroit, Michigan artist Charles Alexander, a longtime activist in his local community.

Finally, the many local groups and activities you'll find here—like the Michigan Womyn's Music Festival, the Connecticut Gay Men's Chorus, Chicago's Artemis Singers, and the Detroit Women's Coffeehouse—will welcome your participation.

SPOTLIGHT

## LESLIE-LOHMAN GAY ART FOUNDATION

"We celebrate the whole range of lesbian and gay art," says Wayne Snellen, director of the Leslie-Lohman Gay Art Foundation. "From high art to hot art," is how *Advocate* contributor Joe E. Jeffreys put it, explaining that the foundation's holdings "serve as a means of battling the right-wing attacks on homoerotic art."

In an April 1992 interview with Jeffreys, foundation president Charles Leslie explained that gay art, to him, "is art that is politically repressed because of its perceived sexual content ... art that is officially despised because of what it possibly seems to be as well as what it clearly is in some cases." He

## CANADA

### ALBERTA

**Healing Words Bookstore**
Carolyn Anderson
705 1520—4 Street SW
Calgary, AB T2R 1H5

**Orlando Books**
10640 Whyte Ave.
Edmonton, AB T6E 2A7
Bookstore.

**Woman to Womon Books**
106-12404-114 Ave.
Edmonton, AB T5M 3M5
Mail-order bookstore.

**A Woman's Place Bookstore**
1412 Centre St. South
Calgary, AB T2G 2E4

### BRITISH COLUMBIA

**Bookmantel**
Bonnie Murray, Cynthia Brooke
1002 Commercial Dr.
Vancouver, BC V5L 2R2
Bookstore.

**Chief's Mask Bookstore**
Renee Richards
73 Water St.
Vancouver, BC V6B 1A1

**Everywoman's Books**
635 Johnson St.
Victoria, BC V8W 1M7
Bookstore.

**Little Sister's Book & Art Emporium**
Jannine Fuller
1221 Thurlow St.
Vancouver, BC V6E 1X4

**Vancouver Women's Bookstore**
315 Cambie St.
Vancouver, BC V6B 2N4

**Women in Print**
3566 West 4th Ave.
Vancouver, BC V6R 1N8
Bookstore.

**Women's Work**
291 Wallace St.
Nanaimo, BC V9R 5B4
Bookstore.

added, "Unless there is the element of taboo that offends the art establishment bourgeoisie—which is the entire American art establishment—then it is not what we are interested in salvaging."

Leslie and his lover, Frederic Lohman, are longtime advocates of gay art who began displaying and selling art in 1969, when they opened the first New York City gallery dedicated to gay arts in their SoHo loft. Although that venture, having moved to a formal gallery, eventually closed in 1981, they continued their work in the arts. In 1990 they founded the Leslie-Lohman Gay Art Foundation as a tax-exempt, nonprofit corporation "to preserve and protect works of art whose very existence is endangered by societal sexual prejudices." In addition to sponsoring gallery exhibitions of lesbian and gay erotic art, the foundation manages and preserves a permanent collection of

## ONTARIO

### Food for Thought: Women's Connection

RR#1
Bloomfield, ON K0K 1G0
Bookstore.

### Glad Day Bookshop

598a Yonge St.
Toronto, ON M4Y 123

### mother tongue books/femmes de parole

1067 Bank St.
Ottawa, ON K1S 3W9
Bookstore.

### The Northern Woman's Bookstore

65 S. Court St.
Thunder Bay, ON P7B 2X2

### Ottawa Women's Bookstore/Librairie des Femmes D'Ottawa

272 Elgin St.
Ottawa, ON K2P 1M2

### Pink Triangle Press

Ken Popert, Publisher
Fred Lee, Office Administrator
PO Box 7289, Sta. A
Toronto, ON, Canada M5W 1X9
phone: (416) 925-6665
fax: (416) 925-6674
Offers *XTRA!*, a biweekly paper for Toronto's gay and lesbian communities.

### Queer Press

Regan McClure, Coordinator
PO Box 485, Sta. P
Toronto, ON, Canada M5S 2T1
Nonprofit publisher of new Canadian lesbian and gay writers. Accepts unsolicited manuscripts; query first with outline. Reaches market through commission representatives, direct mail, and distributors.

### Toronto Women's Bookstore

73 Harbord St.
Toronto, ON M5S 1G4

### Women's Bookstop

333 Main St. West
Hamilton, ON L8P 1K1

### Womansline Books

711 Richmond St.
London, ON N6A 3H1
Bookstore.

### WomenSource

Annie Wilcox
PO Box 1742

works by living artists and the estates of artists and collectors, and it sponsors discussion groups, forums, panels, and lectures.

The gallery and archive currently reside in donated space—the basement at 127 Prince Street in the SoHo district—but, says Leslie, "we envision a future in which we will have a fully constituted museum." Their permanent collection includes between 200 and 300 works, including those by erotic illustrator Blade (Neal Bate), cowboy painter Delmas Howe, abstract expressionist Gerhardt Leibman, photographers Robert Mapplethorpe and Bruce of Los Angeles, and many others. Among their contemporary displays have been works by gay artists Patrick Angus, Jeffrey Byrd, and Don Herron, and lesbian artists Avital Greenberg, Becki Jayne Harrelson, and Gail S. Goodman.

Kingston, ON K7L 5J6
Mail-order bookstore.

### QUEBEC

**L'Androgyne**
3636 boul. St.-Laurent
Montreal, QUE H2X 2V4
Bookstore.

### SASKATCHEWAN

**Cafe Browse**
269 Third Ave. South
Saskatoon, SK S7K 1M3
Bookstore.

**One Sky Books**
259A 3rd Ave. South
Saskatoon, SK S7K 1M3
Bookstore.

## ENGLAND

**Silver Moon**
68 Charing Cross Rd.
London WC2H 0BB
Mail-order bookstore for books from the United Kingdom.

## RUSSIA

**Moscow Union of Lesbians in Literature and Art**
Lyudmila Ugolkova, Chairwoman
ulitsa Chernyakhovskogo 15,
Bldg. 4, Apt. 134
Moscow 127951, Russia
phone: 095 1521657
fax: 095 28430380
Founded in 1991, the Moscow Union comprises lesbians in Russia who are interested in the arts and promotes the involvement of lesbians in the arts. The union's journal, *Adelfe,* is published annually.

## UNITED STATES

### ALABAMA

**Lodestar Books**
2020 11th Ave. S.
Birmingham, AL 35205
Bookstore.

**Opening Books**
202 Goldsmith St. SE
Huntsville, AL 35801
Bookstore.

**Rainbows Ltd. Inc.**
4321 University Dr., Ste. 400B
Huntsville, AL 35816
Bookstore.

*Cowboy painting by Delmas Howe, courtesy Leslie-Lohman Gay Art Foundation.*

## ALASKA

### Bona Dea: The Women's Bookstore (Alaska Women's Bookstore)
2440 E. Tudor Rd. #304
Anchorage, AK 99507
New Age/Wiccan Bookstore.

## ARIZONA

### Antigone Books
411 N. 4th Ave.
Tucson, AZ 85705
Bookstore.

### Aradia Bookstore
PO Box 266
116 W. Cottage
Flagstaff, AZ 86001

### Ferrari Publications, Inc.
Marianne Ferrari, Editor and Publisher
Sharon Rosen, Manager
PO Box 37887
Phoenix, AZ 85069
phone: (602) 863-2408
fax: (602) 439-3952
Ferrari publishes worldwide gay and lesbian travel guidebooks to the United States, Canada, Caribbean, Europe, Mexico, Australia, New Zealand, and Tahiti. Specializes in covering gay and lesbian events and tours. Reaches market through direct mail, wholesalers, and retailers.

## ARKANSAS

### The Women's Project
2224 Main St.
Little Rock, AR 72206
Bookstore.

## CALIFORNIA

### Alamo Square Distributors
Bert Herrman, Senior Partner

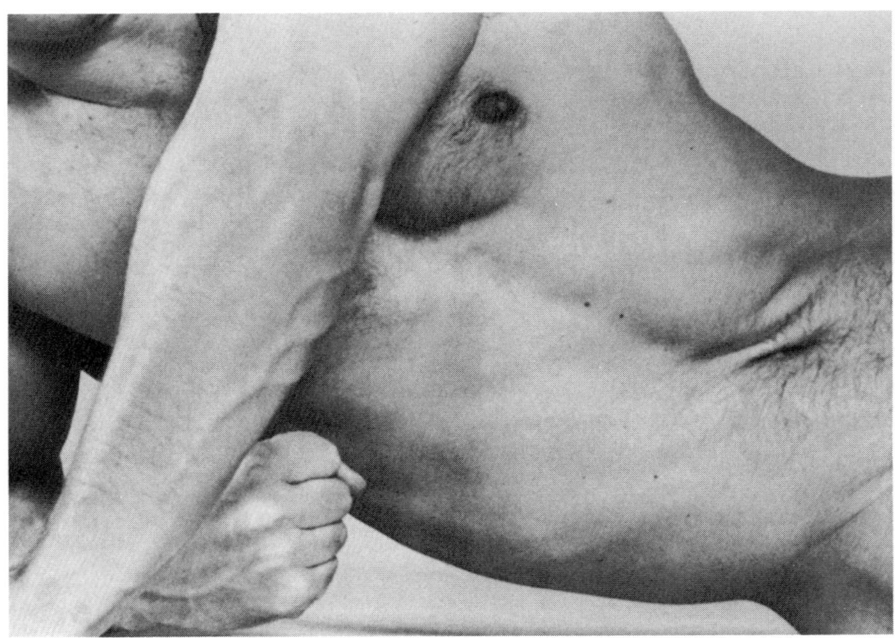

*Photo by John Lesnick, courtesy Leslie-Lohman Gay Art Foundation.*

Emily Tilles, Managing Partner
PO Box 14543
San Francisco, CA 94114
phone: (415) 252-0643
Affiliated with Alamo Square Press, Alamo Square Distributors is a wholesaler that represents smaller gay and lesbian presses. Reaches market through direct mail and telephone sales.

## Alamo Square Press

Bert Herrman, President
PO Box 14543
San Francisco, CA 94114
phone: (415) 252-0643
fax: (415) 863-7456
Alamo Square Press publishes on matters of interest to gay men and lesbians. Does not accept unsolicited manuscripts. Reaches market through direct mail, telephone sales, and distributors, including InKoBook, Bookpeople Inc., and New Leaf Distributing Co.

## Artists Confronting AIDS (ACA)

James Carroll Pickett, Executive Officer
1616 Garden St.
Glendale, CA 91201-2614
phone: (213) 250-4487
Founded in 1985, the ACA comprises individuals working to confront stereotypes and humanize AIDS through the creative and performing arts. ACA's *Purple Circuit Directory* lists gay and lesbian theaters and producers and is published annually.

## Bay Area Women's Philharmonic

330 Townsend
San Francisco, CA
phone: (415) 543-2297
The Bay Area Women's Philharmonic is the first professional orchestra in the United States to be dedicated to promoting women composers, conductors, and performers. Founded in 1980, the Women's Philharmonic has won numerous awards from ASCAP and the American Symphony Orchestra League for "adventuresome programming in contem-

porary music" and has presented works by more than 50 women composers. The group's National Women Composers Resource Center is dedicated to moving works by past and present women composers into the mainstream orchestral repertoire.

### *La Bella Figura*
PO Box 411223
San Francisco, CA 94141-1223
Quarterly literary magazine for Italian-American lesbians.

### Boadecia's Books
398 Colusa Ave.
North Berkeley, CA 94707
Bookstore.

### Books 'n Birds
2358 Market St.
San Francisco, CA 94114
Bookstore.

### Choices Books and Music
901 De La Vina
Santa Barbara, CA 93101
Bookstore.

### Circus of Books
4001 Sunset Blvd.
Los Angeles, CA 90029
Bookstore.

### Clothespin Fever Press
5529 N. Figueroa
Los Angeles, CA 90042
phone: (213) 254-1373
Founded in 1986, this lesbian/feminist press publishes the newsletter *Lesbian Line* and books including *A Dyke's Bike Repair Handbook.*

### Crossing Press
John Gill and Elaine G. Gill, Co-Publishers
PO Box 1048
Freedom, CA 95019
phone: (408) 722-0711
phone: (800) 777-1048
fax: (408) 722-2749
Crossing Press publishes general fiction and nonfiction, including books on homosexuality and feminism, and offers postcards and calendars. Reaches market through commission representatives, direct mail, trade sales, and wholesalers and distributors, including Baker & Taylor Books, Ingram Book Co., Bookpeople Inc., and InKoBook.

*"FEmenINE," photograph by Remsen Wolff, courtesy Leslie-Lohman Gay Art Foundation.*

### Damron Co., Inc.
Gina M. Gatta, President
Robert Ian Philips, Editor
PO Box 422458
San Francisco, CA 94142-2458
phone: (415) 255-0404
phone: (800) 462-6654
fax: (415) 703-9049
Formerly known as Bob Damron Enterprises, Damron publishes "the largest selling, most widely circulated gay travel guide on the market. Lists bars, baths, hotels, restaurants, etc. in the U.S., Canada, Puerto Rico, Virgin Islands, Costa Rica, and Mexico which cater to and are frequented by gays and lesbians." Reaches market through commission representatives and direct mail.

### Dan Brown Books
416 Dorado Ter.
San Francisco, CA 94112
phone: (415) 585-3410
Dan Brown Books publishes and reprints gay titles. Reaches market through InKo-Book.

### A Different Drummer Bookstore
1027 N. Pacific Coast Hwy A
Laguna Beach, CA 92651

# SPOTLIGHT
## WORD IS OUT

Specializing in books for women and for the gay, lesbian, bisexual, and transgendered communities, Boulder, Colorado's Word Is Out Women's Bookstore opened in November 1994. With 3,000 titles (mostly new, plus some used, along with music, magazines, jewelry, buttons, bumper stickers, cards, and other gift items), the store is still small, but it's growing and strives to reach out to the community.

"My intention," explains owner Louise Knapp, "is that the store serve as a community center for women and the queer community"—a role adopted by

**A Different Light—SF**
Richard LaBonte
489 Castro St.
San Francisco, CA 94114
Bookstore.

**A Different Light—WH**
8853 Santa Monica Blvd.
West Hollywood, CA 90069
Bookstore.

**Down There Press**
Joani Blank, Publisher
Leigh Davidson, Managing Editor
938 Howard St.
San Francisco, CA 94103
phone: (415) 974-8985
fax: (415) 974-8989
Affiliated with Open Enterprises, Inc., Down There Press publishes exclusively sexual self-help books for adults and children. Accepts unsolicited manuscripts; send query letter with table of contents and sample chapters first. Reaches market through direct mail, Bookpeople, InKoBook, Pacific Pipeline, the distributors, New Leaf Distributing Co., and Baker & Taylor Books.

***Feminist Bookstore News***
PO Box 882554
San Francisco, CA 94188
phone: (415) 626-1556
Trade magazine, founded in 1976, for booksellers, librarians, and publishers interested in books by and about women.

**Gaia Bookstore**
Patrice Wynne
1400 Shattuck Ave.
Berkeley, CA 94709

**Gay Sunshine Press/Leyland Publications**
Winston Leyland, Publisher
PO Box 410690
San Francisco, CA 94141
phone: (707) 996-6082
fax: (707) 996-8418
Publishes books specializing in gay male themes. Reaches market through direct mail and wholesalers and distributors, including InKoBook and Bookpeople Inc.

**GLB Publishers**
W. L. Warner, Owner/Publisher
935 Howard St., Ste. B
San Francisco, CA 94103
phone: (415) 243-0229
fax: (415) 243-0885
GLB publishes fiction, nonfiction, and poetry by and for the gay, lesbian, and bisexual communities. Accepts unsolicited manuscripts; author shares cost of printing and promotion. Reaches market through direct mail and trade sales.

many a gay bookstore. Displays of local artists' works, readings and book signings, book group meetings, and bulletin board notices for housing, job, and other networking opportunities contribute to the store's community outreach.

"For many people new to the area, Word Is Out is the only visibly gay-friendly business they're able to find easily," says Knapp. "I have created a map of other businesses and agencies of interest, and the store often serves as a sort of 'welcome wagon' to the community."

Though Knapp is the sole proprietor and only full-time staff person, she credits her partner and several volunteers with providing a great deal of help. The lesbian-owned store is open from 10 a.m. to 6 p.m. Tuesday through Saturday, and from noon to 5 p.m. Sunday, and is wheelchair accessible.

**Glen Park Books**
Pat Cull
2788 Diamond
San Francisco, CA 94131
New Age/Wiccan Bookstore.

**Gualala Books**
PO Box 765
39141 Highway One
Gualala, CA 95445
Bookstore.

**Her Body Books**
433 South Beverly Drive
Beverly Hills, CA 90212
Bookstore.

**Her Body Books #2—West Hollywood**
8721 Beverly Blvd.
Los Angeles, CA 90048
Bookstore.

**HerBooks**
Irene Reti, Publisher
PO Box 7467
Santa Cruz, CA 95061
phone: (408) 425-7493
HerBooks publishes books on lesbianism and feminism with a Jewish emphasis. Reaches market through commission representatives, direct mail, trade sales, InKoBook, and Bookpeople.

**Herland Book/Cafe**
Kayla Rose
902 Center St.
Santa Cruz, CA 95060
Bookstore.

**Lioness Books**
2224 J. St.
Sacramento, CA 95816
Bookstore.

**Mama Bears**
6536 Telegraph Ave.
Oakland, CA 94609
Bookstore.

***Mama Bears News and Notes***
6536 Telegraph Ave.
Oakland, CA 94609
Publishes reviews of lesbian fiction and nonfiction and other women's and children's books, spirituality, recovery, psychology, women's studies, and Third World women.

**Marcus Books**
1712 Fillmore
San Francisco, CA 94115
Bookstore.

**Midea Books**
849 Almar Ave., Ste. C-285
Santa Cruz, CA 95060
Mail-order bookstore.

### Modern Times Bookstore
888 Valencia St.
San Francisco, CA 94110

### M.O.O.C.H. Motivational Organization of Curious Humanity
Tom Church
PO Box 410086
San Francisco, CA 94141
phone: (415) 776-0409
M.O.O.C.H. publishes booklets on homosexuality and the magazines *The Moocher's Periodical* and *M.O.O.C.H.* Accepts unsolicited manuscripts. Reaches market through direct mail.

### Moonyean
1130 Baywood Dr. #61
Petaluma, CA 94954
Mail-order bookstore.

### Obelisk: The Bookstore
1029 University Ave.
San Diego, CA 92103

### Page One—Books By & For Women
1200 E. Walnut
Pasadena, CA 91106
Bookstore.

### Pearls
224 Redondo Ave.
Long Beach, CA 90803
Bookstore.

### Persona Press
N. A. Diaman, President
PO Box 14022
San Francisco, CA 94114
phone: (415) 775-6143
Persona Press publishes works of fiction with homosexual content and reaches its market through Bookpeople, InKoBook, Turnaround Distribution, and Alamo Square Distributor.

### Pride Products
296 W. 2nd St.
Pomona, CA 91766
Gift shop.

### Raven in the Grove
505 Lighthouse Ave., Ste. 103
Pacific Grove, CA 93950
Bookstore.

### *Sinister Wisdom: Journal for the Lesbian Imagination in the Arts and Politics*
PO Box 3252
Berkeley, CA 94703
Quarterly magazine, founded in 1976.

### Sisterhood Bookstore
1351 Westwood Blvd.
Los Angeles, CA 90024

### Sisterspirit
175 Stockton Ave.
San Jose, CA 95126
Bookstore.

### Stepping Stones
The Artifactory
226 Hamilton Ave.
Palo Alto, CA 94301
Bookstore.

### Third Woman Press
Norma Alarcon, Editor and Publisher
Chicano Studies
University of California
Dwinelle Hall 3412
Berkeley, CA 94720
(510) 642-0240
Publishes works by and about U.S. Latinas and Third World women in general.

### Travellin' Pages
1174 East Ave.
Chico, CA 95926
Bookstore.

### True Hearts
20786 Bear Valley Rd., Ste. J
Apple Valley, CA 92307
Bookstore.

### Two Sisters Bookshop
605 Cambridge Ave.
Menlo Park, CA 94025

### Valley Women Books and Gifts
1118 N. Fulton St.
Fresno, CA 93728

### Waterwomen Books
3022 Ashbrook Court
Oakland, CA 94601
phone: (415) 532-3545

Publishes a lesbian photo album and provides consultation on self-publishing, production, and marketing.

### West Berkeley Women's Books
2514 San Pablo Ave.
Berkeley, CA 94702
Bookstore.

### Wild Iris Bookstore
Genevieve Beenen
143 Harvard Ave., Ste. A
Claremont, CA 91711

### Woman in the Moon Publications (W.I.M.)
SDiane Bogus, Publisher
PO Box 2087
Cupertino, CA 95015-2087
phone: (408) 738-4623
fax: (408) 738-4623
Woman in the Moon publishes feminist and lesbian poetry, and offers mail-order directories, mailing lists, book reviews, and self-publishing consulting. W.I.M. sponsors two poetry contests; inquire for guidelines. Reaches market through direct mail, telephone and trade sales, and trade shows.

## COLORADO

### The Book Garden—A Women's Store
2625 E. 12th Ave.
Denver, CO 80206

### Beebo's Books
925 Spruce St.
Louisville, CO 80027
Bookstore.

### Category Six Books
1029 E. Eleventh Ave.
Denver, CO 80218
Bookstore.

### Gena Rose Press
Vicki P. McConnell, Owner
2424 Franklin, No. B
Denver, CO 80205
phone: (303) 830-2157

### Hue-Man Experience
911 Twenty-third St.
Denver, CO 80205

*Barbara Grier and Donna J. McBride of Naiad Press.*

Bookstore.

### Out Back Books
69 Elk Park Dr.
Pine, CO 80470
Mail-order bookstore.

### A Quiet Corner Bookstore
803 E. Mulberry St.
Fort Collins, CO 80524

### Word Is Out Women's Bookstore
Louise Knapp, Owner
1731 15th St.
Boulder, CO 80302
phone: (303) 449-1415
fax: (303) 449-7605

## CONNECTICUT

### Bloodroot Restaurant and Bookstore
85 Ferris St.
Bridgeport, CT 06605

### Connecticut Gay Men's Chorus
PO Box 8824
New Haven, CT 06532-0824

### Golden Thread Booksellers
915 State St.
New Haven, CT 06511

### InKoBook (Inland Book Co.)
140 Commerce

*The staff of Naiad Press, clockwise from left: Barbara Grier, LeeAnn Day, Alex Jaeger, Arden Singletary, Maria Douglas, Rita Reese, Amy McDonald, and Donna McBride. (Photo by Beatrice Queral.)*

East Haven, CT 06512
phone: (203) 467-4257
phone: (800) 243-0138
fax: (203) 469-7697
e-mail: http://outpost.callnet.com/outpost.hml
InKoBook, formerly known as Inland Book Company or InBook Distribution, is a distributor and wholesaler that carries more than 2,000 publishers on a non-exclusive basis and 85 publishers on an exclusive basis, and acts as primary trade distributor for approximately 65 others. Inland distributes books about homosexuality, feminism, political science, and literature, and reaches its market through direct mail and telephone sales. Among the publishers InKoBook represents are: Africa World Press; Alyson Publications; Asylum Arts Publishing; Bay Press; Bishop Books; Broken Moon Press; Cane Hill Press; Cheshire Iguana; Cleis Press; Curbstone Press; Dalkey Archive Press; Eclipse Books; ECW Press; Firebrand Books; Franklin Square Press; Gang of Seven; Goodwood Press; gynergy books/Ragweed Press; Hysteria; Literary Press Group; LongRiver Books; New Society Publishers; New Victoria; Press Gang; Second Story Press; See Sharp Press; Society for American Baseball Research; South End Press; Spinsters Book Co.; SteerForth Press; Tailisman House; Talong Books; Torrance Publishing; White Pine Press; Zephyr Press; Zoland Books Inc.; Bruno Gmunder Verlag; Marion Boyars Publishing; Jon Carpenter Publishing; Cassell Publishing; GMP Publishers; Green Print; International Books; Janssen Verlag; Scarlet Press; Millivres Books; and SpinFex.

**The Reader's Feast**
529 Farmington Ave.
Hartford, CT 06105
Bookstore.

## SPOTLIGHT

## BARBARA GRIER and NAIAD PRESS

Barbara Grier has devoted much of her career to writing, editing, and publishing articles and books pertaining to lesbians and lesbianism. Writing under her own name as well as various pseudonyms, she contributed a wealth of material to the pioneer lesbian periodical the *Ladder,* also serving as the publication's editor from 1968 until 1972. Later, she and her companion, Donna J. McBride, cofounded Naiad Press, which has grown to become the world's largest lesbian book publisher.

Born November 4, 1933, in Cincinnati, Ohio, Grier became aware of her homosexuality in her youth. Beginning at the age of eight, she fell in love repeatedly with slightly older girls as her family moved to various locations

### DELAWARE

**Lambda Rising—Rehoboth**
39 Baltimore Ave.
Rehoboth, DE 19971
Bookstore.

### DISTRICT OF COLUMBIA

***Lambda Book Report***
Lambda Rising, Inc.
1625 Connecticut Ave. NW
Washington, DC 20009
phone: (202) 462-7924
Review of contemporary gay and lesbian literature; founded in 1987.

**Lambda Rising—DC**
Deacon Maccubbin
1625 Connecticut Ave. NW
Washington, DC 20009
Bookstore.

**Lammas Women's Books & More**
1426 21st St. NW (at P)
Washington, DC 20036
Bookstore.

**SisterSpace & Books**
1354 U St. NW
Washington, DC 20009
Bookstore.

### FLORIDA

**Brigit Books**
3434 4th St. N. #5
St. Petersburg, FL 33704
Bookstore.

**Caroline Street Books**
800 Caroline St. #7
Key West, FL 33040
Bookstore.

**Iris Books**
802 West University Ave.
Gainesville, FL 32601
Bookstore.

**Lambda Passages**
7545 Biscayne Blvd.
Miami, FL 33138
Bookstore.

**Lavenders**
5600 Trail Blvd. #4
Naples, FL 33963
Bookstore.

***Lesbian Periodicals Index***
Box 10543

throughout the country. When she was 12 and her family was living in Detroit, Michigan, she told her mother of her sexual orientation. Her sympathetic mother explained the term "lesbian" and later joked that she had read Radclyffe Hall's *The Well of Loneliness* while she was pregnant with Grier and that she had marked her daughter.

During her childhood Grier became an avid reader, but she did not become seriously interested in lesbian fiction until age 16 when she found *The Well* in the library. She believes literature is the most important part of coming out—in helping to find an identity and a sense of connectedness to the lesbian past. Asked in an October 1976 *Christopher Street* interview if she had been frightened off by the negative descriptions of homosexuality that she read in early books, she replied "No," adding, "I've always felt very good about myself."

Tallahassee, FL 32302
phone: (904) 539-5965
List of nearly 40 libraries and archives with extensive holdings of lesbian periodicals. Principal content is subject and author indexes of articles, drawings, poems, and stories in lesbian journals.

**Naiad Press, Inc.**
Barbara Grier, C.E.O.
PO Box 10543
Tallahassee, FL 32302
phone: (904) 539-5965
phone: (800) 533-1973
fax: (904) 539-9731
Naiad Press, one of the premier publishers of lesbian literature, also offers video cassettes. Accepts unsolicited manuscripts; query first. Reaches market through direct mail, trade sales, wholesalers, and distributors, including Blackwell North America, John Coutts Library Services, Baker & Taylor, InKoBook, Bookpeople, and Ingram Book Co.

**On the Move (Mobile Bookstore)**
PO Box 2985
St. Petersburg, FL 33731

**Orlando Gay Chorus**
c/o David Schuler
PO Box 3103
Orlando, FL 32802-3103

**Out & About Books**
930 North Mills Ave.
Orlando, FL 32803
Bookstore.

**Outbooks**
Robert Sonneken
1239 E. Las Olas Blvd.
Ft. Lauderdale, FL 33301
Bookstore.

**Rubyfruit Books**
666 W. Tennessee St. #4
Tallahassee, FL 32304
Bookstore.

**Silver Chord**
10901 Lillian Hwy
Pensacola, FL 32506
Bookstore.

**STARbooks Press**
Patrick J. Powers, President
2516 Ridge Ave.
Sarasota, FL 34235
phone: (813) 957-1281
fax: (813) 954-5083
Affiliated with Woldt Publishing Corp., STARbooks Press publishes gay and lesbian fiction and nonfiction. Also offers cards, calendars, and videos. Reaches market

When she was 18, she became the companion of an older, married librarian. They ran off to Denver for two years before spending some 20 relatively isolated years in or near Kansas City, Kansas, where they both worked for the public library. Grier also began a more than 15-year association with the *Ladder,* the pioneering lesbian periodical that started in San Francisco in 1956 as a 12-page mimeographed newsletter. While Grier worked for the *Ladder,* the periodical expanded before its demise in 1972 to a 56-page magazine with some 3,800 subscribers.

Grier's work with the *Ladder* commenced several months after the periodical's debut as she began submitting book reviews. From 1957 until 1972 she wrote a column called "Lesbiana," a breezy and to-the-point summary of current lesbian literature. She also created a series called "Living Propaganda," and she wrote an entire issue alone. In addition, she contributed to

through direct mail, trade sales, and wholesalers.

**Three Birds Bookstore and Coffee Room**
1518 7th Ave.
Tampa, FL 33605

**Tomes and Treasures**
202 South Howard Ave.
Tampa, FL 33606
Bookstore.

**Woldt Publishing Group**
Patrick J. Powers, President
2516 Ridge Ave.
Sarasota, FL 34235
phone: (813) 957-1281
Woldt publishes literature of interest to gay men, and also publishes calendars and cards. Accepts unsolicited manuscripts. Provides direct mail service. Reaches market through direct mail and InKoBook.

## GEORGIA

**Charis Books and More**
1189 Euclid Ave., NE
Atlanta, GA 30307
Bookstore.

**DreamWeaver**
306 W. St. Julian
Savannah, GA 31401
Bookstore.

**Outwrite Bookstore**
Philip Rafshoon
931 Monroe Dr., Ste. 108
Atlanta, GA 30308

**Spike's Stuff**
307 Adair St. C4
Decatur, GA 30030
Gift shop.

## HAWAII

**Book Exchange**
74-5588 Pawai Pl., Bldg. K
Kailua, Kona, HI 96740
Bookstore.

## ILLINOIS

**Artemis Singers**
PO Box 578296
Chicago, IL 60657
phone: (312) 764-4465
Lesbians in the Chicago, Illinois area with an interest in choral music founded the

other periodicals, including *ONE Magazine* and the *Mattachine Review.* From October, 1965, until March, 1970, *Tangents* carried her "Reader at Large" column, which summarized the gay literature of the day. When preparing this work, later reprinted by *Tangents* in the form of two pamphlets, Grier attempted to feature titles that appealed to a variety of tastes. She culled reviews in various publications, looking for telltale signs of often obscure books that might be of interest, and hunted down those that were, informing her readers without pedantry or condescension how the subject was treated. From 1966 to 1967 she became fiction and poetry editor for the *Ladder,* before assuming editorship from 1968 until 1972. From 1970 until 1972, she was the magazine's publisher.

In time Donna McBride came to work on the *Ladder* and a love blossomed between her and Grier. Ending her longtime relationship with the librarian,

Artemis Singers in 1980. The group performs three to six concerts each year.

### Back to the Source
1831 Camp Ave.
Rockford, IL 61103
Bookstore.

### A Book for All Seasons
105 S. 3rd St.
Bloomingdale, IL 60108
Bookstore.

### *Hot Wire: The Journal of Women's Music and Culture*
5210 N. Wayne
Chicago, IL 60640
phone: (312) 769-9009
Founded in 1985, *Hot Wire* covers contemporary and historical women in the arts, including writers, musicians, comediennes, and actresses.

### Institute of Lesbian Studies
Ann Seawall, Coordinator
PO Box 25568
Chicago, IL 60625
The Institute of Lesbian Studies publishes on lesbian theory for classroom use in women's studies, lesbian studies, feminist theory, and philosophy. Reaches market through direct mail, trade sales, and distributors, including InKoBook and Bookpeople.

### Jane Addams Book Shop
208 North Neil St.
Champagne, IL 61820

### Once Upon a Time Alternative Books & Gifts
311 N. Main St.
Bloomington, IL 61701

### People Like Us Books
Carrie Barnett
3321 N. Clark St.
Chicago, IL 60657
Bookstore.

### Prairie Moon Ltd.
8 North Dunton Ave.
Arlington Heights, IL 60005
Bookstore.

### Pride Agenda Bookstore
PO Box 3508
Oak Park, IL 60303

### Women & Children First
5233 N. Clark St.
Chicago, IL 60640
Bookstore.

## INDIANA

### Aquarius Books Inc.

Grier eventually moved with McBride to the rural town of Bates City, Missouri. Following the relocation, their lives became more social, with more travel and speaking engagements. After years of city living, Grier and McBride lived on a five-acre farm (called 20 rue Jacob in honor of American author Natalie Barney's Paris address). Together they raised trees, learned the joys of gardening, and continued the search for lesbian literature.

Grier and McBride's work for the *Ladder* ended in 1972, when the magazine folded. The periodical's long-anonymous financial supporter withdrew her funding after the magazine's focus switched from lesbian to lesbian-feminist issues. In 1973 Grier and McBride started Naiad Press with the assistance of two older women, just retired, who supplied the start-up funds for the lesbian/feminist publishing house. Naiad's first book was 1974's *Latecomer* by Sarah Aldridge. For nine years Grier and McBride did all work for Naiad Press

732 Whitethorn Pl.
Bloomington, IN 47403
Bookstore.

**Dreams and Swords**
6503 Ferguson St.
Indianapolis, IN 46220
Bookstore.

## IOWA

**Crystal Rainbow**
1025 W. 4th St.
Davenport, IA 52802
Bookstore.

## KANSAS

**Visions & Dreams Bookstore/Freedom Cafe**
2819 E. Central
Wichita, KS 67214

## LOUISIANA

**Faubourg Marginy Bookstore**
600 Frenchman St.
New Orleans, LA 70116

**Moore Magic**
1212 Royal St.
New Orleans, LA 70116
Bookstore.

## MAINE

**Womankind Gifts**
Nancy Bouchard
48 Cushing St.
Brunswick, ME 04011
Gift shop.

## MARYLAND

***Alternative Press Index***
PO Box 33109
Baltimore, MD 21218
phone: (410) 243-2471
Founded in 1969, the *Alternative Press Index* costs $35 for a subscription of four issues per year.

***Belles Letters: A Review of Books by Women***
11151 Captain's Walk Ct.
North Potomac, MD 20878
phone: (301) 294-0278

while holding down regular jobs. The publishing house has since grown into a considerable business, with successful books like Jane Rule's *Outlander* and *Desert of the Heart,* Sheila Ortiz Taylor's *Faultline,* and Katherine V. Forrest's *Curious Wine.*

Naiad Press became a major force in aiding the development of new genres in lesbian literature, including mysteries, westerns, science fiction, and erotic fiction (as opposed to erotic stories about lesbians written by and for heteromales). The publisher also helped create today's market, in which lesbians are among the nation's top book purchasers. When Naiad Press issued Rosemary Curb and Nancy Manahan's controversial book *Lesbian Nuns: Breaking Silence,* the publicity helped the publisher gain a larger customer base, with most new patrons also ordering heavily from the house's substantial backlist. Naiad Press attempts to keep virtually all back titles in print—

Quarterly magazine ($20 per year) promoting the writing of women. Includes retrospectives, interviews, rediscoveries, and reviews of current titles and reissues. Publishes personal essays and poetry.

### Lambda Rising—Baltimore
241 W. Chase St.
Baltimore, MD 21201
Bookstore.

### Lammas—Baltimore
1001 Cathedral St.
Baltimore, MD 21202
Bookstore.

### New Poets Series, Inc.
Clarinda Harriss Raymond, Editor and Publisher
541 Piccadilly Rd.
Baltimore, MD 21204
phone: (410) 828-0724
Publishes books by promising poets with no previous books published. Accepts unsolicited manuscripts with a self-addressed, stamped envelope. Distributes for Salmon Publishing and Galway (Ireland). Reaches market through library lists. Distributed by Blackwell North America, Inc., Bookman, and Baker & Taylor Books.

## MASSACHUSETTS

### Alyson Publications, Inc.
Sasha Alyson, President
40 Plympton St.
Boston, MA 02118
phone: (617) 542-5679
Alyson publishes books for a gay and lesbian readership. Accepts unsolicited manuscripts; must query with outline first, and include a self-addressed, stamped envelope. Reaches market through direct mail, trade sales, and distributors, including InKoBook, Bookpeople Inc., and InKoBook.

### *Bay Windows*
1523 Washington St.
Boston, MA 02118
phone: (617) 266-6670
Weekly magazine, founded in 1983, covering gay male and lesbian literature. Subscriptions are $35.

### Crone's Harvest
761 Centre St.
Jamaica Plain, MA 02130
Bookstore.

### Fag Rag Books
E. Carlotta
PO Box 331, Kenmore Sta.
Boston, MA 02215

an unusual practice but one driven by the memory of days when positive literature about lesbians was almost non-existent. Grier is resolved that every young lesbian coming out should have ready access to a wide variety of books that support her sexual orientation.

In 1980 McBride and Grier moved Naiad Press to Tallahassee, Florida. Naiad Press began receiving hundreds of visitors each year—to many lesbians the publishing complex is like a shrine or a mecca. In addition, a number of Naiad Press books were optioned for film. Two have reached the screen—*Desert of the Heart* (as *Desert Hearts*) and *Claire of the Moon*.

Starting her career in lesbian literature at a time when such material was thought to be very scarce, hard to find, often illegal, usually buried in symbolism or euphemism, and most often extremely negative, Grier has made a substantial contribution to the field. Through her work as reviewer and

phone: (617) 492-7713
Fag Rag Books is an offshoot of the gay male quarterly *Fag Rag*.

### Fighting Words Press

Dorian Gregory, Editor
124 Williams St.
Northampton, MA 01060
phone: (413) 586-0450
Publishes feminist literature for a predominantly lesbian and feminist audience. Accepts unsolicited manuscripts. Reaches market through direct mail, telephone sales, and Baker & Taylor Books.

### Food for Thought Books

106 N. Pleasant St.
Amherst, MA 01002
Bookstore.

### Gaylactic Network (GN)

Michael Wadley, Executive Officer
PO Box 127
Brookline, MA 02146
The gay, lesbian, and bisexual individuals and other members of the Gaylactic Network are interested in science fiction, fantasy, and horror. Founded in 1987, GN promotes the genres in all media, specifically material dealing with homosexuality, and provides a network for shared information and interests. With 315 members and 13 local branches, GN produces an electronic bulletin board called Gaylactic Network Echo on FidoNet, and a bimonthly newsletter called the *Gaylactic Gayzette* that contains short stories, book reviews, and artwork. The *Gaylaxians International Member Directory,* published annually, contains membership and organizational listings, with quarterly updates. The group's Gaylaxicon convention occurs annually.

### Glad Day

673 Boylston, 2nd Floor
Boston, MA 02116
Bookstore.

### Good Gay Poets

Charles Shively and Michael Bronski, Collective Members
PO Box 277, Astor Station
Boston, MA 02123
phone: (617) 492-7713
Good Gay Poets publishes books of poetry by lesbians and gay men. The press is collectively run and operated; income is supplemented by grants and benefits.

### Lunaria

90 King St.
Northampton, MA 01060
Bookstore.

anthologist, and finally and importantly as a publisher, she has helped create vast, diverse, readable, and positive lesbian literature. Her research, started back in those dark days, produced massive card files "overflowing with unworked information—probably three thousands cards," she related at the Second Annual Lesbian Writer's Conference in Chicago in 1978. Describing "notes on women I've personally not had time to research fully, or even at all," she explained that all her subjects "need to be talked about because all the women out there are really waiting to hear.... There are many women to find, many lesbians to write about and for.... We have to go out on the hills and listen for the fine wild sweet singing of our past and record it for our future."

Grier decided to donate these files and other private papers, along with the records of Naiad Press and her collection of well more than 15,000 books

**Madwoman Press**
Diane Benison, President
PO Box 690
Northboro, MA 01532
fax: (508) 393-8305
Madwoman publishes lesbian fiction, nonfiction, and humor. Accepts unsolicited manuscripts. Reaches market through direct mail, trade sales, and wholesalers and distributors, including InKoBook and Bookpeople Inc.

**New Herizons Books & Gifts**
376 W. Boylston
Worcester, MA 01606
Bookstore.

**New Words Bookstore**
186 Hampshire St.
Cambridge, MA 02139

**Now Voyager**
PO Box 551
357 Commercial St.
Provincetown, MA 02657
Bookstore.

**Pride's of Provincetown**
Box 511
Provincetown, MA 02657
Gift shop.

**Radzukina's**
714 North Broadway
Haverhill, MA 01832
Bookstore.

**Recovering Hearts Book and Gift Store**
Leslie McGrath
2 & 4 Standish St.
Provincetown, MA 02657

**Third Wave Feminist Booksellers**
90 King St.
Northampton, MA 01060
Bookstore.

**Union Park Press**
William A. Koelsch, Publisher
PO Box 2737
Boston, MA 02208
phone: (617) 423-3427
Publishes Boston and New England gay authors writing nonfiction of regional and general interest.

**Wild Iris**
7 Old South St.
Northampton, MA 01060
Gift shop.

**Womencrafts Inc.**
PO Box 190
376 Commercial St.

(including many books about gay males which she collected until 1968), to the new Gay and Lesbian Center at the San Francisco Main Public Library. She had been contacted by several primarily male gay archives and had investigated some one hundred institutional library archives interested in receiving the collection before making her decision. An 18-wheel semi-trailer was used to send the first batch, appraised at $400,000. Funds have been raised from the Xerox Corporation and the National Endowment for the Humanities for de-acidification and to guarantee its preservation in perpetuity. Much of her periodical collection had already been shipped to the June Mazer Lesbian Collection in West Hollywood.

In 1996, Naiad Press celebrates its 23rd birthday and the publication of over 350 books. Twenty-eight new titles are being released and the press has begun a new association with Northern Arts Entertainment, one of the

Provincetown, MA 02657
Bookstore.

## MICHIGAN

### Chosen Books
120 W. 4th St.
Royal Oak, MI 48067
phone: (810) 543-5758
Gay male and lesbian bookstore.

### Common Language
215 S. Fourth Ave.
Ann Arbor, MI 48104
Women-owned bookstore serving the feminist, lesbian, and gay communities.

### Community Newscenter
330 East Liberty
Ann Arbor, MI 48104
phone: (313) 663-6168
Bookstore.

### Crazy Wisdom Bookstore
206 N. Fourth Ave.
Ann Arbor, MI 48104
phone: (313) 665-2757
Holistic, metaphysical, and psychological bookstore.

### Detroit Together Men's Chorus
2441 Pinecrest
Ferndale, MI 48220
phone: (810) 280-3872 or (419) 726-4830
The chorus performs choral music.

### Detroit Women's Coffeehouse Red Door
First Unitarian Universalist Church
Forest & Cass Streets
Detroit, MI
phone: (313) 341-7749
Hosts monthly entertainment, women's music, and feminist poetry and readings.

### Earth & Sky
6 Jefferson SE
Grand Rapids, MI 49503
Bookstore.

### Falling Water Books and Collectables
213 S. Main St.
Ann Arbor, MI 48104
phone: (313) 747-9810

### Great Lakes Gaylaxians
1106 E. Fifth St.
Royal Oak, MI 48067
Local chapter of the Gaylactic Network (see Massachusetts listing) for gay and lesbian science fiction fans.

### Great Lakes Men's Chorus
PO Box 336

United States' leading independent distributors of art and specialty films. Together, Northern Arts Entertainment/Naiad Press has created a new video label for the distribution of lesbian-themed movies. The movie adaptation of Mindy Kaplan's *Devotion,* released in January 1996, was the first title in the joint venture, followed by the award-winning *Costa Brava (Family Album),* a 92-minute feature film shot in Barcelona, Spain, in English, and *Meeting Magdalene,* a 34-minute U.S. feature film.

Grier and McBride plan to partially retire from Naiad Press on January 3, 2000, when the former will be 67 years old. Both believe that the publishing house will continue to thrive long after their total departure sometime in the year 2005.

*By Jim Kepner*

Royal Oak, MI 48068
phone: (810) 399-SING

**It's Your Pleasure**
3228 Glade St.
Muskegon, MI 49444
Bookstore.

**Mad River Press**
PO Box 1762
East Lansing, MI 48826
Publishes "Letters from Harriet." Reaches market through direct mail.

**Michigan Womyn's Music Festival**
PO Box 22
Walhalla, MI 49458
phone: (616) 757-4766
Annual event each August for women.

**Middleground Books & Gifts**
17550 Woodward Ave.
Detroit, MI 48203
phone: (313) 869-6841

**Pandora Books for Open Minds**
226 W. Lovell
Kalamazoo, MI 49007
Bookstore.

**Read Between the Lines**
Audrey Kowalski
341 N. Main St.
Milford, MI 48381
New Age/Wiccan Bookstore.

**The Real World Emporium**
1214-16 Turner St.
Lansing, MI 48906
Bookstore.

**Sistrum: Lansing Women's Chorus**
phone: (517) 649-8957

**Sons & Daughters**
962 Cherry St. SE
Grand Rapids, MI 49506
phone: (616) 459-8877
Bookstore and coffeehouse.

**Speculators, Inc.**
Stacey Chandler, President
Liza Cheuk May Chan, Vice President
PO Box 99038
Troy, MI 48099
phone: (810) 879-9772
fax: (810) 362-6133
Speculators publishes humorous books for lesbians and how-to books. Does not accept unsolicited manuscripts. Reaches market through direct mail, trade sales, and wholesalers and distributors, including Bookpeople Inc. and InKoBook.

**Sweet Violets Bookstore**
413 North Third St.
Marquette, MI 49855

### Triangle World
3101 S. Westnedge Ave.
Kalamazoo, MI 49005
phone: (616) 373-4005
Bookstore.

### Triple Goddess
Dawne Botke
2142 Hamilton Rd.
Okemos, MI 48864
New Age/Wiccan Bookstore.

### Western Michigan Music Society
980 128th St.
Grant, MI 49327
phone: (616) 834-5103

### A Woman's Prerogative Bookstore & Cafe
Kelly Smith and Amy Blake
175 W. Nine Mile
Ferndale, MI 48220
phone: (810) 545-5703

## MINNESOTA

### Amazon Bookstore
1612 Harmon Place
Minneapolis, MN 55403

### At Sara's Table Coffeehouse and Bookstore
728 E. Superior St.
Duluth, MN 55804

### A Brother's Touch
2327 Hennepin Ave.
Minneapolis, MN 55405
Bookstore.

### Database of Third World Women's Literary Works
Barbara Fister, Bibliographic Instruction Librarian
Gustavus Adolphus College
St. Peter, MN 56082
phone: (507) 933-7553
Contains a list of more than 600 novels, short story collections, plays, collections of poetry, and personal narratives derived from Third World women writers.

### Healing Touch
Mary Jo Majerus
20 SW 2nd Ave S-14
Rochester, MN 55902
Bookstore.

### Minnesota Women's Press Bookstore
Glenda Martin
771 Raymond
St. Paul, MN 55114

### Spinsters Ink
Joan M. Drury, Publisher and Owner
Rhonda Lundquist, General Manager
32 East First St., Ste. 330
Duluth, MN 55802
phone: (218) 727-3222
phone: (800) 301-6860
fax: (218) 727-3119
Publishes fiction and nonfiction by women, with an emphasis on work by feminists. Accepts unsolicited manuscripts; call for manuscript guidelines. Reaches market through direct mail, trade sales, and InKo-Book.

### Womyn's Braille Press
Marj Schneider, Executive Director
PO Box 8475
Minneapolis, MN 55408
phone: (612) 872-4352
Publishes feminist literature in braille and on audio cassettes for blind or printdisabled people only. All materials are available for purchase or loan. Also publishes a quarterly newsletter in braille, tape, and large or small print. Reaches market through advertising and word of mouth.

## MISSOURI

### Left Bank Books
Kris Kleindienst
399 N. Euclid
St. Louis, MO 63108
Bookstore.

### Our World Too
11 S. Vandeventer
St. Louis, MO 63108
Bookstore.

## MONTANA

### Barjon's
Barbara E. Shenkel
2718 Third Ave. N
Billings, MT 59101
Bookstore.

## NEVADA

### Get Booked
4643 Paradise Rd.
Las Vegas, NV 89109
Bookstore.

### Grapevine Books
Katherine Engblom
1450 S. Wells Ave.
Reno, NV 89502
Bookstore.

## NEW HAMPSHIRE

### Carolyn's Rainbow's End
Carolyn Haneisen
25 Melbourne St. #1
Portsmouth, NH 03801
Bookstore.

## NEW JERSEY

### Light Cleaning Press
Rita Karman, Editor
PO Box 14
Guttenberg, NJ 07093
phone: (201) 868-8106
Publishes poetry with a feminist, lesbian, spiritual, or astrological interest. Formerly called Karmic Revenge Laundry Shop Press.

### Pandora Book Peddlers
9 Waverly Place
Madison, NJ 07940
Bookstore.

### Rainbow Connection
Denville Commons
3130 Route 10 West
Denville, NJ 07834
Bookstore.

### Thunder Road Book Club and Press
PO Box 70
Hackettstown, NJ 07840
Mail-order bookstore.

## NEW MEXICO

### Full Circle
2205 Silver SE
Albuquerque, NM 87106
Bookstore.

### Sisters & Brothers Bookstore
4011 Silver Ave. SE
Albuquerque, NM 87108

## NEW YORK

### A-C Book Service
Albert J. Berube, Manager
60 St. Felix St.
Brooklyn, NY 11217-1206
phone: (718) 855-0600
A-C Book Service is a distributor formed as a nonprofit company to offer hard-to-obtain books on subjects usually not adequately served. The service provides low-cost publishing and distribution for books about homosexuality and religion, and reaches its market through direct mail.

### A.I.R. Gallery
Sarah Savidge, Director
63 Crosby St.
New York, NY 10012
phone: (212) 966-0799
Nonprofit cooperative gallery for women artists.

### Alternate Universe Gaylaxians (AUG)
Joe Leonard, President
PO Box 66054, Ft. Orange Sta.
Albany, NY 12206
This local branch of the Gaylactic Network includes gay and lesbian science fiction fans in the Albany, New York area. AUG provides social activities and a forum for the exchange of ideas on science fiction and imaginative media/literature. The group meets monthly and publishes a newsletter called *The Alternate Universe.*

## Belhue Press

Hugh H. Young, Publisher
Tom Laine, Promotion Editor
2501 Palisade Ave., Ste. A1
Bronx, NY 10463-6133
phone: (718) 884-6606
fax: (718) 884-6606
Publishes poetry, science fiction, and short stories for gay male readers. Also offers posters and cards. Accepts unsolicited manuscripts; include a self-addressed, stamped envelope. Reaches market through direct mail, telephone sales, trade sales, and wholesalers and distributors, including Baker & Taylor Books, InKoBook, Bookpeople, Alamo Square Book Distributors, and TurnAround (UK and Europe).

## Black Books Plus

702 Amsterdam Ave.
New York, NY 10025
Bookstore.

## A Different Light—NYC

Roz Parr
151 West 19th St.
New York, NY 10011
Bookstore.

## Eve's Garden

D. Williams & M. Corbett
119 W. 57th St. #420
New York, NY 10019
Gift shop.

## Firebrand Books

Nancy K. Bereano, Publisher/Editor
141 The Commons
Ithaca, NY 14850
phone: (607) 272-0000
Firebrand publishes books on lesbianism and feminism. Reaches market through direct mail, InKoBook, and In Book.

## Galiens Press

Assotto Saint, Publisher and Editor
PO Box 20171, London Terrace Sta.
New York, NY 10011
phone: (212) 242-3578
Publishes the writings of gay black men. Accepts unsolicited manuscripts only from gay black writers. Reaches market through direct mail, trade sales, and distributors, including InKoBook, Bookpeople, Inc., and Bookslinger.

## Gay Presses of New York

Felice Picano, Editor-in-Chief
PO Box 294
Village Station, NY 10014
phone: (212) 691-9066
fax: (212) 629-5191
Gay Presses of New York publishes works of fiction of interest to gay audiences, primarily novels but also short stories. Reaches market through direct mail and trade sales.

## Gayellow Pages

Frances Green, Publisher
PO Box 533, Village Sta.
New York, NY 10014-0533
phone: (212) 674-0120
Formerly known as Renaissance House, Gayellow Pages publishes well-known regional directories of gay and lesbian services, and distributes for other publishers.

## Kitchen Table/Women of Color Press

PO Box 908
Latham, NY 12110
Kitchen Table is a cooperative with a commitment to publishing and distributing the work of Third World women of all racial/cultural heritages, sexualities, and classes. Collective members are: Myrna Bain, Cherrie Moraga, Mariana Romo-Carmona, and Barbara Smith.

## Leslie-Lohman Gay Art Foundation (LLGAF)

Charles Leslie, President
Wayne Snellen, Director
127 Prince St., Basement (Gallery)
131 Prince St. (Mail)
New York, NY 10012
phone: (212) 673-7007
fax: (212) 260-0363
The Leslie-Lohman Gay Art Foundation, founded in 1990, promotes and protects artwork with gay subject matter. The foundation maintains a permanent collection, archival storage, and three galleries that are open to the public, and it sponsors exhibits and shows annually. *The Archive* newsletter appears quarterly.

## My Sister's Words

Mary Ellen Kavanaugh
304 N. McBride St.

## SPOTLIGHT
## CHARLES ALEXANDER

Detroit, Michigan artist Charles Alexander, who has also written for the *Detroit Free Press* and the local gay papers *Ten Percent, Between the Lines,* and *Metro Gay Times,* has been out since 1954 and has lent his talents to numerous community organizations. A board member of the Detroit Area Gay/Lesbian Council and Affirmations Lesbian/Gay Community Center, and an advisory board member of Michigan's Triangle Foundation, Alexander helped found GLEAM (Gay/Lesbian Educators Association of Michigan) and Just Us (formerly called Unlimited Seniors). His award-winning artwork has been displayed locally at venues including the Detroit Artists Market.

Syracuse, NY 13203
Bookstore.

### New York Feminist Art Institute
91 Franklin
New York, NY 10013
phone: (212) 219-9590
School and resource center for women in the arts in the tristate area of New York City. Offers classes and workshops, special events and symposia, exhibitions and performances. Rents studio space at affordable rates to emerging artists, and sponsors annual benefit.

### Oscar Wilde Memorial Bookshop
15 Christopher St.
New York, NY 10014

### Pagan Press
John Lauritsen, Proprietor and Director
26 St. Mark's Pl.
New York, NY 10003
phone: (212) 674-3321
Pagan Press publishes scholarly books of interest to gay men. Does not accept unsolicited manuscripts. Reaches market through direct mail and wholesalers and distributors, including InKoBook.

### Panacea Books Ltd.
39 North Main St.
Port Chester, NY 10573
Bookstore.

### Rising Tide Press
Lee Boojamra, President
Alice Frier, Vice President
5 Kivy St.
Huntington Station, NY 11746
phone: (516) 427-1289
phone: (800) 648-5333
Rising Tide Press publishes mysteries, science fiction, romance, fantasy, and other fiction books for lesbian readers. Accepts unsolicited manuscripts. Reaches market through wholesalers, distributors, and direct sales to individuals and bookstores.

### A Room of Our Own
Elizabeth Shipley
511 9th St. #1
Brooklyn, NY 11215
Bookstore.

### Silkwood Books
633 Monroe Ave.
Rochester, NY 14607
Bookstore.

### Syracuse Gay and Lesbian Chorus
c/o Barbara L. Allen
PO Box 6796
Syracuse, NY 13217-6796

Alexander wrote the following thoughts on gay art and his own art for the Michigan paper *OUTSpoken,* where it was first printed in the December 1995 issue:

"I do not believe there is such a thing as gay art. To be sure, there is homoerotic art, as evidenced in the work of Michelangelo, Aubrey Beardsley, Charles Demuth, Paul Dadmus, David Hockney.... But gay art with a capital "G"? No....

"Robert Mapplethorpe is certainly identified as a gay artist, but only a small percentage of his output is sexually overt. If you look at those photographs with sexual content, are they unmistakably gay? I think not. Mapplethorpe's artistry transcends labels....

"For myself, I do not make gay art, although I do draw upon a creative psyche that is both masculine and feminine, anima bracketed with animus.

### *13th Moon: A Feminist Literary Magazine*

SUNY—Albany
English Department
Albany, NY 12222
Founded in 1973, *13th Moon* is an eclectic literary publication containing feature articles, poetry, fiction, art, and reviews. The journal particularly solicits feminist and working-class lesbian literature.

### T'n'T Classics Inc.

Francine L. Trevens, President
PO Box 1243, Ansonia Sta.
New York, NY 10023
phone: (213) 736-6279
fax: (212) 695-3219
T'n'T Classics, which absorbed the gay theater publisher JH Press, publishes gay plays and literature. Accepts unsolicited manuscripts. Reaches market through direct mail and wholesalers and distributors, including InKoBook and Baker & Taylor Books.

### Womankind Books

5 Kivy St.
Huntington Sta., NY 11746
Mail-order bookstore.

## NORTH CAROLINA

### The Bag Lady

Hope Swann
2914 Selwyn Ave.
Charlotte, NC 28209
Gift shop.

### *Ladyslipper Catalog*

Ladyslipper, Inc.
Durham, NC 27715
phone: (800) 634-6044
listen line: (919) 644-1942
The *Ladyslipper Catalog* sells well over a thousand selections of women's music, from soul to rock to African to Latina to country to folk to music that cannot be categorized. The catalog also carries a selection of videos, audio and print books, songbooks, "Babyslipper" selections for children, and "Mehn's Music."

### Lesbian Thesbians

c/o Laurie Wolf
PO Box 3295
Durham, NC 27715-3295

### Malaprop's Bookstore/Cafe

61 Haywood St.
Asheville, NC 28801

Because I work as closely to the subconscious as possible, my work seems to appeal to those who dip into the same collective unconscious as I. It is a bisexual wellspring.

"Much of my art is metaphysical in content, dealing with spiritual themes in an erotic manner. The sexual and the spiritual are two sides of the same coin. I have been in several religious art exhibits and won several prizes. I find this rather amusing because my religious art is also satiric....

"I have donated a great deal of my art to raise money for our community. I firmly believe that if one has a gift or a talent, such should be used to abet our common struggle.... We need gays and lesbians and bisexuals who are willing to give the three T's of the highly successful religious right—Time, Talent, and Tithe—and to use these resources as a means to achieving our civil rights as soon as possible."

**Rising Moon Books & Beyond**
316 East Blvd.
Charlotte, NC 28203
Bookstore.

**White Rabbit Books—Charlotte**
843 Central Ave.
Charlotte, NC 28204
Bookstore.

**White Rabbit Books—Greensboro**
1833 Spring Garden St.
Greensboro, NC 27403
Bookstore.

**White Rabbit Books—Raleigh**
Jim Baxter
309 W. Martin St.
Raleigh, NC 17601
Bookstore.

## OHIO

**Crazy Ladies Bookstore**
4039 Hamilton Ave.
Cincinnati, OH 45223

**Fan the Flames Feminist Book Collective**
3387 North High St.
Columbus, OH 43202
Bookstore.

**For Women Only**
13479 Howard Rd.
Millfield, OH 45761
Bookstore.

**Gifts of Athena**
2199 Lee Rd.
Cleveland Heights, OH 44118
Bookstore.

**An Open Book**
749 North High St.
Columbus, OH 43215
Bookstore.

**People Called Women**
3153 W. Central Ave.
Toledo, OH 43606
Bookstore.

**Pink Pyramid**
George Vancouver/Gary Allgeier
36A West Court St.
Cincinnati, OH 45202
Bookstore.

**Prime of Life**
Karen Boyle
623 Neely Manor

E. Palenstine, OH 44413
Mail-order bookstore.

### Tallula's
6725 W. Central Ave., Ste. N
Toledo, OH 43617
Gift shop.

## OKLAHOMA

### Herland Sister Resources Inc.
2312 NW 39th
Oklahoma City, OK 73112
Bookstore.

## OREGON

### Baba Yaga's Dream
Teri Chiacchi & Dawn Lamp
1235 Willamette St.
Eugene, OR 97401
Gift shop.

### Blue Earth
8215 SE 13th Ave.
Portland, OR 97202
Bookstore.

### Calyx Books
Margarita Donnelly, Managing Editor
PO Box B
Corvallis, OR 97339
phone: (503) 753-9384
Calyx publishes books, posters, art cards, and calendars by women and issues *Calyx: A Journal of Arts and Literature by Women.* Accepts unsolicited manuscripts; query for guidelines.

### Green Gables Bookstore
156 SW Coast St.
Newport, OR 97365

### In Her Image
3208 SE Hawthorne
Portland, OR 97214
phone: (503) 231-3726
Art gallery that features feminist art and maintains a small art publishing operation.

### In Other Words Women's Books & Resources
3734 SE Hawthorne Blvd.
Portland, OR 97214
Bookstore.

### Mother Kali's Books
720 E. 13th Ave.
Eugene, OR 97401
Bookstore.

### Widdershins: Books By, For & About Women
PO Box 42395
Portland, OR 97242
Mail-order bookstore.

### Womanshare Books
Billie Mericle, Secretary/Treasurer
PO Box 681
Grants Pass, OR 97526
phone: (503) 862-2807
Womanshare Books publishes work by women.

## PENNSYLVANIA

### Book Gallery
N. Whitehead
19 West Mechanic St.
New Hope, PA 18938
Bookstore.

### Bookwoman Books
Dorothy Kunzig
PO Box 67
Media, PA 19063
Mail-order bookstore.

### Cleis Press
Felice Newman, Publisher
PO Box 8933
Pittsburgh, PA 15221
phone: (412) 937-1555
fax: (412) 937-1567
e-mail: cleis@english-server.hss.cmu.edu
Cleis, a publisher of lesbian and gay titles, is represented to booksellers by Publishers Group West and distributed by Baker & Taylor, Blackwell North America, BookPeople, Brodart, Ingram, and other wholesalers.

### Gertrude Stein Memorial Bookshop
1003 E. Carson
Pittsburgh, PA 15203

### Giovanni's Room
345 South 12th St.
Philadelphia, PA 19107

Bookstore.

### Her Story Bookstore
K. L. Snyder
2 West Market St.
Hallam, York City, PA 17406

### Mogul Book and FilmWorks
Vincent Risoli
PO Box 2773
Pittsburgh, PA 15230
phone: (412) 461-0705
Publishes books on film, homosexuality, and fiction. Reaches market through direct mail and telephone sales.

### Saint Elmo's
Bill Nist
2214 E. Carson
Pittsburgh, PA 15203
Bookstore.

### Sappho's Garden
Connie & Jill
34 E. Ferry St.
New Hope, PA 18938
Bookstore.

### Sidewalk Revolution Press
PO Box 9062
Pittsburgh, PA 15224
phone: (212) 316-7601
Publishes lesbian feminist poetry.

### An Uncommon Vision
Janet Miller
1425 Gerywall Ln.
Wynnewood, PA 19096

## SOUTH CAROLINA

### Avalon
Marie Mocerino
2435 E. North St. #315
Greenville, SC 29615
Gift shop.

### Bluestocking Books
1215 Pulaski St.
Columbia, SC 29201
Bookstore.

### Equilibrium: Celebrating Girls and Young Women
1836 Ashley River Rd. #109
Charleston, SC 29407
Mail-order bookstore.

## SOUTH DAKOTA

### Oriana's Bookcafe
PO Box 479
359 Main St.
Hill City, SD 57745

## TENNESSEE

### Meristem
930 Cooper St.
Memphis, TN 38104
Bookstore.

## TEXAS

### Book Woman
918 W. 12th St.
Austin, TX 78703
Bookstore.

### Celebration!
108 W. 43rd St.
Austin, TX 78751
Bookstore.

### Crossroads Market—Dallas
Thomas Kane
3930 Cedar Springs Rd.
Dallas, TX 75219
Bookstore.

### Crossroads Market—Houston
610 W. Alabama
Houston, TX 77006
Bookstore.

### Liberty Books
1014-B N. Lamar Blvd.
Austin, TX 78703
Bookstore.

### Inklings: An Alternative Bookshop
1846 Richmond Ave.
Houston, TX 77098

### Liberal Press
Royal Reepe, Publicity
PO Box 140361
Las Colinas, TX 75016-0361

phone: (817) 483-9945
phone: (214) 686-5332
Affiliated with Publishers Associates, Liberal Press is a liberal, academic, and scholarly publisher emphasizing women, politics, gays, and social welfare. Distributes for Liberal Arts Press, Monument Press, Tanglewüld, and Ide House. Reaches market through direct mail, trade sales, and wholesalers.

### Rainbow Gifts
Kim Speights
3509 Beechwood Dr.
Texarkana, TX 75501
Gift shop.

### Textures
Martha A. Cabrera
5309 McCullough
San Antonio, TX 78212
Bookstore.

### Washington Square Cafe & Bookstore
1607 S. Washington
Amarillo, TX 79102

## UTAH

### A Woman's Place Bookstore #1
Foothill Village
1400 Foothill Dr., Ste. 236
Salt Lake City, UT 84108

### A Woman's Place Bookstore #2
Cottonwood Mall
4835 Highland Dr. #1205
Salt Lake City, UT 84117

### A Woman's Place Bookstore #3
PO Box 680196
1890 Bonanza Dr.
Park City, UT 84060

### A Woman's Place Bookstore #4
1182 East Draper Pkwy.
Draper, UT 84020

## VERMONT

### Everyone's Books
23 Elliot
Battleboro, VT 05301
Bookstore.

### Heartland Books
Linda Weiss
PO Box 1105
East Corinth, VT 05040
Mail-order bookstore.

### New Victoria Publishers, Inc.
Claudia Lamperti, Editor
Beth Dingman, Vice President
PO Box 27
Norwich, VT 05055-0027
phone: (802) 649-5297 or (800) 326-5297
fax: (802) 649-5297
e-mail: newvic@tele.com
A feminist literary and cultural organization that publishes fiction with lesbian/feminist content. Offers an audio tape. Accepts unsolicited manuscripts; send sample chapter and outline along with self-addressed, stamped envelope. Reaches market through direct mail and distributors.

## VIRGINIA

### Bad Habits Etc.
6123 Sewells Pt. Rd.
Norfolk, VA 23513
Bookstore.

### Max Images
808 Spotswood Ave.
Norfolk, VA 23517
Bookstore.

### Out of the Dark
Betsy Ashby
530 Randolph Rd.
Newport News, VA 23601
New Age/Wiccan Bookstore.

### Outright Books
9229 Granby St.
Norfolk, VA 23503
Bookstore.

### The Purple Moon
810 Caroline St.
Fredericksburg, VA 22401
Bookstore.

## WASHINGTON

### Beyond the Closet Bookstore
1501 Belmont Ave.
Seattle, WA 98122

### New Woman Books
Sherry Thompson
326 W. Meeker
Kent, WA 98032
Bookstore.

### Red and Black Books
432 15th Ave.
Seattle, WA 98117
Bookstore.

### Weaved Words
Terry Ames & Albertha Moses
2411 Walnut St.
Everett, WA 98201
Mail-order bookstore.

## WISCONSIN

### A Different World Bookstore
414 E. Grand Ave.
Beloit, WI 53703

### Rainbow Revolution Bookstore
PO Box 441
122 5th Ave. So.
Lacrosse, WI 54601

### A Room of One's Own
317 West Johnson St.
Madison, WI 53703
Bookstore.

# ONLINE RESOURCES

## THE WEB

### ArtAIDS
http://www.illumin.co.uk/artaids/
ArtAIDS is an online art gallery featuring donated work in the form of digital art, video, sound and writings. Throughout the site there are opportunities to donate money to help AIDS victims.

### Isle of Lesbos
http://www.sappho.com/
The Isle of Lesbos Web page is a collection of femme prose. Featured poets include Emily Dickinson and Gertrude Stein.

### Jeffrey
http://www.datalounge.com/Jeffrey
Film clips, reviews, and production notes are available from *Jeffrey*, the 1995 critically acclaimed comedy. This breakthrough film romanticized gay relationships without exploitation.

### LaFemme
http://www.webcom.com/~femme
LaFemme has created an online maze that is more confusing than entertaining. But the gem at this site is LaJava Femme, a collection of lesbian art, entertainment, and literature resources.

### Lambda Literary Awards
http://www.books.com/awards/lambwin.htm
Seaching for a good book? Book Stack Unlimited, an online bookstore, features biographies of authors who have won the Lambda Literary Award. This award honors excellence in gay and lesbian literature.

## ONLINE SERVICES

### Lambda Rising Online
AOL: lambda rising
Lambda Rising is an online gay/lesbian bookstore. Stop by to browse through books and other items with a gay or lesbian theme. Online orders are accepted.

From all corners of the earth, from all walks of life, from all spiritual backgrounds and from every generation, spanning the multitude of skin hues and personal histories, we form a community. What a relief it is to discover that we are not alone, that others share our hopes and fears, that there is a phone number we can call or an Internet source we can tap or a physical place we can go for support or for fun. What a joy to celebrate with our sisters and brothers in a Pride rally. What a comfort to know that, somewhere, you belong.

Within our community, we often disagree with each other. There's the old separatist-versus-mainstream debate: Should we work independent from, or together with, the mainstream? Does our uniqueness—whatever makes us separate and special—best defines us and our contribution to the world at large, or should we highlight those qualities that show how similar we are to non-queers?

Which leads to the terminology debate: Is "queer" a good, brief-but-inclusive term, or does it carry too many historically negative connotations? Does "gay" define us all? How about the clinical "homosexual" and "bisexual"? Can we lump "transsexual" and "transvestite" together under one "transgender" category? Because we've come to tend toward inclusion rather than exclusion, the unwieldy "lesbian-gay-bisexual-transgender" label (often in shorthand as *lesbigay* or *lgbt*) is becoming the term of choice. "Our community," in a pinch, often suffices nicely.

Political debates, naturally, arise as well. Gay Republicans, represented by the Log Cabin Federation, seek to wrest their party from dangerous, ultra-conservative right-wing opinions and policies, while others believe the Democratic Party or even a third party is the answer.

To "out" or not to out: another debate. How best to fight and prevent AIDS: another debate. To serve the military openly or not to tell; to reform or abandon our churches; to marry or not to marry: still more debates.

So we debate, we disagree, we argue—and we compromise, learn a little, reaffirm our bonds, and strengthen the diverse community we've built.

And we did build this lesbigaytrans community. Although people like us have always existed, in all cultures all over the world, we did not always have this sense of community to support and connect us. It was only after a same-sex orientation was defined scientifically in the 19th century that people began to organize to end the social and legal discrimination we faced. In 1897, the Scientific Humanitarian Committee in Berlin became the first homosexual rights group in the world. Twenty-seven years later, Chicago's Society for Human Rights became the first formally organized U.S. group advocating gay support and understanding—sort of. (Its mission, according to Barry D. Adam in *The Rise of a Gay and Lesbian Movement,* was to protect people who were abused and faced legal discrimination because of their "mental and physical abnormalities.") The 1950s saw the formation of two more civil rights organizations in California, the Mattachine Society for gay men, and Daughters of Bilitis for lesbians.

By 1969, 50 lesbian and gay organizations existed in the United States. Public awareness grew and the civil rights movement gained momentum, and four years later there were 800; a decade later that number had more than tripled. Today, an estimated 3,000 lesbian, gay, bisexual, and transgender organizations are active in the United States and Canada, including at least 65 community centers.

This chapter lists those community centers, as well as telephone information lines, state and neighborhood Pride committees, and ethnic and social groups, large and small. In addition, "spotlight" features describe the recent formation of the National Association of Lesbian and Gay Community Centers, dedicated to nurturing new centers and strengthening the links among existing ones; Affirmations Lesbian and Gay Community Center in Ferndale, Michigan; the national gay social fraternity Delta Lambda Phi, with at least 18 chapters and colonies across the United States; and Detroit's inspirational Men of Color Motivational Group.

## BRAZIL

### Lesbian Information Network

Miriam Martinho
Caixa Postal 65092
Sao Paulo, SP 01390-970
phone: 11 2512838
fax: 11 2845610
e-mail: outroolhar@ax.apc.org
Comprised of women between the ages of 20 and 50 years old, the Lesbian Information Network strives to create a network of contacts for lesbians; to minimize marginalization and isolation of lesbians; to provide venues for interaction and expression of opinions, feelings, and creativity; and to increase public awareness of the causes and effects of discrimination against women, especially lesbians. The group, founded in 1990, maintains a speakers' bureau, disseminates information, and holds books, periodicals, video recordings, and other archival

materials about homosexuality. The network, which meets semiannually, publishes a quarterly bulletin called *Um Outro Olhar.*

## CANADA

### BRITISH COLUMBIA

#### Vancouver Gay & Lesbian Center

1170 Bute St.
Vancouver, BC V6E1Z6
phone: (604) 684-6869

### ONTARIO

#### Human Sexuality Program

Toronto Board of Education
155 College Street
Toronto, ON M5T 1P6
phone: (416) 397-3755

#### Lesbian & Gay Ottawa—Hull

Box 2919, Station D
Ottawa, ON KIP 5W9
phone: (613) 238-1717

#### Pink Triangle Services

PO Box 3043, Station D
Ottawa, ON K1P 6H6
phone: (613) 828-4759

## COSTA RICA

#### Grupo Lesbico Feminista Costarricense—las Entendidas (GLFC)

Calle 15, Avenida 6
Apartamentos Blancas Umana 1
Apartado 1057
San Jose, Costa Rica
phone: 5513849

The women in GLFC defend the lesbian identity by fighting socio-cultural stereotypes. Founded in 1986, GLFC seeks to provide opportunities for lesbians to interact and communicate; conducts support groups for victims of incest and alcohol abuse; organizes workshops and recreation activities; offers medical, legal, and psychological help; maintains a specialized documentation center; and publishes a quarterly bulletin, *Boletina.*

*The epitome of community: Hundreds of thousands gather on the Mall during the 1987 March on Washington for Lesbian and Gay Rights. (Photo by Ron Thomas; courtesy UPI/Bettman.)*

## ENGLAND

#### Ligo Samseksamaj Geesperantistoj (LSG)

Peter A. Danning, Honorary Secretary
c/o Peter A. Danning
G/F 68 Church Rd.
Richmond, Surrey TW10 6LN
phone: 181 9482256

Ligo Samseksamaj Geesperantistoj is a network of organizations and individuals in 44 countries who speak Esperanto—a language derived as much as possible from the chief European languages—and are either homosexual or sympathetic to homosexuals. Founded in 1977, the group fosters international communication and support. Group members offer travel accommodations or introductions to suitable clubs and act as interpreters for visiting members. LSG's newsletter, *FORUMO,* appears bimonthly.

**SPOTLIGHT**

## NATIONAL ASSOCIATION of COMMUNITY CENTERS

Following years of loose affiliation, lesbian and gay community centers from across the U.S. have united in coalition, providing a grassroots base for national organizing. The National Association of Lesbian and Gay Community Centers aims to nurture new centers, to further link existing ones, and to coordinate nationwide efforts among them.

Formally established shortly before its first official meeting at the National Gay and Lesbian Task Force's November 1995 *Creating Change* conference in Detroit, NALGCC represents at least 65 LGB centers, with estimated staffing of nearly 500 people and combined budgets of $30 million. The umbrella

The group's annual meeting takes place the last week of July in conjunction with the World Esperanto Congresses.

### NORTHERN IRELAND

#### Lesbian Line

Box 44
Belfast, Antrim
phone: 1232 238668
Lesbian Line offers advice, support, and information to lesbian women in Northern Ireland, provides a safe place for lesbian women to develop friendships, and sponsors lesbian-oriented social events.

## UNITED STATES

### ALASKA

#### Arctic Gay/Lesbian Association (AGLA)

Box 82290
College, AK 99708
AGLA promotes understanding and sponsors educational programs within the College, Alaska area on issues of sexual orientation. The group was formerly known as Identity.

### ARIZONA

#### Lesbian, Gay, Bi Community Center

422 N. 4th Ave.
Tucson, AZ 85705
phone: (602) 624-1779

### ARKANSAS

#### University of Arkansas Gay and Lesbian Student Association

Alan Brewer, President
Arkansas Union 517
Fayetteville, AR 72701
phone: (501) 575-5255
The students, faculty, staff, and nonstudents in the Gay and Lesbian Student Association provide education on issues affecting the gay/lesbian community. Founded in 1982, the group seeks to reduce prejudice and stereotyping; offers support and advocates on behalf of gays and lesbians; and sponsors cultural events, a speakers' bureau, workshops, and AIDS education.

### CALIFORNIA

#### Bill Wilson Center

3490 The Alameda

organization grew out of ad hoc meetings held among LGB center leaders at various conferences since 1987.

As one of its first major pursuits, the association will launch a sweeping voter registration project in 1996. The massive, non-partisan campaign intends to rally gay and lesbian voters throughout the country. Similar to traditional registration campaigns conducted by the League of Women Voters, as well as the more strategic mobilizing of the Christian Coalition, the registration drive will give new visibility to lesbians and gays as a voting constituency.

According to Richard Burns, executive director of the Lesbian and Gay Community Services Center in New York City and one of NALGCC's founders, community centers represent a significant "untapped" resource within the lesbian and gay movement. He suggests that national groups headquartered

Santa Clara, CA 95050
phone: (408) 243-0222

### Billy DeFrank Lesbian & Gay Community Center

175 Stockton Avenue
San Jose, CA 95126-2760
phone: (408) 293-2429

### Fresno Lesbian and Gay Pride Committee

c/o Elizabeth B. Maines
2703 N Van Ness Blvd.
Fresno, CA 93704-5550

### Gay Asian-Pacific Support Network

c/o Peter Corpus
PO Box 461104
Los Angeles, CA 90046-9104

### Gay & Lesbian Community Services Center

1625 North Schrader Blvd.
Los Angeles, CA 90028
phone: (213) 993-7451 or (213) 993-7450
Founded in 1971, the Los Angeles Center is the largest of the nations's gay and lesbian community centers.

### G/L Resource Center

126 E. Haley St., Ste. A-17
Santa Barbara, CA 93101
phone: (805) 963-3636

### Gay Pride Celebration Committee of San Jose

William Kiley, President
265 Meridan Ave., Ste. 6
San Jose, CA 95126-2906
phone: (408) 235-1034
e-mail: SJPRIDE@VV.com
The committee, founded in 1986, supports and promotes Gay Pride in San Jose, California. The group donates money to local gay charities, educates the public and promotes civil liberties; and sponsors a festival, parade, and street party. The journal *Pride Guide* appears annually.

### Lesbian, Gay, Bisexual & Transgendered Community Center

PO Box 8280
Santa Cruz, CA 95061-8280
phone: (408) 425-LGBC

### Lesbian and Gay Men's Center

PO Box 3357
San Diego, CA 92163
phone: (619) 692-2077

in Washington have a limited capacity for addressing local needs. "Community centers are engines of the gay and lesbian grassroots movement," he says. "NALGCC will provide a critical boost to the efforts aimed at local municipalities, school boards, and state legislatures."

*By Tim Retzloff. First printed in* Between the Lines, *January 1996.*

### Men of All Colors Together: A Gay Multiracial Organization for All People, Los Angeles Chapter

Paul Cloutier, Co-Chair
c/o MACT/LA
7985 Santa Monica Blvd., Ste. 109-136
Los Angeles, CA 90046
phone: (213) 664-4716
A local chapter of the National Association of Black and White Men Together: A Gay Multiracial Organization for All People, the Los Angeles chapter comprises black, white, and other men who are gay or bisexual. The group provides support and encourages equality; engages in cultural, educational, political, and social activities; sponsors other local gay groups; conducts charitable activities; and publishes a monthly newsletter and information on AIDS.

### Pacific Center for Human Growth—Berkeley

Robert Fuentes, Board Chair
2712 Telegraph Ave.
Berkeley, CA 94705
phone: (510) 548-8283
fax: (510) 548-2938
The Pacific Center for Human Growth, founded in 1973, comprises gay, lesbian, bisexual, transsexual, and transvestite individuals in the San Francisco Bay area of California. The center promotes positive lifestyles for members; provides support, referrals, information, outreach, and counseling to members; conducts weekly support group meetings; maintains a speakers' bureau; operates an HIV/AIDS counselor and advocacy program; and provides training to organizations, schools, and other nonprofits.

Pacific Center for Human Growth—Walnut Creek
1250 Pine Street, Suite 301
Walnut Creek, CA 94596
phone: (510) 939-7711

### Palm Springs Lesbian/Gay Pride (PSLGP)

Richard Black, President
PO Box 2116
Cathedral City, CA 92235
phone: (619) 321-6500
fax: (619) 770-9850
Founded in 1992, Palm Springs Lesbian/Gay Pride supports and promotes gay and lesbian rights, awards grants to local gay charities, and sponsors the annual two-day Gay Pride festival.

### San Jose State University Gay, Lesbian and Bisexual Alliance (GLBASJSU)

Nicole Matos, Co-President
1 Washington Sq.
SAS Box 55
San Jose, CA 95192-0038
phone: (408) 236-2002
Students, staff, and faculty at San Jose State University united to provide a "safe environment" for lesbians, gays, bisexuals, and supportive non-gays to socialize. Founded in 1971, the alliance works to increase understanding between gays and non-gays; maintains a speakers' bureau; sponsors Pride Week and a film festival; conducts a residence hall outreach program; and offers voice mail referral to switchboards and local organizations.

### Spectrum Center for Lesbian, Gay, and Bisexual Concerns

Lea Brown, Program Director
1000 Sir Francis Drake Blvd.
San Anselmo, CA 94960
phone: (415) 457-1115
fax: (415) 457-2838

*Terry Chisholm is president of Delta Lambda Phi at Eastern Michigan University.*

Founded in 1982, Spectrum provides nonjudgmental support and advocacy for the lesbian/gay/bisexual community in Marin County, California. The center conducts support groups and publishes a semiannual newsletter.

### Stonewall Alliance of Chico

Eric S. Ruben, Executive Officer
PO Box 8855
Chico, CA 95927-8855
phone: (916) 893-3336
The Stonewall Alliance of Chico, founded in 1990, serves the gay, lesbian, and bisexual communities of the northern Sacramento Valley. The alliance operates a community services center and publishes a quarterly newsletter, *Centerstone*.

### Trikone

Dipti Ghosh and Tinku Ali Ishtiag, Co-chairs
Box 21354
San Jose, CA 95151
phone: (408) 270-8776
fax: (408) 274-2733
e-mail: trikone@rahul.net
WEB site: http://www.rahal.net//trikone
Trikone is a support group for gay or lesbian persons from southern Asia. Founded in 1985, the group seeks to help participants come to terms with their sexual orientation. Trikone networks with homosexual groups around the world and is compiling material for a gay/lesbian archives to document the history of homosexuality in the area. *Trikone Magazine,* which appears quarterly, includes personal stories, interviews, news about gay and lesbian South Asians, letters, personal ads, and resource listings.

## COLORADO

### Colorado State University Student Organization of Gays, Lesbians, and Bisexuals (SOGLB)

Randy McCrillis
Box 206

## SPOTLIGHT
## DELTA LAMBDA PHI

Delta Lambda Phi is a frat whose members like to have parties for the sake of having parties. They enjoy helping local charities in their communities, planning social events and fund-raisers, and just hanging out and relaxing with fellow brothers. That is what being part of a fraternity is all about. The guys in the Delta Lambda Phi house are like the guys in any frat across the nation with one exception. Most are gay or bisexual.

Established in Washington, D.C., in 1987, Delta Lambda Phi National Social Fraternity was created to offer the kind of opportunity that many gay men on college campuses never had: a fraternity that would not discriminate on the basis of sexual orientation. Enrollment is not limited to only gays and

Ft. Collins, CO 80523
phone: (303) 491-7232
SOGLB provides social, cultural, and political support to gays, lesbians, and bisexuals in the Fort Collins area. Formerly known as the Ft. Collins Gay and Lesbian Alliance Activities Center (FCGLAAC), the group works to educate people about gay, lesbian, and bisexual issues; sponsors Gay Awareness Week annually, in April; and publishes a quarterly newsletter.

### Gay, Lesbian and Bisexual Community Services Center of Colorado
PO Drawer 18E
Denver, CO 80218-0140
phone: (303) 831-6268

### Lamda Community Center
1691 Saulsbury Court
Loveland, CO 80538
phone: (970) 635-9863

### McMaster Center
301 S. Union
Colorado Springs, CO 80910
phone: (719) 578-3160

## CONNECTICUT

### Triangle Community Center
PO Box 4062
East Norwalk, CT 06855
phone: (203) 853-0600

## DISTRICT OF COLUMBIA

### Delta Lambda Phi National Social Fraternity
Chris Hunt, Extensions Chair
Washington, DC
phone: (800) 587-FRAT
National social fraternity for gay and bisexual men.

### National Coming Out Day (NCOD)
Wesley Combs, Project Director
PO Box 34640
Washington, DC 20043-4640
phone: (202) 628-4160 or (800) 866-6263
fax: (202) 347-5323
National Coming Out Day is a project of the Human Rights Campaign (see **Legal Issues and Political Action**) that works to increase the gay/lesbian community's visibility and demonsrate its diversity by coordinating National Coming Out Day, an annu-

bisexuals, though. Straight men are welcome. Delta Lambda Phi is based on the Greek model that rules all fraternities, and they have rushes, pledge programs, secret initiation ceremonies, a crest, and rituals like any other Greek frat.

Members find Delta Lambda Phi a place on a college campus where a gay man can be himself and not have to worry about hiding his sexual orientation for fear of being shunned, a place to count on peers for support and friendship, and most importantly, a place where gay men can come together to build strong and lasting friendships based on respect, loyalty, and trust.

Describing the diverse membership of the Eastern Michigan University chapter—students of all ethnicities, foreign students, rural and big city dwellers, a member of a campus military group, and a varsity athlete, among others—chapter president Terry Chisholm told Nancy Costello of the Michigan

al campaign taking place on October 11; encouraging gay and lesbian individuals to "come out" to friends, family, and coworkers; and coordinating a national public relations campaign. NCOD offers support and technical assistance to local gay/lesbian organizations; makes available shirts, posters, and buttons to organizations for wholesale distribution and retail; conducts national and local educational programs and activities; maintains a speakers' bureau; and publishes *Out and About.*

## FLORIDA

### The Alliance for Learning About Sexual Orientation (ALSO)

PO Box 7382
Sarasota, FL 34278-7382
phone: (813) 252-ALSO

### Black and White Men Together/South Florida (BWMTSF)

Roland Wilkins
PO Box 15581
Miami, FL 33101-5581
phone: (305) 463-4528 or (305) 751-3318
The South Florida chapter of the national group includes men of all races working together to understand racial and cultural differences and to celebrate diversity. The chapter's annual recognition award honors individuals who promote better understanding, fellowship, and friendship among gay men of all races and nationalities. The group's newsletter, *Chiaroscuro,* appears bimonthly.

### Florida State University Lesbian Gay Bisexual Student Union (LGBSU)

Lisa Pontoriero
PO Box 65914
Tallahassee, FL 32313
phone: (904) 644-8804
Founded in 1973 and comprised of gay and lesbian students at Florida State University and the neighboring community, LGBSU provides education on gay and lesbian issues and support.

### Gay Information Services of Pinellas (GISP)

PO Box 14323
St. Petersburg, FL 33733
phone: (813) 586-4297
hotline: (813) 229-8839
Since 1983, Gay Information Services has provided information, referral, and support to the gay and lesbian community in the

newspaper *Between the Lines,* "We have conservative gays and outrageous flamboyant queens. There's a little attitude here and there, but we get along."

The EMU chapter joined the national frat in December 1995, having existed for two years as Chi Theta Sigma, a gay fraternity that started out closeted until members insisted on going public. Having changed its name upon joining the national fraternity, Delta Lambda Phi hopes soon to be included in university-sanctioned Greek groups like the Interfraternity Council. "EMU

Pinellas County, Florida area (Tampa Bay and surrounding areas). The group has also been known as The Line.

### Gay/Lesbian Community Services of Central Florida

Lara Anderson, Director
PO Box 533446
Orlando, FL 32853-3446
phone: (407) 425-4527

## GEORGIA

### Atlanta Gay and Lesbian Community Center

63 Twelfth Street
Atlanta, GA 30309
phone: (404) 876-5372

### The Gay Center

63 12th Street
Atlanta, GA 30309
phone: (404) 876-5372

### Georgia Girth and Mirth

PO Box 190972
Atlanta, GA 31119-0972

## HAWAII

### Gay & Lesbian Community Services Center

1820 University Avenue, 2nd Floor
Honolulu, HI 96822
phone: (808) 951-7000

### Pride Parade and Rally Council

William Woods, President
PO Box 37083
Honolulu, HI 96837-0083
phone: (808) 532-9000
Founded in 1989, the council promotes the annual Gay and Lesbian Pride Parade and Rally in Hawaii, and donates funds to gay rights causes.

## ILLINOIS

### Coalition for Positive Sexuality

3712 North Broadway, Box 191
Chicago, IL 60613
phone: (312) 604-1654

### Horizon Community Services

961 West Montana Street
Chicago, IL 60614
phone: (312) 472-6469

### North Suburban Gays (NSG)

Scott Ohlman, President
c/o Ken Ayers
Box 465
Wilmette, IL 60091-0465
phone: (708) 251-8853
Founded in 1981, North Suburban Gays serves as a social and educational forum for gay men and lesbians from the northern suburbs of Chicago. The newsletter *Northern Lites* appears monthly.

## INDIANA

### Ball State University Lesbian, Bisexual, Gay Student Association (LBGSA)

Kerry Poynter, President
Student Center
Box 16
Muncie, IN 47306

would welcome it," Greek affairs advisor Bob Gordon told Costello. "I look forward to them making a positive impact on campus."

Since the first chapter was established in Washington, D.C., more than 18 other chapters and colonies (a colony is a future chapter) have sprung up around the country. The West Coast has the highest number of chapters, but chapters can be found in Arizona, Michigan, Minnesota, and Wisconsin as well.

*By Eric Dobson*

phone: (317) 28-LBGSA
Founded in 1974, LBGSA provides opportunities for anonymous, safe, and friendly interaction for gay, lesbian, and bisexual students, and works to develop social and political awareness among members. Affiliated with the National Gay and Lesbian Task Force, the group meets weekly and publishes a newsletter called *Family Values*.

### Crisis Center for Human Understanding

101 North Montgomery Street
Gary, IN 46403
phone: (219) 938-7070

### Gays and Lesbians at Notre Dame/St. Mary's College

John Blandford, Co-Chair
PO Box 194
Notre Dame, IN 46556-0194
phone: (219) 287-6665
Students, faculty, and staff members at Notre Dame and St. Mary's colleges in Indiana united to improve conditions for gay and lesbian students. Founded in 1984, the group works to combat homophobia and heterosexism through support, education, and fellowship.

### Purdue LesBiGay Network

Lupita Acosta, President
Box 512 PMU
Purdue University
West Lafayette, IN 47907
phone: (317) 496-1647
Founded in 1992 as the Purdue Gay Alliance, the Purdue LesBiGay Network is a social, political, and educational organization for gay, lesbian, bisexual, and transgender students, faculty, and staff at Purdue University and interested individuals.

## IOWA

### Gay and Lesbian Resource Center (GLRC)

Michael J. Current, Executive Director
PO Box 7008
Des Moines, IA 50309-7008
4211 Grand Ave.
Des Moines, IA 50312
phone: (515) 281-0634
Founded in 1985, the Gay and Lesbian Resource Center promotes public understanding and acceptance of gay and lesbian people. The center conducts networking activities within the community; assists in improving access to supportive human services; maintains a phone line, library, and speakers' bureau; sponsors support groups, an anti-violence project, and youth services; and offers HIV/AIDS educational programs. The *GLRC Report* is published monthly.

### Iowa State University Lesbian/Gay/Bisexual Alliance (LGBA)

Michael Selha, President
39 Memorial Union
Iowa State University
Ames, IA 50011
phone: (515) 294-2104
fax: (515) 294-5239
Founded in 1983 and comprised of lesbians, gay men, bisexuals, and heterosexual supporters at Iowa State University, LGBA offers support for members; provides public information and educational forums on les-

bian, gay, and bisexual issues; and publishes a weekly newsletter called *Queen Bits* and a monthly magazine called *Alloy.*

### University of Iowa Gay People's Union (PSNLGBC)

Jason Wiley, Spokesperson
SAC/IMU
University of Iowa
Iowa City, IA 52242
phone: (319) 335-3251
Gayline: (319) 335-3877
The Gay People's Union, founded in 1970, includes gay, lesbian, and bisexual individuals in Iowa City and Coralville, Iowa. The union serves as a forum for discussion of common concerns among members; seeks to address homophobia on the University of Iowa campus; conducts protests and social gatherings; holds semi-monthly support group meetings; sponsors Iowa City Pride Week; and publishes the *Gay Iowan* newsletter.

## KANSAS

### Lesbian, Bisexual and Gay Services of Kansas

Mr. Joe Cuevas and Ms. Sam Korshin, Directors
Matt Hydeman, Office Coordinator
Box 13, Kansas Union
Lawrence, KS 66045
phone: (913) 864-3091
e-mail: lbgsok@ukanaix.cc.ukans.edu
Gays, lesbians, bisexuals and their supporters make up the group, which used to be called Gay and Lesbian Services of Kansas. Founded in 1970, the group seeks to educate the public on gay and lesbian issues, reduce homophobia, and provide a safe environment for gays, bisexuals, and lesbians. The group meets every Thursday and publishes a monthly newsletter, *Vanguard.*

## LOUISIANA

### Lesbian & Gay Community Center of New Orleans

816 North Rampart Street
New Orleans, LA 70116
phone: (504) 522-1103

### Louisiana State University Gay and Lesbian Student Association (GLSA)

PO Box 16031
Baton Rouge, LA 70893-6031
Founded in 1972, GLSA promotes awareness and understanding of homophilic issues; conducts political, social, and educational activities; and sponsors fundraising programs.

## MAINE

### Alliance for Sexual Diversity (Powers House)

Libby Stuart, Coordinator
96 Falmouth St.
Portland, ME 04103
phone: (207) 874-6596
The Alliance for Sexual Diversity is a college-based organization for lesbian feminists, gays, and bisexuals. Founded in 1976, the alliance seeks to educate the campus community on homophobia and provides outreach and networking services.

### Ingraham

PO Box 5370, Station A
Portland, ME 04101
phone: (207) 774-HELP
Referral service.

### Outright (Central Maine)

PO Box 802
Auburn, ME 04212
phone: (207) 783-2557

### Outright (Portland)

PO Box 5077
Portland, ME 04101
phone: (207) 828-6560

## MARYLAND

### Gay and Lesbian Community Center of Baltimore (GLCCB)

Jack Travis, President
Michael Linemann, Center Coordinator
241 W. Chase St.
Baltimore, MD 21201
phone: (410) 837-5445
hotline: (410) 837-8888 (7-10 p.m.)

hotline: (410) 837-8529
fax: (410) 837-8512
Individuals at the Baltimore center work to enhance and unite the gay and lesbian community through the achievement of equality, human dignity, and respect for diversity. The center, founded in 1977, offers preventive health education programs; operates the William Wolfe Institute for Gay and Lesbian Studies and various social/support groups for women, men, and youth; and sponsors the Baltimore Gay-Lesbian Pride Parade and Festival and other gay/lesbian cultural events. The group publishes the *Baltimore Gaypaper* semi-monthly and a directory, *Focus Guide*, annually.

## MASSACHUSETTS

### Boston University Lesbian/Gay/Bisexual Alliance

Kelly Dunn, President
Student Activities Office
George Sherman Union
775 Commonwealth Ave.
Boston, MA 02215
phone: (617) 353-9808
Founded in 1969, the Alliance includes college students, faculty, and staff of Boston University. The group offers campus educational programs on gay/lesbian issues; provides a social outlet for gay/lesbian students; addresses harassment and discrimination issues; sponsors speakers and dances; and meets weekly.

### GAMIT—Gays, Lesbians, Bisexuals, and Friends at MIT

Thomas E. Wilhelm, General Coordinator
Massachusetts Institute of Technology 50-306
Walker Memorial
142 Memorial Dr.
Cambridge, MA 02139
phone: (617) 253-5440
Founded in 1969, GAMIT is a support group that fosters acceptance of homosexual and bisexual students in the greater Boston/Cambridge area. The group sponsors frequent social events and meets weekly.

### Gay Community News Prisoner Project (GCNPP)

Tatiana Schreiber, Director
25 West St.
Boston, MA 02111-1213
phone: (617) 426-4469
The Gay Community News Prisoner Project supports prisoners by providing them with pen pals, book donations, and information on topics like AIDS. The project, founded in 1980, seeks to educate the gay community about inequities in the justice system, including bias against prisoners who are incarcerated because they cannot afford adequate legal assistance, racism in the prison system, and anti-gay bias in prisons. The project publishes a weekly newspaper for members.

### Gay and Lesbian Information Services

West Greenfield, MA
phone: (413) 731-5403

### Gay, Lesbian and Straight Society (GLASS)

86 Washington St.
Greenfield, MA 01060

### Northeastern University Bisexual, Lesbian, & Gay Association (NUBILAGA)

Ell Student Center, Rm. 260
360 Huntington Ave.
Boston, MA 02115
phone: (617) 373-2738
Founded in 1974, the association provides a supportive social atmosphere and promotes the concerns of the gay community. NUBILAGA sponsors social outings, day trips, extended trips, and community related activities, and publishes the newsletter *Bay Windows* and the *Gay Yellow Pages* directory.

## MICHIGAN

### Affirmations Lesbian and Gay Community Center

Julie Enszer, Executive Director
195 W. Nine Mile Rd.
Ferndale, MI 48220
phone: (810) 398-7105
hotline: (800) 398-GAYS
fax: (810) 541-1943
e-mail: affirmglcc@aol.com

Founded in early 1989 as a telephone support line staffed by volunteers, Affirmations has grown into a 1,700-member community center. Affirmations provides support toward the development of a positive self image for individual gay, lesbian, and bisexual people and for the community as a whole. The center maintains a speakers' bureau and hosts Town Hall meetings, regular social activities, and holiday events. Group services include personal growth and educational groups, peer support groups for adults and youth, and a mentorship project for lesbian and gay youth. The group also publishes a monthly newsletter and community calendar and a community directory. Affirmations' Bayard Rustin Resource Center houses books, magazines, newspapers, and videos, and its Pittman/Puckett Art Gallery features works by artists in the lesbian, gay, and bisexual communities.

### Ambitious Amazons/Lesbian Connection/Lesbian Center

PO Box 811
East Lansing, MI 48826
phone: (517) 371-5257

### Billionaire Boys Club

PO Box 439431
Detroit, MI 48243

### Black Gay Men Together

Ann Arbor, MI
phone: (313) 936-1809

### Black Lesbian Womyn and Gay Men in Struggle

Ann Arbor, MI
phone: (313) 936-1809

### Black and White Men Together (BWMT)

PO Box 248831
Detroit, MI 48224
phone: (313) 864-1154
Sponsors travel events, dinners, bar nights, and parties.

### Capitol Men's Club

PO Box 18062
Lansing, MI 48901
phone: (517) 484-6342 or (517) 336-0965
Publishes a bi-monthly newsletter and sponsors four parties a year, plus various other social activities.

### Crossroads

PO Box 1245
Royal Oak, MI 48068
phone: (810) 357-3267
Social and educational meetings for people who cross dress.

### Detroit Area Gay/Lesbian Council (DAG/LC)

Lee Holmberg, President
29209 Northwestern Highway
Office No. 507
Southfield, MI 48043-1024
phone: (810) 988-0242
or
PO Box 4425
Troy, MI 48009
phone: (810) 853-2488
The council, founded in 1981, serves as a clearinghouse for sharing information and the activities of different organizations, and sponsors the annual Pridefest. The council's community calendar appears monthly.

### Detroit Studs 30

PO Box 52035
Livonia, MI 48152
phone: (313) 471-0341
Leather group.

### Forum Foundation/Living Well Conference

21700 Northwestern Highway
Suite 840
Southfield, MI 48075
phone: (810) 582-1588
Foundation and annual workshop conference serving the lesbian and gay community.

### Friends North

Box 562
Traverse City, MI 49685-0562
phone: (616) 946-1804
Friends North, organized in 1986, provides a support group for gays, lesbians, and their friends in northwestern Michigan. The group sponsors social activities, networking, and referrals; provides a Community

Needs Fund for financial assistance; and sponsors speakers and workshops. Formerly known as Dignity of Northern Michigan, Friends North publishes a bimonthly newsletter called *Networking 45 Degrees North.*

### Friends Southwest

PO Box 2391
Kalamazoo, MI 49003
phone: (616) 345-9399
Social support group for gays and lesbians in southwestern Michigan.

### Gay Connection

PO Box 1806
Royal Oak, MI 48068
(810) 644-7077
Socialization and discussion of topics related to the gay lifestyle.

### Gay and Lesbian Alano Club

PO Box 1000
Dearborn, MI 48121-1000
(313) 545-0132 or (313) 886-6422

### Gays and Lesbians Older and Wiser (GLOW)

1010 Wall St.
Ann Arbor, MI 48109
Social support group.

### Girth and Mirth

PO Box 39523
Redford, MI 48239
phone: (313) 531-3907 or (313) 531-0733
Social and educational group for big men and their admirers.

### Just Us

PO Box 20703
Ferndale, MI 48220
phone: (810) 681-4791 or (810) 588-4743
Social/support group for seniors.

### Kalamazoo Gay-Lesbian Resource Center

Jim Knox, Assistant Secretary
PO Box 1532
Kalamazoo, MI 49005-1532
phone: (616) 345-7878 or (616) 345-2437
The Kalamazoo resource center provides support and services to gay and lesbian people. The center operates the Lesbian-Gay Resource Line and the Resource Center Youth Support Group, and publishes a quarterly newsletter that features news and resources for lesbian and gay people in South West Michigan.

*Detroit's Men of Color Motivational Group rallies at the 1993 March on Washington for Lesbian and Gay Rights. (Photo by Pam Mc Intosh.)*

### Kindred Souls

PO Box 43650
Detroit, MI 48226
phone: 882-9854
Collective of over 30 African American women artists.

### Lambda Car Club

23072 Beech St.
Dearborn, MI 48124
phone: (313) 563-5824

### Lavender Morning

D. Iffland, Executive Officer
PO Box 729
Kalamazoo, MI 49005
Founded in 1980, Lavender Morning provides services and programs for feminists and lesbians in the Kalamazoo, Michigan area. The *Lavender Morning* newsletter appears monthly.

## SPOTLIGHT
## MEN of COLOR

"We can be, we will be, we must be—the best we can be." So states the Men of Color Motivational Group, a Detroit-based network for African American men. An irrepressibly energetic, optimistic, and fun group, Men of Color focuses on self-esteem, self-awareness, and education in supporting African American men with HIV and AIDS. In addition to their "Motivational Tuesday" meetings, Men of Color sponsors Arms of Love, a weekly support group for gay men with HIV/AIDS, and Angels Without Wings, a hospital visitation program to assist in patients' physical needs as well as boost morale and provide encouragement.

Founded several years ago, Men of Color did not begin as an explicitly gay organization. Its membership "snowballed," according to co-founder Charles

### Lesbian Alliance
PO Box 6423
East Lansing, MI 48826
phone: (517) 372-2882
Social, political, educational activities for lesbians.

### Lesbian Gay Community Network of Western Michigan
909 Cherry St. SE
Grand Rapids, MI 49506-1403
phone: (616) 458-3511 or (616) 241-4297
The Network promotes greater public acceptance of gay and lesbian lifestyles.

### LG Society
PO Box 6184
Jackson, MI 49204
(517) 783-6874
Weekly support group for lesbians, gays, and bisexuals.

### Men of Color Motivational Group (MOC)
mailing address: PO Box 11499
Detroit, MI 48211
meetings: St. Matthew's & St. Joseph's Church
8850 Woodward, Detroit, MI
colorline: (313) 691-1486
Men of Color Motivational Group strives to empower African American men by providing information, insight, and knowledge on day-to-day issues in the African American community. MOC advocates positive health strategies and the dissemination of culturally sensitive and non-biased information. Although the needs of the African American male is its primary focus, MOC wlecomes the participation of all community-minded individuals. MOC sponsors the New Generations gay youth support group, a Bible study, weekly motivational meetings, and two programs, Angels Without Wings hospital visitation program and Arms of Love support group, for African American men with HIV and AIDS.

### Mensa G-Sig
5000 Town Center #3104
Southfield, MI 48075
phone: (810) 356-8484

### PRIDE Community Center
PO Box 7014
Flint, MI 48507
phone: (810) 238-9854

### Rainbow Oasis Center
PO Box 492
Saline, MI 48176
This community center is still in formation.

Coleman, when word of mouth sent mostly gay, bisexual, and transgendered men with HIV or AIDS to the group's weekly meetings. Co-founder Cornelius Wilson estimated that 95 percent of the membership, including the group's founders, was gay or bisexual. "We were always open to whoever wanted to come in," Wilson told interviewer Charles Gervin in the December 1995 issue of Michigan's *OUTSpoken* newspaper. But "we needed to come out ourselves," and as more out members joined the group, it seemed the sensible decision.

In the same interview, co-founder Sean Parker explained why Men of Color focuses on motivation and self-esteem as factors that affect AIDS care and prevention: "If you believe you are worthy and are loved, [that] in turn leads out to taking steps to change behavior.... We were telling people that were already infected that you can go to your doctor's appointments and

**South East Michigan Pride (SEMP)**
PO Box 1915
Royal Oak, MI 48068
phone: (810) 825-6651
Sponsor of annual Pride celebration in greater Detroit.

**Sunshine Partners**
PO Box 2191
Ann Arbor, MI 48106
phone: (313) 665-6363
Gay men's naturalist social club.

**Tribe Men's Club**
PO Box 07247
Detroit, MI 48207
Leather club.

**Western Michigan Lambda Car Club**
PO Box 1100
Grand Rapids, MI 49501-1100

**Women Together**
Lathrup Village, MI
phone: (810) 548-0220
Weekly social and support meetings.

## MINNESOTA

**Gay/Lesbian Community Action Council (GLCAC)**
Ann Marie De Groot, Executive Director
310 E. 38th St.
Minneapolis, MN 55409
phone: (612) 822-0127
hotline: (800) 800-0907
fax: (612) 822-8786
e-mail: glcacmpls@aol.com
GLCAC is a service and advocacy organization providing community education, organizing, advocacy, social services, and telephone counseling for gays and lesbians.

## MISSOURI

**Gay & Lesbian Services**
132 W. 61st Terrace
Kansas City, MO 64113
phone: (816) 822-8204

**Men of All Colors Together, Kansas City Chapter (MACT/KC)**
Box 412432
Kansas City, MO 64141
The Kansas City chapter of the National Association of Black and White Men Together: A Gay Multiracial Organization for All

take your medications and make decisions for longevity and quantity and quality of life, and at the same time telling people that were not infected that you are worthy of not being infected."

Parker added: "Many people didn't have a safe place to go to talk about family issues, employment issues, or job issues and feel good about themselves. We want to provide that place. An African American gay male helping another was without parallel."

In addition to their focus on HIV/AIDS care and prevention, Men of Color uses their Motivational Tuesdays to provide "more positive and creative venues to the bars. We are here to educate, empower, and motivate ourselves to our fullest potential through workshops, open forums, guest speakers, [and] reference materials." Men of Color also sponsors a Bible Study for all religious faiths, and a new gay youth support group called New Generations.

People conducts cultural, educational, political, and social activities as a means of dealing with racism, sexism, and homophobia. MACT/KC publishes a newsletter and meets monthly.

### Pride—St. Louis (SLLGPCC)

Carol Robinson, President
3810 S Broadway
St. Louis, MO 63118
phone: (314) 772-8888
Formerly known as the St. Louis Lesbian/Gay Pride Celebration Committee, the individuals and organizations of Pride—St. Louis are united to plan and coordinate the annual St. Louis Lesbian and Gay Pridefest and other events. The group meets semimonthly January through March, then weekly April through June.

### Triangle Coalition of the University of Missouri (TRICOMU)

University of Missouri—Columbia
A022 Brady Commons
Columbia, MO 65211
phone: (314) 882-4427
TRICOMU, founded in 1978, acts as social and support group; operates a speakers' bureau; conducts fundraising activities for AIDS projects; and sponsors Gay, Lesbian, Bisexual Pride Month each April. The group was formerly known as the Gay and Lesbian Alliance of the University of Missouri.

## MONTANA

### PRIDE

2001 Porter Ave.
Butte, MT 59701
phone: (406) 723-6656

## NEVADA

### Gay and Lesbian Community Center of Southern Nevada

c/o David Green
PO Box 60301
Las Vegas, NV 89160-0301

## NEW HAMPSHIRE

### Monadnock Gay Men (MGM)

Dr. Kenneth E. DeVoid Jr., Executive Officer
Box 1124
Keene, NH 03431
phone: (603) 357-5544
MGM is a social support group for gay men in New Hampshire, southeastern Vermont, and northwestern Massachusetts. Founded

in 1984, MGM publishes a monthly newsletter.

### Seacoast Gay Men (SGM)

Box 1394
Portsmouth, NH 03802-1394
phone: (603) 430-4052
SGM is a social group of gay men in Portsmouth, New Hampshire, southern Maine, and northern Massachusetts. The group sponsors discussions, films, presentations, and suppers, and publishes a monthly newsletter, *Identity*.

### Seacoast Outright

4 Bayview Road
Durham, NH 03824
phone: (603) 868-2468

### Women in Touch (WIT)

Mona Jewell, Executive Officer
Box 3541
Nashua, NH 03061
phone: (603) 883-9228
Women in Touch, established in 1983, promotes networking and social support in a chemical free environment. The group presents annual Gay and Lesbian Community Awards and publishes a newsletter.

## NEW JERSEY

### Gay Activist Alliance in Morris County (GAAMC)

Gary Wyssling, President
Box 137
Convent Station, NJ 07961
phone: (201) 285-1595
fax: (201) 538-8882
e-mail: gaamc@eies.hjit.edu
GAAMC, founded in 1972, promotes political, health, and social awareness and programs for gay men and lesbians. The alliance provides a helpline, women's network, men's rap group, and information and referral services, and publishes the monthly newsletter *Challenge* and the annual *New Jersey Pride, Guide to Gay New Jersey.*

### New Jersey Lesbian and Gay Coalition

Laura Pople, President
PO Box 1431
New Brunswick, NJ 08903
phone: (908) 828-6772
Founded in 1972, the New Jersey Lesbian and Gay Coalition comprises gay and lesbian organizations statewide. The coalition acts as a clearinghouse for information on gay and lesbian issues; conducts educational, lobbying, and political action activities; sponsors the New Jersey Pride Parade; and presents Lesbian and Gay Achievement Awards at its annual banquet.

## NEW YORK

### Bronx Lesbians United in Sisterhood Blues Foundation

c/o Lisa A. Winters
2081 Cruger Ave., Ste. 1M
Bronx, NY 10462-2331

### Capitol District Community Center

PO Box 131
Albany, NY 12201
phone: (518) 438-0546

### Columbia Lesbian, Bisexual and Gay Coalition (LBGC)

Columbia University
303 Earl Hall
New York, NY 10027
phone: (212) 854-1488
Gay, lesbian, and bisexual students, faculty, and staff of Columbia University. Founded in 1967, LBGC attempts to present as complete a view as possible of the contemporary social, educational, and political gay experience, and aims to create a gay community at Columbia that will enable its members to relate to each other as people in an unoppressive atmosphere; promote among homosexuals, bisexuals, and heterosexuals alike an enlightened understanding of homosexuality free of the taboos, misconceptions, and stigmatization of a sexist society; and fight against the oppression of gay persons, in and out of Columbia. LBGC sponsors discussions as well as many social activities for gay people on campus; conducts a monthly dance to bring together the gay youth of New York City and surrounding areas; holds a weekly Gay Issues Rap Group on issues and problems; and distributes literature to educate the public.

The group maintains a speakers' bureau, biographical archives, and library of 500 volumes on gay life.

## Empire State Pride Agenda

611 Broadway, Rm. 907A
New York, NY 10012-2608

## Gay Alliance of Genesee Valley (GAGV)

179 Atlantic Avenue
Rochester, NY 14607-1255
phone: (716) 244-8640

## Gay and Lesbian Switchboard of Long Island (GLSBLI)

PO Box 1312
Long Island, NY 11779
phone: (516) 737-1615
Offers peer counseling information & referral.

## Gays and Lesbians in Brookhaven (GLIB)

John B. Deitz, Secretary
PO Box 203
Brookhaven, NY 11719
phone: (516) 286-6867
GLIB, an offspring of the National Gay and Lesbian Task Force, provides a supportive environment for gays, lesbians, and their friends where issues affecting the gay and lesbian community can be discussed, and publishes *GLIB News.*

## Heritage of Pride (HOP)

Janice Thom and Arthur Finn, Co-coordinators
154 Christopher St., Ste. 1D
New York, NY 10036
phone: (212) 807-7433
fax: (212) 807-7436
Founded in 1984, Heritage of Pride includes gay, lesbian, bisexual, transgender, and straight individuals. The group works to organize the annual Gay & Lesbian Pride Weekend in New York City, which includes a march, rally, festival, and dance. HOP meets monthly at the Lesbian & Gay Community Services Center at 208 West 13th Street and publishes a quarterly newsletter, *Lavender Line.*

## Ithaca Lesbian, Gay, and Bisexual Task Force (ILGBTF)

PO Box 283
Ithaca, NY 14851-0283
phone: (607) 277-4614
Founded in 1985, the Ithaca task force seeks to advance the status of gay, lesbian, and bisexual people. The group provides advocacy and education programs; sponsors a speaker's bureau; offers information and referral services; and publishes a monthly bulletin and quarterly journal called *Outlines.*

## Lesbian and Gay Community Services Center

Richard Burns, Executive Director
208 W. 13th St.
New York, NY 10011
phone: (212) 620-7310
The Community Center is host to numerous organizations and functions, and maintains a library and archives.

## National Association of Lesbian and Gay Community Centers (NALGCC)

c/o Lesbian and Gay Community Services Center
Benjamin Stilp, Director of Communications
208 W. 13th St.
New York, NY 10011
phone: (212) 620-7310
The National Association of Lesbian and Gay Community Centers was formed in 1995 to encourage the establishment and growth of lesbian and gay community centers throughout the United States. The existing 65 lesbian and gay community centers across America act as engines of progressive social change through a national network of local grassroots organizations with estimated combined annual budgets of $30 million.

## The Neutral Zone

162 Christopher Street
New York, NY 10014
phone: (212) 924-3294

## Sex Information & Education Council of U.S. (SIECUS)

130 West 42nd Street, Suite 2500

New York, NY 10036
phone: (212) 819-9770

## NORTH CAROLINA

### Alternative Resources of the Triad

PO Box 4442
Greensboro, NC 27404
phone: (910) 274-2100

### Lesbian and Gay Cultural Organization

c/o Tom Warshaulk
428 Park Ave.
Charlotte, NC 28203-0000

### Our Own Place (OOP)

Alice Stark, Director
c/o Janet Reed
PO Box 11732
Durham, NC 27703
phone: (919) 286-9966
Our own place promotes networking, exchanging information, developing community projects, and educational and social programs for lesbians. The weekly meetings may include lectures and social activities.

### OutFit

PO Box 5978
Asheville, NC 28813
phone: (704) 277-7815

### OutRight!

PO Box 3203
Durham, NC 27715-3203
phone: (919) 286-2396

## OHIO

### Bowling Green State University Lesbian and Gay Alliance (LGA)

Marlene Bomer, Secretary
University Hall Box 22
Bowling Green, OH 43403-0001
phone: (419) 372-0555
Support group for gays, lesbians, bisexuals, supportive heterosexuals, and gay and lesbian transgenders on the Bowling Green State University campus and surrounding communities. Founded in 1984, LGA sponsors panels and groups; makes available information and referral services; conducts social and recreational activities; and meets weekly.

### Case Western Reserve University Gay-Lesbian-Bisexual Alliance (GLBA)

Thwing Center, Student Activities Office
Cleveland, OH 44106-7103
phone: (216) 368-2679
fax: (216) 368-8840
e-mail: xx425@po.cwru.edu
Founded in 1978, GLBA includes university faculty, staff, and students interested in meeting gays, lesbians, and bisexuals and understanding current lesbigay issues. The group sponsors the annual Coming Out Day Dance and publishes a weekly newsletter.

### Columbus Association of Black and White Men Together/DRS (CABWMT)

Richard Hanson, Co-Chairperson
Box 151276
Columbus, OH 43215
phone: (614) 221-2734
The Columbus chapter of the National Association of Black and White Men Together: A Gay Multiracial Organization for All People is an interracial support group for gay men in central Ohio.

### Gay & Lesbian Community Center of Greater Cleveland

PO Box 6177
1418 West 29th Street
Cleveland, OH 44101
phone: (216) 522-1999

### Kent State University Lesbian, Gay, Bisexual Union (LGBU-Kent)

Alyssa Noel Lamb, President
Kent Student Center, Rm. 235
Box 17
Kent, OH 44242
phone: (216) 672-2068
hotline: (216) 672-2068
The Lesbian, Gay, Bisexual Union includes students and individuals from the local community interested in offering education, support, and social activities for Kent State University students who are gay.

Founded in 1970, the group was formerly called the Kent Gay Liberation Front and focuses on political issues affecting the community.

### Lorain County Gay/Lesbian Information Center

PO Box 167
Lorain, OH 44052
phone: (216) 988-5326

### Stonewall Union

Ann Santilli, President
PO Box 10814
Columbus, OH 43201
phone: (614) 299-7764
fax: (614) 299-4408
The Stonewall Union, established in 1981, comprises gay and lesbian individuals and couples in central Ohio who support gay rights and the organizations that also support those rights. The union promotes the empowerment of members; provides social activities and referrals for the gay community; and sponsors the annual Gay Fest. The group publishes the monthly *Stonewall Union Journal* and two annual directories, *Lavender Listings* and the *Ohio Guide*.

## OREGON

### Capitol Forum (CF)

Box 406
Salem, OR 97308
Capitol Forum, founded in 1977, is a social service organization serving the gay and lesbian community.

### Deschutes County Coalition for Human Dignity

Bend, OR
phone: (503) 383-4861

### Oregon State University Gay and Lesbian Association

Brian Parks, Director
c/o Lesbian, Gay, Bisexual Alliance Student Activities Center
Corvallis, OR 97331
phone: (503) 737-6363
Gays, lesbians, bisexuals, and their friends at Oregon State University. The Gay and Lesbian Association, founded in 1976, provides support to those just learning about their sexual orientation; seeks to present a positive image of gays and lesbians; and sponsors Gay Pride Week at Oregon State University, a speakers' bureau, and educational forums.

### Outside In

1236 SW Salmon
Portland, OR 97205
phone: (503) 223-4121, ext. 35

### Phoenix Rising

620 SW Fifth
Portland, OR 97204
phone: (503) 223-8299

## PENNSYLVANIA

### The Attic

Voyage House
1431 Lombard Street
Philadelphia, PA 19146
phone: (215) 545-2910

### Closet Culture

PO Box 10274
Erie, PA 16504-0274
phone: (814) 825-6131

### 40 Acres of Change

201 South 12th Street
Suite 1R
Philadelphia, PA 19107
phone: (215) 627-6233

### Free Spirit

PO Box 113, Kerr Station
Bloomsburg, PA 17815

### Unity, Inc.

1207 Chestnut
Suite 209
Philadelphia, PA 19107
phone: (215) 851-1912

## RHODE ISLAND

### The Way Out

Providence, RI
phone: (401) 861-5969

## TENNESSEE

### The Center for Lesbian & Gay Community Services

703 Berry Road
Nashville, TN 37204-2803
phone: (615) 297-0008

### Nashville Lesbian, Gay, and Bisexual Pride Committee

c/o Robert D. Adams
PO Box 41653
Nashville, TN 37204-1653

## TEXAS

### Austin Community College Gay Students Organization

Cathe Wooton, President
Austin Community College
Austin, TX 78767
phone: (512) 469-9012

### Coalition of Lesbian/Gay Student Groups (CLGSG)

PO Box 190712
Dallas, TX 75219
phone: (214) 521-5342
Founded in 1989, the coalition includes lesbian, gay, and bisexual student groups from area colleges and universities. The coalition hosts an annual Fall Conference, quarterly meetings, and an annual Summer Leadership Retreat.

### Gay and Lesbian Alliance of Central Texas

PO Box 9081
Waco, TX 76714-9081

### San Antonio Lambda Students Alliance

PO Box 12715
San Antonio, TX 78212
phone: (210) 733-1225

## UTAH

### Utah Stonewall Center

770 South 300 West
Salt Lake City, UT 84101
phone: (801) 539-8800

*Julie Enszer, executive director of Affirmations Lesbian and Gay Community Center in Ferndale, Michigan. (Photo courtesy* Between the Lines.)

## WASHINGTON

### Associated Lesbians of Puget Sound (ALPS)

PO Box 20424
Seattle, WA 98102
phone: (206) 233-8145
Founded in 1980, ALPS is a social and educational network for lesbians and conducts fundraising activities for other lesbian organizations. The *ALPS Newsletter* is published monthly.

### Gay and Lesbian Association (GALA)

Alex MacMath, President
NE 729 Thatuna, Ste. 211
Pullman, WA 99163
phone: (509) 335-4311
Founded in 1978 for gays and lesbians and their friends, GALA provides educational, political, social, and supportive programs to the gay, lesbian, and heterosexual communities of the Palouse. GALA meets the first and third Tuesday of the month; offers

## SPOTLIGHT

## AFFIRMATIONS LESBIAN AND GAY COMMUNITY CENTER

One of approximately 50 community centers in the United States, Affirmations resembles its cousins nationwide in its history and focus. Founded in early 1989 as a telephone support line staffed by volunteers, Affirmations has grown into a 1,700-member center based in Ferndale, a Detroit, Michigan suburb that is known for welcoming gay people. Through members, volunteers, and its board of directors, Affirmations offers community outreach, education, a lesbian/gay helpline, a host of discussion groups and other group services, and youth services—all to support "the development of a

referrals and resource information; operates a speakers' bureau; maintains a lending library; publishes a monthly newsletter, *The Key*.

### Lesbian Resource Center (LRC)

Valerie Reuther, Executive Director
1808 Bellevue Ave., Ste. 204
Seattle, WA 98122
phone: (206) 322-3953
Established in 1971, the Lesbian Resource Center provides classes, support groups, workshops, social activities, and information on housing, employment, and lesbian community groups and events. The Center, which has also been known as Pacific Women's Resources and the Gay Women's Alliance, operates a lending library and a speakers' bureau and represents the lesbian community in areas of political and social concern. The *Lesbian Resource Center Community News,* covering community and center events, appears monthly.

### Seattle Central Community College Gay/Lesbian Student Organization

Vincent A.G. Diana, Advisor
1701 Broadway SAC 350
Seattle, WA 98122
phone: (206) 587-6924
Also known as the Triangle Club, the Gay/Lesbian Student Organization includes gay and lesbian students united for support and social and political activity, and meets weekly during the school year.

### Tacoma Lesbian Concern (TLC)

Mary DeSanto, Treasurer
Box 947
Tacoma, WA 98401
phone: (206) 472-0422
TLC is a charitable, educational, and support group for lesbians in the South Puget Sound area. Founded in 1981, TLC supports the local YWCA and AIDS foundation, sponsors two annual camping trips and a winter retreat, and publishes the monthly *TLC Newsletter* and a directory, the *Resource List for Puget Sound Area.*

## WISCONSIN

### Cream City Foundation (CCF)

William Frank, President
PO Box 204
Milwaukee, WI 53201
phone: (414) 265-0880
The Cream City Foundation, founded in 1981, provides financial, medical, and other support for gays and lesbians in Wisconsin. CCF also offers art and educational programs, and sponsors the Milwaukee

positive self image for individual gay, lesbian, and bisexual people and for the community as a whole."

Affirmations' executive director, Julie Enszer, told Melanie Eversley of the *Detroit Free Press* in October 1995 that, "in the past, a lot of the work we've done has been with people who are just coming out or who are at a crisis point in their lives. Now, as we grow, we [also] respond to emerging events," such as hate crimes against lesbians and gay men, including the recent murders of two gays in the Detroit area. One man, Gary Rocus, was beaten to death in November 1994. In an incident that drew headlines and outrage nationwide, Scott Amedure was shot to death in March 1995 by a friend, Jonathan Schmitz, after revealing his crush on Schmitz during a taping of the "Jenny Jones" television show. "More and more," said Enszer,

Gay/Lesbian Cable Network. The *CCF Update Newsletter* appears quarterly.

### Gay People's Union of Milwaukee (GPU)

Michael Lisowski, President
Box 208
Milwaukee, WI 53201
phone: (414) 562-7010
Founded in 1971, the Gay People's Union provides resources, referrals, and counseling to interested individuals, and operates a 24-hour hotline.

### Madison Community United

Sande Janagold, Acting Director
PO Box 310
14 W. Mifflin, Ste. 103
Madison, WI 53703
phone: (608) 255-8582
gay hotline: (608) 255-4297
lesbian hotline: (608) 255-0743
Madison Community United is a gay and lesbian social service agency funded by Community Shares of Wisconsin, the City of Madison Dane County, foundations, and contributions. Founded in 1978, the agency works to create a safe and positive environment through political advocacy, community outreach and education, support groups, social events, and speakers' bureau. The *Unity Newsletter* is published quarterly.

# ONLINE RESOURCES

## THE WEB

### Canadian Gay, Lesbian & Bisexual Resource Directory

http://www.cglbrd.com/
Whether a tourist or resident, you can locate businesses and services in Canada for the gay, lesbian, and bisexual community online. This Web site features information on more than 1,200 items, from hotels to religious organizations. The directory is searchable.

### FatGiRL

http://www.fatgirl.com/
In a society that applauds super-thin cover models, it's refreshing to find a Web page where big is beautiful. This irreverent e-zine celebrates and appreciates overweight lesbian women with poetry, editorials, and commentary.

### Gai Pied

http://www.gaipied.fr/
Gai Pied is a rebellious French magazine for the European gay community. A language dictionary will help you translate the Gai Pied Guide to gay places in France, Belgium, and Switzerland, which is especially useful if you're planning a trip to Europe.

"Affirmations is emerging as a voice to speak to those issues to help not only gay and lesbian people, but also to speak to the broader community." Citing the Religious Right's increasing power in legislation and the media as a major external threat to the lesbian and gay community, explained Michigan's *Between the Lines* newspaper in its coverage of the national 1995 *Creating Change* conference, Enszer said the community "must commit itself to building lasting institutions." She insisted: "If we are to be successful, to sustain ourselves and to provide ongoing, meaningful services, we have to institutionalize." In addition to continuing Affirmations' current social and support funtions, with a special focus on youth programs, Enszer would like to expand its community education and advocacy functions.

### Gay Daze

http://www.gaydaze.com

Each day, a new melodrama unfolds on the Web soap opera Gay Daze. Tune in to follow the events in the lives of the characters—one lesbian and five gay men—in downtown Los Angeles.

### Gay and Lesbian Star Trek Home Page

http://ccnet.ccnet/com/gaytrek

Science-fiction fans gather on the Gay and Lesbian Star Trek Home Page to relive their favorite episodes—and to write a few homosexual characters into the plot.

### Gay Source

http://www.gaysource.com/

Featuring dramatic graphics, Gay Source delivers a first-class gay and lesbian e-zine. Don't miss the Voices page, where notable public figures speak out.

### Gays

http://www.gays.com

The Gays Web site claims to offer "everything for gays on the Web" but offers little more than an online mail and matchmaking service. If you're looking for an erotic video, lingerie, or a romantic relationship, you'll find it here.

### International Association of Lesbian and Gay Pride Coordinators

http://www.tde.com/~ialgpc

The homosexual community proudly participates in Gay Pride parades, rallies, and other events nationwide. The International Association of Lesbian and Gay Pride Coordinators keeps an updated calendar of these events on this Web page.

### Lesbian.org

http://www.lesbian.org/

This not-for-profit group seeks to promote Internet visibility of lesbian interests. To achieve this goal, a team of volunteers will create a Web presence for any lesbian-oriented nonprofit or activist group.

### Lesbians and Gays of New York (LGNY)

http://gravity.fly.net/~lgny

From politics to entertainment, LGNY captures the pulse of New York City's gay community in print. The monthly magazine hits the Web with an interface that is appropriately vibrant yet surprisingly easy to navigate, unlike the streets of New York. The Web version features news, current events, and night club information.

### Out and Proud

http://www.catalog.com/outproud/index2.htm

As part of its current outreach and education program, Affirmations maintains a speakers' bureau and hosts Town Hall meetings, regular social activities, and holiday events. Group services include personal growth and educational groups, peer support groups for adults and youth, and a mentorship project for lesbian and gay youth. The group also publishes a monthly newsletter and community calendar, and a community directory. Affirmations' Bayard Rustin Resource Center houses books, magazines, newspapers, and videos, and its Pittman/Puckett Art Gallery features works by artists in the lesbian, gay, and bisexual communities.

The Out and Proud Web page offers support to men who are acknowledging and accepting their emerging homosexuality or bisexuality. As they "come out," they can turn to this Web page for advice from gay psychologist Dr. Martin Rochford.

### PrideNet

http://www.pridenet.com/
As a full-service site, PrideNet offers an overwhelming collection of information, articles, and resources for the gay and lesbian community. The two most impressive PrideNet features are The Pink Pages, an international directory of gay and lesbian businesses; and G-Spot, a searchable database of homosexual clubs, restaurants, and entertainment around the world.

### Queer Resources Directory

http://www.qrd.org/QRD/
The Queer Resources Directory is the quintessential archive of gay and lesbian information on the Internet. Bookmark this vast directory of cultural, business, political, religious, and youth-oriented sites.

### Texas Triangle

http://www.outline.com/triangle/hp.html
Texas Triangle is "the state's gay news source," available every Thursday both in print and on the Web. With a no-nonsense objective approach, the publication presents world, national, state, and local news relevant to the gay community, as well as cultural, humorous, and editorial pieces.

### West Hollywood

http://www.geocities.com/cgi-bin/main/WestHollywood
Why not spend the day sightseeing in West Hollywood? This Web site takes you on a virtual tour through gay, lesbian, and bisexual pages that originate in West Hollywood, California.

## ONLINE SERVICES

### Gay and Lesbian BB

Prodigy: gay bb
Prodigy's Gay and Lesbian Bulletin Board provides an open forum for the discussion of any topic of interest within the homosexual community. Regular participants are generally warm and nonjudgmental, although prejudicial comments are occasionally posted.

### Gay and Lesbian Forum

AOL: GLCF
At the Gay and Lesbian Forum, users will find support conferences, a chat room, and many active message boards. The forum also contains a map that indicates where all gay and lesbian information is located on America Online.

### Open Human Sexuality Forum

CompuServe: hsx100

Within the Open Human Sexuality Forum, the Gay Alliance acts as a support group for the gay community. You'll find an archive of popular message threads in the file library, as well as articles, poetry, and event announcements.

### PlanetOut

MSN: PlanetOut

MSN's PlanetOut megaforum is one of the richest gay and lesbian sites online. With lush graphics, this comprehensive service spans social, political, and leisure interests. Jam-packed chat rooms and bulletin boards are evidence of the forum's healthy membership.

## USENET

### Bisexuals

soc.bi

Bisexuals can meet here to exchange experiences, analyze relationships, and discuss the problems of discrimination they face.

### Homosexual Sex

alt.sex.homosexual

News and views of the homosexual world are discussed, challenged, and defended. This moderately active group receives crossposts from many other homosexual, political, and religious newsgroups.

### Homosexuality

alt.homosexual

Is homosexuality natural? The state of homosexuality in today's society is discussed in this open forum, where heated debates are commonplace.

### Members of the Same Sex

soc.motss

For those who prefer same-sex partners, this forum is a close-knit group of regular users who discuss issues affecting the homosexual community—gay rights, dating, romance, discrimination, and HIV/AIDS.

### Same-Sex Personal Ads

alt.personals.motss

Browse through personal ads from gays and lesbians around the world. Messages vary in their form and content, from blatant requests for sex to heartfelt pleas for loving relationships.

### Same-Sex Unions

alt.sex.motss

This newsgroup is for members of the same sex who want to discuss sexual relationships. But heated debates occur when critics post messages attacking homosexual lifestyles.

## THE NET AND BBS

### Eye Contact

modem: 415-703-8200

telnet: bbs.eyecon.com

Almost anything goes on Eye contact, an exclusively gay and lesbian BBS located in San Francisco. Log on for uncensored chat and matchmaking. Eye Contact has local access numbers across the country. You may also connect to the BBS via telnet.

### Gaze Support BBS

modem: 503-238-0680

telnet: gaze.com

The Gaze Support BBS in Portland, Oregon, strives to be "the source" for global gay life information. You will find events calendars, entertainment, book reviews, and message conferences from FidoNet and Usenet online. You may also connect to The Gaze Support via telnet.

### Lesbian-Studies

mailing list: majordomo@queernet.org

Results of lesbian studies are often posted on this mailing list for lesbian and bisexual scholars. To subscribe, send an e-mail message to the address above. In the body of your message, type only *subscribe lesbian-studies.*

### Lesbigay Freenet

telnet: freenet2.carleton.ca

path: Login: Guest/Go:glb

A division of the National Capital Freenet in Ottawa, Lesbigay Freenet offers an active message board for the homosexual community. Topics of discussion include equality, support for parents and friends of gays or lesbians, spirituality, and entertainment. For dial-up access by modem, call (613) 520-1130.

Family—it's a loaded word.

We all come from somewhere. Biological parents and maybe a couple siblings, an adoptive family, maybe step-relatives too—or maybe it was an aunt or uncle or grandparent who raised us. Whoever it may have been, those are the people who gave us our first notion of *family*. And those are the people, so often, whose opinions most matter when we first begin to realize—at age 12, 20, or 60—that we are lesbian or gay, bisexual or transgendered.

Some of us, thankfully, are accepted wholeheartedly. Others of us, sadly, are rejected outright. Many of us receive some mixture of those responses—which may change over time, which may result in some family members drawing closer while others keep their distance, or which may take the form of an understood tolerance—as long as we don't discuss our homosexuality, our partners, or the nature of our relationships.

And so we find support and understanding within our next family, which we've come to call our "chosen family." With our lesbian, gay, bisexual, and transgendered sisters and brothers, we link arms and sing our chosen song—"We Are Family"—and we mean it.

Many of us, in addition, establish new family units—as partners or parents or both—and the word *family* takes on an added dimension. Many of us long for our unions to be recognized formally, legally, in our own homeland, so we wait with bated breath as Hawaii's Supreme Court decides the constitutionality of same-sex marriages in that state—and, by extension, in other states too. Many of us, parents already, fear the whims of a bigoted judicial system that may decree us unfit parents simply by reason of our sexual orientation. Still others, wishing to raise children, struggle through a legal system that passively overlooks or actively denies our right to build a family.

The organizations listed in this chapter encompass our many notions of family. Our beloved PFLAG—Parents, Families, and Friends of Lesbians and Gays—based in Washington, D.C., has hundreds of chapters throughout North America. It remains one of the most compassionate and committed sources of understanding and education for our parents and families, and of active support for the gay and lesbian community.

In addition to listing local PFLAG chapters, we describe the group's Project Open Mind campaign, which addresses the extent to which hateful speech promotes devastatingly hateful actions. Other organizations in this chapter, like Gay and Lesbian Parents Coalition International, also based in Washington, D.C., focus on the concerns of lesbian and gay parents and their children. In addition, you'll read about one city's steps toward securing benefits for domestic partners.

## CANADA

### ONTARIO

#### Gay Fathers of Toronto

Brian Moore, Coordinator
PO Box 187, Sta. F
Toronto, ON, Canada M4Y 2L5
phone: (416) 975-1680
Gay Fathers of Toronto publishes books for homosexual men who are fathers, as well as a newsletter for its members and supporters.

## UNITED STATES

### ALABAMA

#### Gay and Lesbian Parents Coalition International—Gulf Coast

PO Box 1990
Semmes, AL 36575
Local chapter of the Washington, D.C.-based Gay and Lesbian Parents Coalition International.

### ALASKA

#### Anchorage Lesbian Moms Group

Alaska Women's Center
2440 E. Tudor, Box 304
Anchorage, AK 99507

#### PFLAG—South Central Alaska

PO Box 203231
Anchorage, AK 99520-3231
Support and education group; for more details, see listing for national chapter under District of Columbia.

#### PFLAG—Fairbanks

3135 Forrest Dr.
Fairbanks, AK 99709
Support and education group; for more details, see listing for national chapter under District of Columbia.

### ARIZONA

#### PFLAG—Phoenix

PO Box 37525
Phoenix, AZ 85069
Support and education group; for more details, see listing for national chapter under District of Columbia.

#### PFLAG—Prescott

920 E. Goodwin St., Ste. A
Prescott, AZ 86303
Support and education group; for more details, see listing for national chapter under District of Columbia.

#### PFLAG—Tucson

PO Box 36264
Tucson, AZ 85740-6264
Support and education group; for more details, see listing for national chapter under District of Columbia.

## SPOTLIGHT

# PFLAG'S PROJECT OPEN MIND

Founded in 1981 and representing more than 50,000 families, Parents, Families, and Friends of Gays and Lesbians (PFLAG) is one of the most respected and effective grassroots organizations in the United States. With affiliates in more than 380 cities across the United States and 11 other countries, PFLAG is devoted to providing support to gays and lesbians and their families, educating the ill-informed public, and advocating the rights of all regardless of their sexual orientation.

Project Open Mind is one of the many ways PFLAG has brought its concerns before the public. Project Open Mind consists of two 30-second television

## ARKANSAS

### PFLAG—Little Rock

PO Box 251191
Little Rock, AR 72225
Support and education group; for more details, see listing for national chapter under District of Columbia.

### PFLAG—Northwest Arkansas

PO Box 2897
Fayetteville, AR 72702
Support and education group; for more details, see listing for national chapter under District of Columbia.

## CALIFORNIA

### Alternative Family Project (AFP)

Cheryl Deaner, Project Coordinator
745 Taravel St., No. 300
San Francisco, CA 94116
phone: (415) 566-5683
The Alternative Family Project provides affordable therapy to non-traditional families, especially families with gay, lesbian, bisexual, or transgendered members. Founded in 1993, AFP conducts educational and research programs, provides advocacy services for government and media, compiles statistics, and maintains a speakers' bureau. In addition to a biweekly support group meeting, AFP sponsors an annual Family Day conference.

### Children of Lesbians and Gays Everywhere (COLAGE)

2300 Market Street, Suite 165
San Francisco, CA 94114
phone: (415) 861-KIDS

### Gay and Lesbian Parents of Los Angeles

7985 Santa Monica Blvd., Ste. 109-346
West Hollywood, CA 90046
phone: (213) 654-0307
This local chapter of Gay and Lesbian Parents Coalition International is a support group for gay parents, their current and former partners and spouses, and their children in Los Angeles County. The group's newsletter is published monthly.

### PFLAG—Central Coast

PO Box 3313
San Luis Obispo, CA 93403
Support and education group; for more details, see listing for national chapter under District of Columbia.

### PFLAG—Chico

555 Vallombrossa, Ste. 73

announcements, coupled with community outreach programs, public speaking engagements, and events. The first 30-second spot features a young girl with a handgun contemplating suicide while Rev. Pat Robertson, Senator Jesse Helms, and Rev. Jerry Falwell demean and condemn homosexuals and their "sickness." The second spot features a man being chased by a mob shouting taunts such as "Queer" and "Fag" as Robertson and Falwell again lash out at homosexuals with hateful words.

The main goal is to provide a hard-hitting, emotionally compelling national TV ad campaign portraying the hurtful and deadly consequences brought on by the anti-gay rhetoric of Falwell, Helms, Robertson, and others in positions of power and authority. A young person feeling alone and abandoned cannot be helped by Falwell's words: "God hates homosexuality." And a group seeking to justify its intolerance and violent actions need only to

Chico, CA 95926
Support and education group; for more details, see listing for national chapter under District of Columbia.

**PFLAG—Claremont/Pomona Valley Area**
607 Leyden Lane
Claremont, CA 91711-4236
Support and education group; for more details, see listing for national chapter under District of Columbia.

**PFLAG—Danville/San Ramon**
PO Box 3315
San Ramon, CA 94583
Support and education group; for more details, see listing for national chapter under District of Columbia.

**PFLAG—Eureka**
5755 Dow's Prairie Rd.
McKinleyville, CA 95521
Support and education group; for more details, see listing for national chapter under District of Columbia.

**PFLAG—Fresno**
PO Box 27382
Fresno, CA 93729-7382
Support and education group; for more details, see listing for national chapter under District of Columbia.

**PFLAG—Hayward**
PO Box 3493
Hayward, CA 94544
Support and education group; for more details, see listing for national chapter under District of Columbia.

**PFLAG—Idyllwild**
PO Box 485
Idyllwild, CA 92549
Support and education group; for more details, see listing for national chapter under District of Columbia.

**PFLAG—Long Beach**
PO Box 8221
Long Beach, CA 90808
Support and education group; for more details, see listing for national chapter under District of Columbia.

**PFLAG—Los Angeles**
PO Box 24565
Los Angeles, CA 90024
Support and education group; for more details, see listing for national chapter under District of Columbia.

hear Robertson: "Many of those people involved with Adolf Hitler were Satanists, many of them were homosexuals. The two things seem to go together."

"The damage caused by these attacks," says PFLAG Executive Director Sandra Gills, "affects every community—large and small."

The groundbreaking ads first started airing in November 1995 in Washington, D.C., and three other pilot cities: Houston, Tulsa, and Atlanta. The two spots drew a hailstorm of opposition from Pat Robertson and his Christian Broadcasting Network. CBN claimed the spots were "defamatory" to Robertson, and a lawyer for the network threatened TV stations and networks with lawsuits if they ran the spots.

"Apparently," contends PFLAG in a later public service announcement,

**PFLAG—Marin County**
PO Box 1626
Mill Valley, CA 94941
Support and education group; for more details, see listing for national chapter under District of Columbia.

**PFLAG—Mid-Peninsula**
PO Box 8265
Stanford, CA 94305
Support and education group; for more details, see listing for national chapter under District of Columbia.

**PFLAG—Modesto**
PO box 4311
Modesto, CA 95353
Support and education group; for more details, see listing for national chapter under District of Columbia.

**PFLAG—Monterey County**
PO Box 9052
Monterey, CA 93942
Support and education group; for more details, see listing for national chapter under District of Columbia.

**PFLAG—Palm Springs**
244 Pinyon Crest
Mt. Center, CA 92561
Support and education group; for more details, see listing for national chapter under District of Columbia.

**PFLAG—Oakland**
100 Monte Cresta Ave., Ste. 209
Oakland, CA 94611-4802
Support and education group; for more details, see listing for national chapter under District of Columbia.

**PFLAG—Orange County/Santa Ana**
PO Box 28662
Santa Ana, CA 92799-8662
Support and education group; for more details, see listing for national chapter under District of Columbia.

**PFLAG—Pasadena**
300 Cherry
Pasadena, CA 91105
Support and education group; for more details, see listing for national chapter under District of Columbia.

**PFLAG—Pleasanton/Dublin/Livermore**
1452 Parkview Ct.
Pleasanton, CA 94566

"Robertson and Falwell and their friends see nothing wrong with broadcasting their discriminatory language on their own programs. But they threaten legal action when their words are linked to the climate of intolerance they help create."

"We are condemning hate speech," says PFLAG President Mitzi Henderson. "America should hold its leaders accountable to a higher standard."

PFLAG contends the spots are honest and important to the issues they represent. The two spots are among the first such efforts to address gay and lesbian hate on a national TV level.

Despite the pilot cities cancelling any further plans to air the spots, PFLAG reports that Project Open Mind is a success and has had a huge impact on the gay community and the way the public views gays and lesbians.

Support and education group; for more details, see listing for national chapter under District of Columbia.

**PFLAG—Redlands**
1 E. Olive Ave.
Redlands, CA 92373
Support and education group; for more details, see listing for national chapter under District of Columbia.

**PFLAG—Riverside**
3891 Ridge Rd.
Riverside, CA 92506
Support and education group; for more details, see listing for national chapter under District of Columbia.

**PFLAG—Sacramento**
PO Box 661855
Sacramento, CA 95866
Support and education group; for more details, see listing for national chapter under District of Columbia.

**PFLAG—San Diego**
PO Box 82762
San Diego, CA 92138
Support and education group; for more details, see listing for national chapter under District of Columbia.

**PFLAG—San Francisco**
PO Box 640223
San Francisco, CA 94164-0223
Support and education group; for more details, see listing for national chapter under District of Columbia.

**PFLAG—Santa Barbara**
PO Box 41152
Santa Barbara, CA 93140-1152
Support and education group; for more details, see listing for national chapter under District of Columbia.

**PFLAG—Santa Cruz County**
849 Almar, Ste. C-222
Santa Cruz, CA 95060-5856
Support and education group; for more details, see listing for national chapter under District of Columbia.

**PFLAG—Sonoma County**
PO Box 1266
Healdsburg, CA 95448
Support and education group; for more details, see listing for national chapter under District of Columbia.

**PFLAG—South Bay**
Pete Koopman
PO Box 2718
Sunnyvale, CA 94087

"The project has gained a lot of attention because of the legal threats put forth by the Christian Broadcasting Network," says PFLAG Communications Director Rob Banaszak. "Project Open Mind has always been a campaign of public education and awareness that involves much more than the advertisements. The whole message of the campaign goes way beyond the television advertisement."

Project Open Mind is a continuing endeavor. Even though it was met with strong opposition when it began, that same opposition has helped to bring a higher level of understanding to the campaign's main points: that hateful speech promotes violent actions, and that as long as there exist hate speech and violence toward those who differ from the majority, equality for all cannot be had.

*By Eric Dobson*

phone: (408) 270-8182
The South Bay chapter of PFLAG (see the national description under District of Columbia for more information) comprises parents and other family members of gay and lesbian individuals. The group provides support and assistance to gay and lesbian people and their families, conducts educational programs, and publishes the quarterly newsletter *PFLAGPole*. For more details, see listing for national chapter under District of Columbia.

### PFLAG—Stockton
PO Box 77725
Stockton, CA 95267
Support and education group; for more details, see listing for national chapter under District of Columbia.

### PFLAG—Ventura County
PO Box 5401
Ventura, CA 93005
Support and education group; for more details, see listing for national chapter under District of Columbia.

### PFLAG—Walnut Creek
PO Box 94
Walnut Creek, CA 94597
Support and education group; for more details, see listing for national chapter under District of Columbia.

### PFLAG—Yolo County
17801 County Rd. 97
Woodland, CA 95695
Support and education group; for more details, see listing for national chapter under District of Columbia.

### PFLAG—Yreka
420 Jackson St.
Yreka, CA 96097
Support and education group; for more details, see listing for national chapter under District of Columbia.

### Youth and Family Assistance
609 Price Ave. #205
Redwood City, CA 94063
phone: (415) 366-8401 or (415) 367-9687

## COLORADO

### Gay and Lesbian Parents of Denver
PO Drawer E
Denver, CO 80203

Local chapter of Gay and Lesbian Parents Coalition International, based in Washington, D.C.

### PFLAG—Boulder

PO Box 19696
Boulder, CO 80308-2696
Support and education group; for more details, see listing for national chapter under District of Columbia.

### PFLAG—Collegiate Peaks

PO Box 516
Hartsell, CO 80449
Support and education group; for more details, see listing for national chapter under District of Columbia.

### PFLAG—Colorado Springs

PO Box 10076
Colorado Springs, CO 80917
Support and education group; for more details, see listing for national chapter under District of Columbia.

### PFLAG—Denver

PO Box 18901
Denver, CO 80218
Support and education group; for more details, see listing for national chapter under District of Columbia.

### PFLAG—Durango

203 W. 22nd St.
Durango, CO 81301-4617
Support and education group; for more details, see listing for national chapter under District of Columbia.

### PFLAG—Evergreen/Mountain Area

PO Box 265
Evergreen, CO 80439
Support and education group; for more details, see listing for national chapter under District of Columbia.

### PFLAG—Fort Collins

2607 Gilpin Ave.
Loveland, CO 80538
Support and education group; for more details, see listing for national chapter under District of Columbia.

### PFLAG—Grand Junction

Cindy Werner, President
PO Box 4904
Grand Junction, CO 81502-4904
phone: (970) 242-8965
The Grand Junction chapter of PFLAG (see the national description under District of Columbia for more information) provides support services and programs for homosexuals and their families and friends, and promotes equal rights and opportunities for homosexuals.

### PFLAG—Longmont

PO Box 611
Longmont, CO 80502
Support and education group; for more details, see listing for national chapter under District of Columbia.

### PFLAG—Pueblo

PO Box 4484
Pueblo, CO 81006
Support and education group; for more details, see listing for national chapter under District of Columbia.

### PFLAG—San Luis Valley

PO Box 1[illegible]81
Alamosa, CO 81101
Support and education group; for more details, see listing for national chapter under District of Columbia.

### PFLAG—Summit County

PO Box 1350
Dillon, CO 80435-1350
Support and education group; for more details, see listing for national chapter under District of Columbia.

## CONNECTICUT

### PFLAG—Coventry

PO Box 752
Coventry, CT 06238-3200
Support and education group; for more details, see listing for national chapter under District of Columbia.

### PFLAG—Hartford

49 Beechwood Ln.
South Glastonbury, CT 06073-2201
Support and education group; for more details, see listing for national chapter under District of Columbia.

### PFLAG—Madison/Shoreline

66 Bower Rd.
Madison, CT 06443
Support and education group; for more details, see listing for national chapter under District of Columbia.

### PFLAG—Southwestern Connecticut

Joan Rolnick, President
PO Box 16703
Stamford, CN 06905
phone: (203) 544-8724 or (203) 322-5380
The Southwestern Connecticut chapter of PFLAG (see the national description under District of Columbia for more information) is a support group for parents and friends of lesbians and gay men. PFLAG promotes gay rights, AIDS research, and laws that will help to eliminate anti-gay hate crimes; sponsors youth and educational outreach programs; and maintains a support group for spouses and ex-spouses of members. The group's newsletter appears bimonthly.

### PFLAG—Tri-State

PO Box 278
Salisbury, CT 06068-0278
Support and education group; for more details, see listing for national chapter under District of Columbia.

## DISTRICT OF COLUMBIA

### Gay and Lesbian Parents Coalition International (GLPCI)

Tim Fisher, Executive Director
Box 50360
Washington, DC 20091
phone: (202) 583-8029
phone/fax: (201) 783-6204
GLPCI acts as clearinghouse for information concerning gay and lesbian parenting. Founded in 1979, the coalition has 106 local branches that strive to teach society that parenting and homosexuality are compatible. GLPCI supports the passage of legislation created to eliminate discrimination due to sexual orientation; coordinates the establishment of support groups for parents and children; conducts educational outreach programs to teach professionals and the public the joys, challenges, and special concerns related to gay parenthood; and maintains a speakers' bureau and the annual College Scholarship Fund. Formerly known as the Gay Fathers Coalition, GLPCI also runs the program Children of Lesbians & Gays Everywhere (COLAGE). The coalition publishes a bulletin called *Agenda* and a quarterly newsletter that highlights news, books, movies, and other resources of interest to gay and lesbian parents, as well as the annual *Bibliography of Books for Children of Lesbian and Gay Parents;* the teen newsletter *Just for Us;* the *Fun Pages* for children aged six to 12; and guides and information packets.

### Parents, Families, and Friends of Lesbians and Gays (National PFLAG)

Sandra Gillis, Executive Director
1101 14th St. NW, Ste. 1030
Washington, DC 20005
phone: (202) 638-4200
fax: (202) 638-0243
e-mail: pflagntl@aol.com
Parents, Families, and Friends of Lesbians and Gays, known affectionally as "P-FLAG," was founded in 1981 to promote the health and well-being of gay, lesbian, and bisexual persons, and their families and friends. With 30,000 members and 350 local chapters, PFLAG works to educate the public, end discrimination, and secure equal civil rights. Among the booklets the group publishes are *Be Yourself,* a coming-out guide for youth; *Coming Out for Parents; Homosexuality and Biology; Is Homosexuality a Sin?* and *Opening a Straight Spouse's Closet.* PFLAG also publishes a recommended reading list and a pamphlet called "10 Simple Things You Can Do to End Homophobia." The quarterly *PFLAG Pole Newsletter* covers both regional and national news. The International Convention of Parents, Families, and Friends of Lesbians and Gays takes place every Labor Day weekend in Washington, D.C.

### PFLAG—Washington, DC

PO Box 28009
Washington, DC 20038
Support and education group; for more details, see listing for national chapter under District of Columbia.

## DELAWARE

### PFLAG—Northern Delaware

PO Box 26049
Wilmington, DE 19899
Support and education group; for more details, see listing for national chapter under District of Columbia.

## FLORIDA

### Family Resources, Inc.

5959 Central Ave.
PO Box 13087
St. Petersburg, FL 33733
phone: (813) 893-1150

### Gay and Lesbian Parents Coalition International—Central Florida

PO Box 561504
Orlando, FL 32856-1504
Support group for parents and their children; for more details, see listing for national chapter under District of Columbia.

### PFLAG—Daytona Beach

199 N. Timberland Dr.
New Smyrna Beach, FL 32168
Support and education group; for more details, see listing for national chapter under District of Columbia.

### PFLAG—Ft. Lauderdale

8747 SW 52nd St.
Cooper City, FL 33328
Support and education group; for more details, see listing for national chapter under District of Columbia.

### PFLAG—Ft. Myers

5100-318 S. Cleveland Ave.
Ste. 219
Ft. Myers, FL 33907
Support and education group; for more details, see listing for national chapter under District of Columbia.

### PFLAG—Gainesville/Ocala

PO Box 140176
Gainesville, FL 32606
Support and education group; for more details, see listing for national chapter under District of Columbia.

### PFLAG—Lakeland

519 Cresap St.
Lakeland, FL 33801-4709
Support and education group; for more details, see listing for national chapter under District of Columbia.

### PFLAG—Sarasota

PO Box 7382
Sarasota, FL 34278-7382
Support and education group; for more details, see listing for national chapter under District of Columbia.

### PFLAG—South Florida

7652 Mansfield Hollow
Delray Beach, FL 33446
Support and education group; for more details, see listing for national chapter under District of Columbia.

### PFLAG—Tampa

16301 Sonsoles Dr.
Tampa, FL 33613
Support and education group; for more details, see listing for national chapter under District of Columbia.

### PFLAG—Tri-County

PO Box 12267
Brooksville, FL 34614
Support and education group; for more details, see listing for national chapter under District of Columbia.

## GEORGIA

### PFLAG—Atlanta

PO Box 8482
Atlanta, GA 31106-0482
Support and education group; for more details, see listing for national chapter under District of Columbia.

## HAWAII

### PFLAG—Kailua-Kona

74-5615 Luhia St., D2
Kailua-Kona, HI 96740
Support and education group; for more details, see listing for national chapter under District of Columbia.

### PFLAG—Oahu
2085 Ala Wai Blvd.
Twin Towers, Ste. 16-3
Honolulu, HI 96815
Support and education group; for more details, see listing for national chapter under District of Columbia.

## IDAHO

### PFLAG—Eastern Idaho
PO Box 50191
Idaho Falls, ID 83405-0191
Support and education group; for more details, see listing for national chapter under District of Columbia.

### PFLAG—Treasure Valley
3773 Cayuga Pl.
Boise, ID 83709
Support and education group; for more details, see listing for national chapter under District of Columbia.

### PFLAG—Twin Falls
1434 Pole Line Rd. E.
Twin Falls, ID 83301
Support and education group; for more details, see listing for national chapter under District of Columbia.

## ILLINOIS

### PFLAG—Chicago
PO Box 11023
Chicago, IL 60611-0023
Support and education group; for more details, see listing for national chapter under District of Columbia.

### PFLAG—Collinsville
114 Westridge
Collinsville, IL 62234
Support and education group; for more details, see listing for national chapter under District of Columbia.

### PFLAG—Downer's Grove
PO Box 105
Downer's Grove, IL 60516
Support and education group; for more details, see listing for national chapter under District of Columbia.

### PFLAG—Northern Illinois
112 E. Taylor St.
De Kalb, IL 60115
Support and education group; for more details, see listing for national chapter under District of Columbia.

### PFLAG—Southern Illinois
505 Orchard Dr.
Carbondale, IL 62901
Support and education group; for more details, see listing for national chapter under District of Columbia.

## INDIANA

### Gay and Lesbian Parents Coalition International—Indianapolis
PO Box 831
Indianapolis, IN 46206
Support group for parents and their children; for more details, see listing for national chapter under District of Columbia.

### PFLAG—Evansville
PO Box 113
Evansville, IN 47701
Support and education group; for more details, see listing for national chapter under District of Columbia.

### PFLAG—Indianapolis
PO Box 441633
Indianapolis, IN 46206
Support and education group; for more details, see listing for national chapter under District of Columbia.

### PFLAG—South Bend
PO Box 4195
South Bend, IN 46634
Support and education group; for more details, see listing for national chapter under District of Columbia.

### PFLAG—Terre Haute
135 Aikman Pl.
Terre Haute, IN 47803
Support and education group; for more details, see listing for national chapter under District of Columbia.

## IOWA

### PFLAG—Cedar Valley

514 W. 4th St.
Cedar Falls, IA 50613-2804
Support and education group; for more details, see listing for national chapter under District of Columbia.

### PFLAG—Central Iowa

804 15th St.
Des Moines, IA 50265-3425
Support and education group; for more details, see listing for national chapter under District of Columbia.

### PFLAG—Waterloo

317 Hartman Ave.
Waterloo, IA 50701
Support and education group; for more details, see listing for national chapter under District of Columbia.

## KANSAS

### PFLAG—Hays

2910 Country Ln.
Hays, KS 67601-1710
Support and education group; for more details, see listing for national chapter under District of Columbia.

### PFLAG—Wichita

PO Box 686
Wichita, KS 67201-0686
Support and education group; for more details, see listing for national chapter under District of Columbia.

## KENTUCKY

### PFLAG—Lexington

PO Box 55484
Lexington, KY 40555-5484
Support and education group; for more details, see listing for national chapter under District of Columbia.

### PFLAG—Louisville

PO Box 5002
Louisville, KY 40255-0002
Support and education group; for more details, see listing for national chapter under District of Columbia.

### PFLAG—Paducah

2942 Clay St.
Paducah, KY 42001-4133
Support and education group; for more details, see listing for national chapter under District of Columbia.

## LOUISIANA

### PFLAG—Baton Rouge

PO Box 65398
Baton Rouge, LA 70896
Support and education group; for more details, see listing for national chapter under District of Columbia.

### PFLAG—Lafayette

PO Box 31078
Lafayette, LA 70593
Support and education group; for more details, see listing for national chapter under District of Columbia.

## MAINE

### PFLAG—Andy Valley

6 Lemieux St.
Lewiston, ME 04240
Support and education group; for more details, see listing for national chapter under District of Columbia.

### PFLAG—Hallowell

23 Winthrop St.
Hallowell, ME 04347
phone: (207) 623-2349
The Hallowell chapter of PFLAG (see the national description under District of Columbia for more information) comprises parents and friends of lesbians and gays who are organized to lobby for gay rights. PFLAG encourages the parents of gays and lesbians to accept their children to the best of their ability.

### PFLAG—Portland

PO Box 8742
Portland, ME 04104
Support and education group; for more details, see listing for national chapter under District of Columbia.

## MARYLAND

### PFLAG—Baltimore

PO Box 5637
Baltimore, MD 21210-0610
Support and education group; for more details, see listing for national chapter under District of Columbia.

### PFLAG—Eastern Shore

PO Box 171
Stevensville, MD 21666
Support and education group; for more details, see listing for national chapter under District of Columbia.

## MASSACHUSETTS

### Alyson Wonderland

Karen Barber, Associate Publisher
40 Plympton St.
Boston, MA 02118
phone: (617) 542-5679
phone: (800) 825-9766
fax: (617) 542-9189
An imprint of Alyson Publications, Alyson Wonderland publishes books for children of gay and lesbian parents.

### PFLAG—Amherst

PO Box 2025
Amherst, MA 01004
Support and education group; for more details, see listing for national chapter under District of Columbia.

### PFLAG—Berkshire County/South

29 Stringer Ave.
Lee, MA 02138-9569
Support and education group; for more details, see listing for national chapter under District of Columbia.

### PFLAG—Boston

PO Box 44-4
West Somerville, MA 02144
Support and education group; for more details, see listing for national chapter under District of Columbia.

### PFLAG—Canton/Southeast

PO Box 187
Stoughton, MA 02072
Support and education group; for more details, see listing for national chapter under District of Columbia.

### PFLAG—Cape Cod/Brewster

PO Box 1167
Orleans, MA 02653
Support and education group; for more details, see listing for national chapter under District of Columbia.

### PFLAG—Cape Cod/Falmouth

PO Box 839
West Falmouth, MA 02574
Support and education group; for more details, see listing for national chapter under District of Columbia.

### PFLAG—Concord Area

PO Box 344
Stow, MA 01775
Support and education group; for more details, see listing for national chapter under District of Columbia.

### PFLAG—Hingham

510 Main St.
Hingham, MA 02043
Support and education group; for more details, see listing for national chapter under District of Columbia.

### PFLAG—Metro-West/Framingham

22 Caroline St.
Wellesley, MA 02181
Support and education group; for more details, see listing for national chapter under District of Columbia.

### PFLAG—Pioneer Valley

PO Box 55
South Hadley, MA 01075-0055
Support and education group; for more details, see listing for national chapter under District of Columbia.

### PFLAG—Springfield

PO Box 625
West Springfield, MA 01089
Support and education group; for more details, see listing for national chapter under District of Columbia.

### PFLAG—Worcester

c/o United Congregational Church

## SPOTLIGHT

## PARTNERSHIP BENEFITS

"A marriage license does not a family make," says the Detroit (Michigan) City Council, and therefore the council is considering extending the advantages of marriage to couples who can't or don't acquire that license.

Within a few weeks the council will debate an ordinance that enables "committed partners" to register and be recognized by the city as a family unit.

Who will benefit? Obviously, lesbian and gay couples, and that community is active in supporting the ordinance. But the new law would save Grandma, too, from living in sin. Widowed seniors often choose to live together because remarrying would cancel their pensions. The ordinance would also

6 Institution Rd.
Worcester, MA 01609
Support and education group; for more details, see listing for national chapter under District of Columbia.

## MICHIGAN

### Domestic Partnership Task Force
Cindy Tobias, Co-Chair
phone: (313) 331-6728
Carlie Steen, Co-Chair
phone: (313) 224-2939

### Gay and Lesbian Parents Association
PO Box 2694
Southfield, MI 48037
phone: (810) 891-7292
Holds monthly meetings at Affirmations Community Center in Ferndale, Michigan.

### Our Kids
c/o Pandora's Books and Music
226 West Lovell
Kalamazoo, MI 49007
phone: (616) 385-2654
Group for gay and lesbian parents and their children.

### PFLAG—Ann Arbor
c/o Karen E. Baker
PO Box 7471
Ann Arbor, MI 48107-7471
phone: (313) 741-0659 or (313) 769-1684
The Ann Arbor chapter of PFLAG (see the national description under District of Columbia for more information) provides support services and programs for homosexuals and their families and friends, and promotes equal rights and opportunities for homosexuals.

### PFLAG—Detroit
Karen Fenwick, President
PO Box 145
Farmington, MI 48332
phone: (810) 478-8408
hotline: (810) 656-2875
The Detroit branch of PFLAG (see the national description under District of Columbia for more information) comprises parents and families of lesbians and gay people in the Detroit area who are united as a support group for others. The group meets the second Sunday of the month, and the newsletter *Parents FLAG/Detroit* is published monthly.

### PFLAG—Flint
PO Box 90722

serve straight couples who, for whatever reason, choose not to seek the blessing of the church or the state.

Supporters of the ordinance say it's necessary to accommodate changing living patterns and experiences of family. Only a quarter of "families" in the United States consist of the traditional married woman, man and kids. The U.S. Census estimates that 4.2 million households consist of unmarried couples—gay or straight.

"Going into the 21st century we need to recognize and support all kinds of families," Domestic Partnership Task Force Co-Chair Cindy Tobias explains. "The city has always been a place of diversity and support for all kinds of differences, and this is another way that we can do that."

A Task Force fact sheet puts it more simply: "Legally recognizing the union

Burton, MI 48509
phone: (313) 631-4910 or (313) 653-0460
Support and education group; for more details, see listing for national chapter under District of Columbia.

### PFLAG—Grand Rapids
PO Box 6226
Grand Rapids, MI 49506-4823
phone: (616) 285-9133
Support and education group; for more details, see listing for national chapter under District of Columbia.

### PFLAG—Grand Traverse Area
PO Box 1705
Acme, MI 49610
phone: (616) 947-4462
Support and education group; for more details, see listing for national chapter under District of Columbia.

### PFLAG—Jackson
PO Box 4065
Jackson, MI 49204
Support and education group; for more details, see listing for national chapter under District of Columbia.

### PFLAG—Kalamazoo
PO Box 1201
Portage, MI 49081-1201
phone: (616) 327-8107 or (616) 345-1713
Support and education group; for more details, see listing for national chapter under District of Columbia.

### PFLAG—Lansing
PO Box 35
Okemos, MI 48805
phone: (517) 349-3612
Support and education group; for more details, see listing for national chapter under District of Columbia.

### PFLAG—Tri-Cities
PO Box 834
Bay City, MI 48707-0834
phone: (517) 893-2475
Support and education group that serves Bay City, Midland, and Saginaw; for more details, see listing for national chapter under District of Columbia.

### PFLAG—Upper Peninsula
PO Box 2754
Iron Mountain, MI 49801
phone: (906) 774-1343
Support and education group; for more details, see listing for national chapter under District of Columbia.

of two people who love and are committed to each other strengthens their bond and provides for long term stability."

Rabbi Arnold Sleutelberg of Royal Oak, Michigan, says it's a simple matter of human rights: "The rights, responsibilities, benefits, and obligations should be the same no matter who one chooses as a life companion."

The ordinance would give domestic partners visitation rights at city hospitals and jails and access to certain city records. And city employees (those not under union contracts) could declare their partners as dependents for purposes of health insurance benefits.

Scores of cities and a few states have already adopted such ordinances, from such gay centers as West Hollywood, California, to the more staid Minneapolis and Vermont. In Michigan, Ann Arbor and East Lansing allow residents

## MINNESOTA

### PFLAG—Alexandria

12556 E. Lake Miltona Dr. NE
Miltona, MN 56354
Support and education group; for more details, see listing for national chapter under District of Columbia.

### PFLAG—Duluth

612 First Bank Pl.
Duluth, MN 55802-2056
Support and education group; for more details, see listing for national chapter under District of Columbia.

### PFLAG—Northfield

5048 Ebel Way
Northfield, MN 55057
Support and education group; for more details, see listing for national chapter under District of Columbia.

### PFLAG—St. Paul/Minneapolis

PO Box 8588
Minneapolis, MN 55408-0588
Support and education group; for more details, see listing for national chapter under District of Columbia.

### PFLAG—Rochester

2205 Elton Hills Dr. NW
Rochester, MN 55901-1564
Support and education group; for more details, see listing for national chapter under District of Columbia.

### PFLAG—St. Cloud

402 Eighth Ave. S
St. Cloud, MN 56302
Support and education group; for more details, see listing for national chapter under District of Columbia.

### Queer Parents

PO Box 124
Mankato, MN 56002-0124

## MISSOURI

### Gay and Lesbian Parents Coalition—Kansas City

6241 Blue Ridge Blvd.
Kansas City, MO 64113
Support group for parents and their children; for more details, see listing for national chapter under District of Columbia.

### PFLAG—Kansas City

PO Box 414101
Kansas City, MO 64141-4101

to officially register their partnerships, and Ann Arbor city employees have partner health benefits....

Outside these oases of enlightenment, however, non-married partners are excluded from a long list of privileges that married ones take for granted: family sick leave; child custody; bereavement leave; visitation rights in hospitals and jails; the automatic right to inherit if the partner dies without a will; the right to authorize emergency medical treatment; even family discounts on an employer's products.

Heading the list, of course, is medical insurance, which, for those who still have it, makes up a growing portion of a worker's total compensation. The National Gay and Lesbian Task Force argues that excluding gay and lesbian couples from coverage is "the same as advertising a job in the paper saying,

Support and education group; for more details, see listing for national chapter under District of Columbia.

## MONTANA

### PFLAG—Montana

38 Sloway W
St. Regis, MT 59866
Support and education group; for more details, see listing for national chapter under District of Columbia.

## NEBRASKA

### PFLAG—Holdrege/Kearney

1320 Eighth Ave.
Holdrege, NE 68949
Support and education group; for more details, see listing for national chapter under District of Columbia.

### PFLAG—Lincoln

PO Box 4374
Lincoln, NE 68505-1819
Support and education group; for more details, see listing for national chapter under District of Columbia.

### PFLAG—Omaha

2912 Lynwood Drive
Omaha, NE 68123-1957
phone: (402) 291-6781
Support and education group; for more details, see listing for national chapter under District of Columbia.

## NEVADA

### PFLAG—Las Vegas

PO Box 20145
Las Vegas, NV 89112-0145
Support and education group; for more details, see listing for national chapter under District of Columbia.

### PFLAG—Reno/Sparks

1685 Whitewood Dr.
Sparks, NV 89434
Support and education group; for more details, see listing for national chapter under District of Columbia.

## NEW HAMPSHIRE

### PFLAG—Concord Area

158 Liberty Hill Rd.
Bedford, NH 03110

'Salespeople wanted: Salary for heterosexuals $12 an hour; salary for gays and lesbians $7.20.'"

"The ironic thing," according to Task Force member Julie Enszer, who heads Affirmations Gay and Lesbian Community Center in Ferndale, "is that when these benefits for domestic partners come in force, they end up being taxable."

The IRS does not tax benefits for *dependents*—but domestic partners are not legally dependents. "So from an equity perspective, domestic partnership still is not the complete remedy economically," says Enszer.

On the other side of the issue, of course, are those who want to condemn "alternative life styles." Some local governments or employers don't want to offend those who see domestic partnership as "an onslaught on the family," as one consultant put it.

Support and education group; for more details, see listing for national chapter under District of Columbia.

### PFLAG—Manchester

PO Box 386
Manchester, NH 03105
Support and education group; for more details, see listing for national chapter under District of Columbia.

### PFLAG—Monadnock Area

Willard Farm Rd.
New Ipswich, NH 03071
Support and education group; for more details, see listing for national chapter under District of Columbia.

### PFLAG—Seacoast Area

18 Hobbs Rd.
Kansington, NH 03833-5510
Support and education group; for more details, see listing for national chapter under District of Columbia.

## NEW JERSEY

### PFLAG—Asbury Park

PO Box 1542
Asbury Park, NJ 07712
Support and education group; for more details, see listing for national chapter under District of Columbia.

### PFLAG—Bergen County

44 Kira Lane
Ridgewood, NJ 08840
Support and education group; for more details, see listing for national chapter under District of Columbia.

### PFLAG—Mays Landing

103 Dover Ave.
Mays Landing, NJ 08330
Support and education group; for more details, see listing for national chapter under District of Columbia.

### PFLAG—North Jersey

Norma Brewster, President
Box 244
Belleville, NJ 07109
hotline: (201) 267-8414
The North Jersey chapter of PFLAG (see the national description under District of Columbia for more information) educates the public about gay people and helps parents cope with the realization their child is gay. The group meets the second Sunday of each month and publishes a monthly newsletter.

*Don Robinson, Dave Scott, Bubba Adams, and T. J. Fay Fikker attend the massive marriage ceremony during the October 1987 March on Washington, D.C. (Photo by Ron Bennett; courtesy UPI/Bettmann.)*

## NEW MEXICO

### PFLAG—Albuquerque

1907 Buena Vista SE, Ste. 75
Albuquerque, NM 87106-4178
Support and education group; for more details, see listing for national chapter under District of Columbia.

### PFLAG—Santa Fe

PO Box 16498
Santa Fe, NM 87506
Support and education group; for more details, see listing for national chapter under District of Columbia.

## NEW YORK

### The Center for Children & Families, Inc.

133 West 46th Street
New York, NY 10036
phone: (212) 354-SAFE

### PFLAG—Albany

PO Box 12531
Albany, NY 12212-2531
Support and education group; for more details, see listing for national chapter under District of Columbia.

### PFLAG—Binghamton

Box 728
Westview Station
Binghamton, NY 13905-4631
Support and education group; for more details, see listing for national chapter under District of Columbia.

### PFLAG—Brooklyn

7304 Fifth Ave., Ste. 307
Brooklyn, NY 11209

In Washington, D.C., a gay department store employee filed a discrimination complaint because the store denied his partner a family discount card. The store got heat from both sides, with the gay community threatening a boycott and the Christian right weighing in. "The classic quote," said the store's vice president, "was that we were 'contributing to the downfall of Judeo-Christian values.'"

The store changed its policy—this was more than five years ago—and as far as anyone can tell, the state of morality in Washington is no worse than it was before.

Morals aside, money is always an issue. Far more employers have consented to allow sick or bereavement leave for domestic partners—relatively low-cost items—than have gone all the way to offer health benefits. (East

Support and education group; for more details, see listing for national chapter under District of Columbia.

### PFLAG—Buffalo/Niagara

PO Box 861
Buffalo, NY 14225
Support and education group; for more details, see listing for national chapter under District of Columbia.

### PFLAG—Ithaca

PO Box 24
Willeysville, NY 13864
Support and education group; for more details, see listing for national chapter under District of Columbia.

### PFLAG—Jamestown

414 Palmer St.
Jamestown, NY 14701
Support and education group; for more details, see listing for national chapter under District of Columbia.

### PFLAG—Long Island

109 Browns Rd.
Huntington, NY 11743
Support and education group; for more details, see listing for national chapter under District of Columbia.

### PFLAG—Mohawk Valley

423 Fiore Dr.
Utica, NY 13502
Support and education group; for more details, see listing for national chapter under District of Columbia.

### PFLAG—New York City

Richard Ashworth, President
Box 553
Lenox Hill Sta.
New York, NY 10021-0034
phone: (212) 463-0629 or (516) 889-6619
The New York City branch of PFLAG (see the national description under District of Columbia for more information) includes parents, friends, and relatives of gays and lesbians. The group helps parents accept their children's homosexuality, provides education to the public, and publishes a pamphlet called *Can We Understand?* and a monthly newsletter. The group meets the fourth Sunday of the month.

### PFLAG—Poughkeepsie/Mid-Hudson

PO Box 880
Pleasant Valley, NY 12569
Support and education group; for more details, see listing for national chapter under District of Columbia.

Lansing is one example.) Employers have argued that their costs would soar, raising the specter of AIDS, or that employees would claim fake partners, to do an uninsured friend a favor.

Experience has shown these fears groundless, however. In fact, according to Hewitt Associates, a benefits consulting firm, domestic partners may actually be cheaper to insure than spouses: most employed domestic partners are young, and therefore healthier than the average, and most, both gay and straight, are childless—no pregnancy claims.

When partner coverage was established for city employees in Berkeley, San Francisco, and Seattle, insurers demanded a surcharge or a back-up fund. In all three cities the surcharge was later refunded to the city or the back-up fund dismantled, because it was not needed. In Seattle, domestic partners

**PFLAG—Rochester**
179 Atlantic Ave.
Rochester, NY 12309
Support and education group; for more details, see listing for national chapter under District of Columbia.

**PFLAG—Syracuse**
232 E. Onondaga St.
Syracuse, NY 13202
Support and education group; for more details, see listing for national chapter under District of Columbia.

**PFLAG—Westchester County**
3 Leatherstocking Lane
Mamaroneck, NY 10543
Support and education group; for more details, see listing for national chapter under District of Columbia.

## NORTH CAROLINA

**Gay and Lesbian Parents Coalition—Charlotte**
PO Box 221841
Charlotte, NC 23222
Support group for parents and their children; for more details, see listing for national chapter under District of Columbia.

**PFLAG—Charlotte**
5815 Charing Place
Charlotte, NC 28211
Support and education group; for more details, see listing for national chapter under District of Columbia.

**PFLAG—Dallas/Western Piedmont**
PO Box 722
Dallas, NC 28034
Support and education group; for more details, see listing for national chapter under District of Columbia.

**PFLAG—Flat Rock/Hendersonville**
Route 2, Box 105-L
Flat Rock, NC 28731
Support and education group; for more details, see listing for national chapter under District of Columbia.

**PFLAG—Raleigh/Durham**
PO Box 10844
Raleigh, NC 27605-0844
Support and education group; for more details, see listing for national chapter under District of Columbia.

**PFLAG—Western North Carolina**
PO Box 5978

have averaged less expense than either employees or spouses. Total costs to the city increased only 1.3 percent.

In any case, the experience nationally is that only a small number of employees sign up for the new benefits. Apple Computer, for example, reported only 42 employees out of 4,700. If the employer allows opposite-sex partners to sign up as well, the numbers rise moderately.

This is because, overall, two-thirds of those who register as domestic partners are heterosexual. Although the most organized and visible activists on the issue have been lesbian and gay, it's "hets" who have benefited most.

Most employers or city governments who have adopted domestic partner language have included definitions and safeguards. The draft Detroit ordinance has the two partners sign, in front of a notary, that they live together and

Asheville, NC 28813-5978
Support and education group; for more details, see listing for national chapter under District of Columbia.

## NORTH DAKOTA

### PFLAG—Central Dakota
PO Box 2491
Bismarck, ND 58502-2491
Support and education group; for more details, see listing for national chapter under District of Columbia.

### PFLAG—Fargo/Moorhead
1709 Sixth Ave. S
Fargo, ND 58103
Support and education group; for more details, see listing for national chapter under District of Columbia.

### PFLAG—Grand Forks
3210 Cherry
Grand Forks, ND 58501
Support and education group; for more details, see listing for national chapter under District of Columbia.

## OHIO

### PFLAG—Akron
PO Box 3204
Cuyahoga Falls, OH 44223
Support and education group; for more details, see listing for national chapter under District of Columbia.

### PFLAG—Athens Area
40011 Carpenter Hill Rd.
Pomeroy, OH 45769
Support and education group; for more details, see listing for national chapter under District of Columbia.

### PFLAG—Cleveland
14260 Larchmere Blvd.
Shaker Heights, OH 44120
Support and education group; for more details, see listing for national chapter under District of Columbia.

### PFLAG—Columbus
PO Box 340101
Columbus, OH 43234
Support and education group; for more details, see listing for national chapter under District of Columbia.

### PFLAG—Dayton
175 Park Meadows Dr.
Yellow Springs, OH 45387
Support and education group; for more details, see listing for national chapter under District of Columbia.

that they "are in a relationship of mutual support, caring and commitment (and) intend to remain in such a relationship." If they break up, they must sign a termination statement, and they may not register a new partnership for six months.

*By Jane Slaughter.*

*First published in* Metro Times, *February 14–20, 1996.*
*Reprinted with permission.*

### PFLAG—Greater Cincinnati

PO Box 19634
Cincinnati, OH 45219-0634
Support and education group; for more details, see listing for national chapter under District of Columbia.

### PFLAG—Lorain County

730 Park Ave.
Amherst, OH 44001
Support and education group; for more details, see listing for national chapter under District of Columbia.

### PFLAG—Miami Valley/Northwest Ohio

Dan Neiswonger, Chair
PO Box 45
Greenville, OH 45331-0045
phone: (513) 548-6730
This local branch of PFLAG (see the national description under District of Columbia for more information) includes friends and relatives of gays who want a better understanding of the homosexual lifestyle. The group attempts to offer an understanding about the history of the gay community and its importance; offers educational and counseling services; and works to improve the emotional health of individuals and enhance and preserve family relationships. The group was formerly known as the Great Lakes Regional chapter of the National Federation of Friends and Relatives of Gays.

### PFLAG—Portsmouth

11 Offnere St.
Portsmouth, OH 45662
Support and education group; for more details, see listing for national chapter under District of Columbia.

### PFLAG—Toledo

1719 Greenwood
Toledo, OH 43605
Support and education group; for more details, see listing for national chapter under District of Columbia.

### PFLAG—Youngstown

2201 Goleta Ave.
Youngstown, OH 44504
Support and education group; for more details, see listing for national chapter under District of Columbia.

## OKLAHOMA

### PFLAG—Tulsa

PO Box 52800
Tulsa, OK 74152
Support and education group; for more details, see listing for national chapter under District of Columbia.

## OREGON

### PFLAG—Ashland

PO Box 13
Ashland, OR 97520
Support and education group; for more details, see listing for national chapter under District of Columbia.

### PFLAG—Bandon

535 Ninth St., Ste. A-12
Bandon, OR 97411

Support and education group; for more details, see listing for national chapter under District of Columbia.

### PFLAG—Bend

1937 NW West Hills Ave.
Bend, OR 97701
Support and education group; for more details, see listing for national chapter under District of Columbia.

### PFLAG—Eugene/Springfield

PO Box 11137
Eugene, OR 97440-3337
Support and education group; for more details, see listing for national chapter under District of Columbia.

### PFLAG—Grants Pass

PO Box 555
Wilderville, OR 97543
Support and education group; for more details, see listing for national chapter under District of Columbia.

### PFLAG—Hood River

PO Box 321
Hood River, OR 97031
Support and education group; for more details, see listing for national chapter under District of Columbia.

### PFLAG—Klamath Falls

2306 Marina Dr.
Klamath Falls, OR 97601
Support and education group; for more details, see listing for national chapter under District of Columbia.

### PFLAG—Linn-Benton

1687 NW Division St.
Corvallis, OR 97330
Support and education group; for more details, see listing for national chapter under District of Columbia.

### PFLAG—Ontario

450 Bar-O Dr.
Ontario, OR 97914
Support and education group; for more details, see listing for national chapter under District of Columbia.

### PFLAG—Pendleton

1805 Southgate
Pendleton, OR 97801
Support and education group; for more details, see listing for national chapter under District of Columbia.

### PFLAG—Roseburg

1567 NW Lester St.
Roseburg, OR 97470
Support and education group; for more details, see listing for national chapter under District of Columbia.

### PFLAG—Salem

PO Box 121
Gates, OR 97346
Support and education group; for more details, see listing for national chapter under District of Columbia.

## PENNSYLVANIA

### Custody Action for Lesbian Mothers (CALM)

Rosalie G. Davies, Coordinator
PO Box 281
Narberth, PA 19072
phone: (610) 667-7508
fax: (610) 667-0978
CALM was established in 1974 to provide free legal and counseling services for lesbian mothers seeking child custody. The group's primary commitment is to aid the mother in keeping her children; its broader goal is to bring cases to court so the attitudes of judges and the courts may be challenged. Volunteers (usually lesbian mothers) advise mothers of their options, provide them with support and understanding, and accompany them through all phases of the legal process. CALM supports litigation addressing constitutional rights on the basis of sexual preference, and maintains nationwide contact with lesbian mother groups and attorneys who are either providing a similar counseling service or doing research in this area.

### PFLAG—Central Pennsylvania

Jackie Schulze, Contact
960 Century Dr.
PO Box 2001
Mechanicsburg, PA 17055
phone: (717) 795-0330
fax: (717) 795-0353

The Central Pennsylvania chapter of PFLAG (see the national description under District of Columbia for more information) comprises parents and friends of gay and lesbian persons. The group seeks to improve family relationships, educate the public about homosexuality, and influence anti-discriminatory laws and policies. Its newsletter appears monthly.

### PFLAG—Central Susquehanna

RD 2, Box 1955
Milton, PA 17847
Support and education group; for more details, see listing for national chapter under District of Columbia.

### PFLAG—Erie

1106 Oregon
Erie, PA 16505
Support and education group; for more details, see listing for national chapter under District of Columbia.

### PFLAG—Franklin Area

7430 Nyesville Rd.
Chambersburg, PA 17201
Support and education group; for more details, see listing for national chapter under District of Columbia.

### PFLAG—Lancaster/Red Rose

2112-13 Stone Mill Rd.
Lancaster, PA 17603-6073
Support and education group; for more details, see listing for national chapter under District of Columbia.

### PFLAG—Lehigh Valley

2040 Lehigh St., Ste. 710
Easton, PA 18042
Support and education group; for more details, see listing for national chapter under District of Columbia.

### PFLAG—Northeastern Pennsylvania

107 Butler St.
Forty Fort, PA 18704
Support and education group; for more details, see listing for national chapter under District of Columbia.

### PFLAG—Philadelphia

PO Box 15711
Philadelphia, PA 19103
Support and education group; for more details, see listing for national chapter under District of Columbia.

### PFLAG—Pittsburgh

PO Box 223
Monroeville, PA 15146
Support and education group; for more details, see listing for national chapter under District of Columbia.

### PFLAG—York

c/o Lutheran Social Services
1050 Pennsylvania Ave.
York, PA 17404
Support and education group; for more details, see listing for national chapter under District of Columbia.

## RHODE ISLAND

### PFLAG—East Bay

85 Roseland Terr.
Tiverton, RI 02878
Support and education group; for more details, see listing for national chapter under District of Columbia.

## SOUTH CAROLINA

### PFLAG—Charleston Area

PO Box 30734
Charleston, SC 29417-0734
Support and education group; for more details, see listing for national chapter under District of Columbia.

### PFLAG—Columbia

493 Hickory Hill Dr.
Columbia, SC 29210
Support and education group; for more details, see listing for national chapter under District of Columbia.

### PFLAG—Greenville

801 Butler Springs Rd.
Greenville, SC 29615
Support and education group; for more details, see listing for national chapter under District of Columbia.

## TENNESSEE

### PFLAG—Greater Chattanooga

PO Box 17252
Chattanooga, TN 37415
Support and education group; for more details, see listing for national chapter under District of Columbia.

### PFLAG—Memphis

1303 Calais Rd.
Memphis, TN 38120
Support and education group; for more details, see listing for national chapter under District of Columbia.

### PFLAG—Nashville

135 Holly Forest
Nashville, TN 37221-2226
Support and education group; for more details, see listing for national chapter under District of Columbia.

## TEXAS

### Gay and Lesbian Parents Coalition—Dallas

PO Box 820492
Hurst, TX 76182
Support group for parents and their children; for more details, see listing for national chapter under District of Columbia.

### Gay and Lesbian Parents Coalition—San Antonio

2839 NW Military Dr., Ste. 508
San Antonio, TX 78231
Support group for parents and their children; for more details, see listing for national chapter under District of Columbia.

### PFLAG—Austin

PO Box 9151
Austin, TX 78766-9151
Support and education group; for more details, see listing for national chapter under District of Columbia.

### PFLAG—Dallas

c/o Pat Stone
PO Box 38415
Dallas, TX 75238-0415
Support and education group; for more details, see listing for national chapter under District of Columbia.

### PFLAG—Denton

PO Box 51096
Denton, TX 76206
Support and education group; for more details, see listing for national chapter under District of Columbia.

### PFLAG—El Paso

PO Box 1761
El Paso, TX 79949
Support and education group; for more details, see listing for national chapter under District of Columbia.

### PFLAG—Fort Worth

PO Box 48612
Fort Worth, TX 76148
Support and education group; for more details, see listing for national chapter under District of Columbia.

### PFLAG—Houston

PO Box 692444
Houston, TX 77269-2444
Support and education group; for more details, see listing for national chapter under District of Columbia.

### PFLAG—San Antonio

PO Box 790093
San Antonio, TX 78279
Support and education group; for more details, see listing for national chapter under District of Columbia.

## UTAH

### PFLAG—Salt Lake City

3363 Enchanted Hills Dr.
Salt Lake City, UT 84121-5465
Support and education group; for more details, see listing for national chapter under District of Columbia.

## VERMONT

### PFLAG—Barre/Montpelier

15 Vine St.
Northfield, VT 05663

Support and education group; for more details, see listing for national chapter under District of Columbia.

### PFLAG—Brattleboro

409 Hillwinds
Brattleboro, VT 05301
Support and education group; for more details, see listing for national chapter under District of Columbia.

### PFLAG—Burlington

23 Birchwood Lane
Burlington, VT 05401
Support and education group; for more details, see listing for national chapter under District of Columbia.

## VIRGINIA

### PFLAG—Charlottesville

301 Monte Vista Ave.
Charlottesville, VA 22903
Support and education group; for more details, see listing for national chapter under District of Columbia.

### PFLAG—Richmond

PO Box 36392
Richmond, VA 23235-8008
Support and education group; for more details, see listing for national chapter under District of Columbia.

### PFLAG—Roanoke/Western Virginia

12 Lakeshore Terr.
Hardy, VA 24101-3501
Support and education group; for more details, see listing for national chapter under District of Columbia.

## WASHINGTON

### Family Services, Eastside

11911 N.E. First
Bellevue, WA 98005
phone: (206) 451-2869

### Lavendar Families Resource Network

Jenny Sayward
PO Box 21567
Seattle, WA 98111
phone: (206) 325-2643
Also known as the Lesbian Mothers National Defense Fund, the network was founded in 1974 and provides legal, emotional, and financial support for lesbian and gay parents involved with custody problems. The fund monitors and reports on judicial and legislative activities and decisions that affect gay and lesbian parents; conducts specialized education; provides alternative conception and adoption information, an information bank, and a lawyer referral service; and maintains a speakers' bureau. The quarterly newsletter, *Mom's Apple Pie,* reports on lesbian and gay custody cases, current legislation, and other issues surrounding lesbian parenting.

### Legal Marriage Alliance of Washington

1202 E. Pike, #1190
Seattle, WA 98122-3934
phone: (206) 689-6280
Web site: http://www.eskimo.com/~demian/lma.html
Lesbian and gay couples and supporters working together to prepare the community and the general public for the impact on Washington state of the expected decision by the Hawaii Supreme Court on same-sex marriages.

### Partners Task Force for Gay & Lesbian Couples

Box 9685
Seattle, WA 98109-0685
phone: (206) 935-1206
e-mail: demian@eskimo.com
Web site: http://www.eskimo.com/~demian/partners.html

### PFLAG—Bremerton

2880 NE 72nd St.
Bremerton, WA 98311
Support and education group; for more details, see listing for national chapter under District of Columbia.

### PFLAG—Ellensburg

1106 E. Third Ave.
Ellensburg, WA 98926
Support and education group; for more details, see listing for national chapter under District of Columbia.

### PFLAG—Ephrata

165 D St. SW
Ephrata, WA 98823
Support and education group; for more details, see listing for national chapter under District of Columbia.

### PFLAG—Lewis and Clark

2220 Second Ave.
Clarkston, WA 99403
Support and education group; for more details, see listing for national chapter under District of Columbia.

### PFLAG—Olympia

PO Box 6123
Olympia, WA 98502
Support and education group; for more details, see listing for national chapter under District of Columbia.

### PFLAG—Richland

648 Saint St.
Richland, WA 99352
Support and education group; for more details, see listing for national chapter under District of Columbia.

### PFLAG—Seattle/Tacoma

1202 E. Pike St., Ste. 260
Seattle, WA 98122
Support and education group; for more details, see listing for national chapter under District of Columbia.

### PFLAG—Spokane

PO Box 40122
Spokane, WA 99202-0901
Support and education group; for more details, see listing for national chapter under District of Columbia.

### PFLAG—Vancouver

12102 NW 21st Ave.
Vancouver, WA 98685
Support and education group; for more details, see listing for national chapter under District of Columbia.

### PFLAG—Yakima Valley

732 Summitview, Ste. 584
Yakima, WA 98902
Support and education group; for more details, see listing for national chapter under District of Columbia.

### Vashon Youth and Family Services

PO Box 237
Vashon, WA 98070
phone: (206) 463-5511

## WISCONSIN

### PFLAG—Appleton/Fox Cities

PO Box 75
Little Chute, WI 54140-0075
Support and education group; for more details, see listing for national chapter under District of Columbia.

### PFLAG—Lakeshore/Sheboygan

831 Union Ave.
Sheboygan, WI 53081
Support and education group; for more details, see listing for national chapter under District of Columbia.

### PFLAG—Madison

Box 1722
Madison, WI 53701
phone: (608) 273-1208 or (608) 255-0533
The Madison Chapter of PFLAG (see the national description under District of Columbia for more information) acts as a support group for parents, family members, and friends of lesbians and gays, and attempts to provide an understanding and acceptance of the individual's sexual orientation.

### PFLAG—Milwaukee

c/o Lutheran Campus Ministries
3074 N. Maryland
Milwaukee, WI 53211
Support and education group; for more details, see listing for national chapter under District of Columbia.

## WYOMING

### PFLAG—Casper

404 S. McKinley St.
Casper, WY 82601-2916
Support and education group; for more details, see listing for national chapter under District of Columbia.

### PFLAG—Jackson

PO Box 2704
Jackson, WY 83001
Support and education group; for more details, see listing for national chapter under District of Columbia.

# ONLINE RESOURCES

## THE WEB

### Equal Marriage Rights Home Page

http://nether.net/~rod/html/xub/marriage.html
Supporters of the legalization of same-sex marriage will find much fuel for their cause here. The Equal Marriage Rights Home Page details the progress of same-sex legislation throughout the United States.

### Lesbian and Gay Families

http://www.casti.com/QRD/family/lgb.family.bibliography
Nothing flashy, just a helpful list of books, articles, and videos—for both adults and children—that support lesbian/gay families.

### Partners Task Force for Gay & Lesbian Couples

http://www.eskimo.com/~demian/partners.html
This award-winning site offers dozens of survey results, reports, articles, and links to other sources of information about same-sex couples and the struggle for legally recognized gay marriage.

## USENET

### MARRIAGE

mailing list: majordomo@abacus.oxy.edu
The MARRIAGE listserv is for the exchange of news and opinions relating to same-sex marriage. To subscribe, send an e-mail message to the address above. The subject of you message should be *subscribe marriage.*

### Parents, Families, and Friends of Lesbians and Gays

mailing list: majordomo@pflag.casti.com
This unmoderated discussion list is a support forum for the friends and family members of homosexuals. To subscribe, send an e-mail message to the address above. The body of your message should contain only *subscribe pflag-talk.*

# HEALTH and HIV/AIDS

For lesbians and gay men, support from one another and from sympathetic members of the medical community has helped many during times of crisis to secure visitation and other rights with loved ones, to find supportive therapy and recovery counseling, and to cope with HIV/AIDS as it affects us or those we love.

The AIDS pandemic, in particular, affected the LGBT community like none other in history. Unlike the disease's initial progression in the rest of the world (according to the World Health Organization in 1993, 75% of people with HIV worldwide were infected through heterosexual sex), in North America it became first and most widely evident among gay men, affecting them in horrifying numbers. Although the rate of transmission among gay men has decreased progressively since 1989, its devastating effects on the gay community continue—as do the positive effects of the community's response.

The broad and heartfelt reaction of lesbians and gay men to the AIDS crisis helped unify their political efforts; spurred new, dramatic and highly effective methods of political action; helped educate gays and straights alike on prevention, treatment, and compassion; and encouraged more and better testing and treatment options. The work is not done; the crisis is not over. But consider how far we have come.

The men and women who formed the AIDS Coalition to Unleash Power (ACT UP)—one of many groups dedicated to addressing the AIDS pandemic—realized there was no time to resolve personal or philosophical differences before setting in motion steps to curb the crisis. One method ACT UP used to great effect was the zap—a small, focused action by just a few people. ACT UP was not the first or last group to use this tactic, but as the one that "produced the largest grassroots, democratic, and most effective organizing in the history of both the gay and feminist movements," according to ACT UP cofounder Sarah Schulman, the group used the method often and effectively. The group wasn't perfect, Schulman writes in her 1994 book *My American History*, but it's probably "safe to say that most of the substantial progress that has been made in this country on behalf of people with AIDS"—such as needle exchange programs, condom distribution, developing and quickly releasing new and alternative treatments, improving pediatric care, changing the disease's official definition so more women could receive benefits, reforming insurance policies, and so on—"can be traced to ACT UP."

ACT UP is by no means the only AIDS action or awareness group out there. National groups like Project Inform of San Francisco, the Lambda Legal Defense and Education Fund in New York, the National AIDS Hotline, and many others provide information about AIDS prevention and treatment, legal support, financial aid, political advocacy, and other help to those affected by HIV/AIDS. The NAMES Project Foundation and its local chapters have created probably the most brilliant and moving commemoration to those who have died of AIDS: the AIDS Memorial Quilt, which is displayed in portions throughout the country and will be presented in its entirety—covering more than 27 acres—in Washington, D.C., in October 1996.

The National Lesbian and Gay Health Foundation, the Association of Lesbian and Gay Psychiatrists, the International Advisory Council for Homosexual Men and Women in Alcoholics Anonymous, the National Gay and Lesbian Domestic Violence Victims' Network, Senior Action in a Gay Environment (SAGE), and many other groups offer treatment, counseling, advocacy, and other support in all aspects of physical and mental health.

Local groups, as well, offer lesbian- and gay-friendly health, counseling, and referral services. For people with HIV/AIDS, groups like the Midwest AIDS Prevention Program (described in this chapter) provide buddy programs, hospital visitation, home and transportation help, counseling, fundraisers and financial assistance, legal advice, community education, and numerous other support programs.

Although this chapter is broad-ranging, we realize it is not comprehensive. If a support or health program for your area is not listed in this chapter, please call your local medical center, women's clinic, or lesbian/gay community center, who may know of even more programs than we list here.

# CANADA

## ONTARIO

### AIDS Committee of London
343 Richmond St., Ste. 200
London, ON N6A 3C2
phone: (519) 434-1601

### AIDS Committee of Windsor
2090 Wyandotte St. E
Windsor, ON N8Y 4R8
phone: (519) 973-0222

*Two men supporting ACT UP participate in the 1994's Stonewall 25 march in New York City. (Photo copyright Reuters/Bettmann.)*

## ENGLAND

### Gemma

Elsa Beckett, Coordinator
BM Box 5700
London WC1N 3XX
phone: 171 4854024
Gemma works toward diminishing the isolation of homosexual and bisexual women with disabilities through a pen-, tape-, phone-, and braille-friend network. Founded in 1976, Gemma also provides information on other lesbian groups and helplines. The group publishes a magazine called *Facets* and a quarterly newsletter, and meets the second Sunday of each month.

## UNITED STATES

### NATIONAL

### National AIDS Hotline

English: (800) 342-AIDS
Spanish: (800) 334-SIDA
hearing impaired: (800) AIDS-TTY
A project of the National Centers for Disease Control, Atlanta, Georgia.

### ALABAMA

### AIDS Hotline (Statewide)

phone: (800) 228-0469

### Live and Let Live Alcoholics Anonymous

PO Box 55372
Birmingham, AL 35255

### ALASKA

### AIDS Hotline (Statewide)

phone: (800) 478-2437

## SPOTLIGHT

# THE QUILT

*"Powerful and impressive, the AIDS Memorial Quilt has educated millions about HIV and AIDS. It is both a lasting memorial to those who have died and a compassionate cry for humanity to pay attention to the AIDS crisis." — California Senator Dianne Feinstein*

The AIDS Memorial Quilt is the largest on-going community arts project in the world. Each of the 32,000 colorful panels in the Quilt was made to remember the life of a person lost to AIDS. Panels are three feet by six feet—the size of a human grave. As the epidemic claims more lives, the Quilt continues to grow: Over 50 new memorial panels are added each week. The Quilt stands for more than the tens of thousands of people whose names

## ARIZONA

### AIDS Hotline (Statewide)
phone: (602) 265-3300

### Community AIDS Council
3136 N. 3rd Avenue
Phoenix, AZ 85013
phone: (602) 264-5437

### HIV/AIDS Prevention Program
1825 E. Roosevelt
Phoenix, AZ 85006
phone: (602) 506-6853

### Lesbian Resource Project
PO Box 26031
Tempe, AZ 85285-6031

### New Creations
1029 E. Turney
Phoenix, AZ 85014
Recovery services.

### People with AIDS Coalition—Arizona
801 W. Congress
Tucson, AZ 85745

## ARKANSAS

### AIDS Hotline (Statewide)
phone: (800) 448-8305

### Women's Project
2224 Main St.
Little Rock, AR 72206

## CALIFORNIA

### ACT UP—Golden Gate
519 Castro St., #93
San Francisco, CA 94114
phone: (415) 252-9200
fax: (415) 252-9277
Web site: http://www.creative.net/~actupgg/
The Golden Gate chapter of the AIDS Coalition to Unleash Power says in its statement of purpose: "ACT UP Golden Gate is a diverse, non-partisan group of individuals, united in anger and committed to direct action to end the AIDS crisis. We are engaged in a battle to reform the research and treatment of HIV and its associated opportunistic diseases, intensify HIV education and prevention efforts, and revolutionize the health care delivery system in this country. The HIV pandemic crosses all racial, age, sexual, cultural, and class

are sewn into the fabric. It stands, as well, for the sorrow, anger, love, and hope of people who make the panels.

The origin of the NAMES Project, which sponsors the Quilt, can be traced to June of 1987, when a small group of strangers gathered in a San Francisco storefront to document the lives they feared history would neglect. Their goal was to create a memorial for those who had died of AIDS, and to thereby help people understand the devastating impact of the disease. This meeting of devoted friends and lovers served as the foundation of the NAMES Project AIDS Memorial Quilt.

Nearly a decade later, the Quilt is a powerful visual reminder of the AIDS pandemic—"one of the great memorials of our time, and one of history's most powerful works of political art," according to George Shaekelford, curator of the Houston, Texas Museum of Fine Arts. More than 31,000 individual

boundaries, and we are committed to involving all affected communities in this fight. The fight against the HIV pandemic is our highest priority."

### ACT UP—Long Beach
5595 E. Seventh St., #174
Long Beach, CA 90804
Local chapter of the AIDS Coalition to Unleash Power.

### ACT UP—Los Angeles
3924 W. Sunset Blvd., #2
Los Angeles, CA 90029
Local chapter of the AIDS Coalition to Unleash Power.

### ACT UP—Sacramento
Lambda Community Center
1931 L St.
Sacramento, CA 95814
Local chapter of the AIDS Coalition to Unleash Power.

### ACT UP—San Francisco
333 Valencia St.
San Francisco, CA 94103
Local chapter of the AIDS Coalition to Unleash Power.

### AIDS Foundation—San Diego
4080 Centre Street
San Diego, CA 92103
phone: (619) 686-5024

### AIDS Hotline (Statewide)
phone: (800) 922-2437

### AIDS Project—Central Coast
Gay & Lesbian Resource Center
126 E. Haley St., Ste. A-17
Santa Barbara, CA 93101
phone: (805) 963-3636

### AIDS Project—East Bay
565 16th St.
Oakland, CA 94612

### American Indian AIDS Institute
333 Valencia St., Ste. 400
San Francisco, CA 94103
phone: (415) 626-7639

### Bay Area Physicians for Human Rights (BAPHR)
4111 18th St.
San Francisco, CA 94114
phone: (415) 558-9353
The Bay Area Physicians for Human Rights are graduates of and students in approved schools of medicine and osteopathy, dentists, and podiatrists. The group's objectives

three-by-six-foot memorial panels, each one commemorating the life of someone who has died of AIDS, have been sewn together by friends, lovers, and family members. The NAMES Project Foundation coordinates displays of portions of the Quilt worldwide.

The Quilt was conceived in November of 1985 by longtime San Francisco gay rights activist Cleve Jones. Since the 1978 assassinations of gay San Francisco Supervisor Harvey Milk and Mayor George Moscone, Jones had helped to organize the annual candlelight march honoring these men. As he was planning for the 1985 march, he learned that the number of San Franciscans lost to AIDS had passed the 1,000 mark. He was moved to ask each of his fellow marchers to write on placards the names of friends and loved ones who had died of AIDS. At the end of the march, Jones and others stood on ladders, above the sea of candlelight, taping these placards to the walls of

are to improve the quality of medical care for gay and lesbian patients; to educate physicians, both gay and nongay, in the special problems of gay and lesbian patients; to educate the public about health care needs of the homosexual; to maintain liaison with public officials about gay and lesbian health concerns; and to offer the gay and lesbian physician support through social functions and consciousness-raising groups. The group, which was founded in 1977, sponsors research into medical problems and issues that are of special interest to homosexual patients; provides a medical and physician referral service and monthly educational programs; operates a speakers' bureau; and compiles statistics. Membership is concentrated in the San Francisco Bay Area. The bimonthly *BAPHRON* newsletter features medical-related human rights issues, especially gay and lesbian rights and public policy on AIDS. The group has also published a monograph called *Medical Evaluation of Persons at Risk of HIV Infection* and hosts an annual symposium.

### Gay and Lesbian Medical Association

Benjamin Schatz, Executive Director
211 Church St., Ste. C
San Francisco, CA 94114
phone: (415) 255-4547
fax: (415) 255-4784

The Gay and Lesbian Medical Association includes physicians and medical students. Founded in 1981 and with 21 local branches, the association seeks to eliminate discrimination on the basis of sexual orientation in the health professions; promotes unprejudiced medical care for gay and lesbian patients; maintains a referral and support program for HIV infected physicians; sponsors an annual symposium on lesbian and gay health issues; offers support to homosexual physicians; encourages research into the health needs of gays and lesbians; maintains a liaison with medical schools and other organizations concerning needs of gay patients and professionals; fosters communication and cooperation among members and other groups and individuals supportive of gay and lesbian physicians; and offers a referral service. Formerly known as the American Association of Physicians for Human Rights, the Gay and Lesbian Medical Association bestows annual achievement and recognition awards and publishes a quarterly newsletter that covers the activities of the association, the medical community, and the public regarding lesbian and gay health issues.

the San Francisco Federal Building. The wall of names looked to Jones like a patchwork quilt.

Inspired by this sight, Jones made plans for a larger memorial. A little over a year later, he created the first panel for the NAMES Project AIDS Memorial Quilt in memory of his friend Marvin Feldman. In June of 1987, Jones teamed up with several others to formally organize the NAMES Project Foundation.

Public response to the Quilt was immediate. People in each of the U.S. cities most affected by AIDS—New York, Los Angeles, and San Francisco—sent panels to the San Francisco workshop in memory of their friends and loved ones. Generous donors rapidly filled "wish lists" for sewing machines, office supplies, and volunteers. Lesbians, gay men, and their friends were especially supportive.

### Lesbian and Gay Caucus of Public Health Workers (LGCPHW)

Donald Gabard, Ph.D.
2341 Hidalgo Ave.
Los Angeles, CA 90039
phone: (213) 664-9002
LGCPHW is a caucus of the American Public Health Association and represents public health workers in the fields of administration, government, direct care, and teaching. The caucus, founded in 1975, promotes the dissemination of information on the health needs of lesbians, gay men, and bisexuals, and serves as a support network for gay public health workers. The caucus believes homophobia interferes with the proper delivery of health care to gays, lesbians, and bisexuals and restricts or eliminates their contributions as health workers, and causes physical and mental health problems. The group holds scientific sessions on gay and lesbian health issues at its annual meeting, held in conjunction with APHA and the National Gay Health Coalition.

### Lesbian-Gay Health and Health Policy Foundation

c/o Shane S. Que Hee
PO Box 168
Los Angeles, CA 90024-0000

### Lesbian Health Project—Los Angeles

8240 Santa Monica Blvd.
West Hollywood, CA 90046

### Lesbian Health Project—San Diego

PO Box 3357
San Diego, CA 92163-3357

### Lobby for Individual Freedom and Equality (LIFE)

Laurie McBride, Executive Director
926 J St., Ste. 522
Sacramento, CA 95814
phone: (916) 444-0424
fax: (916) 444-3059
LIFE, founded in 1986, works to coordinate, develop, and promote the statewide agenda of gay, lesbian, and HIV-affected Californians. Its newsletter, *LIFELINES,* is published quarterly.

### Mobilization Against AIDS

584-B Castro St.
San Francisco, CA 94114
phone: (415) 863-4676

### NAMES Project Foundation

Michael Berg, President

As awareness of the Quilt grew, so did participation. Hundreds of individuals and groups from all over the world sent panels to San Francisco to be included in the Quilt. On October 11, 1987, the NAMES Project displayed the Quilt for the first time on the National Mall in Washington, D.C., during the National March on Washington for Lesbian and Gay Rights. It covered a space larger than a football field and included 1,920 panels. Half a million people visited the Quilt that weekend.

The overwhelming response to the Quilt's inaugural display led to a four-month, 20-city, national tour for the Quilt in the spring of 1988. The tour raised nearly $500,000 for hundreds of AIDS service organizations. More than 9,000 volunteers across the country helped the seven-person traveling crew move and display the Quilt. Local panels were added in each city, tripling the Quilt's size to more than 6,000 panels by the end of the tour.

310 Townsend St., Ste. 310
San Francisco, CA 94107
phone: (415) 882-5500
fax: (415) 882-6200
e-mail: info@aidsquilt.org
Web site: http://www.aidsquilt.org/
Sponsors and coordinates displays of the AIDS Memorial Quilt, including a complete display of the Quilt—15 city blocks of fabric—planned for October 1996 in Washington, D.C. According to the group's extensive Web site, "The Quilt is a patchwork of lives, made up of 3′ by 6′ panels, each remembering a person lost to AIDS. The Quilt is art that heals—and anyone can add to it. It grows larger every day. The Quilt makes you think—it's a tool for learning about AIDS. The Quilt is the icon of the epidemic—it turns despair into action in communities all over the world."

## NAMES Project—Inland Empire

1240 Palmyrita Avenue, Suite E
Riverside, CA 92507
phone: (909) 784-2437
Web site: http://www.aidsquilt.org/
Sponsors and coordinates displays of the AIDS Memorial Quilt.

## NAMES Project—Long Beach

996 Redondo Ave., Suite 230
Long Beach, CA 90804
phone: (310) 493-2305
Web site: http://www.aidsquilt.org/
Sponsors and coordinates displays of the AIDS Memorial Quilt.

## NAMES Project—Los Angeles

7985 Santa Monica Blvd., #260
West Hollywood, CA 90046
phone: (213) 653-6263
Web site: http://www.aidsquilt.org/
Sponsors and coordinates displays of the AIDS Memorial Quilt.

## NAMES Project—Orange County

PO Box 4577
Garden Grove, CA 92686
phone: (714) 490-3880
Web site: http://www.aidsquilt.org/
Sponsors and coordinates displays of the AIDS Memorial Quilt.

## NAMES Project—San Diego

3305 Adams Ave., #6E
San Diego, CA 92116
phone: (619) 492-8452
Web site: http://www.aidsquilt.org/
Sponsors and coordinates displays of the AIDS Memorial Quilt.

## NAMES Project—Ventura County

PO Box 7336
Ventura, CA 93006

The Quilt returned to Washington, D.C., in October of 1988, when 8,288 panels were displayed on the Ellipse in front of the White House. Celebrities, politicians, families, lovers, and friends read aloud the names of the people represented by the Quilt panels. The reading of names is now a tradition followed at nearly every Quilt display.

In 1989 a second NAMES Project tour of North America brought the Quilt to 19 additional cities in the United States and Canada. That tour and other 1989 displays raised nearly a quarter of a million dollars for AIDS service organizations. In October of that year, the Quilt was again displayed on the Ellipse in Washington, D.C.

By 1992, the AIDS Memorial Quilt included panels from every U.S. state and 28 countries. In October of that year, the entire Quilt returned to Washington, D.C., this time in the shadow of the Washington Monument. To reflect

phone: (805) 650-9546
Web site: http://www.aidsquilt.org/
Sponsors and coordinates displays of the AIDS Memorial Quilt.

### National Association of Lesbian and Gay Alcoholism Professionals

1147 S. Alvarado St.
Los Angeles, CA 90006

### National Lawyers Guild AIDS Network

558 Capp St.
San Francisco, CA 94110

### National Native American AIDS Prevention Center

3515 Grand Ave., Ste. 100
Oakland, CA 94610
hotline: (800) 283-2437

### National Task Force on AIDS Prevention

631 O'Farrell St.
San Francisco, CA 94109
phone: (415) 749-6714

### ONE, Incorporated (OI)

David G. Cameron, President
PO Box 19028A
1130 Arlington Ave.
Los Angeles, CA 90019-3515
phone: (213) 735-5252
Founded in 1952, ONE, Inc. is comprised of corporate trustees. ONE provides group therapy, individual counseling, and referrals to gays and lesbians; offers some programs for transsexuals and transvestites; provides college-level courses, lectures, and panels under a state-authorized M.A. and Ph.D. degree program at the ONE Institute of Homophile Studies. The group also sponsors a placement service; participates with public and community committees; compiles statistics and bibliographies; and operates a speakers' bureau. ONE publishes *ONE Calendar* nine to ten times per year, and *ONEletter* monthly.

### Project Inform (PI)

1965 Market St., Ste. 220
San Francisco, CA 94103
state hotline: (800) 344-7422
national hotline: (800) 822-7422
Web site: http://hivnet.org/inform-www/
Project Inform's goals are "to inform the HIV-infected (and all those at risk) of life-saving strategies like early diagnosis and early intervention; to give people and their physicians the means to make informed choices about the most promising treatment options; and to change research and regula-

the global nature of the AIDS pandemic, this display was titled the "International Display."

In January 1993, the NAMES Project was invited to march in President Bill Clinton's inaugural parade. Over 200 volunteers, including representatives of national AIDS organizations and Leanza Cornett, Miss America 1993, carried Quilt panels down Pennsylvania Avenue in the parade. Also in January 1993, the NAMES Project board of directors selected Anthony Turney as executive director. Turney is former deputy chairman of the National Endowment for the Arts, and former executive director of the Dance Theatre of Harlem.

Today there are more than 40 NAMES Project chapters in the United States and 32 independent Quilt initiatives from around the world. Since 1987, more than 5.5 million people have visited the Quilt in thousands of displays

tory policies which delay or prevent access to treatment." Originally meant to be a short-term project, Project Inform was founded in 1985 to create a community-based research study of the effect of AIDS treatments that were in common use. PI subsequently created printed materials, a hotline service, and regular public town meetings. PI's Treatment Hotline is the only nationwide hotline service devoted exclusively to a broad range of treatment issues—from passing along the latest in treatment news, to debunking the latest in treatment hype. *PI Perspective,* published three times yearly, analyzes AIDS treatment and research, along with the political, scientific, and regulatory issues that affect the lives of people with HIV. The *PI Briefing Paper,* a newsletter, also comes out three times yearly and augments the *PI Perspective* with legislative updates, reports on late-breaking news and developments, and updates on current drugs in development and standards of care. PI also publishes regular fact sheets and discussion papers. PI's advocacy programs include the PI Treatment Action Network, which coordinates and unites people throughout the United States to address issues affecting research, access to treatment, and health care. In addition, PI conducts ethical reviews of community-based research projects and otherwise supports or monitors research developments.

### San Francisco AIDS Foundation

25 Van Ness Ave., Ste. 660
San Francisco, CA 94102

### Spencer Recovery Center

343 W. Foothill Blvd.
Monrovia, CA 91016

### Stop AIDS Los Angeles

G/L Community Services Center
1625 N. Hudson Ave.
Los Angeles, CA 90028

### Stop AIDS Project—San Francisco

Fredric Sonenberg, Executive Director
201 Sanchez St.
San Francisco, CA 94114
phone: (415) 575-1545
fax: (415) 252-5352
Web site: http://www.stopaids.org/
The mission of the Stop AIDS Project is to develop and implement a community organizing project for self-identified gay and bisexual men in San Francisco which seeks to reduce HIV transmission and lessen the adverse effects of the HIV epidemic on the community.

worldwide. Through such displays, the NAMES Project Foundation has raised over $1,600,000 for AIDS service organizations throughout North America.

The Washington, D.C. displays of October 1987, 1988, 1989, and 1992 are the only ones to have featured the Quilt in its entirety. Plans are underway to display the entire NAMES Project AIDS Memorial Quilt in Washington, D.C. over Columbus Day weekend in 1996. The NAMES Project estimates that by that time, the Quilt will include as many as 45,000 panels and cover more than 27 acres, or roughly the size of 29 football fields.

The Quilt is the largest example of a community art project in the world. It has redefined the tradition of quiltmaking in response to contemporary circumstances. The Quilt was nominated for a Nobel Peace Prize in 1989. "Common Threads: Stories from the Quilt" won the Academy Award as the best feature-length documentary film of 1989. *A Promise to Remember,* a

**Women Organized to Respond to Life Threatening Diseases (WORLD)**
PO Box 11535
Oakland, CA 94611

**Women's Cancer Research Center**
3023 Shattuck Ave.
Berkeley, CA 94705

**Youth Advocates Teen HIV Program**
555 Cole Street, Suite 6
San Francisco, CA 94117
phone: (415) 386-9398

## COLORADO

**ACT UP—Denver**
432 Broadway, #100
Denver, CO 80209
Local chapter of the AIDS Coalition to Unleash Power.

**AIDS Hotline (Statewide)**
phone: (800) 252-2437

**Lavender Project**
Presbyterian—St. Luke's Medical Center
1719 E. 19th Ave.
Denver, CO 80218

**National Gay and Lesbian Domestic Violence Victims' Network**
Sharon F. Daugherty II
3506 S. Ouray Cir.
Aurora, CO 80013
The network was formed in 1990 as a support group for people abused by gay or lesbian partners, and promotes victim advocacy. The group maintains a speakers' bureau and has published a book, *Closeted Screams: A Service Provider Handbook for Same-Sex Domestic Violence Issues,* for $19.95.

**People with AIDS Coalition—Colorado**
PO Box 300339
Denver, CO 80203

**Women's HIV Outreach Program**
Boulder County Health Department
3450 North Broadway
Boulder, CO 80304
phone: (303) 441-1244

## CONNECTICUT

**AIDS Hotline (Statewide)**
phone: (800) 342-2437

collection of letters to the NAMES Project written by panelmakers, was published by Avon in July 1992.

### AIDS Project—Greater Danbury
PO Box 91
Newton, CT 06801

### AIDS Project—Greater New Britain
PO Box 1214
New Britain, CT 06053

### AIDS Project—Hartford
30 Arbor St.
Hartford, CT 06105

### AIDS Project—New Haven
PO Box 636
New Haven, CT 06503

### NAMES Project—Connecticut
216 Lakeview Avenue
Waterbury, CT 06705
phone: (203) 591-1886
Web site: http://www.aidsquilt.org/
Sponsors and coordinates displays of the AIDS Memorial Quilt.

## DELAWARE

### AIDS Delaware
601 Delaware Ave.
Wilmington, DE 19801
phone: (302) 652-6776
fax: (302) 652-5150
Formerly known as Delaware Lesbian & Gay Health Advocates.

### AIDS Hotline (Statewide)
phone: (800) 422-0429

## DISTRICT OF COLUMBIA

### ACT UP—Washington, DC
1339 14th St. NW, #5
Washington, DC 20005
Local chapter of the AIDS Coalition to Unleash Power.

### AIDS Action Council
1875 Connecticut Ave. NW, Ste. 700
Washington, DC 20009
The AIDS Action Council lobbies at the national level for AIDS program and research funding.

### AIDS Hotline (Statewide)
phone: (202) 332-2437

### International Advisory Council for Homosexual Men and Women in Alcoholics Anonymous (IAC)
PO Box 90
Washington, DC 20044-0090
Established in 1980, this advisory council supports groups within Alcoholics Anonymous World Services that are specifically composed of gays and lesbians. The council's purpose is to serve the gay and lesbian members of AA and to provide advice and support to other members of AA. As it works for unity and service with AA to benefit both the gay and lesbian members and AA, the council advocates freedom in communication as an important aid to recovery and provides alcoholism professionals with information about gay and lesbian AA groups for use in counseling lesbian and gay alcoholics. The council's committees include Group Needs, Lesbian Outreach, Literature, Loners, and Public Information. Its newsletter appears four times each year, and the group also publishes an annual world directory of gay/lesbian AA groups and a semiannual calendar of events.

### Lesbian Health Project
Whitman-Walker Clinic
1407 S St. NW
Washington, DC 20009

### Mautner Project for Lesbians with Cancer
Susan Hester and Deb Morris, Contacts
PO Box 90437
Washington, DC 20090

### NAMES Project—National Capital Area
1613 "K" Street, NW

Washington, DC 20006
phone: (202) 296-2637
Web site: http://www.aidsquilt.org/
Sponsors and coordinates displays of the AIDS Memorial Quilt.

### National AIDS Fund
1400 I St., Ste. 1220
Washington, DC 20005-2208

### National AIDS Minority Information and Education
Howard University
2139 Gerogia Ave. NW, Ste. 3B
Washington, DC 20001

### National Association of People with AIDS (NAPWA)
1413 K St. NW, 8th F.
Washington, DC 20005
phone: (202) 898-0414 or (800) 338-2437
Founded in 1983, NAPWA represents Americans affected by HIV/AIDS and profides information and education services, treatment partnerships, and other forms of assistance.

### National Lesbian and Gay Health Association (NLGHA)
Christopher J. Portelli, Executive Director
1407 S St., NW
Washington, DC 20009
phone: (202) 797-3536
fax: (202) 797-3504
The NLGHA membership includes 20,000 lesbian, gay, and nongay health professionals providing care to lesbians and gay men, and individuals concerned with the accessibility and quality of health care for lesbians and gay men. The purpose of the association, which formed in 1994 by the merger of the National Lesbian and Gay Health Foundation and the National Alliance of Lesbian and Gay Health Clinics, is to develop and coordinate interdisciplinary health programs and activities. NLGHA seeks to develop a healthier environment for all lesbians and gay men and to further the delivery of appropriate health care to them. The group promotes research on issues of lesbian and gay health care; serves as liaison among members, health agencies, and other private and governmental bodies; facilitates networking among national lesbian and gay health organizations; provides educational and consultative service to associations, hospitals, institutions, and schools regarding lesbian and gay health issues; conducts training programs on gay health issues; and assists in local conferences. NLGHA's annual Paroski Scholarship is designated for currently enrolled medical students who are interested in and dedicated to the advancement of lesbian and gay health. The group publishes a quarterly newsletter, *Check-up,* and sponsors the annual Lesbian and Gay Health Conference and National AIDS/HIV Forum.

### National Minority AIDS Council
300 I St. NE, Ste. 400
Washington, DC 20002-4389
phone: (202) 544-1076

### National Resource Center on Women and AIDS
2000 P St. NW, Ste. 508
Washington, DC 20036

### National Women and HIV/AIDS Project
PO Box 53141
Washington, DC 20009

## FLORIDA

### AIDS Hotline (Statewide)
phone: (800) 352-2437

### Health Crisis Network
5050 Biscayne Blvd.
Miami, FL 33137-3241

### Lesbian Educational AIDS Resource Network
14002 Clubhouse Circle, #205
Tampa, FL 33524

### People of Color AIDS Coalition
PO Box 14365
Tallahassee, FL 32317

### People with AIDS Coalition—Broward County
2294 Wilton Dr.
Fort Lauderdale, FL 33305

**People with AIDS Coalition—Jacksonville**
1628 San Marco Blvd., Ste. 5
Jacksonville, FL 32207

**People with AIDS Coalition—Key West**
709 Olivia St.
Key West, FL 33040

**People with AIDS Coalition—Miami**
3890 Biscayne Blvd.
Miami, FL 33137

**People with AIDS Coalition—West Palm Beach**
2580 Metrocentre Blvd.
West Palm Beach, FL 33407

**Tampa AIDS Network**
11215 N. Nebraska Ave., #B3
Tampa, FL 33612
phone: (813) 979-1919, ext. 225

## GEORGIA

**ACT UP—Atlanta**
44 Twelfth St. NE
Atlanta, GA 30309
Local chapter of the AIDS Coalition to Unleash Power.

**AIDS Hotline (Statewide)**
phone: (800) 551-2728

**Atlanta Lesbian AIDS Project**
PO Box 5409
Atlanta, GA 30307

**Feminist Women's Health Center**
580 14th St. NW
Atlanta, GA 30318
AIDS hotline: (404) 888-9991

**National AIDS Information Clearinghouse**
National Centers for Disease Control
Atlanta, GA
hotline: (800) 458-5231

**Rainbow Wellness Center**
1718 Reynolds St., Ste. 300
Waycross, GA 31502

## HAWAII

**AIDS Foundation of Hawaii**
PO Box 88980
Honolulu, HI 96815

**AIDS Hotline (Statewide)**
phone: (800) 922-1313

**Kapiolani Women and Children Center**
1319 Punahou St., 6th Fl.
Honolulu, HI 96826
Sponsors the AIDS Education Project.

**NAMES Project—Honolulu**
758 Kapahulu Avenue
Honolulu, HI 96816-1135
phone: (808) 948-1481
Web site: http://www.aidsquilt.org/
Sponsors and coordinates displays of the AIDS Memorial Quilt.

## IDAHO

**AIDS Hotline (Statewide)**
phone: (208) 345-2277

## ILLINOIS

**AIDS Foundation of Chicago**
1332 N. Halstead Rd., Ste. 303
Chicago, IL 60622

**AIDS Hotline (Statewide)**
phone: (800) 243-2437

**Chicago Lesbian Community Cancer Project**
PO Box 46352
Chicago, IL 60646

**Families' and Childrens' AIDS Network (FCAN)**
721 N LaSalle St., Ste. 301
Chicago, IL 60610

**Kindheart Women's Center**
2214 Ridge Ave.
Evanston, IL 60201

**NAMES Project—Chicago**
4334 North Hazel, Suite 212
Chicago, IL 60613
phone: (312) 472-4460
Web site: http://www.aidsquilt.org/

Sponsors and coordinates displays of the AIDS Memorial Quilt.

### National AIDS Brigade
1610 W. Highland, #77
Chicago, IL 60660

### Stop AIDS Chicago
909 W. Belmont
Chicago, IL 60657

### Stop AIDS Chicago—African-American Office
2154 East 71st St.
Chicago, IL 60649

### Stop AIDS Chicago—Latino/Latina-American Office
1352 N. Western Ave.
Chicago, IL 60622

## INDIANA

### AIDS Hotline (Statewide)
phone: (800) 848-2437

### Crisis Center for Human Understanding
101 N. Montgomery St.
Gary, IN 46403
Offers recovery services.

### NAMES Project—Indianapolis
3951 N. Meridian St., #101
Indianapolis, IN 46268
phone: (317) 920-1200
Web site: http://www.aidsquilt.org/
Sponsors and coordinates displays of the AIDS Memorial Quilt.

## IOWA

### AIDS Hotline (Statewide)
phone: (800) 445-2437

### Emma Goldman Clinic for Women
227 N. Dubuque
Iowa City, IA 52245

### NAMES Project—Cedar Valley
2034 Merner Avenue
Cedar Falls, IA 50613
phone: (319) 266-7903
Web site: http://www.aidsquilt.org/
Sponsors and coordinates displays of the AIDS Memorial Quilt.

## KANSAS

### AIDS Hotline (Statewide)
phone: (800) 232-0040

## KENTUCKY

### AIDS Hotline (Statewide)
phone: (800) 654-2437

## LOUISIANA

### AIDS Hotline (Statewide)
phone: (800) 922-4379

### People with AIDS Coalition—New Orleans
704 N. Rampart
New Orleans, LA 70116

## MAINE

### ACT UP—Portland
142 High St., Suite 222
Portland, ME 04101
Local chapter of the AIDS Coalition to Unleash Power.

### AIDS Hotline (Statewide)
phone: (800) 851-2437

### AIDS Project—Portland
PO Box 5305
Portland, ME 04104
22 Monument Square, 5th Fl.
Portland, ME 04101
phone: (207) 774-6877

### NAMES Project—Portland
PO Box 10248
Portland, ME 04104
phone: (207) 774-2198
Web site: http://www.aidsquilt.org/
Sponsors and coordinates displays of the AIDS Memorial Quilt.

### People with AIDS Coalition—Maine
377 Cumberland Ave.
Portland, ME 04101

## SPOTLIGHT
## CRAIG COVEY and MAPP

Speaking of his recent candidacy for public office, Craig Covey explained, "I go into this knowing full well, in effect, I'm a pioneer." Indeed he is, in more ways than one. Covey ran for a City Council position in Ferndale, Michigan, in 1995 as the first openly gay candidate to run for office in Metro Detroit. He didn't win the election, but he did receive one-third of the votes. Although Covey received a large number of votes from the significant lesbian and gay community in Ferndale and in areas where he went door-to-door campaigning, he also showed the public that he was concerned with the entire community. Public safety, crime, and downtown development

## MARYLAND

### AIDS Hotline (Statewide)
phone: (800) 638-6252

### National AIDS Information Clearinghouse
PO Box 6003
Rockville, MD 20849-6003
hotline: (800) 458-5231

### National Institute of Allergic and Infectious Diseases (NIAID)
900 Rockville Pike
Bethesda, MD 29892
hotline: (800) TRIALS-A
NIAID's hotline offers information about clinical drug trials.

### People with AIDS Coalition—Baltimore
101 W. Read St., Ste. 808
Baltimore, MD 21201

## MASSACHUSETTS

### Act Up—Boston
PO Box 483
Kendall Square Station
Cambridge, MA 02142
phone: (617) 49-ACTUP
e-mail: contact@actup.or
Web site:
http://www.tcp.com:8000/qrd/aids/attitude-ACTUP.BOSTON
ACT UP—Boston meets every Tuesday in the Boston Living Center, 140 Clarendon St., 7th floor, at 7 p.m. The group's *Attitude!* newsletter is published over the Internet at the address above.

### ACT UP—Provincetown
PO Box 1619
Provincetown, MA 02657
Local chapter of the AIDS Coalition to Unleash Power.

### AIDS Hotline (Statewide)
phone: (800) 235-2331

### AIDS Project—Worcester
305 Shrewsbury St.
Worcester, MA 01604

### Association of Gay and Lesbian Psychiatrists (AGLP)
24 Olmstead St.
Jamaica Plain, MA 02401
phone: (617) 522-1267
AGLP consists of gay, lesbian, and bisexual members of the American Psychiatric Association and other psychiatrists throughout

were a few of the issues Covey addressed. As Covey wrote in the Michigan gay newspaper *Between the Lines,* "The campaign was very successful. We managed to present the gay community in a whole new light."

Another area in which Covey pioneers is AIDS awareness. Covey founded the Midwest AIDS Prevention Project (MAPP) in 1988 and serves as its president. MAPP is a non-profit organization that focuses on developing and spreading safe sex education and AIDS prevention. As an activist and an educator Covey has traveled across Michigan speaking to groups, such as high schools, colleges, churches, and community groups. Working closely with the Michigan Department of Public Health, MAPP's reach is broad while also trying to target high-risk groups. In the past seven years MAPP has reached over a quarter of a million people and has provided more than three thousand educational

North America. The association's objectives are to provide support and encouragement for gay and lesbian psychiatrists; serve as a vehicle for the promotion of social and legal equality for all gay people; further the understanding of members, colleagues, and the public in matters relating to homosexuality; promote improved mental health services for gays and lesbians; and encourage research in areas related to homosexuality. AGLP provides, by mail, referrals to private gay-sympathetic therapists; conducts seminars and exhibits; maintains a speakers' bureau; and presents papers and panels. Founded in 1975, the 500-member group has also been known as the Caucus of Gay, Lesbian, and Bisexual Members of the American Psychiatric Association. The quarterly AGLP newsletter includes book reviews, a calendar of events, and obituaries.

### Boston Women's Health Book Collective

240-A Elm St.
Somerville, MA 02144

### NAMES Project—Boston

PO Box 498
Boston, MA 02117
phone: (617) 262-6263
Web site: http://www.aidsquilt.org/

Sponsors and coordinates displays of the AIDS Memorial Quilt.

### Stop AIDS Boston

40 Plympton St.
Boston, MA 02118

### Women's Center

46 Pleasant St.
Cambridge, MA 02139

## MICHIGAN

### ACT UP—Ann Arbor

Ann Arbor, MI
phone: (313) 662-6282.

### AIDS Awareness Advocacy Center

Reach, Inc.
1840 Midland
Detroit, MI 48238
phone: (313) 869-2600
The center offers direct services to mothers and their children.

### AIDS Care Connection of United Community Services

4221 Cass Ave.
Detroit, MI 48201
phone: (313) 993-1320
Case management system.

AIDS programs. They have provided safer sex workshops, AIDS information displays, teen peer training, and theater productions, and the group publishes a catalogue with a wide range of posters, brochures, and safer sex items.

Covey has been and still is a leading activist for AIDS and also for civil rights for lesbians and gays. Covey's move into the political field seemed like a natural progression. "As more people run, it can only help our efforts," Covey explains. "It's part of the effort to familiarize the community that gay and lesbian people are among them, working among them every day."

*By Lisa Breck*

### AIDS Consortium of Southeastern Michigan

1150 Griswold, #1400
Detroit, MI 48226
phone: (313) 496-0140
The consortium is a case management system staffed by nurses and social workers.

### AIDS Hotline (Statewide)

phone: (800) 872-2437

### AIDS Interfaith Network—Detroit

16260 Dexter
Detroit, MI 48221-9998
phone: (313) 863-5700
The network provides referrals to HIV/AIDS-sensitive clergy of all denominations.

### AIDS Law Center

Linda D. Bernard, President & CEO
Wayne County Neighborhood Legal Services
65 Cadillac Square, Ste. 3802
Detroit, MI 48226
phone: (313) 962-0466, ext. 348
for hearing impaired: (313) 868-8045
The AIDS Law Center provides compassionate legal services to AIDS/HIV-positive residents of Southeastern Michigan and their families and/or significant others. Programs include a client education project, community education project, and youth education project.

### AIDS Legal Coalition and Referral Service of Michigan

916 Ford Building
615 Griswold
Detroit, MI 48226
phone: (313) 964-4188
Refers people with HIV/AIDS to attorneys for help with legal problems.

### AIDS Resource Center

PO Box 6603
Grand Rapids, MI 49516
1414 Robinson Rd.
Grand Rapids, MI 49506
phone: (616) 459-9177
The AIDS Resource Center provides a buddy program, food bank, transportation, chores, emergency financial assistance, information, and referrals.

### Arab Community Center Economic Social Services (ACCESS)

9708 Dix Ave.
Dearborn, MI 48120
phone: (313) 842-0700 or (313) 842-7010
ACCESS offers prevention educational seminars, counseling and testing, referrals, bilingual educational materials (Arabic/English), street outreach, and follow-up services for people with HIV/AIDS.

### Battle Creek Cares

PO Box 989
Battle Creek, MI 49016
phone: (800) 944-2437
Offers HIV/AIDS support and education.

### Berrien County AIDS Coalition

769 Pipestone
PO Box 706
Benton Harbor, MI 49022

## Community Health Awareness Group (C-HAG)

3028 East Grand Boulevard
Detroit, MI 48202
phone: (313) 872-2424
Offers counseling and testing, community outreach education, family skills building education, support services, and adolescent outreach.

## Department of Social Services

Ken Pape, AIDS Coordinator
Executive Office Plaza
North Tower, 11th Fl.
1200 Sixth St.
Detroit, MI 48226
phone: (313) 256-1380 or (313) 256-1377
Offers an insurance assistance program for people with AIDS, client advocacy, information, and referrals.

## Friends—Detroit

1419 W. Warren
Detroit, MI
phone: (800) 350-PWAS
Self-empowerment group for people with AIDS.

## Friends—Saugatuck

PO Box 20580
Fenville, MI 49020
phone: (616) 543-8310
Self-empowerment group for people with AIDS.

## Grand Rapids Minority AIDS Project

PO Box 1064
Grand Rapids, MI 49501
phone: (616) 452-AIDS

## Healing Ourselves Through Prevention Education Services (HOPES)

4458 Joy Rd.
Detroit, MI 48208
(313) 896-0233

## Health Emergency Lifeline Program (HELP)

18040 Coyle
Detroit, MI 48235
phone: (313) 837-2590
fax: (313) 837-2534

*Craig Covey, founder of the Midwest AIDS Prevention Project. (Photo courtesy* Between the Lines.*)*

HELP offers financial assistance to people with AIDS.

## Herman Keifer Institute

Detroit Health Department
1151 Taylor
Detroit, MI 48202
phone: (313) 876-0756
Anonymous AIDS testing site.

## HIV/AIDS Advocacy Program (HAAP)

29200 Vassar Blvd., Ste. 501
Livonia, MI 48152
phone: (313) 442-0520
HAAP provides legal information and assistance with litigation on discrimination and insurance issues relevant to HIV/AIDS.

## HIV/AIDS Resource Center (HARC)—Jackson

209 E. Washington Ave., Ste. 233
Jackson, MI 49201
phone: (517) 784-4515
HARC was established by volunteers in 1986 to provide HIV-related services to the community through compassionate direct care,

prevention, and outreach activities. HARC's services include support groups, information and referral, advocacy, buddy programs, housekeeping, a food bank, respite work, hospital visitation, transportation services, emergency financial assistance, and community education.

## HIV/AIDS Resource Center (HARC)—Ypsilanti

3975 Clark Rd., Ste. 203
Ypsilanti, MI 48197
phone: (313) 572-9355
fax: (313) 572-0554
HARC was established by volunteers in 1986 to provide HIV-related services to the community through compassionate direct care, prevention, and outreach activities. HARC's services include support groups, information and referral, advocacy, buddy programs, housekeeping, a food bank, respite work, hospital visitation, transportation services, emergency financial assistance, and community education.

## Kalamazoo AIDS Resource and Education Services (KARES)

628 South Park St.
Kalamazoo, MI 49007
phone: (616) 381-2437
KARES offers a buddy program, support groups, care coordination, prevention education, speakers, emergency financial assistance, and transportation assistance.

## Lansing Area AIDS Network (LAAN)

PO Box 14215
Lansing, MI 48901
phone: (517) 351-0303
LAAN provides support, education, and buddy services for people with HIV/AIDS and their friends and families.

## Latino Family Services

3815 West Fort St.
Detroit, MI 48216
phone: (313) 841-7380
Latino Family Services is a bilingual, bicultural program that offers counseling and support groups, youth services, and AIDS/HIV counseling and support.

## Men of Color Motivational Group

PO Box 11499
Detroit, MI 48211
phone: (313) 691-1486
Offers support for men of color with HIV/AIDS.

## Michigan Jewish AIDS Coalition (MJAC)

c/o Temple Israel
5725 Walnut Lake Rd.
West Bloomfield, MI 48323
phone: (810) 661-5700
MJAC offers service and referrals to Jewish people affected by AIDS.

## Midwest AIDS Prevention Project (MAPP)

Craig Covey, President
702 Livernois
Ferndale, MI 48220
phone: (810) 545-1435
MAPP focuses on AIDS education and prevention.

## NAMES Project—Metro Detroit

PO Box 1953
Royal Oak, MI 48068
phone: (313) 371-9599
or
PO Box 303
Taylor, MI 48480
phone: (313) 753-9117 or (313) 285-1517
Web site: http://www.aidsquilt.org/
Sponsors and coordinates displays of the AIDS Memorial Quilt.

## NAMES Project—Thumb Area

3075 Strawberry Lane
Port Huron, MI 48060
phone: (810) 982-6361
Web site: http://www.aidsquilt.org/
Sponsors and coordinates displays of the AIDS Memorial Quilt.

## Northern AIDS Awareness Community Education Services (NAACES)

PO Box 803
Prudenville, MI 48651
phone: (517) 366-4443

## People with AIDS Coalition—Grand Rapids
PO Box 1247
Grand Rapids, MI 49501
phone: (616) 363-7689

## Rainbow House
PO Box 463
Kalamazoo, MI 49005
phone: (616) 381-4611
The Rainbow House is a 14-room residential facility for people with AIDS.

## Simon House
16260 Dexter
Detroit, MI 48221
phone: (313) 863-1400
Simon House provides housing for HIV-positive mothers and children.

## Steppin' Out Foundation
405 S. Washington, Ste. B
Royal Oak, MI 48067
phone: (810) 541-6900

## Wellness HIV/AIDS Services
PO Box 438
Flint, MI 48501
phone: (810) 232-0888
fax: (810) 232-2418
Provides information and referrals, support services advocacy, and benefits counseling.

## Wellness House of Michigan
PO Box 03827
Detroit, MI 48203
phone: (313) 342-1230
Wellness House is a residence for people with AIDS.

## Wellness Networks
845 Livernois
Ferndale, MI 48220
phone: (810) 547-3783
hotline: (800) 872-AIDS
hearing impaired: (800) 332-0849
Wellness Networks is a statewide, community-based AIDS organization that provides the Michigan AIDS hotline, support groups, a buddy system, and other services.

## Wellness Networks—Grand Traverse
PO Box 1632
Traverse City, MI 49685
phone: (616) 947-1110

## Wellness Networks—Huron Shores
PO Box 663
Alpena, MI 49707
phone: (517) 356-0035

## Wellness Networks—Huron Valley
PO Box 3242
Ann Arbor, MI 48106
phone: (313) 572-9355

## Wellness Networks—Tri-Cities
PO Box 6361
Saginaw, MI 48603
phone: (517) 771-0802

## Women and AIDS Committee
Detroit Health Department
1151 Taylor
Detroit, MI 48202
phone: (313) 876-0982

# MINNESOTA

## AIDS Hotline (Statewide)
phone: (800) 248-2437

## Minnesota AIDS Project
109 South Fifth St.
Marshall, MN 56258
phone: (800) 243-7321

## NAMES Project—Twin Cities
PO Box 16408
Minneapolis, MN 55416
phone: (612) 373-2468
Web site: http://www.aidsquilt.org/
Sponsors and coordinates displays of the AIDS Memorial Quilt.

## Womyn's Braille Press
Marj Schneider, Executive Director
PO Box 8475
Minneapolis, MN 55408
phone: (612)872-4352
Publishes feminist literature in braille and on audio cassettes for blind or print-disabled people only. All materials are available for purchase or loan. Also publishes a quarterly newsletter in braille, tape, and large or small print. Reaches market through advertising and word of mouth.

**Youth and AIDS Project**
428 Oak Grove Street
Minneapolis, MN 55403
phone: (612) 627-6820

## MISSISSIPPI

**AIDS Hotline (Statewide)**
phone: (800) 537-0851

**Camp Sister Spirit**
PO Box 12
Ovett, MS 39464

## MISSOURI

**AIDS Hotline (Statewide)**
phone: (800) 533-2437

**AIDS Project—Ozarks**
1722-LL S. Glenstone Ave.
Springfield, MO 65804

**Four State Community AIDS Project**
Cheryl Tullis, Director
PO Box 3476
Joplin, MO 64803

**Live and Let Live Alcoholics Anonymous**
PO Box 411111
Kansas City, MO 64141-1111

**NAMES Project—Metro St. Louis**
PO Box 11251
Clayton, MO 63105
phone: (314) 997-9897 ext. 43
Web site: http://www.aidsquilt.org/
Sponsors and coordinates displays of the AIDS Memorial Quilt.

## MONTANA

**AIDS Hotline (Statewide)**
phone: (800) 233-6668

## NEBRASKA

**AIDS Hotline (Statewide)**
phone: (800) 782-2437

## NEVADA

**AIDS Hotline (Statewide)**
phone: (800) 842-2437

**NAMES Project—Southern Nevada**
1120 Almond Tree Ln., Ste. 207
Las Vegas, NV 89104
phone: (702) 226-2701
Web site: http://www.aidsquilt.org/
Sponsors and coordinates displays of the AIDS Memorial Quilt.

## NEW HAMPSHIRE

**AIDS Hotline (Statewide)**
phone: (800) 872-8909

## NEW JERSEY

**AIDS Hotline (Statewide)**
phone: (800) 624-2377

**NAMES Project—New Jersey**
PO Box 716
New Brunswick, NJ 08903
phone: (908) 739-4863
Web site: http://www.aidsquilt.org/
Sponsors and coordinates displays of the AIDS Memorial Quilt.

**People with AIDS Coalition—New Jersey**
1576 Palisades Ave.
Ft. Lee, NJ 07024

**Women's Center of Monmouth County**
1 Bethany Rd., Ste. B3-A42
Hazlet, NJ 07730-1606

## NEW MEXICO

**AIDS Hotline (Statewide)**
phone: (800) 545-2437

**Live and Let Live Alcoholics Anonymous**
PO Box 674
Santa Fe, NM 87504

**NAMES Project—Santa Fe**
8 Monte Alto Circle

Santa Fe, NM 87505
phone: (505) 466-2211
Web site: http://www.aidsquilt.org/
Sponsors and coordinates displays of the AIDS Memorial Quilt.

## NEW YORK

### ACT UP—New York
135 W. 29th St., 10th Fl.
New York, NY 10001
Web site: http://www.actupny.org
Local chapter of the AIDS Coalition to Unleash Power.

### AIDS Center of Queens County
9745 Queens Boulevard
Rego Park, NY 11374
phone: (718) 896-2500

### AIDS Hotline (Statewide)
phone: (800) 541-2437

### AIDS National Interfaith Network
475 Riverside Dr., 10th Fl.
New York, NY 10115
phone: (212) 239-0700
The network provides referrals to HIV/AIDS-sensitive clergy of all denominations.

### American Civil Liberties Union

### Lesbian and Gay Rights/AIDS Project
132 W. 43rd St.
New York, NY 10036

### American Foundation for AIDS Research (AmFAR)
733 Third Ave., 12th Fl.
New York, NY 10017-3204
phone: (212) 682-7440 or (800) 39-AMFAR

### Brooklyn AIDS Task Force
465 Dean St.
Brooklyn, NY 11217
Also supports the Women's AIDS Video Enterprise (WAVE).

### Community Health Project
208 W. 13th St.
New York, NY 10011

### Gay Men's Health Crises Action
129 W 20th St.
New York, NY 10011-3629
Also maintains an archive of AIDS-related material.

### Lambda Legal Defense and Education Fund (LLDEF)
Kevin M. Cathcart
666 Broadway, Suite 1200
New York, NY 10012
phone: (212) 995-8585
fax: (212) 995-2306
The Lambda Legal Defense and Education Fund, founded in 1973, defends the civil rights of gay persons and people with AIDS in areas such as employment, housing, education, child custody, and the delivery of medical and social services. LLDEF engages in test case litigation as counsel or co-counsel, and files briefs as "a friend of the court" to present statistical and educational information and to help inform the court of the needs of gay men and lesbians and people with AIDS. The fund also provides resources and assistance to attorneys working on behalf of gay clients; maintains a national network of cooperating attorneys; helps inform the gay community about its rights and recent legal developments; and educates the public and the legal community about issues and concerns of gay persons and people with AIDS. LLDEF operates a speakers' bureau; sponsors seminars; compiles statistics; and maintains files containing court decisions and copies of briefs and pleadings. The group's Jay C. Lipner Liberty Award annually recognizes service in combatting AIDS and AIDS discrimination, and the Lambda Liberty Award is given for service in the Gay/Lesbian Community. The *Lambda Update* newsletter reports on the court cases in which LLDEF is involved, and on issues of concern to the organization and its 22,000 members.

### Lesbian AIDS Project
129 W. 20th St.
New York, NY 10010

### Lesbian Health Project
Community Health Project
208 W. 13th St.
New York, NY 10011

### Life Force: Women against AIDS
165 Cadman Plaza East, Room 310
Brooklyn, NY 12201

### NAMES Project—Long Island
PO Box 7
Greenport, NY 11944
phone: (516) 477-2447
Web site: http://www.aidsquilt.org/
Sponsors and coordinates displays of the AIDS Memorial Quilt.

### NAMES Project—New York City
75 Varick St., Suite 1404
New York, NY 10013
phone: (212) 226-2292
Web site: http://www.aidsquilt.org/
Sponsors and coordinates displays of the AIDS Memorial Quilt.

### NAMES Project—Syracuse
PO Box 805
Syracuse, NY 13201
phone: (315) 425-8695
Web site: http://www.aidsquilt.org/
Sponsors and coordinates displays of the AIDS Memorial Quilt.

### Office of Gay and Lesbian Health Concerns
NYC Department of Health
125 Worth St., #67
New York, NY 10013

### Open Mind Group Alcoholics Anonymous
PO Box 395, Ellicott Sta.
Buffalo, NY 14205

### People of Color in Crisis
462 Bergen St.
Brooklyn, NY 11217

### People with AIDS Coalition—Long Island
1170 Route 109
Lindenhurst, NY 11757

### People with AIDS Coalition—New York
50 W. 17th St., 8th Fl.
New York, NY 10011

### People with AIDS Health Group
150 West 26th St., Ste. 201
New York, NY 10001
phone: (212) 255-0520

### Prostitutes of New York (PONY)
25 W. 45th St.
New York, NY 10036

### Senior Action in a Gay Environment (SAGE)
Arlene Kochman, Executive Director
305 7th Ave., 16th Fl.
New York, NY 10001
phone: (212) 741-2247
fax: (212) 366-1947
Founded in 1977, SAGE comprises professional social workers and trained volunteers, including doctors, lawyers, psychologists, gerontologists, and others who are dedicated to meeting the needs of older gays and lesbians and ending the isolation that has kept them separate from each other, from other gays, and from the larger community. Centered in the New York City area, the 4,000-member group provides a friendly visitor homebound program; information and referrals in legal matters and assessments; individual and group counseling, including bereavement services; and social activities to reduce loneliness, rebuild relationships, and establish supportive connections with the gay and lesbian community. SAGE also provides in-service training for agency members and institutions serving older gays; educates professionals and the public with regard to lesbian and gay aging; sponsors an AIDS Service Program for the Elderly; and conducts weekly workshops and training programs for volunteers and social service agencies interested in issues of lesbian and gay aging. The SAGE Bulletin is published monthly, and the SAGE North America conference occurs annually. Membership fees are $35 annually for individuals, or $50 annually for families.

### Women and AIDS Resource Network
30 Third Ave., #212
Brooklyn, NY 11217

### Women and AIDS Women's Center
2271 Second Ave.
New York, NY 10035

### Women in Crisis
360 W 125th St.
New York, NY 10027

## NORTH CAROLINA

### AIDS Hotline (Statewide)
phone: (800) 342-2437

### NAMES Project—Charlotte
PO Box 9392
Charlotte, NC 28299
phone: (704) 376-2637
Web site: http://www.aidsquilt.org/
Sponsors and coordinates displays of the AIDS Memorial Quilt.

### North Carolina Lesbian and Gay Health Project
PO Box 9203
Durham, NC 27715

## NORTH DAKOTA

### AIDS Hotline (Statewide)
phone: (800) 472-2180

## OHIO

### AIDS Foundation of Miami Valley
PO Box 3539
Dayton, OH 45401
A service and prevention organization.

### AIDS Holistic Services
655 N. Main St.
Akron, OH 44312

### AIDS Hotline (Statewide)
phone: (800) 332-2437

## OKLAHOMA

### AIDS Hotline (Statewide)
phone: (800) 535-2437

### NAMES Project—Tulsa Area
4154 S. Harvard, Suite H-1
Tulsa, OK 74135
phone: (918) 748-3111
Web site: http://www.aidsquilt.org/
Sponsors and coordinates displays of the AIDS Memorial Quilt.

## OREGON

### ACT UP—Columbia
PO Box 6352
Portland, OR 97228
Local chapter of the AIDS Coalition to Unleash Power.

### AIDS Hotline (Statewide)
phone: (800) 777-2437

### Live and Let Live Club
PO Box 11261
Portland, OR 97211-0261

### NAMES Project—Portland
PO Box 5423
Portland, OR 97228
phone: (503) 650-7032
Web site: http://www.aidsquilt.org/
Sponsors and coordinates displays of the AIDS Memorial Quilt.

## PENNSYLVANIA

### ACT UP—Philadelphia
PO Box 15919
Philadelphia, PA 19103-0919
phone: (215) 731-1844
Web site: http://www.critpath.org/~russell/actup/
ACT UP—Philadelphia meets every Monday night at the Church of Saint Luke and the Epiphany, 330 South 13th St., Center City Philadelphia, at 7:45 p.m.

### AIDS Hotline (Statewide)
phone: (800) 662-6080

### AIDS Project—Centre County
301 S. Allen St., Ste. 102
State College, PA 16801
phone: (814) 235-4655

### Association for Gay, Lesbian, and Bisexual Issues in Counseling (AGLBIC)
Robert Rohde, Treasurer
Box 216
Jenkintown, PA 19046

AGLBIC includes counselors and personnel and guidance workers who are concerned with lesbian and gay issues. Founded in 1974 as the Caucus of Gay Counselors, the association seeks to eliminate discrimination against and stereotyping of gay and lesbian individuals, particularly gay counselors; works to educate heterosexual counselors on how to overcome homophobia and to best help homosexual clients; provides a referral network and support for gay counselors and administrators; and encourages objective research on gay issues. AGLBIC publishes a quarterly newsletter and an annotated bibliography of basic resources for counselors working with gay, lesbian, and bisexual clients.

### NAMES Project—Philadelphia
PO Box 15935
Philadelphia, PA 19103
phone: (215) 735-6263
Web site: http://www.aidsquilt.org/
Sponsors and coordinates displays of the AIDS Memorial Quilt.

### NAMES Project—Pittsburgh
PO Box 98248
Pittsburgh, PA 15227
phone: (412) 343-9846
Web site: http://www.aidsquilt.org/
Sponsors and coordinates displays of the AIDS Memorial Quilt.

### NAMES Project—Susquehanna Valley
1906 North Second Street
Harrisburg, PA 17102
phone: (717) 234-0629
Web site: http://www.aidsquilt.org/
Sponsors and coordinates displays of the AIDS Memorial Quilt.

### Planned Parenthood
1144 Locust Street
Philadelphia, PA
phone: (215) 351-5514

## PUERTO RICO

### AIDS Hotline (Statewide)
phone: (800) 765-1010

## RHODE ISLAND

### AIDS Hotline (Statewide)
phone: (800) 726-3010

### NAMES Project—Rhode Island
PO Box 2591
Newport, RI 02840
phone: (401) 847-7637
Web site: http://www.aidsquilt.org/
Sponsors and coordinates displays of the AIDS Memorial Quilt.

## SOUTH CAROLINA

### AIDS Hotline (Statewide)
phone: (800) 332-2437

## SOUTH DAKOTA

### AIDS Hotline (Statewide)
phone: (800) 592-1861

## TENNESSEE

### AIDS Hotline (Statewide)
phone: (800) 525-2437

### Suicide and Crisis Intervention
PO Box 40068
Memphis, TN 38174

## TEXAS

### ACT UP—Austin
PO Box 13322
Austin, TX 78711
Local chapter of the AIDS Coalition to Unleash Power.

### AIDS Foundation of Houston
3202 Wesleyan Annex
Houston, TX 77027

### AIDS Hotline (Statewide)
phone: (800) 299-2437

### American Institute for Teen AIDS Prevention
6032 Jacksboro Hwy., Ste. 100
Fort Worth, TX 76136
phone: (817) 237-0230

### Lambda Adult Children of Alcoholics
PO Box 191025
Dallas, TX 75219

### Lesbian Health Initiative
PO Box 130158
Houston, TX 77219-0158

### NAMES Project—Dallas Metroplex
PO Box 190869
Dallas, TX 75219-0869
phone: (214) 520-7397
Web site: http://www.aidsquilt.org/
Sponsors and coordinates displays of the AIDS Memorial Quilt.

### NAMES Project—Ft. Worth/Tarrant County
1418 Milam Street
Fort Worth, TX 76112-3339
phone: (817) 336-2637
Web site: http://www.aidsquilt.org/
Sponsors and coordinates displays of the AIDS Memorial Quilt.

### NAMES Project—Houston
PO Box 66595
Houston, TX 77266
phone: (713) 526-2637
Web site: http://www.aidsquilt.org/
Sponsors and coordinates displays of the AIDS Memorial Quilt.

### People with AIDS Coalition—Houston
1475 W. Gray, Ste. 163
Houston, TX 77019

## UTAH

### AIDS Hotline (Statewide)
phone: (800) 366-2437

### NAMES Project—Salt Lake City
c/o Utah AIDS Foundation
1408 S. 1100 E.
Salt Lake City, UT 84151
phone: (801) 487-2323
Web site: http://www.aidsquilt.org/
Sponsors and coordinates displays of the AIDS Memorial Quilt.

### People with AIDS Coalition—Utah
1406 South 1100 East, Ste. 107
Salt Lake City, UT 84105-2435

## VERMONT

### AIDS Hotline (Statewide)
phone: (800) 882-2437

## VIRGIN ISLANDS

### AIDS Hotline (Statewide)
phone: (800) 773-2437

## VIRGINIA

### AIDS Hotline (Statewide)
phone: (800) 533-4138

### Lesbian, Gay and Bisexual People in Medicine (LGBPM)
c/o American Medical Student Association
1902 Association Dr.
Reston, VA 22091
phone: (703) 620-6600
fax: (703) 620-5873
LGBPM is a standing committee of the American Medical Student Association that includes physicians, physicians in training, and others who are interested in gay/lesbian issues. The committee was founded in 1976 to improve the quality of health care for gay patients, and to improve working conditions and professional status of gay health professionals and students. The group, which has 35 local chapters, administers educational workshops for health professionals; designs training materials; conducts research on the health problems of gay people and surveys on admissions, hiring, and promotion policies of medical schools and hospitals; provides referrals; sponsors support groups for gay professionals to meet, socialize, and organize; presses for legislative and political action to end discrimination against gay people; and maintains a speakers' bureau.

### NAMES Project—Central Virginia
PO Box 15451
Richmond, VA 23227

phone: (804) 346-8047
Web site: http://www.aidsquilt.org/
Sponsors and coordinates displays of the AIDS Memorial Quilt.

### National AIDS Bereavement Center
1953 Columbia Pike, #24
Arlington, VA 22204

### Triangle Services Recovery Center
1610 Meadowlake Dr.
Norfolk, VA 23518

## WASHINGTON

### ACT UP—Seattle
1202 E. Pike St., Ste. 814
Seattle, WA 98122
Local chapter of the AIDS Coalition to Unleash Power.

### AIDS Hotline (Statewide)
phone: (800) 272-2437

### NAMES Project—Seattle
1201 E. Pike Street, #1122
Seattle, WA 98122
phone: (206) 285-2880
Web site: http://www.aidsquilt.org/
Sponsors and coordinates displays of the AIDS Memorial Quilt.

### People of Color Against AIDS Network
1200 S. Jackson, Ste. 25
Seattle, WA 98144

### Seattle Bisexual Women's Network
PO Box 30645
Seattle, WA 98103-0645

### Seattle Lesbian Cancer Project
2732 NE 54th St.
Seattle, WA 98105

### Spokane County Health District AIDS Program
1101 West College Avenue, Room 401
Spokane, WA 99201-2095
phone: (509) 324-1547

### Stonewall Recovery Services
430 Broadway Ave East
Seattle, WA 98102
phone: (206) 461-4546

## WEST VIRGINIA

### AIDS Hotline (Statewide)
phone: (800) 642-8244

### NAMES Project—Upper Ohio Valley
34 Edgelawn Avenue
Wheeling, WV 26003
phone: (304) 242-9443
Web site: http://www.aidsquilt.org/
Sponsors and coordinates displays of the AIDS Memorial Quilt.

## WISCONSIN

### ACT UP—Milwaukee
PO Box 1707
Milwaukee, WI 53201
Local chapter of the AIDS Coalition to Unleash Power.

### AIDS Hotline (Statewide)
phone: (800) 334-2437

### Disabled Womyn's Educational Project
Catherine Odette, Executive Officer
PO Box 8773
Madison, WI 53708-8773
phone: (608) 256-8883
e-mail: SLKARON@facstaff.wisc.edu
Founded in 1988, the Disabled Womyn's Educational Project comprises lesbians with disabilities. The project promotes members' interests by supporting legislation sensitive to members' needs. The group also maintains a speakers' bureau and book, periodical, and artwork holdings. Their newsletter, *Dykes, Disability, and Stuff,* is published quarterly and is available in various formats, including audiocassette, braille, DOS diskette, large print, modem transfer, and audio tape.

## WYOMING

### AIDS Hotline (Statewide)

phone: (800) 327-3577

# ONLINE RESOURCES

## THE WEB

### ACT UP—New York

http://www.actupny.org/
"Silence = Death" is the motto of ACT UP (AIDS Coalition to Unleash Power). Users empower those with the deadly virus by giving them a voice and a platform to use it. The ACT UP Web page calls on everyone to spread the word about AIDS prevention.

### AIDSBytes

http://www.clients.anomtec.com/Aids-Bytes/
This online educational resource explains the medical terminology surrounding AIDS and HIV.

### AIDS Housing Corporation

http://www.ahc.org/infoweb/agencies/ahc
The AIDS Housing Corporation is a private business in Boston that supports housing programs for people with HIV or AIDS. Discover how the firm's efforts help housing developments literally get off the ground.

### ArtAIDS

http://www.illumin.co.uk/artaids/
ArtAIDS is an online art gallery featuring donated work in the form of digital art, video, sound, and writings. Throughout the site there are opportunities to donate money to help AIDS victims.

### The Body

http://www.thebody.com/
This multimedia AIDS and HIV information resource disseminates articles from experts in the fields of medicine, law, politics, religion, and sports, and a political action archive provides users with opportunities to join the fight for better laws to help AIDS victims. The Body also offers a unique service to people who are interested in learning privately about AIDS. With confidential IDs provided by the site, users can participate anonymously in Usenet newsgroups dealing with AIDS. The page aims to educate HIV/AIDS patients, as well as their caretakers and families.

### CDC National AIDS Clearinghouse

http://cdnac.aspensys.com:86/
The Center for Disease Control presents this comprehensive AIDS/HIV online archive. In addition to disease prevention and care reports, the CDC posts daily summaries of AIDS/HIV news. Users also can order publications online and get details on outreach programs.

### HIV Database

http://www.hiv-web.lanl.gov/
HIV is the subject of the Human Retro Viruses and AIDS Database. The Los Alamos National Laboratory maintains this database of its research on the HIV virus. Findings are published for the scientific community but are also available to the general public.

### Safer Sex Page

http://www.cmpharm.ucs.edu/~troyer/safe sex.html
People of all sexual preferences will benefit from The Safer Sex Page, which promotes the practice of safe sex in preventing the spread of AIDS.

### WHO Global Programme on AIDS

http://gpawww.who.ch/gpahome.htm
In 1995, the World Health Organization received 1,291,810 reports of AIDS cases from 193 countries. The number, posted online, climbs daily. Find out what the current global statistics are at this site and read about sexually transmitted diseases, as well as women and AIDS.

## ONLINE SERVICES

### Human Sexuality

CompuServe: hsx
CompuServe's Human Sexuality forum (go *hsx*) is an authoritative resource that provides information for people of all sexual preferences. Users will find the ABCs of Sexual Terms, a library of commonly asked questions, and a keyword search, but the question-and-answer columns are the real meat of this forum. Here, experts give pub-

lic answers to posted questions. A special section addresses gay, lesbian, and bisexual concerns. Users can also access the Open Human Sexuality forum (go *hsx100*)and the Adult Human Sexuality forum (go *hsx200*), which offer message boards and file libraries.

### Personal Empowerment Network

AOL: pen

The AIDS, HIV Info and Support folder contains a plethora of health and medical information regarding the disease. But the most useful area is the message board, which offers support to, and coping suggestions for, AIDS sufferers.

## USENET

### Medical Discussion on AIDS

sci.med.aids

Participants take a scientific look at the AIDS epidemic on this Usenet newsgroup. Much discussion is devoted to new drugs, their effectiveness, and their side effects, as well as possible cures.

## THE NET AND BBS

### AIDS Information Newsletter

gopher: gopher.niaid.nih.gov

path: AIDS/VA AIDS Information Newsletter

The San Francisco VA Medical Center publishes the biweekly *AIDS Information Newsletter* online. The publication takes a scientific view of the AIDS epidemic. Recent articles have covered safe sex, women and the HIV infection, and HIV/AIDS in health care.

### CDC Daily Report

gopher: gopher.niaid.nih.gov

path: AIDS/CDC Daily Summaries

In its daily reports, the CDC provides "a national reference, referral and distribution service for HIV- and AIDS-related information." Reports cover daily news updates, as well as statistical information on HIV infection cases.

### Disease/Pregnancy Prevention

gopher: gopher.uiuc.edu

path: Univ. of Illinois/Campus services/Health Services/Health Information/Sexuality/Disease/Preg Prev

Online pamphlets explain how to use a condom or latex square correctly to prevent the transmission of HIV and other sexually transmitted diseases. Do you think you already have the answers? Take the Condom Quickie Quiz to test your knowledge.

# POLITICAL ACTION

Gay, lesbian, bisexual, and transgendered people are not yet recognized as full-fledged citizens of our countries. Yes, we can and do vote. Yes, we can and do own property. Yes, we can and do form domestic partnerships, raise our families, earn a living, and serve in the military. But our domestic partnerships are not legally recognized as marriages, our children can be and have been taken from us, our health care benefits rarely extend to our partners and their children as they would to heterosexual spouses and step-children, we can legally be fired from our jobs simply for being gay or lesbian, and we can be removed from military service (or prevented from serving) for refusing to hide or lie about our personal relationships. Our rights are not equal to those of heterosexual citizens; "liberty and justice for all" is enacted as "liberty and justice for some."

The organizations and individuals in this chapter are dedicated to changing the laws and guaranteeing equal rights for lesbian, gay, bisexual, and transgendered people. Some, like the Lesbian Avengers and Queer Nation, stage dramatic actions or tightly focused "zaps" to draw attention to a specific cause. Others, like the Gay and Lesbian Victory Fund, support gay and gay-friendly candidates for public office. Still others, including the International Lesbian and Gay Association, the Human Rights Campaign, Lambda Legal Defense and Education Fund, the National Gay and Lesbian Task Force, and more, support a broad range of political lobbies, educational programs, and international, national, and local campaigns dedicated to securing and ensuring liberty and justice for all.

## ARGENTINA

**International Lesbian and Gay Association—Argentina**
c/o CHA, CC45
Suc 37
Buenos Aires, 1437
The International Lesbian and Gay Association works to end discrimination and gain equal rights for the gay and lesbian community in Argentina. The association publishes the *ILGA Bulletin* and the *Pink Book.*

# SPOTLIGHT
## THE LESBIAN AVENGERS

On Gay Pride Day in June 1993, six experienced political activists distributed 8,000 fluorescent green notes in New York City that said, "Lesbians! Dykes! Gay Women! We want revenge and we want it now," and invited interested women to come to a meeting. Fifty showed up, and since then similar groups have gathered throughout the world as Lesbian Avengers.

Lesbian Avengers organize for action and visibility, and they focus on the specifics. They meet to plan their goals ("Who are we trying to reach? What is our message?"), logistics ("What are the time, date, place and length of the action? Do these choices make sense given the goals and message of

## BELGIUM

### International Lesbian and Gay Association (ILGA)—Belgium

Andy Quan, Coordinator
81, rue Marche-au-Charbon
Brussels, B-1000
phone: 2 5022471
fax: 2 5022471
e-mail: ilga@gn.apc.org
ILGA is a multinational association, operating in English, French, and Spanish, that comprises gay and lesbian groups in 60 countries. With a membership of 400, ILGA fights discrimination against homosexuals in all sectors and promotes the recognition of lesbian and gay rights by applying pressure on governments, international groups, and the media. Founded in 1978, ILGA serves as an information clearinghouse on gay oppression and liberation issues. The association's committees cover ableism, Africa, AIDS, asylum, Christian churches, gays and lesbians in military, health, immigration, Latin America, and youth. ILGA also sponsors various projects, including the Council of Europe/CSCE, European Community, Homosexual Prisoners, Iceberg Project on Discrimination of Lesbians and Gays, ILGA Pink Book Project, ILGA Project on Amnesty International, Twinning, United Nations, and WHO; and study groups covering Asia, community centres, culture, and Eastern Europe. The association publishes press releases, an annual conference report, the *ILGA Bulletin,* and the *ILGA Pink Book.* ILGA's annual conference takes place in June or July.

## CANADA

### ONTARIO

### Spirited People of the 1st Nations

Art Zoccole, President
2 Carlton St., Ste. 1419
Toronto, ON M5B 1J3
phone: (416) 944-9300
fax: (416) 944-8381
Spirited People of the 1st Nations works to represent lesbian and gay Native Americans throughout Canada. Founded in 1989, the 185-member group also provides support to those infected with the HIV-virus. The group's newsletter, *Sacred Fire,* appears quarterly, and its general assembly takes place every June in Toronto, Ontario.

## ENGLAND

### Lesbian Avengers—London

The Wheel

the action? How much space do we have? Will the action take place inside or outside? Will we have to contend with security?", and tactics ("What type of action are we planning: symbolic, disruption/interference, education?")—and then they stage their action.

The Lesbian Avengers handbook, published both on the Internet and within Avenger cofounder Sarah Schulman's book *My American History,* cautions Avengers to "avoid old, stale tactics at all costs. Chanting, picketing and the like alone no longer make an impression; standing passively and listening to speakers is boring and disempowering." Instead, the founders say, "look for daring, new participatory tactics depending on the nature of your action. New York Avengers have staged overnight encampments, surprised politicians with daring zaps in the halls of the Plaza Hotel, invaded the offices of *Self* magazine, marched down Fifth Avenue at rush hour with

4 Wild Ct., off Kingsway
London WC2B 4AU
Web site: http://www-dept.cs.ucl.ac.uk/students/S.Stumpf/LA.html
Formed in July 1994, the London Lesbian Avengers have already organized more than 50 actions, zaps, demonstrations, protests, and parties.

## MEXICO

### International Gay and Lesbian Association—Mexico

Apartado Postal 1-1693
Mexico City, 06030
The International Gay and Lesbian Association represents the interests of gays and lesbians in Mexico, working to abolish discrimination against homosexuals and to gain equal rights in legislation for gays and lesbians. The association publishes a bulletin five times per year, as well as the *Pink Book.*

## SPAIN

### Comite Reivindicativo Cultural de Lesbianas (CRECUL)

Elena Criado de Leon
Barquillo 44, 2 izquierda
Madrid, E-28004
phone: 91 3193689 or 91 4296241
CRECUL works to increase awareness of problems lesbians face. Founded in 1991, the group seeks to end sexual and gender discrimination in the workplace, provides legal advice and encourages lesbians to work for their rights, and seeks to create a new social definition of lesbians that will allow them total equality. CRECUL also conducts public educational and informational sexuality programs; collects and disseminates summaries of films, books, and art works relevant to lesbians; and researches the history of lesbians and lesbianism. The group's magazine, *Mujeres y Punto,* is published quarterly.

## UNITED STATES

### CALIFORNIA

### American Civil Liberties Union Gay Rights Chapter

1663 Mission St., #460
San Francisco, CA 94103
phone: (415) 621-2493
The ACLU Gay Rights Chapter conducts activities to promote and protect civil liberties

flaming torches, and handed out balloons that said 'Ask about lesbian lives!' to school children in an anti-gay district. What is the visual design of the action going to be? It should let people know clearly and quickly who we are and why we are there. The more fabulous, witty and original the better. New York Avengers have used a wide range of visuals such as fire eating, a 12-foot shrine, a huge bomb and a ten-foot plaster statue."

The Lesbian Avengers chapter of London, England, which organized about a year after the original group began in New York, staged more than 50 actions, zaps, demonstrations, protests, and parties in its first two years of existence. An August 1995 action with a sibling group, Outrage!, received television and newspaper coverage and drew attention to "the frightening issue of ex-gay groups," as the Avengers newsletter described. For the action, members of the Lesbian Avengers and Outrage! stormed into a

and gay rights; lobbies on behalf of members; sponsors ad hoc programs and activities; and conducts monthly board meetings.

### Gay and Lesbian Alliance of the Desert (GLAD)

Richard Black, President
PO Box 861
Cathedral City, CA 92235-0861
phone: (619) 322-8769
fax: (619) 324-7193
GLAD was established in 1989 to support and promote gay and lesbian rights. The alliance sponsors support groups, counseling, and town meetings with elected officials, and publishes a monthly newsletter.

### International Gay and Lesbian Human Rights Commission (IGLHRC)

Julie Dorf, Executive Director
1360 Mission St., Ste. 200
San Francisco, CA 94103
phone: (415) 255-8680
fax: (415) 255-8662
e-mail: IGLHRC@IGC.APC.ORG
The action society of the International Gay and Lesbian Association, the International Gay and Lesbian Human Rights Commission mobilizes gay and lesbian activists worldwide and operates in many languages, including Croatian, English, Japanese, Portuguese, Romanian, Russian, Spanish, and Vietnamese. Founded in 1990, the commission monitors, documents, exposes, and mobilizes response to human rights violations against lesbians, gays, bisexuals, and people with HIV and AIDS worldwide. IGLHRC promotes the repeal of sodomy laws; advocates AIDS education and prevention; acts as a clearinghouse for information on gay and lesbian human rights violations; conducts volunteer training workshops; offers educational presentations and internships; and organizes speaking tours of foreign-born activists. The group's annual Felipa da Souga Awards recognize gay and lesbian activists from around the world. IGLHRC's bimonthly newsletter *Emergency Response Network* addresses the group's letter-writing campaign, and printed and online reports cover issues concerning gays and lesbians in various regions or countries around the world.

### National Center for Lesbian Rights (NCLR)

Kate Kendall, Interim Director and Legal Director
870 Market St., Ste. 570

church where Living Waters, a Christian Evangelical group that focuses on curing people of their homosexuality, was meeting. For nearly an hour the Lesbian Avengers and Outrage! members blew whistles, released stink bombs, and chanted, "We are not sick, we don't need healing!" After being forced outside, the members continued to chant and sing gay hymns, while one activist posed in front of a large pink cross to symbolize her crucifiction for being queer. Media coverage, including a documentary of "ex-gay" groups in the United States and England, was immediate and extensive—a prime goal of Avenger actions.

San Francisco, CA 94102
phone: (415) 392-6257
fax: (415) 392-8442
Founded in 1977 as the Lesbian Rights Project, the National Center for Lesbian Rights is a legal resource center specializing in sexual orientation discrimination cases, particularly those involving lesbians. The center's activities include legal counseling and representation, community education, workshops on legal issues for lesbians, and technical assistance. The group provides legal services to lesbians on issues of custody and foster parenting, employment, housing, the military, and insurance, and publishes *Lesbian and Gay Parents' Legal Guide to Child Custody; Lesbian Mother Litigation Manual; Lesbians Choosing Motherhood: Legal Issues in Donor Insemination; Preserving and Protecting the Families of Lesbians and Gay Men;* and *Recognizing Lesbian and Gay Families: Strategies for Extending Employment Benefits.* The *NCLR Newsletter* comes out three times a year.

### National Organization for Men against Sexism (NOMAS)

54 Mint St., Ste. 300
San Francisco, CA 94103
phone: (415) 546-6627
NOMAS is an activist organization supporting a broad range of positive changes for men. According to the group's statement, "NOMAS is pro-feminist, gay-affirmative, and working to enhance the quality of men's lives. We feel that working to make this nation's ideals of equality substantive is the finest expression of what it means to be men." Members include both men and women. A national organization since 1982, the group's history began with the first National Men & Masculinity Conference in 1975. The organization had two name changes, from the National Organization for Men to the National Organization for Changing Men, before becoming NOMAS. The group's newsletter, *Brother,* lists national, regional, and local men's events. *Changing Men* magazine offers in-depth coverage of anti-sexist men's issues and writing.

### Radical Women

Nancy Reiko Kato, Organizer
523-A Valencia St.
San Francisco, CA 94110
phone: (415) 864-1278
Radical Women comprises women with a socialist-feminist political orientation who believe that women's leadership is decisive for basic social change. Radical Women works toward reform in the ares of lesbian rights, reproductive rights, child care, affirmative action, divorce, police brutality, rape, women of color, and working women. The group opposes the efforts of conservative anti-feminist groups. Founded in 1967, Radical Women supports nine local groups.

## COLORADO

### Ground Zero

PO Box 1982
Colorado Springs, CO 80901
phone: (719) 635-6086

## SPOTLIGHT URVASHI VAID

In the preface to her book *Virtual Equality,* Urvashi Vaid quotes Allen Ginsberg when she vows, "America, I'm putting my queer shoulder to the wheel." Since her first political act at age 10—writing a letter to Richard Nixon—Vaid has kept her shoulder at that wheel.

Vaid, an attorney and the former executive director for the National Gay and Lesbian Task Force (NGLTF), has lead an undeniably out and active life, having been involved in the lesbian and gay movement for more than 15 years. While in college, where she says she "learned all the tools of activism," she organized feminist conferences and helped establish an anti-apartheid group. Vaid later became involved with Lesbians United in

fax: (719) 635-6106
e-mail: grndzeroco@aol.com
Ground Zero promotes the civil rights of the gay, lesbian, transgendered, and bisexual community. The 750-member group, founded in 1992, strives to sustain the separation of church and state concerning governmental issues. Ground Zero conducts charitable, research, and educational programs; maintains a speakers' bureau; and compiles statistics. Membership fees are $20. The group's holdings include archival materials and books, periodicals, clippings, and audio and video recordings about gay, lesbian, bisexual, religious, and civil rights. *Ground Zero News* appears monthly.

## DISTRICT OF COLUMBIA

### Bisexual and Radical Feminists (BARF)
1400 L St. NW
Washington, DC 20043

### Gay and Lesbian Victory Fund
1012 14th St. NW, #707
Washington, DC 20005
phone: (202) 842-8679
The Victory Fund is a Political Action Committee benefitting openly gay and lesbian candidates for public office.

### Gays and Lesbians for Individual Liberty
David Morris, President
PO Box 65743
Washington, DC 20035

### Human Rights Campaign (HRC)
Elizabeth Birch, Executive Director
1101 14th St. NW, Ste. 200
Washington, DC 20005
phone: (202) 628-4160
Formerly known as the Human Rights Campaign Fund, HRC was founded in 1980 to advance the cause of lesbian and gay civil rights by lobbying Congress and political candidates who support gay and lesbian civil rights and increased funding for women's health concerns and AIDS research, education, and treatment. In 1992 the 80,000-member group provided more than $700,000 in financial contributions to supportive congressional candidates. In terms of civil rights, HRC encourages legislative protection for lesbian and gay men in employment, housing, public accomodations, military service, and immigration matters; recognition of the legitimacy of gay and lesbian families; and the repeal of laws criminalizing gay and lesbian Americans. The campaign also works for the elimination of anti-gay violence and collects

Non-Nuclear Action (LUNA), the non-profit newspaper *Gay Community News,* and the American Civil Liberties Union (ACLU), and she co-founded the lesbian direct-action group LIPS and worked with the National Prison Project to focus attention on prisoners with HIV and AIDS. Vaid spent six and a half years with NGLTF, coordinating media events and creating relationships with various interest groups and grassroots activists as public information director, then focusing on fundraising as executive director. Soon after she retired in 1993, *Time* magazine named Vaid one of their "Fifty for the Future" selection of promising young leaders. Vaid continues to act in support of the community, appearing recently at NGLTF's 1995 Creating Change conference, which was held in Detroit, Michigan, for activists nationwide.

Vaid's experiences and observations in gay activism—she specifically recalls her elation after Bill Clinton's election, then disillusionment as he (like

data detailing crimes committed against gay men and lesbians. HRC, which has absorbed the Gay Rights National Lobby and National Coming Out Day campaign, regularly presents a recognition award for contributions to the advancement of gay and lesbian civil rights. HRC publishes a bimonthly newsletter called *Capitol Hill Update* and a quarterly newsletter called *Momentum,* which details legislative issues pertaining to gay and lesbian rights.

## Human Rights Campaign Fund's Field Division (HRCFFD)

Elizabeth Birch, Director
1101 14th St. NW, Ste. 200
Washington, DC 20005
phone: (202) 628-4160
Founded in 1987 as a project of the Human Rights Campaign (see above entry), the Field Division lobbies Congress to prevent the enactment of national legislation adversely affecting the civil rights of gay and lesbian individuals and AIDS patients; to encourage funding for AIDS education, patient care, and research; and to support legislation favorable to gays, lesbians, and AIDS patients. Formerly known as the Fairness Fund or the Mobilization Project, the HRC Field Division conducts Speak Out mail campaign that directs messages to senators and representatives prior to legislative action on gay/lesbian, AIDS, or choice issues; organizes a support network on the state, congressional district, and local levels; and maintains a congressional alert system to inform local leaders and organizations about legislative developments.

## Log Cabin Federation (LCF)

PO Box 65822
Washington, DC 20035
phone: (202) 347-5306 or (202) 488-1561
The Log Cabin Federation, founded in 1987 and formerly known as United Republicans for Equality and Privacy, seeks to unite all gay and lesbian Republicans. The federation works to ensure equality for gay and lesbian individuals, especially in the Republican party. The group confronts the "reactionary religious right in the Republican party and the irresponsible extremists of the left in the gay community"; supports Republican candidates for office at all governmental levels; conducts fundraising and lobbying activities; sponsors outreach programs; and operates a speakers' bureau.

## National Association of Social Workers National Committee on Lesbian and Gay Issues (NASW)

Sheldon Goldstein, CEO

others before him) abandoned the community that had supported him—informed her 1995 book, *Virtual Equality: The Mainstreaming of Gay & Lesbian Liberation*. Just as "virtual reality" is a state in which things appear to be real but are not, "virtual equality," according to Vaid, is "a state of conditional equality based more on the appearance of acceptance by straight America than on genuine civic parity." The gay community has indeed gained visibility, power, and political access (and thus the appearance of equality), but prejudice and stigmatization still persist, and gay, lesbian, bisexual, and transgendered people still maintain a second-class status. In *Virtual Equality,* which documents the advancements made during this century, Vaid shows that the lesbian and gay community still has a long way to go to achieve true equality, but that equality is nonetheless a realistic goal. "My hope," she writes, "is to bring about a rethinking of our approach to the dilemmas gay people face."

*By Lisa Breck*

750 1st St. NE, Ste. 700
Washington, DC 20002-4241
phone: (202) 336-8287
This committee of the National Association of Social Workers seeks to ensure equal employment opportunities for lesbian and gay individuals. The committee informs the NASW about domestic, racial, and antigay violence; civil rights; and family and primary associations. The group encourages the NASW to support legislation, regulations, policies, judicial review, political action, and other activities that seek to establish and protect equal rights for all persons without regard to their affectional and/or sexual orientation. The committee also advises government bodies and political candidates regarding the needs and concerns of social workers and lesbian and gay people; reviews proposed legislation; and publishes *Lesbian and Gay Issues: A Resource Manual.*

## National Coalition for Black Lesbians and Gays

Washington, DC
phone: (202) 389-1094

## National Gay and Lesbian Task Force (NGLTF)

Melinda Paras, Executive Officer
2320 17th St. NW
Washington, DC 20009
phone: (202) 332-6483
fax: (202) 332-0207
Web site: http://www.ngltf.org/
NGLTF, founded in 1973, is dedicated to the elimination of prejudice against persons based on their sexual orientation. The 18,000-member task force lobbies U.S. Congress; organizes on the "grass roots" level; demonstrates and engages in direct action for gay freedom and full civil rights; works with the media to cover gay issues and the lives of gay people; and assists other associations and foundations in working effectively with the homosexual community. NGLTF also represents the national gay/lesbian community on AIDS policy issues and works for a responsible, nondiscriminatory national AIDS policy; strives to reform sodomy law and repeal the military policy against homosexuals; offers technical assistance, leadership training, education, and resource support; and maintains a speakers'

*Urvashi Vaid, former director of NGLTF, and Tim McFeely, former director of the Human Rights Campaign, speak with a reporter during the national 1995 Creating Change Conference. (Photo Courtesy* Between the Lines.)

bureau. Among NGLTF's publications are *Anti-Gay/Lesbian Victimization; Anti-Gay Violence: Causes, Consequences, Responses; Dealing with Violence: A Guide for Gay and Lesbian People; Gay and Lesbian Rights Protections in the U.S.;* the semiannual *Campus Organizing Newsletter;* and the quarterly *NGLTF Task Force Report,* which describes the activities of the task force and governmental actions that affect gays and lesbians. NGLTF sponsors the national Creating Change Conference every November.

### National Latino Lesbian and Gay Organization (LLEGO)

PO Box 44483
Washington, DC 20026
phone: (202) 544-0092

### People for the American Way

2000 M St. NW, Ste. 400
Washington, DC 20036
phone: (202) 467-4999

### Queer Nation

Box 34773
Washington, DC 20043
Founded in 1991, Queer Nation is dedicated to the "subversion of heterosexism and homophobia in all of its various cultural, political, and economic manifestations." The group uses nonviolent actions to "celebrate and flaunt sexual diversity"; organizes press conferences, candlelight vigils, marches, and protests; and conducts charitable, educational, and research programs. The group, which meets the first and third Monday of the month, has no elected officials or hierarchy of power.

## GEORGIA

### Atlanta Lesbian Feminist Alliance

Box 5502
Atlanta, GA 30307
phone: (403) 378-9769

## SPOTLIGHT
## SARAH SCHULMAN

Since the publication of her first novel, *The Sophie Horowitz Story,* in 1984, Schulman's fiction and essays have provided a constant reminder to writers and readers of the possibilities and responsibilities of lesbian and gay fiction. Throughout all of her writing, Schulman explores the interaction between the nature of art and the reality of politics, examining not only the inherent tensions present there but the inescapable interdependency as well. In Schulman's writing and vision, good, truthful art and politics are inextricably bound together.

Sarah Schulman was born in New York City in 1958 into a Jewish, middle-class professional family. A Fulbright fellow in 1984, Schulman received the

The Atlanta Lesbian Feminist Alliance provides social, political, educational, cultural, and recreational activities. The group maintains a library covering women's theory, lesbianism, and feminism, and publishes *Atalanta* monthly.

### HAWAII

#### Hawaii Equal Rights Marriage Project

Gay/Lesbian Community Center
1820 University Ave.
Honolulu, HI 96822

### KENTUCKY

#### Gays and Lesbians United for Equality

PO Box 992
Louisville, KY 40201-0992

### MASSACHUSETTS

#### Gay and Lesbian Advocates and Defenders (GLAD)

Amelia Craig, Executive Director
PO Box 218
Boston, MA 02112
phone: (800) 455-GLAD or (617) 426-1350
fax: (617) 426-3594
e-mail: GLAD@AOL.COM

Attorneys in GLAD volunteer time to defend the civil rights of lesbians, gay men, and people with HIV. Founded in 1978, GLAD operates the AIDS Law Project and a speakers' bureau, and conducts educational programs, impact litigation, and advocacy programs. Although the group's activities are based in the New England area, it provides information and referrals nationwide. The newsletter, *GLAD Briefs,* includes information on recent cases, legislation affecting civil rights issues, and organization activities.

### MICHIGAN

#### AIDS Law Center

Linda D. Bernard, President & CEO
Wayne County Neighborhood Legal Services
65 Cadillac Square, Ste. 3802
Detroit, MI 48226
phone: (313) 962-0466, ext. 348
for hearing impaired: (313) 868-8045

The AIDS Law Center provides compassionate legal services to AIDS/HIV-positive residents of Southeastern Michigan and their families and/or significant others. Pro-

American Library Association's Gay Book Award in 1988. From an early age she has been involved in progressive politics and grassroots movements for social change: the women's movement, reproductive rights, lesbian and gay liberation, tenants rights, and most recently, AIDS work and lesbian empowerment. In 1986, with Jim Hubbard, she founded the New York Lesbian and Gay Experimental Film Festival; the following year she became a founding member of ACT UP; and in 1992 she helped found the Lesbian Avengers.

After working for years as a waitress and writing essays, reviews, and news for the lesbian and gay press, Schulman published her first novel, *The Sophie Horowitz Story,* about a lesbian reporter attempting to track down two radical feminist bank robbers who have recently resurfaced after 10 years underground. Although Schulman relied upon the detective story genre to move her plot along, the novel is also a meditation on the state of lesbian

grams include a client education project, community education project, and youth education project.

### AIDS Legal Coalition and Referral Service of Michigan

916 Ford Building
615 Griswold
Detroit, MI 48226
phone: (313) 964-4188
Refers people with HIV/AIDS to attorneys for help with legal problems.

### Libertarians for Gay and Lesbian Concerns (LGLC)

James Hudler, International Coordinator
PO Box 447
Chelsea, MI 48118
phone: (313) 475-9792
Libertarians for Gay and Lesbian Concerns, founded in 1981, serves as a network for gay libertarians; seeks to improve awareness of gay concerns within the libertarian movement; and provides libertarian outreach to gays and lesbians. The *LGLC Newsletter* is issued quarterly.

### Palmer Fund

PO Box 1137
Royal Oak, MI 48068-1137
The Palmer Fund is a foundation serving the gay and lesbian community.

### Triangle Foundation

Jeffrey Montgomery, President
19641 W. Seven Mile Rd.
Detroit, MI 48219-2721
phone: (313) 537-3323
hate reports: (313) 533-1166 or (517) 753-9823
fax: (313) 537-3379
Web site: http://www.tri.org
The Triangle Foundation works in advocacy, education, non-discrimination, and anti-violence. Among other activities, the foundation fields up to 50 calls per week for victim assistance and responds to press inquiries about gay/lesbian-related media stories.

## NEBRASKA

### Coalition for Gay and Lesbian Civil Rights

PO Box 94882
Lincoln, NE 68509-4882

## NEW YORK

### American Civil Liberties Union (ACLU)

politics and sexuality, as well as the potential of writing as a tool for social change. In her 1986 novel, *Girls, Visions and Everything* (the title comes from a passage in *On the Road* by Jack Kerouac), Schulman sets the action in a lesbian community on New York's lower East Side. Schulman examines the idea of pursuing personal freedom in a city, and a country, that is becoming increasingly hostile and dysfunctional.

All of Schulman's novels take place in Manhattan, and in them the city becomes a microcosm of social ills as well as a metaphor for the political and moral corruptions of the broader culture. Schulman insists on exploring the individual's responsibility to her community as well as to the world. In an interview in *Women's Review of Books* she states, "I write about New York City. New York is a very stratified city and your layer of protection determines your sense of responsibility ... because that is the disease of how

Ira Glasser, Executive Director
132 W. 43rd St.
New York, NY 10036
phone: (212) 944-9800
The ACLU champions the rights set forth in the Bill of Rights of the U.S. Constitution: freedom of speech, press, assembly, and religion; due process of law and fair trial; and equality before the law regardless of race, color, sexual orientation, national origin, political opinion, or religious belief. The ACLU's activities include advocacy and public education, and it sponsors litigation projects on topics such as gay and lesbian rights, women's rights, and children's rights. Founded in 1920, the group maintains a library of more than 3,000 volumes, supports 50 state and 200 local groups, and publishes *Civil Liberties Alert* monthly and policy statements, handbooks, reprints, and pamphlets.

### Astraea Foundation

Katherine Acey, Executive Director
116 East 16th St., 7th Fl.
New York, NY 10003
Astraea was the first lesbian foundation in America and provides funding to lesbian projects, organizations, initiatives, and resources throughout the United States. Astraea aims to "build a diverse and empowering network of resources that celebrates and safeguards *our* lives." Originally founded as a regional women's foundation in 1979, Astraea "came out" as the lesbian action foundation in 1990.

### Lambda Legal Defense and Education Fund (LLDEF)

Kevin M. Cathcart
666 Broadway, Suite 1200
New York, NY 10012
phone: (212) 995-8585
fax: (212) 995-2306
The Lambda Legal Defense and Education Fund, founded in 1973, defends the civil rights of gay persons and people with AIDS in areas such as employment, housing, education, child custody, and the delivery of medical and social services. LLDEF engages in test case litigation as counsel or co-counsel, and files briefs as "a friend of the court" to present statistical and educational information and to help inform the court of the needs of gay men and lesbians and people with AIDS. The fund also provides resources and assistance to attorneys working on behalf of gay clients; maintains a national network of cooperating attorneys; helps inform the gay community about its rights and recent legal developments; and educates the public and the legal communi-

Americans live, people don't care about something unless it affects them personally. So marginal people know how they live and how the dominant culture lives. Dominant culture people know only how they live. The people who have the most power have the least information and the smallest sense of responsibility."

This view is manifest in Schulman's next three novels, *After Delores, People in Trouble,* and *Empathy*. In *Empathy,* the main character, Anna O., attempts to make sense of a modern world in which the three mainstays of contemporary thinking—psychoanalysis, communism, and capitalism—are all proven failures. *Empathy* deals with some of the themes of the earlier novels—social responsibility, minoritization, urban decay—but investigates them further through formal invention in an attempt to completely link the personal (and the psychological) with the political. Schulman also views the

ty about issues and concerns of gay persons and people with AIDS. LLDEF operates a speakers' bureau; sponsors seminars; compiles statistics; and maintains files containing court decisions and copies of briefs and pleadings. The group's Jay C. Lipner Liberty Award annually recognizes service in combatting AIDS and AIDS discrimination, and the Lambda Liberty Award is given for service in the Gay/Lesbian Community. The *Lambda Update* newsletter reports on the court cases in which LLDEF is involved, and on issues of concern to the organization and its 22,000 members.

## Lesbian Avengers—New York

208 W. 13th St.
New York, NY 10011
phone: (212) 967-7711, ext. 3204
Web site: http://www.cc.columbia.edu/~vk20/lesbian/avenger.html

Lesbian Avengers is a direct action group focused on issues vital to lesbian survival and visibility. Founded in 1993, it has developed the Lesbian Avenger Civil Rights Organizing Project (LA CROP), which has organized against homophobic legislation in Maine and Idaho, and the FREE NY Project, which is fighting for lesbian and gay rights in New York State. The group sponsors a Dyke March each June—held on the Saturday before Sunday's regular Pride March—and publishes the *Lesbian Avenger Handbook.* Local Avengers chapters exist throughout the world.

## Lesbian Feminist Liberation (LFL)

Eleanor Cooper, Spokeswoman
Lesbian & Gay Community Services Center
208 W. 13th St.
New York, NY 10011
phone: (212) 924-2657
fax: (212) 620-7310

The Lesbian Feminist Liberation promotes lesbian and women's rights by working to change the attitudes and institutions that limit or deny women the control of their own lives and bodies. Founded in 1973, the group's activities include forming coalitions with feminist and gay groups; lobbying; direct confrontation tactics (such as nonviolent demonstrations and sit-ins); and educational programs. The group also conducts dances, concerts, sports events, and conferences.

## Women's Action Coalition

High School for the Humanities
351 W. 18th St.
New York, NY 10011
phone: (212) 967-7711

work as a challenge to the false linearity of the "coming-out novel," attempting to address the creation of lesbian identity formally as well as in the content of the novel.

In *My American History: Lesbian and Gay Life During the Reagan/Bush Years,* Schulman collects and adds commentary and updates to her nonfiction writing from 1981 through 1993. The collection "documents a radical political history that most people—gay or straight—never knew happened," writes lesbian activist Urvashi Vaid in the book's foreword. Describing "the lesbian-led Seneca Women's peace encampment, the raid on the New York City bar Blues in 1983, the closing of the bathhouses in 1985, the dyke-baiting and defunding of the National Coalition Against Sexual Assault by Ed Meese, the direct action in Congress in 1983 to protest the Human Life Amendment restricting abortion, the 1991 Outwrite conference, the Dyke March at the

WAC is "an open alliance of women committed to direct action on issues affecting the rights of all women." WAC "insists on economic parity and representation for all women, and an end to homophobia, racism, religious prejudice, and violence against women." WAC also "insists on every woman's right to health care, child care, and reproductive freedom" and seeks to "launch a visible and remarkable resistance." WAC organizes and participates in demonstrations and rallies for women's rights.

## OHIO

### Stonewall Cincinnati Human Rights Organization

Shirley Lesser, Executive Officer
Box 954
Cincinnati, OH 45201
phone: (513) 541-8778
The Stonewall Cincinnati Human Rights Organization includes individuals and businesses promoting non-discrimination on the basis of sexual orientation. The 800-member group, founded in 1981, sponsors educational and political activities; is involved in voter registration; maintains political action committee; and publishes the monthly *Stonewall Newsletter.*

## OREGON

### Electronic Political Action in the Gay Environment

PO Box 19851
Portland, OR 97280-0851

## RHODE ISLAND

### Rhode Island Alliance for Lesbian and Gay Civil Rights

PO Box 5758
Providence, RI 02903-0758

## TEXAS

### Old Lesbians Organizing for Change (OLOC)

Vera Martin, Coordinator
PO Box 980422
Houston, TX 77098
phone: (713) 661-1482; (510) 439-8003
OLOC's membership of 1,000 consists of lesbians 60 years or older. Founded in 1989, OLOC serves as a network to reduce ageism by exchanging information on the diversity

1993 March on Washington," and about 50 other events, Vaid continues, Schulman "writes with a confidence that leaves her insights ringing like bells in your head."

Schulman's fiction addresses the very pertinent question of how we might be able to live responsibly and fruitfully in a politically corrupt world. Her political commentary tells us what has been done, what it's meant, and what remains to be accomplished. Her work with ACT UP and the Lesbian Avengers, as well as other social action groups, has been a major influence on her writing. Her role as an artist has been guided by her political actions and ideals, and she steadfastly refuses to view "art" and "artists" as separate from or above political concerns.

*By Michael Bronski*

of races, ethnicities, class backgrounds, and histories of its members. Formerly known simply as Old Lesbians Organizing, OLOC also publishes educational materials on ageism and how to combat discrimination, including the biennial *Facilitator's Handbook: Confronting Ageism for Lesbians 60 and Over*. The group's annual membership fee is $10.

### Tarrant County Lesbian/Gay Alliance (TCLGA)

1219 6th Ave.
Ft. Worth, TX 76104-4308
phone: (817) 877-5544
fax: (817) 877-1626
TCLGA works to ensure the protection of the civil rights of lesbians and gay people. The group provides community education, voter forums, and legal defense in discrimination cases; maintains a speakers' bureau and referral service; and publishes *Alliance News* monthly. The group meets the third Thursday of the month.

## WASHINGTON

### Stonewall Committee for Lesbian/Gay Rights (SCLGR)

Chris Smith, Chairperson
6727 Seward Park Ave., South
Seattle, WA 98118
phone: (206) 722-0938
fax: (206) 723-7691
The Stonewall Committee for Lesbian/Gay Rights, founded in 1981, seeks to advance gay and lesbian rights through education, coalition-building, and direct action. SCLGR meets the second and fourth Thursday of the month.

## WISCONSIN

### Disabled Womyn's Educational Project

Catherine Odette, Executive Officer
PO Box 8773
Madison, WI 53708-8773
phone: (608) 256-8883
e-mail: SLKARON@facstaff.wisc.edu
Founded in 1988, the Disabled Womyn's Educational Project comprises lesbians with disabilities. The project promotes members' interests by supporting legislation sensitive to members' needs. The group also maintains a speakers' bureau and book, periodical, and artwork holdings. Their newsletter, *Dykes, Disability, and Stuff,* is published quarterly and is available in various formats, including audiocassette, braille, DOS

diskette, large print, modem transfer, and audio tape.

# ONLINE RESOURCES

## THE WEB

### Amy's Obsession

http://www.best.com/~agoodloe/home.html

The objects of Amy Goodloe's obsessions range from feminism to the Internet. Goodloe has collected an impressive list of lesbian-oriented Internet resources on literature and women's rights.

### Equal Marriage Rights Home Page

http://nether.net/~rod/html/sub/marriage.html

Supporters of the legalization of same-sex marriage will find much fuel for their cause here. The Equal Marriage Rights Home Page details the progress of same-sex legislation throughout the United States.

### National Gay and Lesbian Task Force

http://www.ngltf.org/

Since 1973, the National Gay and Lesbian Task Force (NGLTF) has fought for gay and lesbian civil rights. This progressive organization serves as a resource center for grassroots organizations nationwide. The NGLTF Web page offers press releases, a task force officer list, and an event schedule.

### NOW and Lesbian Rights

http://www.now.org/issues/lgbi.html

The National Organization for Women (NOW) has played a major role in the feminist movement for almost 30 years. The group actively campaigns for equal rights for people of all genders, races, and sexual preference. Keep up with NOW's recent actions for lesbian rights on this Web page.

## ONLINE SERVICES

### American Civil Liberties Union (ACLU)

AOL:ACLU

The ACLU forum on America Online provides extensive information on the status of gay and lesbian rights in America today. Of special note is the 1995 Docket of the ACLU Lesbian and Gay Rights Project found in the ACLU Briefing Paper folder.

### National Gay and Lesbian Task Force

AOL:NGLTF

AOL's National Gay and Lesbian Task Force brings together a wide variety of gay, lesbian, bisexual, and transgender resources. The Gay and Lesbian Alliance Against Defamation and the National Lesbian and Gay Journalist Association are just two of the local and national organizations represented.

## USENET

### Homosexual Politics

alt.politics.homosexuality

On this newsgroup, such issues as gay rights and the legalization of same-sex marriages receive a lot of attention from political and religious groups, as well as from homosexual rights activists.

# and ARCHIVES

How do others view us? How do we see ourselves?

The organizations, library archives, and media outlets in this chapter attempt to monitor, record, and positively influence how the mass media represents lesbians, gay men, bisexuals, and transgendered individuals.

Some organizations, like the Gay and Lesbian Alliance Against Defamation (GLAAD) and People for the American Way, target media and public defamation of gay and lesbian individuals and seek to replace the negative images with fair and accurate depictions of the gay community. To accomplish this, GLAAD and its allies identify and respond to public expressions of homophobia and bring instances of gay defamation to the attention of the gay community, while also promoting fair and accurate images of gays and lesbians by convincing those in the broadcasting and publishing fields to devote time and space to gay-related issues, events, and groups. People for the American Way tracks and documents anti-gay activity in its annual publication *Hostile Climate: A State by State Report on Anti-Gay Activity*.

Large and small library archives throughout the world, many listed in this chapter, serve an important historical function by collecting, storing, and lending hundreds of thousands of books, journals, newspapers, videos, and other memorabilia both by and about the LGBT community.

Finally, lesbian- and gay-owned media outlets, from local newspapers to national magazines to broadcast shows (like New York's DYKE TV, profiled here), report and comment on the news that affects the community from a gay point of view.

## SPOTLIGHT

## DYKE TV

"Pro-lesbian, pro-female and thoroughly engaging," according to the *Bay Area Reporter,* DYKE TV is a stylish and dynamic television magazine show that airs twice a month in more than 50 cities. Regular features on the program include a news segment covering current stories that are relevant to lesbian lives from a lesbian perspective, and "Eyewitness," an in-depth look at an issue of particular interest to the lesbian community. Other features include interviews with lesbian artists showcasing examples of their work; "I Was a Lesbian Child," which features home movies and childhood photos revisited from lesbian voices; and political commentary, lesbian herstory, health, gossip, sports news, workplace issues, "dyke-on-the-street" interviews, and more.

## AUSTRALIA

### Darling House Community Library

Stephen B. Leahy, Library Officer
64 Fullarton Rd.
Norwood, SA 5067
phone: 8 3621611
fax: 8 3631046
Founded in 1984, the Darling House Community Library was formerly called the AIDS Council of South Australia Library. The library holds 2,300 books; 30 bound periodical volumes; 500 reports; 300 archives; 2,000 journal reprints; and subscriptions to 120 journals on the subjects of acquired immune deficiency syndrome, gay and lesbian issues, self help (health), injecting drug use, counseling, and gay and lesbian literature. The library is open to the public with restrictions.

## BELGIUM

### Lesbisch Doe Front (LDF)

Postbus 621
Ghent, B-9000
phone: 9 2216331
Founded in 1986, LDF provides information to individuals and the public regarding lesbian issues, and sponsors the annual Lesbian Day assembly.

## CANADA

### BRITISH COLUMBIA

### Out on the Shelves/The Gay and Lesbian Library

Peter Thompson
1170 Bute St., 2nd Fl.
Vancouver, BC V6E 1Z6
phone: (604) 684-5307
fax: (604) 684-5309
e-mail: CORINNEP@SFU.CA
Founded in 1979, Out on the Shelves collects materials on gay and lesbian studies. Holdings include 5,000 books; video recordings; audio recordings; clipping files; and subscriptions to 15 journals and five newspapers. The library is open to the public.

### Special Libraries Cataloguing, Inc./Special Collection

J. McRee Elrod, Director
4493 Lindholm Rd., R.R. No. 1
Victoria, BC V9B 5T7
phone: (604) 474-3361
fax: (604) 474-3362
e-mail: ub652@freenet.victoria.bc.ca

The show has reported on Camp Sister Spirit under siege, lesbians in the military, the murder of Brandon Teena in Nebraska, and the activities of the Christian Right, and has featured filmmakers like Cheryl Dunye, performers including Phranc and the Five Lesbian Brothers, writers Jewelle Gomez and Dorothy Allison, and comediennes Kate Clinton and Marga Gomez.

The series was created in 1993 by three women—playwright and Lesbian Avenger cofounder Ana Maria Simo, theater director and producer Linda Chapman, and independent film and videomaker Mary Patierno—who consider the show "a blueprint for community-oriented lesbian television, broadcast throughout the country to enhance lesbian visibility and empowerment." Grassroots media activism at its best, DYKE TV intends to "incite, subvert, provoke, and organize."

Founded in 1979, this special collection of Special Libraries Cataloguing is devoted to gay literature. The collection's holdings include 1,000 books, 20 reports, and subscriptions to three journals. The collection is open to the public.

## MANITOBA

### Council on Homosexuality and Religion/Library

Leslie Corrin, Executive Director
PO Box 1912
Winnipeg, MB R3C 3R2
phone: (204) 284-5208 or (204) 474-0212
fax: (204) 478-1160

Founded in 1978, the library of the Council on Homosexuality and Religion gathers materials on homosexuality, sexuality, religious attitudes, and the history of sexuality. Holdings include 3,500 books; 60 bound periodical volumes; 150 reports; 4,500 archival items; 350 audiovisual items; and subscriptions to six journals and 20 newspapers. The library is open to the public.

### Winnepeg Gay/Lesbian Resource Centre

Leslie Corrin, Director
One 222 Osborne St. South
Winnipeg, MB R3L 1Z3
phone: (204) 474-0212
fax: (204) 478-1160

Founded in 1973, the Winnepeg Gay/Lesbian Resource Centre collects materials on homosexuality, lesbianism, gay liberation, sexuality, sexual minorities, and other gay-related issues. The centre's holdings include the Manitoba Gay and Lesbian Archives (45 meters of files); 3,200 books; 45 VF drawers of correspondence, reports, and news clippings; 160 audiotapes; 150 videotapes; 1,100 photographs; 700 posters; and subscriptions to 10 journals and 35 newspapers. The library is open to the public.

## ONTARIO

### Canadian Lesbian and Gay Archives

James Fraser Library
Harold Averill, President
Box 639, Sta. A
Toronto, ON M5W 1G2
phone: (416) 777-2755
fax: (416) 251-8285

Founded in 1973, the Canadian Lesbian and Gay Archives of the James Fraser Library focus on homosexuality, lesbianism, bisexuality, the gay liberation movement, and censorship. The archives' special collections

Executive Producer Cyrille Phipps, a fine arts graduate of the School of Visual and Performing Arts at Syracuse University, says she's thrilled to continue her long-standing relationship with grassroots media at DYKE TV. "It's a refreshing perspective on lesbians. We are the only national show to reflect lesbians as individuals as well as part of the community." Emphatically, she adds, "Where else do you see such a realistic portrayal of lesbians on television? Nowhere."

If the key to realistic portrayals of lesbians is diversity, then the key to diversity at DYKE TV lies in further developing its outreach program. "As an African American and West Indian woman of color I am happy to see other women of color on staff. DYKE TV has made great strides to avoid tokenism and alienation, but there is always room for improvement," says Phipps. "We are planning a major outreach program to lesbian organizations of

include records of lesbian and gay organizations and individuals (260 linear meters); 2,000 sound recordings; 2,000 posters; and 1,000 artifacts, including baseball uniforms, T-shirts, banners, pins, and matchbook covers. The archives also hold 5,000 books; 8 linear meters of clippings; 380 hours of audiotapes; 450 films; 120 hours of videotapes; 4,000 lesbian and gay periodical titles; 2,000 other periodical titles; 5,000 photographs; 10,000 vertical files; and subscriptions to 350 journals and other serials. Special indexes include a card index to published material; partial index to *Body Politic;* partial index to clippings; and finding aids and inventories to some archival holdings, poster collection, and photo collection. The library is open to the public and publishes the newsletter *Gay Archivist.*

### *Canadian Woman Studies (les cahiers de la femme)*

Luciana Ricciutelli, Editor
Inanna Publications, Inc.
York University
212 Founders College
4700 Keele St.
North York, ON M3J 1P3
Quarterly feminist journal containing articles, book and film reviews, and new fiction and poetry by Canadian writers (English and French). Founded in 1978.

### Canadian Women's Movement Archives (Archives Canadiennes du Mouvement des Femmes)

University of Ottawa/Library Network
Christine Banfill, Head of Archives and Special Collections
65 University, Rm. 603
Ottawa, ON K1N 9A5
phone: (613) 564-8129
fax: (613) 564-5871
Founded in 1977, the Canadian Women's Movement Archives holds 750 periodicals and newsletters, 2,500 group files, individual files, ephemera, buttons, T-shirts, photographs, slides, tapes, and subscriptions to 150 journals and 20 newspapers on the subjects of women's groups, lesbian groups, women's conferences, festivals, demonstrations, and issues in Canada from 1960 to the present. The archives are open to the public.

### *GenderTrash*

PO Box 500-62
552 Church St.
Toronto, ON M4Y 2E3

color in an effort to make diversity as much a focus as, say, distribution and fundraising. Diversity will be an ongoing process, a thread throughout the organization."

Outreach goes hand in hand with education. DYKE TV offers eight-week workshops in video production to the New York lesbian community through grants from the Manhattan Neighborhood Network, one of the public access stations that airs DYKE TV. Phipps expects to expand the educational and outreach department by providing not only individuals in the lesbian community with access to training, but entire organizations. DYKE TV–inspired educational programs located throughout the country is a dream that could become a reality.

Phipps asks everyone to support DYKE TV as it grows but continues to nurture and respect its roots. "We need the community of lesbians, women at

### *Lexicon*

PO Box 459, Station P
Toronto, ON M5S 2S9

### *XTRA! Your Gay & Lesbian Guide to Toronto*

Dayne Ogilvie, Editor
David Walberg, Publisher
Pink Triangle Press
45 Charles St.
Toronto, ON M4Y 1R9
phone: (416) 925-6665
fax: (416) 925-6503
Newspaper covering the newest entertainment opportunities for Toronto's gay and lesbian communities. Founded in 1984, appears semimonthly.

## QUEBEC

### *Attitude*

617 St. Remi, #205
Montreal, PQ H4C 3G7

### *RG*

Alain Bouchard, Editor
CP 5245, Succursale C
Montreal, PQ H3A 1G9
Publication focusing on gay and lesbian issues. Founded in 1982, appears monthly.

# UNITED STATES

## ARIZONA

### Equality Public News Service

7239 S. 43rd Pl.
Phoenix, AZ 85040-6318

## CALIFORNIA

### *Aché*

PO Box 6071
Albany, CA 94706
Journal for lesbians of African descent.

### *The Advocate*

Richard Rouilard, Editor in Chief
Liberation Publications, Inc.
6922 Hollywood Blvd., 10th Fl.
Los Angeles, CA 90028
phone: (213) 871-1225
fax: (213) 467-6805
National gay and lesbian news and lifestyle magazine. Founded in 1967, *Advocate* appears biweekly.

### *AdvocateMEN*

Jeff Yarbrough, Editor
Liberation Publications, Inc.
6922 Hollywood Blvd., 10th Fl.

large, gay men, and people in general to back us as we continue to develop a network, a coalition that begins with a safe environment to express our ideas, feelings, and thoughts," she says. "We must always have a venue that affirms, empowers, and reflects."

DYKE TV is produced almost exclusively by the volunteer efforts of more than 350 talented women, and is funded by several foundations and businesses, including Art Matters, Inc., the Astrea Foundation, the Creative Time/City-wide Fund, the HDJM Charitable Living Trust Grant, An Uncommon Legacy Foundation, the North Star Fund, the New York State Council on the Arts/Media Program, and the Bay Area Women's Fund of Our Own. Lesbians in cities nationwide have formed independent groups to produce segments, following DYKE TV's encouragement to all lesbians to "pick up a video camera and aim."

Los Angeles, CA 90028
phone: (213) 871-1225
fax: (213) 467-6805
Magazine featuring gay, male erotica. Founded in 1984, appears monthly.

### *Anything That Moves: Beyond the Myths of Bisexuality*
Bay Area Bisexual Network
2404 California St., Box 24
San Francisco, CA 94115
phone: (415) 703-7977

### *Bay Area Reporter*
395 Ninth St.
San Francisco, CA 94103-3831
Alternative newspaper for the San Francisco community.

### *Black Lace*
Alycee J. Lane, Editor
PO Box 83912
Los Angeles, CA 90083-0912
phone: (213) 410-0808
fax: (213) 410-9250
Magazine published by and for African American lesbians. Includes erotica and politically focused articles and analysis. Founded in 1991, *Black Lace* appears quarterly.

### Blanche M. Baker Memorial Library
ONE, Inc.
Luis Balmaseda, Librarian
1130 Arlington Ave.
Los Angeles, CA 90019
phone: (213) 735-5252
Founded in 1953, the Blanche M. Baker Memorial Library collects materials about homosexuality, the homophile movement, the gay liberation movement, gay and lesbian literature, and women's and lesbian studies. The library's holdings include 20,000 titles; 60 VF drawers of other catalogued items; archival collections of many organizations; personal papers; foreign language periodicals; and subscriptions to 200 journals and 46 newspapers. The library is open to qualified scholars by appointment only.

### *BLK*
PO Box 83912
Los Angeles, CA 90083-0912
phone: (310) 410-0808
fax: (310) 410-9250
Magazine for the black lesbians and gay men.

### *Cauldron*
PO Box 14779
Long Beach, CA 90803-1345

Development Director Maria Petulla, a liberal studies graduate of Hofstra University, is initiating a standardized fundraising plan for DYKE TV. "Now that the organization has carved its creative niche," she says, "we can focus on a strategic plan in which fundraising will work in tandem with—but will never overshadow—production. Both will have primary functions." Petulla launched a major donor campaign in March 1996 and plans to network with other activist, community, and professional organizations so that people of all ages, races, and ethnicities will have the opportunity to support DYKE TV. Petulla calls hers a mission for support. "Volunteers are encouraged to help out in the office or produce a segment," she suggests, "and members of the community are welcomed to become a local business sponsor or send a donation." She stresses, "We must increase every effort to provide a means for all lesbians to see reflections of themselves in the media. Our lives depend on it."

### *Community Yellow Pages*

Jeanne Cordova, Publisher
2305 Canyon Dr.
Los Angeles, CA 90068

### *Curve*

Frances Stevens, Publisher
FRS Enterprises
2336 Market St., #15
San Francisco, CA 94107
phone: (415) 863-6538
fax: (415) 863-1609
Known as *Deneuve* until a French actress (whose name happens also to be Deneuve) raised a fuss, *Curve* is a national lesbian magazine covering news, politics, sports, arts, entertainment, and trends, and it includes fiction, poetry, and profiles. Founded in 1991, the magazine appears bimonthly.

### *Dyke Review Magazine*

584 Castro St., #456
San Francisco, CA 94114
phone: (415) 621-3769

### *The Family Next Door*

PO Box 21580
Oakland, CA 94620
phone: (510) 482-5778
Newsletter for lesbian and gay parents and their friends.

### *Feminist Bookstore News*

PO Box 882554
San Francisco, CA 94188
phone: (415) 626-1556
Trade magazine, founded in 1976, for booksellers, librarians, and publishers interested in books by and about women.

### *Freshmen*

Liberation Publications, Inc.
6922 Hollywood Blvd., 10th Fl.
Los Angeles, CA 90028
phone: (213) 871-1225
fax: (213) 467-6805
Magazine featuring gay, male erotica. Founded in 1991, appears monthly.

### Gay & Lesbian Alliance Against Defamation—San Francisco Bay Area Chapter (GLAAD/SFBA)

Kristy Billuni, Managing Director
1360 Mission St., Ste. 200
San Francisco, CA 94103
phone: (415) 861-2244
fax: (415) 861-4893
Web site: http://www.glaad.org/glaad/glaad.html
The San Francisco Bay Area chapter of GLAAD strives for fair treatment of gays and lesbians in the San Francisco Bay area. Founded in 1988, three years after the

Based in New York and nationally cablecast in more than 50 U.S. cities, DYKE TV has been screened at film festivals around the globe, including the New York New Festival and lesbian and gay film festivals in Baltimore, Chicago, London, Paris, and elsewhere.

national New York City chapter, the group confronts homophobic defamation, stereotypical portrayal, and heterosexist omission to ensure the dignity of lesbian, gay, and bisexual people; provides educational programs and information and referral services; maintains a speakers' bureau; publishes the weekly "Media Watch Column" and a monthly newsletter called *Update;* and maintains the Project 21 Internet database.

## Gay and Lesbian Center

Jim Van Buskirk, Librarian
San Francisco Main Public Library
100 Larkin
San Francisco, CA 94102
phone: (415) 557-4499 or (415) 557-4400
Holdings include records of lesbian publisher Naiad Press and more than 15,000 books donated by Naiad founder Barbara Grier.

## *Gay & Lesbian Periodicals Directory*

New Vista Publishing
770 Sycamore Ave., #J-437
Vista, CA 92083
phone: (619) 727-8718

## Gay Media Task Force (GMTF)

Newton E. Deiter, Ph.D., Executive Director
71-426 Estellita Dr.
Rancho Mirage, CA 92270
phone: (619) 568-6711
fax: (619) 568-3241
The purpose of the Gay Media Task Force, established in 1972, is to provide resources and consultative services to the media relative to the gay and lesbian community. The task force actively monitors the media; works with authors to promote accuracy in nonfiction works concerning gays; and represents gays before Congress, the Federal Communications Commission, and other decision-making bodies on issues brought to the task force's attention by members of the gay community throughout the United States.

## *Genre*

8033 Sunset Blvd., #1
Los Angeles, CA 90046
phone: (213) 874-1300
Magazine of lifestyle, fashion, and entertainment for gay men. Founded in 1990, appears quarterly.

## *Girlfriends Magazine*

3415 Cesar Chavez, Ste. 101
San Francisco, CA 94110
phone: (415) 648-9464
Web site: http://www.best.com/~agoodloe/girlfriends/
Bimonthly magazine for and about lesbians; portions appear online.

## *Girljock*

Rox-A-Tronic
PO Box 882723
San Francisco, CA 94188
phone: (510) 452-2085
fax: (415) 282-6833
Quarterly publication focusing on the lives of women athletes and their admirers, founded in 1990.

## Institute for Advanced Study of Human Sexuality

Exodus Trust Archives of Erotology
Dr. Ted McIlvenna, Director
1523 Franklin St.
San Francisco, CA 94109
phone: (415) 928-1133
fax: (415) 928-8061
Founded in 1976, the archives collect works about human sexuality and include two special collections: the Lyle Stuart Library of Sexual Science and the Harry Mohne Collection. The Exodus Trust Archives include 60,000 books; 12,000 bound periodical volumes; 189,000 films; 500 slides; 16,000 videotapes; 50,000 periodicals; 25,000 mag-

azines and special photographs; videotapes of all lectures given at the institute; and 10 unbound volumes of American and European journals on homosexuality. The archives also subscribe to 15 journals and five newspapers. The library is not open to the public, but researchers may submit a formal written request for access to the library.

### *In Touch for Men*

Tom Quinn, Publisher
In Touch International
13122 Saticoy St.
North Hollywood, CA 91605-3402
phone: (818) 764-2288
fax: (818) 764-2307
Magazine for gay men. Founded in 1973, appears monthly.

### June Mazer Lesbian Collection

Degania Golove, Coordinator
626 N. Robertson Blvd.
West Hollywood, CA 90069
phone: (213) 659-2478
Founded in 1987, the June Mazer Collection holds 3,000 books, 700 periodical titles, three VF drawers of manuscripts, one VF drawer of archives, one VF drawer of dissertations, audiocassettes, and videotapes on lesbian history, culture, thought, organizations, writers, writings, and the arts. Special collections include the Margaret Cruikshank Collection, Lillian Faderman Collection, Reid/Hyde papers, Sue Prosin papers, Joanne Parrent papers, Diana Press Archive, Telewoman archive, and SCWU archive. The collection is open to the public. Publishes *In the Life* newsletter.

### *Kuumba*

PO Box 83912
Los Angeles, CA 90083
phone: (310) 410-0808
Poetry journal for black lesbians and gay men.

### *Lesbian Contradiction*

Jan Adams, Editor
LesCon
584 Castro St., Ste. 356
San Francisco, CA 94114-2512
Subtitled "A Journal of Irreverent Feminism," *Lesbian Contradiction* is a newspaper that presents commentary, analysis, and humor. Founded in 1982, appears quarterly.

### *The Lesbian News*

Deborah Bergman, Editor and Publisher
PO Box 1430
Twentynine Palms, CA 92277
phone & fax: (619) 367-3386
Magazine of lesbian-oriented articles, features, and cartoons. Founded in 1975, appears monthly.

### California School of Professional Psychology

Los Angeles Campus Library
Tobeylynn Birch, Library Director
1000 S. Fremont Ave.
Alhambra, CA 91803-1360
phone: (818) 284-2777
fax: (818) 284-1682
e-mail: csppabir@class.org
Founded in 1970, the Los Angeles Campus Library of the California School of Professional Psychology's holdings include 20,000 books; 2,000 bound periodical volumes; 4,000 microfiche; 1,800 dissertations; 80 reels of microfilm; 450 audiotapes; 125 videocassettes; 7 films; 8 CD-ROMs; and subscriptions to 350 journals and other serials in the subjects of psychology, women's issues, homosexuality and lesbianism, and minority mental health. The library is open to the public for reference use only.

### Media Fund for Human Rights (MFHR)

R. J. Curry, Executive Director
PO Box 8185
Universal City, CA 91608
phone: (818) 902-1476
MFHR is an educational foundation of the Gay and Lesbian Press Association that seeks to reeducate the media and the American public about gays; utilize the media to change attitudes that deny gays full benefits of citizenship; enable gays to report their news; and promote the accessibility of gay history nationwide.

### *Mom Guess What Newspaper*

Linda Birner, Publisher
1725 L Street
Sacramento, CA 95814-4023

## SPOTLIGHT
## HOSTILE CLIMATE

Montana: The State Senate requires anyone violating the state's "deviant sexual conduct" law (which includes homosexual activity) to register with police. Maine, Oregon, Washington and Idaho: Religious right activists campaign to pass statewide anti-gay initiatives restricting the rights of lesbians and gays. Texas: A Church in Austin was expelled from the Austin Baptist Association for ordaining a gay man as a deacon. Ohio: A student at a Toledo Catholic high school was punished for wearing a "Boycott Homophobia" T-shirt.

Michigan: Scott Amedure, a gay Pontiac man, was murdered after revealing his crush on a straight acquaintance during a "Jenny Jones" taping. Also, the

phone: (916) 441-6397
Gay newspaper with a political emphasis. Founded in 1978, appears semimonthly.

### New College Library
New College of California
50 Fell St.
San Francisco, CA 94102-5298
phone: (415) 241-1376
Founded in 1971, the New College Library collects materials on law, alternative humanities, psychology, poetics, women's studies, homosexuality/lesbianism, minorities, multicultural issues, and social action. The library's holdings include 30,000 books, unbound periodicals, and subscriptions to 40 serials. The library is open to the public.

### *On Our Backs*
Debi Sundahl, Editor
526 Castro St.
San Francisco, CA 94114
phone: (415) 861-4723
Subtitled "Entertainment for the Adventurous Lesbian," *On Our Backs* contains fiction, features, columns, and pictorials. Founded in 1984, appears bimonthly.

### Out on the Screen
Morgan Rumpf, Executive Director
8455 Beverly Blvd, No. 309
Los Angeles, CA 90048
phone: (213) 951-1247
fax: (213) 951-9721
Out on the Screen, formerly known as the Gay and Lesbian Media Coalition, sponsors an annual film festival and publishes the catalog *Outfest: The Los Angeles Gay and Lesbian Film Festival.*

### *OUT/LOOK*
Jan Zita Grover, Editor
1255 Post St., #948
San Francisco, CA 94109
phone: (415) 626-7929
The national and gay quarterly was founded in 1988 and appears quarterly.

### *OutNOW!*
45 N. First St., Ste. 124
San Jose, CA 95113
Web site: http://www.outnow.com/
Biweekly newspaper.

### *Radiance: The Magazine for Large Women*
PO Box 30246
Oakland, CA 94604
phone: (510) 482-0680

### *San Diego Gay Times*
Roland deBeque, Editor
PO Box 34624
San Diego, CA 92163-4624

Saugatuck City Council rejected a proposal to extend civil rights protections to gays and lesbians.

That's just a few of the 180 anti-gay incidents nationwide compiled by People for the American Way, according to its third annual issue of *Hostile Climate,* a report documenting anti-gay discrimination.

In the two years since the first report was released, there has been a staggering increase in the number and breadth of anti-gay incidents fueled by hate speech and ignorance as well as by numerous measures in Congress and state legislatures that would infringe on gay rights.

As a result, American Way has challenged Sens. Bob Dole (R-Kansas) and Phil Gramm (R-Texas) and other political figures to "condemn in no uncertain terms the hate-filled language and anti-gay legislative agenda advocated

phone: (619) 299-6397
fax: (619) 299-3430
Newspaper serving the San Diego gay community. Founded in 1988, appears every Thursday.

### *San Diego Lesbian Press*
PO Box 16388
San Diego, CA 92176-6388
Newspaper providing a forum and focus for lesbian ideas and issues. Appears bimonthly.

### *San Francisco Bay Times*
Kim Corsaro, Editor
288 7th St.
San Francisco, CA 94103
phone: (415) 626-8121
fax: (415) 626-0629
Newspaper and calendar of events for Bay Area lesbian, bisexual, and gay communities. Founded in 1979, appears semimonthly.

### *Shamakami*
PO Box 460456
San Francisco, CA 94146-0456
For South and Southeast Asian lesbian and bisexual women.

### *Sinister Wisdom*
Elana Dykewomon, Editor
PO Box 3252
Berkeley, CA 94703
Subtitled "A Journal for the Lesbian Imagination in the Arts and Politics," *Sinister Wisdom* was founded in 1976 and appears quarterly.

### *TenPercent*
Lenore Schatz, Editor
ASUCLA Communications Board
University of California, Los Angeles
308 Westwood Plaza
112 I Kerckhoff Hall
Los Angeles, CA 90024
phone: (213) 206-6168
fax: (213) 206-0906
Subtitles "UCLA's Lesbian, Gay and Bisexual Magazine," *TenPercent* was founded in 1979 and appears six times per year.

### This Way Out
PO Box 38327
Los Angeles, CA 90038
phone: (213) 469-5907
Weekly radio show distributed to more than 60 stations in six countries.

### *Trikone*
Arvnd Kumar, Cofounder
Sandip Roy, Editor
PO Box 21354
San Francisco, CA 95151

by the Christian Coalition, The Traditional Family Values Coalition and their allies."

For the first time in more than a decade the American political system is largely controlled by people who firmly believe in "traditional family values." Many gay activists believe one of the key factors behind the rise of anti-gay activity stems from the emergence of this new ultraconservative majority.

"The political government world is really the thing that has the most direct effect on our everyday lives, and if things are getting bad for us in that realm, it's very, very serious and that causes a great deal of problems," notes Jeff Montgomery of Detroit's Triangle Foundation. "Their rhetoric gets quite a bit of play and it can be very dangerous. (It's) translated by the followers of those people into violence and very ugly activities."

phone: (408) 270-8776
Web site: http://www.rahul.net./trikone/
*Trikone*, pronounced "tree cone," is the Sanskrit word for "triangle." Mailed free to the Indian subcontinent, the quarterly magazine was founded as a newsletter in 1986 by two gay Indian men who sought to connect with others like them. *Trikone* points out that, when the newsletter was founded, there were "no gay groups, no gay political organizations and no gay channels of communication" in South Asian countries, including India, Pakistan, Afghanistan, Bangladesh, Bhutan, Burma, Maldives, Nepal, Sri Lanka, and Tibet. The newsletter quickly reached those countries and American immigrants from South Asia and, as founder Arvnd Kumar told syndicated columnist Deb Price, "became a catalyst for groups to form all over the world."

### *Update*

Tom Ellerbrock, Editor and Publisher
Dawn Media
PO Box 33148
San Diego, CA 92163-3148
phone: (619) 229-0500
fax: (619) 229-6907
General circulation newspaper serving the gay community. Founded in 1979, appears every Wednesday.

### *Wishing Well Magazine*

Laddie Holser, Editor and Publisher
Laddie's Ventures II
PO Box 713090
Santee, CA 92072-3090
phone: (619) 443-4818
Confidential correspondence/meeting service for women who love women. Formed in 1974, appears bimonthly.

### Women's Resource Center Library

Dorothy Lazard, Libary Coordinator
250 Golden Bear Ctr.
University of California
Berkeley, CA 94720
phone: (510) 642-4786 or (510) 642-9078
Founded in 1973, the Women's Resource Library collects materials on women's studies, women and work, financial aid, comparable worth, women of color, and international issues. Its special collections include the Catherine Scholten Collection on Women in American History (100 books); Bea Bain Collection on the Women's Movement (100 books); Margaret Monroe Drews Collection of Working Papers (the status of women in the U.S., 1950—1970; 12 VF drawers); Constance Barker Collection on Lesbian History (700 books); and women's movement magazines of the 1970s. Holdings

All too often, corporations, elected and spiritual leaders and non-profit organizations—the very groups and individuals that should be leading the charge for equal justice—are the source of the strife, according to the report. It cites evangelist Pat Robertson as an example.

"It's not a question of denying anybody any rights," insists Robertson. "It's a question of giving special rights to people on account of how they perform sex acts. It has nothing to do with being good to people of this persuasion. It's giving them special privileges."

That kind of rhetoric simply fuels the hate parade, adds Montgomery. "Gay people aren't looking for anything special or anything different," he says. "What we're trying to do is have our citizenship recognized, and have access to the rights, or equal rights, as any other citizen of the state or the

include 3,000 books; 20,000 other uncatalogued items; and subscriptions to 60 journals and other serials. The library is open to the public for reference use only.

## DISTRICT OF COLUMBIA

### Gay and Lesbian Alliance Against Defamation—National Capitol Area (GLAAD/NCA)

Cathy Renna, Co-Chair
c/o Chris Vaughan
PO Box 57044
Washington, DC 20037-0044
phone: (202) 429-9500
The National Capitol Area chapter of GLAAD, founded in 1990 (five years after the national New York City chapter), advocates fair and accurate representation of the gay, lesbian, and bisexual community in mainstream media, and conducts media education concerning gay, lesbian, and bisexual issues. The *GLAAD Rag* appears monthly.

### *Lambda Book Report*

Jim Marks, Editor
Lambda Rising, Inc.
1625 Connecticut Ave. NW
Washington, DC 20009-1013
phone: (202) 462-7924
fax: (202) 462-7257
Bimonthly magazine subtitled "A Review of Contemporary Gay and Lesbian Literature," founded in 1987. Associated with Lambda Rising Bookstore; sponsor of the annual Lambda Literary Awards (Lammies).

### *Metro Arts & Entertainment Weekly*

724 Ninth St. NW, Ste. 429
Washington, DC 20001

### *off our backs: a women's newsjournal*

2423 18th St. NW, 2nd Fl.
Washington, DC 20009
phone: (202) 234-8072
fax: (202) 234-8092
Monthly feminist magazine featuring articles by, for, and about women, founded in 1970.

### People for the American Way: Your Voice Against Intolerance

Tom Andrews, President
2000 M St. NW, Ste. 400
Washington, DC 20036
phone: (202) 467-4999
e-mail: pfaw@pfaw.org

country.... What people like Pat Robertson want is a special right to discriminate against us."

Meanwhile, *Hostile Climate* reports several success stories as well, especially stories about the work of broad community coalitions—including churches and labor, business, minority and civic organizations—and ongoing evidence that the average American still holds fairness and tolerance in high regard.

*By Eric Dobson. First published in* Metro Times, *February 7–13, 1996. Reprinted with permission.*

People for the American Way is a 300,000-member, non-partisan constitutional liberties organization. The group tracks and documents anti-gay activity in its annual publication *Hostile Climate: A State by State Report on Anti-Gay Activity.*

### *The Washington Blade*

Lisa M. Keen, Editor
1408 U St. NW, 2nd Fl.
Washington, DC 20009
phone: (202) 797-7000
fax: (202) 797-7040
Subtitled "The Gay Weekly of the Nation's Capital," the *Washington Blade* is a tabloid presenting gay and lesbian community and national news. Founded in 1969.

### *Youth Magazine*

PO Box 34215
Washington, DC 20043-4215

## FLORIDA

### *esto no tiene nombre*

4700 N.W. Seventh St., 463
Miami, FL 33126
phone: (305) 541-6097
Revista de lesbianas latinas.

### Gay and Lesbian Alliance Against Defamation—Florida Chapter

PO Drawer 2969
Winter Park, FL 32790-2969

### *Hers*

PO Box 8362
Longboat Key, FL 34228

### *Our World*

Richard Valdmanis, Editor
Our World Publishing Corp.
1104 N. Nova Rd., Ste. 251
Daytona Beach, FL 32117
phone: (904) 441-5367
fax: (904) 441-5604
Subtitled "the international gay travel magazine," *Our World* was founded in 1989.

### *The Weekly News (TWN)*

Steven Biller, Editor
901 N.E. 79th St.
Miami, FL 33138
phone: (305) 757-6333
fax: (305) 756-6488
Gay newspaper on news and issues. Founded in 1977.

## GEORGIA

### *Amethyst*

75 Bennett St. NW, #N-1
Atlanta, GA 30309
phone: (404) 609-0590
Literary journal for lesbians and gay men.

### *EtCetera Magazine*

Jack Pelhaw, Editor
427 Moreland Ave., Ste. 700
Atlanta, GA 30307
phone: (404) 525-3821
fax: (404) 525-1908
Magazine for gays and lesbians. Founded in 1985, appears monthly.

### *Iris Literary Review*

PO Box 7263
Atlanta, GA 30357
(404) 337-0061
Gay men's literary magazine.

### *Sage*

PO Box 42741
Atlanta, GA 30311
phone: (404) 223-7528
Scholarly journal for black women.

## HAWAII

### *Gay Community News*

PO Box 37803
Honolulu, HI 96837

### *Island Lifestyle Magazine*

2851-A Kihei Pl.
Honolulu, HI 96816

## IDAHO

### *Diversity*

PO Box 323
Boise, ID 83701

## ILLINOIS

### ALA Gay/Lesbian/Bisexual Book Awards Committee

John DeSantis, Chairperson
Dartmouth College Library
HB 6025
Hanover, NH 03755-3525
phone: (603) 646-3605
fax: (603) 646-3702
e-mail: jcdesantis@dartmouth.edu
According to Awards Committee member Michael A. Lutes, "The American Library Association's Gay/Lesbian/Bisexual Book Award is the longest standing award of its kind, having been established in 1971 by members of the library profession to honor outstanding works by or about lesbians, gay men, or bisexuals. The awards are announced in April of the year following the current year: two awards are given, one for nonfiction and one for fiction."

### ALA Gay & Lesbian Task Force Clearinghouse

JoAnn Segal, Associate Director for Programming
c/o American Library Association
Office of Library Outreach Services
50 E. Huron
Chicago, IL 60611
phone: (312) 944-6780
Founded in 1970, the ALA Gay & Lesbian Task Force's Clearinghouse holds 2,000 books, pamphlets, and periodicals about homosexuality, lesbianism/feminism, and gay rights. The Clearinghouse also sells *Gay Bibliography* and other titles. For further information about the task force, which is affiliated with the American Library Association's Social Responsibilities Round Table, write to GLTF c/o Roland Hansen, Secretary/Treasurer, 3824 N. Fremont, Chicago, IL 60613.

### *Daughters of Sarah*

PO Box 411179
Chicago, IL 60641-1179
Magazine for Christian feminists.

### *Gay Chicago Magazine*

Ralph Paul Gernhardt, Publisher
Ultra Ink, Inc.
3121 N. Broadway
Chicago, IL 60657
phone: (312) 327-7271
fax: (312) 327-0112
Entertainment magazine for the gay community. Founded in 1976, appears weekly.

### Hammond Library/Chicago Theological Seminary

Rev. Neil W. Gerdes, Librarian
5757 S. University Ave.
Chicago, IL 60637
phone: (312) 752-5757
fax: (312) 752-5925
Founded in 1855, the Chicago Theological Seminary's Hammond Library holds 110,155 volumes, 12,000 volumes of church records from Midwest Congregational churches and societies, 785 microforms, 705 audio-visual programs, and subscriptions to 225 journals and other serials. The library's subjects include gay/lesbian studies as well as theology, the Bible, social ethics, personality and religion, Congregational Church histo-

ry, sociology and religion, sexuality and religion, psychology and religion, and African American religion. The library is open to the public with approval of librarian.

### *Windy City Times*

Jeff McCourt, Publisher
970 W. Montana
Chicago, IL 60614
phone: (312) 935-1790
fax: (312) 935-1853
Weekly gay and lesbian community newspaper, founded in 1985.

### *Women's Music Plus*

5210 Wayne
Chicago, IL 60640
phone: (312) 769-9009
fax: (312) 728-7002
Annual directory listing contact information for more than 4,000 individuals and groups involved in feminist or lesbian culture. Includes performers, festivals, writers, publications, radio, film/video, craftswomen, cartoonists, photographers, bookstores, agents, etc. Each includes women's music sampler CD. Founded in 1977.

## IOWA

### *Common Lives/Lesbian Lives*

PO Box 1553
Iowa City, IA 52244
phone: (319) 335-1486

### *Gay & Lesbian Resource Center Report*

Claire Hueholt, Editor
4211 Grand
Des Moines, IA 50312
phone: (515) 279-2110
Monthly newspaper for the gay and lesbian community of central Iowa.

## LOUISIANA

### Homosexual Information Center/Library

Leslie Colfax, Librarian
115 Monroe St.
Bossier City, LA 71111
phone: (318) 742-4709
Founded in 1952, the Homosexual Information Center Library holds 9,800 books and bound periodical volumes; 32 VF drawers of manuscripts, clippings, pamphlets, documents; and 86 legal briefs and court opinions; and subscribes to 32 journals and 21 newspapers. The library's holdings are devoted to homosexuality, civil liberties, censorship, sexual freedom, lesbiana, prostitution, and abortion, and its Homosexual Movement Collection features papers from 1948 to the present. The center is open to the public and publishes *Directory of Homosexual Organizations; Seeds of the American Sexual Revolution; Prostitution is Legal; HIC Newsletter; Selected Bibliography of Homosexuality;* and selected bibliographies, reading lists, subject heading guides, and a list of other publications, all available upon request. The Homosexual Information Center is supported by the Tangent Group. Founded in 1965 and based in Universal City, California, the Tangent Group conducts charitable programs, maintains a speakers' bureau, and supports the Committee to Fight Exclusion of Homosexuals from the Armed Forces. The Tangent Group/Homosexual Information Center's annual meeting takes place each July in Los Angeles.

### *The Second Stone*

Jim Bailey, Editor and Publisher
Bailey Communications
PO Box 8340
New Orleans, LA 70182
phone & fax: (504) 891-7555
Newspaper for gay and lesbian Christians. Founded in 1988, appears bimonthly.

## MARYLAND

### *Amazon Times*

Charlotte Zinser, Editor
PO Box 135
Owings Mills, MD 21117
Publication featuring dialogue on all topics of interest to lesbians. Founded in 1990, appears quarterly.

### *Baltimore Alternative*

6619 Frederick Rd.
Baltimore, MD 21228-3530

### *Baltimore Gay Paper*

Mike Chase, Editor
PO Box 22575
Baltimore, MD 21203
phone: (410) 837-7748
fax: (410) 837-8512
Newspaper publishing news and articles of interest to the Baltimore gay and lesbian community. Founded in 1979, appears semimonthly.

### *In the Family*

Laura Markowitz, Editor
Box 5387
Takoma Park, MD 20913
Quarterly magazine about family issues targeted toward a les/bi/gay/trans audience and the therapists who serve them.

### *Tribe: An American Gay Journal*

Columbia Publishing
234 E. 25th St.
Baltimore, MD 21218
phone: (410) 366-7070

## MASSACHUSETTS

### *Bad Attitude*

Jasmine Sterling, Editor
PO Box 390110
Cambridge, MA 02139
phone: (508) 372-6247
Journal for women who are interested in lesbian lifestyles; features erotic fiction. Founded 1984, appears bimonthly.

### *Bay Windows*

Jeff Epperly, Editor
South End News
1523 Washington St.
Boston, MA 02118
phone: (617) 266-6670
fax: (617) 266-5973
Magazine covering gay male and lesbian literature. Founded in 1983, appears weekly.

### *Fag Rag*

PO Box 15331
Boston, MA 02215
phone: (617) 661-7534

### *Gay Community News*

Bromfield Street Educational Foundation
29 Stanhope St.
Boston, MA 02116
phone: (617) 262-6969
Newspaper covering news, reviews, and commentary for the lesbian and gay community, with feminist and anti-racist commentary. Founded in 1973, appears weekly.

### Gay Community News Library

Bromfield Street Educational Foundation
29 Stanhope St.
Boston, MA 02116
phone: (617) 262-6969
Founded in 1973, the Bromfield Street Educational Foundation publishes the *Gay Community News* and produces the Outright Conference. The *Gay Community News* Library, which contains news and features of interest to lesbians and gays, as well as the online Alternative Press Index, is open to the public with some restrictions.

### *Harvard Gay & Lesbian Review*

Richard Schneider, Editor
HGLR-W
Box 180722
Boston, MA 02118
e-mail: hglr@aol.com
Web site: http://www.hglc.org./hglc/review.htm
Quarterly journal containing discussion and analysis of contemporary gay, lesbian, and bisexual ideas and literature. Founded in 1994 by the Harvard Gay & Lesbian Caucus (which has no affiliation with Harvard University).

### *Hikane: The Capable Womon*

PO Box 841
Great Barrington, MA 02130
Magazine serving as a networking/grassroots tool for disabled lesbians and their wimmin allies. Available in print, cassette, and braille. Founded in 1989, appears quarterly.

### *Provincetown Advocate*

PO Box 93
Provincetown, MA 02657

### *Sojourner: The Women's Forum*

Karan Kahn, Editor
42 Seaverns Ave.
Boston, MA 02130-2355
phone: (617) 524-0415

Magazine covering political, cultural, and social issues from a wide range of feminist perspectives. Founded in 1975, appears monthly.

### *Trivia: A Journal of Ideas*

PO Box 9606
Amherst, MA 01059-9606
Journal for feminists and lesbians.

### *Woman of Power: A Magazine of Feminism, Spirituality, and Politics*

Charlene McKee, Editor
PO Box 2785
Orleans, MA 02653
phone: (508) 240-7877
Quarterly magazine containing articles, interview, profiles, art, poetry, and photographs; each issue explores a special theme. Founded in 1984.

### *Women's Review of Books*

Wellesley College Center for Research on Women
Wellesley, MA 02181
phone: (617) 283-2555

## MICHIGAN

### *Between the Lines*

Susan Horowitz and Jan Stevenson, Publishers
Pride Access Corp.
33523 Eight Mile Rd., Ste. 185, A-3
Livonia, MI 48152
phone: (810) 615-7003
fax: (810) 615-7018
e-mail: Pridepblis@aol.com
Subtitled "Michigan's Community News for Lesbians, Gays, Bisexuals & Friends," *Between the Lines* appears monthly.

### *Cruise*

19136 Woodward Ave.
Detroit, MI 48203
phone: (313) 369-1901 or (313) 169-1900
Weekly gay/lesbian magazine.

### *Lavender Morning*

PO Box 729
Kalamazoo, MI 49005
Monthly newsletter for women.

### *Lesbian Connection*

Helen Diner Memorial Women's Center
PO Box 811
East Lansing, MI 48823
phone: (517) 371-5257
Free national newsletter by, for, and about lesbians, and edited by the Ambitious Amazons. Founded in 1974, appears bimonthly.

### *METRA*

Garry Hoffman, Editor
PO Box 71844
Madison Heights, MI 48071-0844
Bi-weekly community and entertainment guide for the Great Lakes region. METRA also sponsors two gay/lesbian picnics each year.

### *Metro Times*

Desiree Cooper, Editor
733 St. Antoine
Detroit, MI 48226
phone: (313) 961-4060
Local alternative/entertainment weekly newspaper, appearing each Wednesday.

## MINNESOTA

### *Equal Time*

Nancy Walker, Publisher
Lavendar, Inc.
310 E. 38th St., #207
Minneapolis, MN 55409
phone: (612) 823-3836
fax: (612) 823-2615
Newspaper for gay, lesbian, and bisexual communities. founded in 1982, appears weekly.

### *Hurricane Alice: A Feminist Quarterly*

Martha Roth, Executive Editor
Hurricane Alice Foundation
207 Lind Hall
Church St. SE
Minneapolis, MN 55455
phone: (612) 625-1834
Feminist journal covering works of culture, prose, poetry, and artwork. Founded in 1983, appears quarterly.

### *The James White Review*

Philip Wilkie, Publisher
PO Box 33565, Butler Quarter Sta.

Minneapolis, MN 55403
phone: (612) 339-8317
Gay men's literary journal containing poetry, short stories, book reviews, and art. Founded in 1983, appears quarterly.

### *Maize: A Lesbian Country Magazine*

Word Weavers
PO Box 8742
Minneapolis, MN 55408
Quarterly magazine focusing on the rural lesbian experience and strategies for economic survival and community building. Topics include food, shelter, agriculture, environmental issues, and healing arts. Contains essays, news, book reviews, interviews, and how-to articles.

### Quatrefoil Library

Edward Swanson, Executive Director
1619 Dayton Ave., Ste. 105
St. Paul, MN 55104-6206
phone: (612) 641-0969
Founded in 1983, the Quatrefoil Library is devoted to gay, lesbian, and other sexual minority materials. The library holds 7,000 books; 30 bound periodical volumes; unbound newspapers and magazines from 1946 to the present; 150 videotapes; 200 audiotapes; 100 sound recordings; six file cabinets of clippings; a button collection; clothing; art work; the *Out and About Theater* archives; posters; and subscriptions to 40 journals and other serials. The library is open to the public and publishes a newsletter.

## NEW YORK

### *B.G. (Black & Gay)*

Box 1511, Cooper Sta.
New York, NY 10276
phone: (212) 629-1887 or (800) 688-5401

### *Christopher Street*

PO Box 1475
New York, NY 10008
phone: (212) 627-2120
Literary magazine for gay men and lesbians.

### *Colorlife! Magazine*

2840 Broadway, Box 287
New York, NY 10025
phone: (212) 222-9794
Magazine for the lesbian/gay/bisexual people of color community.

### DYKE TV

Cyrille Phipps, Executive Producer
Sang-Froid
PO Box 55, Prince St. Sta.
New York, NY 10012
phone: (212) 343-9335
fax: (212) 343-9337
e-mail: dyketv@echonyc.com
Web site: http://www.dyketv.org/
DYKE TV is a cable access, biweekly television show and non-profit organization. By lesbians, for lesbians, it seeks to combat invisibility, isolation, and negative stereotypes, and to produce positive, realistic images of lesbian lives. Founded in June of 1993, DYKE TV is a forum for creative expression providing information, opinion, activism, and social change for the lesbian community and the world at large.

### Empty Closet Newspaper

Rochester, NY
phone: (716) 244-9030

### Gay Alliance of the Genesee Valley Inc./Library

Horace Lethbridge, President
Marta Maletski, Librarian
179 Atlantic Ave.
Rochester, NY 14607
phone: (716) 244-8640
fax: (716) 244-8246
Founded in 1974, the library of the Gay Alliance of Genesee Valley holds 1,400 books, along with periodicals and newspapers, and subscribes to five journals and six newspapers. The library features gay and lesbian literature, history, male and female fiction, feminism, sex, religion, and philosophy. The library is open to the public and publishes *Empty Closet* monthly.

### Gay Cable Network

150 W. 26th St., #703
New York, NY 10001
phone: (212) 727-8850
fax: (212) 229-2347

## Gay and Lesbian Alliance Against Defamation—New York (GLAAD/NY)

Mark Johnson, Executive Director
150 W. 26th St., Ste. 503
New York, NY 10001
phone: (212) 807-1700
fax: (212) 807-1806
e-mail: glaad@glaad.org

Founded in 1985, GLAAD seeks to oppose media and public defamation of gay and lesbian individuals through education; replace "bigoted and misinformed representations" of lesbians and gays with accurate images of the gay community; and organize the gay community to respond to defamation and assert its right to be treated with dignity. GLAAD works to identify and respond to public expressions of homophobia and bring instances of gay defamation to the attention of the gay community, and to counter attacks on the legal rights and physical well-being of gays and lesbians in the media. The 10,000-member alliance promotes fair and accurate images of gays and lesbians by convincing those in the broadcasting and publishing fields to devote time and space to gay-related issues, events, and groups; monitors and reports occurrences of defamation in the media; offers suggestions and editorial style guidelines for news stories; encourages members of the gay community to voice their protest against those responsible for gay defamation; and works to attain national media attention for civil rights battles fought by gays. The group also operates MediaGrams campaign and PhoneTree, through which members telephone television and radio stations to protest media defamation and bigotry; sponsors fundraising events; and produces "Naming Names," a weekly radio and television commentary on the portrayal of the gay community in the press. The GLADD Media Award is presented annually. GLAAD meets the first Wednesday of the month and publishes the bimonthly *GLAAD Bulletin*, the weekly *GLAAD Tidings*, and the *Images* newsletter, and the *Media Guide to the Lesbian and Gay Community*.

## *Gayellow Pages*

Frances Green, Editor
PO Box 533, Village Sta.
New York, NY 10014-0533
phone: (212) 674-0120

Classified directory of gay and lesbian information sources, services, community centers, businesses, and entertainment venues througout the United States and Canada.

## *Heresies*

Jean Casella, Managing Editor
Heresies Collective, Inc.
PO Box 1306, Canal St. Sta.
New York, NY 10013
phone: (212) 227-2108

Periodical containing essays, poetry, short fiction, satire, criticism, letters, interviews, page art, photography, and visual art by women. Founded in 1977, appears once or twice a year.

## Lesbian Herstory Archives

Lesbian Herstory Educational Foundation, Inc.
PO Box 1258
New York, NY 10116
phone: (212) 768-3953

Founded in 1974, the Lesbian Herstory Archives collect material dealing with women's and lesbian history and culture. Special collections include a manuscript collection; oral history collection; international lesbian collection; lesbian organizations (files on 500 groups); biographical collection (files on 1500 individuals); art and music collection; and button, T-shirt, and photography collections. The archives include 12,000 books; 30 bound periodical volumes; 500 unbound periodical volumes; 700 tapes; 500 subject files; dissertations, and subscriptions to 200 journals and 50 newspapers. The archives are open to the public by appointment. The archives publishes the *L.H.A. Newsletter*, occasional bibliographies, and indexes of periodical holdings and organization holdings.

## *Honcho Magazine*

Stan Leventhal, Editor
MMG, Inc.
462 Broadway, Ste. 4000
New York, NY 10013
phone: (212) 966-8400
fax: (212) 966-9366

Magazine for adult gay men. Founded in 1977, appears monthly.

### *HX (Homo Xtra)*
Two Queens, Inc.
19 West 21st St., #703
New York, NY 10010
phone: (212) 627-0747
fax: (212) 627-5280
Weekly magazine for gays in New York City.

### *Journal of Gay and Lesbian Social Services*
Jim J. Kelley, Editor
The Haworth Press
10 Alice St.
Binghamtom, NY 13904-1580
phone: (607) 722-2077
fax: (607) 722-1424
Journal that aims to promote the well-being of homosexuals and bisexuals in society. Founded in 1993, appears quarterly.

### *Journal of Homosexuality*
John De Cecco, Editor
The Haworth Press
10 Alice St.
Binghamtom, NY 13904-1580
phone: (607) 722-2077
fax: (607) 722-1424
Journal devoted to theoretical, empirical, and historical research on homosexuality, heterosexuality, sexual identity, social sex roles, and the sexual relationships of both men and women. Founded in 1974, appears quarterly.

### *Mandate Magazine*
Stan Leventhal, Editor
MMG, Inc.
462 Broadway, Ste. 4000
New York, NY 10013
phone: (212) 966-8400
fax: (212) 966-9366
Magazine for adult gay men. Founded in 1975, appears monthly.

### *Ms. Magazine*
Marcia Ann Gillespie, Editor
Lang Communications, Inc.
230 Park Ave., 7th Fl.
New York, NY 10169
phone: (212) 551-9595
fax: (212) 551-9384
Bimonthly feminist magazine, founded in 1972.

### *On the Issues*
97-77 Queens Blvd.
Forest Hills, NY 11374
phone: (718) 275-6020
Feminist magazine featuring political, social, and ethical concerns.

### *Out Magazine*
Michael Goff, Editor
The Soho Building
110 Greene St., Ste. 800
New York, NY 10012-3836
phone: (212) 334-9119
Web site: http://www.out.com
Called "America's Most Widely Read Gay and Lesbian Magazine," *Out* was founded in 1992 and appears 10 times per year.

### *Playguy Magazine*
Stan Leventhal, Editor
MMG, Inc.
462 Broadway, Ste. 4000
New York, NY 10013
phone: (212) 966-8400
fax: (212) 966-9366
Magazine for adult gay men. Founded in 1975, appears monthly.

### *Project X Magazine*
37 W. 20th St., #1007
New York, NY 10011
phone: (212) 366-6603
Magazine for LGBT youth.

### World Congress of Gay & Lesbian Jewish Organizations/Resource Library
Bill Wahler, Executive Director
Box 3345
New York, NY 10008
Founded in 1980, the WCGLJA Resource Library collects materials on gay Jewish ideas, feminism, and gay consciousness. Holdings include journal articles; newsletters; religious and liturgical materials. The library is not open to the public.

## NORTH CAROLINA

### *Q News*
4037 E. Independence Blvd.
Charlotte, NC 28205

## OHIO

### *Stonewall Union Reports Newspaper*

PO Box 10814
Columbus, OH 43201

## OKLAHOMA

### *Tulsa Family News*

PO Box 4140
Tulsa, OK 74159-0140

## OREGON

### *CALYX: A Journal of Art and Literature by Women*

PO Box B
Corvallis, OR 97339
phone: (503) 753-9384
fax: (503) 753-0515
Semiannual journal containing poetry, prose, art and book review, translations, and photography by women artists and writers. Founded in 1976.

### *Just Out*

PO Box 15117
Portland, OR 97215

### *The Lavender Network*

Inga Sorensen, Editor
PO Box 10262
Eugene, OR 97440
phone: (503) 485-7285
fax: (503) 485-6120
Subtitled "Oregon's Newspaper for Gays, Lesbians and Bisexuals," *The Lavender Network* appears monthly.

## PENNSYLVANIA

### *Au Courant*

Scott Mallinger, Editor and Publisher
PO Box 42741
Philadelphia, PA 19101
phone: (215) 790-1179
fax: (215) 790-9721
Newspaper for the gay and lesbian community. Founded in 1982, appears weekly.

### *BiFocus*

PO Box 30372
Philadelphia, PA 19103

### Contemporary Culture Collection

Temple University/Central Library System
13th & Berks Sts.
Philadelphia, PA 19122
phone: (215) 204-8667
fax: (215) 204-5201
e-mail: whitetm@astro.ocis.temple.edu
Founded in 1969, Temple University's Contemporary Culture Collection includes materials on social change, peace and disarmament, small press poetry, fringe politics, alternative life styles, animal rights, feminism, and gays and lesbians. Its special collections include counter culture and peace movement newspapers from the Vietnam era; early second wave feminist publications and literary chapbooks; the Liberation News Service Archive (160 linear feet); the Youth Liberation Archive (40 linear feet); Committee of Small Press Editors and Publishers Archive (32 linear feet); small presses archives (83 linear feet); personal papers of poet Lyn Lifshin (36 linear feet); and the Philadelphia Gay and Lesbian Task Force archive (20 linear feet). The collection's holdings include 8,000 books and pamphlets; 4,000 periodical, newspaper, and newsletter titles; 730 reels of microfilm; 70 linear feet of ephemera; and subscriptions to 290 journals and 90 newspapers. The collection is open to the public for reference use only.

### *PGN*

Tommi Avicolli, Editor
254 S. 11th St.
Philadelphia, PA 19107
phone: (215) 625-8501
fax: (215) 925-6437
Newspaper for the gay community. Founded in 1976, appears weekly.

## RHODE ISLAND

### Rhode Island Gay and Lesbian News Bureau

187 Narragansett St.
Cranston, RI 02905-4109

## TENNESSEE

### *RFD: The Country Journal for Gay Men Everywhere*

PO Box 68

Liberty, TN 37095-0068
phone: (615) 536-5176
Founded in 1974, appears quarterly.

## TEXAS

### Charles Botts Memorial Library

Metropolitan Community Church of the Resurrection
Rev. Carolyn Mobley, Library Committee Chairperson
1919 Decatur
Houston, TX 77007
phone: (713) 861-9149
fax: (713) 861-2520
Founded in 1977 and formerly known as the MCC Library, the Charles Botts Memorial Library features materials dealing with homosexuality, religion, and self-help psychology. The library's collection on all aspects of homosexuality includes 10,000 books; total holdings include 15,000 volumes; 20,199 periodicals, and subscriptions to 1,000 journals and other serials. The library is open to the public with restrictions. A special catalog of gay and lesbian books is available in the Charles Botts Memorial Library, which also features an index of gay-related news clippings from local and non-local newspapers, and an index of obituaries of gay men and women in Houston who have died since 1980.

### *Houston Voice*

811 Westheimer, Ste. 105
Houston, TX 77067

## VIRGINIA

### *Blue Ridge Lambda Press*

PO Box 237
Roanoke, VA 24002

### *IRIS: A Journal about Women*

Rebecca Hyman, Managing Editor
University of Virginia
Women's Center
PO Box 323, HSC
Charlottesville, VA 22908
phone: (804) 924-4500
Twice-yearly journal focusing on the political, academic, social, and artistic concerns of women. Founded in 1980.

## WASHINGTON

### *Guide Magazine*

Roger Sandon, Editor
One in Ten Publishing Co.
1535 11th Ave., Ste. 200
PO Box 23070
Seattle, WA 98102
phone: (206) 323-7374
fax: (206) 324-8124
Magazine for and about gay people in the Pacific Northwest. Founded in 1986, appears monthly.

### *NorthWest Gay & Lesbian Reader*

Ron Whiteaker, Editor and Publisher
1501 Belmont Ave.
Seattle, WA 98122
phone: (206) 322-4609
Bimonthly publication featuring poetry, fiction, and community information for gays and lesbians. Founded in 1988.

### *Seattle Gay News*

1605 12th Ave., Ste. 31
Seattle, WA 98122
phone: (206) 324-4297
Web site: http://electra.cortland.com/sgn/

### *Sound Out*

PO Box 1844
Olympia, WA 98507
phone: (206) 705-1294
Gay, lesbian, and bisexual journal. Founded in 1992, appears monthly.

### *Twist Weekly*

Mark Karten, Editor and Publisher
Triangle Media
600 First Ave., #227A
Seattle, WA 98104-2221
phone: (206) 343-0311
fax: (206) 343-0545
Weekly publication focusing on gay issues.

### *Women's Work*

602 Avenue A
Snohomish, WA 98290
phone: (206) 568-5914

## WISCONSIN

### *Dykes, Disability & Stuff*

Disabled Womyn's Educational Project
PO Box 8773
Madison, WI 53708
Magazine for lesbians and disability advocates, containing information on health, disability, and illness issues related to women. Founded in 1987.

### *Solitary*

PO Box 6091
Madison, WI 53716
phone: (608) 244-0072
Quarterly spirituality/pagan journal.

### *The Wisconsin Light*

D. Terry Boughver, Editor
1843 N. Palmer
Milwaukee, WI 53212
phone: (414) 372-2773
fax: (414) 372-1840
Statewide newspaper for the gay/lesbian community. Founded in 1987, appears biweekly.

# ONLINE RESOURCES

## THE WEB

### Gay & Lesbian Web Alliance

http://colossus.net/glwa/glwa/
As the home page says, this is "the place for gays, lesbians, and their friends to share community news and business." The site features action alerts to provide information that users can respond to, plus archives of postings about a variety of topics.

### Girlfriends

http://www.best.com/~agoodloe/girlfriends/
Written for and about lesbians, *Girlfriends* takes a homosexual viewpoint on current issues. Although very little of this printed publication appears on the Web, the magazine's irreverent attitude can be found here. Online users can subscribe, write a letter to the editor, and check out the table of contents for the next issue.

### Lambda Literary Awards

http://www.books.com/awards/lambwin.htm
Searching for a good book? Book Stack Unlimited, an online bookstore, features biographies of authors who have won the Lambda Literary Award. This award honors excellence in gay and lesbian literature.

### Out.com

http://www.out.com
A leading magazine for the gay and lesbian community, *Out* now has a place of its own on the Web. Out.com features reader forums, gossip, editorials, and entertainment information.

### OutNOW! Alive

http://www.outnow.com/
A biweekly newspaper published in California, *OutNOW!* extends its circulation to Web users. This newsworthy site recaps the top national and state news of the lesbian and gay community.

### Project 21/GLAAD/SFBA

Kristy Billuni, Managing Director
1360 Mission St., Ste. 200
San Francisco, CA 94103
phone: (415) 861-2244
fax: (415) 861-4893
http://www.glaad.org/glaad/glaad.html; or Gopher: zooey.outright.com 70; choose Project21
The Project 21 database, maintained by the San Francisco Bay Area chapter of GLAAD (see GLAAD entries under New York and California) provides fair, accurate, and unbiased information regarding the nature and diversity of sexual orientation, with emphasis on the gay/lesbian life style. Main files include: Project 21 Brochure; APA Statement on L/G/B Youths in Schools; Another PenPal Service; Book Banning and Burning; Books for Gay Youth; Call to Teachers; Chelsea House YA Series; Gay Teen Pen Pal Program; L/G/Bi Students' Bill of Rights; Lesbian, Gay & Bisexual Resource Lists; NEA Action Sheet; PFLAG Statement on Health/Sex Education; Resources for GLB Youth & Adults; SFUSD Anti-Slur Program; TA's Guide for Overcoming Homophobia in the Classroom; text of Idaho's antigay Proposition 1; The Essential Queer Youth

Magazine; The Invisible Minority in Our Schools.

## Q San Francisco

http://www.qsanfrancisco.com
*Q San Francisco* is a lifestyle magazine for gay and lesbian residents of the Bay city. The Web provides an excellent forum for the magazine's infamous QSF Guide, a resource for social life and culture in San Francisco.

## Queer Press International

http://www.cyberzine.org/html/GLAIDS/QPI/qpipage.html
Queer Press International gathers LGBT news from around the world, representing both gay/lesbian media and general media. The site also features an AIDS Daily Summary.

## Queer Resources Directory

http://vector.casti.com/QRD/.html/QRD-home-page.html
e-mail: disc@vector.casti.com
The Queer Resources Directory, established in 1991, is an electronic library with news clippings, political contact information, newsletters, essays, images, and every other kind of information resource of interest to the GLB community. Information, provided by QRD staff members, is stored both for the use of casual network users and serious researchers alike. Main files include: QRD FAQ; QRD Vision Statement; New Items; HIV and AIDS Information; Stonewall 25; Europride, the Gay Games and Other Queer Happenings; Images; Queer Organizations; Homosexuality and Religion; Queer Youth; Polls and Surveys; Queer Families; Legal Transcripts and Other Policies; and Community Resources.

## Queer Studies Information Center

http://csun.edu/~hfphi002/nethot.html#referendias
Maintained by the CSU Northridge Lesbian, Gay & Bisexual Communities' Resource Center, the Queer Studies Info Center contains links to dozens of Web sites dealing with educational organizations, books on the Net, films and videos, magazines and other periodicals, arts organizations, museums, libraries, and other reference sources.

# THE NET AND BBS

## Gay TV

mailing list: carolm10@aol.com
Distributed once a week, this mailing list outlines which television programs will deal with homosexuality. The schedule and program descriptions are culled from many TV publications and promotions. To subscribe, send a message to the address above. In the body of your message, request to be added to this publicly distributed list.

## Gender and Sexuality Collection

gopher: english.hss.cmu.edu/
path: Gender
The English department and Carnegie Mellon University has compiled a series of articles on gender studies. The works come from a variety of sources—student papers, Usenet posts, university studies, and government agencies. Of special interest is the recorded history of homosexuality.

# RELIGION

Human beings are spiritual creatures. It is our nature to wonder who we are, how we got here, where we're going, and why; it is our nature to marvel at creation and at whatever force—God or Goddess, Chance or Fate—brought it about.

Human beings are also social creatures. We tend to gather, to share, to find things in common and celebrate them together. When we share a common spirituality and express it through common creeds or rituals, we call it our religion.

Most religious people would say their faith sustains, guides, or comforts them. But what touches us so deeply can hurt equally profoundly. The same church or temple that nurtured and comforted us as children, that embraced us in adolescence, seems to turn away, calling our love an "abomination," when we realize we're gay. Why does that happen? Other biblical "abominations" (and there are quite a few) include remarriage after divorce and eating the meat of pigs and other animals deemed unclean. So why do so many divorced and remarried people, who may well have had bacon for breakfast or ham on Easter Sunday, and who probably don't consider their own actions "abominations," still consider homosexuality an abomination?

A lot of people are asking that question. Many lesbians, gays, bisexuals, and transsexuals abandon their religious faiths. Others, like the Radical Faeries, form new spiritual groups. Still others, representing numerous religious groups—Jewish, Catholic, Lutheran, Methodist, Presbyterian, Quaker, Unitarian Universalist, United Church of Christ, and others—have formed support and educational groups within or alongside their denominations. In addition, more than 25 lesbian and gay synagogues exist in the United States, and the Metropolitan Community Church, founded by the Rev. Troy Perry in 1968 for the LGBT community and supporters, now has nearly 300 churches throughout the world.

In 1995 Detroit's Auxiliary Bishop Thomas Gumbleton received the Bridge Building award from New

Ways Ministry, a Maryland-based organization that helps minister to gay Catholics and their families, for his support of gay and lesbian Catholics. You'll read about Gumbleton in this chapter, as well as an explanation, written by Rachel Pollack and Cheryl Schwartz in their book *The Journey Out,* of some of the biblical passages that refer to homosexuality.

# CANADA

## MANITOBA

### Council on Homosexuality and Religion

Rev. A. E. Millward, President
PO Box 1661
Winnipeg, MB R3C 2Z6
phone: (204) 284-5208, (204) 474-0212, (204) 945-6660
fax: (204) 478-1160

The Council on Homosexuality and Religion works for the fair representation of gays and lesbians in religion and religious programs. The group, which was founded in 1978, provides peer counseling programs and information line services; provides a forum for discussion on issues affecting homosexuals; maintains a resource center; produces a cable television show entitled "Coming Out"; and publishes the pamphlets *What the Bible Says to Homosexuals* and *Your Questions Answered About Homosexuality.* The council also presents an annual "Twinkie" award for the homophobe of the year.

### Lutherans Concerned/North America (LC/NA)—National Canadian Chapter

1-120 Donald St., Box 22034
Winnipeg, MB R3C 4K6

LC/NA includes Lutherans and other Christians who are either gay or lesbian, and supportive heterosexuals. Lutherans Concerned was founded in 1974 to create a climate of justice, reconciliation, and understanding among all men and women, regardless of affectional preference. The association, with 26 local chapters and 2,000 members, encourages gay/lesbian members to remain within local congregations; seeks to identify supportive Lutheran congregations; works toward the unity of gay Lutherans and nongay supporters, thereby fostering mutual education and affirmation as an extension of the healing ministry of the church; encourages the church to honestly, objectively, and openly deal with the concerns, problems, and needs of gay people within the church and those who have left because of the failure of the church to understand them; provides gay individuals with opportunities for Christian social activities, peer counseling, and worship; organizes visits to church offices and provides them with a variety of resource materials; sponsors study sessions and research and fundraising activities; monitors the gay and mainstream press; maintains a speakers' bureau and task forces on women and Lutheran church bodies; and publishes the *Concord* quarterly. The group's biennial Jim Seifkes Justice Maker award recognizes the extraordinary contributions of heterosexual persons to the lesbian and gay community.

## ONTARIO

### Metropolitan Community Church of Windsor

PO Box 2052
Windsor, ON N8Y 4R5

# UNITED STATES

## ALABAMA

### Integrity—Alabama

PO Box 530785
Birmingham, AL 35253-0785

## SPOTLIGHT
# BISHOP THOMAS GUMBLETON

He wanted gay and lesbian Catholics, so used to feeling undesirable in the sacred confines of a church, to know they were welcome and blessed. How to do it, he wondered, beyond just words?

Across a specially made bishop's miter—the ornamental, double-peaked headdress of a dignitary of the Catholic Church—Detroit [Michigan] Auxiliary Bishop Thomas Gumbleton wore a pink triangle.

Marked with the symbol used by Nazis to identify homosexual prisoners in World War II concentration camps and now adopted in the United States by

## ALASKA

### Lamb of God Metropolitan Community Church

PO Box 142095
Anchorage, AK 99514-2095

## ARIZONA

### Dignity/Integrity—Phoenix (DIP)

PO Box 60953
Phoenix, AZ 85082
phone: (602) 258-2556
Founded in 1977, Dignity/Integrity of Phoenix includes gays and lesbians who are members of the Roman Catholic and Episcopal Churches, along with supportive individuals. The group publishes *The Phoenix*.

### Integrity—Tucson

Grace St. Paul's Church
2331 E. Adams St.
Tucson, AZ 85719

### Mishpachat Am

PO Box 7731
Phoenix, AZ 85011

## ARKANSAS

### Dignity—Little Rock

Bill Branch, Executive Officer
PO Box 3015
Little Rock, AR 72203
phone: (501) 758-3512
The Little Rock chapter of Dignity/USA includes Catholics and other interested individuals. The support group for gays and lesbians, founded in 1985, sponsors an AIDS Ministry, conducts charitable activities, and meets every Tuesday.

## CALIFORNIA

### Affirmation/Gay and Lesbian Mormons—National Chapter

Scott McKay, Executive Director
PO Box 46022
Los Angeles, CA 90046
phone: (213) 255-7251
phone: (714) 998-2052
Affirmation includes members of the Church of Jesus Christ of Latter Day Saints, commonly referred to as the Mormon church, and friends, relatives, and interested individuals. The group was founded in 1977 to promote understanding, tolerance, and acceptance of gay men and lesbians as full,

*"We must become an open church," says Bishop Thomas Gumbleton. (Photo by George Waldman. Courtesy Detroit Sunday Journal.)*

equal, and worthy members of the church and society. Affirmation maintains that homosexuality and homosexual relationships can be consistent with and supported by the gospel of Jesus Christ. The group, which has 15 local chapters, fosters affirmation, self-acceptance, and self-worth among members; encourages members' continued spiritual development, participation in church activities, prayer, and the practice of Christian behavior; assists members in dealing with personal problems, the church, employers, family, social contacts, and work associates, and in reconciling sexual orientation with traditional Mormon beliefs and other belief systems as they relate to homosexuality; seeks to educate church members and the public regarding the realities and implications of homosexuality; provides a forum for dialogue and social interaction among members, church leaders, and peers; seeks to stimulate cultural exposure, emotional stability, and intellectual development among individuals of similar heritage and background; sponsors lectures, seminars, service projects, and social events; and operates a speakers' bureau to provide discussion on topics such as AIDS, education, and outreach. The group's monthly newsletter, *Affinity*, contains topical articles, personal stories, pen pal listings, and a directory. Affirmation's annual conference usually takes place in October.

## American Baptists Concerned (ABC)—National Chapter

Rick Mixon, Co-Chair
13318 Clairepointe Way
Oakland, CA 94619-3531
phone: (510) 465-8652

ABC includes homosexual, bisexual, and heterosexual clergy and laypersons affiliated with the American Baptist Churches/U.S.A. (ABC/USA). Founded in 1972, ABC works to unite gay individuals supporters of gay rights, Gumbleton entered Minneapolis' Basilica of St. Mary for Mass and a "listening session" for gay Catholics. The miter was a gift that Gumbleton wore "to show solidarity and connect the church institutionally to them and their lives."

That gesture [in late 1994] at a symposium for gay Catholics is an example of how Gumbleton, virtually alone among the country's 400 Catholic bishops, publicly challenges church teaching that homosexual relationships are sinful.

"We must become an open church that truly respects each person and accepts them in the way God made them," Gumbleton said last month when he was honored by a national group helping gay Catholics.

Gumbleton received a blitz of publicity, including an eight-minute story on National Public Radio, for the award he received from New Ways Ministry.

and their families and friends within ABC/USA for mutual assistance, support, and education; and seeks to persuade ABC/USA to forthrightly address and deal with the questions and needs of its practicing and nonpracticing gay members. American Baptists Concerned holds educational workshops; provides speakers; and publishes *Voice of the Turtle* quarterly.

### Beth Chayim Chadashim
6000 W. Pico Blvd.
Los Angeles, CA 90035
Gay and lesbian synagogue formed in 1973.

### Congregation Kol Ami
8400 Sunset Blvd., #2A
West Hollywood, CA 90069

### Dignity—Long Beach
PO Box 92375
Long Beach, CA 90809
phone: (310) 984-8400

### Dignity—Los Angeles
PO Box 42040
Los Angeles, CA 90042
phone: (213) 344-8064

### Dignity—Sacramento
c/o Kevin Shellooe
8220 Inskip Drive
Sacramento, CA 95828
phone: (916) 689-1736

### Dignity—San Diego
PO Box 33367
San Diego, CA 92163
phone: (619) 645-8240
The San Diego chapter of Dignity/USA comprises gays and lesbians who are members of the Roman Catholic Church. Founded in 1971, the group provides community services to AIDS victims; participates in annual gay pride festivities; maintains spiritual support/awareness program; and publishes *Dimensions* monthly.

### Dignity—San Francisco
1329 Seventh Avenue
San Francisco, CA 94122
phone: (415) 681-2491

### Dignity—San Jose
Bill Welch, Director
PO Box 2177
Santa Clara, CA 95055
phone: (408) 977-4218
The San Jose chapter of Dignity/USA includes gays, lesbians, friends, families, and loved ones in the Roman Catholic tradition. Dignity promotes spiritual development, committed relationships, personal growth, and social justice via prayer, dis-

Attending the ceremony was his younger brother Dan Gumbleton, whose coming out as a gay man influenced the bishop.

Unnoticed, however, was that Gumbleton's award came as the Vatican considers whether to censure the two founders of New Ways Ministry, who were recently investigated by a Vatican-appointed commission chaired by Gumbleton's superior, Detroit Cardinal Adam Maida.

New Ways Ministry, a Maryland-based organization that gives seminars on ministering to gay Catholics and their families, gave Gumbleton its Bridge Building award in the same Washington, D.C., hotel that was hosting the annual meeting of the National Conference of Catholic Bishops. About nine other bishops attended the ceremony.

Also watching Gumbleton receive the award were the founders of New Ways

cussion groups, social activities, speakers, information, and networking. The group offers ministry, holy union services, and AIDS/HIV educational outreach, and sponsors an information booth at the annual Gay Pride Celebration. The group, founded in 1983, also offers a 24-hour hotline, sponsors a monthly potluck supper and weekly gatherings, and publishes *The Catalyst* quarterly.

## Emergence International
PO Box 9161
San Rafael, CA 94912-9161
Christian Scientists supporting lesbians, gay men, and bisexuals.

## HerBooks
Irene Reti, Publisher
PO Box 7467
Santa Cruz, CA 95061
phone: (408)425-7493
HerBooks publishes books on lesbianism and feminism with a Jewish emphasis. Reaches market through commission representatives, direct mail, trade sales, InKo-Book, and Bookpeople.

## Kol Simcha
PO Box 1444
Laguna Beach, CA 92652

## Long Beach Lesbian and Gay Havurah
3801 E. Willow St.
Long Beach, CA 90815

## National League for Social Understanding (NLSU)
Rev. Jerome Stevens, Vice President
4470-107 Sunset Blvd., Ste. 293
Los Angeles, CA 90027
phone: (213) 664-6422
The National League for Social Understanding strives to encourage all people to cooperate and relate positively to one another. Founded in 1961, NLSU participates in marches for gay and lesbian rights and other civil rights projects; conducts an AIDS education program; maintains a speakers' bureau; presents forums and classes for spiritual and psychological growth and insight, and publishes a newsletter and booklets.

## Reconciled in Christ Program
2800 Buena Vista Way
Berkeley, CA 94708
phone: (510) 841-6990
Lutheran lesbian- and gay-affirmative program.

Ministry, the Rev. Robert Nugent and Sister Jeannine Gramick, the subjects of Maida's investigation.

It's the first time that other bishops have stood supporting a bishop who has been so courageous on this issue," said Nugent. "It's a breakthrough on these issues in the Catholic hierarchy."

Maida was at the Vatican at the time and did not attend the bishops conference. He had little comment about Gumbleton's award.

Maida's investigation, completed last January [1995], did not extend to Gumbleton's participation in the organization. The cardinal has never prohibited or questioned Gumbleton's involvement in New Ways activities, according to Gumbleton.

**Seventh Day Adventist Kinship International (SDAKI)—National Chapter**
Darin Olson, President
PO Box 3840
Los Angeles, CA 90078
phone: (213) 588-7672
SDA Kinship International, founded in 1976, includes Seventh-day Adventist gay men and lesbians and their friends. The 1,000-member group, which was formed by the merger of Orion and SDA Kindred, works to heighten understanding of homosexuality and related issues; provides educational materials and speakers; offers AIDS education and support services; and conducts charitable programs. SDA Kinship International publishes a pen pal list for members, *Kinship Kontact*, and the monthly newsletter *SDA Kinship Connection*, which includes reports on organization activities, book reviews, and gay/lesbian news briefs.

**Sha'ar Zahav**
220 Dancers St.
San Francisco, CA 94114

**Shalom Chavurah**
PO Box 11686
Costa Mesa, CA 92627

**Triangles**
Unitarian Universalist Church
505 East Charleston Road, Room 13
Palo Alto, CA 94306
phone: (415) 324-2674

**United Lesbian and Gay Christian Scientists (ULGCS)—National Chapter**
Pastor John W. Vondouris, Founder
PO Box 2171
Beverly Hills, CA 90213
phone: (213) 654-4867
ULGCS works to "stimulate confrontation with the church policy of censorship," to challenge the church to publish diverse opinions on controversial topics, and to try to help overcome stereotypes that incite anger and hatred against homosexuals. Founded in 1979, the 25,000-member gruop conducts research on Christian Science and being gay; compiles statistics; operates a charitable program, phone referral service, speakers' bureau, and extensive library of information on HIV/AIDS, gay issues, the Bible, and Christian Science; conducts support groups and AIDS education programs; and plans to establish a museum. ULGCS is related to the group Affirmation/Gay and Lesbian Mormons. The *Faith and Under-*

"We don't talk about the substance of what I do," said Gumbleton of his relationship with Maida. "I'd be happy to talk some of these things through."

Maida's investigation of the New Ways founders "was a very deliberate focus on their teachings and writings," said Ned McGrath, a spokesman for the Archdiocese of Detroit. "It was not an investigation of people who go to their meetings or get awards from New Ways Ministry."

The emphasis was on whether their writings and seminars adhered to the church's teachings on homosexual behavior. The commission—Maida and two theologians—conducted three interviews with Nugent and Gramick in Detroit in mid-1994. Vatican officials have not yet acted on the commission's recommendations, which have not been made public.

*standing Newsletter* appears monthly. The national group meets each June.

### Unity Fellowship Church Movement/Minority AIDS Project

Bishop Carl Bean, D.M., Founder
5149 W. Jefferson Blvd.
Los Angeles, CA 90016
phone: (213) 936-4948
fax: (213) 936-4973
The Unity Fellowship Church Movement consists of Christian gay and lesbian individuals who are interested in the teachings of liberation theology from the King James version of the Bible. Founded in 1985, the 3,000-member group conducts special programs for imprisoned people and youth and publishes the bimonthly *Liberator* newsletter.

### Universal Fellowship of Metropolitan Community Churches (UFMCC)—National Chapter

Rev. Troy D. Perry, Moderator
5300 Santa Monica Blvd., Ste. 304
Los Angeles, CA 90029
phone: (213) 464-5100
fax: (213) 464-2123
The Universal Fellowship is a Christian group ministering to primarily gay/lesbian communities in 17 countries through worship services and social action. Founded in 1968, the 32,000-member fellowship maintains the Board of World Church Extension; conducts research and educational programs, including operation of the Samaritan College; maintains a speakers' bureau; and bestows the biennial Human Rights Award. The fellowship's departments and subgroups include People of Colors, AIDS Ministry, and Women's Secretariat. The quarterly newsletter *Alert* covers AIDS legislation, education, research, and treatment. Other publications include the semiannual *Directory of Congregations and Clergy,* the quarterly *Global Outreach,* and the monthly newsletter *Keeping in Touch.*

### Voice & Vision: Lutheran Lesbian & Gay Ministry

152 Church Street
San Francisco, CA 94114
phone: (415) 553-4515

### Yachad

PO Box 3457
San Diego, CA 92163

The Vatican could allow Nugent and Gramick to continue their ministry and writings for homosexual Catholics, but possibly require them to change their emphasis. Or they could be forbidden from writing or speaking on the topic. The pair no longer direct New Ways, although they still participate.

In an August interview on the archdiocese's cable television program, Maida said Nugent's and Gramick's outreach to the gay community "is a very important work."

"The work that they're trying to do in the name of the church is very much needed and, quite honestly, I'm very supportive of those who would reach out and help" gay Catholics, Maida said.

"It becomes a problem, however, because it's one thing to have an orientation," Maida said. "It's another to act out. It is our belief in the church

## COLORADO

### Dignity—Denver
PO Box 3072
Denver, CO 80204
phone: (303) 322-8485

### Dignity—Southern Colorado
PO Box 1172
Colorado Springs, CO 80901
phone: (719) 635-5773

### Tikvat Shalom
PO Box 6694
Denver, CO 80206

### Voices of Faith for Human Rights
Chris Moore, Equality Colorado
PO Box 300476
Denver, CO 80203
phone: (303) 839-5540
Works with interfaith religious communities to challenge the religious right.

## CONNECTICUT

### Am Segulah
PO Box 271522
West Hartford, CT 06127

### Dignity—Hartford
Ann Percikal, President
PO Box 72
Hartford, CT 06141
phone: (203) 296-9229
The Hartford chapter of Dignity/USA, for lesbian and gay Catholics, meets for worship and works for social justice for all minorities, particularly within the Catholic Church. Founded in 1975, the group publishes a monthly newsletter called *The Good Word.*

### Dignity—New Haven
Paul Scarbrough, President
134 Washington Street, D205
Norwalk, CT 06854
phone: (203) 855-0377
The New Haven chapter of Dignity/USA, which includes lesbian and gay Catholics and their friends, provides opportunities for fellowship and prayer and conducts social activities. Founded in 1977, the group publishes a bimonthly newsletter.

## DISTRICT OF COLUMBIA

### Bet Mishpachah
PO Box 1410
Washington, DC 20013

that the activity, the (homosexual) sex act, is wrong. The question arises to what extent when you minister to somebody, do you try to help them and to what extent do you perhaps condone or even encourage homosexual activity."

Nugent said the commission that investigated him addressed questions such as whether New Ways refers to theologians whose opinions about homosexual behavior differ from church teachings.

"We do say what the church teaches: that homosexual behavior is objectively immoral, because it's outside the sacrament of marriage and not for procreation," said Nugent. "We also say that some theologians say, in some circumstances, homosexual behavior might not be immoral."

"If there's confusion, we're willing to clear it up," said Nugent. "But I think they're nervous that we're educating people. And there's fear that people

### Dignity/USA—National Chapter

Marianne Duddy, President
1500 Massachusetts Ave. NW, Ste. 11
Washington, DC 20005
phone: (202) 861-0017 or (800) 877-8797
fax: (202) 429-9808
e-mail: dignity@aol.com

Dignity/USA includes gay men and lesbians who are members of the Roman Catholic church; individuals of other religious affiliations; theologians, priests, and nuns. The organization, founded in 1968 by an Augustinian priest, believes that gay, lesbian, and bisexual Catholics are members of Christ's mystical body and numbered among the people of God; that it is the right, duty, and privilege for a gay, lesbian, or bisexual person to live the sacramental life of the church; that gay men and lesbians can express their sexuality in a manner that is consonant with Christ's teaching; and that sexuality should be exercised in an ethically responsible and unselfish way. Dignity and its 88 local chapters seek to unite all gay, lesbian, and bisexual Catholics; develop leadership; and be an instrument through which gay Catholics may be heard by the church and society. Dignity works in the areas of spiritual development, education, and social events, and operates Dignity's Prison Ministry and National AIDS Project. The group publishes *Theological Pastoral Resources: A Collection of Articles on Homosexuality from a Catholic Perspective* and the quarterly *Dignity/USA Journal.*

### Dignity—Washington

Bernie Delia, President
PO Box 53001
Washington, DC 20009
phone: (202) 387-4516

The Washington, D.C. chapter of Dignity includes gays and lesbians who are members of the Roman Catholic Church. Dignity offers assistance to organizations serving the poor, AIDS victims, and the homeless; participates in gay pride activities; conducts charitable activities; sponsors annual community dinners and monthly potlucks; and publishes a monthly newsletter.

### Integrity—National Chapter

Fred Ellis, President
PO Box 19561
Washington, DC 20036
phone: (404) 892-3143

Integrity was founded in 1974 for gay and lesbian Episcopalians/Anglicans and supporters. The group's objectives are to minister to the spiritual needs of gay men and lesbians; work for full participation of gay people in church and society; promote the study of human sexuality within a Christian

will make up their own minds or come to a conclusion that's different from what the Catholic church teaches.

Gumbleton maintains that "church teaching can evolve" about homosexuality, and that his main concern is making sure gay Catholics find support and solace from their church.

Gumbleton works hard at helping families accept gay sons and daughters. His zeal stems from personal experience. About 15 years ago, Dan Gumbleton, a social worker and counselor in California, revealed in letters to his eight siblings and his mother that he was gay.

The bishop didn't say much to his brother at the time. He almost wished Dan had kept quiet, and he worried a little whether there would be repercussions from the church. He didn't discuss it with his mother until years later.

context. Integrity, with 58 local chapters, distributes educational materials for clergy and lay persons; offers counseling, AIDS ministries, and worship services; and publishes an annual directory, biennial handbook, and quarterly newsletter called *The Voice of Integrity,* which includes book reviews, a calendar of events, chapter news, and membership directory updates. The national group convenes annually except in national church convention years.

## FLORIDA

### Beth Rachameem
3817 Creek Way Ct.
Plant City, FL 33567

### Dignity—Fort Lauderdale
Bill Farrington, President
PO Box 22884
Fort Lauderdale, FL 33335
phone: (305) 463-4528
The Fort Lauderdale chapter of Dignity/USA, a social and support group for gay and lesbian Roman Catholics and their friends, publishes a monthly newsletter.

### Dignity—Orlando
Orlando, FL 32861
phone: (407) 898-9335

### Dignity—Palm Beach
PO Box 3014
Tequesta, FL 33469
phone: (407) 751-3468

### Dignity—Tampa Bay
Randy Strebing, President
PO Box 24806
Tampa, FL 33623
phone: (813) 238-2868
Founded in 1975, the Tampa Bay chapter of Dignity/USA is a support group for gay and lesbian members of the Roman Catholic Church and their families and friends. The group conducts outreach programs to people with AIDS and the homeless and poor, and publishes the monthly newsletter *Reflections.*

### Etz Chaim
19094 W. Dixie Hwy.
North Miami Beach, FL 33180

### Yeladim Shel Yisrael
2677 Forest Hill Blvd., Ste. 106
West Palm Beach, FL 33406

## GEORGIA

### Bet Haverim
PO Box 54947
Atlanta, GA 30308

Helen Gumbleton, then 87 and in failing health because of heart ailments, brought it up. She wanted to know if Dan would go to hell because he was gay.

God made us the way we are, Gumbleton told his mother, and God accepts us the way we are.

The bishop told this story in Chicago when he addressed a New Ways Ministry symposium attended by about 500 Catholics, many of them gay, in April 1992. Since then, he has spoken at other seminars, including an October retreat in Connecticut for parents of gay Catholics.

"I tell them it's OK to love their child, that he or she is not evil and will not go to hell," says Gumbleton. He chides himself now for letting his mother fret so long in silence and confusion.

### Dignity—Atlanta

Joan Perez, President
PO Box 14342
Atlanta, GA 30324
phone: (404) 409-0203
Gay Catholics, also known as Dignity/Atlanta, comprises gays and lesbians who are members of the Roman Catholic Church. Founded in 1975, the group conducts fundraising activities and monthly potluck dinners, and publishes the monthly newsletter *Gay Catholics.*

### Presbyterians for Lesbian/Gay Concerns—Atlanta Chapter

James Earhart, Coordinator
PO Box 8362
Atlanta, GA 30306
phone: (404) 373-5830 or (800) 270-2168
The Atlanta Chapter of Presbyterians for Lesbian and Gay Concerns was founded in 1987 and seeks an increased inclusion of gays and lesbians in the Presbyterian Church, U.S.A. The group publishes a monthly newsletter called *More Light Update.*

## HAWAII

### Dignity—Honolulu

PO Box 3956
Honolulu, HI 96812
phone: (808) 536-5536

### Dignity—Maui

PO Box 2068
Kihei, Maui, HI 96753
phone: (808) 874-3950

## ILLINOIS

### Affirmation: United Methodists for Lesbian, Gay and Bisexual Concerns (AUMLGBC)—National Chapter

Mike Troyer
PO Box 1021
Evanston, IL 60204
phone: (847) 711-9590
Affirmation includes gay, lesbian, bisexual, and heterosexual individuals concerned with opening the United Methodist Church to all people. Founded in 1976, Affirmation is a branch of the Reconciling Congregation Program that seeks to affirm the presence of and provide ministry for all individuals in the United Methodist Church community regardless of race, class, age, sex, or sexual orientation; enlist the cooperative efforts of other supportive United Methodist groups; act upon opportunities of ecumeni-

"I'm sure she was afraid of what I, the bishop, might say," says Gumbleton. "I didn't have the sense to see how much my mom must have been struggling."

Gumbleton doesn't hesitate to point out what he sees as contradictions in the church's teachings. While the church seems to concede that many homosexuals are born as such, it considers their sexual expression sinful.

"Gay people are going to have to work out how to enter into relationships. I encourage them into moving toward the most healthful place—psychologically, mentally and spiritually—they can come to in their personal developments," says Gumbleton.

Gumbleton has a folder stuffed with letters from grateful gay Catholics and their relatives. One New York man wrote him after learning Gumbleton had

cal and interfaith action; and conduct educational and informational services. Affirmation also operates the justice ministry, which works on behalf of discriminated individuals, and sponsors a biennial retreat. The *Affirmation Newsletter* appears quarterly.

### Congregation Or Chadash

656 W. Barry Ave.
Chicago, IL 60657

### Dignity—Chicago

3023 N. Clark Street, #237
Chicago, IL 60657
phone: (312) 296-0780

### Integrity of Chicago

Dan Wall, Executive Officer
Box 2516
Chicago, IL 60690
phone: (312) 348-6362
Founded in 1975, Integrity of Chicago is a ministry of gay and lesbian Christians and their families. The group publishes *Integrity/Chicago News Notes.*

### Lutherans Concerned/North America (LC/NA)—National U.S. Chapter

Lynn Mickelson, Secretary
PO Box 10461
Ft. Dearborn Station
Chicago, IL 60610-0461
LC/NA includes Lutherans and other Christians who are either gay or lesbian, and supportive heterosexuals. Lutherans Concerned was founded in 1974 to create a climate of justice, reconciliation, and understanding among all men and women, regardless of affectional preference. The association, with 26 local chapters and 2,000 members, encourages gay/lesbian members to remain within local congregations; seeks to identify supportive Lutheran congregations; works toward the unity of gay Lutherans and nongay supporters, thereby fostering mutual education and affirmation as an extension of the healing ministry of the church; encourages the church to honestly, objectively, and openly deal with the concerns, problems, and needs of gay people within the church and those who have left because of the failure of the church to understand them; provides gay individuals with opportunities for Christian social activities, peer counseling, and worship; organizes visits to church offices and provides them with a variety of resource materials; sponsors study sessions and research and fundraising activities; monitors the gay and mainstream press;

worn the pink triangle on his miter.

"Two days later, a daughter called to say she was gay," the man wrote. "My mind in a flash went back and I realized there was nothing I could say which would change her lifestyle and anger would only alienate her," the man wrote.

"My sincere thanks to you for helping. Jesus was not a legal technician and you are not either. Jesus was full of compassion and so are you," the man wrote.

*By Patricia Montemurri. First printed in* Detroit Sunday Journal, *December 3, 1995.*

maintains a speakers' bureau and task forces on women and Lutheran church bodies; and publishes the *Concord* quarterly. The group's biennial Jim Seifkes Justice Maker award recognizes the extraordinary contributions of heterosexual persons to the lesbian and gay community.

### More Light Churches Network

600 W. Fullerton Pkwy.
Chicago, IL 60614-2690
phone: (312) 338-0452
Lesbian- and gay-affirmative Presbyterian program.

### Presbyterians for Lesbian, Gay, and Bisexual Concerns—Champaign Chapter (PLGBCC)

Charles A. Sweitzer and Stephen Showmaker, Executive Officers
McKinley Memorial Presbyterian Church
809 S. 5th St.
Champaign, IL 61820
phone: (217) 344-0297
The Champaign Chapter of PLGBC includes ministers, elders, deacons, and other members of the Presbyterian Church organized to raise the concerns of lesbian, gay, and bisexual people, along with their families and friends within the Presbyterian Church.

### Reconciling Congregation Program (RCP)

Mark Bowman, Executive Officer
3801 N. Keeler Ave.
Chicago, IL 60641-3007
phone: (312) 736-5526
fax: (312) 736-5475
RCP comprises United Methodist congregations seeking to affirm the participation of gay and lesbian members in church affairs and to resolve differences and problems between the United Methodist Church and homosexuals in the U.S. The Reconciling Congregation Program, founded in 1984, provides a network of support and assistance to local congregations wishing to include gay and lesbian persons in their worship and administration. RCP publishes the *List of Reconciling Congregations;* the quarterly journal *Open Hands,* which focuses on themes of concern to lesbians and gay men in the United Methodist church; and the brochures *How to Become a Reconciling Congregation* and *Reconciling Congregation Program.* RCP also produces the videotape *Casting Out Fear.*

## INDIANA

### Dignity—Central Indiana

PO Box 431
Indianapolis, IN 46206
phone: (317) 251-0860

### Dignity—Fort Wayne

PO Box 11988
Fort Wayne, IN 46862
phone: (219) 484-6492

### Dignity—Lafayette
PO Box 4665
Lafayette, IN 47903
phone: (317) 463-7449

## IOWA

### Lutherans Concerned—Bettendorf
PO Box 773
Bettendorf, IA 52722

## KANSAS

### L'Cha Dodi
5801 W. 115th St., #203
Oakland Park, KS 66211

## KENTUCKY

### B'Nai Shalom
PO Box 4012
Louisville, KY 40204

### Dignity—Lexington
533 Cane Run Road
Lexington, KY 40505
phone: (606) 299-4458

### Dignity—Louisville
PO Box 4778
Louisville, KY 40204
phone: (502) 473-1458

### Lutherans Concerned (LC)
Jim Okywe, Coordinator
PO Box 7692
Louisville, KY 40257-0692
phone: (502) 897-5719
Lutherans Concerned of Louisville provides support for gay, lesbian, and bisexual persons and their families in the Lutheran churches of Southern Indiana and Greater Louisville area. Founded in 1981, LC publishes a monthly newsletter called *Juncture* that contains international news of importance to mainline Protestant bisexual, gay, and lesbian people.

### Presbyterians for Lesbian/Gay Concerns—Louisville Chapter
Nick Wilkerson, Coordinator
1435 S. 3rd St.
Louisville, KY 40208
phone: (502) 635-7003
Founded in 1982, the Louisville Chapter of Presbyterians for Lesbian and Gay Concerns provides support and fellowship for gay and lesbian members of the Presbyterian Church in the greater Louisville, Kentucky area and southern Indiana. The group works to change congregational and public attitudes on their demonstrations and policies, and publishes a monthly newsletter.

## LOUISIANA

### Jewish Gay & Lesbian Alliance
1228 Bourbon St., Apt. D
New Orleans, LA 70116-2554

## MAINE

### Am Chofshi
RR1, Box 686
South Harpswel, ME 04079

### Dignity—Maine
PO Box 8113
Portland, ME 04104
phone: (207) 878-0546

## MARYLAND

### Adath Rayoot
Box 22575
Baltimore, MD 21203

### Dignity—Baltimore
PO Box 1243
Baltimore, MD 21203
phone: (410) 325-1519

### New Ways Ministry (NWM)
Rev. Robert Nugent & Sister Jeannine Gramick, Founders
Francis De Bernardo, Program Director
4012 29th St.
Mount Rainier, MD 20712
phone: (301) 277-5674
fax: (301) 864-6894
Established in 1977, New Ways is a Catholic gay/lesbian ministry group that attempts to provide adequate and accurate information concerning homosexuality in the Roman

## SPOTLIGHT
## KEEPING the FAITH

For their informative, compelling, and touching book for and about lesbian, gay, and bisexual teens, called *The Journey Out,* Rachel Pollack and Cheryl Schwartz interviewed numerous young people. "Of all the subjects we raised in our interviews," they write, "the one which elicited the saddest responses and revealed the most frustration and anxiety among our young respondents was the subject of religion and spirituality." What follows is excerpted directly from their chapter on religion and spirituality:

*"Nothing can replace church; only my sexuality makes it impossible to go. I don't pray, I don't meditate and I don't read the Bible anymore." —Lynn, 16*

Catholic Church and in society; assesses personal and communal attitudes about homosexuality; and offers pastoral resources and antidotes to the fears, myths, and prejudices affecting the lives of gay and lesbian persons in the church and society. New Ways Ministry promotes theological dialogue; describes and promotes civil rights for homosexual people; provides consulting services; conducts specialized education and research programs; and sponsors a speakers' bureau. The group also bestows the triennial Bridge Building Award; publishes a quarterly newsletter called *Bondings;* and publishes *Building Bridges: Gay and Lesbian Reality and the Catholic Church, Prayer Journey for Persons with AIDS,* and *Voices of Hope.*

### MASSACHUSETTS

**Am Tikva**
PO Box 11
Cambridge, MA 02238

**Dignity—Boston**
PO Box 408
Boston, MA 02117
phone: (617) 421-1915

**Dignity—Fall River**
PO Box 627
Fall River, MA 02722
phone: (508) 992-9273

**Dignity—Provincetown**
160 West Central Street
Natick, MA 01760
phone: (508) 653-5405

**Interweave: Unitarian Universalists for Lesbian, Gay, Bisexual, and Transgender Concerns (UULGC)—National Chapter**
Barb Reeve, Contact
25 Beacon St.
Boston, MA 02109
phone: (617) 742-2100
fax: (617) 367-3237
Interweave works to foster the creation of a self-affirming, self-determining, and mutually supportive community for gay, lesbian, bisexual, and transgender people within the Unitarian Universalist denomination, and works for the development of a society "where none need fear persecution or alienation." The group, founded in 1971 and with 40 local chapters, maintains a speakers' bureau and lists of recommended reading and films; conducts educational programs; and bestows the annual Mark Dewolfe Award recognizing contributions in

*"Look, I don't always worry about the future. But I worry about today. Deep down in my heart, I want to be able to go to church—to know that God still loves me. After all, God loved me before I came out. Why can't He love me today?" —Kevin, 17*

Many young people seem to have lost their faith and run away from any involvement with their religious institutions upon discovering their homosexuality. They believe that by accepting their homosexuality they ceased to be acceptable to their church or synagogue. Not only is this sad, and in some cases tragic, it's also not true....

While many religious communities and institutions are debating their church's policies on homosexuality, some religious organizations are taking the debate into the larger community. Today, the most vocal group denouncing

the area of gay, lesbian, bisexual, and transgender concerns. Interweave also publishes a quarterly newsletter, *Interweave World*, and meets every February and June.

### Lutherans Concerned—New England

Ken Westhassel
96 Hemenway St., No. 1
Boston, MA 02115
phone: (617) 536-3788
The New England chapter of Lutherans Concerned, which was founded in 1977 and includes Lutherans and other sympathetic individuals, is a religious social activist group working within the Lutheran Church toward greater understanding of homosexual Lutherans' needs.

### Open and Affirming Program

PO Box 403
Holden, MA 01520
phone: (508) 856-9316
Lesbian- and gay-affirmative program within the United Church of Christ.

### United Church Coalition for Lesbian/Gay Concerns—Massachusetts Chapter

69 Monadnock Road
Worcester, MA 01609-1714
phone: (508) 755-0005

## MICHIGAN

### Agape Community Church

16801 Plymouth Rd.
Detroit, MI 48227
phone: (313) 255-1728

### Aware

PO Box 7824
Grand Rapids, MI 49510
phone: (616) 456-6174
Organization for Christian reform.

### Beit Chayim

PO Box 7292
Ann Arbor, MI 48107

### Canterbury House Open House

Lord of Light Lutheran Church
801 South Forrest
Ann Arbor, MI 48104
phone: (313) 665-0606
Holds weekly meetings and an open house for gay and lesbian people.

### Church of the Good Shepherd

2145 Independence Boulevard
Ann Arbor, MI 48106
phone: (313) 971-6133
Interracial/intercultural congregations.

homosexuals is the radical Christian right, a group of people from a variety of churches with a biblical literalist tradition and a political agenda of seeing their beliefs enforced by government. Biblical literalists believe that all evil in the world can be overcome by reading the Bible and following it word for word in the most literal sense, as if it were a legal document. The radical Christian right can quote chapter and verse from the Bible to justify their beliefs about how life should be lived not just by members of their churches but by everyone. They believe simply that homosexuality is an abomination, that all homosexuals are damned, and that all homosexuals are a threat to "traditional" American families. They base their beliefs on their interpretation of a handful of biblical passages, texts which other religious institutions also use in their debates on homosexuality. So let's go right to the source of the controversy.

**Dignity—Detroit**
Jim Holubila, President
PO Box 32874
Detroit, MI 48232
phone: (313) 961-4818
*Sunday Mass:*
Most Holy Trinity Church
6th and Porter Streets
Detroit, MI
The Detroit chapter of Dignity/USA includes gay and lesbian members of the Roman Catholic church united to represent the interests of the gay and lesbian community in the church and society. Founded in 1974 by six young men and a determined priest, Dignity Detroit has grown to more than 100 active members. The group conducts charitable activities, participates in the annual Gay/Lesbian Pride Celebration, and publishes a monthly newsletter and weekly *Sunday Bulletin.*

**Dignity—Flint**
PO Box 585
Flint, MI 48501
phone: (313) 238-9854

**Dignity—Grand Rapids**
PO Box 1373
Grand Rapids, MI 49501
phone: (616) 454-9779

**Dignity—Greater Lansing**
PO Box 1265
East Lansing, MI 48826
phone: (517) 321-4841

**Divine Peace Metropolitan Community Church**
PO Box 71938
Madison Heights, MI 48071
phone: (313) 544-8335

**Evangelicals Concerned**
PO Box 6011
Grand Rapids, MI 49516

**First Unitarian Universalist Church**
4605 Cass Ave.
Detroit, MI 48201
phone: (313) 833-9107

**Full Truth Fellowship of Christ Church**
4458 Joy Rd.
Detroit, MI 48208
phone: (313) 896-0233
Christian Church serving the African American gay/lesbian community.

One of the passages in the Old Testament that is most often cited as condemnation of homosexuality is Leviticus 18:22, which says, "You shall not lie with a male as with a woman; it is an abomination." A few verses later, Leviticus 20:13 adds the penalty: "If a man lies with a male as with a woman, both of them have committed an abomination; they shall be put to death, their blood is upon them." For biblical literalists, there's no way to argue with that. But if you do take this injunction literally, wouldn't you need to take every other command in the Bible equally literally? There also is a passage in the Old Testament that prescribes the death penalty for people who loan money at interest (Ezekiel 18:5–18). Should bankers be cast out of the flock? Should they even be allowed to live? And what about the many practices the Old Testament condones that are not acceptable today, such as slavery, animal sacrifice, polygamy, and treating women as property?

**Gay and Lesbian Acceptance Reorganized Church of Jesus Christ of Latter Day Saints**
PO Box 4721
East Lansing, MI 48826

**Lutherans Concerned—Great Lakes**
PO Box 8417
Liberty Station
Ann Arbor, MI 48107-8417
phone: (313) 475-3684 or (810) 268-4287
Serves southeast Michigan and northwest Ohio.

**Metropolitan Community Church of Detroit**
Mark G. Bidwell, Pastoral Leader
*mailing address:*
PO Box 836
Royal Oak, MI 48068-0836
*church office:*
Affirmations Community Center
195 West Nine Mile Rd., #210
Ferndale, MI 48220
phone: (810) 399-7741

**Metropolitan Community Church of Muskegon**
PO Box 5095
North Muskegon, MI 49445
phone: (616) 861-5275

**Phoenix Community Church/United Church of Christ**
PO Box 2222
1758 North 10th St.
Kalamazoo, MI 49003
phone: (616) 381-3222
Spiritual, personal, and political worship Sunday evenings.

**Presbyterians for Lesbian & Gay Concerns—Detroit**
PO Box 1004
Royal Oak, MI 48068
phone: (810) 255-7059

**Reconciliation Metropolitan Community Church**
PO Box 1259
Grand Rapids, MI 49501
phone: (616) 364-7633

**Redeemer Metropolitan Community Church**
1665 North Chevrolet
Flint, MI 48504
phone: (810) 238-6700

**Simcha**
PO Box 652
Southfield, MI 48037
phone: (313) 353-8025

Should these practices be allowed according to the teachings given by the Bible?

Obviously, biblical literalists are selective in what biblical laws they choose to follow. It is simply not possible to live in modern times in the same way that people lived thousands of years ago. As the Reverend Elder Dr. Charles Arehart of the Metropolitan Community Church of the Rockies states, "Religious belief has always had a historical relationship to a particular time and culture."

We should consider the laws of Leviticus in terms of the time when they were first applied. The Israelites were then a scattered group of tribes. They were traveling in search of a homeland, surrounded by hostile peoples against whom they had to defend themselves and their religious beliefs.

According to the group's literature: "The Jewish word 'Simcha' means a joyous event, a great pleasure, a celebration. Simcha originated as a group of friends who had the desire to bring into harmony our Gay and Lesbian lives and our Jewish heritage. We have grown into an extended family of women and men sharing a sense of culture and religious values, representing diverse Jewish religious and ethnic traditions." Simcha offers monthly social events, cultural and religious activities, a monthly Oneg Shabbat, Passover Seder and holiday celebrations, speakers and seminars, education and outreach through a speakers' bureau, and an annual "Bagels and Bobkas" membership drive. Simcha is affiliated with the World Congress of Gay and Lesbian Jews.

### Tree of Life Metropolitan Community Church

PO Box 2598
Ann Arbor, MI 48106
phone: (313) 485-3922

## MINNESOTA

### Brethren/Mennonite Council for Lesbian and Gay Concerns (BMC)—National Chapter

Jim Sauder, Staff Coordinator
PO Box 6300
Minneapolis, MN 55406
phone: (612) 305-0315
e-mail: BMCouncil@aol.com.us

BMC includes Brethren and Mennonite lesbians and gays and their parents, spouses, relatives, and friends. Founded in 1976, BMC offers support to gay people of the Brethren and Mennonite church denominations and fosters dialogue between them and nongay church members. The council believes that the traditional attitude of the church toward homosexuals is inconsistent with the Christian ideal, and seeks to disseminate accurate information from biblical studies, social sciences, and theology regarding homosexuality. BMC also maintains a speakers' bureau and publishes a newsletter, *Dialogue,* that includes articles about AIDS, theology and homosexuality, convention proceedings, and a calendar of events.

### Dignity—Twin Cities

PO Box 3565
Minneapolis, MN 55403
phone: (612) 827-3103

### Keshet

3500 Holmes Ave.
Minneapolis, MN 55408

Because their numbers were so few, God's injunction to "be fruitful and multiply" had to be taken very seriously. In numbers they would find strength; it was a matter of simple survival. The Israelites also believed that men were solely responsible for procreation, that sperm contained all the elements of life; women were merely the "vessel" in which the seed grew. So "spilling the seed," through masturbation or nonreproductive sex, was a grave sin. It was also important for the Israelites to separate themselves from the more widely followed pagan religions of the times, some of which incorporated homosexual rituals in their fertility rites. Participating in male homosexual acts (the Bible never directly mentions female homosexuality) wasn't just against Israelite law, it was also seen as a rejection of their small, struggling community. Given our current understanding of human reproduction, the probable genetic basis of homosexuality, and the fact that overpopulation is far more

## MISSISSIPPI

### Integrity—Mississippi
PO Box 68314
Jackson, MS 39286-9998

## MISSOURI

### Dignity—St. Louis
PO Box 23093
St. Louis, MO 63156
phone: (314) 997-9897

### St. Louis Gay and Lesbian Chavurah, Central Reform Congregation
77 Maryland Pl.
St. Louis, MO 63108

## MONTANA

### Affirmation—Bozeman
1000 N. 17th Ave., #29
Bozeman, MT 59715

## NEBRASKA

### Mishpachat Chaverim
959 S. 51st St.
Omaha, NE 68107

### Presbyterians for Lesbian/Gay Concerns—Nebraska Chapter
Cleveland Evans, Coordinator
3810 S. 13th St., No. 22
Omaha, NE 68107-2260
phone: (402) 733-1360
The Nebraska Chapter of Presbyterians for Lesbian and Gay Concerns includes lesbian and gay Presbyterians and their supporters in Nebraska and western Iowa. Founded in 1987, the group promotes fellowship and understanding of homosexuality within the Presbyterian church, and meets the last Saturday of the month.

## NEVADA

### Dignity—Las Vegas
PO Box 70424
Las Vegas, NV 89170
phone: (702) 369-8127

## NEW HAMPSHIRE

### Dignity—New Hampshire
PO Box 7
Manchester, NH 03105
phone: (603) 647-0206

of a threat today than underpopulation, homosexuality can no longer be perceived as a threat to or a rejection of the community.

The other most widely cited biblical condemnation is the story of Sodom and Gomorrah, which first appears in Genesis (18:16–19:29). When two male angels travel to Sodom to try to find ten righteous people and so prevent the city's destruction by God, they spend the night as Lot's guests. A mob gathers demanding to "know" the angels, that is to rape them. So as not to violate the laws of hospitality, Lot instead offers the mob his two virgin daughters to do with as they please. The Christian radical right says that the mob's homosexual desire is "the sin of Sodom"—leaving out that their intent was rape. Yet when the story of Sodom is told elsewhere in the Old Testament, other explanations of Sodom's sin are given. In Ezekiel 16:49,

## NEW JERSEY

### Dignity—Metro New Jersey

PO Box M
550 Ridgewood Road
Maplewood, NJ 07040
phone: (201) 857-4040
Founded in 1976, the Metro New Jersey chapter of Dignity/USA includes gays and lesbians who are members of the Roman Catholic Church. The group sponsors an annual St. Patrick's Day dinner and other charitable events, and publishes the monthly newsletter *Ichthus*.

### Dignity—New Brunswick

PO Box 10781
New Brunswick, NJ 08906
phone: (908) 254-7942
The New Brunswick, New Jersey chapter of Dignity/USA includes gays and lesbians who are members of the Roman Catholic Church. The group publishes the monthly newsletter *Kairos* and meets several times a month.

### New Jersey Lesbian and Gay Havurah

PO Box 10494
Menlo Park, NJ 08818

### The Oasis

Harker McHugh, Director
24 Rector St.
Newark, NJ 07102
phone: (201) 621-8151
fax: (201) 622-3503
Founded in 1989, The Oasis is a support group for gays and lesbians operated in conjunction with the Episcopal church. Oasis offers social and religious programs and publishes a quarterly newsletter called *Wellspring*.

### Presbyterians for Lesbian, Gay, and Bisexual Concerns (PLGBC)—National Chapter

James D. Anderson, Communications Secretary
PO Box 38
New Brunswick, NJ 08903-0038
phone: (908) 249-1016
e-mail: PresbyNet
PLGBC, which has 20 local chapters, includes ministers, elders, deacons, and other members of the Presbyterian Church. The group was founded in 1974 to raise the concerns of lesbian and gay people and their parents, families, and friends within the Presbyterian church. PLGBC seeks to explore the mission and ministry of the church in support of lesbian and gay people both inside and outside the Presbyterian church; promotes the belief that the

Ezekiel says, "Behold, this was the guilt of your sister Sodom: she and her daughters had pride, surfeit of food, and prosperous ease, but did not aid the poor and needy." In the books of Isaiah and Jeremiah, the sins of Sodom are described as arrogance, adultery, insincere religious practices, political corruption, oppressions of the poor, and neglect of the fatherless and the widowed. The term *sodomy* for the sexual act between men is nowhere used in the Bible; it was first invented by biblical scholars in the first century A.D.

In the New Testament, Jesus in Luke 10:10–13 speaks of inhospitality to the messengers of God as the sin that will bring down God's vengeance as it was brought down on Sodom. And what does Jesus say about homosexuality? Absolutely nothing. Jesus welcomed all people and made love and compassion the basis for his discipleship: "A new commandment I give to you, that

"Church of Jesus Christ is the church for all people of God," whatever their sexual orientation; sponsors educational projects with local Presbyterian congregations; and organizes conferences and synod and presbytery groups that meet for worship, planning, support, study, action, and celebration. The group bestows the Inclusive Church Award annually to an individual or organization working for the full inclusion of lesbian and gay Christians in the Presbyterian Church. The group's video *More Light Churches* shows how a congregation can become a "More Light Church" welcoming lesbian and gay people into full membership and participation, and the *More Light Update* newsletter appears monthly. PLGBC's annual conference is held in conjunction with the annual General Assembly of the Presbyterian Church (U.S.A.). PLGBC is affiliated with the National Gay and Lesbian Task Force and the International Gay and Lesbian Association.

## NEW MEXICO

### Dignity—New Mexico

Steve Getman, Contact
PO Box 27294
Albuquerque, NM 87125
phone: (505) 880-9031
The New Mexico chapter of Dignity/USA includes gay and lesbian Catholics and their friends. Founded in 1984, the group publishes a monthly newsletter and conducts educational programs, social activities, and a worship service the first Sunday of each month.

## NEW YORK

### Axios USA—National Chapter

Nicholas Zymaris, President
PO Box 990
Village Station
New York, NY 10014-0990
phone: (718) 805-1952 or (212) 989-6211
Axios USA includes gay and lesbian Christians who belong to, have been educated and reared in, or have converted to the Eastern Christian tradition. Founded in 1980, Axios USA seeks to address the issue of human sexuality within Eastern Christianity; to affirm that gay men and women can live an active life of prayer and witness; to find spiritual strength, stability, and well-being; to bridge the gulf between the church community and the gay community through dialogue, prayer, service, and education; to provide comfort, help, and

you love one another; even as I have loved you.... By this all men will know that you are my disciples, if you have love for one another" (John 13:34–35).

In the New Testament, it is the teachings of St. Paul, particularly in Romans 1:26–27 and 1 Corinthians 6:9–11, that are most often cited against homosexuality. In both passages, however, there is some debate about whether the Greek words in the original text can even be translated as "homosexual" (they are not done so in either the King James version or the Revised Standard version). Many scholars believe that the words used in Corinthians refer to the idolatrous practice of temple prostitution, not to homosexuality at all. And in the passage from Romans, Paul regards "homosexuality" as a punishment accorded to idolaters and those who were unfaithful to God—it is not the sin but its consequence. Paul may also have foreseen that this passage

support of our brothers and sisters and their families in realizing the joys and responsibilities of God's gift of sexuality; to protect against stigmatization, repression, and acts of intolerance; to serve others in acts of charity and love as individuals and as a group; to study rich and varied heritages and traditions; to find a true sense of appreciation for each other; and to achieve a spirit of fun and enjoyment in our development. Axios USA holds membership meetings, prayer, Vespers, discussions, and an annual Christmas Party. The group sponsors the AIDS Ministry and Network, conducts research, maintains a speakers' bureau, offers educational programs, and publishes a newsletter that contains theological, hagiographics, and other articles of interest to Eastern and Orthodox Christians.

### Conference for Catholic Lesbians (CCL)

Karen Doherty, Board Member
PO Box 436
Planetarium Station
New York, NY 10024
phone: (718) 680-6107 or (212) 663-2963
fax: (212) 268-7028
The Conference for Catholic Lesbians comprises women of Catholic heritage and their non-Catholic women friends who recognize the importance of the Catholic tradition in shaping their lives, but who seek to develop and nurture a spiritual life that enhances and affirms their lesbian identity. Founded in 1982, CCL provides a forum for exploring spirituality through liturgies and rituals; promotes Catholic lesbian visibility and community; advocates women's and lesbian rights and social justice issues in the church and society; serves as a support network worldwide; and sponsors lectures, retreats, and conferences. The newsletter *Images* appears quarterly.

### Congregation Beth Simchat Torah

57 Bethune St.
New York, NY 10014-1791
phone: (212) 929-9498

### Congregation B'nai Jesurua, Gay and Lesbian Committee

152 W. 89th St.
New York, NY 10024

### Dignity—Big Apple

PO Box 1028
New York, NY 10011
phone: (212) 620-0369

### Dignity—Brooklyn

PO Box 021313

could be used to unfairly condemn others, as he followed it with, "You have no excuse, O man, whoever you are, when you judge another; for in passing judgement upon him you condemn yourself" (Romans 2:1).

The teachings of Paul should also be understood in the light of his belief that Jesus was returning—not in millennia, but any day. Procreation was no longer necessary; preparing for the Lord's imminent return was his priority. Dr. Charles Arehart comments, "To put it simply, Paul believed that if you put your earthly interests above your spiritual relationship with God, then you are tempted away from God. Paul even believed it was better not to marry; his distant second choice was to marry if you can't control yourself."

It is always necessary for you—for all people—to remember that the writers of and the commentators on the Bible were, first of all, mere human beings,

Brooklyn, NY 11202
phone: (718) 769-3447

**Dignity—Buffalo**
PO Box 75
Ellicott Station
Buffalo, NY 14205
phone: (716) 833-8995

**Dignity—Capital District**
PO Box 11204
Loudonville, NY 12211
phone: (518) 458-8095

**Dignity/Integrity—Mid-Hudson**
PO Box 356
Lagrangeville, NY 12540
phone: (914) 724-3209

**Dignity—Mid-New York**
PO Box 352
Utica, NY 13503
phone: (315) 738-0599

**Dignity—Nassau**
PO Box 48
East Meadow, NY 11554
phone: (516) 781-6225

**Dignity—New York**
PO Box 1554
FDR Station
New York, NY 10150
phone: (212) 866-8047

**Dignity/Integrity—Rochester**
17 South Fitzhugh Street
Rochester, NY 14614
phone: (716) 262-2170

**Dignity—Queens**
Bill Foote, President
4230 Hampton St.
Flushing, NY 11373-2664
phone: (718) 565-2171

**Dignity—Suffolk**
Kathleen Kane, President
PO Box 1336
Patchogue, NY 11772
phone: (516) 654-5367
The Suffolk chapter of Dignity/USA, a support group for gay and lesbian Catholics, conducts social and religious activities and publishes *Sound* bimonthly.

**Evangelicals Concerned (EC)—National Chapter**
Dr. Ralph Blair, Founder and President
311 E. 72nd St., No. G-1
New York, NY 10021
phone: (212) 517-3171
Evangelicals Concerned is a task force and ministry founded in 1976 during the national convention of the National Associ-

and secondly, almost exclusively men. They are, as all humans are, fallible and subject to the misinformation and emotional and prejudicial attitudes of their own time and culture. "Who today would share Paul's anti-Semitic attitude, his belief that the authority of the state was not to be challenged or that all women ought to be veiled?" asks Bishop John S. Spong of the Episcopal Diocese of Newark, New Jersey.

In various historical times, the Bible has been used to foster peace—but also, unfortunately, persecution. It was the most devout Catholics who ordered the expulsion, torture, and burning of Jews, homosexuals, and heretics during the Spanish Inquisition, justifying their actions by the Bible. Many people in the past have claimed righteousness as the basis for unrighteous actions, in direct opposition to the Judeo-Christian tradition, and

ation of Evangelicals, although there is no official affiliation between the two organizations. Members of EC, both homosexual and heterosexual, are concerned with "the lack of preparation for dealing realistically with homosexuality in the evangelical community and about the implications of the Gospel in the lives of gay men and lesbians." EC consults with leaders of the religious and secular communities; maintains a speakers' bureau; makes referrals for counseling; holds Bible studies and worship services; and published educational materials and a quarterly newsletter.

### Radical Faeries
PO Box 1251
Canal Street Station
New York, NY 10013

### World Congress of Gay and Lesbian Jewish Organizations (WCGLJO)
William W. Wahler, Executive Director
PO Box 3345
New York, NY 10008-3345
phone: (201) 798-6383
fax: (201) 798-2506
The world congress serves as umbrella organization for Jewish gay and lesbian organizations, synagogues, and social groups worldwide. Founded in 1980, the group provides educational outreach to the nongay community; operates a speakers' bureau; conducts charitable programs; maintains a reference library of Jewish liturgy sensitive to gay and lesbian concerns; publishes the semiannual newsletter *Digest;* and hosts a biennial international conference.

## NORTH CAROLINA

### Dignity—Triangle
PO Box 51129
Durham, NC 27717
phone: (919) 744-1591

### Gay Baha'i Fellowship
PO Box 2623
Asheville, NC 28802

### Lesbian and Gay Shabbat
807 Onslow St.
Durham, NC 27705

## OHIO

### Central United Methodist Church
701 W. Central
Toledo, OH 43610
phone: (419) 241-7729

regrettably, many still do. But the Bible is not theirs alone to interpret. The Bible is above all else a testament to love: God's all-inclusive love for each of us, our love for God and for each other.

Many different religions have organizations for gay members.... But if you are in a church or synagogue that treats you with hostility, that denies your existence or asks that you lead your life as a lie, that promotes harassment, homophobia, and hatred amongst its members, it may not be worth keeping it in your life. As the Reverend Elder Dr. Arehart says, "It hurts your relationship with God to be constantly at war with yourself. And being at war with yourself means living a life of pretense, not being true to yourself, keeping part of yourself hidden from God."

Jesse, 17, says, "I seem to have lost whatever spirituality I once had when

### Chevrei Tikva
Becky Streem, President
PO Box 18120
Cleveland, OH 44118
phone: (216) 932-5551
Chevrei Tikva provides religious, social, and educational activities for gay and lesbian Jews in northeastern Ohio. Founded in 1983, the group is a member of the World Congress of Gay and Lesbian Jewish Organizations and the Union of American Hebrew Congregations. Chevrei Tikva publishes a monthly newsletter and sponsors Shabbat services the first and third Friday of the month.

### Dignity—Cincinnati
PO Box 983
Cincinnati, OH 45201
phone: (513) 557-2111

### Dignity—Cleveland
PO Box 91697
Cleveland, OH 44101
phone: (216) 229-2138

### Dignity—Dayton
PO Box 55
Dayton, OH 45401
phone: (513) 277-7706
The Dayton chapter of Dignity/USA includes gay and lesbian members of the Roman Catholic church united to represent the interests of the gay and lesbian community in the church and society. Founded in 1975, Dignity publishes a bimonthly newsletter and *The Pilgrim*.

### Dignity—Greater Columbus
PO Box 02001
Columbus, OH 43202
phone: (614) 451-6528

### Dignity—Toledo
PO Box 1388
Toledo, OH 43603
phone: (419) 242-9057

### Presbyterians for Lesbian, Gay, and Bisexual Concerns—Covenant Region (PLGCCR)
Arthur L. Kaltenborn, Coordinator
1370 Athena Dr.
Kent, OH 44240
phone: (216) 673-7642
Founded in 1975, the Covenant Region chapter of PLGBC includes ministers, deacons, and members of the Presbyterian Church in Michigan and Ohio. The group ministers to the needs of homosexuals within the church; provides fellowship and mutual support; and sponsors education to end homophobia within the church.

I left my religion, as if I also left behind everything I had learned in church all the years I attended with my family." Even if, after recognizing your sexuality, you feel you cannot attend your family church, you don't have to lose your spirituality. "Spirituality," says Rabbi Susan Freeman of Congregation B'nai Israel in Northampton, Massachusetts, "is a way of doing and being that connects you to something greater. It is those moments of connection that elevate you from the mundane to the more meaningful. It is a way of life that prescribes a personal moral and ethical relationship to God."

Rabbi Freeman, like other thoughtful, concerned leaders of many religious faiths, believes that whether you are a Buddhist, Christian, Jew, Catholic, or member of any other religion, you can find an accepting religious community.

"The great message of Scripture is of a God of unbounded love for the human family," says Bishop Stanley E. Olson, retired pastor and bishop of

**United Church Coalition for Lesbian/Gay Concerns (UCCL/GC)—National Chapter**
Jan Griesinger, Director
18 N. College St.
Athens, OH 45701
phone: (614) 593-7301
UCCL/GC includes both laity and clergy of the United Church of Christ. Founded in 1973, the group provides confidential counseling, support, and referrals; acts as advocate for gay, lesbian, and bisexual concerns within the church and society; encourages communication between individuals and organizations; and wishes to perpetuate the belief that all persons are loved by God and have much to offer regardless of sexual orientation. The newsletter, *Waves*, is published three times a year.

## OKLAHOMA

**Dignity/Integrity—Oklahoma City**
PO Box 25473
Oklahoma City, OK 73125
phone: (405) 424-5147

**Dignity—Tulsa**
PO Box 701044
Tulsa, OK 74101
phone: (918) 298-4648

## OREGON

**Dignity—Portland**
PO Box 6708
Portland, OR 97228
phone: (503) 295-4868

**Dignity—Willamette Valley**
PO Box 532
Salem, OR 97308
phone: (503) 363-0006

**People of Faith Against Bigotry**
Dan Stutesman, AFSC
2249 E. Burnside
Portland, OR 97214
phone: (503) 230-9429
Multi-faith coalition that helped successfully challenge the religious right in Oregon.

## PENNSYLVANIA

**Bet Tikva**
Persad Center
5150 Penn Ave.
Pittsburgh, PA 15224-1627

the Evangelical Lutheran Church in America. And this love is unqualified, freely given to all God's children.

As long as you maintain your ability to question, to search for your own answers, and to believe, you will be able to find a spiritual community that will welcome you. Accepting yourself as a sexual being does not mean surrendering your life as a spiritual being. The sense of belonging, of support, and of community that religious groups may provide can be an invaluable help to you in your journey toward self-acceptance. It's important not to let the inhumane words and actions of a few keep you from fully exercising and exploring your own spirituality.

*By Rachel Pollack and Cheryl Schwartz. First printed in* The Journey Out, *published by Viking, 1995.*

**Beth Ahavah**
PO Box 7566
Philadelphia, PA 19101

**Dignity—Central Pennsylvania**
Clair E. Gunnet, Jr., President
PO Box 297
Federal Square Station
Harrisburg, PA 17108
phone: (717) 652-7683
The Central Pennsylvania chapter of Dignity/USA includes gays and lesbians who are members of the Roman Catholic Church, and their friends. The group was founded in 1975 and publishes *The Keystone.*

**Dignity—Erie**
PO Box 3746
Erie, PA 16508
phone: (814) 864-4627

**Dignity—North Central Pennsylvania**
94 Kinsey Street
Montgomery, PA 17752
phone: (717) 547-1329

**Dignity—Northeast Pennsylvania**
c/o Fran Molinaro
PO Box 437
Hamlin, PA 18427
phone: (717) 347-0090

**Dignity—Philadelphia**
PO Box 53348
Philadelphia, PA 19105
phone: (215) 546-2093

**Dignity—Pittsburgh**
PO Box 362
Pittsburgh, PA 15230
phone: (412) 371-4240

**Friends for Lesbian and Gay Concerns (FLGC)**
Bruce Grimes, Editor
PO Box 222
Sumneytown, PA 18084
FLGC comprises gay and lesbian Quakers united to provide support for one another and encourage personal spiritual growth. Founded in 1973, Friends seeks to broaden acceptance and understanding by the Quaker faith; conducts workshops and seminars at various Quaker meetings in America and Canada; and publishes *Each of Us Inevitable,* which contains the group's keynote addresses; *History of Gay Rights Movement in the Religious Society of Friends; Inclusive Minutes on Marriage by Religious Society of Friends;* and a quarterly newsletter. A con-

ference for women takes place each summer, and a conference for men each fall.

### Metropolitan Community Church—Allentown
1345 Linden #3
Allentown, PA 18102
phone: (215) 439-8755

### Metropolitan Community Church—Harrisburg
PO Box 11543
Harrisburg, PA 17108
phone: (717) 236-7387

## RHODE ISLAND

### Dignity—Providence
Ron Coepeau-Cross, President
PO Box 2231
Pawtucket, RI 02861
phone: (401) 727-2657
Dignity of Providence includes gay men and lesbians in Rhode Island and parts of Massachusetts and Connecticut united to show a gay presence in the Roman Catholic Church. Founded in 1973, the Dignity chapter conducts charitable activities, sponsors an annual retreat, and publishes a newsletter called *Gaudeamus.*

## SOUTH CAROLINA

### Unitarian Universalist Church
251 E. Henry St.
Spartanburg, SC 29303

### Unitarian Universalist Fellowship
2701 Heyward Street
Columbia, SC 29205
phone: (803) 799-0845

## TENNESSEE

### Gays Rejoicing and Affirmed in a Catholic Environment (GRACE)
6 S. McLean, #402
Memphis, TN 38104

## TEXAS

### Congregation Beth El Binah
PO Box 191188
Dallas, TX 75219

### Dignity—Austin
Cynthia Barnette, Presiding Officer
PO Box 2666
Austin, TX 78768
phone: (512) 918-1707
The Austin chapter of Dignity includes gays and lesbians who are members of the Roman Catholic Church. Founded in 1978, Dignity offers monthly masses, conducts charitable and social activities, and publishes a quarterly newsletter.

### Dignity—Dallas
PO Box 190133
Dallas, TX 75219
phone: (214) 521-5342

### Dignity—Houston
PO Box 66821
Houston, TX 77266
phone: (713) 880-2872

### Dignity—San Antonio
PO Box 12544
San Antonio, TX 78212
phone: (210) 558-3287

### Mishpachat Alizim
PO Box 960136
Houston, TX 77298

## UTAH

### Affirmation—Salt Lake City
PO Box 526175
Salt Lake City, UT 84152

## VERMONT

### Dignity—Vermont
PO Box 782
Burlington, VT 05402

## VIRGINIA

### Dignity—Norfolk
PO Box 434
Norfolk, VA 23501
phone: (804) 625-5337

### Dignity—Northern Virginia

PO Box 10037
Main Station
Arlington, VA 22210
phone: (703) 912-1662

### Dignity/Integrity—Richmond

c/o Joe Hilterman
1611 Carlisle Avenue
Richmond, VA 23231
phone: (804) 226-8140

## WASHINGTON

### Dignity—Seattle

PO Box 20325
Seattle, WA 98102
phone: (206) 325-7314

### Tikvah Chadashah

PO Box 2731
Seattle, WA 98111

## WISCONSIN

### Dignity/Integrity—Madison

PO Box 730
Madison, WI 53701
phone: (608) 836-8886
Dignity/Integrity of Madison is a social and support group for gay and lesbian Christians, along with their friends and families. Associated with the national groups Dignity/USA and Integrity, the Madison chapter conducts charitable programs and publishes the quarterly newsletter *Identity*.

### Dignity—Milwaukee

Chuck Bowe, Executive Officer
PO Box 597
Milwaukee, WI 53201
phone: (414) 444-7177
The Milwaukee chapter of Dignity/USA includes gay and lesbian members of the Roman Catholic Church united to represent the interests of the gay and lesbian community in the church and society. Founded in 1975, Dignity/Milwaukee participates in the Cream City Foundation and Milwaukee AIDS Project; sponsors Pride Week and a weekly Sunday Mass and Social; and publishes a bimonthly newsletter.

# ONLINE RESOURCES

## THE WEB

### Evangelical Network

http://metro.turnpike.net/D/Deacon/index.html
The Evangelical Network (TEN) is a fundamental Christian organization open to all ministries and people, especially in the gay community. Cristo Press, the publishing arm of TEN, offers booklets online that interpret biblical passages and preach acceptance for homosexuals as well as heterosexuals.

# RECREATION

The hundred or so organizations listed in this chapter represent only a fraction of the clubs, associations, teams, and groups in North America—not to mention worldwide—for athletic lesbians, gay men, and bisexuals—and, of course, their admirers.

The groups in this chapter offer something for everyone, representing every interest and every level of ability. Front Runners, named after the book about a gay runner, hosts events for runners, joggers, walkers, and cyclers in several cities; the New York chapter sponsors the five-mile Lesbian and Gay Pride Race in Central Park each year during Gay Pride Week. International Gay and Lesbian Aquatics, founded by aquatics competitors at Gay Games II in San Francisco, boasts several member organizations for swimmers worldwide. The Gay and Lesbian Tennis Alliance, which manages and sanctions the gay tennis circuit, sponsors 23 tournaments annually in the United States, Canada, Australia, and the United Kingdom. Local associations like Indy OUTfields promote numerous recreational activities through already-established groups, such as bowling, camping, caving, diving, hiking, hot air ballooning, martial arts, mini golf, motorcycling, mountain biking, racquetball, rock climbing, running, soccer, softball, swimming, tennis, volleyball, and walking.

The International Gay Rodeo Association, with more than 20 member groups, appeals to cowpokes of any gender, and those who like to celebrate in style after the rodeo can find kindred spirits through the International Association of Gay and Lesbian Country Western Dance Clubs or the International Association of Gay Square Dance Clubs.

For outdoor lovers who prefer non-competitive action, groups like the Chiltern Mountain Club (whose Web site features a seemingly infinite amount of information on outdoor clubs worldwide), the Gay and Lesbian Sierrans, and more than a hundred others represented by the International Gay and Lesbian Outdoors Organization (IGLOO), offer camping, hiking, climbing, biking, boating, rollerblading, and a host of other activities. Several lesbian and gay campsites and travel associations are listed here as well, along with publications dealing with lesbian and gay sports, recreational activities, and travel.

We also offer a brief history of the Gay Games, which will take place next in Amsterdam in 1988 and expects to draw more than 12,000 athletes competing in 30 competitive sports, plus demonstration sports. "Friendship '98" is destined to be the biggest Gay Games to date, and will also feature a cultural program including music, dance, fine arts, theater, and film.

# AUSTRALIA

## NEW SOUTH WALES

### Sydney Gay & Lesbian Mardi Gras

PO Box 557
Newtown, NSW 2042

### Sydney Gay Sports Association/Team Sydney

PO Box 1037
Darlinghurst, NSW 2010

### Wett Ones Swimming Club

Bob McInnes and Marcus Tate, Contacts
PO Box 458
Newtown, NSW 2042
phone: 61 2 358 5572
fax: 61 2 358 1873
e-mail: mtate@ozemail.com.au
Web site: http://www.kwic.net./lgb-sports/teams/WettOnesSwim/
Australia's first gay and lesbian swimming club was formed in 1991 after swimmers returned from Gay Games III in Vancouver. Wett Ones, which has about 70 members, is affiliated with the Australian Union of Senior Swimmers (AUSSI) and competes in masters competitions and open ocean water swims off Sydney's beaches.

# CANADA

## ONTARIO

### Downtown Swim Club

Box 1112, Station F
Toronto, ON M4Y 2T8
phone: (416) 925-9872
e-mail: beadie@astral.magic.ca or wearing@epas.utoronto.ca
Web site: http://www.kwic.net/lgb-sports/teams/TorontoSwim/team.html
The Downtown Swim Club, a member of International Gay and Lesbian Aquatics and Masters Swim Ontario, was founded in March 1987 and has participated in three Gay Games and most annual IGLA meets. The club also hosts its own annual meet, coinciding with Toronto's Lesbian/Gay Pride Day celebrations.

### Rainbow Boating Association

Box 40012
280 Viewmount Ave.
Toronto, ON M6B 4K4
phone: (416) 760-4080

### Team Toronto

PO Box 1121SM-F
Toronto, ON M9Y 2T8

## QUEBEC

### A Contre-courant Swim Club

Montreal, PQ
phone: (514) 522-9323
Web site: http://www.kwic.net/lgb-sports/teams/MontrealSwim/team.html
A Contre-courant is a swim club that belongs to International Gay and Lesbian Aquatics. Organized by Gay Games athletes Yves Leclerc and Sylvain Dugas after the 1990 Gay Games III, the club was originally called Montreal Equipe Natation. A Contre-courant regularly participates in gay and lesbian competitions in North America and

# SPOTLIGHT GAY GAMES

The Gay Games—an Olympic-type competition for gay and lesbian athletes—were first held in San Francisco in 1982. Conceived by Dr. Thomas Waddell, a former Olympic decathelete, the Games have grown over the years, from a 14-sport competition in 1980 to a 31-sport program in 1994. The Games, like the Olympics, are held every four years and draw competitors from all over the world.

The initial competition was called "Challenge '82" and drew more than 1,300 athletes from 12 countries. Originally called the Gay Olympics, the event was forced to change its name after a protest from the United States Olympic

has recently begun to compete in Europe as well. About 110 members participate in eight workouts per week, from the beginner to the advanced level. The group publishes a newsletter called *l'eAU COURANTe.*

### Team Montreal/Equipe Montreal

CP726 SVCC Tour de la Bourse
Montreal, PQ H4Z 1J9

## ENGLAND

### Ishigaki Ju-Jitsu Club

Rick, Publicity/Liaison
phone: 0171 232 2895
Chris Denning, Web coordinator
cdenning@cygnet.co.uk
Web site: http://www.cygnet.co.uk/~cdenning/ishigaki.html
The Ishigaki Ju-Jitsu Club ("Ishigaki" means "stone wall" in Japanese) is run by gay people and is suitable for everyone, regardless of age or gender. As the club's organizers stress, "We are conscious of the popular and unfortunate image that martial art has with many people and we strive to foster a more caring and positive attitude in our club. The techniques we use are practical and realistic, and relate directly to real-life situations and dangers. Our style does not rely on aggression nor brute force; instead, ju-jitsu displaces and uses the force of the attacker.

## FRANCE

### Comité Gai Paris Ile-de-France (CGPIF)

BP 120
75623 Paris
phone: 1 47 00 60 03
The sports association CGPIF is preparing for 1998's Gay Games V in Amsterdam and for 1997's EuroGames in Paris. The association includes individual associations for various sports, including volleyball, basketball, running (Front Runners of Paris), badminton, karate (Karaboom), swimming, pétanque, and others.

### Karaboom

chez M. Oliver Wehlmann
49, bd. Voltaire
75011 Paris
phone: 1 43 57 78 35
e-mail: Wehlmann@Imaginet.Fr
Web site: http://fglb.qrd.org:8080/fqrd/assocs/karaboom/
Karaboom is a karate club that is open to everyone, regardless of gender, experience, or age. Karaboom is a member of the *Comité*

Committee (USOC). A legal battle ensued, and the United States Supreme Court ruled in the USOC's favor in 1987, prohibiting the gay and lesbian competition from using the Olympics name.

Gay Games II—dubbed "Triumph '86"—was also held in San Francisco, and saw 3,482 athletes from 16 nations compete. This gathering held the distinction of being the largest international athletic competition to take place in North America in 1986. It was also the last Gay Games that Waddell attended before dying of AIDS in 1987.

Vancouver, British Columbia, was the site of the third Gay Games. At the Games' largest gathering to date, more than 7,000competitors from 30 countries participated in 26 sports. These Games, which included a celebration of gay and lesbian arts in addition to athletic competition, were viewed by 50,000 spectators. In addition, many of the athletic events were officially

*gai Paris Ile-de-France* (CGPIF). The group, which has about 30 members, has three classes each week from September to June.

## NETHERLANDS

### Gay Games Amsterdam 1998

Joed Elich, Board Member
PO Box 2837
NL 1000 CV Amsterdam
phone: 31 20 620 1998
fax: 31 20 626 1998
e-mail: Joed.Elich@gaygames.nl
e-mail: Marjo.Meijer@gaygames.nl (president)
e-mail: Marc.Janssens@gaygames.nl (secretary)
Web site: http://www.kwic.net/lgb-sports/gaygames/index.html

### Gay Integration through Sports and Activities Holland (GISAH)

European Gay & Lesbian Sports Federation
Breedstratt 28
2513 TT Den Haag
Web site: http://www.gaysport.org/gisah/
The GISAH foundation, based in Den Haag (The Hague), was established in 1990. GISAH's purpose is "to promote the integration of gay men and lesbians into sports and to tackle the problem of discrimination based on sexual preference in sports. We try to attain these goals through, among other ways, establishing, stimulating, and supporting (inter)national sports and cultural festivals in Den Haag."

## SOUTH AFRICA

### Cape Organisation for Gay Sports (COGS)

3 Bateleur Pl.
21 Bateleur Crescent
Table View 7441
phone: 27-21 557-7195
e-mail: ro@global.co.za
"We do a day hike almost every Sunday in our summer, a weekend or five-day hike about once a month, also have a social braai (barbeque) each month, and arrange block bookings for gay-themed films and plays for our members." The COGS newsletter is published every other month and lists gay support and service organizations and activities.

### The Organisation for Gay Sports (TOGS)

PO Box 462
Melville 2109

recognized by their respective sanctioning bodies for the first time in Gay Games history.

In 1994, the Gay Games and Cultural Festival continued to grow, again attracting record numbers of both participants and spectators. More than 500,000 fans watched as 11,000 athletes and 2,500 artists from 44 countries gathered in New York City to take part in the week-long festivities. "Unity '94" boasted 31 sporting events—including same-sex pairs figure skating—and held its closing ceremonies in Yankee Stadium. President Bill Clinton and New York Governor Mario Cuomo were among those offering their support to Gay Games IV.

The fifth edition of the Gay Games is scheduled to take place in Amsterdam, Holland, August 1–8, 1998. "Friendship '98" is destined to be the biggest Gay Games to date, and will include 30 competitive sports—ranging from

TOGS organizes hiking, running, squash, and tennis activities.

## UNITED STATES

### ARIZONA

#### Ferrari Publications, Inc.

Marianne Ferrari, Editor and Publisher
Sharon Rosen, Manager
PO Box 37887
Phoenix, AZ 85069
phone: (602) 863-2408
fax: (602) 439-3952
Ferrari publishes worldwide gay and lesbian travel guidebooks, including *Places of Interest, Places for Men, Places of Interest to Women,* and *Inn Places,* for the United States, Canada, the Caribbean, Europe, Mexico, Australia, New Zealand, and Tahiti. Specializes in covering gay and lesbian events and tours. Reaches market through direct mail, wholesalers, and retailers.

### CALIFORNIA

#### Barnacle Busters

PO Box 461510
West Hollywood, CA 90046
phone: (310) 451-2111
e-mail: Gaydivers@aol.com
Lesbian and gay scuba diving club.

#### Bay Area Boxing Club

San Francisco, CA
phone: (415) 585-2365
The Bay Area Boxing Club, for lesbians and gay men, sponsors two tournaments each year. For the winter event, called the Rainbow Gloves Tournament, boxers come from throughout the country to compete.

#### Damron Co., Inc.

Gina M. Gatta, President
Robert Ian Philips, Editor
PO Box 422458
San Francisco, CA 94142-2458
phone: (415) 255-0404 or (800) 462-6654
fax: (415) 703-9049
Formerly known as Bob Damron Enterprises, Damron publishes travel guides including the *Damron Address Book,* "the largest selling, most widely circulated gay travel guide on the market. Lists bars, baths, hotels, restaurants, etc. in the U.S., Canada, Puerto Rico, Virgin Islands, Costa Rica, and Mexico which cater to and are frequented by gays and lesbians." Reaches market through commissioned representatives and direct mail.

karate and tennis to ballroom dancing and chess—in addition to demonstration sports. The cultural program will feature a wide variety of events, including music, dance, fine arts, theater, and film. In all, more than 12,000 athletes are expected to participate in Gay Games V.

*By Dean Dauphinais*

### Different Strokes Swim Team—San Diego

San Diego, CA
phone: (619) 525-SWIM
e-mail: bandit5972@aol.com or sbe@cwsl.edu
Web site: http://www.kwic.net/lgb-sports/teams/SanDiegoSwim/team.html
Different Strokes began in the mid-1980s and works out at the Coronado Municipal Pool in Coronado, California.

### Federation of Gay Games

Susan Kennedy and Gilles Pettigrew, Co-Presidents
584 Castro, Ste. 343
San Francisco, CA 94114
Web site: http://www.eor.com/fgg/purpose.htm
The Federation of Gay Games is a nonprofit organization whose purpose "is to foster and augment the self-respect of lesbians and gay men throughout the world and to engender respect and understanding from the non-gay world, primarily through an organized international participatory athletic and cultural event held every four years, and commonly known as the Gay Games." For information about Gay Games V, which will take place in Amsterdam in 1988 and expects to draw at least 12,000 athletes, contact either the Federation or Gay Games Amsterdam in the Netherlands.

### Gay & Lesbian Sierrans—Bay Chapter

6014 College Ave.
Oakland, CA 94618
Member of the grassroots, environmental organization, the Sierra Club.

### Gay & Lesbian Sierrans—Loma Prieta Chapter

3921 E. Bayshore Rd.
Palo Alto, CA 94303
phone: (408) 450-0402
Web site: http://www.qrd.org/qrd/usa/california/ gl.sierrans.loma.prieta.chapter
The Gay & Lesbian Sierrans (GLS) is part of the Loma Prieta Chapter of the Sierra Club, one of the oldest and most respected grassroots environmental organizations in the world. GLS of Loma Prieta began in 1991 as an offshoot of the the San Francisco Bay Chapter GLS. GLS sponsors activities including day hikes, camping trips, bike rides, game nights, and holiday events, and participates in gay and lesbian pride festivals in San Jose and San Francisco. The group describes itself as "a friendly, relaxed group of lesbians and gay men who enjoy outdoor adventures and camaraderie on the San Francisco Peninsula and in the San Francisco South Bay (San Jose area). As we grow, we hope to develop new programs (e.g., trail maintenance, monthly educational programs on conservation-related issus) and subcommittees (e.g., membership, publicity, and conservation) to encourage your participation in, and appreciation of, the outdoors, and to educate ourselves on current environmental issues and how we can be involved."

### Gay & Lesbian Sports Alliance of Greater Los Angeles

c/o Gay & Lesbian Community Services Center
1625 N. Schrader Blvd.
Los Angeles, CA 90028
phone: (310) 515-3337
e-mail: powell@mizar.usc.edu
Web site: http://www.webcom.com/~bkm/sa.html

"The Gay & Lesbian Sports Alliance of Greater Los Angeles was formed in August 1991 to promote recreational and competitive sports within the community. The Alliance does not organize any sports, but instead acts as a source of information for who's playing what, when and where. The Alliance is busiest during the Gay Games, held every four years. In New York (in 1994), for example, the group coordinated housing for more than 200 athletes of Team LA."

## Gay & Lesbian Tennis Federation of San Francisco

Dan Hess, President
2215-R Market St., Ste. 109
San Francisco, CA 94114
e-mail: SFGLTFER@aol.com
Web site: http://www.slip.net/~gltf/
Sponsors the U.S. Gay Open Tennis Championships, which began in 1981 and is the largest and longest-running international gay tennis tournament. For more information about the tournament, which takes place in May, contact tournament director Dennis Fitzgerald via e-mail at DFitzge892@aol.com.

## Gay Recreation Plus of San Francisco

355 Noe St.
San Francisco, CA 94114-1618

## *Girljock*

Rox-A-Tronic
PO Box 882723
San Francisco, CA 94188
phone: (510) 452-2085
fax: (415) 282-6833
Quarterly publication focusing on the lives of women athletes and their admirers, founded in 1990.

## Golden Gate Wrestling

63 Whitney St.
San Francisco, CA 94131-2742

## Golden State Gay Rodeo Associaion—Greater Los Angeles Chapter

8033 Sunset Blvd., #41
Los Angeles, CA 90046
phone: (310) 498-1675
e-mail: gsgraglac@aol.com
Founded in 1984; member of the International Gay Rodeo Association.

## Great Outdoors—Antelope Valley

PO Box 5044
Lancaster, CA 92529-5044
phone: (805) 265-1871

## Great Outdoors—Inland Empire

PO Box 56586
Riverside, CA 92517
phone: (909) 792-2255

## Great Outdoors—Los Angeles

PO Box 1318
Studio City, CA 91614
phone: (818) 763-4496

## Great Outdoors—Orange County/Long Beach

PO Box 30171
Long Beach, CA 90803
phone: (714) 665-7377

## Great Outdoors—Pamona/San Gabriel Valley

PO Box 2516
Covina, CA 91722-8516
phone: (818) 964-8075

## Great Outdoors—San Diego

3211 Gergory St.
San Diego, CA 92104
phone: (619) 563-8960

## Great Outdoors—Santa Barbara

PO Box 21051
Santa Barbara, CA 93121
phone: (805) 564-3646

## Marin Hike and Bike Club

PO Box 2471
Mill Valley, CA 94942
phone: (415) 457-1115, ext. 230
Web site: http://www.microweb.copm/rogm/marin-hike&bike-club.html
Social and outdoor club for gays and lesbians "in association with Spectrum Center for Gay, Lesbian, and Bisexual Concerns" that offers regular hikes and mountain bike trips.

## Rainbow Cyclists—San Diego

PO Box 3344
San Diego, CA 92163
Web site: http://www.liscom.com/rainbow-cyclist/
Rainbow Cyclists is a bicycle club for gay and lesbian riders of all ability levels. Founded in 1988, the club publishes a bimonthly newsletter.

## SAGA North Ski Club

PO Box 14384
San Francisco, CA 94114-0384
phone: (415) 995-2772
e-mail: SAGANorth@aol.com
Web site: http://users.aol.com/saganorth/sagaski1.html
Founded in the early 1980s, SAGA is a predominantly gay and lesbian winter downhill ski club. Sponsors both winter and summer trips to Lake Tahoe and ski resorts outside California and (occasionally) outside the United States. Publishes the monthly newsletter *Snowflurries*.

## Team San Francisco

2215R Market St.
San Francisco, CA 94114

## Undersea Expeditions

San Diego, CA
phone: (619) 270-2900
e-mail: UnderseaX@aol.com
Undersea Expeditions sponsors gay and lesbian scuba diving expeditions.

## Volleyball Organization in Los Angeles (VOILA)

Doug Walters, Commissioner
Lance Laforteza, Assistant Commissioner
8424A Santa Monica Blvd., Ste. 244
West Hollywood, CA 90069
phone: (310) 289-4423
e-mail: LLaforteza@aol.com
Web site: http://www.webcom.com/~bkm/sa_orgs/woila/index.html
VOILA was formed to provide a source of volleyball venues for gay and lesbian players and to host a high quality tournament in Los Angeles. The group, whose main sponsor is the Lambda Alumni Association of the University of California at Los Angeles, usually holds its annual tournament in early autumn at UCLA's Pauley Pavilion.

## West Hollywood Aquatics

West Hollywood, CA
phone: (310) 288-6555
Web site: http://www.kwic.net/lgb-sports/teams/WH2O/team.html
West Hollywood Aquatics includes gay and straight women and men swimmers and water polo players. The group, which is a member of the International Gay and Lesbian Aquatics, "grew out of a group of swimmers training for Gay Games I in 1982. The 20 swimmers on the original roster ranged in age from 22 to 46 (19 men and one woman). By Gay Games IV in 1994, the team grew to over 120 members."

## WOMBATS (Women's Mountain Bike and Tea Society)

Box 757
Fairfax, CA 94978
phone & fax: (415) 459-0980
Web site: http://www.wombats.org/
The WOMBATS (that's Women's Mountain Bike and Tea Society) are a group of women with a great sense of humor and a love of cycling. Based in Fairfax, California, WOMBATS has regional chapters in the San Francisco Bay Area and Los Angeles, California; Dallas, Texas; Hilo, Hawaii; and Clinton Township, Michigan.

# COLORADO

## Aspen Gay & Lesbian Community Ski Club

PO Box 3143
Aspen, CO 81612
phone: (303) 925-9249

## Bicycle Boys from Hell

168 W. Maple Ave.
Denver, CO 80233

## Colorado Outdoor and Ski Association

PO Box 18598
Denver, CO 80218-0598
phone: (303) 355-5029
e-mail: cosa@tde.com
Web site: http://www.tde.com/~cosa/

"Founded in December 1986 to provide its members with the opportunity to meet other gays and lesbians who share their interests in the outdoors in a casual, enjoyable, and healthy atmosphere." Most group trips involve Alpine skiing, while other trips include river rafting, camping, hiking, climbing, biking, four wheeling, Nordic skiing, snow boarding, and more.

### Dyke Bike Club

PO Box 4959
Boulder, CO 80306

### International Gay Rodeo Association

Executive Office
900 E. Colfax Ave.
Denver, CO 80218
phone: (303) 832-IGRA
The International Gay Rodeo Association has 21 member associations throughout the United States and Canada, including the Golden State Rodeo Association, Colorado Gay Rodeo Association, Arizona Gay Rodeo Association, and British Columbia's Northwest Gay Rodeo Association.

## CONNECTICUT

### Northeast Women's Musical Retreat

PO Box 550
Branford, CT 06405

### *Out & About Travel Newsletter*

542 Chapel St.
New Haven, CT 06511
phone: (800) 929-2268

## DISTRICT OF COLUMBIA

### Adventuring

PO Box 18118
Washington, DC 20036
phone: (703) 521-0290
e-mail: erewhon@access.digex.net or adventuring@glib.org
Web site: http://access.digex.net/~erehwon/
Adventuring, an all-volunteer gay and lesbian outdoor club, organizes activities in the Washington, D.C., area and posts an events schedule online and in its monthly newsletter.

### Capital Tennis Association

Jim Wang, President
Andy Morris, Social Committee
Washington, DC
e-mail: JWang1060@aol.com
e-mail: andy.morris@washingtondc.ncr.com
The Capital Tennis Association has more than 140 members and sponsors tennis leagues, socials, tournaments, and instruction throughout the year.

## FLORIDA

### International Gay Travel Association

PO Box 4974
Key West, FL 33041
phone: (800) 448-8550
e-mail: IGTA@aol.com
Founded in 1983, IGTA is a network of travel agents, tour operators, owners and managers of hotels, guest houses, resorts, and other accommodations, and other travel professionals.

### *Our World Travel Magazine*

1104 N. Nova Rd., #251
Daytona Beach, FL 32117
phone: (904) 441-5367
Monthly magazine featuring places of interest to lesbian and gay travelers.

### Sunshine Athletic

PO Box 14481
Fort Lauderdale, FL 33302

## GEORGIA

### Atlanta Gaymes/Team Atlanta

2221 Peachtree Rd. NE, Ste. D369
Atlanta, GA 30309

### Gay and Lesbian Tennis Alliance

PO Box 82262
Atlanta, GA 30354
e-mail: GLTASAN@aol.com
Web site: http://www.kwic.net/lgb-sports/umbrella/glta.html
GLTA is "the international organization that manages and sanctions the gay tennis cir-

cuit around the world. With 23annual tournaments in the U.S., Canada, Australia, and the U.K., the GLTA is the fastest growing gay sport in the 1990s. The GLTA represents tennis in the Federation of Gay Games, and drew 700 players in the 1994 Gay Games in New York."

### International Gay & Lesbian Football Association (IGLFA)

1445 Monroe Dr. NE, #D-8
Atlanta, GA 30324
phone: (404) 876-6010
e-mail: iglfa@aol.com
Web site: http://www.kwic.net/lgb-sports/umbrella/iglfa.html
IGLFA states as its purpose: "To foster and augment the self-respect of gay men and lesbians throughout the world and engender respect and understanding from the non-gay world through the medium of football (soccer)," and "to establish an international network of football clubs and to promote physical and tactical understanding of the game of football." IGLFA organizes international and regional tournaments and helps develop gay soccer clubs around the world, and publishes a quarterly newsletter.

## HAWAII

### Organization of Hawaii Arts & Athletics

PO Box 90543
Honolulu, HI 96835

## ILLINOIS

### Chicago Smelts

Chicago, IL
phone: (312) 409-4974
Web site: http://www.kwic.net/lgb-sports/teams/SmeltsSwim/team.html
Club member of International Gay and Lesbian Aquatics.

## INDIANA

### Indy OUTfields

Mike Naylor
133 W. Market St.
Indianapolis, IN 46204-2801
phone: (317) 541-1371
e-mail: Mmalkmus@Iquest.net
Web site:
http://www.chiltern.org/chiltern/igloo/clubs/indy.html
Indy OUTfields is a gay and lesbian athletic/outdoor association that promotes numerous recreational activities and already-established groups, including bowling, camping, caving,diving, hiking, hot air ballooning, martial arts, mini golf, motorcycling, mountain biking, racquetball, rock climbing, running, soccer, softball, swimming, tennis, volleyball, and walking.

### National Women's Music Festival

PO Box 1427
Indianapolis, IN 46206-1427
phone: (317) 927-9355

### Travel Club of Indiana

City Centre Box 128
Monroe City, IN 47557
phone: (812) 743-2919
Nonprofit organization that sponsors and leads trips worldwide; publishes a newsletter.

## KANSAS

### Topeka Outdoor Group Adventures (TOGA)

PO Box 1224
Topeka, KS 66601
phone: (913) 986-6398

## MASSACHUSETTS

### Chiltern Mountain Club

PO Box 407
Boston, MA 02117-0407
phone: (617) 859-2843
e-mail: chiltern@chiltern.org
http://www.actwin.com/chiltern/index.html
Chiltern is one of the world's largest gay, lesbian, and bisexual outdoor sports organizations. The volunteer group has about 1,200 members in the New England area, and its Web site can point you to outdoor clubs worldwide. Chiltern sponsors outdoor

sports activities of all kinds, including hiking, backpacking, canoeing, camping, biking, rollerblading, and volleyball. In addition to day and weekend trips throughout the year, Chiltern hosts a camping weekend twice a year for several hundred members. Trips are listed in the monthly newsletter.

### *The Guide*
PO Box 593
Boston, MA 02199
phone: (617) 266-8557
*The Guide* contains travel information, directories and maps for bars and community centers, and news for the United States and Canada.

### Stonewall Climbers
PO Box 445
Boston, MA 02124
Lesbian and gay rock climbers and cavers.

## MICHIGAN

### Ann Arbor Queer Aquatics Swim Club (A2QUA)
Ann Arbor and Royal Oak, MI
phone: (313) 663-0036

### BTI Bowling League
Detroit, MI
phone: (313) 979-8943
Gay & lesbian bowling league, meeting each Sunday at the State Fair Lanes in Detroit from September through May.

### Front Runners of Royal Oak
Royal Oak, MI
phone: (810) 737-0284

### Grand Rapids Rivermen
PO Box 3497
Grand Rapids, MI 49501

### Male Tent & Trailer Campers
16117 Masonic Blvd.
Fraser, MI 48026
phone: (313) 293-6512
Sponsors camping and other outdoor activities.

### Metro Detroit Softball League
781 E. Webster
Ferndale, MI 48220
phone: (810) 886-3356

### Michigan Womyn's Music Festival
PO Box 22
Walhalla, MI 49458
phone: (616) 757-4766
Annual event each August for women.

### Muskegon Area Canoeists, Hikers & Outdoor Lovers (MACHO)
phone: (616) 998-0752

### Team Great Lakes
195 W. Nine Mile Rd., #106
Ferndale, MI 48220
phone: (810) 547-4692
Fund raiser for participants at the Gay Games.

## MINNESOTA

### Outwoods
PO Box 8855
Minneapolis, MN 55408
phone: (612) 825-1953

## NEW JERSEY

### Campfest
Rural Route 5, Box 185
Franklinville, NJ 08322
phone: (609) 694-2037
Womyn's music festival.

### Womongathering: The Festival of Womyn's Spirituality
Rural Route 5, Box 185
Franklinville, NJ 08322
phone: (609) 694-2037

## NEW YORK

### Front Runners New York
PO Box 87, Ansonia Sta.
New York, NY 10023
phone: (212) 724-9700
Web site: http://www.tiac.net/users/kaz/frny.html
"Front Runners New York, Inc., was founded in 1979 to promote running as a sport among gay men and lesbians. FRNY is the largest of the Front Runner organizations

throughout the United States, as well as one of the largest lesbian and gay groups in the New York metropolitan area. Our purpose is to provide encouragement and support to gay men and lesbians who are interested in running, race walking, track & field, bi/triathlons, and cycling." The regular "fun runs," running classes, and special runs are open to beginners and experienced runners, members or not, as are the group's social activities. FRNY sponsors the five-mile Lesbian and Gay Pride Race in Central Park each year during Gay Pride Week.

### *Gayellow Pages*

Frances Green, Editor
PO Box 533, Village Sta.
New York, NY 10014-0533
phone: (212) 674-0120
Classified directory of gay and lesbian information sources, services, community centers, businesses, and entertainment venues througout the United States and Canada.

### Hikin' Dykes

500 West End Ave.
New York, NY 10024

### International Gay and Lesbian Aquatics (IGLA)

450 Broome St., #4W
New York, NY 10013
Web site: http://www.kwic.net/igla.html
IGLA was founded by aquatics competitors at Gay Games II in San Francisco, and hosted it first meet in San Diego in 1987. The group's purpose is "to promote participation in aquatic sports among lesbian and gay men and friends of our community," and "to ensure maintenance of the highest standards for aquatic competitions and international standards for all Gay Games and IGLA Championships." ILGA representatives can be found in at least 10 cities worldwide.

### Metropolitan Tennis Group

332 Bleecker St.
New York, NY 10014
phone: (212) 802-4768
e-mail: geostar@dorsai.org
The nonprofit Metropolitan Tennis Group offers its members opportunities to play recreational and competitive tennis in New York, New Jersey, and Connecticut. The group also sponsors the annual Liberty Open in July (one of more than 20 tournaments sponsored by the Gay and Lesbian Tennis Alliance) at the USTA National Tennis Center—a competition that drew almost 200 participants from around the world in 1995. In addition, the Metropolitan Tennis Group hosts monthly parties at the USTA National Tennis Center (home of the US Open).

### *Odysseus Travel Planner*

PO Box 1548
Port Washington, NY 11050-0306
phone: (516) 944-5330
Travel guide listing accomodations and gay resorts in the United States and internationally.

### Village Dive Club

461 W. 49th St.
New York, NY 10019
phone: (718) 847-1779

## NORTH CAROLINA

### Wilderness Network of the Carolinas

PO Box 78081
Greensboro, NC 27404

## OHIO

### Ohio Lesbian Festival

Lesbian Business Association
PO Box 02086
Columbus, OH 43202
phone: (614) 267-3953

### Team Dayton

1455 Cory Dr.
Dayton, OH 45406

### Wheel Cool

2304 South Ave.
Toledo, OH 43609

## OKLAHOMA

### OK Spoke Club

PO Box 9165
Tulsa, OK 74157

## OREGON

### The Adventure Group

PO Box 2201
Portland, OR 97208-2201
phone: (503) 452-5680
Web site:
http://www.teleport.com/~hunt/ag/ag.shtml

The Adventure Group organizes hiking, mountain biking, skiing, camping, snowshoeing, horseback riding, whitewater rafting, and other non-competitive outdoor activities in northwest Oregon and southwest Washington. Loosely organized in the mid-1980s, the group organized more formally in 1994 and now has more than 120 members, participates in activities with other gay outdoor groups, and publishes a monthly newsletter.

## PENNSYLVANIA

### International Assoication of Gay & Lesbian Martial Arts

311 Barren Hill Rd.
Conshohocken, PA 19428

### Wilderness Womyn

6914 Ridge Ave.
Philadelphia, PA 19128

## TEXAS

### International Association of Gay and Lesbian Country Western Dance Clubs (IAGLCWDC)

c/o Paul G. Ross
3115 Houston Ave.
Houston, TX 77009-6736
Web site: http://ourworld.compuserve.com/homepages/Hanknit

The association promotes the appreciation of country western dance.

### Lambda Mermaids

PO Box 190869
Dallas, TX 75219
phone: (214) 521-5342

### Oak Lawn Soccer Club

834 S. Montclair Ave.
Dallas, TX 75208-5856
phone: (214) 942-9537
e-mail: astrojet@aol.com
Web site: http://www.kwic.net/lgb-sports/teams/DallasSoccer/index.html

"The Oak Lawn Soccer Club is a nonprofit, predominantly gay & lesbian organization formed to provide its members a gay-friendly atmosphere in which to play and enjoy the game of soccer. We field teams in local mainstream leagues and play in local, regional, and international tournaments, both gay and mainstream. As a member of the International Gay & Lesbian Football Association, we participate in its activities and will be hosting the 1996 international championship."

## VERMONT

### Just Women Travel

275 Jacksonville Stage Rd.
Brattleboro, VT 05301
phone: (802) 257-0152

## WASHINGTON

### Bottom Dwellers

PO Box 530515
Seattle, WA 98122-0553
phone: (206) 233-1311

Lesbian and gay scuba diving club.

### Team Seattle

1202 East Pike, #515
Seattle, WA 98122
phone: (206) 322-7769
e-mail: teamseattle@eor.com

"Team Seattle exists to facilitate, provide, and promote opportunities for lesbians, gays, and their friends in all sports at all levels of ability, and to foster their physical and emotional health and well-being. We accomplish this mission primarily by providing an inter-sports resource network for athletes and sports leaders, by organizing Seattle's team to the Gay Games, and by producing the Northwest Gay/Lesbian Summer and Winter Sports Festivals. Team Seattle was founded in 1986."

## WISCONSIN

### Milwaukee Gamma

R. Grunke, Treasurer
Box 1900
Milwaukee, WI 53201-1900
phone: (414) 963-9833
Milwaukee Gamma, founded in 1978, is an outdoor, social, and sports group for gay individuals from the Milwaukee area. The 200-member group's newsletter appears monthly, and its annual banquet takes place in November.

# ONLINE RESOURCES

## THE WEB

### Adventuring

http://access.digex.net/~erehwon/
Adventuring, a gay and lesbian outdoor club, has packed this Web page with details of its weekend outings. The group organizes activities in the Washington, D.C., area and posts an events schedule online.

### Chiltern Mountain Club

http://www.actwin.com/chiltern/index.html
With more than 1,200 members, the Chiltern Mountain Group organizes outdoor activities for New England—area gays and lesbians virtually every weekend. This page allows users to read about the hiking, skiing, and canoeing trips the group is currently offering. Don't feel left out if you don't live on the East Coast: The Chiltern Mountain Web page offers a search engine to help you find a club in your area.

### CyberQueer Lounge

http://www.cyberzine.org/html/GLAIDS/Sports/sportspage.html
The CyberQueer Lounge Sports and Square Dancing page offers links to dozens of lesbian and gay sports and dancing clubs.

### The Gay and Lesbian Travel Web

http://www.cts.com/~drcarr/gay_travel/
The Gay and Lesbian Travel Web page is still being developed but promises to deliver an important service in identifying homosexual travel tours, cruises, and accommodations.

### International Association of Gay Square Dance Clubs (IAGSDC)

e-mail: bobbers630@aol.com
http://molscat.giss.nasa.gov/IAGSDC/.html
The database contains contact information for some member and non-member clubs in the United States and Canada. The database also provides times and dates for association-wide conventions and related events, as well as a listing of other square dance resources available via the Internet. Main files include: IAGSDC Conventions and Related Events; Information about IAGSDC Clubs (including listings by state or province); and Other Square Dance Resources.

### International Gay & Lesbian Outdoors Organization (IGLOO)

http://www.access.digex.net/~erewhon/igloo.html
IGLOO is "the largest all-volunteer lesbigay outdoors network. Our membership is comprised of over 100 groups worldwide (and growing) which sponsor high adventure outdoor activities. Member groups swap newsletters and ideas and periodically join in combined adventure." IGLOO lists contact information for its member groups at its Web site.

### MiCasa SuCasa International Gay Home Exchange

http://www.well.com/user/homeswap
Wherever you travel, you have a friend. Members of this large international travel network open their homes to vacationing fellow members. Referrals and membership details are available online.

Within companies, geographical areas, and industries, gays, lesbians, bisexuals, transgendered people, and their allies are organizing to muster support for one another. From judges to postal employees to entertainers, from nurses to pilots to architects, LGBT professionals are using their talents to support one another and the community at large.

Some groups, like Across America Real Estate Network and North Carolina Gay and Lesbian Attorneys, support lesbian and gay professionals by providing referrals to interested parties. Connecticut's Robert Donnell Productions and New York's Stonewall Business Group have taken this idea a step further by creating regional and national business expositions to promote business activity within the lesbian and gay community.

Other groups, like Digital Queers, use their talents specifically to help the LGBT community. Digital Queers, a philanthropic group of computer professionals, supplies funding, time, and expertise to help LGBT organizations go online. The American Library Association (ALA) was the first professional organization to establish a gay and lesbian subgroup, the Gay and Lesbian Task Force, in 1970. ALA's Gay and Lesbian Task Force helps get more and better materials about gays into libraries and out to patrons, and also helps deal with discrimination against gay people in libraries. The Gay, Lesbian, and Straight Teachers Network, meanwhile, addresses issues of homophobia and heterosexism in public, private, and parochial schools throughout the United States. And the Gay Officers Action League; Gay, Lesbian, and Bisexual Veterans of Greater New York; and other such groups challenge homophobia and its repercussions in the police force and the military.

These groups and others within mainstream companies are having a positive effect. "Surprisingly," according to Melinda Paras, executive director of the National Gay and Lesbian Task Force (NGLTF), "some of the most dramatic changes are happening in the workplace." Paras was quoted in the April 22, 1996, issue of the *San Francisco Examiner,* which reported on the fifth annual Conference on Lesbian, Gay, and Bisexual Workplace Issues in San Francisco. Paras added: "The corporate boardroom is far outpacing the halls of government when it comes to recognition of gays." While states rush to introduce legislation banning non-discrimination policies that include homosexuals and denying the recognition of same-sex marriages, more than 400 corporations have adopted non-discrimination policies that do include gays and lesbians, and many have also extended health care and other benefits to domestic partners. Progress is underway, and groups like those in this chapter will ensure that the progress continues.

## AUSTRALIA

### Digital Queers—Australia

Web site: http://www.geko.com.au/digiqueers/

Digital Queers is a group of computer professionals who help LGBT groups go online by donating time, products, expertise, or funding. According to its Web site, DQ also "encourages its members to develop their careers through training and networking," "demystifies queers in the workplace by being out—and professional—role models," and "organises great parties and other social events to raise money to help the queer community."

## CANADA

### ONTARIO

### Gay and Lesbian Organization of Bell Enterprises (GLOBE)

552 Church St.
Toronto, ON M4Y 2E3

### Lambda Ottawa

PO Box 1445, Station B
Ottawa, ON K1P 5P6
phone: (613) 233-8212

### Toronto Women for Recreation and Business

552 Church St.
Toronto, ON M4Y 2E3
phone: (216) 925-9872

## UNITED STATES

### ALABAMA

### Alabama Gay and Lesbian Organization of Professionals

PO box 914
Huntsville, AL 35804
phone: (205) 517-6127

### CALIFORNIA

### Apple Lambda

Apple Computer, Inc.
20525 Mariani Ave.
Cupertino, CA 95014

Apple Lambda is Apple Computer's lesbian and gay employee support, education, and advocacy group.

### Bay Area Physicians for Human Rights (BAPHR)

4111 18th St.
San Francisco, CA 94114
phone: (415) 558-9353

The Bay Area Physicians for Human Rights are graduates of and students in approved schools of medicine and osteopathy, dentists, and podiatrists. The group's objectives are to improve the quality of medical care for gay and lesbian patients; to educate physicians, both gay and nongay, in the special problems of gay and lesbian patients; to educate the public about health care needs of the homosexual; to maintain liaison with public officials about gay and lesbian health concerns; and to offer the gay and lesbian physician support through social functions and consciousness-raising groups. The group, which was founded in 1977, sponsors research into medical problems and issues that are of special interest to homosexual patients; provides a medical and physician referral service and monthly educational programs; operates a speakers' bureau; and compiles statistics. Membership is concentrated in the San Francisco Bay Area. The bimonthly *BAPHRON* newsletter features medical-related human rights issues, especially gay and lesbian rights and public policy on AIDS. The group has also published a monograph called *Medical Evaluation of Persons at Risk of HIV Infection* and hosts an annual symposium.

### Digital Queers—Los Angeles

3175 S. Hoover St., Box 344
Los Angeles, CA 90007
e-mail: la@dq.org
Digital Queers is a group of computer professionals who help LGBT groups go online.

### Digital Queers—San Francisco

584 Castro St., Ste. 150
San Francisco, CA 94114
phone: (415) 252-6282
e-mail: DQSF-Info@queernet.org or Diqueers@aol.com
Digital Queers is a group of computer professionals who help LGBT groups go online.

### Employee Association of Gay & Lesbian Employees at MCA/Universal (EAGLE)

100 Universal Plaza Bldg.
Universal City, CA 91608

### Gay and Lesbian Medical Association

Benjamin Schatz, Executive Director
211 Church St., Ste. C
San Francisco, CA 94114
phone: (415) 255-4547
fax: (415) 255-4784
The Gay and Lesbian Medical Association includes physicians and medical students. Founded in 1981 and with 21 local branches, the association seeks to eliminate discrimination on the basis of sexual orientation in the health professions; promotes unprejudiced medical care for gay and lesbian patients; maintains a referral and support program for HIV infected physicians; sponsors an annual symposium on lesbian and gay health issues; offers support to homosexual physicians; encourages research into the health needs of gays and lesbians; maintains a liaison with medical schools and other organizations concerning needs of gay patients and professionals; fosters communication and cooperation among members and other groups and individuals supportive of gay and lesbian physicians; and offers a referral service. Formerly known as the American Association of Physicians for Human Rights, the Gay and Lesbian Medical Association bestows annual achievement and recognition awards and publishes a quarterly newsletter that covers the activities of the association, the medical community, and the public regarding lesbian and gay health issues.

*Piles of signs at the 1993 March on Washington support open gay and lesbian service in the U.S. military. (Photo by Pam Mc Intosh.)*

### Gay and Lesbian Postal Employees Network (GLPEN)

Jeff Perez

## SPOTLIGHT
# CREATING CHANGE at WORK

Historically, work has been the last place queers have come out. Fear of coming out at work, possibly resulting in harassment or even losing one's job, has reinforced the decision to stay in the closet. As a last frontier of coming out, workplace organizing will be one of the main areas of activity for the queer community in the coming years, according to speakers at the Creating Change conference held November 10–12, 1995, in Detroit, Michigan. The conference, sponsored by the National Gay and Lesbian Task Force (NGLTF), offered sessions on workplace topics including organizing employee groups, working with organized labor, equal employment opportunity,

PO Box 282982
San Francisco, CA 94128-2982
phone: (415) 873-4308
GLPEN promotes educational and social interaction among gay and lesbian employees of the U.S. Postal Service.

### Hollywood Supports

Richard Jennings, Executive Director
8455 Beverly Blvd., Ste. 305
Los Angeles, CA 90048
phone: (213) 655-7705
fax: (213) 655-0955
e-mail: HSupports@aol.com
Web site: http://www.hsupports.org/hsupports/hs_home.html
"Hollywood Supports was launched in the fall of 1991 by leading entertainment industry figures to counter workplace fear and discrimination based on HIV status and sexual orientation." Hollywood Supports sponsors the "Day of Compassion," an annual (June 21st) television event in which cable networks, national talk shows, and daytime soap operas feature programming and public service announcements "aimed at increasing AIDS awareness and modeling compassion for people affected by HIV and AIDS." The group's model policy for extending group health care benefits to employees' same-sex partners has been adopted by MCA/Universal, Viacom Inc., HBO, Warner Bros., Time Inc., Sony Pictures, Paramount Pictures, CAA, William Morris, the Writers Guild's Industry Health Fund, Ticket Master, Lucas Films, E! Entertainment, and Capital Cities/ABC. Hollywood Supports also offers seminars on "AIDS in the Workplace" and "Sexual Orientation in the Workplace," a "Guide to Starting an Employee Support Group Organizing Around Gay & Lesbian Workplace Issues," and other support and educational programs for people in the entertainment industry.

### International Association of Lesbian and Gay Judges

c/o Stephen M. Lachs
5683 Holly Oak Dr.
Los Angeles, CA 90068-2521

### International Association of Lesbian and Gay Pride Coordinators (IAL/GPC)

M. Levine
PO Box 584
San Francisco, CA 94114
e-mail: ialgpc@tde.com
Web site: http://www.tde.com/~ialgpc

domestic partner benefits, and socially responsible investing. Strategies for furthering queer issues in the workplace include educating employees and management, organizing shareholder influence, and mobilizing consumers.

Sean O'Brien Stub, the New York author of *Cracking the Corporate Closet,* moderated a workshop in which activists shared their ideas and experiences. Scott Fearing, of the Gay and Lesbian Community Action Council in Minneapolis, talked of the importance of finding a corporate "angel," a high-ranking executive who will advocate on behalf of queer employees, whether or not they are unionized. Martha Grevatt, a union activist from Cleveland, said the ideal situation would be "pressure from above and below" to achieve improvements in the work environment.

Working with employees and management brings pressure to change from within an organization. Other participants discussed ways to bring outside

IAL/GPC is a "nonprofit organization made up of many cities producing Gay and Lesbian Pride events worldwide." The group was founded in 1981 in Boston, Massachusetts, and holds a yearly conference in October. IAL/GPC publishes the *Global Pride Calendar* listing pride events around the world.

### Lesbian and Gay Caucus of Public Health Workers (LGCPHW)

Donald Gabard, Ph.D.
2341 Hidalgo Ave.
Los Angeles, CA 90039
phone: (213) 664-9002
LGCPHW is a caucus of the American Public Health Association and represents public health workers in the fields of administration, government, direct care, and teaching. The caucus, founded in 1975, promotes the dissemination of information on the health needs of lesbians, gay men, and bisexuals, and serves as a support network for gay public health workers. The caucus believes homophobia interferes with the proper delivery of health care to gays, lesbians, and bisexuals and restricts or eliminates their contributions as health workers, and causes physical and mental health problems. The group holds scientific sessions on gay and lesbian health issues at its annual meeting, held in conjunction with APHA and the National Gay Health Coalition.

### National Organization of Gay & Lesbian Scientists and Technicians

PO Box 91803
Pasadena, CA 91109
phone: (818) 791-7689

### United Airlines Gay & Lesbian United Employees (GLUE)

108 Delores St.
San Francisco, CA 94103

### *Victory*

2312 N St.
Sacramento, CA 95816
phone: (916) 444-6894
Magazine for lesbian and gay entrepreneurs.

### Walt Disney Lesbian and Gay United Employees (LEAGUE)

Garrett Hicks, Contact
500 S. Buena Vista St.
Burbank, CA 91521
phone: (818) 544-3363

pressure to bear. Shelley Alpern of Franklin Research and Development Corporation and the Wall Street Project, which coordinates efforts by socially conscious investors to influence target companies, discussed several methods. Shareholder lobbying and initiatives have called attention to anti-queer policies at companies such as Cracker Barrel. Also, consumer actions, from letter-writing campaigns to boycotts, were presented as useful.

Participants discussed positive versus negative approaches to influencing decision makers. Gary Hickox, a corporate executive from Bridgewater, New Jersey, said working with issues of economics rather than principle will be most effective. "Where we hit people is in their pocketbook," Hickox said.

Negative strategies such as consumer boycotts can hurt a company, but also hurt a company's queer employees. Positive strategies allow employees to remain loyal while working to convince the company that supporting queer

## COLORADO

### The Colorado Business Council

PO Box 57555
Denver, CO 80248-0794
phone: (303) 595-8042

### Coors Lesbian and Gay Employee Resource (LAGER)

PO Box 643
Golden, CO 80403

### Lesbian, Bisexual, and Gay United Employees at AT&T (LEAGUE)

Margaret Burd, Co-Chair
11900 N. Pecos St., No. 30H-078
Denver, CO 80234-2703
phone: (303) 538-4430
fax: (303) 538-3564
LEAGUE includes individuals employed at or retired from AT&T or any of its subsidiaries. Established in 1987, the group fosters the value of mutual respect and appreciation of cultural differences among employees; offers educational programs and support groups to address issues that affect lesbian, gay, and bisexual employees, and their friends and families; acts as an information clearinghouse on homosexuality, bisexuality, and lesbian and gay issues; and provides referral services to support groups and community and service organizations. LEAGUE's Professional Development Conference occurs annually.

## CONNECTICUT

### National Gay & Lesbian Business and Consumer Expos

Robert Donnell Productions
30 Tower Ln.
Avon, CT 06001
phone: (800) 243-9774 or (860) 677-0094
fax: (860) 677-6869
e-mail: rdpsteven@aol.com
Web site: http://www.gaysource.com/expo/index.html
When Robert Donnell Productions, a company that produces 20 trade shows a year, joined forces with Steven Levenberg, director of New York's Stonewall Business Group, Inc., the two organized regional and national expositions to promote business activity within the gay and lesbian community.

## DISTRICT OF COLUMBIA

### National Gay Pilots Association

PO Box 27542
Washington, DC 20038-7542

employees is best for the bottom line, whether in recruiting the best employees to selling to the queer market. Steven Horn, manager of community and governmental programs for IBM in Southfield, Michigan, reminded participants that there are many issues companies must consider in deciding policies. "This is only one thing; there's a lot of other [stuff] out there," Horn said. Horn suggested that advocates will be most successful if they keep in mind the full range of concerns companies must consider when trying to change policies.

The goals of these various strategies may vary by workplace and change over time. Alice McKeage, one of the founders of Ford GLOBE (Gay, Lesbian or Bisexual Employees) in Dearborn, shared in another workshop that although the organization has not yet reached its current goal of getting Ford Motor Corporation to add sexual orientation to its equal opportunity policy, it has

The National Gay Pilots Association includes gay and lesbian pilots and non-pilots interested in aviation.

### National Lesbian and Gay Health Association (NLGHA)

1407 S St. NW
Washington, DC 20009
phone: (202) 939-7880
fax: (202) 234-1467
NLGHA offers a "single, comprehensive resource for physical and mental health-related issues, advocacy, education, technical assistance, and research, as well as a powerful voice for educating public health officials and leaders of the importance of lesbian and gay health." NLGHA was formed in 1994 by a merger between the National Lesbian and Gay Health Foundation (which was founded in 1980, developed a network of more than 20,000 health educators and health care providers, and helped establish the National Association of People With AIDS, the National Association of Lesbian and Gay Alcoholism Professionals, and other groups), and the National Alliance of Lesbian and Gay Health Clinics (founded in 1992 by 11 lesbian and gay health centers or clinics). NLGHA hosts an annual Lesbian and Gay Health Conference and AIDS/HIV Forum that includes symposia, workshops, networking sessions, community forums, and other programs.

### National Lesbian and Gay Journalists Association

Roy Aarons, President
1718 M St. NW, #245
Washington, DC 20036
phone: (202) 588-9888
The National Lesbian and Gay Journalists Association, which has 16 local chapters, serves as a support group for gays and lesbians in the media industry. Recently relocated from California to Washington, DC, the group seeks to encourage fair coverage of gay issues, conducts workshops and seminars, and bestows the annual Award for Journalistic Excellence. The *Alternatives* newsletter appears quarterly.

### United States Federal Employees: Gay, Lesbian, or Bisexual Employees (GLOBE)

PO Box 45237
Washington, DC 20026-5237
phone: (202) 986-1101

## FLORIDA

### Digital Queers—Florida

Richard Sullivan

made great strides in educating employees and management, and has helped create a more safe and supportive environment for queer Ford employees. McKeage believes that Ford GLOBE has achieved a high level of success in its first 18 months by starting small and working toward progressively higher goals.

Sue Spielman and Liz Winfeld of Natick, Massachusetts, the authors of *Straight Talk about Gays in the Workplace,* gave a workshop on domestic partner benefits, another common goal. Spielman and Winfeld believe economic arguments favor implementation of equal benefits. Winfeld cited a U.S. Department of Commerce study that estimated the cost of replacing an employee is five times greater than the cost of changes to retain an employee. Winfeld and Spielman's own studies show adding coverage for domestic partners raises the overall cost of benefits by less than one percent.

*By Lee Gasaway. First printed in* Between the Lines, *December, 1995. Reprinted with permission.*

PO Box 173131
Tampa, FL 33672
phone: (813) 833-2507
e-mail: Digi Q FL@aol.com
Digital Queers is a group of computer professionals who help LGBT groups go online.

### Tampa Bay Business Guild

Jim Scarborough, Secretary/Treasurer
1222 S. Dale Mabry, Ste. 656
Tampa, FL 33629-5009
phone: (813) 237-3751
Founded in 1982, the Tampa Bay Business Guild includes business owners, consumers, and professionals united to improve business and cultural opportunities in the gay and lesbian community. The guild conducts fundraisers benefitting support groups for people with AIDS, publishes an annual directory and a monthly newsletter, and meets the first Tuesday of the month.

## GEORGIA

### Digital Queers—Atlanta

PO Box 7806
Atlanta, GA 30357-1806
e-mail: DQAtlanta@aol.com
Web site: http://www.casti.com/dq/html/chapters/dqat.html
Digital Queers is a group of computer professionals who help LGBT groups go online.

## ILLINOIS

### Gay, Lesbian, and Bisexual Employees of Ameritech (GLEAM)

PO Box 14308
Chicago, IL 60614

### Gay & Lesbian Building and Trade Professionals Directory (GLBTP)

Stuart Keeshin, SUBA Internet Center
Chicago, IL
phone: (312) 494-2646
e-mail: keeshin@suba.com
Web site: http://www.suba.com/~glbtp/
GLBTP is an informal network for community referrals in the Chicago area for openly gay and lesbian professionals in the building industry, including architects, carpenters, computer applications specialists, electricians, furniture manufacturers and vendors, home inspectors, interior and exte-

rior designers, kitchen and bath designers, millwork, painters, plumbers, real estate workers, insurance and legal services, telephone and security systems, zoning and land use experts, and other building and trade specialists.

### Gay and Lesbian Task Force/American Library Association (GLTF/ALA)

Roland C. Hansen, Co-Chair
Social Responsibilities Round Table
Office of Library Outreach Services
50 E. Huron
Chicago, IL 60611
phone: (312) 280-4294 or (800) 545-2433
fax: (312) 280-3256
The American Library Association (ALA) was the first professional organization to establish a gay and lesbian subgroup, back in 1970. The Gay and Lesbian Task Force is a division of the ALA's Social Responsibilities Round Table. The group's purposes are to help get more and better materials concerning gays into libraries and out to patrons and to deal with discrimination against gay people in libraries. The task force, which has also been known as the Task Force on Gay Liberation and the Gay Task Force of ALA, maintains an information clearinghouse and bestows the annual Gay/Lesbian/Bisexual Book Award—the longest standing award of its kind—to honor books relating to the gay experience. The *GLTF Newsletter* appears quarterly.

### Out at Work (or Not)

Jason Cohen, Contact
PO Box 359
Chicago, IL 60690-0359
(312) 794-5218
This association of Chicago-area companies and organizations publishes a newsletter and resource directory.

## MASSACHUSETTS

### Provincetown Business Guild

PO Box 421
Provincetown, MA 02657
phone: (508) 487-2313

## MICHIGAN

### Detroit Bar Guild

PO Box 20595
Ferndale, MI 48220
Organization of Detroit area gay/lesbian bars.

### Ford GLOBE

Alice McKeage, Cofounder
Dearborn, MI
Founded in 1994, Ford GLOBE is the group for Gay, Lesbian, or Bisexual Employees of Ford Motor Company.

### Gay/Lesbian Educators Association of Michigan (GLEAM)

PO Box 271
Royal Oak, MI 48068
phone: (810) 755-7445

### Motor City Business Forum

29209 Northwestern Hwy., #609
Southfield, MI 48034
phone: (810) 546-9347
Professional and social organization for lesbians and gay men.

### National Lesbian and Gay Journalists Association—Detroit

phone: (313) 998-0752
Member chapter of the National Lesbian and Gay Journalists Association, located in Washington, DC.

### Our Little Group

Ann Arbor, MI
phone: (313) 662-8941
Professional men's group.

## NEVADA

### Lambda Business Association of Las Vegas

1350 E. Flamingo Rd., Ste. 370
Las Vegas, NV 89119
phone: (702) 593-2875

## NEW YORK

### Center for Lesbian and Gay Studies (CLAGS)

Martin Duberman, Executive Officer
CUNY Graduate Center
33 W. 42 St.
New York, NY 10036
phone: (212) 642-2924
fax: (212) 642-2642
Founded in 1986, CLAGS promotes gay/lesbian studies at the university level. CLAGS encourages the development of scholarship, courses, and degree programs in gay/lesbian studies; works to recognize the contributions of lesbians and gay men in the arts and sciences; and maintains a speakers' bureau and lesbian/gay collection at The Mina Rees Library of The Graduate School, City University of New York. CLAGS also sponsors awards, including the annual Constance Jordan Award, the CUNY Student Papers Awards, the Ken Dawson Award for persons in the field of lesbian/gay studies, the Open Meadows Foundation Award, and the annual Rockefeller Residency Fellowship in the Humanities for research in gay and lesbian studies.

### Gay, Lesbian, and Bisexual Veterans of Greater New York (GLBVGNY)

German Lopez
346 Broadway, Ste. 811
New York, NY 10013
phone: (212) 368-5072
GLBVGNY was founded in 1984 for gays and lesbians who have served in the U.S. Armed Forces. Formerly known as the Gay Veterans Association, the group advocates and works to secure equal rights and privileges for all veterans regardless of sexual orientation; aims to ensure that all veterans may participate in any and all veterans' activities; serves as a forum to aid, support, and bring together gay veterans; seeks cooperation with other gay and veterans' organizations in an effort to broaden their constituency; offers services to gay veterans, including counseling and psychotherapy, programs aiding homeless veterans, and monitoring AIDS patients in Veterans' Administration hospitals; and monitors and attempts to influence legislation affecting gay and lesbian veterans and active military personnel. The monthly newsletter *On Alert* includes a calendar of events. The group meets the third Monday of each month.

### Gay, Lesbian & Straight Teachers Network (GLSTN)

122 W. 26th St., Ste. 1100
New York, NY 10001
phone: (212) 727-0135
e-mail: glstn@glstn.org
Web site: http://www.glstn.org/freedom/
GLSTN is "a national federation of local groups working to address issues of homophobia and heterosexism in K–12 public, private, and parochial school." The group's goal is "to create a school environment in which every member of the school community is valued and respected, regardless of sexual orientation." GLSTN was founded in 1990 by teachers in the Boston, Massachusetts, area, and has more than 20 local chapters throughout the United States. The group was instrumental in leading Massachusetts to become the first state to ban discrimination on the basis of sexual orientation in its public schools.

### Gay Officers Action League (GOAL)

Jeffrey Jackson
PO Box 2038, Canal St. Sta.
New York, NY 10013
phone: (212) 996-8808
e-mail: goalgaz@aol.com
GOAL is a professional and fraternal organization of gay or lesbian active and former employees of the police department and criminal justice system in New York City. The group, which was founded in 1982 and meets the second Tuesday of the month, bestows awards, maintains a speakers' bureau, and publishes the *GOAL Gazette*.

### Gay Pilots Association—New York

Dennis or Jerry, Contacts
c/o Lesbian and Gay Community Services Center
208 W. 13th St.
New York, NY 10011
phone: (718) 459-6168

The Gay Pilots Association includes gay and lesbian pilots and non-pilots interested in aviation.

### Lavender Lamps: National Lesbian and Gay Nurses Association

c/o Lesbian and Gay Community Services Center
208 W. 13th St.
New York, NY 10011
phone: (718) 933-1158 or (212) 355-7178
Lavender Lamps offers education, outreach, and support.

### Lesbian and Gay Labor Network of New York

PO Box 1159, Peter Stuyvesant Sta.
New York, NY 10009
Works for lesbian and gay rights in unions.

### Lesbian and Gay Law Association of Greater New York (LeGaL)

799 Broadway, Ste. 340
New York, NY 10003
phone: (212) 353-9118
fax: (212) 353-2970
e-mail: le-gal@interport.net
Web site: http://www.interport.net/~le-gal
LeGaL's mission is "to promote the expertise and advancement of lesbian and gay legal professionals."

### Lesbian & Gay Teachers Association

c/o Lesbian and Gay Community Services Center
208 W. 13th St.
New York, NY 10011
phone: (718) 596-1864

### New York CyberQueers

c/o Lesbian and Gay Community Services Center
208 W. 13th St.
New York, NY 10011
e-mail: nycq@aol.com or nycq@nycnet.com
New York CyberQueers includes lesbian, gay, bisexual, and transgender computer professionals.

### New York Network of Business and Professional Organizations

332 Bleeker St., #G32
New York, NY 10014
phone: (212) 517-0771
The New York Network provides networking and mutual support opportunities for lesbian and gay businesses and professionals in the New York area.

### New York Stonewall Business Group

Steven Levenberg, Director
PO Box 613, FDR Sta.
New York, NY 10012
phone: (212) 629-1764

### Organization of Lesbian and Gay Architects and Designers

c/o Gary Rosard
185 W Houston St., Apt. 5H
New York, NY 10014-4825
phone: (212) 475-7652
The Organization of Lesbian and Gay Architects and Designers includes professionals and students of all design disciplines.

### Outmusic

c/o Lesbian and Gay Community Services Center
208 W. 13th St.
New York, NY 10011
phone: (212) 330-9197
Outmusic is an organization of lesbian and gay musicians, composers, and lyricists.

### Psychologists for Human Dignity (PHD)

c/o Lesbian and Gay Community Services Center
208 W. 13th St.
New York, NY 10011
phone: (212) 505-8024

### Publishing Triangle

PO Box 114, Prince St. Sta.
New York, NY 10012
phone: (212) 572-6142

### Stonewall Business Association (SBA)

c/o Lesbian and Gay Community Services Center
208 W. 13th St.

New York, NY 10011
phone: (212) 629-1764

### Women Playwrights Collective

c/o Lesbian and Gay Community Services Center
208 W. 13th St.
New York, NY 10011
phone: (212) 885-1119

### *Working It Out*

PO Box 2079
New York, NY 10108
phone: (212) 769-2384
fax: (212) 721-2680
Newsletter about gay and lesbian employment issues.

## NORTH CAROLINA

### Across America Real Estate Network

Mark Kasper, Owner/Broker
908 Elizabeth Dr.
Yaupon Beach, NC 28465
phone: (800) 449-7350
fax: (910) 278-4119
e-mail: aaren@wilmington.net
Web site: http://www.wilmington.net/businesses/rs/aaren/
Across America is a nation-wide relocation referral source for relocating lesbians and gay men. Across America matches home buyers with sellers at no cost to its clients.

### North Carolina Gay and Lesbian Attorneys (GALA)

PO Box 2164
Durham, NC 27702
e-mail: ncgala@aol.com
Web site: http://users.aol.com/ncgala/index.htm
NC-GALA, formed in 1994, is a voluntary, nonprofit professional organization for lesbian, gay, and bisexual attorneys in North Carolina. The group, which is open to licensed attorneys, law students, and non-lawyers, provides visibility, advocacy, and referrals for the lesbian, gay, and bisexual communities.

## PENNSYLVANIA

### Gay & Lesbian Organizations Bridging Across the Land (GLOBAL)

PO Box 42406
Philadelphia, PA 19101-2406
GLOBAL includes individual and group members throughout the United States.

### Lesbian, Bisexual and Gay United Employees at AT&T (LEAGUE)

c/o Donald C. Dennis
4979 Lanark Rd.
Center Valley, PA 18034-9529

## TEXAS

### Federal Gay, Lesbian, and Bisexual Employees of Texas

c/o Robert Lemond
PO Box 50961
Dallas, TX 75250-0961

### Stonewall Business Society—Austin

PO Box 49976
Austin, TX 78765
phone: (512) 707-3794

### Stonewall Business Society—Dallas

PO Box 191343
Dallas, TX 75219
phone: (214) 526-6216

## VIRGINIA

### Lesbian, Gay and Bisexual People in Medicine (LGBPM)

c/o American Medical Student Association
1902 Association Dr.
Reston, VA 22091
phone: (703) 620-6600
fax: (703) 620-5873
LGBPM is a standing committee of the American Medical Student Association that includes physicians, physicians in training, and others who are interested in gay/lesbian issues. The committee was founded in 1976 to improve the quality of health care

for gay patients, and to improve working conditions and professional status of gay health professionals and students. The group, which has 35 local chapters, administers educational workshops for health professionals; designs training materials; conducts research on the health problems of gay people and surveys on admissions, hiring, and promotion policies of medical schools and hospitals; provides referrals; sponsors support groups for gay professionals to meet, socialize, and organize; presses for legislative and political action to end discrimination against gay people; and maintains a speakers' bureau.

## WASHINGTON

### Digital Queers—Northwest

1202 E. Pike St., Ste. 972
Seattle, WA 98122-3934
phone: (206) 860-6900
e-mail: dqnw@aol.com
Web site: http://www.eor.com/dqnw/
Digital Queers is a group of computer professionals who help LGBT groups go online.

### Gay, Lesbian & Bisexual Employees at Microsoft (GLEAM)

Microsoft Corp.
1 Microsoft Way, Bldg. 1-1
Redmond, WA 98052-6399

### Greater Seattle Business Association (GSBA)

Jeff Calley, President
2033 6th Ave., Suite 804
Seattle, WA 98121
phone: (206) 443-4722
fax: (206) 441-8262
The Greater Seattle Business Association, founded in 1981, acts as a clearinghouse for the exchange of ideas and networking for the purpose of strengthening and supporting our businesses and to create a strong voice in the lesbian/gay community and the community at large. The association's annual business directory lists business and non-profit organizations that are owned or served by the gay/lesbian or gay-friendly population. The group also publishes a monthly newsletter and meets the second Wednesday of the month.

### Northwest Gay & Lesbian Employee Network

830 19th Ave.
Seattle, WA 98122

### *Women's Work*

602 Avenue A
Snohomish, WA 98290
phone: (206) 568-5914

# ONLINE RESOURCES

## THE WEB

### Digital Queers

http://www.dq.org/dq
Digital Queers is a philanthropic group of computer professionals who raise money to equip gay, lesbian, bisexual, and transgender organizations with hardware and software. Their fundraising efforts have enabled many groups, including the NGLTF and GLAAD, to go online. This Web page offers information about how other organizations may donate to, or benefit from, Digital Queers projects.

### Gay Workplace Issues Homepage

http://www.nyu.edu/pages/sls/gaywk/gay-wkpl.html
This site, which offers samples from Annette Friskopp and Sharon Silverstein's book *Straight Jobs, Gay Lives,* about lesbian and gay workplace issues, provides a directory of professional associations, employee groups, and other organizations throughout the United States and Canada, along with other information of interest to lesbian, gay, and bisexual professionals.

### Veterans for Human Rights

http://nehalem.rain.com/VFHR/
With a mission to end discrimination against openly homosexual Americans, Veterans for Human Rights focuses mainly on gays in the military. The Web page issues a call to action against anti-gay/lesbian legislation and asks volunteers to join the fight.

## USENET

### Lesac-Net

mailing list: majordomo@queernet.org

The Lesac-Net mailing list gives lesbian and bisexual women in academia the opportunity to network and share resources. To subscribe, send an e-mail message to the address above. In the body of your message, type only *subscribe Lesac-net.*

Adolescence—growing up, making friends, falling in love, disagreeing with your parents, finding someone to sit with in the cafeteria, wearing the right clothes, finding an after-school job, learning to drive a car—is tough enough.

Now consider these facts:

30% of all adolescents who complete suicide—more than 5,000 annually in the United States—do so because they are gay or lesbian, or think they may be. That's more than 1,500 deaths each year, at least four kids each day, from self-hatred, isolation, fear, and despair brought on by external and internal homophobia.

Lesbian and gay youths are two to three times more likely than their heterosexual peers to attempt suicide. A 1991 study of young gay and bisexual men showed that 30% had attempted suicide once, and 13% reported multiple attempts. A 1981 study reported that 53% of transsexual youths had attempted suicide.

80% percent of lesbian and gay youth report serious isolation.

60% of adolescent HIV/AIDS cases are among gay, lesbian, and bisexual youth.

50% of gay and lesbian youth are rejected by their parents because of their sexual orientation.

Nearly 50% of all homeless youth are lesbian, gay, bisexual, or transgendered.

40% of LGBT youth have been assaulted by peers or family members.

25% drop out of school.

Sexual minority youth are much more likely than their heterosexual peers to retreat into substance abuse, increased sexual activity, pregnancy, truancy, running away, and suicide.

And it's not because they're sinful, crazy, perverted, or sick. They're not. It's because they're alone, confused, scared, often abused, and afraid to speak to parents, teachers, counselors, religious leaders, siblings, friends—in short, anyone—for fear of absolute rejection.

Lesbian, gay, bisexual, transgendered, and questioning young people have learned to hide their thoughts—to keep silent—because they've observed that most people do not discuss homosexuality at all. Those who do mention homosexuality do so, too often, to condemn it—and the gay men and lesbians themselves—as sinful, perverted, or disgusting.

Silence, especially in the face of such vehement and often violent hatred, will help no one, least of all a young lesbian, gay, bisexual, or transgendered person who is certain that she or he is alone in the world. Thankfully, hundreds of youth support organizations—unheard of only 15 years ago—now exist to help young lesbians and gays and to educate others about their concerns.

Literature from the Hetrick-Martin Institute, the oldest and largest organization helping lesbian, gay, and bisexual youth, elegantly expresses its call to help these young people: "Lesbian, gay, and bisexual youth need to know that they are not alone. They are in our families, schools, social service agencies, and churches and synagogues. They are our sons and daughters, nieces and nephews, students, clients, and neighbors.

"To reach out to these young people, we need to break the silence about their existence. All young people need to know that some people fall in love with members of the same sex. No young person should be made to feel bad or ashamed for having these feelings."

Since 1979, the Hetrick-Martin Institute has been helping young people and their families through numerous support, counseling, and educational programs. In this chapter you'll read about the institute and its life-saving works. You'll also learn about the Bridges Project of the American Friends Service Committee, a vast network of resources and information for LGBT youth and the educators, human service providers, religious people, parents, and others who work with sexual minority youth. A smaller, local youth support group, Windfire, is described here as well.

Right up front, here are some national, toll-free hotlines to remember:

1-800-347-TEEN is the Indianapolis Youth Group hotline, operating from 7 p.m. to 10 p.m. Monday through Thursday, and from 7 p.m. to midnight Friday through Sunday.

1-800-96-YOUTH is the OutYouth Austin hotline, operating from 5:30 p.m. to 9:30 p.m. every day.

1-800-621-4000 and 1-800-621-0394 (for hearing impaired) are the National Runaway Switchboard hotlines, operating 24 hours each day.

1-800-342-AIDS (English language), 1-800-344-SIDA (Spanish language), and 1-800-243-7889 (for hearing impaired) are the National AIDS Hotline numbers, run by the Centers for Disease Control in Atlanta, Georgia.

# CANADA

## BRITISH COLUMBIA

### Vancouver Gay & Lesbian Center
1170 Bute St.
Vancouver, BC V6E1Z6
phone: (604) 684-6869

## ONTARIO

### AIDS Committee of London
343 Richmond Street, Suite 200
London, ON N6A 3C2
phone: (519) 434-1601

### Coaliton for Bisexual, Lesbian and Gay Youth in Peel
Peel Health Department
3038 Hurontario Street, 3rd Floor
Mississauga, ON L5B 3B9
phone: (905) 791-7800

### Kensington Youth Theater and Employment Skills
457 Richmond St. W., Basement
Toronto, ON M51X9
phone: (416) 504-6070

### LesBi Youth Peer Support (LYPS)
519 Church Street
Toronto, ON M4Y 2C9
phone: (416) 925-9872

### Lesbian, Gay, Bisexual Youth Line
PO Box 62, Station F
Toronto, ON M4Y 2L4
phone: (416) 962-YOUTH

### Lesbian, Gay & Bisexual Youth Program
Central Toronto Youth Services
65 Wellesley Street East, Suite 300
Toronto, ON M4Y 1G7
phone: (416) 924-2100

### Lesbian, Gay and Bisexual Youth of Toronto
519 Church Street
Toronto, ON M4Y 2C9
phone: (416) 971-LGYT

*An attendee of the April 1993 Youth Empowerment Speakout, sponsored in part by the Bridges Project of AFSC, joins more than 1,500 members of the Youth Contingent at that year's March on Washington. (Photo courtesy Bridges Project of AFSC.)*

### Lesbian & Gay Ottawa—Hull
Box 2919, Station D
Ottawa, ON KIP 5W9
phone: (613) 238-1717

### Lesbian & Gay Students of the Toronto Board of Education
Toronto Board of Education
Human Sexuality Program
155 College Street
Toronto, ON M5T 1P6
phone: (416) 397-3755

### Lesbian & Gay Youth—Kingston
PO Box 120
Kingston, ON K7L46
phone: (613) 545-2960

### Mississauga Lesbian, Gay, Bisexual Peer Student Support Group
Peel Health Department
3038 Hurontario Street, 3rd Floor

## SPOTLIGHT
## BRIDGES PROJECT of AFSC

AFSC, the American Friends Service Committee, is an independent Quaker organization that was founded in 1917 to build "a just and peaceful world." Since the mid-1970s AFSC has worked to end discrimination against gay men and lesbians, and in the mid-1980s the group began to address some of the specific issues faced by gay and lesbian youth. After releasing the first resource guide written for people working with these youth, *Bridges of Respect: Creating Support for Lesbian and Gay Youth,* in 1989, the overwhelming response to this much-needed information prompted AFSC to create the Bridges Project.

Mississauga, ON L5B 3B9
phone: (416) 925-9872

**One in Ten**
2090 Wyandotte St. E
Windsor, ON N8Y 4R8
phone: (519) 973-0222

**Peel Bisexual, Gay and Lesbian Youth Drop-in**
Emerald Building
10 Kingsbridge Garden Circle
Mississauga, ON
phone: (416) 925-9872

**Pink Triangle Youth**
Pink Triangle Services
PO Box 3043, Station D
Ottawa, ON K1P 6H6
phone: (613) 828-4759

## NETHERLANDS

**International Gay & Lesbian Youth Organization**
PO Box 542
NL-100 AM Amsterdam
Specifically for people 26 and under, the organization offers an international pen pal program.

## UNITED STATES

### ARIZONA

**HIV/AIDS Prevention Program**
1825 E. Roosevelt
Phoenix, AZ 85006
phone: (602) 506-6853

**Phoenix Gay and Lesbian Youth Group**
PO Box 80174
Phoenix, AZ 85060
phone: (602) 280-9927

**Valley Youth Group/Community AIDS Council**
3136 N. 3rd Avenue
Phoenix, AZ 85013
phone: (602) 264-5437

**Wingspan Youth Group**
Lesbian, Gay, Bi Community Center
422 N. 4th Ave.
Tucson, AZ 85705
phone: (602) 624-1779

### CALIFORNIA

**AIDS Foundation San Diego**
4080 Centre Street

The Bridges Project, based in Philadelphia, Pennsylvania, is a nationwide network of programs and organizations that support LGBT youth. The project's main goals are to help community workers, educators, health and human service providers, parents, religious leaders, and organizations and programs that work with sexual minority youth, and to encourage all other youth-serving organizations to respond to the needs of LGBT youth. To accomplish these goals, the Bridges Project has established a national Advisory Committee and a national database of resources and organizations, along with two publications, to offer useful, up-to-date information on LGBT youth issues.

The resource guide, *Bridges of Respect,* is now available in Spanish and as an audio recording. Written specifically for those seeking to support lesbian and gay youth, the guide presents a powerful analysis of the effects of

San Diego, CA 92103
phone: (619) 686-5024

**Bill Wilson Center**
3490 The Alameda
Santa Clara, CA 95050
phone: (408) 243-0222

**Billy DeFrank Lesbian & Gay Community Center**
175 Stockton Avenue
San Jose, CA 95126-2760
phone: (408) 293-2429

**Central City Hospitality House Youth Program**
288 Turk Street
San Francisco, CA 94102
phone: (415) 776-2102

**Children of Lesbians and Gays Everywhere (COLAGE)**
2300 Market Street, Suite 165
San Francisco, CA 94114
phone: (415) 861-KIDS

**Contra Costa Youth Group**
Pacific Center for Human Growth
1250 Pine Street, Suite 301
Walnut Creek, CA
phone: (510) 939-7711

**Diamond Street Youth Shelter**
536 Central Ave.
San Francisco, CA 94117
phone: (415) 567-1020

**Gay and Lesbian Adolescent Social Services (GLASS)**
650 N. Robertson Blvd.
Suite A
West Hollywood, CA 90096
phone: (310) 358-8727

**Gay Youth Alliance/San Diego**
Phill Rector, Ph.D., Senior Advisor
PO Box 83022
San Diego, CA 92138-3022
phone: (619) 233-9309
The Gay Youth Alliance serves gay, lesbian, and bisexual youths aged 24 and under in San Diego County, California. Founded in 1983, the alliance seeks to provide a safe, supportive, friendly, and nurturing environment for members to discuss important issues and socialize. The 70-member group, which meets at 3916 Normal Street in San Diego, also maintains a speakers bureau to educate teachers, parents, and counselors about the special needs and concerns of its members. Its newsletter, *I AM R U,* appears quarterly.

homophobia on young people, and offers creative ideas and approaches to effecting change.

The group's quarterly newsletter, *Crossroads,* provides practical information on national and local events and resources. Each topic-specific issue includes articles from around the country written both by youth and by those working with youth.

In addition, the Bridges Project helps support national youth projects by working with young people and youth-serving organizations across the United States. One such endeavor was the Youth Empowerment Speakout, YES, which attracted almost 600 young people on April 24, 1993. During the

**Gay Youth Community Coalition**
PO Box 846
San Francisco, CA 94101-0846

**G/L Resource Center**
126 E. Haley St., Ste. A-17
Santa Barbara, CA 93101
phone: (805) 963-3636

***insideOUT: The Essential Queer Youth Magazine***
PO Box 460268
San Francisco, CA 94146-0268
e-mail: InsideOUT@aol.com
Web site: http://www.youth.org/io
Includes photos, articles, letters, articles from youth nationwide.

**Lambda Youth Network**
PO Box 7911
Culver City, CA 90233
This is one of the largest pen-pal programs available, with thousands of youth participants nationwide.

**Larkin Street Youth Center**
1044 Larkin Street
San Francisco, CA 94109
phone: (800) 669-6196

**Lavender Youth Recreation & Information Center (LYRIC)**
123 Collingwood St.
San Francisco, CA 94114
phone: (415) (703) 6150

**Lesbian, Gay, Bisexual & Transgendered Community Center**
PO Box 8280
Santa Cruz, CA 95061-8280
phone: (408) 425-LGBC

**Lesbian and Gay Men's Center**
PO Box 3357
San Diego, CA 92163
phone: (619) 692-2077

**Lyric Youth Talk Line and Info Line**
phone: (415) 863-3636 or (800) 246-7743
San Francisco, CA
The Talk Line is a way for young people, 23 and under, to learn about homosexuality, bisexuality, or gender identity, or to talk with other young people who understand and are ready to listen.

**National Gay Youth Network (NGYN)**
M. Nulty, Executive Officer
PO Box 846
San Francisco, CA 94101-0846
NGYN comprises gay youth support groups, gay student unions and their sponsors, and other interested groups. Founded in 1979, the 350-member group serves as a networking resource for the exchange of information among members. The network also conducts research and educational programs

three-hour forum, the youth shared their hopes and concerns, and the following day more than 1,500 young people and supporters marched as a youth contingent in the March on Washington for Equal Rights and Liberation.

In addition to its work with LGBT youth, AFSC sponsors a Lesbian, Gay, and Bisexual Rights Task Force, formed in 1976. Among other initiatives, the Task Force has prompted AFSC to join in lawsuits supporting the rights of lesbian mothers and challenging sodomy laws; produced a series of publications on gay rights; created the People of Color Against AIDS Network in Seattle, Washington; and is working with coalitions in five states to oppose anti-gay ballot initiatives.

and sponsors a recognition award. In addition to the *Gay Youth Community News,* which includes book reviews, resources, and news articles, and the *We Are Here Guide,* which offers an annotated bibliography, state by state resources, and articles, NGYN publishes *Helping Gay Youth: Problems and Possibilities, How to Involve Others, How to Start a Youth Group in Your Area, Media Handbook,* and *Stages of Homosexuality.*

**!OutProud!, The National Coalition for Gay, Lesbian & Bisexual Youth**
PO Box 24589
San Jose, CA 95154-4589
phone: (408) 269-6125

**Pro Active Youth Job Training Program**
c/o Community United Against Violence
973 Market Street, Suite 500
San Francisco, CA 94103
phone: (415) 777-5500

**Project Eden**
409 Jackson Street
Hayward, CA 94544
phone: (510) 247-8200

**Project FOCYS**
Lynn Marie, Director
1710 South Amphlett Boulevard, Suite 210
San Mateo, CA 94402
phone: (415) 349-7969

**Project Teens**
One East Olive Avenue
Redlands, CA 92373
phone: (909) 335-2005

**Rainbow's End**
Spectrum Center
1000 Sir Francis Drake Boulevard, Room 10
San Anselmo, CA 94960
phone: (415) 457-1115

**Triangles**
Unitarian Universalist Church
505 East Charleston Road, Room 13
Palo Alto, CA 94306
phone: (415) 324-2674

**Voice & Vision: Lutheran Lesbian & Gay Ministry**
152 Church Street
San Francisco, CA 94114
phone: (415) 553-4515

**Walnut Creek Youth Group**
Pacific Center for Human Growth
1250 Pine Street, Suite 301
Walnut Creek, CA 94596
phone: (510) 939-7711

**Young Lesbians**
Pacific Center for Human Growth
2712 Telegraph Avenue
Berkeley, CA 94705
phone: (510) 548-8283

### Youth Advocates Teen HIV Program
555 Cole Street, Suite 6
San Francisco, CA 94117
phone: (415) 386-9398

### Youth and Family Assistance
609 Price Ave. #205
Redwood City, CA 94063
phone: (415) 366-8401 or (415) 367-9687

### Youth Networks
2215 Market St., Suite 479
San Francisco, CA 94114-1612

### Youth Outreach
c/o Gay & Lesbian Community Services Center
1625 North Schrader Blvd.
Los Angeles, CA 90028-9998
phone: (213) 993-7451

### Youth Services Department—The Center
1625 N. Schrader Blvd., Suite 205
Los Angeles, CA 90028-9988
phone: (213) 993-7450
Among other programs, the Youth Services Department offers a pen pal program for LGBT folks 23 and under. Young people who contact the program are given a start-up list of five to seven people to write to, along with a free newsletter and more lists later on, if desired. The program requests a $5 voluntary donation each year.

### Youth Visibility Project
The Gay & Lesbian Alliance Against Defamation
1360 Mission Street, Suite 200
San Francisco, CA 94103
phone: (415) 861-2244

## COLORADO

### Gay, Lesbian and Bisexual Community Services Center of Colorado
PO Drawer 18E
Denver, CO 80218-0140
phone: (303) 831-6268

### Lamda Community Center
1691 Saulsbury Court
Loveland, CO 80538
phone: (970) 635-9863

### McMaster Center
301 S. Union
Colorado Springs, CO 80910
phone: (719) 578-3160

### Oasis: Coming Out Boulder
3450 North Broadway
Boulder, CO 80304
phone: (303) 441-1244

### Youth Services Program
PO Drawer 18-E
Denver, CO 80218-0140
phone: (303) 831-6268

## CONNECTICUT

### Bisexual Gay Lesbian Active Dialogue for Youth
c/o AIDS Project New Haven
PO Box 636
New Haven, CT 06503
phone: (203) 624-0947

### Danbury Gay, Lesbian & Bisexual Youth Group
105 Garfield Avenue
Danbury, CT 06810
phone: (203) 798-0863

### Inner City Youth Project
Metropolitan Community Church of Hartford
1841 Broad Street
Hartford, CT 06114-1780
phone: (203) 724-4605

### OUT-SPOKEN
c/o Triangle Community Center, Inc.
PO Box 4062
East Norwalk, CT 06855
phone: (203) 853-0600

### Your Turf
Metropolitan Community Church of Hartford
1841 Broad Street
Hartford, CT 06114-1780
phone: (203) 724-4605

## DELAWARE

### AIDS Delaware
601 Delaware Ave.

Wilmington, DE 19801
phone: (302) 652-6776
fax: (302) 652-5150
Formerly known as Delaware Lesbian & Gay Health Advocates.

## DISTRICT OF COLUMBIA

### Center for Youth Development
1255 23rd Street NW, Suite 400
Washington, DC 20037

### National Advocacy Coalition on Youth and Sexual Orientation
Rea Carey, Coalition Coordinator
1711 Connecticut Ave. NW, Ste. 206
Washington, DC 20009-1139
phone: (202) 319-7596
Formed in 1992, the national coalition includes more than 70 organizations and receives most of its support from New York's Hetrick-Martin Institute, the oldest and largest lesbian, gay, and bisexual youth organization in the United States. The coalition raises awareness of the existence and needs of lesbian and gay youth on a nationwide level, and includes its young members in the administration of the organization.

### National Network for Youth
1319 F Street NW, Suite 401
Washington, DC 20004
phone: (202) 783-7949

### Sexual Minority Youth Assistance League
333-1/2 Pennsylvania Ave. SE, Third Floor
Washington, DC 20003-1148
phone: (202) 546-5940

## FLORIDA

### The Alliance for Learning About Sexual Orientation (ALSO)
PO Box 7382
Sarasota, FL 34278-7382
phone: (813) 252-ALSO

### COMPASS Youth Program
1700 N. Dixie Hwy.
West Palm Beach, FL 33406
phone: (407) 833-3638

### Delta Youth Alliance
PO Box 536012
Orlando, FL 32853
phone: (407) 236-9415

### Family Resources, Inc.
5959 Central Ave.
PO Box 13087
St. Petersburg, FL 33733
phone: (813) 893-1150

### Gay/Lesbian Adolescents Surviving in Polk County
4815 Country Road 542 East
Lakeland, FL 33801

### Gay/Lesbian Community Services of Central Florida
Lara Anderson, Director
PO Box 533446
Orlando, FL 32853-3446
phone: (407) 425-4527

### GLB Youth Group of South Florida
PO Box 398651
Miami Beach, FL 33239-8651
phone: (305) 736-8248 (voice mail)

### Jacksonville Area Sexual Minorities Youth Network (JASMYN)
PO Box 23778
Jacksonville, FL 32241
Gay youth information line: (904) 565-1668

### Project YES (Youth Empowerment & Support)
6750 Southwest 59th Street
Miami, FL 33143
phone: (305) 284-0026

### Queer Youth
PO Box 12971
Gainesville, FL 32604-0971

### Rainbow's End Youth Group
Tampa AIDS Network
11215 N. Nebraska Ave., #B3
Tampa, FL 33612
phone: (813) 979-1919, ext. 225

## SPOTLIGHT
# THE HETRICK-MARTIN INSTITUTE

"I was scared," says Lisa, age 15. "I was tired of running from my family, my school, myself. I felt desperate and had no place to go. The Hetrick-Martin Institute found me and saved my life."

Outraged at the prevalence of violence and discrimination against lesbian and gay youth, Drs. Emery S. Hetrick and A. Damien Martin, a psychiatrist and educator, established the Hetrick-Martin Institute in New York City in 1979 to provide a nurturing environment for sexual minority youth. The non-profit institute is now the oldest and largest organization in the United States devoted to helping lesbian, gay, and bisexual youth. Each year, the

**Respect Every Single Person Especially Children and Teens (RESPECT)**
PO Box 5218
Daytona Beach, FL 32118
phone: (904) 257-7071

**True Expressions**
315 South Tessler Drive
St. Petersburg Beach, FL 33706
phone: (813) 367-5964

**Youth Group**
4611 South University Drive, Suite 469
Ft Lauderdale, FL
phone: (305) 581-7138

### GEORGIA

**Atlanta Gay and Lesbian Community Center**
63 Twelfth Street
Atlanta, GA 30309
phone: (404) 876-5372

### HAWAII

**Gay & Lesbian Community Services Center**
1820 University Avenue, 2nd Floor
Honolulu, HI 96822
phone: (808) 951-7000

**Gay & Lesbian Teen Discussion Group**
Honolulu, HI
phone: (808) 951-8607

**Gay & Lesbian Youth Support**
2146 Damon St.
Honolulu, HI 96822
phone: (808) 955-4080

**Lesbian, Gay, Bisexual and Transexual Teen Support Group**
Wailuku, HI
phone: (808) 575-2681

**Maui Lesbian/Gay Youth Project**
Box 356, Ste. 171
Paia Maui, HI 96779

### ILLINOIS

**Coalition for Positive Sexuality**
3712 North Broadway, Box 191
Chicago, IL 60613
phone: (312) 604-1654

**Horizons Youth Group**
Horizon Community Services
961 West Montana Street

institute serves more than 7,000 young people with direct social services, trains more than 2,000 professionals in working with lesbian, gay, and bisexual youth, and provides outreach services to more than 5,000 homeless youth.

"Lesbian, gay, and bisexual youth are everywhere," the founders remind us. "They're our nieces and nephews, our clients, our children, our students, our neighbors. Because homosexuality is often treated with hostility—or at best with silence—they all suffer. Sadly, many who make their way to social-service programs—counseling centers, foster and group homes, homeless shelters, or drug rehabilitation programs—are frequently spurned."

Though the institute began as a "safety net" for those young people, it has grown to become much more. An after-school drop-in center provides a

Chicago, IL 60614
phone: (312) 472-6469

**Neon Street Center for Homeless Youth**
4822 North Broadway
Chicago, IL 60640
phone: (312) 271-6366

**Pride Youth**
1779 Maple Street
Northfield, IL 60093
phone: (708) 441-9880

**Prism Youth Network**
PO Box 784
Oak Park, IL 60603
phone: (708) FUN-FIND or (708) 386-3463

## INDIANA

**Crisis Center for Human Understanding**
101 North Montgomery Street
Gary, IN 46403
phone: (219) 938-7070

**Indianapolis Youth Group**
Jeff Werner, Executive Director
PO Box 20716
Indianapolis, IN 46220-0716
phone: (317) 541-8726
hotline: (800) 347-TEEN
fax: (317) 545-8594
The Indianapolis Youth Group conducts healthy recreational activities for gay, lesbian, and bisexual youth under the age of 21, and offers a national youth hotline.

**IYG—Evansville**
PO Box 2901
Evansville, IN 47728
phone: (800) 347-TEEN

## IOWA

**Gay & Lesbian Youth in Discussion & Education**
c/o Gay & Lesbian Resource Center
4211 Grand Avenue
Des Moines, IA 50312
phone: (515) 281-0634

**United Action for Youth**
410 Iowa Avenue
Iowa City, IA 52240
phone: (319) 338-7518

**Young Women's Resource Center**
554 28th Street
Des Moines, IA 50312-5222
phone: (515) 244-4901

safe place where lesbian, gay, and bisexual youth can develop meaningful friendships with other youth who understand what it's like to grow up gay. At the drop-in center they can join support groups, participate in programs like photography, writing, computers, theater, television production, or HIV/AIDS education, and attend field trips.

The institute's Harvey Milk School, established in 1985 with the New York City Board of Education, is the nation's first alternative high school for youth who are not able to complete their education because of anti-gay harassment. One of 25 alternative city high school programs, the Harvey Milk School enrolls a maximum of 30 students per year. While there, the students—who enter with varying academic backgrounds—receive academic help, develop positive feelings about learning, and succeed at school—often for the first time.

## KENTUCKY

### Louisville Youth Group

PO Box 4664
Louisville, KY 40204
phone: (502) 894-9787

## LOUISIANA

### Youth Services Program

Lesbian & Gay Community Center of New Orleans
816 North Rampart Street
New Orleans, LA 70116
phone: (504) 522-1103

## MAINE

### AIDS Project

22 Monument Square, 5th Fl.
Portland, ME 04101
phone: (207) 774-6877

### Ingraham

PO Box 5370, Station A
Portland, ME 04101
phone: (207) 774-HELP
Referral service.

### Outright (Central Maine)

PO Box 802
Auburn, ME 04212
phone: (207) 783-2557

### Outright (Portland)

PO Box 5077
Portland, ME 04101
phone: (207) 828-6560

## MARYLAND

### Sufficient As I Am

Baltimore Gay & Lesbian Community Center
241 W. Chase St.
Baltimore, MD 21201
phone: (410) 837-5445

## MASSACHUSETTS

### Alyson Publications Letter Exchange

40 Plympton St.
Boston, MA 02118
Alyson Publications, a gay and lesbian publisher of books for adults and children, offers a Letter Exchange free for people 21 and under.

### Boston Alliance of Gay and Lesbian Youth (BAGLY)

PO Box 814
Boston, MA 02103

According to the institute's executive director, Frances Kunreuther, "The Harvey Milk School re-opens the door to school for lesbian and gay youth, and offers them an education in an environment that is safe and supportive. Whenever possible, Harvey Milk School students are mainstreamed back into their community high schools."

The Hetrick-Martin Institute also offers individual and family counseling. Young people receive help understanding and accepting their sexual orientation, as well as dealing with family, friends, school, relationships, health, jobs, or any other challenge confronting them, while families can receive counseling to help them accept their children's sexual identities.

The institute's Project First Step provides street outreach, hot meals, clothing, showers, and a safe social environment for homeless youth who have

phone: (800) 42-BAGLY or (800) 422-2459

**CAPE & Islands Gay & Lesbian Youth Group**
Drawer 78
Yarmouth Port, MA 02675
phone: (508) 362-2492

**Framingham Regional Alliance of Gay & Lesbian Youth**
PO Box 426
Framingham, MA 01701-0003
phone: (508) 655-7183

**Gay and Lesbian Information Services**
West Greenfield, MA
phone: (413) 731-5403

**Gay, Lesbian and Straight Society (GLASS)**
FCAC Youth Program
86 Washington St.
Greenfield, MA 01060

**Gay, Lesbian, Undecided, Bisexual Youth (GLUB)**
Woman Services of Western Massachusetts
Pittsfield, MA 01201
phone: (413) 499-2425
hotline: (413) 443-0089

**Pioneer Valley Youth Support Group**
PO Box 202
Hadley, MA 01035
phone: (413) 584-4213

**South Shore Alliance of Gay and Lesbian Youth (SSHAGLY)**
18 Milford Street, Suite 2
Boston, MA 02118
617-338-7082

**Supporters of Worcester Area Gay and Lesbian Youth**
PO Box 592
Westside Station
Worcester, MA 01602
phone: (508) 755-0005

**Youth and Young Adult Outreach Program**
United Church Coalition for Lesbian/Gay Concerns
69 Monadnock Road
Worcester, MA 01609-1714
phone: (508) 755-0005

been rejected by their families or who have left home to avoid abuse. The program also offers health care, education, legal assistance, and counseling to help the young people leave the streets, as well as referrals to other sources.

As a leader in local and state coalitions on HIV/AIDS and youth and peer education, the institute encourages young people to reach out to their peers on issues of human sexuality and HIV/AIDS. The institute also places young people in internship programs to help them find role models and learn job skills. The newsletter *HMI Report Card* is distributed to interested parties, and a comic book called *Tales of the Closet* addresses issues such as isolation, family, violence, health, and pride.

## MICHIGAN

### Affirmations Lesbian and Gay Community Center

195 West Nine Mile Road, Suite 110
Ferndale, MI 48220
phone: (810) 398-7105
hotline: (800) 398-GAYS
fax: (810) 541-1943
e-mail: affirmglcc@aol.com
Affirmations provides Saturday peer support groups for people 21 years and younger, along with peer education, a youth speakers' bureau, and a mentorship project.

### Gay Lesbian Youth Positive Support, Resource, and Peer Group

PO Box 759
Douglas, MI 48915
phone: (616) 857-1864

### Kalamazoo Gay Lesbian Resource Center Youth Group

PO Box 1532
Kalamazoo, MI 49005-1532
phone: (616) 345-7878

### Michigan Alliance for Lesbian and Gay Youth Services (MALGYS)

617 North Jenison
Lansing, MI 48915
phone: (517) 484-0946
Statewide network of lesbian and gay youth service agencies.

### Ozone House Gay & Lesbian Youth Group

608 N. Main Street
Ann Arbor, MI 48104
phone: (313) 662-2265
Ozone House provides individual and family counseling, independent living programs, and emergency food, clothing, and shelter.

### PRYSM

Gateway Community Services
910 Abbott Road, Suite 100
East Lansing, MI 48823
phone: (517) 351-4000

### Windfire (Grand Rapids)

6457 28th St. SE
Grand Rapids, MI 49546
phone: (616) 949-4078
Windfire meets weekly to enjoy activities centered around social interaction, and includes separate groups for male and female participants. The group also provides AIDS education and risk assessment, plus "no name required" AIDS testing and counseling. In addition to its youth programs, Windfire offers educational programs for schools, counselors, therapists, teachers, parent groups, and other organizations.

### Windfire (Kalamazoo)

c/o WMU Alliance for Lesbian and Gay Support

"Through direct service, education, and advocacy," according to Kunreuther, "the Hetrick-Martin Institute is committed to creating a world where lesbian, gay, and bisexual youth can grow successfully into adulthood and find understanding and respect from the larger society."

According to the kids, it works.

Says Carlos, age 17, "I have grown at HMI. I can be me there. They've helped me to see that I am a good person, that I have something to give to my community and my world."

Faunce Student Services
Kalamazoo, MI 49008
phone: (616) 387-1000

**Windfire (Traverse City)**
Crisis Center
PO Box 562
Traverse City, MI 49685
phone: (616) 922-4800

**Young Detroit Health Center, Herman Keifer Complex**
1151 Taylor
Detroit, MI 48202
(313) 876-4130
General medical care and HIV testing for young persons aged 13 to 24. Testing is low-cost or free to all young people, regardless of residency.

## MINNESOTA

**District 202 Youth Center**
2524 Nicollet Avenue South
Minneapolis, MN 55404
phone: (612) 871-5559

**Lutheran Social Services Street Program**
1299 Arcade Street
St. Paul, MN 55416
phone: (612) 774-9507

**The Marshall GLBT Youth Group**
Minnesota AIDS Project
109 South Fifth St.
Marshall, MN 56258
phone: (800) 243-7321

**Minnesota Task Force for Gay and Lesbian Youth**
PO Box 8588
Minneapolis, MN 55408
phone: (612) 451-7996

**SO WHAT IF I AM**
The Bridge, Inc.
2200 Emerson Avenue South
Minneapolis, MN 55405
phone: (612) 377-8800

**Storefront/Youth Action**
7145 Harriet Avenue South
Richfield, MN 55423
phone: (612) 861-1675

**Youth and AIDS Project**
428 Oak Grove Street
Minneapolis, MN 55403
phone: (612) 627-6820

## MISSOURI

**Gay & Lesbian Services**
132 W. 61st Terrace
Kansas City, MO 64113
phone: (816) 822-8204

**Growing American Youth**
c/o Our World Too, Inc.
11 South Vandeventer

St. Louis, MO 63108
phone: (314) 533-5322

## MONTANA

### PRIDE

2001 Porter Ave.
Butte, MT 59701
phone: (406) 723-6656

## NEBRASKA

### Gay and Lesbian Youth Talkline

PO Box 94882
Lincoln, NE 68509
phone: (402) 473-7932

### Support Group for Lesbigay Youth

c/o PFLAG
2912 Lynwood Drive
Omaha, NE 68123-1957
phone: (402) 291-6781

## NEVADA

### Gay Youth Outreach Program

University of Nevada (Reno)
Mailstop 058
Reno, NV 89557
phone: (702) 784-1944

## NEW HAMPSHIRE

### Seacoast Outright

4 Bayview Road
Durham, NH 03824
phone: (603) 868-2468

### Southern New Hampshire Alliance of Gay and Lesbian Youth

207 Union Square, Suite 3
Milford, NH 03055

## NEW JERSEY

### Gay and Lesbian Youth in New Jersey (GALY-NJ)

Charlie Signorino, Co-Director
PO Box 137
Convent Station, NJ 07961-0137
help line: (201) 285-1595

GALY-NJ is for adolescents aged 16-21 who are self-identified as lesbian, gay, or bisexual. The group, founded in 1989, seeks to provide a safe space for gay and lesbian youth where they can meet to gain a better understanding of themselves, interact socially with peers, and build self-esteem without undue pressures. Its newsletter, *YouthWatch*, appears quarterly for educators and youth services providers. The group's meetings take place on Saturdays.

### Planned Parenthood

437 East State Street
Trenton, NJ 08608
phone: (609) 599-4881

### Rainbow Place of South Jersey

1103 North Broad Street
Woodbury, NJ 08096
phone: (609) 848-2455

## NEW MEXICO

### One in Ten

c/o Common Bond Inc.
PO Box 26836
Albuquerque, NM 87108-2643
phone: (505) 266-8041

## NEW YORK

### Bisexual, Gay and Lesbian Youth of New York

Lesbian and Gay Community Services Center
208 West 13th Street
New York, NY 10011-7799
phone: (212) 620-7310

### Comprehensive Adolescent Young Adult Care Center (CAYACC)

St. Luke's—Roosevelt Hospital
411 West 114th Street, Suite 2D
New York, NY 10025
phone: (212) 523-6306

### Gay, Lesbian & Bisexual Youth Group

c/o AIDS Center of Queens County
9745 Queens Boulevard
Rego Park, NY 11374
phone: (718) 896-2500

## Gay and Lesbian Switchboard of Long Island (GLSBLI)

PO Box 1312
Long Island, NY 11779
phone: (516) 737-1615
Offers peer counseling information & referral.

## Gay & Lesbian Young Adult Support Group

c/o Capitol District Community Center
PO Box 131
Albany, NY 12201
phone: (518) 438-0546

## Gay & Lesbian Youth of Buffalo

190 Franklin Street
Buffalo, NY 14202
phone: (716) 855-0221

## Gay and Lesbian Youth Services of Western New York

190 Franklin Street
Buffalo, NY 14202
phone: (716) 855-0221

## Hetrick-Martin Institute

Frances Kunreuther, Executive Director
2 Astor Place
New York, NY 10003-6998
phone: (212) 674-2400
TTY: (212) 674-8695
fax: (212) 674-8650
The Hetrick-Martin Institute—the oldest and largest lesbian, gay, and bisexual youth organization in the United States—informs and educates the public and youth service agencies about the needs of gay and lesbian youth. The group, which was founded in 1979, coordinates existing services and provides direct service to gay and lesbian youth, including group and individual counseling and referral, outreach services to homeless youth, and education on human sexuality and AIDS. The institute helped establish and continues to sponsor the Harvey Milk School, a New York City high school for gay and lesbian students named after slain San Francisco, California, city supervisor and gay activist Harvey Milk. The institute also sponsors the National Advocacy Coalition on Youth and Sexuality and presents an annual recognition award. The group publishes its newsletter, the *HMI Report Card*, quarterly, as well as a comic book series called "Tales of the Closet," a directory called *You Are Not Alone: National Directory of Lesbian, Gay, and Bisexual Youth Organizations*, and fact sheets on lesbian, gay, and bisexual youth.

## Lesbian & Gay Youth Program of Central New York

c/o Lambda Youth Services
PO Box 6103
Syracuse, NY 13217-6103
or
826 Euclid Ave.
Syracuse, NY 13210
phone: (315) 422-9741

## Lesbian & Gay Youth of Rochester

c/o Gay Alliance of Gennessee Valley (GAGV)
179 Atlantic Avenue
Rochester, NY 14607-1255
phone: (716) 244-8640

## The Neutral Zone

162 Christopher Street
New York, NY 10014
phone: (212) 924-3294

## Ninety-Second Street Y, Teen Division

1395 Lexington Avenue
New York, NY 10128
phone: (212) 996-1100

## Pride for Youth

Middle Earth Crisis Center
2740 Martin Avenue
Bellmore, NY 11710
phone: (516) 679-9000

## Pride in da Bronx c/o YAADA

2488 Grand Concourse
Suite 326
Bronx, NY 10458
phone: (718) 364-9529

## Project Reach Anti-Discrimination Space

1 Orchard Street, 2nd floor
New York, NY 10002
phone: (212) 966-4227

## SPOTLIGHT

### WINDFIRE

Windfire, a social and support group for lesbian and gay youth, uses as its symbol the phoenix. As the group's mission statement explains, "The phoenix is a mythological bird that would consume itself by fire, then rise from its own ashes young and beautiful to live full and whole again. At Windfire we believe that lesbian and gay youth can rise up, as the phoenix, from the ashes of misunderstanding, loneliness and despair to live free, whole and beautiful again."

Recognizing that one in four families has a gay or lesbian family member; that young people hurt by homophobia may retreat into destructive activities such as running away, substance abuse, truancy, increased sexual

**SAFESPACE**
The Center for Children & Families, Inc.
133 West 46th Street
New York, NY 10036
phone: (212) 354-SAFE

**Sex Information & Education Council of U.S. (SIECUS)**
130 West 42nd Street, Suite 2500
New York, NY 10036
phone: (212) 819-9770

**StreetWorks**
545 Ace Avenue, 22nd Floor
New York, NY 10018
phone: (212) 695-2220

**TRUST**
c/o CANDLE
30 Parrott Road
West Nyack, NY 10994-1028
phone: (914) 634-6677

**YES Community Counseling Services**
30 Broadway
Massapequa, NY 11758
phone: (516) 799-3000

**Youth Communication**
144 West 27th Street
New York, NY 10001
phone: (212) 242-3270, ext. 102

**Youth Enrichment Services**
Lesbian & Gay Community Services Center
208 West 13th Street
New York, NY 10011-7799
phone: (212) 620-7310

### NORTH CAROLINA

**Chapel Hill High School**
High School Road
Chapel Hill, NC 27516
phone: (919) 929-2106

**Gay & Lesbian Adolescent Support System**
Alternative Resources of the Triad
PO Box 4442
Greensboro, NC 27404
phone: (910) 274-2100

**OutFit**
PO Box 5978
Asheville, NC 28813
phone: (704) 277-7815

**OutRight!**
PO Box 3203
Durham, NC 27715-3203
phone: (919) 286-2396

activity, teen pregnancy, or suicide; and that more than 5,000 adolescents complete suicide annually in the United States—an estimated third of them gay or lesbian youth—Windfire hopes to ease the process of coming out.

As a private, non-profit group for young people ages 13 through 22 years, Windfire meets weekly in three Michigan cities to enjoy activities centered around social interaction—with special emphasis on self-improvement and self-understanding—and includes separate groups for male and female participants. The group also provides AIDS education and risk assessment, plus "no name required" AIDS testing and counseling. Windfire's "ground rules" include confidentiality, using first names or nicknames only, discouraging stereotypical names and references, and fostering respect for the diversity of all people.

**A Safer Place Youth Network**
PO Box 12831
Raleigh, NC 27605-2831
phone: (919) 851-9544 or (919) 851-7427

**STANDOUT**
PO Box 53751
Fayetteville, NC 28309
phone: (910) 487-6535

**Time Out Youth**
4037 E. Independence Blvd.
Suite G33
Charlotte, NC 28205
phone: (704) 537-5050

## OHIO

**Central United Methodist Church**
701 W. Central
Toledo, OH 43610
phone: (419) 241-7729

**Cincinnati Youth Group**
PO Box 19852
Cincinnati, OH 45224
phone: (513) 721-2912

**Kaleidoscope Youth Coalition**
PO Box 8104
Columbus, OH 43201
phone: (614) 447-7199

**Northwest Ohio Gay/Lesbian Youth Group**
Central United Methodist Church
701 West Central Ohio
Toledo, OH 43610
phone: (419) 241-7729

**Pride and Respect for Youth in a Sexual Minority**
Gay & Lesbian Community Center of Greater Cleveland
PO Box 6177
Cleveland, OH 44101
phone: (216) 522-1999

**PRISM**
Akron, OH
phone: (216) 253-3652 (voice mail)

**Rainbow's End Youth Group**
Lorain County Gay/Lesbian Information Center
PO Box 167
Lorain, OH 44052
phone: (216) 988-5326

In addition to its youth programs, Windfire offers educational programs for schools, counselors, therapists, teachers, parent groups, and other organizations.

**United Church Coalition for Lesbian/Gay Concerns (National Office)**
18 North College Street
Athens, OH 45701
phone: (614) 593-7301

**Youth Rap Group**
140 Foster Park Road
Amherst, OH
phone: (216) 960-2050

**Youth Rap Group**
The Center
1418 West 29th Street
Cleveland, OH
phone: (216) 522-1999

**YouthQuest**
PO Box 3032
Dayton, OH 45401-3032
phone: (513) 449-8249

## OKLAHOMA

**Lesbian, Gay & Bisexual Youth Support Program**
Youth Services of Tulsa
302 South Cheyenne
Tulsa, OK 74103
phone: (918) 582-0061

**National Resource Center for Youth Services**
202 West 8th Street
Tulsa, OK 74119-1419
phone: (918) 585-2986

## OREGON

**Awakenings Youth Group**
3576 NE Schuyler
Portland, OR 97212
phone: (503) 281-2385

**Bend Youth Services**
Deschutes County Coalition for Human Dignity
Bend, OR
phone: (503) 383-4861

**Oregon Sexual Minority Youth Network (OSMYN)**
PO Box 162
Portland, OR 97207-0162
phone: (503) 243-0538

**Outreach to Rural Youth Project**
PO Box 25791
Portland, OR 97225
phone: (503) 292-3454

**Outside In**
1236 SW Salmon
Portland, OR 97205
phone: (503) 223-4121, ext. 35

**Phoenix Rising**
620 SW Fifth
Portland, OR 97204
phone: (503) 223-8299

**Southern Oregon Youth Outreach**
2371 Voorhies Road
Medford, OR 97501

## PENNSYLVANIA

**The Attic**
Voyage House
1431 Lombard Street
Philadelphia, PA 19146
phone: (215) 545-2910

**Bi, Gay, Lesbian Youth Association of Harrisburg (BI-GLYAH)**
PO Box 872
Harrisburg, PA 17108

**Bridges Project of American Friends Service Committee**
Jenie Hall, Director
1501 Cherry Street
Philadelphia, PA 19102
phone: (215) 241-7133

The Bridges Project, a branch of the Quaker organization American Friends Service Committee, is a national network of resources and information for LGBT youth and the community workers, educators, health and human service providers, parents, religious leaders, and others who work with sexual minority youth. Publishes a resource guide, *Bridges of Respect,* and the quarterly newsletter *Crossroads.*

**Closet Culture**
PO Box 10274
Erie, PA 16504-0274
phone: (814) 825-6131

**Eagles Perch**
c/o Metropolitan Community Church
PO Box 11543
Harrisburg, PA 17108
phone: (717) 236-7387

**40 Acres of Change**
201 South 12th Street
Suite 1R
Philadelphia, PA 19107
phone: (215) 627-6233

**Gay, Lesbian and Bi Youth Alliance**
PO Box 31
Lancaster, PA 17608-0031
phone: (717) 397-0691

**Gay, Lesbian and Bi Youth Group**
1514 North Second Street, Lower Level
Harrisburg, PA
phone: (717) 234-0328

**Growing Alternative Youth**
4120 Brownsville Rd.
Pittsburgh, PA 15227
phone: (412) 884-5223

**Metropolitan Community Church**
1345 Linden #3
Allentown, PA 18102
phone: (215) 439-8755

**Penguin Place Youth Group**
201 South Camac Street
Philadelphia, PA 19107
phone: (215) 732-2220

**Planned Parenthood**
1144 Locust Street
Philadelphia, PA
phone: (215) 351-5514

**Q-Youth**
c/o AIDS Project
301 S. Allen St. Suite 102
State College, PA 16801
phone: (814) 235-4655

**SMYLE**
44 North Queen Street
Lancaster, PA
phone: (717) 656-4152

**Unity, Inc.**
1207 Chestnut
Suite 209
Philadelphia, PA 19107
phone: (215) 851-1912

## RHODE ISLAND

**The Way Out**
Providence, RI
phone: (401) 861-5969

**Youth Pride Inc.**
PO Box 603017
Providence, RI 02906
phone: (401) 421-5626

## SOUTH CAROLINA

**Gay/Lesbian/Bisexual Youth Circle**
141 South Shandon Street, Suite A
Columbia, SC 29205
phone: (803) 771-7713

**Saturday Mornings OUT**
c/o Unitarian Universalist Fellowship
2701 Heyward Street
Columbia, SC 29205
phone: (803) 799-0845

## TENNESSEE

**Gay Teens Memphis**
Memphis, TN
phone: (901) 761-1444

### One in Ten Youth Services
c/o The Center for Lesbian & Gay Community Services
703 Berry Road
Nashville, TN 37204-2803
phone: (615) 297-0008

## TEXAS

### Gay, Lesbian & Bisexual Young Adults
PO Box 190712
Dallas, TX 75219
phone: (214) 521-5342

### The Gay Youth Project
Corpus Christi, TX
phone: (512) 850-2940

### Hope House Transitional Living Shelter
PO Box 35466
Dallas, TX 75235
phone: (214) 351-1901

### Houston Area Teenage Coalition of Homosexuals
PO Box 66574
Houston, TX 77266-6574
phone: (713) 942-7002

### LAMBDA Services—Youth OUTreach
PO Box 31321
El Paso, TX 79931-0321
phone: (915) 562-GAYS

### Out Youth Austin
425 Woodward Street
Austin, TX 78704 7213
phone: (512) 326-1234 or (800) 96-YOUTH
Out Youth Austin provides weekly support groups, HIV services, social activities, community and youth education, referral services, a drop-in center, and a toll-free helpline for LGBT youth.

### San Antonio Lambda Students Alliance
PO Box 12715
San Antonio, TX 78212
phone: (210) 733-1225

### StreetWise Houston
527 Spring Drive
Pasadena, TX 77504
phone: (713) 942-9884

### Teen Project
3327 Winthrop, Suite 243
Fort Worth, TX 76116
phone: (817)763-8382

## UTAH

### Cache Valley Gay and Lesbian Youth
395 West 200 North
Logan, UT 84322

### Utah Gay and Lesbian Youth Group—Stonewall Youth Services
Utah Stonewall Center
770 South 300 West
Salt Lake City, UT 84101
phone: (801) 539-8800

## VIRGINIA

### Out Youth of the Blue Ridge
717 Rugby Rd.
Charlottesville, VA 22903

### Outright
TRUST
404 Elm Avenue, SW
Roanoke, VA
phone: (540) 344-0790

### Project: LIFEGUARD
Jody Wheeler
Whitman Walker Clinic of Northern Virginia
426 Washington Blvd., Ste. 102
Arlington, VA 22201
(703) 358-9550
Project: LIFEGUARD is a peer-led intervention and education program in which young people talk to each other about AIDS and the cofactors that relate to HIV prevention or infection, such as self-esteem, drug abuse, communication, and risk reduction.

### Richmond Organization for Sexual Minority Youth (ROSMY)
Jon Klein, Director

PO Box 5542
Richmond, VA 23220-0542
office phone: (804) 353-1699
support line: (804) 353-2077
The Richmond Organization seeks to provide support and accurate information about human sexuality to gay, lesbian, bisexual, transvestite, and transsexual youth from 14 to 21, and to their families. Educates counselors, teachers, parents, and human services workers about the needs of sexual minority youth, and works to bannish the unfair treatment of these young people. Weekly support groups are run by trained adult facilitators. The *ROSMY Newsletter* appears quarterly.

### Young People's Support Group
Lynchburg, VA 24503
phone: (804) 845-5783

### Youth Out United
485 S. Independence Blvd., Suite 111
Virginia Beach, VA 23452
phone: (804) 490-6658

## WASHINGTON

### Family Services, Eastside
11911 N.E. First
Bellevue, WA 98005
phone: (206) 451-2869

### Gay, Lesbian and Bisexual Youth Program and Infoline
American Friends Service Committee
814 NE 40th
Seattle, WA 98105
phone: (206) 632-0500

### Lambert House Gay, Lesbian & Bisexual Youth Center
1818 15th Avenue
Seattle, WA 98122
phone: (206) 322-2735

### Lesbian Youth Group
Lesbian Resource Center
1808 Bellevue Ave., Ste. 204
Seattle, WA 98122
phone: (206) 322-3953

### Oasis Gay, Lesbian and Bisexual Youth Association
Tacoma-Pierce County Health Dept.
3629 South D Street
Tacoma, WA 98408-6897
phone: (206) 591-6060

### Odyssey
Spokane County Health District AIDS Program
1101 West College Avenue, Room 401
Spokane, WA 99201-2095
phone: (509) 324-1547

### Snohomish County GLB Youth Support Group
Snohomish County Health District
3020 Rucker Avenue, Suite 206
Everett, WA 98201-3971
phone: (206) 339-5251

### Stonewall Recovery Services
430 Broadway Ave East
Seattle, WA 98102
phone: (206) 461-4546

### Stonewall Youth
PO Box 7383
Olympia, WA 98507
phone: (206) 705-2738

### Vashon Youth and Family Services
PO Box 237
Vashon, WA 98070
phone: (206) 463-5511

### Youth Advocates, Inc.
2317 East John Street
Seattle, WA 98112
phone: (206) 322-7838

### Youth Care
333 First Avenue W
Seattle, WA 98119
phone: (206) 282-1288

### Youth Eastside Services
16150 NE 8th
Bellevue, WA 98008
phone: (206) 747-4937

## WEST VIRGINIA

### Gay & Lesbian Oriented Youth
PO Box 9725
Casper, WY 82609-0721
phone: (307) 577-7969

### Young, Gay and Proud
PO Box 3642
Charleston, WV 25336-3642
phone: (304) 340-3690

## WISCONSIN

### Briarpatch, Inc.
512 East Washington Avenue
Madison, WI 53704
phone: (608) 251-6211

### 18—21 Year Old Social Group for Lesbigay People
Gay/Bi Men's Activities Organization
14 West Mifflin, Suite 103
Madison, WI 53703
phone: (608) 256-2667

### Gay Youth Milwaukee (GYM)
Michael S. Lisowski, Director
Box 09441
Milwaukee, WI 53209
phone: (414) 265-8500
Gay Youth Milwaukee, founded in 1979, is a discussion, support, counseling, and advocacy group for gays, lesbians, and bisexual teens 18 and under. It meets the first and third Saturdays of the month.

### Madison Community United (The United)
PO Box 310
14 W. Mifflin, Ste. 103
Madison, WI 53701
phone: (608) 255-8582

### Teens Like Us
512 East Washington
Madison, WI 53703
phone: (608) 251-6211

### University of Wisconsin—Milwaukee
1402 Well St.
Onalaska, WI 54650
phone: (608) 783-1242

# ONLINE RESOURCES

## THE WEB

### Oasis
http://www.cyberspace.com/outproud/oasis
Oasis, the e-zine for gay and lesbian teenagers, features poetry, stories, and commentary by and about homosexual teens struggling to accept their sexuality in a homophobic world. Written pieces from readers are readily accepted.

### Queer Resources Directory
http://www.qrd.org/QRD/
Containing information about gay, lesbian, bisexual, and transgender lifestyles, the QRD offers an enormous number of articles, essays, clippings, newsletters, images, and contact information. Materials fall under several subject headings, including politics, media, religion, youth, culture, and business. Links to other Internet sites are included as well. Users also can access the Queer Resources Directory by ftp at *ftp.qrd.com* and by gopher at *gopher.qrd.com*.

### The Ultimate Gay Youth Page
http://www.bridge.net/~puente/
newlife.html
Web cruising folks should check out this Web site for a vast list of referrals and descriptions of where to go on the World Wide Web for LGBT youth information.

# USENET

### Support for Homosexual Youth
soc.support.youth.gay-lesbian-bi
Considering the heated discussions that occur in the majority of homosexual newsgroups, it is indeed a surprise to find this gem. The group is a warm, caring environment for homosexual youth to support one another.

# GEOGRAPHIC INDEX

## ARGENTINA



## AUSTRALIA

### New South Wales



### South Australia



## BELGIUM



## BRAZIL



## CANADA

### Alberta



### British Columbia



### Manitoba



### Ontario

### Quebec



### Saskatchewan



## COSTA RICA



## ENGLAND

## Arkansas



## California

## Colorado

## Connecticut



## Delaware



## District of Columbia

## Florida

## Georgia



## Hawaii



## Idaho



## Illinois

## Indiana

## Maryland



## Massachusetts

## Michigan

## Minnesota



## Mississippi



## Missouri

## Montana



## Nebraska



## Nevada



## New Hampshire



## New Jersey

## New Mexico



## New York

## North Carolina



## North Dakota



## Ohio

## Oklahoma



## Oregon

## Pennsylvania

## Rhode Island



## South Carolina



## South Dakota



## Tennessee



## Texas

## Utah



## Vermont

## Virginia



## Washington

### West Virginia



### Wisconsin



### Wyoming



## VIRGIN ISLANDS



## ONLINE RESOURCES

### The Web

## Online Services



## Usenet



## The Net and BBS

# INDEX

## B

# C

## D

## E



## F

## G

## H

# I

## J



## K

## L

## M

## N

## O

## P

# Q



# R

## S

## T

## U



## V



## W

## X



## Y



## Z

# **Dear Reader:** We welcome your comments!

RE: **Strength in Numbers**

We would like to know what you think of **Strength in Numbers** and what would make it even more useful for you. Please take a few minutes to fill out and return this card. Thanks for your interest!

Where did you purchase this book? ______

How did you become aware of this book? ______

What feature of the book do you like the most? ______

What feature do you like the least? ______

How would you improve this book? ______

______

Other subject areas of interest ______

❑ Please send me information on other **Visible Ink Press** titles.

Name ______ Phone (____) ______

Street Address ______

City ______ State ______ Zip ______

Age ____ M ____ F ____ Do you own a PC? ____ Do you own a CD-ROM Player? ____

**Visible Ink Press**

In U.S. and Canada: 1-800-776-6265 Fax: (313) 961-6637

# SKI COUNTRY

# Western United States

# Orientation

Schussing the pristine back bowls of **Vail**, cutting through **Snowbird**'s knee-deep powder, admiring the azure expanse of **Lake Tahoe** from the top of a trail at **Heavenly**—experiences such as these characterize skiing in the Western United States, one of the preeminent winter playgrounds in the world. The usually bountiful snowfall (not to worry, an arsenal of artificial snowmakers fills in for Mother Nature's occasional oversights) and diverse terrain create unparalleled skiing opportunities at resorts that vary in style from casual mom-and-pop ski centers that mainly attract weekend crowds to full-service luxury vacation resorts with miles of runs and myriad restaurants and diversions.

Sorting out resort prospects from among the region's 152 ski sites can be frustrating, especially if you're trying to accommodate skiers of varying abilities and interests. This guide to the Western ski country can help you in your search. It presents information on 29 of the area's top ski resorts in an accessible format, along with evaluative reviews of hotels and restaurants, and trail analyses from a skier's point of view.

The prime determinant in planning a successful ski trip can be summed up in three words: location, location, location. If you have only three or four days to spend on the slopes, keeping your transit time to a minimum will maximize your fun. Target areas that are conveniently located near a large airport or gateway, and take into consideration the flight frequencies of major airlines and easy access to ground transportation. Salt Lake City is a good example of a choice hub—it's possible to arrive on a morning plane and be cutting figure-eights by noon at any of the four major resorts situated within an hour's drive of the airport: **Park City**, **Deer Valley**, **Alta**, and Snowbird.

Several stellar Colorado ski areas have overcome the drawbacks of their isolation by offering nonstop flights into small local airports during high season. **Steamboat**, Vail, **Aspen**, and **Crested Butte** all sponsor flights from selected metropolitan areas, allowing direct access to some truly exceptional ski destinations. If you're on a tight schedule, remember that sudden storms can shut down mountain airstrips with very little notice, while the big city airports commonly have facilities to cope with massive quantities of white stuff. Of course, if you're spending a week or more in the snow, the extra day or two of travel time needed to reach the really remote locations—such as **Big Sky**, Montana,

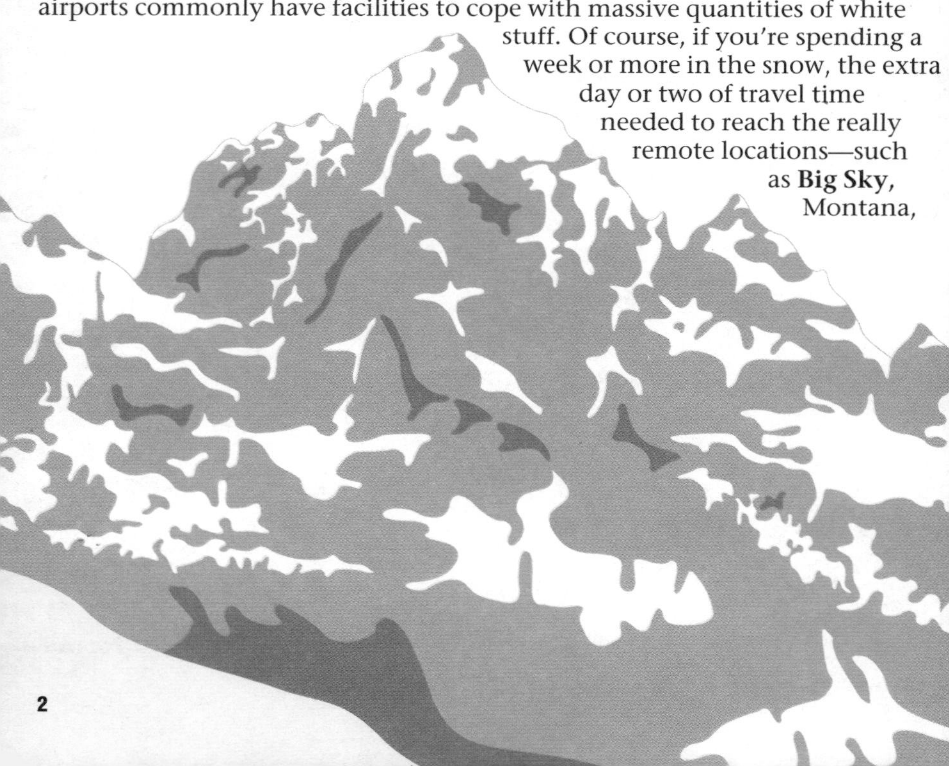

or **Sun Valley**, Idaho—shouldn't prove a problem.

Weather may be a deciding factor in choosing where to ski. Snow in the **Sierra Nevada** of California and the **Cascades** of the Pacific Northwest tends to have a lot of moisture, especially early in the season, and therefore can be a bit difficult to ski. In the **Rockies**, snow doesn't fall in the prodigious amounts that it does farther west, but it's a lot drier and more forgiving. And as a rule, the coastal resorts are immune to the bone-chilling temperatures prevalent inland, particularly in the northern Rocky Mountain states of Wyoming, Montana, and Idaho. The most temperate months here tend to be March and April.

Of course there's more to it than hard pack and pistes. Resorts have come up with both practical and inventive ways to pamper guests. Families will find that certain ski areas cater to them, providing day care for young children, lessons for older kids, and teen team competitions. State-of-the-art teaching techniques and ski school facilities give beginners a jump start. **Winter Park** and Vail, for instance, pride themselves on employing "terrain gardens" that replicate a variety of conditions. And some resorts—among them **Breckenridge, Tiehack,** Park City, and **Northstar**—are especially attractive to neophytes because they offer a large number of beginner runs.

The social climates of resorts can differ substantially. For couples seeking an intimate retreat, Sun Valley, Aspen, **Beaver Creek, Telluride,** and Deer Valley offer romantic inns and restaurants, and après-ski activities (such as moonlit sleigh rides) conducive to cuddling. The chic night spots and convivial watering holes in **Squaw Valley**, Heavenly, Snowbird, and **Keystone** are magnets for skiers looking for a lively social scene.

Even with all these diversions, if the notion of cruising the same slopes for a few days threatens to give you a case of cabin fever, there are multiple-resort destinations that operate free or inexpensive shuttle service between ski sites. The best of these are **Summit County**, with four mountains; Aspen, which also has four peaks; Park City, with three ski areas; and Lake Tahoe, grouping three resorts on the South Shore and a half-dozen on the North Shore.

Just as individual resorts have unique atmospheres, so their environs have specific appeal. Free spirits can kick back with cowboys at **Jackson Hole**, Wyoming, which has as much true grit as the West can muster. Inveterate shoppers with money to burn will attain nirvana in the upscale boutiques of Aspen, while vacationers with healthy hedonistic tendencies can indulge in Steamboat's natural hot springs after a day of running the chutes. And if glitzy nightlife and gambling set your heart racing, Lake Tahoe has enough 24-hour

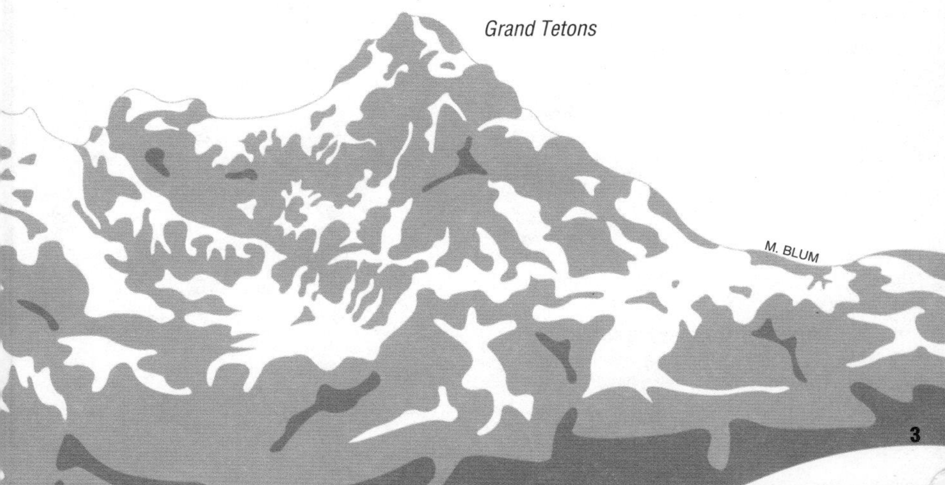

*Grand Tetons*

casinos and cabarets to keep your pulse rate up long after the ski runs close.

Unless you win big at the gambling tables, it pays to know some time-proven tricks to stretch your dollar. In California, incredible weekday deals are available all season long at both Lake Tahoe and **Mammoth**, locations that cater largely to crowds of weekend warriors from San Francisco and Los Angeles. If you arrive on a Sunday night and check out before Friday, for example, it's possible to save up to 50 percent on accommodations, and sometimes 20 percent or more on lift tickets. At the major resorts in Colorado and Utah, frugal skiers opt for the low or shoulder seasons (usually prior to mid-December and after late March) to make the most of their budgets and avoid the high-season crush.

Price considerations are prompting more skiers to consider less prominent resorts that are gaining favor through word of mouth. Ten top picks from **Santa Fe**, New Mexico, to **Alyeska**, Alaska, are briefly profiled in "Ten Up-and-Coming Ski Areas" (see page 216). Whatever your ultimate destination, you'll be rewarded with some of the best skiing on the planet, plus the bonus of Western friendliness and hospitality.

## How To Read This Guide

**Ski Country** ACCESS® Western United States is arranged by resort so you can see at a glance where you are and what is around you. The numbers next to the entries in the following chapters correspond to the numbers on the maps. The text is color-coded according to the kind of place described:

**Restaurants/Clubs:** Red | **Hotels:** Blue
**Shops/ Outdoors:** Green | **Sights/Culture:** Black

### Rating the Resorts

All resorts have different methods of counting the number of trails and rating their difficulty. There is no universally accepted standard in rating terrain difficulty, so a trail rated as expert at one resort might be rated intermediate at another. The trail counts and the breakdown of their difficulty ratings used in this book are based on numbers provided by each resort. Lift-ticket prices are for "regular season" rates, unless otherwise noted, and all prices, for tickets and lessons, were applicable as of press time. Almost all ski areas operate between the hours of 9AM and 4PM during the week; most open at 8:30AM on Saturdays, Sundays, and holidays.

### Rating the Restaurants and Hotels

The restaurant star ratings take into account the quality, service, atmosphere, and uniqueness of the restaurant. An expensive restaurant doesn't necessarily ensure an enjoyable evening; however, a small, relatively unknown spot could have good food, professional service, and a lovely atmosphere. Therefore, on a purely subjective basis, stars are used to judge the overall dining value (see the star ratings at right). Keep in mind that chefs and owners often change, which sometimes drastically affects the quality of a restaurant. The ratings in this guidebook are based on information available at press time.

The price ratings, as categorized at right, apply to restaurants and hotels. These figures describe general price-range relationships between other restaurants and hotels in the area. The restaurant price ratings are based on the average cost of an entrée for one person, excluding tax and tip. Hotel price ratings reflect the base price of a standard room for two people for one night during the peak season.

### Restaurants

| | |
|---|---|
| ★ | Good |
| ★★ | Very Good |
| ★★★ | Excellent |
| ★★★★ | An Extraordinary Experience |
| $ | The Price Is Right |
| $$ | Reasonable |
| $$$ | Expensive |
| $$$$ | Big Bucks |

### Hotels

| | |
|---|---|
| $ | The Price Is Right |
| $$ | Reasonable |
| $$$ | Expensive |
| $$$$ | Big Bucks |

### Map Key

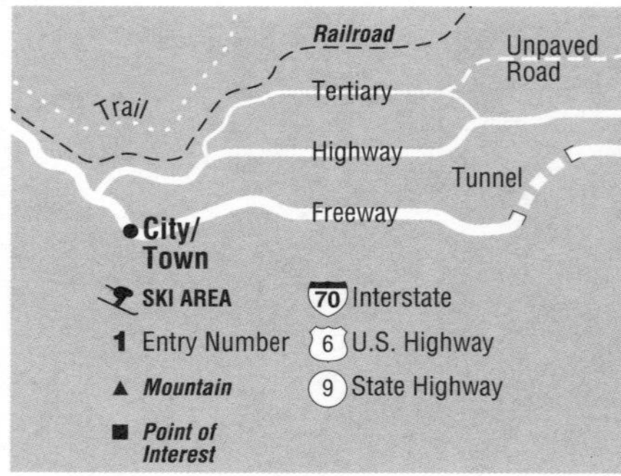

# Ah Schuss—A Beginner's Guide to Ski Lingo

- Alpine Skiing—Downhill skiing (as opposed to cross-country).
- Après-ski—After-skiing social activities, i.e., libations, conversations, and jubilations at the ski lodge.
- Base—Amount of packed snow reported by ski areas.
- Bumps—Slang for moguls.
- Bunny Hill—Easiest hill on the mountain, generally used by beginning skiers.
- Cat Track—A narrow, usually flat trail through the woods that serves as a connector between two major trails.
- Christie—Short for christiania, a ski turn invented in the late 19th century by skiers of Christiania (now Oslo) in Norway. You've performed a successful christie when your skis are parallel after the turn is completed. Variations include the stem christie and wedge christie.
- Chute—Steep and narrow run usually flanked by rocks or trees.
- Corn Snow—Large granules of snow (not unlike kernels of corn) formed when granular snow melts in the sun. The closest thing to fresh powder in the spring.
- Cornice—Overhanging ledge of snow that makes an ideal launching pad for expert skiers negotiating a drop-off.
- Crud—Heavy, slushy, or crusty snow that inhibits good skiing.
- Cruiser—Long, smooth, bump-free run on packed powder.
- DIN (Deutsche Industrial Norm)—Standard for binding manufacturers' calibrations on spring tension (the little chart at the top of the binding indicates how easily the boot will release). Conventional wisdom suggests the higher the DIN, the lower the IQ.
- Download—To ride the chairlift back down the slope, a practice that is usually prohibited. The alternative is a long walk or a free (albeit degrading) sled ride down the mountain courtesy of the ski patrol.
- Face—Usually a steep, open section of a trail.
- Fall Line—Path your ski would take down the mountain if it prereleased at the top of a run.
- G.S. (Giant Slalom)—Form of ski racing that combines elements of both slalom and downhill racing, where a skier must negotiate a series of widely spaced gates by making large radial turns. G.S. also refers to a type of ski and a style of skiing incorporating long, sweeping, high-speed turns.
- Half-pipe—Half-cylindrical form (like a tube cut in half lengthwise) designed exclusively for snowboarders who execute tricks off its edges. A standard-size pipe measures 400 feet long by 75 feet deep with a slope between 19 and 23°.
- Moguls—Bumps of snow caused by the turning action of skiers, usually occurring on steep, ungroomed slopes.
- NASTAR (National Standard Race)—Created by *Ski* magazine in 1969, NASTAR is the largest recreational ski racing program in the world, consisting of giant slalom–type competitions open to the public at most American ski resorts. Participants' times are measured against those of national pacesetters at specific ability levels.
- Powder—Dry, fresh, light snow. Preferred by powderhounds, but often the bane of less experienced skiers because it requires a more difficult technique than does skiing in regular snow.
- Prerelease—When the binding releases from the ski boot without sufficient cause or warning, usually at the worst possible time (e.g., in the middle of a jump).
- Quad—Short for quadruple chair, a four-person chairlift that is either a "fixed model" permanently attached to the cable or a "high-speed detachable," which temporarily releases from the fast-moving cable for loading and unloading passengers.
- Shred—Used to describe the performance of an exceptional skier/snowboarder, as in "That dude shreds!"
- Sitzmark—Depression made in soft snow when a skier falls backward.
- Ski Brake—Spring-loaded device on all modern bindings that stops runaway skis by projecting two prongs into the snow when the binding releases from the boot.
- Slalom—Form of racing in which a skier attempts to negotiate a course of staggered, closely set gates using short radial turns. From an archaic Norwegian word meaning "zigzag."
- Snowcat—Nickname for grooming tractors.
- Snowplow—Basic ski technique where skis are spread into a wedge position (tips together) for easy control of speed and turning.
- Telemarking—A method of skiing in which the boot heel is free to lift up from the ski during a turn, unlike conventional downhill skiing in which the heel is fixed to the ski by the binding. One of the big advantages of a telemark rig is that the free heel makes climbing on skis much easier—a fact appreciated by backcountry skiers. The byword of hardcore telemarkers; "Free the heel and you free the mind."
- Velcro—Sticky patch of snow that unexpectedly retards only one ski, usually resulting in a fall. See "yard sale."
- Yard Sale—Result of a high-speed fall, where a trail of hat, gloves, poles, skis, goggles, and dignity are displayed for all to scrutinize.

# Squaw Valley

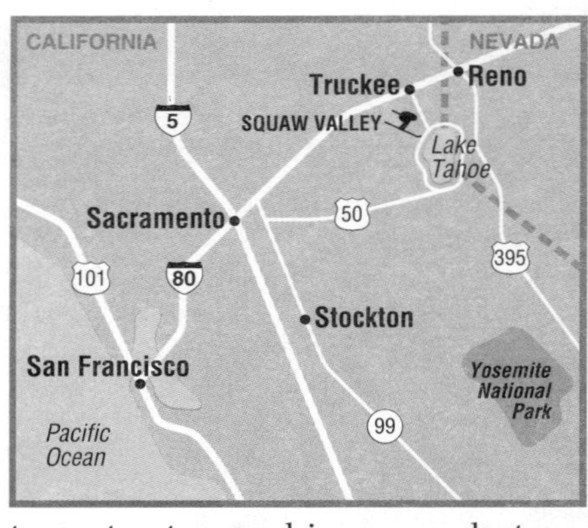


Attitude: No other ski resort in California can compete with Squaw Valley in this arena. Spread over six mountain peaks, five of them exceeding 8,000 feet in height, Squaw Valley attracts the best (and often most demented) skiers from around the world, many of whom graduated from Squaw's intensive racing program. Not only was it the site of the **1960 Winter Olympic Games**, but Squaw also boasts some of the country's gnarliest, wickedest, most gut-wrenching runs, chutes, cornices, and cliffs. Even for the most accomplished, conquering some of the steeper runs here is truly cause for celebration.

Yet, Squaw Valley is not exclusively for pros. In fact, it's geared primarily toward beginner and intermediate skiers. Even the most fear-inducing sections of the resort have been tamed with the addition of a few intermediate-level, bump-free runs. Snowboarders enjoy their own park, complete with jumps, pipes, and chutes (as well as access to the entire ski area), while novices can tumble down acres and acres of wide-open bowls.

Over the past few years, Squaw has invested millions in new lifts, runs, snowmaking equipment, and intensive ski school programs, as well as in such amenities as luxury accommodations, gourmet restaurants, and midmountain lodges. For people who just like to whip through a few runs and spend the rest of a day in other pursuits, there are ice skating and bungee-jumping opportunities, spas, pools, a movie theater, arcades, a 30-foot climbing wall, and enough expensive shops and restaurants to max out even the gold credit cards. And nonskiers can happily lose their shirts, day or night, at casinos located less than an hour from the slopes.

Which isn't to suggest that you'll go broke here. Children under 13 and seniors over 65 can ski all day long for a mere $5, and first-time skiers 13 and over may test out the sport for free through Squaw's "Fun in the Sun" program (ski rental, a lift ticket, and ski orientation are all included). Harried parents can catch their breath thanks to day-care facilities for children up to 12 years of age.

All of these amenities, added to the fact that it's one of the largest ski areas in the US, have earned Squaw Valley world-class credentials. Not bad, when you consider that the resort opened in 1949 with only one chairlift, two rope tows, and a tiny lodge. No wonder the place has an attitude.

**Squaw Valley USA**
**PO Box 2007**
**Olympic Valley, California 96146**

| | |
|---|---|
| **Information** | 916/583.6985 |
| **Central Reservations** | 800/545.4350 |
| **24-Hour Information** | 916/583.6955 |
| **24-Hour Snow Phone** | 916/583.6955 |
| **Road Conditions** | 916/445.7623 |

## Fast Facts

*Area code 916 unless otherwise noted.*

**Ski Season** Mid-November to May, depending on the snowfall; a few runs are open year-round.

**Location** Squaw Valley is eight miles northwest of **Tahoe City**.

## Getting to Squaw Valley

**By air: Reno/Tahoe International Airport,** about 45 miles to the northeast of Squaw, is served daily by **America West, American, Continental, Delta, Northwest, Reno Air, Southwest, United**, and **USAir**. All offer direct flights. Call **Squaw Valley Central Reservations** (see above) to book passage. Shuttle service from **Tours Unlimited** (546.1355) is available from the airport.

**By bus: Greyhound** (800/231.2222) runs buses daily (8AM-11PM) from **Truckee** and **Reno.**

**By car:** All-wheel-drive rental cars are available from several agencies at **Reno/Tahoe International Airport.** Driving from **Reno**, take Interstate 80 West 11 miles to **Truckee,** and then head south on Highway 89 for eight miles. To avoid traffic jams, try to arrive earlier or later than Squaw's regular operating hours.

**All-weather highways:**

Reno—Interstate 80 West to Highway 89 South

Sacramento—Interstate 80 East to Highway 89 South

Greater San Francisco—Interstate 80 East to Highway 89 South

**Driving times from:**

Reno—50 minutes (42 miles)

Sacramento—1.75 hours (96 miles)

Greater San Francisco—3.5 hours (196 miles)

**By train: Amtrak**'s (800/USA.RAIL) *California Zephyr* stops daily in **Reno** and **Truckee**—mornings westbound, evenings eastbound.

## Getting around Squaw Valley

**Tahoe Area Regional Transit** (TART; 581.6365), **North Tahoe's** only public transportation system, operates a handful of buses serving the North Tahoe area from **Sugar Pine Point** to **Incline Village** and **Truckee**. Buses run Monday through Thursday and Sunday from 6:30AM to 6:30PM, Friday and Saturday until 2:30AM. The **Squaw Valley Free Shuttle** (583.6985) provides service between the North Tahoe area and Squaw Valley, leaving from designated stops along the road.

## FYI

# SQUAW VALLEY

**Area** 4,200 acres with open bowl terrain, the most challenging of which is concentrated on the mountain's left flank

Beginner—25 percent

Intermediate—45 percent

Advanced/Expert—30 percent

**Number of Groomed Runs** It varies, depending on the season, although at least 30 percent are groomed at any one time. A daily listing is available at the ticket booth.

**Longest Run** 3.5 miles (Mountain Run)

**Capacity** 49,000 skiers per hour

**Base Elevation** 6,200 feet

**Summit Elevation** 9,050 feet

**Vertical Rise** 2,850 feet

**Average Annual Snowfall** 450 inches

**Snowmaking** 20 percent

**Night Skiing** Weekends and holidays 4PM-9PM

**Lifts** 33 (a 150-passenger cable car, 6-passenger gondola, 3 detachable quads, 8 triple chairs, 15 double chairs, 5 surface lifts)

| Lift Passes | Full Day | Half Day (starts at 1PM) |
|---|---|---|
| **Adult** | $43 | $29 |
| **Child** (12 and under) | $5 | $5 |
| **Senior** (65 and over) | $5 | $5 |
| Nights only: all ages | $8 | |

**Ski School** The ski school office (583.0119) is located just to the left of the main ticket portal, at the end of the parking lot. Group lessons and private instruction (including powder, moguls, and freestyle) are available.

**Kids' Ski School** All children's programs, for ages two to 12, are offered through **Children's World** (583.6985). **Snow School** provides lessons for ages 4 to 6 and **Junior Mountain** helps 7- to 12-year-olds improve their technique.

**Clinics and Special Programs** Squaw offers a variety of adult programs, such as specialized ski clinics, snowboard instruction, and adult racing classes. A free "Fun in the Sun" program is available for first-time skiers ages 13 and older. **Just For Women** is taught by and for women and offers a series of three- and five-day sessions, including video analysis and technical workshops. The **Advanced Skiing Clinic** is for ambitious intermediate and advanced skiers who want to spend three to five days improving their handling of any terrain or snow conditions.

**Races** An electronically timed course is located at the top of **Shirley Lake Express,** near **East Broadway.** The fee is $1 per run, and there are no coaches on hand. Specialty race events include the **Resort at Squaw Creek Celebrity Race** (January) and the **US Pro Tour** (February).

**Rentals** The main rental shop (581.7176) is in the **Clocktower Building,** just to the right of the ticket booths. It's open Monday through Friday 8:30AM to 9PM, and Saturday & Sunday 8AM to 8PM; a credit card or check is required to rent equipment. If you don't like the main shop's ski selection, try renting from the **Squaw Tahoe Resort** (near the base of Big Red Lift) or the **Squaw Valley Inn** (across from the **Gondola Building**). Snowboarders will find the best selection and the friendliest service at **Sno Wave Snowboard Shop and Rentals** (581.5703), located at the entrance to Squaw Valley, off Highway 89.

**Lockers** The main locker room is located to the left of the ticket booths, next to the medical clinic. Overnight ski checks are available. Other coin-operated lockers are scattered throughout the resort: next to **Dave's Deli** in the **Olympic House;** within the **Gondola Building;** and at **High Camp** and **Gold**

**Coast,** 8,200 feet up the mountain.

**Day Care Children's World** (583.6985) is located at the base of Big Red Lift, to the left of the main ticket booths. The **Ten Little Indians** program offers day care only for two-year-olds and the option of a ski lesson for three-year-olds. The center usually opens just before and closes just after the ski runs. For children under two years old, call the **Tahoe Chamber of Commerce** (581.6900) for licensed sitters.

**First Aid** A complete medical center, the **Tahoe-Truckee Medical Group** (583.3439)—which includes family practice, internal medicine, and sports medicine—is in the **Portal Building,** to the left of the main ticket booths. It's open daily from 9AM to 5PM. The closest hospital is **Tahoe Forest** (587.6011 or 800/733.9953), eight miles north of Squaw Valley in **Truckee.**

**Parking** There is free parking at the base. Valet parking is available for a fee.

**Worth Knowing**

- Those taking a break from skiing, permanently or temporarily, can ride the cable car or gondola for $12.
- Squaw boasts the greatest number of skiers (49,000) per hour in the US.

## Rating the Runs

As you can ski nearly all of Squaw's six peaks, for a seemingly infinite number of runs, the local powers that be have chosen not to display *any* runs on the ski guide. Instead, the lifts are rated. This isn't a perfect system, as several intermediate runs start from the top of advanced-rated lifts (it doesn't work the other way)—but at least it's a start.

### ● Beginner

Squaw's heartless designers put **Links,** as well as the other two bunny runs, at the *top* of the mountain, forcing agitated novices to ride a gondola or cable car up 2,000 feet of mostly unskiable terrain. The upside is that Squaw's five beginner lifts are interconnected, so you don't have to keep falling down the same run all day long. And the beginner slopes all eventually lead to both lodges. Although the five runs are basically the same, Links offers the best (read: least crowded) slope.

Wide, flat, and slow, **East Broadway** is often crowded. The course's main draw is its proximity to the **Gold Coast** lodge, where mom and dad can sit on an outside deck and watch their schussing young'ns.

At the end of the day, it's acceptable to download on either the cable car or gondola, but brave new skiers will attempt Squaw's version of The Final Exam and go screaming down **Mountain Run** (the only trail actually named on the area map). It is actually easier than it looks, but can crowd up seriously by late afternoon. And, for those who just can't get enough skiing during the day, there's night skiing on this run as well.

### ■ Intermediate

Located at the bottom of **Granite Chief,** Shirley Lake Express is by far Squaw's best intermediate-level lift. Runs are well groomed and fun, with small hills and several curves. The high-speed, well-cushioned quad is another excellent option.

While all intermediate lifts between **Squaw Peak** and **Emigrant Peak** offer challenging runs (some bordering on the advanced), none of them compare with the trails off of Solitude and Shirley Express.

Skiers and snowboarders blaze from the top of the Emigrant Lift straight down to the base—an intensely long ride (3.5 miles) lined with jumps, drop-offs, and a half-pipe.

### ◆ Advanced

For skiers who can handle any sort of terrain, **Granite Chief** offers everything from steep groomed runs to bumps, tree skiing, hidden chutes, and gnarly cornices. It's also somewhat protected from the wind and ubiquitous snowboarders.

Like Granite Chief, **Silverado** offers a wide variety of advanced runs (chute, trees, bumps) and some shelter from the elements.

Take a left at the top of **Cornice II** and cruise down the wide, semi-steep groomed run on your way back to the lift base. This is perfect for GS skiers.

### ◆◆ Expert

The **West Face** of **KT-22**—the steepest run in North America accessible by chairlift—should be tackled only by experts and the terminally insane.

Located at the top of **Squaw Peak,** off the Headwall Chair (4,900 feet), **Palisades** is renowned for its perfect-10 rating on the Fear Factor. It's also a popular backdrop for the movies of Warren Miller, the most successful ski filmmaker ever.

## Snowboarding

Advanced riders head to the snowboard park, located on **Riviera** next to the **Gold Coast Lodge,** to practice tricks on the tabletops, rail slides, pyramids, and whales. For carvers and more advanced boarders getting the hang of the sport, Squaw's extensive grooming system and open bowls provide plenty of terrain. In addition, Squaw has a snowboard racing team, so there is always an opportunity to pick up a tip or two and see some rad action while just hanging out on the slopes.

For a truly uplifting experience, call Lake Tahoe Balloons (916/544.1221) to schedule a hot-air balloon flight over the lakes, meadows, and forests around Tahoe. The 4.5-hour experience (available year-round, weather permitting) includes shuttle service and champagne brunch. Prices range from $95 to $145.

"As it lay there (Lake Tahoe) with the shadows of the mountains brilliantly photographed upon its still surface, I thought it must surely be the fairest picture the whole earth affords."

## Mountain Highs and Lows

Although **Siberia Express** is supposedly for intermediates, a left turn off the lift is guaranteed to challenge all but the bravest snow warriors. The timid will fare better on the opposite side.

## At the Resort

*Area code 916 unless otherwise noted.*

✦ **Opera House** This octagonal building houses a general store, a movie theater, and a restaurant. ♦ East end of the parking lot

Within the Opera House:

**The General Store** With a modest attempt at being a gourmet deli, this place is perfectly located for an end-of-the-day beer and a snack to pack along for the ride home. The store even rents videos. ♦ Daily 8AM-6PM. 583.3906

**Opera House Cinema** First-run movies play here nightly. A small snack bar is right on the premises for the terminally voracious. ♦ 546.5951

**Backstage Bistro** ★★$$$ Small, intimate, and tastefully decorated (lots of earth tones), this restaurant serves Mediterranean cuisine, including pasta, poultry, lamb, veal, and steak. Its highest recommendation may be that it's frequented by locals. ♦ Daily dinner. 581.0454

✦ **Squaw Tahoe Resort** $$$$ This rather homely looking 27-unit establishment offers a choice of studios or one- and two-bedroom condos, each equipped with a kitchen, fireplace, microwave, washer/dryer, and color TV. Two spas, four saunas, a clubhouse, and covered parking round out the amenities. It's a great deal for groups and families, as the condos comfortably house four to six people. A three-night minimum stay is required during high season and holidays. ♦ Bottom of the Big Red Lift. 583.7226

✦ **Squaw Valley Outfitters** Sandwiched between Squaw's medical office and the main ticket booths, this is the Rodeo Drive version of a skiwear boutique, with high-priced, high-fashion skiwear and mountainwear crammed into a small space. Don't expect to find many snowboarders here, and bring your Gold Card. ♦ Daily 9AM-4PM. 583.6985 ext 117

For a well-rounded Tahoe ski experience, purchase an interchangeable lift ticket good at eight ski areas in North Tahoe, including Squaw Valley, Northstar, Alpine Meadows, and Boreal. Three- to six-day passes start at $117. Call the Tahoe North Visitors Bureau (916/583.3494) for more information.

**Restaurants/Clubs:** Red **Hotels:** Blue
**Shops/ Outdoors:** Green **Sights/Culture:** Black

✦ **Olympic Plaza** The **Gondola Building** is part of this plaza, but the eateries here are what are most popular with weary skiers out for a midday beer and sandwich. ♦ Bottom of the gondola. 583.1588

Within Olympic Plaza:

**Dave's Deli** $ This upscale gourmet place offers pastries, great sandwiches, espressos, and imported cheeses and brews. ♦ Daily 8AM-5PM. 581.1085

**Emily's Garden** ★$ Catering to health-conscious sports types, this cafe serves a spartan selection of pitas, salads, soups, and veggie dishes. ♦ Daily 8AM-5PM. No phone

**Hamburger Express** $ Naturally, all this heart-smart consumption must be balanced by a junk-food joint. This quick stop does it just right, serving America's greasy contribution to the decline of civilization at laughable prices. ♦ Daily 8AM-5PM. 583.1588 ext 337

**Bar One** Upstairs in the **Gondola Building,** this capacious bar showcases huge window vistas of the mountain, in addition to a large sundeck, a big-screen TV, rest rooms, and public phones. ♦ Daily 11AM-5PM. 583.1588 ext 320

✦ **Olympic House** A minimall of sorts, this complex contains shops, boutiques, and cafes. **Crepes Annette** (581.1529) serves gourmet coffees and flavored crepes (try the applesauce and cinnamon or bananas and cream varieties). And on the second floor, the **Sundeck Cafe** (no phone) provides just what its name suggests—a pleasant outdoor retreat, overlooking **Mountain Run**. Food service is cafeteria style. ♦ Next to Olympic Plaza. 583.6985

✦ **Squaw Valley Mall** The unofficial mall tour of Squaw Valley includes this commercial center, where two restaurants and a ski store vie for customers. **Mother Barclay's** (581.3251) is known for its meat loaf, but also serves such lunch items as burgers, sandwiches, pasta, and a variety of soups as well as an all-day breakfast menu. Then there's the **Sport Shop** (583.3356), offering high-performance ski rentals, an overnight ski repair service, and every other item or aid you could possibly require on the mountain. Behind the Sport Shop, **Le Chamois** (583.4505), a small but popular cafe, is about as French as pizza—which just happens to be the best item on the menu. Order a Sierra Nevada Ale to wash down the

Le Chamois

crust. ♦ Between the Olympic Mall and Olympic Plaza. 583.6985

✦ **Cable Car Building** If you've never ridden cable car before, boarding this one is well worth the 20-minute-or-so wait. As you ascend rapidly up 2,000 vertical feet toward **High Camp,** the car operator warns you when your stomach is about to sink—which happens at each support tower, when the car suddenly lists. It's a pleasant and scenic ride for skiers and nonskiers alike. ♦ M-F 9AM-10PM; Sa-Su 8:30AM-10PM. 583.6985

Within the Cable Car Building:

**Headwall Cafe and Climbing Wall** Only in America can you power down a double espresso then clamber up 30 feet of seemingly unassailable wall. Attached safety lines make falling impossible, so this sport is safe for people of any age, sex, and timidity level. ♦ Daily 9AM-4PM. 583.6985

✦ **Squaw Valley Inn** $$$$ Located just steps away from the **Cable Car Building,** this two-story wood-shingled inn was designed originally to house visitors to the **1960 Olympic Winter Games**. The 57 guest rooms and trio of suites won't win any design awards, but they're spacious, clean, and comfortable, each outfitted with two queen-size beds, a color TV, and telephone. Other amenities include hot tubs, a ski and sportswear shop, and the inn's own ski rental and repair shop. ♦ 1920 Squaw Valley Rd. 583.1576, 800/323.ROOM; fax 583.7619

Within the Squaw Valley Inn:

At 1,932 feet in depth, Lake Tahoe is the second deepest lake in the US (Oregon's Crater Lake tops the list) and the eighth deepest in the world. It is about as long as the narrowest part of the English Channel (22 miles). The water it holds could flood the entire state of California to a depth of 14.5 inches or fill a Panama Canal-size trench (700 feet wide and 50 feet deep) that stretches the circumference of the earth. The lake is fed by 63 streams and two hot springs, and an average of 1,400,000 tons of water (or 0.1 inch) evaporates from the lake every day—enough to supply the daily water requirements of 3,500,000 people.

**Benton's** ★★$$$ The meals served here are surprisingly good—in contrast to what you'll find at many of the resort's restaurants. The English Country decor and a menu featuring elements of French, Italian, Greek, Southwestern, and California cuisine make for an eclectic combination. Chef Lewis Radoff's specialties change weekly, to take advantage of seasonal produce and seafood, but you can usually order Greek lamb chops, blackened salmon or halibut, and roasted Long Island duckling in a raspberry sauce. The adjoining **Slopes Bar** hosts a brisk après-ski Happy Hour, with the drink of choice being a steaming hot chocolate and schnapps cocktail. ♦ Daily breakfast, lunch, and dinner. 583.1576

✦ **High Camp Bath and Tennis Club** A year-round multisport facility, accessible by way of the cable car, this is the Disneyland of midmountain lodges. Opulent attractions range from an Olympic-size ice rink (the highest in the world, open year-round) and six tennis courts to a swimming lagoon and a 75-foot bungee jumping platform. Several decks overlook the mountain's ski activity. ♦ 583.6985

✦ **Gold Coast** This three-story, skier-friendly midmountain lodge contains two restaurants (a buffet and a *hofbrau*), two bars, an outdoor barbecue, and carts dispensing crepes, cookies, and, of course, espresso. A small retail store sells mostly souvenir items. The lodge (and especially the bar) works well as a designated meeting place for couples or groups who might find themselves dispersed on the slopes. ♦ Top of the gondola line. 583.6985

✦ **Olympic Village Inn** $$$$ A few minutes walk from the lifts and slightly more expensive than the **Squaw Valley Inn,** this three-story complex is a better lodging choice. Ninety luxury suites are decked out with handsome country furnishings, including a cedar hope chest, large armoire, eiderdown comforter on a queen-size sofa bed, and imported wall coverings. The fully equipped kitchenette is key for those on a tight budget and you can retreat to one of the inn's five outdoor spas after the lifts close down. ♦ 1900 Squaw Valley Rd. 581.6000, 800/845.5243; fax 583.3135

✦ **Squaw Valley Lodge** $$$$ Despite the utilitarian architecture, this 154-room hotel rates a second glance for two reasons: Lift lines are only a few feet away, and a health club with four spas, a sauna, steam room, and heated pool coaxes the tension out of bruised bodies. The completely furnished suites include kitchenettes, goose-down comforters, and color TVs. Maid service, a complimentary ski check, and covered parking all help make your stay more comfortable. Studios sleep four to six people. ♦ 210 Squaw Peak Rd. 583.5500, 800/922.9970; fax 583.0326

✦ **Resort at Squaw Creek** $$$$ The *crème de la crème* of Lake Tahoe's lodging options, this luxury hotel is a multimillion-dollar extravaganza complete with five restaurants and lounges, heated pools and whirlpool spas, an executive fitness center, shopping promenade, ice rink, cross-country ski trails, and (here's the clincher) the Squaw Creek Lift, catering exclusively to the resort and providing access to the entire mountain. The 405 deluxe guest rooms and suites feature custom furnishings, original artwork, mini-bars, and daily maid service. Some also come with fireplaces and full kitchens. In summer, this place is popular with golfers and tennis buffs, thanks to an 18-hole championship golf course designed by Robert Trent Jones Jr., and the **Peter Burwash International Tennis Center**. Yes, it's expensive, but midweek package deals can be fairly reasonable. ♦ 400 Squaw Creek Rd. 583.6300, 800/327.3353; fax 581.6632

***For more information on the Squaw Valley area, see "Beyond the Resorts," page 19.***



## Bests

**Allyson Bolla**
Marketing, Squaw Valley Ski Corporation

Of course I adore the **Squaw Valley** area—the spectacular mountain, the **High Camp** facility, and the surrounding terrain.

We love **Donner Lake,** the **Big Lake,** the fresh streams, and the wildflowers.

**Carol L. Dietrich**
Receptionist/Secretary, Squaw Valley Ski Corporation

**Squaw Valley USA**—The terrain is incredible. . . a mountain with something for everyone. My whole family has a great time, and we all ski at different levels.

**Fire Sign Cafe**—Great place for breakfast on a snowy day, or any day for that matter.

**Sunnyside**—Wonderful food and drinks. My favorite thing to do when I'm flat broke is have their soup and salad for $6.50. I feel so indulgent and still have money left over for skiing.

**Tahoe** is a great place to be—hiking, mountain biking, and running in the summer and ski, ski, ski in the winter. There are lots of outdoor daytime activities and exciting things to do at night.

---

What's in and what's out at Tahoe?

IN

1. Wild and silly hats
2. Bright (neon is coming back) colors in clothing
3. All-mountain, go-anywhere skis
4. Specialty (especially women's) clinics and ski adventure classes
5. Snowboards
6. One-piece ski outfits
7. A ceiling on lift-ticket prices ($50 was most often mentioned)
8. Skinny, lighter-weight ski poles

OUT

1. Camouflage and deer hunter-orange colors in clothing
2. Sack lunches
3. Miniskirts or shorts over tight-fitting jeans
4. Out-of-control skiing
5. Animal fur on hats, collars, and après-ski boots
6. $50 lift-ticket prices
7. Faces covered with colored sunscreens
8. Sunny days (With so much snow in recent seasons, sunny days have become as rare as the perfectly carved turn.)

# Alpine Meadows

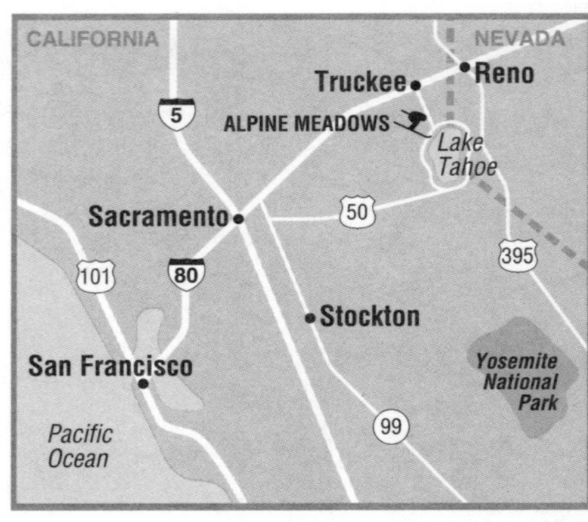


There's no doubt that Alpine stands in philosophical opposition to **Squaw Valley:** No sushi stands, no chichi restaurants, no ice rinks, no aerobics studios, and no chance whatsoever that a deft valet will step forward to save you the hassle of parking your car. All you'll find at Alpine Meadows is one building, 12 lifts, and more than a hundred superlative, sunny trails, bowls, steeps, bumps, cornices, and chutes. Still resisting the invasion of snowboarders, refreshingly underdeveloped (there's nary a condo in sight), and staffed by a family of happily underpaid employees, this resort is a haven for "old school" skiers, to whom only three things matter: skiing, skiing, and skiing.

Because the slopes on Alpine's twin mountain peaks face all directions (there's literally 360-degree exposure, with astonishing views of **Lake Tahoe** from the top of **Scott Peak**), skiers can follow the sun across the mountain, working the eastern faces during morning hours and finishing on the western bowls in the afternoon. And since the majority of lifts here run along the north faces, which hold snow well into June and early July, Alpine is usually the last ski area in California to close, offering ideal spring skiing conditions. Located a mere mile from **Squaw Valley** (in fact, it's possible to ski between the two, if you know where you are going), Alpine shares much of the advanced and expert terrain that has made its neighbor famous. At the same time, it devotes entire peaks to intermediate skiers and has three lifts designed especially for beginners, so no one is left out. The only disadvantage to skiing here is that the majority of Alpine's lifts are slow and outdated. Fortunately, though, upgrading is in the works. Forced by past droughts to beef up its snowmaking abilities, Alpine has risen to the occasion: The resort now guarantees that the majority of its ski runs will be open during the ski season and boasts of snowmaking capabilities from top to bottom.

Since there are no accommodations on-site at Alpine Meadows, the entire area basically shuts down after 5PM. Contented hordes wheel back to lodges along Lake Tahoe or in **Truckee**, perhaps stopping along the way at the **River Ranch Lodge** for an après-ski libation. Alpine's simplicity helps it thrive. Customers here may not be flashy or attitude-enhanced, but they sure are loyal.

**Alpine Meadows Ski Area**
**PO Box 5279**
**Tahoe City, California 96145**

**Information:**...............916/583.4232, 800/441.4423

**24-Hour Snow Phone:** .......................916/581.8374

**Road Conditions:**..............................916/445.7623

## Fast Facts

*Area code 916 unless otherwise noted.*

**Ski Season** Mid-November through end of May

**Location** Alpine Meadows is six miles northwest of Tahoe City.

### Getting to Alpine Meadows

**By air: Reno/Tahoe International Airport,** 46 miles northeast of Alpine, is served daily by **America West, American, Continental, Delta, Northwest, Reno Air, Southwest, United,** and **USAir.** All offer direct flights. **Tours Unlimited** (546.1355) provides shuttle service from the airport.

**By bus: Greyhound** (800/231.2222) runs buses daily (8AM-11PM) from **Truckee** and **Reno.**

**By car:** All-wheel-drive rental cars are available from several agencies at **Reno/Tahoe International Airport.** From **Reno,** take Interstate 80 West 33 miles to **Truckee,** and then head south on Highway 89 for 13 miles. To avoid traffic jams, try to arrive earlier or later than Alpine's operating hours.

**All-weather highways:**

Reno—Interstate 80 West to Highway 89 South

Sacramento—Interstate 80 East to Highway 89 South

Greater San Francisco—Interstate 80 East to Highway 89 South

**Driving times from:**

Reno—55 minutes (46 miles)

Sacramento—2.25 hours (111 miles)

Greater San Francisco—3.5 hours (198 miles)

**By train: Amtrak**'s (800/USA.RAIL) *California Zephyr* stops daily in **Reno** and **Truckee**—mornings westbound, evenings eastbound.

## Getting around Alpine Meadows

**Tahoe Area Regional Transit** (**TART;** 581.6365) operates a handful of public buses daily from 6:30AM to 6:30PM and serves the **North Tahoe** area from **Sugar Pine Point** to **Incline Village** and **Truckee.** Alpine has a free ski shuttle which services most North and West Shore hotels and connects with TART buses.

## FYI

**Area** 2,000 acres with more than 100 runs

Beginner—25 percent

Intermediate—40 percent

Advanced—35 percent

**Number of Groomed Runs** It varies, depending on the season, although at least 30 percent are groomed at any one time.

**Longest Run** 2.5 miles **(High Traverse)**

**Capacity** 16,000 skiers per hour

**Base Elevation** 6,835 feet

**Summit Elevation** 8,637 feet

**Vertical Rise** 1,802 feet

**Average Annual Snowfall** 400 inches

**Snowmaking** 87 percent

**Night Skiing** None

**Lifts** 12 (2 high-speed express quads, 2 triple chairs, 7 double chairs, and 1 surface lift)

| **Lift Passes** | **Full Day** | **Half Day** (starts at12:30PM) |
|---|---|---|
| **Adult** | $43 | $29 |
| **Child** (7-12) | $18 | $12 |
| **Child** (6 and under) | $6 | $6 |
| **Senior** (65-69) | $29 | $29 |
| **Senior** (70 and over) | Free | Free |

Multi-day lift passes are also available: Three-day tickets are $117 for adults, $45 for children; five-day passes are $190 for adults, $70 for children.

**Ski School** The ski school desk (581.8200) is located in the main lodge, on the east side of the bottom floor. Students are divided into beginners and everyone else. The four-hour beginner program starts at 10AM (includes ski equipment and a lift ticket). If you can be ready by 9AM, try the **Early Bird Special.** A two-hour afternoon session starts at noon (includes an afternoon lift ticket). Intermediate skiers and better can take a four-hour group lesson or a two-hour "tune-up" lesson. Private lessons for one or two skiers are available hourly.

**Kids' Ski School Ski Camp** for ages 6 through 12 is offered for all ability levels. Kids ages 4 through 6 can take advantage of a special **Snow School,** offered on a first-come, first-served basis (daily 8:30AM to 9:30AM; afternoon sessions at 12:30PM). The **Hot Shots** program, for intermediate- to advanced-level 4- to 6-year-olds, has the same rates and registration procedures as **Snow School.** Tickets, equipment, lunch, and snacks are included in all sessions. 583.4232.

**Clinics and Special Programs** Offerings include telemark, mogul and powder clinics for advanced skiers; **Women's Weekly Edition Ski Group** exclusively for women; and the **It's Never Too Late** program for adults over 50 who want to learn or improve their skiing. **Create Your Own Clinic** programs can be scheduled with five or more skiers.

**Races** Specialty race events include the **NFL Players Association Challenge** (Feb); **Corporate Ski Challenge** (Mar); NASTAR racing, Saturdays and Sundays; the **Recreational Race Series,** Mondays and Thursdays; a pay-per-race course open most days.

**Rentals** The rental shop (581.8244) is located in the main lodge, on the east side of the bottom floor. There's also a good selection of standard rental equipment, high-performance demos, telemark skis, and the "fat" skis for powder. It's open daily from 8AM to 4:30PM.

**Lockers** Boot and ski lockers are located in the main lodge, just to the right of the ticket windows. Overnight storage and baggage checks are also available on the west side of the lodge's main entrance.

**Day Care** There are no facilities on site. Day care is available, however, at **Squaw Valley,** only six miles away.

**First Aid** A very basic medical stop (581.8211) is located near the main lodge's locker area. The closest hospital is **Tahoe Forest** (587.6011, 800/733.9953), eight miles north of **Squaw Valley,** in **Truckee.**

**Parking** There is free parking at the base.

**Worth Knowing**

- To avoid long lines, try purchasing lift tickets at the **Special Ticket Desk,** right next to the information desk on the east end of the main floor of the main lodge.

## Rating the Runs

### ● Beginner

Located just east of the main lodge, the beginner area is serviced by two chairlifts (Subway and Meadow) and a poma (Tiegel). Warm up on the **Subway** trail, then tumble down **Meadow** for a spell. Skip the poma lift, which is more difficult to use than the chairlift.

### ■ Intermediate

Intermediate skiers simply can't go wrong on any of Alpine's lifts. Since every one provides an adventure, the trick is to find those with the shortest lines.

From the main lodge, take the Weasel Chair over the back side of **Scott Peak.** This gives you access not only to **Lakeview,** but to an entire face of uncrowded, nicely groomed, and wide-open intermediate-level runs, many of which overlook **Lake Tahoe.**

Located to the right of the Sherwood Chair, the **Sherwood** run is perfect for intermediate skiers who favor wide-open terrain with eye-popping views. Entering the open bowl from the short, tree-lined trail gives skiers a pleasant surprise.

Large enough to handle hundreds of people and then some, **Alpine Bowl** also provides access to a half-dozen other intermediate slopes, prolonging the enjoyment with top-to-bottom runs. Reached by the Summit Chair or the Alpine Bowl Chair, this is this resort's most popular run.

### ◆ Advanced

Although it takes a long traverse to reach **Beaver Bowl,** the rewards are epic hidden chutes filled by waist-deep powder and wide expanses of barely tracked snow. If you don't mind hiking, nearby **Estelle Bowl,** with its wicked cornices and steep, nearly untracked chutes, offers a more sublime experience.

After checking out the west end, take **High Traverse** east from the top of Alpine Bowl Chair to the **Sherwood Bowls (Sun Bowl, SP Bowl, Big Bend Bowl)** for wide-open and first-rate schussing. If there's fresh powder, this is the place to make first tracks.

Tree skiers, take heart. The **Lower 40 Face,** just north of the Scott Chair, combines heavy-duty tree dodging with enough open expanses so you can catch your breath.

### ◆◆ Expert

Hellacious, steep, and deep, **Our Father** may be brief and a bit hard to reach, but it's a prime spot for perfecting your jump turns.

If you're into cornice-jumping and don't mind some hiking, **Estelle Bowl** earns at least an 8.5 on the challenge scale. The chest-deep duvet of exceptional powder here is some of the best on the mountain.

Steep and bumpy, with a hairy entrance that demands a few perfect turns, **Scott Chute** is the classic expert run.

### Snowboarding

Not permitted.

## Mountain Highs and Lows

Those who may be tempted by **Wolverine Bowl,** beware. This run looks tame enough from the Summit Lift for intermediate skiers, but its steep and bumpy entrance merits bona fide "advanced" designation.

It's labeled an intermediate course, but unless you can ski bumps, **Yellow Trail** is more appropriate for advanced skiers.

## At the Resort

*Area code 916 unless otherwise noted.*

✦ **Main Lodge** If you can't find what you're looking for here, chances are Alpine Meadows doesn't have it. Aside from a midmountain lodge—**The Chalet**—that offers drinks and dining, this is the only building at the Meadows and the nucleus for everything that goes on. Skiers may be disappointed by Alpine's spartan selection of services, but will appreciate the simplicity of having all the basic needs under one roof. ◆ At the parking lot. 583.4232

Within the Main Lodge:

**Treats** ★$ This junk-food oasis is perfectly located for a morning jolt of caffeine before you hit the slopes. Pick up a frozen yogurt for the ride home. ◆ Daily breakfast, lunch, and dinner. Lower floor. 583.8287

**Breeze Ski and Sport** This is your basic ski shop—and the only one at Alpine. There is a fair selection of the latest skiwear and sundries. Prices can be steep, but there are a few good deals at season's end. ◆ Lower floor. 583.4123

**The Melrose Cafe** $ Formerly **The Cafeteria,** this spot has been remodeled to include five separate restaurant areas. **Pizza Supremo** serves homemade pasta, lasagna, and pizza; **Chili Peppers** is a Mexican stand; **Wong's Deli** specializes in Asian dishes; **Double Diamond Grill** features regular and salmon burgers, sandwiches, chilies, and soups; and **Sweets** is an espresso bar and baked goods stand. Outside is a 7,800-square-foot deck, complete with beer stand, and live jazz and country music. ◆ Daily breakfast, lunch, and dinner. Upper floor. 583.5177

**Kealy's Alpine Bar and Grill** ★$$ This place is for people who ski three runs or so, then retire to someplace far from the hard-core throngs. Serving burgers, salads, sandwiches, and appetizers, this eatery offers the resort's only sit-down service for those who don't mind missing some prime ski time. ◆ Daily lunch and après-ski. Upper floor. 583.5177

**Compactor Bar** Most folks head to Squaw Valley, or on sunny days, retreat to the deck of **The Chalet** for aprés-ski cocktails. But if it's blowing gales outside, a ball game is on, and you need a quick Irish coffee to thaw the chill from your bones, this is the place. Live rock bands often add to the rowdy atmosphere. ◆ Daily 9AM-4PM. Upper floor. 583.5177

✦ **The Chalet** ★★$ This quaint and charming midmountain log cabin is ideal for a brewski and a bowl of homemade soup. A cozy retreat, it offers a secluded setting and fireplace and a variety of reasonably priced Mexican, Chinese, and Italian dishes. Conveniently located at the intersection of **Weasel, Yellow,** and **Scott** Chairs, it epitomizes the local down-home flavor of Alpine Meadows. ◆ Daily breakfast and lunch. 583.8963

***For more information on the Alpine Meadows area, see "Beyond the Resorts," page 19.***

# A Who's Who of Skiing Superstars

Given that Europeans had been schussing the Alps for generations when we first crossed the Delaware, it's no wonder that most of skiing's luminaries hail from across the Atlantic. Furthermore, when you consider that skiing crests in popularity in the US once every four years (when we get summarily creamed by the Austrians, Norwegians, and the Swiss), it's understandable that Americans need a little help recognizing the Michael Jordans of world-class skiing.

## The Legends

**Stein Eriksen** This Norwegian-born racer started earning his stripes in 1950, taking a bronze at the World Championships in **Aspen,** and two years later gold and silver medals at the Olympics. After topping his illustrious career with three gold medals at the **1954 World Championships** in Aare, Sweden, Eriksen moved to the US, where he's currently the Director of Skiing at the **Deer Valley** resort in Utah.

**Jean-Claude Killy** Perhaps the best-known ski racer in history, Killy made his mark at the **1968 Olympic Games** in Grenoble, where he swept the field and took home three gold medals. After an early retirement at age 24, Killy returned to competitive skiing in 1972 to claim the Pro Championship, then settled down in his hometown of Val d'Isère, France, where he worked as co-president of the Albertville Olympic organizing committee for the 1992 winter games. Killy is currently busy promoting his own line of skiwear, which includes high-tech sunglasses that sell for nearly $400 a pair.

**Franz Klammer** Nicknamed "The Kaiser," this charismatic Austrian is considered by some to be the most extraordinary alpine racer of all time, with a gold medal at the **1976 Innsbruck Olympics,** 25 World Cup downhill victories, and five World Cup downhill medals to his credit. The Kaiser retired in 1985, but his heart-stopping Olympic performance is still replayed on television sets worldwide.

**Tamara McKinney** The only American woman to win a World Cup Championship (1983), McKinney's impressive career stats include 18 World Cup wins, four World Championship medals, and an unprecedented nine national titles. By the end of her career, she had tallied more wins than any other US skier except Phil Mahre.

**Phil and Steve Mahre** The best-known American ski racers in history, these twin brothers were at the forefront of international competition for more than a decade, garnering a slew of World Cup victories and Olympic medals. The Mahre brothers now devote their time to auto racing and their namesake ski training centers at **Keystone** and **Arapahoe Basin.**

**Ingemar Stenmark** This soft-spoken Swedish sensation had an unprecedented 86 World Cup wins in slalom and giant slalom between 1974 and 1989. He was literally a one-man team for his country—even his teammates didn't want to race against him!

## The Ones to Watch

**Marc Girardelli** The Legend of Luxembourg, Girardelli's accomplishments include: Ski Racing's Skier of the Year (1985), three-time International Alpine Skier of the Year, leader of all active male skiers with 36 World Cup wins, four-time World Cup overall winner, three slalom titles, a giant slalom prize, a downhill crown, and two silver medals in the **Albertville 1992 Olympics.**

**Tommy Moe** Tommy Moe is America's new superstar following his outstanding success at the **1994 Lillehammer Winter Olympics.** Moe not only clinched the top prize (gold in the Downhill), but he went on to earn a silver in the Super G. He's been sought after by the media ever since, but he continues to earn some top wins on the World Cup circuit.

**Picabo Street** Picabo makes her home in **Sun Valley** and after her success at the Lillehammer Games, where she won a silver medal, the community honored her by naming a street after her.

**Bernard Knauss** Dominating the pro racing scene for the past several years, the Austrian phenomenon consistently wins slalom and giant slalom events. Confident, consistent, and seemingly unbeatable, Knauss has finished first so often he claims it's starting to get boring.

**Glen Plake** Extreme-skier extraordinaire, this Mohawked maniac has made a name for himself by shredding suicidal chutes and otherwise tempting the fates on the slopes.

**Alberto Tomba** Considered the best slalom and giant slalom skier in the world today and the most charismatic downhill racer since Franz Klammer, this Italian superstar's achievements include a double gold medal performance at the **1988 Calgary Olympics,** 19 World Cup wins, the World Cup slalom crown, and the distinction of being the only man ever to win back-to-back Olympic giant slalom gold medals. Relishing his reputation as a playboy and sex symbol, Tomba considers himself "the new messiah of skiing."

**Donna Weinbrecht** The golden girl from West Milford, New Jersey, Weinbrecht put freestyle and American women's skiing in the media limelight by capturing Olympic gold in freestyle moguls at Albertville in 1992. She also holds a career victory record in mogul skiing, accumulating 25 World Cup wins.

## Honorable Mentions

**Diann Roffe-Steinrotter** This longtime US ski racer retired in 1994, but took along the memory of a gold medal at the **1994 Lillehammer Olympics** among many other accomplishments.

**Cristin Cooper** Along with a silver medal for the US at the Olympic games in Sarajevo, Cooper's kudos include five World Cup wins, three World Championship medals, and four national titles.

**Bill Johnson** America's "bad boy" of skiing, Johnson accepted the US's only 1984 Olympic downhill gold and, to the relief of many, was rarely heard from again.

**Scot Schmidt** Less flamboyant than his buddy Glen Plake but equally talented (and nuts), Schmidt's extreme ski stunts are over the edge.

# Northstar-at-Tahoe

If you're determined to tackle the steep and deep, keep looking. If your taste runs to wide-open bowls, chutes, and bumps, keep on driving. But if you prefer a hassle-free ski resort that the whole family can enjoy, Northstar is one of your best choices.

A wide spectrum of terrain at this 2,560-acre winter destination, completely self-contained and located only minutes from **Lake Tahoe**, attracts both new and advanced skiers. Snowboarders are welcome here, as are cross-country and telemark enthusiasts. Northstar claims one of the best ski-instruction programs in the West, with a range of ski, snowboard, and cross-country lessons and clinics. And even nonskiers can find gratification in the form of pony and sleigh rides, saunas and spas, and a host of shops, restaurants, and bars. An excellent licensed day-care center can take charge of youngsters while parents partake of as many activities as possible.

Lodging at Northstar, while a tad expensive, is undeniably convenient, with hotel rooms, condos, and private homes all available for rent and serviced by a free ski shuttle. Resort guests have an added advantage: They can reserve lift tickets in advance, a wise idea during peak season, when Northstar limits ticket sales to reduce the length of lift lines.

While Northstar (jokingly dubbed "Flatstar" by competitors) lacks the true expert terrain that distinguishes neighboring **Alpine Meadows** and **Squaw Valley**, the opening of the impressive "backside" of **Mount Pluto** and seven one-mile–long runs with seriously steep pitches has led advanced skiers to give this resort another try. And for the average skier who enjoys days spent swishing down long, impeccably groomed runs and nights relaxing before the fireplace in a fully stocked condo, Northstar is tough to beat.

---

**Northstar-at-Tahoe**
**PO Box 129**
**Truckee, California 96160**

**Information**........916/562.1010
**Reservations**........800/GONORTH
**24-Hour Snow Phone**........916/562.1330
**Road Conditions**........800/427.7623

## Fast Facts

*Area code 916 unless otherwise noted.*

**Ski Season** Mid-November to mid-April, depending on the snowfall.

**Location** Northstar-at-Tahoe is located off Highway 267, halfway (six miles) between **Truckee** and **North Lake Tahoe**.

### Getting to Northstar-at-Tahoe

**By air: Reno/Tahoe International Airport,** about 45 miles to the northeast of Northstar, is served daily by **America West, American, Continental, Delta, Northwest, Reno Air, Southwest, United,** and **USAir.** All offer direct flights. Northstar books plane reservations (800/466.6784) as well as transportation from the airport (800/786.2376). Shuttle service is available from the airport (587.0257).

**By bus: Greyhound** (800/231.2222) runs buses daily (8AM to 11PM) from **Reno** and **Truckee.**

**By car:** All-wheel-drive rental cars are available from several agencies at **Reno/Tahoe International Airport.** From **Reno,** take Interstate 80 West to the first **Truckee** exit (Highway 267). Turn left toward downtown Truckee, then left again at the stop sign onto 267. Head south six miles. To avoid traffic jams, try to arrive earlier or later than Northstar's operating hours.

**All-weather highways:**

Reno—Interstate 80 West to Highway 267 South

Sacramento—Interstate 80 East to Highway 267 South

Greater San Francisco—Interstate 80 East to Highway 267 South

**Driving times from:**

Reno—45 minutes (40 miles)

Sacramento—1.75 hours (96 miles)

Greater San Francisco—3.5 hours (196 miles)

**By train: Amtrak**'s (800/USA.RAIL) *California Zephyr* stops daily in **Reno** and **Truckee**—mornings westbound, evenings eastbound.

## Getting around Northstar-at-Tahoe

**Tahoe Area Regional Transit** (**TART**; 581.6365) operates a handful of buses serving the **North Lake Tahoe** area from **Sugar Pine Point** to **Incline Village** and **Truckee**. Buses run Monday through Thursday and Sunday from 6:30AM to 6:30PM, Friday and Saturday until 2:30AM. The **Northstar Shuttle** provides free shuttle service (562.2257) to and from most locations in the North Lake Tahoe area.

## FYI

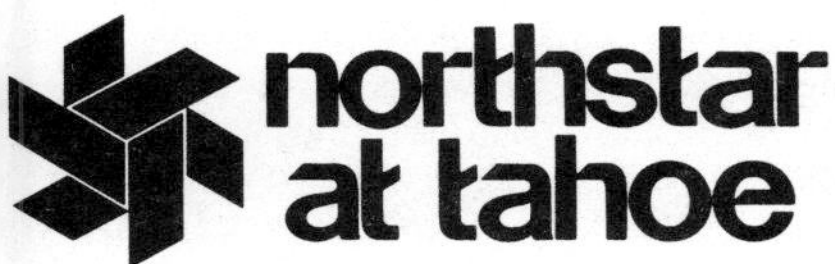


**Area** 2,000 acres shaped like an upside-down pyramid, with most of the 60 runs located at the top

Beginner—25 percent

Intermediate—50 percent

Advanced—25 percent

**Number of Groomed Runs** The majority of Northstar's 60 runs are groomed.

**Longest Run** 2.9 miles **(Village Run)**

**Capacity** 19,400 skiers per hour

**Base Elevation** 6,400 feet

**Summit Elevation** 8,600 feet

**Vertical Rise** 2,200 feet

**Average Annual Snowfall** 400 inches

**Snowmaking** 50 percent

**Night Skiing** None

**Lifts** 11 (1 gondola, 4 express quads, 2 triple chairs, 2 double chairs, and 2 surface lifts)

| **Lift Passes** | **Full Day** | **Half Day** (starts at 12:30PM) |
|---|---|---|
| **Adult** | $42 | $28 |
| **Child** (under 5) | Free | Free |
| **Child** (5-12) | $18 | $12 |
| **Senior** (60-69) | $21 | $21 |
| **Senior** (70 and over) | $5 | $5 |

Under the **Club Vertical** program, each skier wears a wristband containing a pre-programmed computer chip that's scanned at each chairlift. This band allows for a computer record to be made of your accumulated vertical feet and bills you for your lift fee automatically at the lift. Wearers have their own lift gates, save $5 to $10 per day off normal lift-ticket prices, and are awarded bonuses for reaching specific vertical goals (150,000 feet, for instance, earns you a free pizza at nearby **Pedro's Pizza**). The cost of joining for the whole year is around $70 for adults, $50 for children, and it includes one free day of skiing.

**Ski School** There's a ski school booth (562.2471) in the Village and offices located adjacent to the **Midmountain Lodge,** at the top of the gondola line. Two-hour lessons are offered daily at 10AM, noon, and 2PM. Private lessons, three-day programs, and specialized clinics for both children and adults are also available.

**Kids' Ski School** The **Skill Improvement Clinic** (see below) is open to intermediate-level children. There are also basic lessons for all levels.

**Clinics and Special Programs** For intermediate through expert skiers, the **Skill Improvement Clinic** offers 100-minute sessions daily at 10AM, noon, and 2PM. During the week, free one-hour clinics are available for women (Tuesdays), for seniors over 60 (Wednesdays), and for all adults over 13 (Thursdays). Other offerings include breakthrough ski clinics and snowboard clinics. Newcomers can take mountain tours offered free-of-charge daily at 10AM. Meet at the **Information Booth** at the top of the gondola.

**Races** Recreational racing is offered daily from 11AM to 3PM. Sign up at the top of **Main Street Run** (Arrow Express Quad). NASTAR races, in which times are measured against those of the **US Ski Team,** are held Thursdays through Sundays from 1PM to 3PM.

**Rentals** Located at the entrance to **Northstar Village,** the main rental office (562.2248) is open daily from 8AM to 5PM, offering snowboard and standard rental equipment. High-performance demos are also available at the main rental shop and the **Northsport Ski Shop** (562.1010) across the Village. The **Cross Country and Telemark Center** (562.2475), located midmountain, rents high-performance telemark and cross-country skating equipment. A valid driver's license or major credit card is required as a deposit. You must be at least 18 to sign rental vouchers.

**Lockers** Located on both sides of the walkway through the Village, as well as on the ground floor of the **Midmountain Lodge,** and at the **Summit Deck and Grille,** coin-operated lockers take quarters only. A ski/basket check is located across from the **Midmountain Lodge** and next to the **Village Ski Rental Shop** in the Village. Overnight ski storage is available at the midmountain **Dynastar Ski Test Center** for a nominal fee.

**Day Care** Located in the Village's **Clocktower Building, Minors' Camp Child Care** (562.2278), open daily from 8AM to 4:30PM, is a full-service licensed center for kids 2 through 6 years old (they must be toilet-trained). All-day and afternoon child care is available and includes lunch, two snacks, and such activities as art, drama, science, singing, and storytelling. **Ski Cubs** is a learn-to-ski option for 3- to 6-year-olds, and **Super Ski Cubs** is a ski program for 5- to 6-year-olds. (Parents must sign up children for these ski lessons before 9AM daily.) Reservations are recommended at least two weeks in advance, and parents must remain at the resort while the child is in day care.

**First Aid** A first-aid room (562.1010), located on the lower level of the **Midmountain Lodge**, offers only basic care and is open daily from 8AM to 5PM. The nearest hospital is **Tahoe Forest** (587.6011, 800/733.9953), six miles away in **Truckee.**

**Parking** Free parking is available near the base, with shuttle service beyond that. For a fee, you can get preferred parking near the resort entrance.

**Worth Knowing**

- The new Northstar-at-Tahoe **Dynastar Ski Test Center** allows skiers to test several models of Dynastar skis and Lange boots. The ski-in/ski-out test center charges $10 for four hours.
- On Sundays at 2PM, **Mountain Top Church Services** offers interdenominational religious services at the top of Vista Express Quad.

## Rating the Runs

### ● Beginner

Ski classes are held on the exceedingly flat and slow **Woodcutter** run, where neophytes get comfortable with their equipment.

Like Woodcutter, **The Gulch** offers little drama or speed. It's accessible by the Arrowhead Express Quad.

A long, wide, flat, and oh-so-gentle run, **Village Run** is perfect for beginners who dare to strike out on their own. Access is via the gondola.

### ■ Intermediate

When working the Comstock Express Lift, be sure to try **Ax Handle,** a short but semi-steep run. The challenge is brief and the finish is easy.

Don't be intimidated by the cluster of black diamond runs at the top of Comstock Express—they are so short and well groomed that even a weak intermediate can take 'em on. But if you're not yet ready for black diamonds, turn right at the top of Comstock and follow **West Ridge** downhill, exploring a half-dozen intermediate and branching trails, such as **Luggi's** and **Christmas Tree.**

The long groomed **Logger's Loop** runs through the pines and is rarely crowded. The only downside is that you reach it via the painfully slow Forest Chairlift.

### ◆ Advanced

Appropriately named, **Burn Out,** a long, pitched run off the Backside Express Quad, will burn up the thighs of anyone who attempts to ski it nonstop. Along with **Rail Splitter** and **Sierra Grande,** this course is almost always groomed to perfection, making it extremely fast (and dangerous) in icy conditions.

Although Northstar has never been known for its bump runs, **The Rapids,** a top-to-bottom mogul field, will satisfy just about any bump skier. Even pros have been seen here working on their endurance.

When conditions are right, powderhounds turn to Northstar's backside runs (accessible from the Backside Express). If you know what you're doing, it's all smiles to the bottom, especially through the trees between **Iron Horse** and **The Rapids.** If you don't, it's a mouthful of loose teeth. Know your limits.

### Snowboarding

With the entire mountain open to snowboarding combined with the wide diversity of terrain Northstar offers, riders feel right at home here. Freestyle boarders like to rip up the terrain at the area's park on **Pinball** and **Sunshine** where there are machine-made moguls, gaps, and waves as well as quarter-pipes. Riders into carving head straight to the "backside" where seven one-mile–long, wide-open runs allow space for super-wide turns and seriously steep slopes encourage even more challenging carving. Skilled snowboarders like to dip into the trees for fresh snow on powder days.

## Mountain Highs and Lows

Aside from **Flying Squirrel,** when it's bumped out with moguls, all the black diamond runs at the top of Comstock Express and off of **East Ridge** are a disappointment to advanced skiers. Besides being infested with SPOREs (Stupid Persons On Rental Equipment), these runs are so short that, after a few GS turns, your trip is over and it's back in the blue and back in the lift line.

## At the Resort

*Area code 916 unless otherwise noted.*

✦ **The Village** The heart of the Northstar resort, this is where just about everything takes place, from shopping to ski rental to ski school signups. Strategically located between your car and the lifts, it's hard not to drop a few sawbucks here.

Within The Village:

**Activity Center/Guest Services** If you have any questions, the nice people here will answer them. ♦ Daily 9AM-5PM. 562.2286

**Restaurants/Clubs:** Red **Hotels:** Blue
**Shops/ Outdoors:** Green **Sights/Culture:** Black

**Timbercreek Restaurant** ★$$ Formerly **Schaffer's Mill Restaurant,** Northstar's main bar and eatery has a light, contemporary look. Reasonably priced American cuisine includes a decent selection of steaks, pork dishes, pastas, seafood, chicken and vegetarian dishes, as well as salads, gourmet pizzas, sandwiches, and a tempting appetizer menu (go with the roasted garlic and brie). The cozy wood-lined **Alpine Bar** (562.1010), across the Village, is the perfect place for relaxing with an après-ski hot chocolate with Schnapps. ♦ Daily breakfast, lunch, and dinner. 587.0250

**Village Food Company** Have the deli counter folks pack you a lunch for the slopes. Or knock down a cappuccino at the coffee bar and buy the sunscreen you forgot at home. Beer, a decent wine selection, videos, newspapers, magazines, and a small supply of gourmet groceries are also on hand. ♦ Daily 7AM-8PM. 562.2253

**Northsport** The resort's main ski shop is small and expensive, carrying a huge line of souvenir items for children and adults, but a more meager selection of ski gear. Ski repair and tuning are available, along with performance-ski and snowboard rentals. ♦ Daily 9AM-6PM. 562.2268

**Pedro's Pizza** ★$ The pizza is *great,* although pretty good chili and salads can also be had here. Free deliveries are made within the resort on weekends. ♦ Daily lunch and dinner. 562.2245

✦ **Midmountain Lodge** This log-cabinlike structure houses a mediocre cafeteria, an outdoor barbecue (no matter what anybody says, go with the bowl of chili and a large order of fries), and a full bar. Surrounding the lodge is an information booth and ski/basket check, ski school office, and a cross-country center, which houses the **Nordic Cafe** (962.2467). ♦ Daily 8:30AM-4PM. Top of the gondola. 562.1010

✦ **The Recreation Center** This is an ideal spot to work out your skiing kinks. The center provides saunas, an exercise room (complete with stair climbers, rowing machines, and weight-training machines), a children's gameroom, and two outdoor spas. A free shuttle will transport you (or the kids) to the center. There is no admission charge for resort guests. ♦ Daily 2PM-11PM. At the far end of the Village, just past the ticket booths. 562.0320

✦ **Basque Club Restaurant** ★$$ Borrowing on a little local history (Basque shepherds once worked the fields near here), this family-style restaurant serves traditional Basque cuisine in a pleasant setting overlooking scenic Martis Valley. Five-course fixed-price meals may include steak, paella, hare, or lamb. Overall, it's not bad. ♦ Open only during the winter. Dinner. Off Basque Dr, within the resort. 562.2460

✦ **Summit Deck and Grille** ★★$ This open-air facility serves grilled steak, chicken, and interesting salads Southwestern style. There's also a full bar featuring a large selection of microbrewery beers. ♦ Daily 10:30AM-2:30PM; bar until 3:30PM. At the summit of Mount Pluto. 562.2453

✦ **Northstar Sleigh Rides** If there's enough snow on the track, a team of Belgian horses will pull either a four- or a 10-passenger sleigh for a 30-minute ride. Private rides (great for lovers) are also available. ♦ Daily 3PM-7PM Thanksgiving-March. Reservations recommended. Departs from the Basque Club Restaurant on Basque Dr. 562.1230

NORTHSTAR STABLES

✦ **Northstar Stables** Depending on weather and trail conditions, you can take a 45-minute jaunt or for the kids a 15-minute pony ride. ♦ Daily 11AM-4PM. Off Northstar Dr, just past Basque Dr. 562.1230

## Beyond the Resorts

**1 Truckee** A short drive out of **North Lake Tahoe,** this onetime boomtown has been entertaining visitors since 1868, when the First Transcontinental Railroad swept into town from nearby Donner Pass. The railroad brought the timber industry to Truckee, and with it came prosperity; even though logging and trains aren't what they used to be, the town has retained much of its original character. Tourists now stroll by the hundreds down streets formerly trod by timber magnates and their kowtowing disciples. The **Truckee Hotel** (587.4444), even after undergoing a face-lift, still looks much as it did when it opened in 1863. Other 19th-century buildings are now full of trendy emporia, art galleries, pubs, and restaurants. It can all seem a bit kitsch, although the sights, sounds, and smells emanating from the nearby rail yard provide a certain authenticity to this charming Sierra burg, occasionally referred to as "the ghost town that nobody forgot." More modern resources include the swank **Cottonwood** restaurant (587.5711), renowned for its seasonal menu with Southwestern twists (pork loin marinated in tequila, anyone?) and its Saturday night jazzfests; and the down-home **Squeeze Inn** (587.9814), where omelettes come in 57 varieties—all of them large. For more information, call the **Truckee Donner Visitor Center** (587.2757, 800/548.8388 in CA). ♦ Located off I-80, 15 miles north of North Lake Tahoe

**2 Sno Wave Snowboard Shop and Rentals** If you want to "shred proper," bail on the clueless ski resort rental shops and hitchhike to this former gas station. You'll find, if not the best, at least the coolest selection of boards and board gear, as well as apropos shredwear and stickers. ♦ M-Th, Su 8AM-6PM; F-Sa 7:30AM-9PM. Off Hwy 89, at the entrance to Squaw Valley Ski Resort. 581.5705

**3 River Ranch Lodge** $$$$ People who plan to ski at Alpine Meadows won't find more convenient accommodations than these. Not only does this historic lodge boast a great restaurant and the most popular après-ski bar at Tahoe (the circular space cantilevers out over the Truckee River), but its 19 rooms are all tastefully decorated in Early American antiques, with private balconies overlooking the river. The staff is friendly, the continental breakfast complimentary, and there's free shuttle service to both Alpine and Squaw Valley. Oh, and don't forget to ask about special ski packages. ♦ Off Hwy 89 at the entrance to Alpine Meadows Ski Area, 5 miles northwest of North Lake Tahoe. 583.4264, 800/535.9900 in CA; fax 583.7237

Within River Ranch Lodge:

**River Ranch Lodge Restaurant** ★★$$ You won't be disappointed by the Southwestern-flavored meals served here, whether they include fresh seafood, steaks, prime rib, or rack of lamb. This popular après-ski spot is almost always packed. The coziest tables are those near the fireplace. ♦ Daily lunch and dinner. Reservations recommended. 583.4264

**4 Granlibakken** $$$ A European-style resort with saunas, spas, and 120 one- to three-bedroom condominiums offering kitchens, fireplaces, lofts, and decks, this property's main advantage is that it's kid-friendly, with its own small ski hill (ski lift, rentals, and lessons included) and snowplay area. Meanwhile, two cross-country ski trails nearby tempt adult guests. Located only a mile from the Lake Tahoe shoreline in a small, semi-secluded valley, the resort provides a free buffet breakfast as well as transportation to the major ski areas. ♦ End of Granlibakken Rd off W Lake Blvd (Hwy 89), one-half-mile south of the Hwy 89/28 junction, in Tahoe City. 583.4242, 800/543.3221; fax 583.7641

**5 Fire Sign Cafe** ★★$$ A favorite breakfast stop for locals since the late 1970s, this homey little California-country joint makes just about everything from scratch, including blackberry buckwheat pancakes, buttermilk muffins, and fresh-squeezed juices. Try the smoked salmon omelette (owner/chef Bob Young smokes his own fish) or, for lunch, the Cajun and fried chicken sandwiches. Soups, salads, and veggie items are also available. ♦ Daily breakfast and lunch. No smoking. 1785 W Lake Blvd (Hwy 89), 2 miles south of the Hwy 89/28 junction, near Tahoe Park. 583.0871

**6 Sunnyside Lodge** $$ TS Enterprises—which runs Kimo's and Leilani's restaurants on the Hawaiian island of Maui, as well as **Jake's on the Lake** in Tahoe City—specializes in combining exquisite locations with consistent, friendly service and good food. This restored lodge fits the pattern. In summer, locals and drop-bys sip gin-and-tonics on a huge redwood deck. Lakeside guest rooms are each accessorized with decks, but none of the 23 rooms and suites (each decorated in elegant country style, with fireplaces or wet bars) lack fine views. A three-night midweek ski special for two includes breakfast, dinner, and three lift tickets. ♦ 1850 W Lake Blvd (Hwy 89), 2 miles south of the Hwy 89/28 junction, near Tahoe Park. 583.7200, 800/822.2754 (California only); fax 583.2551

Within Sunnyside Lodge:

**Sunnyside Restaurant** ★★$$ Overlooking the lake, the **Chris Craft** dining room serves consistently well-prepared California cuisine. The specialty here is fresh seafood, such as Hawaiian ahi broiled Szechuan style and a broiled swordfish served with papaya-lime butter. Budget-minded types can order off an après-ski bar menu while watching ski flicks beside the fireplace. Live acoustic guitar music lends ambience Wednesday through Saturday. Don't miss the legendary Hula Pie. ♦ Daily dinner; M-Sa lunch and Sunday brunch in summer. Reservations recommended. 583.7200

**7 Bridgetender Tavern and Grill** ★$ This is Tahoe's best bar—bar none. But it's mostly for locals, so don't be surprised if folks stare at you as if you'd sprouted antennae. The tavern's jovial ambience and charming

woodsy interior (notice the tree growing through the bar) make up for the discomfort of being an outsider. Not only does this genuine tavern carry the best beer selection in town, but it also grills a decent burger. ♦ Daily 11AM-2AM. 30 W Lake Blvd (Hwy 89), at the bridge, Tahoe City. 583.3342

**8 Za's** ★★$ The moniker is an abbreviation of "Pizza's," but nothing else about this Italian restaurant comes up short. Very good, very small, very cheap, and very crowded, this is the type of place you wish could relocate to your block. On the menu are scrumptious appetizers (baked polenta with wild mushrooms in a homemade Marsala wine sauce) and salads (smoked chicken with gorgonzola, roasted caramelized walnuts, and roasted red peppers in mixed greens); memorable pastas (try the fettuccine with smoked chicken and fresh artichoke hearts in a garlic cream sauce); and outstanding pizzas, all for less than 10 bucks. The herbed bread is baked fresh daily, sausages are homemade, the cheesecake (sigh) is local, and the majority of menu items are vegetarian, all of which account for the long lines at the door. ♦ M, W-Su dinner. No credit cards accepted. 395 N Lake Blvd (behind Pete 'n' Peter's bar), Tahoe City. 583.1812

**8 Tahoe City Travelodge** $$ In the center of Tahoe City and only 15 minutes from Squaw Valley and Alpine Meadows (via free shuttle), it's hard to go wrong staying here. This 47-room motel boasts a spa and cable TV, as well as a snowmobile course directly behind it. ♦ 455 N Lake Blvd (at the Hwy 89/28 junction), Tahoe City. 583.3766, 800/255.3050; fax 583.5882

**8 Rosie's Cafe** ★★$$ If you're going to spend any time at all in Tahoe City, stop by this venerable landmark for a bite to eat or at least a couple of beers. The menu offers traditional American food as well as a few dishes from left field, such as eggs Sardo (hot buttered artichoke hearts sautéed with scrambled eggs,

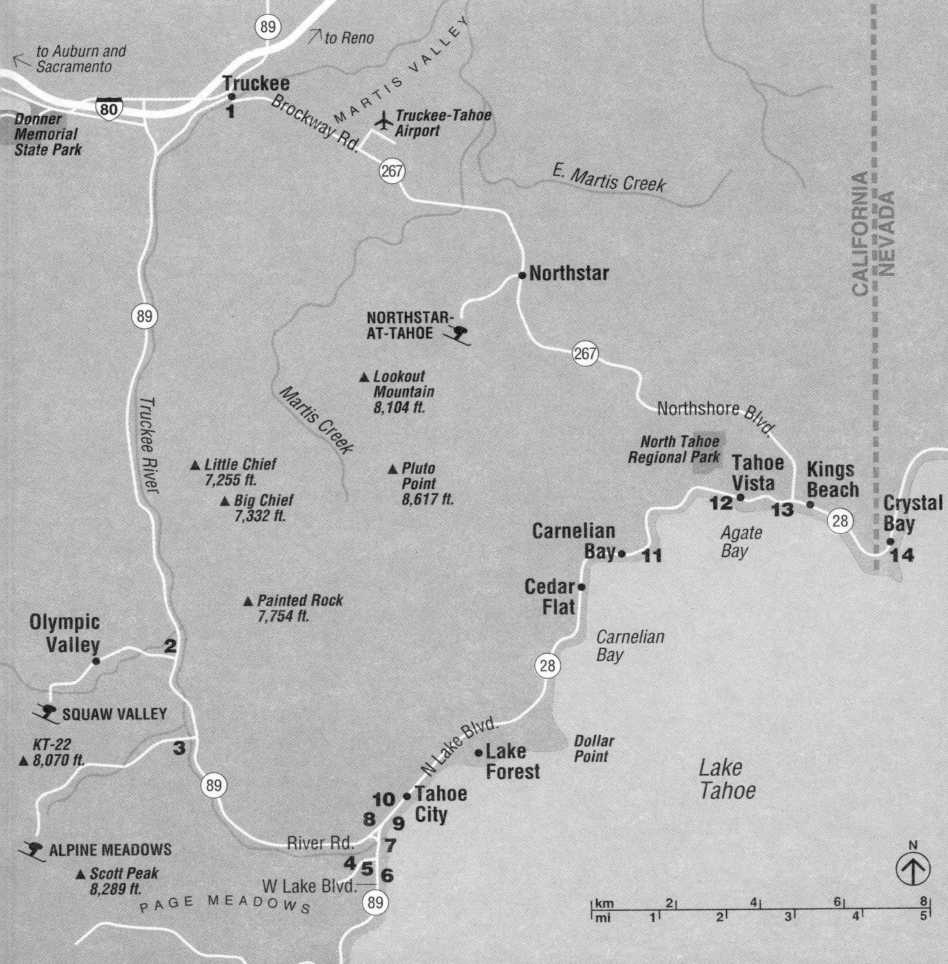

crabmeat, mushrooms, and hollandaise) and Texas Tournedos (filet mignon panfried and served with a tequila-pasilla chili cream sauce). Tuesday is locals night, with a live band and dancing. There is a full bar. ♦ Daily breakfast, lunch, and dinner. 571 N Lake Blvd (next to the big tree), Tahoe City. 583.8504

**8 Rodeway Inn** $$ Boxy and brown, this architecturally uninspired seven-story 51-room inn, in the center of Tahoe City, is convenient to ski areas, and a free shuttle to Squaw Valley stops here twice daily. The midweek ski package includes a lift ticket to Squaw or Alpine Meadows and is the best deal around. Ask for a room near the top, facing the lake. ♦ 645 N Lake Blvd (at the Hwy 89/28 junction), Tahoe City. 583.3711, 800/824.5342 in CA, 800/228.2000; fax 583.6938

**9 Christy Hill** ★★★$$$ Owner/chef Matt Adams provides one of the most romantic fireside settings in the Lake Tahoe area. Matt and his wife, Debbie, prepare seasonal California cuisine (try the Australian lamb loin served with fresh Chilean nectarine and mint chutney, or the sautéed eggplant with fresh oregano, mushrooms, roasted garlic, roma tomatoes, and artichoke hearts). Attentive service and the Adams' friendly conversation complement the cuisine. Arrive before sunset to admire the spectacular view. ♦ Tu-Sa dinner. No smoking. 115 Grove St (turn toward the lake at Tahoe City Pharmacy), Tahoe City. 583.8551

**9 Lakehouse Pizza** ★★$ This is what all pizza joints should be like: cozy, bustling, and blessed with brilliant views. Critics say that this ideal spot serves the best pizza on the lake (as well as good sandwiches and salads), so come by during Happy Hour (4PM to 6PM) and grab a front-row seat for sunset. Takeout is available. ♦ Daily lunch and dinner. 120 Grove St (turn toward the lake at Tahoe City Pharmacy), Tahoe City. 583.2222

**9 Wolfdale's** ★★$$$ Chef/owner Douglas Dale melds Japanese and California cuisines into something he calls "cuisine unique," which translates into entrées such as Alaskan halibut baked in parchment paper served with ratatouille; Australian scallops and prawns; and glazed quail stuffed with fennel sausage over a black olive and spring Napa salad. The spartan à la carte menu changes weekly, with prix-fixe menus available upon request. A full bar is available. ♦ M, W-Su dinner. Reservations recommended. 640 N Lake Blvd (1/2 mile north of the Hwy 89/28 junction), Tahoe City. 583.5700

**9 Jake's on the Lake** ★★$$$ The wizards from TS Enterprises have conjured up a top-notch restaurant at the perfect location, this one recognized for its continental cuisine. Specialties include rack of New Zealand lamb and a sautéed rainbow trout topped with caramelized almonds. Pasta and fresh seafood (swordfish, ahi, lobster) are also recommended. Light eaters and those on tight budgets can dine at the seafood bar in the lounge, where Montana, Tahoe's coolest bartender, holds court. ♦ Daily dinner. Reservations recommended. 780 N Lake Blvd (1/2 mile north of the Hwy 89/28 junction), Tahoe City. 583.0188

**9 Tahoe North Visitors & Convention Bureau** Consider this the local Delphic oracle. You'll find answers to questions about anything in the North Tahoe area. ♦ Daily 8:30AM-5PM; phone assistance daily 7:30AM-7PM. 850 N Lake Blvd (1/2 mile north of the Hwy 89/28 junction), Tahoe City. 583.3494, 800/824.6348

**9 Pierce Street Annex** This is one of the few places in town offering live music and dancing nightly, and the only venue where over-30 types can feel comfortable mingling with hip young thangs. Pool, backgammon, a giant-screen TV, and shuffleboard are all provided for the dance-disadvantaged. ♦ Daily 11:30AM-2AM. 850 N Lake Blvd (behind Safeway, facing the lake), Tahoe City. 583.5800

TAMARACK LODGE MOTEL

**10 Tamarack Lodge Motel** $ It's junky and it's funky, but you sure can't beat the prices, which start at $35 a night. Located just outside of Tahoe City and a short walk from the lake, this 21-room joint has been providing cheap, woodsy lodging for years to people who don't mind crunching a few pinecones to get to their cabin. This place is highly recommended for ski bums and snowboarders. The staffers are a riot. ♦ 2311 N Lake Blvd (1.5 miles north of the Hwy 89/28 junction), Tahoe City. 583.3350

**11 Lakeside Chalet** $$$ If you're big on privacy and romance, reserve one of the seven quaint little lakeside chalets. Each comes with a queen-size bed, stone fireplace, and lakefront perspective, as well as a fully equipped kitchen (with dishwasher), cable TV, and extra foldout bed. ♦ 5240 N Lake Blvd, in Carnelian Bay. 546.5857

**12 Tahoe Vista Inn and Marina** $$$$ This is about as deluxe as it gets at North Lake. Each luxurious suite comes with a spacious living room, fireplace, whirlpool bath, and private lanai overlooking the lake. Reasonably close to the Northstar, Alpine Meadows, and Squaw Valley ski areas and abutting two fine restaurants, this inn is an excellent choice for honeymooners and those accustomed to high-end living. Make your plans early since there are only six rooms altogether. ♦ 7220 N Lake Blvd, at Tahoe Vista. 546.7662, 800/662.3433; fax 546.7963

**12 Captain Jon's Seafood** ★★$$$$ While the sinfully tempting main menu has an excellent salad selection, hold out for chef Geno Duggan's daily seafood specials. Duggan often exceeds expectations with his unique, delicate sauces napping fresh fish. Arrive early and relax at the lakeside cocktail lounge while the sunset unfolds. Valet parking and live music is provided on Saturday night (sorry, no dancing). ♦ Tu-Su dinner. Reservations recommended. 7220 N Lake Blvd, at Tahoe Vista. 546.4819

**12 Le Petit Pier** ★★★$$$$ North Lake Tahoe's most exclusive (and expensive) restaurant boasts an award-winning California and European wine selection to accompany the prix-fixe and à la carte menus. Dishes such as asparagus feuilletage, half-cold lobster bagatelle, and pheasant Souvaroff all merit their devotees. Secluded seating is available for private parties. Otherwise, request a lakeside table. ♦ Daily dinner. Reservations recommended. 7238 N Lake Blvd, at Tahoe Vista. 546.4464

**13 North Tahoe Beach Center** If you need your daily Stairmaster fix or want to steep those aching muscles in a 26-foot Jacuzzi, $7 will get you a day pass here and access to the weight room, arcade, Ping-Pong table, and sauna. ♦ Daily 10AM-10PM. 7860 N Lake Blvd (across from Safeway), Kings Beach. 546.2566

**14 California-Nevada Border** Rumor has it Nevada only earned statehood because President Abraham Lincoln, needing two more Senate votes to pass some crucial legislation, hastily brought it into the Union. Now it serves as a playground for gaming Californians, provides a second chance for struggling entertainers, and sucks up untold millions in gambling and prostitution revenue. Since you're skiing close to the border, you may as well cross into Nevada to sample some of what Lincoln unwittingly helped to create. Casinos at the border between California and Nevada in North Lake Tahoe can't compare to those at South Lake Tahoe, which is 45 miles away. But if you're new to gambling, this is a safe place to start, since the pace is low key and the dealers are generally friendly and helpful (especially during off-hours). The casinos in North Lake Tahoe include: **Cal-Neva Lodge and Casino** (702/832.4000); the **Crystal Bay Club Casino** (702/831.0512); the **Tahoe Biltmore Hotel** (702/831.0660); and the **Hyatt Regency Lake Tahoe** (702/831.1111). Good luck. ♦ On Hwy 28 (N Lake Blvd), at the border between California and Nevada

## From Marginal to Mainstream: Snowboarding Goes Legit

Snowboarding—that rough-hewn hybrid of skiing, surfing, and skateboarding—began as a fringe-element fad in the mid-1980s and has, to the bane of many skiers and the boon of ski resorts, become a permanent fixture among winter sports. Wearing triple-oversize jeans and gaudy shirts (untucked, of course), "boarders," a new generation of youths who are rewriting the tired dogmas of the ski industry and conversing in tongues that would confound veterans of valley speak, could care less that skiers aren't exactly welcoming them onto their coveted trails. The snowboarders know that their money is as green as any skier's: This new influx of paying customers (who now account for 10 to 30 percent of lift-ticket sales) has encouraged all but a handful of resorts nationwide to open their mountains to practitioners of the non-traditional sport. In fact, many areas have gone so far as to construct special snowboard parks replete with half-pipes, jumps, and "boardocross" courses (the snowboard equivalent of motocross), and a few resorts even cater exclusively to the newcomers. Further evidence of the sport's growing acceptance is the plethora of certified snowboard instructors, international competitions, specialty clothing lines, and snowboard magazines that have resulted from a movement that, one could say, is snowballing.

The reasons behind snowboarding's crescendoing popularity? It appeals to surfers and skaters because of its renegade reputation and its physical similarity to their favorite pursuits. The sport also intrigues skiers who have to learn a new modus operandi that's the antithesis of correct skiing technique. Because of their width (approximately nine to 12 inches), snowboards are ideal for carving through both powder and crud, a capability that has convinced many hard-core skiers to assume the sideways stance, strap on a board, swallow some humble pie, and become beginners all over again.

Although novices will undoubtedly suffer bruised fannies and sore wrists, snowboarding is actually easier to master than skiing. Still, it's critical to have the fundamentals down pat before testing your prowess on the board. The snowboard's advantage in powder has proved to have deadly drawbacks: Three boarders in the Lake Tahoe area alone have died from suffocation resulting from headfirst falls into deep powder. Despite the risks, though, the epic experience of gliding effortlessly through untracked powder has been enough to convince 50 million (well, maybe not that many—yet) boarders to leave their skis at home and step on a Sims. Can they all be wrong?

# Heavenly

This is the only American ski area to straddle two states—California and Nevada. Heavenly has a split personality, and a beguiling one at that. It vies in sheer size as one of the largest resorts on the continent, but you'd never know that based on what you see when arriving at the California side: a lumpy mountain face engraved with a steep, nasty run called **Gunbarrel** that gives goosebumps to sane people. Fortunately, what you see is not all you get, not by a long shot. In fact, this unimpressive entrance to the resort conceals a labyrinth of 79 groomed runs on 4,800 acres of skiable terrain. And once you reach the summit (3,500 feet from the bottom) you'll finally gain perspective on how big this place really is. Conclusion? You certainly won't be able to ski it all in one day.

Riding the Heavenly tram to the ski lifts as it climbs the abrupt 1,700-foot slope is similar to rising in a glass-enclosed elevator above the canyons of Manhattan to the top of the World Trade Center. Below you, the **Stateline** casino-hotels resemble diminutive concrete boxes and **Lake Tahoe** takes on the dimensions of a giant indigo bathtub.

First-time skiers at Heavenly, which caters primarily to intermediate- and higher-level skiers, can easily be confused by the maze of runs, access trails, and lifts on the map. Contrary to the usual design of ski areas, where the beginner runs are right up front, Heavenly is an upside-down resort. The cruisin' stuff is at the top, the bruisin' stuff at the bottom—at least to the west, on the California side. On the eastern slopes, in Nevada, it's the other way around.

One way to get your bearings is to ski with a mountain guide or instructor for a while. But if you prefer to go it alone, adopt one of two general strategies for skiing the mountain. If you're entering from the California side closest to town, you can take any one of three chairlifts (West Bowl, Waterfall, and Sky Express) to the summit, do your morning runs on the intermediate slopes there, then skirt across the **Skyline Trail** to the Nevada side for afternoon skiing. Later, you can either return to the California side (leaving by 3:30PM at the latest, before the lifts close) or ski down to one of two Nevada base lodges and take a Heavenly shuttle bus back to your hotel or to the California base.

The second plan involves going directly to the sunny Nevada side in the morning, where you'll find fewer skiers (the entry points are much farther from town), more fall-line skiing, and usually the best snow conditions on the mountain. Snow tends to be drier and better protected here because the slopes face the high desert and storms lose much of their moisture by the time they reach Nevada. In the afternoon, you can work your way across the upper California side, then take the Aerial Tram or the Gunbarrel Chairlift down from midmountain. The reason it's best to download is that there is no easy descent other than via a narrow cat track. Every other marked run is for bump experts. However, taking a ride down isn't exactly a hardship, especially on the chairlift, with Lake Tahoe shimmering beneath your feet.

Skiing isn't the only thing that's top-notch about Heavenly. Attracting visitors from as far afield as Japan and England, the resort has become an international winter playground, and rightly so. The combination of so much prime ski terrain, the beauty of Lake Tahoe, the 24-hour gambling and entertainment options at the Stateline casinos, and other diversions ranging from hot tubs to sleigh rides is unrivaled anywhere in the world. With such diversity, the winter clientele ranges from honeymooners to families, and from lounge lizards to high rollers.

Over the years, the ski area has also hosted many Hollywood luminaries in its annual celebrity professional/amateur race. Leaving their sitzmarks in the snow have been Clint Eastwood, William Shatner, Cheryl Tiegs, George Hamilton, Sonny Bono, John Denver, Susan Anton, Bruce Jenner, Barbi Benton, Michelle Phillips, and Kirstie Ally. You never know who you might run into on the slopes.

Indeed, when not schussing, show-biz people are likely to be performing in one casino theater or another. Imagine tearing up the slopes all day, then consuming a heady performance by Kenny G, Wynona Judd, the Oak Ridge Boys, or Diana Ross at night. **Caesars Tahoe** is the most consistent venue for concerts, followed by **Harrah's Lake Tahoe**, which lately has launched a series of Broadway musicals, **Harvey's**, and **Horizon.** The trick to skiing here is trying not to deplete all your energy on the slopes so that you can do the town at least one night.

As the gateway to Heavenly, **South Lake Tahoe** can outgun most other destination resorts when it comes to meal and lodging prices. This gambling mecca offers a plethora of inexpensive hotels and motels under $50 a night, as well as cheap dining, especially at the famous, stuff-your-face casino buffets. How about a $7.99 all-you-can-eat midweek steak dinner? These places figure they'll attract you with subsidized food prices, then get your extra bucks at the blackjack tables or slot machines. Then again, you might beat the odds and win enough to pay for your entire ski trip.

**Heavenly Ski Area**
**PO Box 2180**
**Stateline, Nevada 89449-9919**

**Information** .................... 916/541.1330 in California
.......................................... 702/586.7000 in Nevada
**Reservations** .................................... 800/2HEAVEN
**Snow Phone** ..................................... 916/541.7544

## Fast Facts

*Area code 916 unless otherwise noted.*

**Ski Season** Mid-November through April

**Location** Situated on the south shore of **Lake Tahoe,** Heavenly is the only bi-state ski resort in the US.

## Getting to Heavenly

**By air: South Lake Tahoe Airport** is seven miles and **Reno/Tahoe International Airport** is 55 miles from Heavenly. Approximately 180 flights land at **Reno/Tahoe International Airport** daily; **America West, American, Continental, Delta, Northwest, Reno Air, Southwest, United,** and **USAir** offer direct flights. **Alpha Air** and **American Eagle** offer nonstop daily flights to **South Lake Tahoe Airport** from **San Jose, San Francisco,** and **Los Angeles.**

**By bus:** The **Tahoe Casino Express** (702/785.2424) offers dependable, luxury bus service with 14 daily scheduled trips to and from **Reno/Tahoe International Airport. Greyhound** (800/231.2222) serves **South Lake Tahoe** with daily buses to and from **Sacramento** and **San Francisco.**

**By car:** Both the **Reno/Tahoe International Airport** and **South Lake Tahoe Airport** have several car-rental agencies that specialize in winterized car rentals, including four-wheel drives with snow tires and front-wheel-drive vehicles equipped with snow chains.

### All-weather highways:

Reno—Highway 395 South to US Highway 50 West

Sacramento—US Highway 50 East

Greater San Francisco—Interstate 80 East to US Highway 50 East

### Driving times from:

Reno—1.25 hours (55 miles)

Sacramento—2 hours (100 miles)

San Francisco—3.5 hours (198 miles)

## Getting around Heavenly

Once you're in Tahoe, Heavenly operates its own free shuttle buses to the ski resort from most **South Lake Tahoe** lodging properties. The buses serve all major routes and run at 20- to 30-minute intervals during peak morning and afternoon hours, operating from 8AM to 5:30PM. They stop at all **Stateline** hotels and along "motel row" on Highway 50 and Pioneer Trail. Apart from the ski buses, several casinos run complimentary shuttle service by van or minivan, upon request, to and from the Stateline gaming area 24 hours a day. Public bus service and private taxi services are also available.

## FYI

Heavenly®
Lake Tahoe

**Area** 4,800 acres of varying terrain, tree, bowl, and groomed surface skiing

Beginner—20 percent

Intermediate—45 percent

Advanced/Expert—35 percent

**Number of Groomed Runs** 79

**Longest Run** 5.5 miles (Nevada side, from the top of the Dipper Chairlift to the bottom of the Galaxy Chairlift)

**Capacity** 33,000 skiers per hour

**Base Elevation** California—6,540 feet Nevada—7,200 feet

**Summit Elevation** 10,040 feet

**Vertical Rise** California—3,600 feet Nevada—2,900 feet

**Average Annual Snowfall** 300 inches

**Snowmaking** 66 percent

**Night Skiing** None

**Lifts** 24 (15 in California and 9 in Nevada); includes 1 aerial tramway, 3 high-speed detachable quads, 8 triple chairs, 7 double chairs, and 5 surface lifts.

| Lift Passes | Full Day | Half Day (starts at 1PM) |
|---|---|---|
| **Adult** | $42 | $29 |
| **Youth** (13-15) | $30 | $25 |
| **Child** (12 and under) | $18 | $12 |
| **Senior** (65 and over) | $18 | $12 |

**Ski School** Four offices are located at **California, Boulder,** and **Stagecoach Base Lodges,** and at the top of the tram. For more information, call 541.1330 ext 6245. For first-time adult skiers, the **Introductory Lesson Package** includes all-day rental equipment, lift tickets, and a three-hour lesson. Also available are two-day (four two-hour sessions) and one-day (two two-hour sessions) classes. There are group lessons for novices (who can turn both ways and stop) to expert skiers, 13 years and up.

**Kids' Ski School** Children's lessons are available for skiers 4 to 12 years old, all ability levels. Programs include lift, lunch, lessons, rental equipment, and games.

**Clinics and Special Programs** The **Monument Peak Mini Clinic** offers one ski run with a coach giving pointers. The certified race staff will help intermediate to expert skiers improve race times with a two-hour session and two timed runs on the coin-operated race course, open daily from 10:30AM to 12:30PM.

**Races** A dual coin-operated course is located on **Canyon** run (California side). Coaches are on hand for pointers. Open to all skiers daily from 10:30AM to 3PM.

**Rentals** Open daily from 8AM to 5:30PM, rental shops are located at all three of the base areas in California (ext 6210) and Nevada (**Boulder** ext 2390; **Stagecoach** ext 2343). A driver's license is required as a guarantee. Package includes skis, boots, and poles that are generally of high quality and well tuned. Children's rentals and high-performance skis and boots are available, too.

**Lockers** Coin-operated lockers are located at **California, Boulder,** and **Stagecoach Base Lodges** and at the top of the tram. Overnight ski checks are available at the **California** and **Boulder Lodges.** Complimentary "Ski Valets"—where you check your skis at an outdoor staff-supervised "corral"—are located at the **California Lodge,** the top of the tram, and the **Boulder Lodge.**

**Day Care** There are no infant care facilities on site. Take children ages 4 to 12 to the **Children's Ski Center** (ext 6217), open daily from 8AM to 4:30PM and located at the west end of the **California Base Lodge** and in the **Boulder Base** area. Half-day care is also available.

**First Aid** A first-aid room (541.6466) is located at the base of the Aerial Tramway; helicopter transportation from the mountain is available for emergencies. The ski patrol and a nurse are on duty during operating hours. **Barton Memorial Hospital** (541.3420), in **South Lake Tahoe,** is six miles away.

**Parking** Free parking is available at all three base areas.

### Worth Knowing

- Check out **Heavenly Mountain Caterers** (542.5153) where you can enjoy a complete catered lunch on "top of the world." Reservations must be placed by 10AM and there is a two-person minimum.

## Rating the Runs

### ● Beginner

Any novice who drives up to the base of the California side for the first time and sees Heavenly's plunging precipices might be tempted to turn tail and run like a rabbit. Although this is not a beginner's mountain, look a little closer and you'll find some bunny hills. Leave the small fry for ski lessons at **Enchanted Forest** on the California side, or at **Boulder Creek Children's Ski Center** on the Nevada side. Also, **West Bowl Poma,** on the California side, accesses a short beginner's trail that's good for kids in front of the base lodge.

On the California side, older novices (including teens and adults) can ride the Aerial Tramway to midmountain, ski **Patsy's,** then take Waterfall Chairlift to **Mombo Trail.** Mombo, however, is not a good place for new skiers at the end of the day, when almost everyone on the mountain comes swooping down in rush-hour mania. Beginners should leave early and return on the Aerial Tramway.

### ■ Intermediate

A good morning romp to get the adrenaline flowing, **Betty's** (California side) also offers *the* designated photo op overlooking **Lake Tahoe** (photographers are on site). Betty's is well groomed, if predictable, and usually has some sugarcoating from nightly snowmaking. Take the Canyon or Ridge Chairlift to access this trail.

Don't let the name deceive you. While **Olympic Downhill** (Nevada side) has been used by World Cup skiers such as Franz Klammer, this run is an expansive ego booster—and probably the least crowded trail on the mountain because it's necessary to pole along a flat access road to reach it. But don't hesitate. Meticulous grooming and Nevada's drier snow make for a forgiving surface, where you can let the boards run and pretend you're a downhill racer.

For a steep pitch and good fall-line skiing—with a few modest bumps occasionally thrown in—**Big Dipper** (Nevada side) gives advanced intermediate skiers a cardiovascular pump that rivals a Jane Fonda workout. Reliably, this run has the best snow at Heavenly, since it's the uppermost intermediate slope facing Nevada's dry, high desert valleys.

### ◆ Advanced

A woman of many moods, **Ellie's** (California side) has about equal amounts of steeps, bumps, and cruising—and she depends on a cloak of natural snowfall for adequate coverage. This run is narrow at the top, wide in the middle, and usually bumped up around the end—which might describe some in-laws you know. Think of her as a late morning wake-up call, though she's not too temperamental for strong intermediates.

### ◆◆ Expert

If you lose it on **Gunbarrel** (California side), you might end up in the lake. This run has the most imposing 1,700 vertical feet at Heavenly (and perhaps in all of the Lake Tahoe ski areas), given that it's one long, steep mogul field. Only hotdoggers and those with elastic legs need apply. If you're a true mountain goat, you can demonstrate your bump-bashing techniques to an appreciative audience of hundreds watching from the Aerial Tramway and Gunbarrel Chairlift above.

An out-of-body (some say out-of-mind) experience can be had on **Milky Way Bowl** (Nevada side). In fact, many claim that skiing through powder doesn't get much better than this. The jump-off point is just below Heavenly's 10,100-foot summit, and would-be *artistes* can use this vast white canvas to ski figure eights. Bring your periscope and snorkel when the white stuff is deep.

Displaying more warning notices than a pack of cigarettes, **Mott Canyon** (Nevada side), a double-diamond run, is serious business. The obstacles are plenty—they're called trees. The object of survival here is to ski the deep powder *between* them. Prepare to confront all of the big nasties—steep bowls, canyons, chutes, and stumps—some 2,000 vertical feet of them. One of the chutes is called **Snake Pit,** and it bites. Wait until after a monster storm to ski Mott Canyon, then make sure that one good turn follows another.

### Snowboarding

Heavenly has always had awesome tree terrain and big vertical for free-riding, but the addition of the new park—with a solid snowmaking system—provides a safe area for big air and rad tricks. The snowboard park, located on **Olympic Downhill** (Nevada) and serviced by the Olympic Double Chair, offers a series of quarter-pipes, gaps, and tabletops as well as open cruising terrain. Riders looking for a fast run on a carving board will find plenty of speed on Olympic Downhill. A favorite among skiers, this run offers an opportunity to fly (you may have to walk to get there, but it's worth it). For powder, it doesn't get any better than on **Milky Way Bowl.** Located near the summit, this bowl provides great terrain for wide sweeping GS turns. **Shred Ready** snowboard lessons are offered for all levels at **Boulder Lodge** and **California Lodge.**

## Mountain Highs and Lows

Listed as an intermediate run (and the easiest way down from the summit), **Ridge Run** (California side) is just a cream puff. Beginners who can do a snowplow can handle the lower two-thirds of this trail, if they access it from Canyon Chairlift. But beware the upper one-third of Ridge, right off the Sky Express Chairlift, which is tricky even for intermediates—it's narrow, congested with fast skiers and shredders, and frequently becomes icy and rutted toward the end of the day.

The map colors it blue, but a lot of skiers who try **Round-a-Bout** (California side) may end up seeing red. This trail is a waste of time for intermediates. A long, winding, uninteresting, narrow cat track leading from California's midmountain to the base lodge, Round-a-Bout is for skiers with time to burn. Unfortunately, aside from taking your chances with the black-diamond advanced and expert runs, it's the only skiable route to the bottom. But consider opting for a third choice: take a few more runs on the good stuff at the top, then download on Gunbarrel Chairlift. The descent on this lift is the most scenic ride in North America, with beautiful sky-blue **Lake Tahoe,** the snow-crested **Sierra** range, and the casinos of **Stateline** unfolding below you in a breathtaking panorama.

## At the Resort

*Resort facilities can be reached by calling the resort's main numbers (916/541.1330 in California; 702/586.7000 in Nevada) unless otherwise noted.*

### Heavenly Facilities (California Side)

✦ **California Base Lodge** This three-story structure houses ticket windows, a ski school, sports store, ski rentals, storage lockers, cafeteria, and bar. ♦ At the base of the California side.

Within the California Base Lodge:

**Heavenly Sport Store** You can find your Heavenly sweatshirt, turtleneck, T-shirt, cap, or a variety of other signature items here. The shop also carries a full line of new skis, boots, poles, plenty of accessories, and high-performance rental equipment. ♦ Daily 7:30AM-5:30PM.

**Heavenly Cafeteria** ★$ There is nothing fancy here, just your basics. The most popular meal is breakfast—scrambled eggs, bacon, sausage, and pancakes. For lunch, burgers, fries, chili, and chef's salads fill the bill. ♦ Daily breakfast and lunch.

**California Bar** This is the prime on-mountain après-ski hangout, and on Thursday through Sunday nights it offers a variety of live music, as well as all of the usual brewskies, nachos, and other munchies. You can hoist your glass to the giant Alaskan brown bear—believed to be the largest stuffed animal of its ilk in North America—that is the centerpiece here. A sushi bar serves a full array of fresh fish and other favorites. ♦ Daily 10AM-7PM.

✦ **Monument Peak Day Lodge** You have to walk all the way across the parking lot to reach the Aerial Tramway, which takes you to a midmountain base area that includes another **Heavenly Sport Store** (with mostly small accessories such as lip balm and sunglasses), a sit-down restaurant, cafeteria, bar, lockers, ski school office, ski rental and repair shop, and sundeck. To reach these facilities, you have to clomp down several flights of stairs in what has become known as "the stairway to hell." ♦ At the top of the tram.

Within Monument Peak Day Lodge:

**Monument Peak Restaurant** ★★$$ The most convenient meal stop on either side of the mountain. Two bonuses are the view of Lake Tahoe, Stateline, and precipitous Gunbarrel slope and the variety of well-prepared items on the menu. Breakfast features omelettes and cold cereals, and lunches include meal-in-a-bowl salads, poached salmon, steak, homemade soups, and gourmet hamburgers. During warm days, you can bask on the sundeck. Nonskiers can ride the tram to the top for about $12. ♦ Daily 11AM-2:30PM.

**Monument Peak Bar** When the blizzards arrive or the wind howls, this is the place to warm up with an Irish coffee. Hot local skiers and celebrities sometimes hang out in this small but scenic bar that carries the usual drinks and toddies. It's a good rendezvous point for the California side. ♦ Daily 10:30AM-5:30PM.

**Monument Peak Cafeteria** ★$ While in the past this place offered few surprises, just the usual hot dogs, hamburgers, chips, and soft drinks, the menu has been expanded to include healthier items such as fresh salads and veggie burgers. On nice days you can eat out on the deck and enjoy the vista of Lake Tahoe. ♦ Daily breakfast and lunch.

✦ **Sky Meadows** ★$ This small snack shack with a relatively spacious outdoor deck offers the basics, including cold sandwiches, liquids, and sweets. Balmy weather brings out the barbecues, and the menu expands to include cook-it-yourself burgers, dogs, and chicken. Although this is a favorite picnic area, there's not much of a view, unless you enjoy people watching in front of the chairlifts. ♦ Daily breakfast and lunch. Bottom of the Sky Chairlift.

### Heavenly Facilities (Nevada Side)

✦ **East Peak Midmountain Lodge** This is the spot where everyone seems to congregate because it's on the sheltered, often sunny Nevada side, and because most people who start skiing in California are ready to move across the state line by lunchtime anyway. What's here is a full-service day lodge with an indoor cafeteria, ski accessory shop, and extensive outdoor deck with cook-it-yourself barbecue facilities and tables. ♦ At the base of Dipper and Comet Chairlifts.

Within the East Peak Midmountain Lodge:

**East Peak Cafeteria** ★★$ Of the on-mountain restaurants, this is the second choice, after **Monument Peak Restaurant** (on the California side). Sheltered in a particularly sunny spot next to a small (usually frozen) lake, this self-serve dispenses the usual burgers and sandwiches but also has a separate pizza stand, wine and cheese bar, deli serving made-to-order sandwiches, and a wide variety of microbrewery beers available. Outside, on the deck, you can grill your own chicken, burgers, and dogs. ♦ Daily breakfast and lunch.

✦ **Stagecoach Base Lodge** A somewhat smaller version of the **California Base Lodge,** this lodge has similar facilities: lift-ticket sales, ski school, cafeteria, ski-rental outlet, and a **Heavenly Sport Store.** The lodge also offers free parking. ♦ Bottom of the Stagecoach Chairlift.

Within the Stagecoach Base Lodge:

**Stagecoach Cafeteria** ★$ Partake of a standard breakfast of eggs, toast, and bacon—or grab a quick burger later in the day at this fuel stop that offers the same fare that's sold at the **Heavenly Cafeteria** on the California side. Inside the cafeteria, a pizza shop called **Slice of Heaven** features homemade pizzas with funky names like "California Dreamin," "Downhill Racer," or "Luigi's Special." And they deliver, too. Because it's more isolated, this Nevada cafeteria tends to be less crowded. ♦ Daily breakfast and lunch.

✦ **Boulder Base Lodge** The largest of the Nevada base lodges, **Boulder** faces beginner and lower-intermediate terrain. It's generally uncrowded, though it has the full array of services, including lift-ticket sales, a ski school, ski-rental shop, first aid, sports shop, cafeteria, and bar. There is also a large outdoor deck, free parking, and a bus stop for Heavenly's free shuttle. ♦ At the base of the Nevada side.

Within the Boulder Base Lodge:

**Boulder Cafeteria** ★$ The cafeteria-style menu allows for a quick pre- or post-slope meal or snack. Choose from the usual staples, such as hot dogs, chili, hamburgers, and fries. For the more unusual try some south-of-the-border fare featuring Jose's black bean soup, seviche, or homemade tamales at the **Black Diamond Cantina** located within this cafeteria. ♦ Daily breakfast and lunch.

Lake Tahoe was discovered by an exploration party consisting of John C. Frémont and guide Kit Carson, on 14 February 1844. But the name "Tahoe" wasn't chosen until more than 20 years later, when a California writer proposed it as an Indian word meaning big water or high water. "Tahoe" was adopted, but no one ever agreed on the definition of the word.

**Restaurants/Clubs:** Red **Hotels:** Blue
**Shops/ Outdoors:** Green **Sights/Culture:** Black

**Boulder Cocktail Lounge** This is an especially lively spot during après-ski hours for some convivial conversation and a steaming Irish coffee. ♦ Daily 10:30AM-6PM.

## Beyond the Resort

**1 Zephyr Cove Snowmobile Center** A favorite activity for skiers resting on an off day, snowmobiling affords picturesque views of Lake Tahoe and the surrounding Sierra peaks. Tours, departing three times a day, last about two hours. Families with children are welcome, guides lead each group, and you can rent one-piece snowmobile suits and boots for a few dollars extra. Zephyr Cove boasts that it is the largest snowmobile center on the West Coast, with one hundred vehicles. Tours lead through US Forest Service land near Lake Tahoe and Carson Valley. The departure point is **Zephyr Cove Lodge,** and shuttle service is available from the casino area. ♦ Daily 9AM-5PM. 760 Hwy 50, 4 miles north of Stateline, Nevada. 702/588.3833

**2 Wild West** At this hot nightspot where the yahoos hang out, people watching is a prime occupation, along with taking Western line-dancing lessons and imbibing cheap beer. As for the soundscape, you can anticipate Top 40 music and, occasionally, live entertainment. ♦ Tu-F 5PM-3AM; Sa 7PM-3AM; Su 7PM-2AM; Happy Hour and buffet F 5PM-9PM. Round Hill Shopping Center on Hwy 50, 2.5 miles north of Stateline, Nevada. 702/588.2175

CHART HOUSE

**3 Chart House** ★$$$ Take a menu similar to that of Sizzler, mark it up 30 to 40 percent, and you have an overpriced restaurant whose major attraction is the lofty view of Lake Tahoe from the flanks of Kingsbury Grade. As long as you realize you're paying for the ambience and not the undistinguished food, you may find the drive here worthwhile. ♦ Daily dinner. Reservations recommended. Kingsbury Grade (off Hwy 207), Nevada. 702/588.6276

WALLEY'S 1862 HOT SPRINGS RESORT

**4 Walley's Hot Springs Resort** Located about 25 minutes over the Kingsbury Grade from South Lake Tahoe, this series of open-air pools is just the ticket to relieve tired ski muscles. Though this resort is more than a century old, the facilities are modern and meticulously clean. Five circular pools, each a different temperature, are situated next to a wildlife area full of ducks and geese. While you're soaking, admire the spectacular view of meringue-tipped peaks. There's also a full fitness club, showers with towels, and a massage center. ♦ Daily 8AM-10PM. Foothill Blvd, two miles north of Hwy 207, near Genoa, Nevada. 702/782.8155

**5 Horizon** $$ Though it's not as tall as the other Big Four casino-hotel properties, and its accommodations are less luxurious, the 539-unit complex has positioned itself as the low-price leader in South Lake Tahoe. A full-service hotel, this property has four restaurants, a cabaret theater that offers "adult" entertainment, and a smattering of shops. The budget-conscious skier can often find promotional rates well below the norm and a midweek buffet dinner that is perhaps the best value in Lake Tahoe. And if you're lucky, you might get to peek inside the **Elvis Suite**—where the King himself stayed when he used to perform in what was once called the **High Sierra Theater,** now the **Grande Lake Theater.** ♦ Hwy 50 (at Lake Pkwy West), Stateline, Nevada. 702/588.6211; fax 702/588.1344

Within Horizon:

**Josh's** ★★★$$ Italian pasta and other continental specialties, as well as many fresh seafood items such as fillet of sole doré, are delicious and reasonably priced. This is the best of the casino-hotel's restaurants. Waiters have that Old World hospitality. ♦ Daily dinner. Reservations recommended. 702/588.6211

**6 Borges Sleigh Rides** This family-owned outfit, which has operated for more than 20 years, offers 35-minute horse-drawn sleigh rides over meadows and along the shoreline of Lake Tahoe every hour on the hour, snow conditions permitting. The driver tells stories of Tahoe, recites poems, and sings songs. ♦ Daily 10AM-4PM. Hwy 50, across from Caesars Tahoe at Lake Pkwy East, Stateline, Nevada. 702/541.2953

CAESARS TAHOE

**7 Caesars Tahoe** $$$ You like Roman orgies? Toga parties? Then you'll love the mood of this casino-resort with 440 suites containing oversize beds and massive, circular bathtubs in the middle of the room—big enough for two. There's plenty of action from the 24-hour casino and the nonstop entertainment. This is Lake Tahoe's only venue for big-name acts such as Kenny G, Huey Lewis and the News, the Moody Blues, and Joe Cocker, who perform nightly in the 1,600-seat **Circus Maximus Showroom.** Amenities run the gamut from an indoor heated pool, saunas, and massage to something called a "Cho-Cho" European-Oriental facial and a fitness club. Bring your own toga. ♦ 55 Hwy 50 (at Lake Pkwy East), Stateline, Nevada. 702/588.3515; fax 702/586.2056

Within Caesars Tahoe:

**Pisces Restaurant** ★★★$$$ If you simply must have fresh seafood in the mountains, and don't mind paying extra for the privilege, this piscatorial dining establishment flies it in daily from San Francisco and other points. A fresh oyster bar also includes Dungeness crab, Maine lobster, and jumbo shrimp. The menu changes daily, according to what's available, featuring such specialties as fresh Hawaiian ahi, coho salmon, swordfish, and bouillabaisse. ♦ M, Th-Su dinner. Reservations recommended. 702/588.3515

LAKE TAHOE

**Planet Hollywood** ★★★$$ Skiers who have visited other locations of this well-known eatery will find little differentiation here apart from distinctive movie memorabilia like Mel Gibsons's motorcycle from *Lethal Weapon III* or the animatronic penguin from *Batman Returns.* The good news is that like the others, this one offers a fun dining experience with inexpensive salads, sandwiches, pastas, burgers, pizza, and fajitas in an environment that allows diners to drift into Hollywood while in ski country. ♦ Daily 11AM-2AM. No reservations accepted. 702/588.7828

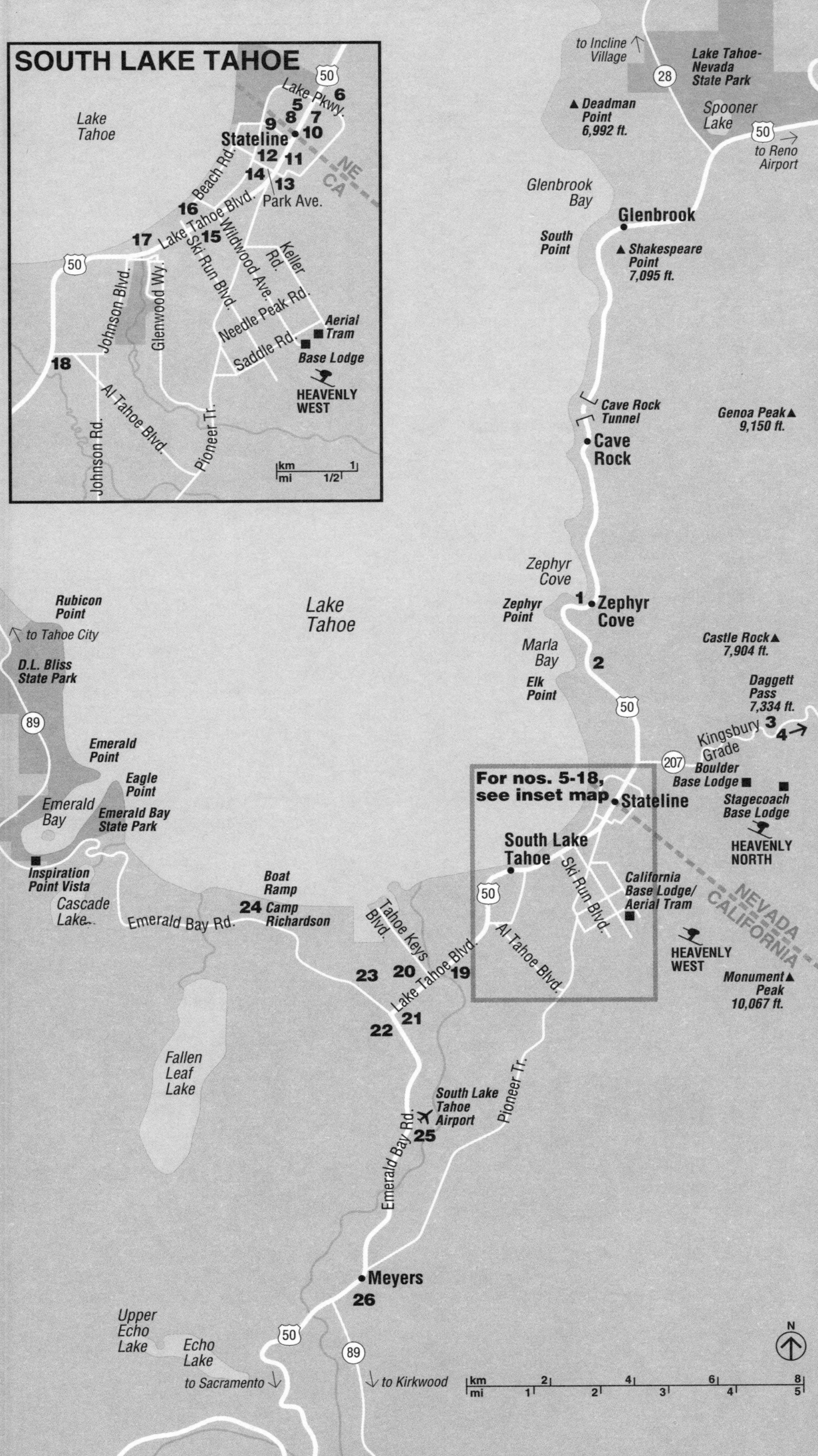
SOUTH LAKE TAHOE
Lake Tahoe
Lake Pkwy.
Stateline
Beach Rd.
Lake Tahoe Blvd.
Park Ave.
Ski Run Blvd.
Wildwood Ave.
Keller Rd.
Needle Peak Rd.
Saddle Rd.
Aerial Tram
Base Lodge
HEAVENLY WEST
Johnson Blvd.
Glenwood Wy.
Al Tahoe Blvd.
Johnson Rd.
Pioneer Tr.
NE
CA
to Incline Village
Lake Tahoe-Nevada State Park
Deadman Point 6,992 ft.
Spooner Lake
to Reno Airport
Glenbrook Bay
Glenbrook
South Point
Shakespeare Point 7,095 ft.
Cave Rock Tunnel
Cave Rock
Genoa Peak 9,150 ft.
Zephyr Cove
Zephyr Point
Castle Rock 7,904 ft.
Marla Bay
Elk Point
Daggett Pass 7,334 ft.
Kingsbury Grade
Boulder Base Lodge
Stagecoach Base Lodge
For nos. 5-18, see inset map
HEAVENLY NORTH
South Lake Tahoe
California Base Lodge/ Aerial Tram
NEVADA
CALIFORNIA
HEAVENLY WEST
Monument Peak 10,067 ft.
Rubicon Point
to Tahoe City
D.L. Bliss State Park
Emerald Point
Eagle Point
Emerald Bay
Emerald Bay State Park
Inspiration Point Vista
Cascade Lake
Emerald Bay Rd.
Boat Ramp
Camp Richardson
Tahoe Keys Blvd.
Fallen Leaf Lake
South Lake Tahoe Airport
Emerald Bay Rd.
Meyers
Upper Echo Lake
Echo Lake
to Sacramento
to Kirkwood
km
mi
N

**Nero's 2000 Nightclub** When you're boogying to a disco beat, who cares if Rome is burning? If you need a rest (after all, you are at 6,000 feet), pull up a spare Corinthian column and find out what the gladiators and lions are up to these days. Live music is offered occasionally. ♦ Cover. Daily 9PM-3AM. 702/588.3515

8 **Harvey's** $$$$ The largest and most modern of the four casino-hotel properties, this is a class act, with spectacular views of Lake Tahoe from 740 spacious guest rooms, dressed up in French provincial decor. Amenities include seven restaurants, a full-size health club, wedding chapel, showroom with live entertainment, and, of course, a sprawling casino. The hotel is known for its exemplary service. ♦ Hwy 50 (just south of the Horizon casino), Stateline, Nevada. 702/588.2411; fax 702/782.4889

Within Harvey's:

**Llewellyn's Restaurant** ★★★$$$ The 19th-floor views—looking out over Lake Tahoe, the snow-crested Sierra, and **Edgewood Golf Club**—almost eclipse the succulent continental cuisine. Daily specials include such gourmet selections as brie soup and sautéed flounder with Champagne cream. ♦ Daily dinner; Sunday brunch. Reservations recommended. 702/588.2411

**Sage Room** ★★★$$$ Flambés such as steak Diane are among the mainstays of this candlelit restaurant, a great place for anniversaries and special occasions. You'll also find specials such as wild-game dishes, soft-shell crab, Great Lakes whitefish, and sautéed lamb roulade. ♦ Daily dinner. Reservations recommended. 702/588.2411

9 **Lone Pine Lodge** $ This small, 20-unit motel is across from **Edgewood Golf Course**. You can count on clean rooms, cable TV, in-room coffee and doughnuts, phones, and a hot tub. ♦ 864 Stateline Ave (one block west of the Stateline casinos), South Lake Tahoe, California. 544.3316

10 **Harrah's Lake Tahoe** $$$$ With 534 rooms, this venerable casino-hotel has long typified high life in the high country. Entertainment is one of the main attractions—Broadway plays and musicals alternate with the occasional celebrity, such as Wynona Judd. And a nightly cabaret combines equal portions of shapely bods, offbeat comics, and magicians. The sum of luxury, every guest room has two bathrooms, each equipped with a miniature color TV. When you're not pursuing other diversions, soak in the indoor swimming pool, get a body massage, work out in a small, but well-equipped, exercise room, or dine in one of the hotel's seven restaurants. ♦ Hwy 50 (across from Harvey's casino), Stateline, Nevada. 702/588.6611; fax 702/586.6607

Within Harrah's Lake Tahoe:

**The Forest Buffet** ★★★$$ Enjoying one of the area's best breakfast buffets, surrounded by a nearly 360-degree view of Lake Tahoe and its mountains, is a delightful way to greet the morning. Made-to-order Belgian waffles and omelettes, complemented by fruit, rolls, potatoes, and other goodies, will pack enough energy to ski **Gunbarrel** at least a couple of times. And the evening buffet is just as sumptuous, with prime rib, seafood on Fridays, and more salads than you can count. Breakfast is an incredible deal at $7.95. ♦ Daily breakfast, lunch, and dinner. 702/588.6611

**Friday's Station** ★★★$$$ Steaks so big they curl over the edge of the plate are the specialties of this high-elevation restaurant on the 18th floor of Harrah's Lake Tahoe. You can order New York steak, filet mignon, and prime rib, as well as an assortment of lamb and veal dishes. But there's plenty of seafood as well: you can dine on seafood crepes, crab legs, salmon, swordfish, and lobster. ♦ Daily lunch and dinner. Reservations recommended. 702/588.6611

11 **Embassy Suites** $$$$ Families are among the main patrons of this 400-room luxury hotel, which is blissfully free of jangling slot machines because it's on the California side of the state line. The eight-story, skylit atrium canopies profuse foliage and babbling brooks—including a Gold Rush–era sluice

box. The large suites comfortably sleep four, with a separate bedroom and living room and TV sets in each. An ample if undistinguished breakfast, served cafeteria style, is included in the room rate for all occupants. Complimentary beverages, including cocktails, are served in the afternoon. Facilities include an indoor pool and sauna, small exercise room, two restaurants, and one of South Tahoe's hottest nightclubs, **Turtles.** ♦ 4130 Lake Tahoe Blvd (right next to Stateline), South Lake Tahoe, California. 544.5400; fax 544.4900

Within Embassy Suites:

**Zackary's Restaurant** ★★★$$$ This restaurant prepares some of the most imaginative cuisine in Lake Tahoe, much of it with an Asian flair. The quiet, elegant atmosphere enhances the superb meals, which include a variety of seafood pasta, sautéed lobster, veal piccata, grilled salmon, and rack of lamb. ♦ Daily lunch and dinner. Reservations recommended

**Turtles Sports Bar and Dance Emporium** Wanna learn how to dance the "snake"? The cocktail waitresses sometimes double as instructors, encouraging even wallflowers to shake their stuff on the circular dance floor, while young deejays ham it up with skits. Within the bar is **Pasquale's,** which serves gourmet pizza made from scratch, cooked in a wood-burning brick oven (try the Thai chicken pizza). And there are plenty of TV screens to watch football games. ♦ Cover. M-F 11AM-2AM; Sa-Su 9AM-2AM; dancing nightly 9PM

**12 Tahoe Tropicana Lodge** $ A 58-unit motel with king- and queen-size beds, showers and tubs, cable TV, and some kitchenettes, this lodging is within walking distance of the Stateline casinos. ♦ 4132 Cedar Ave (off Lake Tahoe Blvd), South Lake Tahoe, California. 541.3911, 800/447.0246; fax 544.2177

**13 Crescent V Shopping Center** This place, which looks like a remnant of the 1950s, before they built enclosed malls, has some interesting stores. The upscale **David Grace** haberdashery (544.1777) carries Ralph Lauren Polo sweaters. There's also a footwear shop, westernwear and boot store, **Bugle Boy** outlet store (542.2121), and the large sporting goods emporium **Sports LTD.** (542.4000), which rents mountain bikes and skis. ♦ 4022 Hwy 50 (at Park Ave), South Lake Tahoe, California

Within Crescent V Shopping Center:

**Sizzler** ★$ For cheap eats, and plenty of them, this place is hard to beat. Steaks from $6 to $12, giant fried shrimp, and the amazing all-you-can-eat salad bar that is a meal unto itself satisfy without denting your pocketbook. ♦ Daily breakfast, lunch, and dinner. 541.8039

**13 Raley's Grocery and Drug Center** This is one of the best supermarkets anywhere and the main reason many skiers choose to dine in rather than eat out. This grocer's strength is its amazing selection of meats, poultry, and seafood, as well as its bakery. But if you need to pick up a video, some windshield de-icer, or cheap pair of gloves, you can do that here as well. ♦ Daily 6AM-11PM. 544.3418

**14 Stateline Cinema** Catch a first-run movie at this large-screen theater. ♦ 293 Park Ave, across from the Crescent V Shopping Center, South Lake Tahoe, California. 541.2121

**15 Fantasy Inn** $$$ This may be the most romantic small hotel in Lake Tahoe. Opened in the summer of 1993, the 56-room, European-style hostelry was designed for couples, so leave the kids at home. While the regular **Princess** rooms have stylish appointments such as sunken bathtubs and mirrored ceilings, there are eight themed suites that are the most distinctive accommodations in the area. They include **Graceland,** complete with Elvis memorabilia and a heart-shaped bed; **Rain Forest,** lush with clinging vines and a jungle motif; and **Romeo and Juliet,** decked out in white satin, lace, and a nine-foot sunken spa. Everyone who checks into a suite gets a complimentary bottle of champagne and two keepsake glasses, along with a basket of treats. There is even a wedding chapel, so you can tie the knot and honeymoon at one stop. There's no restaurant in the hotel. ♦ 3696 Lake Tahoe Blvd (between Wildwood Ave and Ski Run Blvd), South Lake Tahoe, California. 541.6666, 800/367.7736; fax 541.6798

Famous authors who have lived at Lake Tahoe include novelist John Steinbeck, who served as caretaker for an estate at Cascade Lake, just above Tahoe, and Samuel Clemens, better known as Mark Twain, who, with some friends, once accidentally started a forest fire and was fined by a judge.

**16 Tahoe Queen** No, Lake Tahoe does not freeze over in winter, and, yes, you can take a cruise even in the middle of February. Better yet, you can push off from the dock at Ski Run Boulevard to the North Shore in the morning on a stern-wheel steamer (call ahead to find out when this cruise runs), eat a buffet breakfast on the way, and 22 miles later be met at the Tahoe City dock by a shuttle to **Squaw Valley** or **Alpine Meadows** ski areas. You return the same way in the afternoon, only with cocktails and live music. It's a long haul—about two hours each way—but a scenic and relaxing journey. Another option: a two-hour midday cruise to Emerald Bay on an authentic Mississippi paddle-wheeler. The menu for an optional lunch or dinner includes French Quarter beef dip and a Texas-style steak sandwich. There's also a sunset dinner-dance cruise that comes with live music. Red double-decker buses offer free pick-up at most hotels and motels. ♦ End of Ski Run Blvd at the lake shoreline, South Lake Tahoe, California. 541.3364

**17 Lakeland Village Beach & Ski Resort** $$ If your family needs room to roam, but wants the convenience of shuttles to the slopes and the slots, this place—with hotel rooms, studios with Murphy beds, and condominiums containing up to four bedrooms and full kitchens—should fill the bill. The 260-unit resort is surrounded by pine forest and you can walk to Lakeland's private beach, as well as to restaurants and shops. A ski-rental shop, hot tub, heated pools, and saunas are on the premises. ♦ 3535 Hwy 50 (across from Fairway Ave), South Lake Tahoe, California. 544.1685; fax 544.0193

**17 Heidi's** ★★$ The biggest problem with this Old World place is sifting through a menu that's as long as your federal tax form. In the morning, you can't go wrong with much of anything, whether it's some exotic (and copious) omelette combination or the German pancakes. If you eat here before skiing, you can skip lunch. ♦ Daily breakfast and lunch. 3485 Hwy 50 (across from Fairway Ave), South Lake Tahoe, California. 544.8113

**17 South Tahoe Travelodge** $ Part of the franchised chain, this 59-room motel provides comfortable if predictably furnished units with stereo cable TV and in-room coffee brewers. Each unit has an outside entrance. Nonsmoking rooms and baby-sitting services are offered. ♦ 3489 Hwy 50 at Bijou Center (across from Fairway Ave), South Lake Tahoe, California. 544.5266; fax 544.6985

**18 Lucky Food Center** This grocery store, while well stocked, doesn't keep as many gourmet items on hand as Raley's. The big advantage is that it's always open. ♦ Daily 24 hours. 1030 Al Tahoe Blvd (at Hwy 50), South Lake Tahoe, California. 541.5113

**19 Samurai** ★★$$ If you're one of those ski warriors who can negotiate the **Gunbarrel** run and live to tell about it, then you might try this Japanese restaurant where you can test your tolerance for wasabi (green horseradish) and sake. The sushi and sashimi aren't as fresh as you'd find them next to the docks in San Francisco, but you can always play it safe, like many *gaijin,* by ordering tempura, teriyaki, or sukiyaki. ♦ Daily dinner. Reservations recommended for large groups. 2588 Hwy 50 (just before Tahoe Keys Blvd), South Lake Tahoe, California. 542.0300

**20 Tahoe Factory Stores** One of two outlet centers in South Tahoe, this mecca for the spendthrift includes **Leather Loft, Prestige Fragrance, Harve Benard, Ltd.,** and **Hanes-Leggs-Bali.** ♦ M-Sa 10AM-6PM; Su 10AM-5PM. 2501 Hwy 50 (at Tahoe Keys Blvd), South Lake Tahoe, California

If all of the water were drained from Lake Tahoe, it could cover an area the size of California with a layer 14 inches deep, enough to provide everyone in the United States with 50 gallons of water per day for five years.

**21 Factory Stores at the Y** Shopping on the cheap has become a popular pastime at South Lake Tahoe, and this baker's dozen of outlet stores offers impressive bargains. Browsers can mine discounts of 20 to 60 percent off normal retail prices at **Bass Shoes, Van Heusen, Capezio Shoes, Cape Isle Knitter, Great Outdoor Clothing, Geoffrey Beene, Home Again, Levi's,** and **Oneida,** among others. A bus, cab, or the casino shuttle will bring you here. ♦ Daily 9AM-7PM. At the "Y" intersection of Hwys 50 and 89, South Lake Tahoe, California

**21 Act 3 Theaters** When you're craving a tub of popcorn and the latest blockbuster, this movie theater will undoubtedly supply both. ♦ At the "Y" intersection of Hwys 50 and 89, South Lake Tahoe, California. 541.2121

**22 Tahoe Cinema** This single-screen movie theater books first-run flicks, from tearjerkers to action romps. ♦ South Y Shopping Center, 1054 Emerald Bay Rd (at Hwys 50 and 89), South Lake Tahoe, California. 541.2121

**22 Raley's Grocery Center** This is the area's second abundantly stocked Raley's store. ♦ Daily 6AM-11PM. South Y Shopping Center, 1040 Emerald Bay Rd (at Hwys 50 and 89), South Lake Tahoe, California. 541.5160

**23 Cantina Los Tres Hombres** ★★$ Nothing thaws your toes like a bowl of *salsa picante* generously slathered over nachos, enchiladas, tacos, or burritos. This Mexican restaurant, a local favorite, fills rapidly in the evenings, and it's best to arrive early since there's a no-reservation policy except for groups of 10 or more. Most dishes, with the exception of fajitas, are under $10. ♦ Daily lunch and dinner. 765 Emerald Bay Rd (Hwy 89 at 10th St), South Lake Tahoe, California. 544.1233

**24 Camp Richardson Corral Sleigh Rides** Afternoon sleigh rides, some including a steak dinner at a rustic cabin, are available throughout the winter, weather permitting. ♦ Daily 8AM-5PM. Reservations required. Hwy 89, 3 miles north of the "Y" intersection with Hwy 50, South Lake Tahoe, California. 541.3113

**25 Sunset Ranch** Two hundred acres of groomed track beckon to nordic skiers and snowmobilers, though the two hardly seem compatible. Guided snowmobile tours; horse-drawn sleighs; horseback riding; and a snowplay area complete the offerings. ♦ M-F 8AM-6PM; Sa-Su 8AM-8PM. one-quarter-mile south of South Lake Tahoe Airport on Hwy 50, South Lake Tahoe, California. 541.9001

**26 Lake Tahoe Winter Sports Center** Depending on snow conditions, guides will escort groups on two-hour, 25-mile snowmobile tours of the Lake Tahoe high country, including the scenic Hope Valley/Carson Pass area. Tours are tame enough for families with children. Tour leaders make stops to point out areas of interest, and Forest Service roads serve as trails. While snowmobile helmets are provided to all riders, you can rent jumpsuits and boots from the center to stay warm. Free shuttles operate from Stateline to the trailheads. Cross-country skiing also can be arranged here. ♦ Daily 8AM-6PM Nov-Apr. Reservations required. Hwy 50, across from the agricultural inspection station at Meyers, California. 577.2940

## Bests

**Carl Ribaudo**
Director/Management Consultant, Strategic Marketing Group

Best skiing—**Nevada** side of **Heavenly** or **Kirkwood.**

Best dinner—**The Sage Room** at **Harvey's.**

Best place to relax after skiing—**Walley's Hot Springs Resort** in Genoa.

Best local band—**Cosmic Freeway.**

Best aerial view of Lake Tahoe—from Heavenly's **Ridge Run.**

Best summer hangout—**Camp Richardson.**

**Monica Bandows**
Public Relations Manager, Heavenly Ski Resort

I love the **South Shore** of Lake Tahoe for its unique mixture of fine dining and first-class skiing. After a tough day of entertaining the media in the double-diamond chutes of **Mott Canyon,** I like to dazzle our guests with an elegant dinner at **Llewellyn's Restaurant,** located at the top of **Harvey's** casino-hotel. The entrées are spectacular (the views aren't so bad either).

## Kirkwood

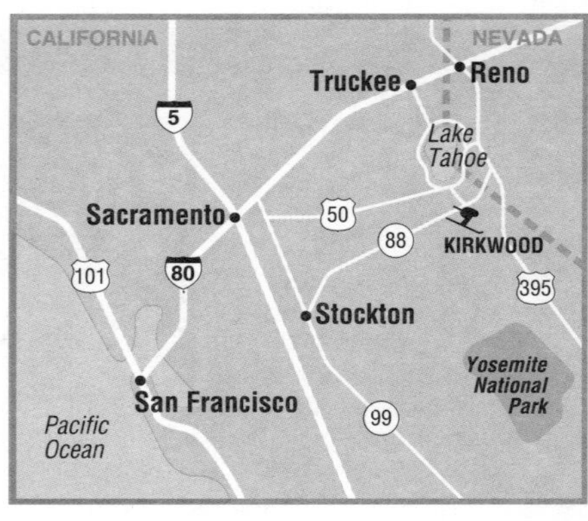


It's where Glen Plake, America's most radical skier and all-around awesome dude (note the Mohawk hairstyle), earned his ski legs trailblazing slopes that most people would describe as unthinkable. It's the same place where Paul Ruff set the world record for ski jumping at 115 feet. And it's where the late speed-skier Steve McKinney burned tracks in the snow while trying to improve on the law of gravity. Considering the steep, volcanic monoliths surrounding this little valley, it's easy to see why extreme skiers have made Kirkwood their stomping grounds of choice.

Yet, for all of its ferocious double-diamond runs, cornices, and chutes, Kirkwood has a tamer side. It boasts the most consistently dependable snow conditions in the **South Lake Tahoe** area. When other ski areas are cranking up their blower guns for nightly assaults on rock-bare slopes, Kirkwood is still cloaked in a generous layer of natural powder, thanks to its high base elevation (7,800 feet) and its position in the storm path. This is the resort that knowledgeable locals head to early in the season to catch first tracks and then late in the spring to carve the final corn snow.

Although the jagged massifs looming over **Kirkwood Meadows** can be intimidating, there is also some gentler terrain here. Beginners have access to their own chairlifts and runs, while intermediate skiers cruise an open bowl and plenty of intimate, sheltered forest. Don't rely too heavily on the resort's trail map for ability levels, because Kirkwood has devised a trail-rating system that bears little resemblance to that used by most Lake Tahoe ski areas.

Located just 30 miles southwest of South Lake Tahoe, Kirkwood is a popular choice for skiers who've come to the area for a few days and are staying elsewhere. Its frequent shuttle buses traveling US 50 (a.k.a. "the Strip") between ski resorts will fetch you there and back without hassle. But because it takes almost two hours to reach Kirkwood from **Reno** (thanks to heavy traffic), and because accommodations are minimal and nightlife nonexistent, this is not generally considered a full-fledged destination resort. Folks come here for seclusion and a family-style environment, not for 24-hour entertainment.

When attacking the slopes at Kirkwood, think of the terrain as five distinct zones. As you drive into the resort, the first zone is the **Timber Creek** area, which consists of flat, well-groomed beginner trails and a few lower intermediate runs. The next zone covers the Cornice and Solitude Lifts, which let you off on mostly strong-intermediate and advanced slopes. Then there's the Wagon Wheel Chair, which is double-diamond stuff and popular with the experts, followed by the buttermilk runs for neophytes and the lower intermediates off the Snowkirk and Caples Crest Chairs. Finally, there's **Sunrise Bowl**—served by two lifts—which offers above-treeline runs for strong intermediates.

If you subscribe to the "follow the sun" theory of skiing a mountain, you'll start your day at Sunrise Bowl, then work your way back over the ridge and across the other zones, ending with the advanced runs off Cornice Chair. Unless you've got rubber ski legs combined with a cast-iron disposition, forget about the couloirs and chutes below **The Sisters.** By day's end, you're ready for the main lodge—**Red Cliffs**—and one final mountain…the heaping plate of nachos and salsa for which Kirkwood is famous.

**Kirkwood Ski Area**
**PO Box 1**
**Kirkwood, California 95646**

**Information**....................................209/258.6000
**Reservations**............209/258.7000, 800/967.7500
**24-Hour Snow Phone**.........................209/258.3000
**24-Hour Road Conditions**.................209/258.3000

## Fast Facts

*Area code 209 unless otherwise noted.*

**Ski Season** Thanksgiving through the end of April

**Location** Kirkwood is 30 miles southwest of **South Lake Tahoe.**

### Getting to Kirkwood

**By air: Reno/Tahoe International Airport,** about 80 miles to the northeast of Kirkwood, is served daily by **American West, American, Continental, Delta, Northwest, Reno Air, Southwest, United,** and **USAir.** All offer direct flights. **Lake Tahoe Airport,** about 25 miles from Kirkwood, is served by **Reno Air,** with flights from **Los Angeles;** and **TransWorld Express,** with flights from **Los Angeles** and **San Francisco.** There is no shuttle or public bus service from either airport to Kirkwood. From **Reno/Tahoe** your best bet would be to take the **Tahoe Casino Express** (702/785.2424) bus to the casino-hotels, then catch a Kirkwood bus. From **Lake Tahoe Airport,** try the **Yellow Cab Company** (916/541.4141) or **Sunshine Cab Company** (916/588.5555).

**By bus: Greyhound** (800/231.2222) serves **South Lake Tahoe** with daily buses from **Sacramento** and **San Francisco.** The nearest drop-off point is **Harrah's Lake Tahoe** near Stateline; from there, you'll be relying again on ski area shuttles.

**By car:** All-wheel-drive rental cars are available from several agencies at **Reno/Tahoe.** Take US Highway 395 South to State Route 88 West. From **Lake Tahoe Airport,** follow State Route 89 South and turn onto State Route 88 West.

**All-weather highways:**

Reno—US Highway 395 South to State Route 88 West

Sacramento—State Route 16 East to State Route 49 South, turning finally onto State Route 88 East

Greater San Francisco—Interstate 580 East to State Route 205 East to Interstate 5 East to State Route 4 East to State Route 88 East

**Driving times from:**

Reno—90 minutes (80 miles)

Sacramento—2 hours (114 miles)

Greater San Francisco—3.5 hours (201 miles)

**By train:** The closest station is in **Reno,** where **Amtrak**'s (800/USA.RAIL) *California Zephyr* stops—mornings westbound, evenings eastbound.

The name "Tahoe" comes from a Washoe Indian term believed to mean "big water," or "high water."

### Getting around Kirkwood

A daily shuttle bus is available from **South Lake Tahoe** lodgings. Reservation calls should originate from the front desk on behalf of guests. Arrive at 9:15AM and depart at 4:30PM. 916/541.7223

## FYI

**Area** 2,300 acres, with some wide, steep bowls, forests, and moguls, in addition to lots of groomed skiing surface

Beginner—15 percent

Intermediate—50 percent

Advanced—20 percent

Expert—15 percent

**Number of Groomed Runs** 68

**Longest Run** 2.5 miles (from **Sunrise Bowl**)

**Capacity** 16,000 skiers per hour

**Base Elevation** 7,800 feet

**Summit Elevation** 9,800 feet

**Vertical Rise** 2,000 feet

**Average Annual Snowfall** 425 inches

**Snowmaking** None

**Night Skiing** None

**Lifts** 11 (7 triple chairs, 3 double chairs, and 1 surface lift)

| **Lift Passes** | **Full Day** | **Half Day** (starts at 12:30PM) |
|---|---|---|
| **Adult** | $40 | $29 |
| **Youth** (13-24) | $30 | $22 |
| **Child** (6-12) | $5 | $5 |
| **Toddlers** (5 and under) | Free | Free |
| **Senior** (60 and over) | $20 | $14 |

**Ski School** The office (258.7245) is located in **Red Cliff Lodge,** at the resort's base area. The **Beginner Special** includes a double-session learn-to-ski lesson (four hours), plus all-day equipment rental and a beginner lift ticket. Group lessons meet daily at 10AM and 2PM. Ninety-minute private lessons are also available.

**Kids' Ski School** The **Mighty Mountain Special** (for ages 4 through 12, all levels) includes four hours of instruction, a child's all-day lift ticket, all-day equipment rental, and lunch.

**Clinics and Special Programs** Meeting three times daily, **Pro-turn** separates skiers into groups (six or fewer per group) according to one of three ability levels. The **Women Only** classes meet near

Chair 5 on Fridays and Saturdays to focus on aspects of skiing most important to women. Skiers 40 and over can try the **Forty Plus** program, offering intermediate and advanced classes on Fridays and Saturdays.

**Races** Daily racing off the Solitude Chair is open to the public, with times announced at the end of each run.

**Rentals** A first-floor office (258.7294) in **Red Cliffs Lodge** offers full-day and half-day rates. Open daily from 8AM to 5PM, the shop carries high-performance skis, as well as demo skis and boots. Some form of identification is required—a driver's license or credit card is acceptable.

**Lockers** You can find coin-operated lockers downstairs in both **Red Cliffs Lodge** and **Timber Creek Lodge**. Basket checks are also available in Red Cliffs (all-day in-and-out privileges).

**Day Care** Parents may drop off children ages 3 to 6 (no diaper-wearers allowed) at the base area, in an office adjacent to **Red Cliffs Lodge.** All-day and half-day stays include lunch. There is also per-hour child care (two-hour minimum).

**First Aid** The **Barton Memorial Clinic at Kirkwood** (592.2151), located on the second floor of **Red Cliffs Lodge,** provides minimal care. The nearest hospital is **Barton Memorial** (916/542.3000) 30 miles away in **South Lake Tahoe.**

**Parking** Free parking is available at the base.

**Worth Knowing**

- You can purchase a five-day, five-resort interchangeable pass that allows you access not only to Kirkwood, but **Heavenly, Alpine Meadows, Northstar,** and **Squaw Valley.** The cost is $185 for all ages.

## Rating the Runs

### ● Beginner

The learning curve is easily mastered on **Graduation.** This forested trail, served by the Bunny Lift, is off the beaten path and reserved entirely for matriculating skiers. Nearby **Timber Creek Lodge,** with a cafeteria specializing in hot dogs, provides sustenance for future hotdoggers. Parents can leave their small fry in ski school here for most of the day.

Close to the main lodge, with a slow lift for neophytes, **Snowkirk** won't induce stage fright. A loop extends the length of the run to a mile, and for the most part, beginners practicing snowplow turns or doing headers into drifts can do so without the scrutiny of onlookers. This isn't a good spot to be at the end of the day, however, when thrillseekers come zooming down from the upper mountain.

### ■ Intermediate

The lone intermediate run off the Reut Chair, **Buckboard** is also the best point from which to view daredevils trying their luck on double-diamond chutes that funnel into a huge ravine from those imposing peaks called **The Sisters.** Buckboard has some good fall-line skiing here, and it's generally uncrowded.

Slicing through the center of **Sunrise Bowl,** wide-open **Elevator Shaft** presents a slight traverse and a few small bumps before it becomes a satin sheet of unadulterated whoopee. Early birds get the best turns, when the morning sun softens up the terrain. Lift lines can be long in the afternoon.

Welcome to a great warm-up run off the Solitude Chair, which serves only cruisin' terrain, most of it meandering through the trees. **Lower Monte Wolfe** is the place to find out if you've got the stuff to move up the mountain to—you guessed it—**Upper Monte Wolfe,** a black diamond run.

### ◆ Advanced

Located on the farthest side of **Sunrise Bowl** is **Larry's Lip,** an open-faced, sparsely vegetated trail presenting only a few benign bumps. You won't want to ski too close to the cliff—it's no-man's-land below.

A nasty-looking black diamond chute, **Sentinel** is really a clean-cut kind of trail that allows strong-intermediate skiers to shine. Groomed regularly, the slope has few moguls and a great pitch. You traverse slightly off the Cornice Chair, take a moderately steep drop from the top, then follow Sentinel as it melds into two lower runs. The trail is marked on the map as "G," as in gee whiz.

### ◆◆ Expert

Link **Thunder Saddle** up with Larry's Lip and Snowkirk to trace Kirkwood's longest run, a total of 2.5 miles. Thunder Saddle is a double-diamond drop-off, leading from **Sunrise Bowl** to **Eagle Bowl,** but even eagles might not dare to ski here. Bail out, if you must, on **Chicken Chute,** which is not shown on the trail map—probably because taking the easy way is nothing to crow about.

You'll be pressing the limits of your ability if you try to challenge **The Wall,** a double-diamond descent, without the nerve of a bomb squad leader and elastic legs. The resort management gives fair warning: there's a skull-and-crossbones sign at the bottom of the Wagon Wheel Chair. The lift unloads on a cornice, and there is little opportunity to say your prayers before taking the plunge. Losing it here means a slide for your life.

## Snowboarding

Snowboarding is permitted on all parts of the mountain. The area has numerous naturally occurring half-pipes and quarter-pipes. The Kirkwood ski school offers private snowboard instruction, but no group lessons. Boards may be rented at the **Red Cliffs** and **Timber Creek** lodges.

## Mountain Highs and Lows

The fact that the trail map shows **Home Run** crossing several other runs ought to be a tip-off to trouble. Indeed, this is no intermediate slope at all, but an access road from **Solitude** to the Timber Creek base area. Other ski resorts would designate trails like this one with broken lines or beginner green. While Home Run is one way to reach the Hole 'n' Wall Chair, most intermediates get there by following **Sentinel** and **Stump Run.**

If you glided down Sentinel and **Larry's Lip,** you might think that other single-diamond runs here would be as easily digested. Wrong. **Olympic** is one tough cookie. It's got more lumps than rocky road ice cream, and skiers without bionic legs will find it hard to swallow.

## At the Resort

*Area code 209 unless otherwise noted.*

✦ **Kirkwood Inn** ★★$ Once a stop for pioneers traveling west from Illinois along the famed Mormon-Emigrant Trail, this rustic 1864 log cabin is a great place to find a hot, filling meal. Small and quaint, with an interior that's dominated by the bar, the inn shows off its past by displaying historic memorabilia. Breakfasts are weighted toward omelettes and waffles (oh, and of course, espresso). Otherwise, look for hamburgers and sandwiches, ribs and homemade soups. Daily specials are posted on a chalkboard. Best bets are the eight-ounce New York steak and Zak's nachos (chili, cheese, salsa, and sour cream). ♦ Daily breakfast, lunch, and dinner. State Route 88, across from Kirkwood entrance. 258.7304

✦ **Kirkwood Stables** What could be more romantic (or more fun for a family) than a horse-drawn sleigh ride? Take your choice of daytime and moonlight rides through picturesque **Kirkwood Meadows.** Specialty excursions include the **Sweetheart's Ride** and the **Sleigh Ride with Bonfire.** ♦ Daily 9AM-5PM. State Route 88, near Kirkwood's entrance. 258.7433

✦ **Timber Creek Lodge** As you drive Kirkwood's entrance road, this is the first base area you see. The lodge includes the ski shop and rentals, ski school, lift-ticket windows, and food services. It also houses the **Mighty Mountain Ski School** for children. ♦ Kirkwood Meadows Dr. 258.7267

Within Timber Creek Lodge:

**Snowshoe Thompson's Bar and Restaurant** ★★$ Next to the beginner hill, this casual spot serves pizza by the slice, salads, sandwiches, and pasta. During the peak season, pizza is also served for dinner. To "beef up" the menu, there's an outdoor barbecue for charbroiling hamburgers and hot dogs. ♦ Daily lunch. 258.6000

✦ **Edelweiss and Thimblewood Condominiums** $$ All rentable accommodations at Kirkwood are of the condo variety. Six condominium complexes are interspersed with restaurants and shops to satisfy residents' basic needs. These two are located across the road from **Timber Creek Lodge** and two chairlifts (Hole 'n' Wall and Bunny)—convenient for beating each morning's rush to the slopes. They're also adjacent to the nordic ski trails in **Kirkwood Meadows.** At Edelweiss, standard units come with one, two, and three bedrooms and lofts. Most are equipped with TVs, and all have phones. Ski bums used to cleaning their own cheap, packed hotel rooms will enjoy Edelweiss's daily maid service. Thimblewood offers one-bedroom condominiums, most with TVs, telephones, and daily maid service. ♦ Kirkwood Village. 258.7000; fax 258.7400

✦ **The Meadows Condominiums** $$ Situated between **Timber Creek Lodge** and Cornice Chair (and within walking distance of both), this 50-unit complex provides deluxe rooms, studios, and one- and two-bedroom units. Each studio boasts a single bathroom, efficiency kitchen, sofa bed, and built-in bunks to sleep as many as four people. Units with one and two bedrooms are also endowed with two bathrooms and full kitchens, with sleeping room for four to six weary skiers. All units include phones, decks or balconies, and underground parking. For TV junkies (gotta keep up with "NYPD Blue," huh?), there is cable reception in most units. Daily maid service prevents empty Cheetos bags from engulfing you. The complex includes a large common room containing a fireplace, a Jacuzzi, laundry facilities, and a gameroom. ♦ Kirkwood Village. 258.7000; fax 258.7400

✦ **Sun Meadows Condominiums** $$ This 30-condo complex is Kirkwood's premium property, directly across from the Solitude and Cornice Chairlifts. It offers deluxe studios, as well as one-, two-, and three-bedroom condominiums (with fireplaces and fully equipped kitchens). Most units feature TVs, and all of them have phones and views of the mountain and meadows. Daily maid service and underground parking are available. ♦ Kirkwood Village. 258.7000; fax 258.7400

Kirkwood, which turned 20 years old during the 1992-93 season, was the last major ski resort to be built in California. It is also the only fully self-contained ski resort in the US, generating all of its own electricity and water, and treating all of its wastewater.

Within Sun Meadows Condominiums:

**Kirkwood General Store and Reservations Office** The reservations office is the check-in point and information hub for Kirkwood Village. Next door, the general store (daily 8AM to 8PM) stocks a few groceries and quotidian sundries, but don't figure on using it to make a five-course dinner for four. The nearest supermarket, in South Lake Tahoe, is 30 miles away. ♦ Daily 8AM-5PM. 258.7000

**Cornice Cafe Restaurant and Bar** ★★$$ Kirkwood's most upscale dining establishment goes heavy on California cuisine. Popular dishes include grilled New York steak with sautéed wild mushrooms and onions, and cannelloni with turkey sausage and sun-dried–tomato marinara. The dining room is large and airy, and the menu includes a decent diversity of premium wines. ♦ Daily lunch and dinner. 258.6000

✦ **Base Camp Condominiums** $ The most spartan and economical property in Kirkwood Village, with 10 one- and two-bedroom units, offers phones, daily maid service, and TVs. ♦ Across the street from Red Cliffs Lodge. 258.7000; fax 258.7400

✦ **Red Cliffs Lodge** This large but undistinguished, three-level day lodge represents the nerve center of the resort's ski operation. Inside, you'll find a full rental and retail shop on the ground floor, ski school offices, rest rooms, and the first-aid office, as well as several places to get nourishment. ♦ Kirkwood Meadows Dr. 258.6000

Within Red Cliffs Lodge:

**The Cafeteria** ★$ As pedestrian as its name suggests, this fuel stop offers hot and cold sandwiches, chili, and daily hot plate specials at lunch, along with complete breakfasts, i.e., the conventional scrambled eggs, bacon, and pancakes. ♦ Daily breakfast and lunch. Second floor. 258.6000

**The Barbecue** ★$$ Chefs grill burgers, 'dogs, ribs, and chicken on the sundeck, while hungry patrons yammer happily away at tables and benches. And if your midafternoon chompfest should turn into a siesta, there are plenty of elevated snowbanks here for cushioning. ♦ Daily lunch (weather permitting). Second floor. 258.6000

**Zak's Bar** ★★★$$ A variety of alcoholic and other beverages help make this a rowdy rendezvous spot after the lifts close, and on weekends and holidays there is also live music to stoke up the crowd. A lot of people like to hang here at day's end, waiting for the flow of traffic to ebb a bit on State Route 88. Zak's is famous for its appetizers, served from food kiosks. The most popular kiosk, **Mexican Cocina,** serves what is arguably the biggest and best plate of nachos in the Lake Tahoe area. Other kiosks serve cold sandwiches, stews, and hearty soups. To make the morning a little more palatable, partake of *caffe lattes* and crusty pastries at **Croissants**

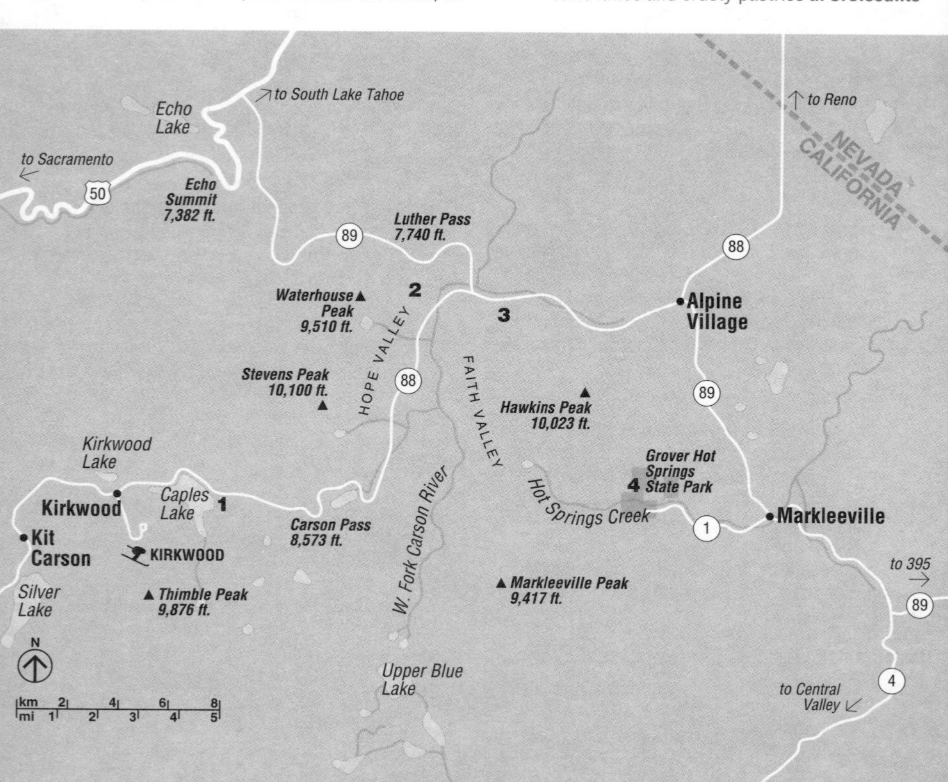

et Café. ♦ Daily 11AM-7PM. Second floor. 258.6000

✦ **Kirkwood Towers** $$ If ski-in, ski-out proximity to the slopes is the most important criterion for you, this is the place. Don't expect anything fancy. Daily maid service, phones, and TVs are staples in most of the 11 rentals. For more entertainment, a bar and grill is located on the building's ground floor. ♦ Adjacent to the **Red Cliff Lodge.** 800/4KIRKWOOD; fax 258.8608

## Beyond the Resort

**1 Caples Lake Restaurant** ★★★$$ Travel writers have this kind of place in mind when they refer to "fine dining in an intimate, rustic atmosphere." Maybe it's the riveting views of Caples Lake that cause them to wax eloquent or just that they've dipped a bit incautiously into the restaurant's store of fine wines. In any case, the cuisine and the atmosphere deserve applause. Fresh salmon, mahimahi, and fettuccine alfredo appear on the menu, along with more pedestrian, but no less savory, dishes such as steak, chicken, and vegetable casserole. ♦ Th-Su dinner. Reservations recommended. State Route 88, 2 miles east of Kirkwood. 258.8888

**2 Husky Express/Sierra Ski Tours** Dogsled rides, like those found in Alaska, allow you a brief spell of fantasy and thrills. The eight-dog sleds carry two passengers apiece (not more than 370 pounds total) through the **Hope Valley.** Dressing *very* warmly is a must, as are advance reservations. ♦ Off State Route 88, near its junction with State Route 89. 800/833.MUSH

**3 Sorensen's** $$ You like rustic? They've got rustic. This resort's 30 cabins, ranging from snug bungalows for two to a replica of a 13th-century Norwegian home (accommodating eight people), cater mostly to "skinny skiers" (cross-country skiers). That's because the Old World layout and nearby trail system are particularly suited to a nordic lifestyle. But because it's close to Kirkwood (just 14 miles away) and its owners take a personal and friendly interest in guests' welfare, downhill aficionados will be happy here, too. A few of the units come with breakfast service included in the price. ♦ 14255 State Route 88, east of State Route 89, Hope Valley, California. 916/694.2203, 800/423.9949

Within Sorensen's:

**Sorensen's Country Cafe** ★★★$ It's quaint and small (only enough room for 28 patrons), but this joint serves delicious and inexpensive homemade cuisine, very much in the California style. Dinners may feature artichoke pasta, fresh salmon or orange roughy, grilled steaks or pork chops, and barbecued chicken. Breakfast is more traditional, offering waffles, quiche, and stuffed ham-and-cheese croissants, while lunches run to soup-and-sandwich combos or beef Burgundy. ♦ Daily breakfast, lunch, and dinner. Main floor. 916/694.2203

**4 Grover Hot Springs State Park** After a long day of skiing, a dip in one of this California park's two concrete mineral springs pools is sure to get your blood circulating again. One pool clocks in at around 103 degrees; the other ranges from 50 to 80 degrees. Swimsuits are required; changing rooms are available. ♦ Admission. Call for winter hours. 3 miles west of Markleeville on Route 1, not far from State Route 88. 916/694.2249

### Bests

**Jim Plake**
Fire Chief, City of South Lake Tahoe Fire Department

**In South Lake Tahoe:**

Best ski area—**Heavenly.** It's the top intermediate/advanced resort.

Best views—Heavenly cannot be beat.

Best runs—in Heavenly: **Gunbarrel, Face** (advanced); in **Kirkwood: The Wall** (Chair 10, advanced).

No lift lines—Chair 10, Kirkwood.

Fastest chair—**Sky Express,** Heavenly (great for advanced/intermediate skiers).

Best après-ski spot—**Heavenly Bar.**

Best casino—**Harvey's.** Be sure to visit a casino if you're not from Tahoe.

Best resort food—Kirkwood (by far).

Most entertaining person to ski with—my son, Glen Plake.

If time and weather permit, take a drive around Lake Tahoe (72 miles); it is an excellent alternative to skiing.

Near Eagle Bowl, Kirkwood has one of only two officially certified speed-skiing courses in the US. The other is at Silverton, Colorado.

# Mammoth Mountain

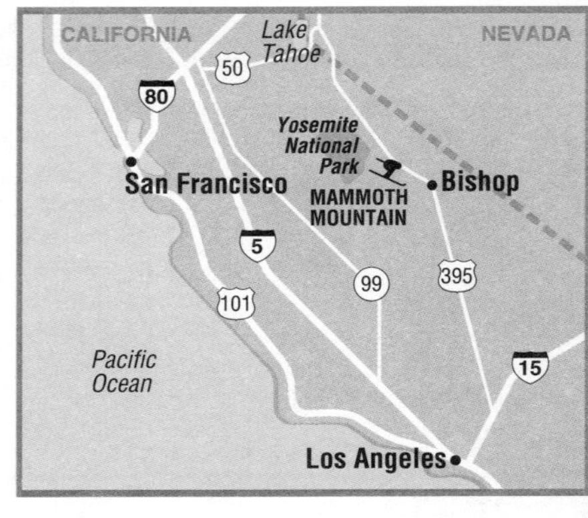


Since he mortgaged his motorcycle for $87 in order to buy his first ski lift in 1955, former downhill and slalom racer Dave McCoy has built up what now ranks as the second-largest resort of its kind in California (after **Heavenly**) and one of the most popular ski areas in the nation—Mammoth Mountain. That single lift has led to the construction of 31 chairs, over 150 runs, and more than 30,000 hotel rooms to service visitors. Aided every winter by a consistently deep snowpack (8 to 12 feet), a 70 percent chance of sunny skies, and a large, friendly staff of 1,800, Mammoth proves the *Field of Dreams* axiom: If you build it, they will come. The resort's 3,500 skiable acres and extraordinarily long season (from November through June or July) now attract downhilling desperados from Southern California in lemminglike hordes—up to 15,000 people a weekend.

Mammoth is located just east of **Yosemite National Park,** near the California-Nevada border. There are other ski areas considerably closer to Los Angeles than this one—**Bear Mountain** and **Ski Summit**, for example—but nothing compares to the Mammoth experience. Dozens of huge, open bowls, a wicked array of chutes and cornices, and myriad tree-lined routes conspire to win the favor of almost every skier living south of **Lake Tahoe**. The greatest number of runs are groomed for intermediate types, but beginners are far from ignored, treated to a generous share of tree-lined slopes and one of the nation's top-ranked ski schools. Advanced and expert skiers will thrill to the near-endless choice of paths, especially when there's (sigh) powder in abundance.

Because of Mammoth's dimensions, its diversity of runs, and its "number 'em as we build 'em" chairlift system (lifts don't have names), first-time visitors will be dazed and confused. After figuring out which color-coded ski shuttle is best and where to stash your stuff (forget about trying to find a free locker on weekends), and then puzzling over why Chair 9 is nowhere near Chair 10, you're still left to decide at which of the seven cafeterias, restaurants, and barbecue stands you should have lunch. And finally, there's that immortal Mammoth worry, brought on by staring over vast sargassos of parking lots: Where *did* you leave your car?

Don't worry. After your first day at this immense, aptly named resort, everything starts to make sense.

Mammoth has managed to eschew ostentation. The main lodge, which is appropriately named the **Main Lodge,** is an exercise in pragmatism, designed to crank thousands of skiers per hour through its labyrinth of levels and hallways, with a minimum of hassle. A sister lodge, **Warming Hut II,** resembles nothing so much as a grounded concrete zeppelin. The satellite town of **Mammoth Lakes** is about as LA-ish as Eugene, Oregon (with the same negligible nightlife), but no one really cares since people come here hell-bent on skiing above all else. And Mammoth is—as its owner would surely testify—the real McCoy.

**Mammoth Mountain Ski Resort**
**PO Box 24**
**Mammoth Lakes, California 93546**

**Information**................619/934.2571, 800/832.7320
.....................................................fax 619/934.0600
**Reservations**....................................800/228.4947
**24-Hour Snow Phone**........................619/934.6166
**24-Hour Road Conditions**..................619/873.6366

## Fast Facts

*Area code 619 unless otherwise noted.*

**Ski Season** November through June

**Location** Mammoth is east of **Yosemite National Park,** near the California-Nevada border.

## Getting to Mammoth Mountain

**By air: Mammoth Lakes Airport,** just eight miles south of town, is served daily by **TW Express.** Flights arrive from the Imperial Terminal at **Los Angeles International Airport (LAX),** as well as from **San Francisco.** For air-and-ski package information and reservations, call 800/221.2000 (California only) or 310/322.9882. Take the shuttle from the airport to Mammoth or hop a cab to the mountain.

**By bus: Greyhound** (800/231.2222) serves the town of **Mammoth Lakes** twice daily from the **Los Angeles** and **Northern California** areas.

**By car:** Rental cars are available at **Mammoth Lakes Airport** through **Mammoth Car Rentals** (800/848.8422). Head northwest from the airport on US Highway 395, then west on State Highway 203 for 7.5 miles.

**All-weather highways:**

Reno—US Highway 395 South to State Highway 203 West

Sacramento—Interstate 80 East or US Highway 50 East, then take US Highway 395 South and State Highway 203 West

Los Angeles—State Route 14 North to US Highway 395 North, and then take State Highway 203 West

Greater San Francisco—Interstate 80 East or US Highway 50 East, then take US Highway 395 South and State Highway 203 West

**Driving times from:**

Reno—3.25 hours (169 miles)

Sacramento—5.5 hours (269 miles)

Los Angeles—6 hours (300 miles)

Greater San Francisco—7 hours (356 miles)

## Getting around Mammoth Mountain

**Mammoth Area Shuttle (MAS)** operates an excellent free four-line shuttle (934.0687) to and from the town of **Mammoth Lakes.** The Red Line provides service around town, while the **Blue, Green,** and **Yellow Lines** service virtually every hotel, as well as all ticket offices and lifts. For more personalized service, call the **KC Cab Company** at 934.4778.

## FYI

**Area** 3,500 acres, arranged in a horseshoe shape, offering ridges, bowls, gulleys, chutes, moguls, and beautifully groomed cruisers

Beginner—30 percent

Intermediate—40 percent

Advanced/Expert—30 percent

**Number of Groomed Runs** It varies, depending on the season, although at least 30 percent are groomed at any one time

**Longest Run** 2.5 miles **(St. Anton)**

**Capacity** 43,000 skiers per hour

**Base Elevation** 7,953 feet

**Summit Elevation** 11,053 feet

**Vertical Rise** 3,100 feet

**Average Annual Snowfall** 335 inches

**Snowmaking** 15 percent

**Night Skiing** None

**Lifts** 31 (2 high-speed quads, 4 quads, 7 triple chairs, 14 double chairs, and 2 surface lifts. A gondola also climbs the mountain in two legs—one going to the **Mid-Chalet,** the second climbing to the top.)

| **Lift Passes** | **Full Day** | **Half Day** (starts at 12:30PM) |
|---|---|---|
| **Adult** | $40 | $30 |
| **Teen** (13-18) | $30 | $25 |
| **Child** (7-12) | $20 | $15 |
| **Toddler** (6 and under) | Free | Free |
| **Senior** (65 and over) | $20 | $15 |

Multi-day tickets (up to 7 days) are also available.

Ticket offices are conveniently located: the **Main Lodge** (both inside and outside the building), the bottom of Chair 2, **Warming Hut II, Mammoth Mountain Inn,** and the **Chair 15 Outpost.** On Saturdays and Sundays, buy tickets also at the bottom of Chairs 4, 20, 21, and 10 (look for the tiny ticket booths along **Minaret Road**).

When signs stating "Please Don't Feed the Coyotes" failed to stop Mammoth Mountain skiers from dropping trails of dog biscuits beneath certain popular chairlifts, the ski patrol tried another tactic: "Please Don't Feed the Coyotes or We'll Shoot You." What finally worked was a poster of a coyote within a bull's-eye and a succinct message about the hazards of feeding wild animals.

**Ski School** Offices are located on the second floor of the **Main Lodge** (934.0685) and at **Warming Hut II** (934.0787). Group lessons begin at 10AM and 1:30PM, lessons range from **A** (beginner) to **G** (expert). Private lessons are available for up to five people at a time, and may be held for one, three, and six hours. Telemark, snowboard, and first-timer classes are also available. For beginners to holy terrors, 13 to 17 years old, **Teen Scene** provides all-day or half-day instruction.

**Kids' Ski School** For children, 4 to 12 years old, **Mammoth Explorers** includes morning, afternoon, or all-day classes (10AM to 3:30PM), with lunch and supervision. Two-day and three-day all-day camps for children, ages 7 to 12, are also available. Prices include equipment rental, lift tickets, and meals.

**Clinics and Special Programs** Slalom and giant slalom classes, 2.5 hours apiece, are available mornings and afternoons. Ski clinics, geared to upper-intermediate and advanced skiers, include five days of lessons and a video analysis of your performance. Advance reservations are required.

**Races** The NASTAR course is open Friday through Sunday, beginning at 1PM, on **Bowling Alley.** Also on this trail is a coin-operated course, open daily from 9AM to 3PM.

**Rentals** Shops are located at the **Main Lodge** (934.0670) and **Warming Hut II** (934.0770), open Monday through Friday from 8AM to 5PM, weekends and holidays from 7:30AM to 5PM. Evening rentals are available Sunday through Thursday at **Warming Hut II.** Photo identification or a credit card is required as a deposit. The standard ski-rental package includes skis, poles, and boots; you can also rent skis alone. Snowboards (with snowboard boots), performance skis, and superior demo skis are available. Children receive a 50-percent discount off all rentals.

**Lockers** Between them, the **Main Lodge** and **Warming Hut II** contain several thousand lockers. They're almost always full on weekends, so secure one early or use the basket check available at both lodges.

**Day Care Small World Day Care Center** (934.0646) can be found at the **Mammoth Mountain Inn,** next to the **Main Lodge,** and is ski-accessible. Children 12 years old and younger will enjoy programs that include art, music, games, reading, and snow activities. Full-day care is available from 8AM to 5PM; half-day 8AM-12:30PM or 12:30PM-5PM.

**First Aid** Ski patrol members and nurses operate medical outposts (934.2571 ext 3376) at the **Main Lodge,** at the top of Gondola 2, at **Warming Hut II,** and at the bottom of Chair 15. Helicopter evacuation is available. **Mammoth Hospital** (934.3311), in **Mammoth Lakes,** is five miles away.

**Parking** Free parking is available at the base, but it fills up quickly and spreads along **Minaret Road.** Numerous free shuttles pick up skiers at designated spots along Minaret. In addition, Mammoth has added an elevated automatic "people mover" to transport skiers to and from parking lots. Two cabins (22-person capacity each) run along an elevated monorail at an average speed of 25 miles per hour.

**Worth Knowing**

- Because of its high-altitude location, Mammoth stays open longer than any other area in California. Sometimes there's skiing into June! Die-hard skiers from the Lake Tahoe region head down to Mammoth in late spring where snow conditions are still winterlike.

## Rating the Runs

### ● Beginner

It's not often that beginners have a choice of tree-lined runs, yet **Road Runner** is but one of three wooded, gently curving trails off Chair 11 and Chair 11B. Later, try nearby **Sesame Street** and **Sesame Street West.**

For beginning beginners, **St. Moritz** is an easy run that would be more satisfying if it weren't so crowded with ski classes. Located just east of the **Main Lodge.**

### ■ Intermediate

If you're in the market for lengthy, peaceful, tree-lined trails, bank on **Wall Street.** Or try its aptly named and equally blue-chip neighbor, **Lost in the Woods.** Both are located just to the right of Chair 10.

Although the ride up Chair 23 will rattle intermediate-level knees a bit, the views from the top of **Road Runner** are worth the annoyance, and the trail down is a piece of cake. (The bottom of this run is beginner territory; see above.)

Intermediates looking for some challenge with banks and turns will enjoy **Hully Gully,** a roller coaster run off Chair 8.

Descending **Sanctuary,** a slightly steep but almost always groomed course, can be purgatory for intermediates. But no sprain, no gain: Success on this run will officially initiate you into the black-diamond crowd. Located to the right of Chair 5, the trail is heavenly for those skiers looking to improve their slalom skills.

### ◆ Advanced

You can't really say you've done Mammoth until you take at least one shot at the gargantuan **Cornice Bowl** or at **Scotty's,** the mother of all ski bowls. When bumps the size of Volkswagen Bugs are in season, this gets to be one heck of a run.

Along with other courses off Chair 19, **Far West** is known for what it *doesn't* have—namely, crowds. When the hoi polloi invade the lower slopes, seek solitude here, on slightly steep, forested runs paralleling the chairlift.

Searching for untracked powder? Try **Santiago,** off Chair 14, on the west side. Not only is the area virtually empty on weekdays, but it offers great tree skiing, too.

An absolutely perfect advanced-level run, **Ricochet** will bring you back again and again. It starts out slightly steep and fast, then mellows into a winding trail that leads back to the lift. Trees scattered halfway down the run will help improve your turning skills.

### ◆◆ Expert

An extended pitch just west of Chair 23, **Wipe Out** calls for some flawless jump turns, as well as some showmanship, since everybody on the lift overhead will be watching your progress. Good luck on this thousand-foot chute.

To escape the crowds, head over to **Avalanche Chutes** on **Lincoln Mountain** (Chair 22)—a great variety of expert terrain, including narrow chutes and precipitous, tree-studded slopes. Lincoln Mountain also provides protection from stormy weather. Why long lines don't gather here is an ongoing Mammoth mystery.

Try **Dragon's Back** for the best place to find untracked snow late in the day. Traverse east off Chair 9 and drop down wherever conditions look good. On powder days, bring a camera to capture the perfect S-turns being carved here.

If you're skiing with people who claim to know this mountain very well, mumble something about **Hole in the Wall** and see if they know what you're talking about. This run is as hard to find as Butch Cassidy's old hideout.

### Snowboarding

Snowboarding is allowed on all of the 150 trails accessed by 31 lifts. Carvers and intermediate boarders find **Stump Alley** great for morning runs on powder days. The **Saddle Bowl** on the backside of Chair 3 provides great GS terrain and a nice, long run to the bottom of Chair 18. Riders also favor the runs near Chairs 9 and 12, particularly **Dragon's Back** (diamond) for its natural half-pipes and gaps. There is an adult snowboard racing program—so it's never too late to start.

## Mountain Highs and Lows

Adventurous novices will enjoy **Easy Rider,** a long, easy glide off of Chair 10. Although it's rated as a blue run (for intermediates), an advanced beginner should be able to handle it with no problem.

The difference between an advanced skier and an expert skier at Mammoth can be judged with one wrong turn (you'll know when it happens). While the majority of expert-level chutes start at the ridgeline, a few manage to sneak their way into advanced runs at midmountain. For example, an advanced skier's peaceful jaunt down tree-lined **Sunshine** (Chair 22) can suddenly turn **Grizzly,** so watch out.

## At the Resort

*Area code 619 unless otherwise noted.*

✦ **Main Lodge** The disjointed floor plan may look like it was conceived by one of Pablo Picasso's abstract-minded disciples, but this building (pictured below) serves its purpose: to feed, outfit, and process thousands of eager skiers every day of the season. The ground floor contains a ticket office, automatic teller machine, and a jillion coin-operated lockers (of which 90 percent will be occupied long before you arrive). More lockers are on the second story, along with a ski school desk, well-stocked ski shop, equipment rental and repair facilities, the race department, ski-bag check, and lost and found. The third floor is devoted to cafeterias that serve basic breakfasts and lunches (ATM cards accepted). You may eat inside, or take your plates onto a huge deck. The gondola departs from the third floor, on the first leg of its two-stage ascent (intermediates unload at the **Mid-Chalet,** while advanced skiers continue to the summit). ♦ M-F 8:30AM-4PM; Sa-Su, holidays 8AM-4PM. End of Minaret Rd. 934.2571

✦ **Mammoth Mountain Inn** $$$ One of the area's nicest lodgings, the inn contains 214 cozy rooms and suites (including apartment units that sleep up to 13 people), many overlooking the slopes. All rooms come with a kitchen, telephone service, cable TV, and queen-size beds. Also available are a whirlpool spa, child care facilities, shuttle bus service, and ski-in/ski-out access. ♦ Across the parking lot from the Main Lodge. 934.2581, 800/228.4947; fax 934.0701

Within the Mammoth Mountain Inn:

**Mountain Side Grill/Dry Creek Lounge** ★$$$ This is an elegant alternative to the cafeteria scene. Take your après-ski cocktail onto the terrace to watch the diehards take a few last runs. The dinner menu includes prime

*Main Lodge*

rib, pasta, lamb, chicken, and seafood. A children's menu is available. ♦ Daily breakfast, lunch, and dinner. 934.0601

✦ **Yodler Restaurant & Bar** $ Okay, so it's just a small step up from the cafeteria food served at the Main Lodge. But the full bar, offering an assortment of steaming coffee drinks, makes all the difference. Lunch consists of burgers, sandwiches, and the like, while dinner ranges from bratwurst to barbecued chicken and lasagna. ♦ Daily breakfast, lunch, and dinner. Across the parking lot from the Main Lodge. 934.0636

✦ **Chair 2 Outpost** You can buy tickets here for immediate mountain access—a major time-saver when overflow crowds descend upon the Main Lodge ticket office. The **Chair 2 Barbecue,** operated out of a weather-beaten hut among the trees at the foot of the lift, is the best sunny-day lunch spot on the mountain. ♦ M-F 8:30AM-4PM; Sa-Su, holidays 8AM-4PM. Bottom of Chair 2, off Minaret Rd. No phone

✦ **Warming Hut II** When you're at Mammoth, one lodge just isn't enough. This has got to be the most utilitarian (translation: homely) ski lodge on the face of the planet, filled with basic necessities such as a ski rental shop, repair shop, and yet another cafeteria. ♦ West end of Mammoth Lakes, off Canyon Blvd. 934.2571

✦ **Chair 15 Outpost** This mini-lodge is perfect for skiers who want to pass on the elaborate rites of preparation and get right to the slopes. ♦ End of Meridian Blvd, on the southwest side of Mammoth Lakes. 934.2571

✦ **Mid-Chalet** There's a small sundries and gift shop here, in case you forgot the sunscreen again, as well as a gondola landing for the midmountain trails. The cafeteria is for people who just can't wait for sustenance; anybody else, though, would be better served (literally) at the **Chair 2 Barbecue.** ♦ M-F 8:30AM-4PM; Sa-Su, holidays 8AM-4PM. Bottom of Chair 3. 934.2571

✦ **Chair 14 Outpost** This place is really indispensable when Mother Nature calls, since the nearest rest room is a good ski-hour away. Hamburgers and hot dogs are available to stave off starvation. ♦ M-F 8:30AM-4PM; Sa-Su, holidays 8AM-4PM. Bottom of Chairs 13 and 14, on the west end of the mountain. 934.2571

> After winning numerous ski-racing trophies and several California slalom titles, Dave McCoy's racing career ended abruptly in the early 1940s when his leg broke in 38 places during a particularly nasty skiing accident. It took five years for the Mammoth founder and owner to recover.

## Beyond the Resort

**1 Tamarack Lodge Resort** $$$ Built in 1924, this isolated complex remains basically unspoiled. Eleven small but quaint rooms are in the central building, and 25 rustic wood cabins, ranging from comfortable to luxurious, are scattered about the six acres surrounding the lodge. Cabins contain wood-burning fireplaces, and no TVs intrude on the mood. Located 2.5 miles from town, Tamarack is not on the local shuttle route, but it's only a short drive to the **Chair 15 Outpost.** The resort also has full-service cross-country skiing with rental and lesson packages. ♦ End of Lake Mary Rd, Twin Lakes. 934.2442, 800/237.6879; fax 934.2281

Within Tamarack Lodge Resort:

**Lakefront Restaurant** ★★★$$$ Lace curtains, fringed lamps, and other antique furnishings set the tone for intimate gourmet dining. The California-French cuisine includes fresh seafood (grilled salmon with ginger, baked Alaskan halibut), rack of New Zealand lamb, sautéed duckling, and pork loin stuffed with spinach and sweet Italian sausage. The wine list is excellent. ♦ Daily breakfast and dinner. Smoking's a no-no here. Reservations recommended. First floor. 934.3534

**2 Jagerhof Lodge** $$$ Impeccably clean and situated within easy walking distance of shops and restaurants, Tony and Marie Campbell's European-style, 24-room inn is great for families—especially those who prefer to do their own cooking (the in-room kitchens are big). You'll enjoy the indoor Jacuzzi and sauna, daily maid service, and color TV. Ski shuttles to the mountain stop nearby. A complimentary breakfast includes juice, coffee, muffins, toast and cereals. ♦ No smoking. 663 Old Mammoth Rd (near Sherwin Creek Rd), Mammoth Lakes. 934.6162, 800/447.7148 in CA

**2 Anything Goes Cafe** ★★$$$ Owners Mary Pipersky and Susan Burgett have spent eight years building up this area's best—and certainly most aromatic—cafe. Breakfast may consist of scalloped potatoes with ricotta and gruyère cheese, or something simpler, like danishes or oatmeal with a hefty mug of gourmet coffee. The lunch menu features

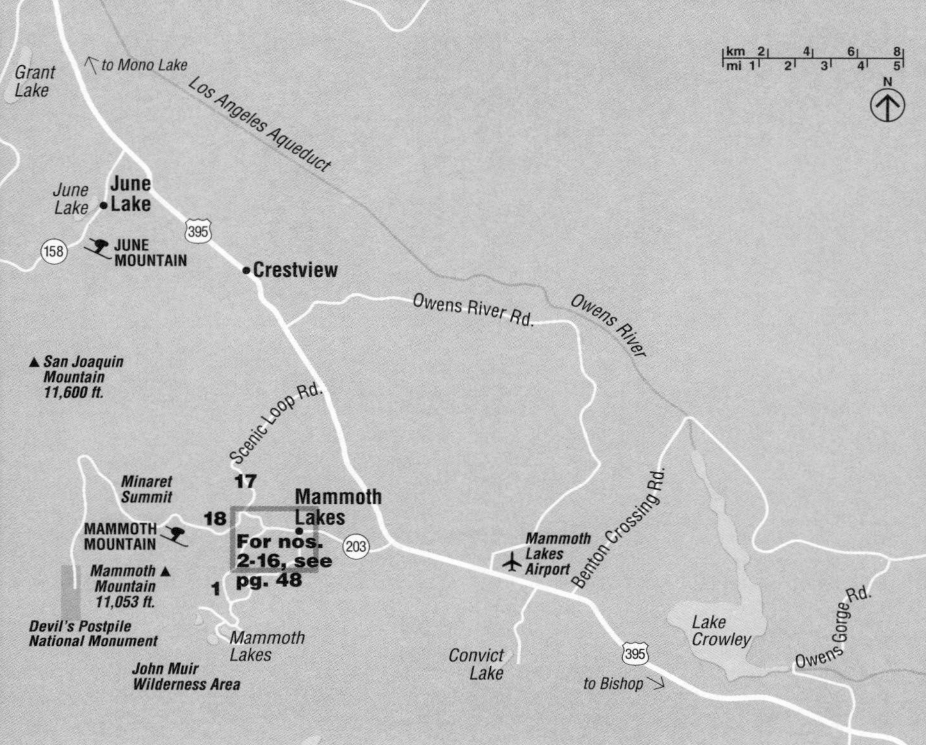


delicious soups, salads, sandwiches, and quiches. Dinner is a casual affair, constructed around Californian-Mediterranean cuisine. Try the Jamaican-spiced Kingston chicken or the Napa pot roast with Merlot sauce. ♦ M, Tu, Th-Su breakfast, lunch, and dinner. No credit cards, but personal checks are accepted. 645 Old Mammoth Rd (near Sherwin Creek Rd), Mammoth Lakes. 934.2424

3 **Natalie's** ★★$$$ What's your pleasure—escargot ravioli? Chicken cordon bleu? Maybe rack of lamb served in a Cabernet rosemary garlic sauce? Offering French country fare in a small (only 10 tables), bright space, owner Randall Sussex wins a following among natives and frequent visitors. Save room for dessert; Natalie's homemade cheesecake and flourless chocolate cake are not to be missed. ♦ Tu, W, F-Su dinner. Reservations recommended. Sherwin Plaza, Old Mammoth Rd (at Chateau Rd), Mammoth Lakes. 934.3902

*Giovanni's*

4 **Giovanni's Pizza** ★★$$ Reasonable prices make this place a local fave. Giovanni's specializes in both traditional and gourmet-style hand-thrown pizzas (don't pass on the clam and garlic variety). Italian dinners, salads, homemade soups, sandwiches, and desserts are also on the menu. Takeout and delivery are available. ♦ M-Su lunch and dinner; dinner only on Sunday. Minaret Village Mall, Old Mammoth Rd (at Meridian Blvd), Mammoth Lakes. 934.7563

5 **Shogun** ★★$$$ At Mammoth's best (and only) Japanese restaurant and sushi bar, the fare leans toward traditional sashimi and teriyaki. The combination dinner for two is a bargain. Karaoke sing-alongs (scheduled on Tuesday and Saturday nights) are a hoot. ♦ Daily dinner. Reservations recommended. Sierra Center Mall, Old Mammoth Rd (at Meridian Blvd), Mammoth Lakes. 934.3970

6 **Roberto's Café** ★★$ Cheap and filling—hey, amigos, what more do you really want from a Mexican restaurant? The tortillas and tamales are homemade, and the fish tacos are at least as good as the ones you inhaled in Tijuana in your college days. Wednesday is Locos Night, noted for its discounted beers. ♦ Tu-Su lunch and dinner. Take-out meals are available. 271 Old Mammoth Rd (at Sierra Nevada Rd), Mammoth Lakes. 934.3667

ROBERTO'S
Café

**Restaurants/Clubs:** Red **Hotels:** Blue
**Shops/ Outdoors:** Green **Sights/Culture:** Black

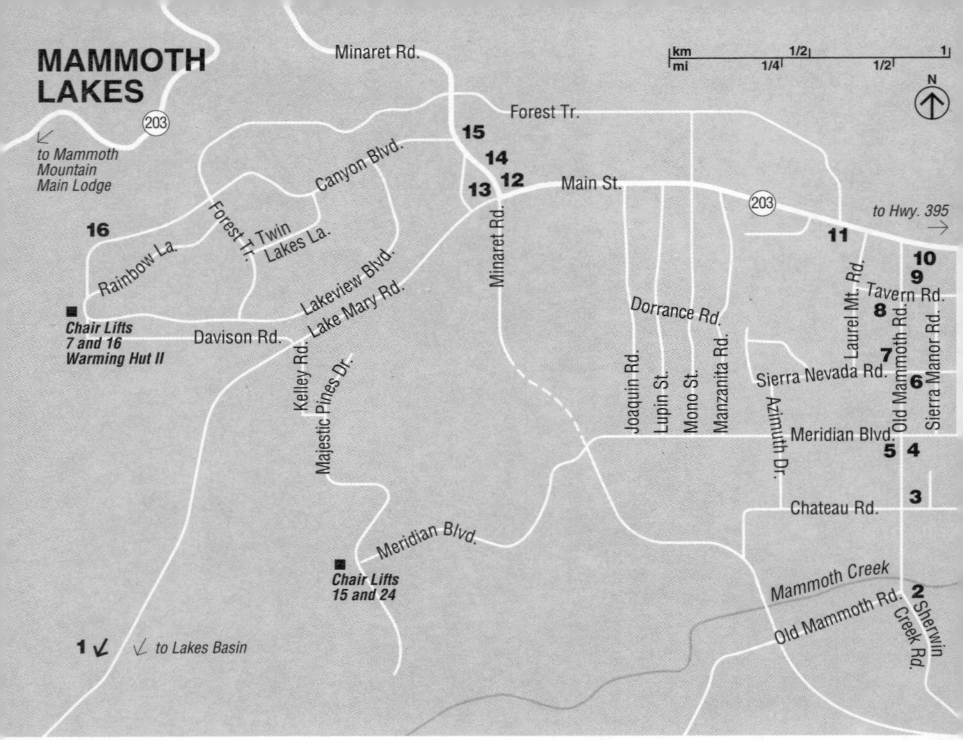

## MAMMOTH LAKES

203
to Mammoth Mountain Main Lodge
Minaret Rd.
Forest Tr.
Canyon Blvd.
Main St.
203
to Hwy. 395
Forest Tr.
Twin Lakes La.
Rainbow La.
Lakeview Blvd.
Lake Mary Rd.
Minaret Rd.
Chair Lifts 7 and 16 Warming Hut II
Davison Rd.
Kelley Rd.
Majestic Pines Dr.
Dorrance Rd.
Joaquin Rd.
Lupin St.
Mono St.
Manzanita Rd.
Azimuth Dr.
Laurel Mt. Rd.
Tavern Rd.
Old Mammoth Rd.
Sierra Manor Rd.
Sierra Nevada Rd.
Meridian Blvd.
Chateau Rd.
Meridian Blvd.
Chair Lifts 15 and 24
Mammoth Creek
Old Mammoth Rd.
Sherwin Creek Rd.
to Lakes Basin

**7** **Ocean Harvest** ★$$$ The fresh seafood (scallops, shrimp, mahimahi, salmon, catfish, swordfish, snapper, and halibut) is nicely charbroiled over mesquite or blackened, Cajun style. But this eatery's real moneymaker is the **Ocean Club,** a basement danceteria serving cheap booze and filled with young men who can't dance. ♦ Daily dinner. Old Mammoth Rd (at Sierra Nevada Rd), Mammoth Lakes. 934.8539

**8** **Chart House** ★★$$$$ Like Chart Houses elsewhere, this one serves consistently good (not to mention *huge*) steak and seafood dinners, and its salad bar is the best in town. ♦ Daily dinner. Reservations recommended. 185 Old Mammoth Rd (at Tavern Rd), Mammoth Lakes. 934.4526

**8** **Good Life Cafe** ★$ The eatery's name clearly signals its bent toward filling but healthy foods. Order a veggie eggs Benedict, homemade soups, veggie burgers, beefless Mexican food, pita sandwiches, or stuffed spuds. For the cholesterol-uninhibited, there are real hamburgers. Takeout is available. ♦ Daily breakfast, lunch, and dinner. Mammoth Mall, Old Mammoth Rd (at Tavern Rd), Mammoth Lakes. 934.1734

**9** **Grumpy's** ★$ Much cheerier than its moniker implies, this is Mammoth's only true sports bar, complete with five big-screen TVs, video games, shuffleboard, foosball, and pool tables. The grub is basic and bows not at all to health-food trends: barbecued ribs, burgers, hot dogs, chili, and damn good steaks. "Grumpy Hour" (a.k.a. Happy Hour) runs from 4PM to 6PM. ♦ Daily 11AM-1AM. 37 Old Mammoth Rd (near Tavern Rd), Mammoth Lakes. 934.8587

**10** **Breakfast Club** ★$ Besides serving freshly baked muffins, pastries, and custom cakes, this place also expedites a no-nonsense, large-portioned, good ol' American breakfast until 1PM—ideal for those who spent last night in a cruel test of liver endurance and bladder capacity. ♦ Daily breakfast. Hwy 203 (Main St) at Old Mammoth Rd, Mammoth Lakes. 934.6944

**10** **Shilo Inn** $$$ What this 70-room hostelry lacks in personality, it more than makes up for in bells and whistles. The suites here come with queen- or king-size beds, along with a convertible sofa; fully equipped kitchenettes; satellite TV and a VCR; and, so you can brag to your buddies back home about those chutes you conquered yesterday, a telephone. Shared amenities are an indoor pool, spa, sauna, steam room, and fitness center. There's covered parking here, as well as a fireplace lounge, ski lockers, and a laundromat for guests. Start your morning with a free continental breakfast and a complimentary copy of *USA Today.* ♦ 2963 Main St (Hwy 203) at Old Mammoth Rd, Mammoth Lakes. 934.4500, 800/222.2244; fax 934.7594

**11** **Slocum's** ★★$$ When locals say they're headed for "the office," they really mean the bar at Slocum's, a "Cheers"-like, wood-lined watering hole. Pastas and pizzas make up the tavern's menu. Beyond the bar, an upscale restaurant serves traditional Italian cuisine, as well as charcoal-grilled steaks, seafood (salmon and lobster), rack of lamb, and veal medaillons. Diners enjoy an extensive selection of fine wines. ♦ Daily 4PM-10PM. 3221 Main St/Hwy 203 (across from Kittredge Sports). 934.7647

**12** **Nevados** ★★$$$ This is the only establishment in Mammoth that even remotely reflects the glitzy tastes of its Angeleno clientele. It presents an eclectic array of items, ranging from steamed Manila clams and baby back ribs with Chinese five-spice marinade to seared ahi, sautéed scallop linguine, and grilled-chicken salad. A commendable wine cellar and a full bar promote politically incorrect discussions about the deliberately underdressed wait staff and the odd interior lighting. ♦ Daily dinner. Main St/Hwy 203 (at Minaret Rd), Mammoth Lakes. 934.4466

**13** **Whiskey Creek** ★★$$$ The decor and menu here look suspiciously like those found at the **Chart House.** But the after-hours spectacle, suited to the 25-and-up crowd, is unlike anything elsewhere in town. Live bands beat the boards every night, egging on the very seriously swinging singles occupying the dance floor. ♦ Daily dinner. Bar open 5PM-1AM; bands start at 9PM. Reservations recommended. Main St/Hwy 203 (at Minaret Rd), Mammoth Lakes. 934.2555

**14** **Alpenhof Lodge** $$ It's obvious from the facade that this lodge has been around for awhile, but it still provides pleasant accommodations with cable TV, phones, a sauna, and spa; a few of its 22 rooms are even endowed with fireplaces. The restaurant doesn't look particularly inviting, but the Austrian-influenced food deserves a taste. Several fine restaurants and groggeries are within easy strolling distance. ♦ 6080 Minaret Rd (near Main St), Mammoth Lakes. 934.6330, 800/828.0371; fax 934.6635

**15** **Berger's** ★★$ Vegetarians should heed the homonymic name of this joint. Come here for huge, meaty sandwiches (try the fresh-roasted turkey sandwich), hefty hamburgers, and dinner entrées of steak, ribs, fish, and chicken. Yes, salads are available, but rabbit cuisine will never make it to the top of the menu at Berger's. ♦ Daily lunch and dinner. Minaret Rd (at Canyon Blvd), Mammoth Lakes. 934.6622

**16** **Austria Hof** $$ The accoutrements make the low prices even more appealing. Consider: queen-size beds, full baths, refrigerators, cable TV, phones, and even hi-fi music are in every room. Other mondo pluses are the communal hot tub, the sauna, and an adjoining German-American restaurant. The slopes (and **Warming Hut II**) can be easily reached on foot, and you can ski back. The exercise will help burn off last night's strudel. ♦ 924 Canyon Blvd (between Forest Tr and Rainbow La), Mammoth Lakes. 934.2764, 800/924.2966; fax 934.1880

**17** **Scenic Loop Sledding Area** Scenic Loop Road, built as an alternative route to Mammoth Mountain in case of some spectacular disaster, also provides access to several popular (though unmarked) sledding and snowplay spots. It's even possible to skate on the numerous lakes dotting the highway, but get recommendations from the Forest Service's visitor center (924.5500) before heading out on the ice. ♦ Scenic Loop Rd, off Hwy 203

**18** **Sledz International Bobsledding** For those who can't get enough thrills, climb into the driver's seat of an Olympic-style bobsled and hurl your mortal bones down a seven-eighths–mile course at up to 35mph. (Brake? What brake?) Speed freaks will prefer the evening run, when the snow freezes up and the course is *much* faster. Children too young to die can bounce down the slope on inner-tubes. ♦ M-F 10AM-6PM; Sa-Su 10AM-7:30PM. Minaret Rd (one-quarter mile below the Chair 4 parking lot). 934.7533

On an average day, the world's largest fleet of modern snowcats—33—barbers more acreage at Mammoth than is groomed at any other ski area in the country.

# Ten Changes That Shook the Ski World

Put yourself in the shoes—or boots—of someone skiing 70 or more years ago: on 10-foot wooden skis, in leather boots, and a full-length, 30-pound fur coat. The relative ease and comfort of skiing today is due to several breakthrough developments that you probably take for granted.

**Metal ski edges:** In 1928, an Austrian salt-mining engineer named Rudolf Lettner came up with the idea of segmented metal edges that would allow the ski edge to flex, without popping off, as the ski flexed. At first not everyone was convinced of the merits of metal edges; beginners were often told not to use them because the possibility of getting sliced and diced made them dangerous.

**Release bindings:** Norwegian Hjalmar Hvam is often credited as the grandfather of the release binding. In fact, numerous inventors tinkered with the concept before Hvam came up with a practical device in the late 1930s. And it wasn't until the mid-1950s that the first reliable release binding was produced by Marker. The release binding has evolved into an extraordinary gizmo, able to sense mechanically when a skier is in trouble and release in various directions: forward, backward, sideways, upward, and combinations thereof.

**Buckle boots:** In the mid-1950s, Henke was the first boot company to come out with a buckle-boot design. When their patent expired in the early 1960s, all the boot companies began substituting buckles for laces. Buckle boots were easier to put on, take off, and adjust than lace-up boots. A few years later, Lange manufactured the first boot made of plastic rather than leather; with various minor refinements made since then, the plastic buckle boot has become the norm.

**Metal and fiberglass skis:** The first patent for a metal ski dates back to 1924. But it wasn't until Howard Head, an aircraft engineer from Baltimore, developed Head skis in the 1950s that the idea of a non-wood ski really took hold. Kneissel developed the first practical plastic ski in the early 1960s, but it was the fiberglass Rossignol Strato a few years later that really opened the floodgates. The use of metal and fiberglass gave ski builders far greater latitude than wood in designing skis to specific performance requirements. Such critical design elements as camber (the arc in the ski from tip to tail), flex, and torsion became controllable in the manufacturing process.

**Ski brakes:** The first ski brakes—devices to keep skis from zooming off down the slopes after bindings released—were developed in the 1950s. Like most prototypes, they didn't work very well, and through the 1960s skiers still used safety straps to prevent runaway skis. But with those straps, a fallen skier could still be conked, in a kind of whiplash effect, by a ski still loosely attached to the boot. By the 1970s, however, workable ski brakes had been developed, devices not only easier to use but safer than "safety" straps.

**Step-in bindings:** Perhaps the first legitimate step-in binding was the Tyrolia Rocket, which hit the ski scene in 1964. At the time, most bindings still used cables attached around the heel, and the way to tighten the cable was to flip down a lever in front of the toe piece; cable bindings had no release capability at the heel. As independent heel units with release mechanisms began evolving, so did the idea of an easy-to-use, step-in/step-out binding.

**Sintered bases:** The first plastic ski bases were developed in the 1940s, heralding an era of ski bases requiring far less maintenance and waxing than wood bases. By the late 1970s a new word entered ski lingo: sintering. Through the miracle of technology, superhard materials were applied to ski bottoms by use of an extreme heating process, further reducing the need for ski-base maintenance. For most recreational skiers today, only periodic edge sharpening is necessary to keep skis running fast and smoothly.

**Functional fabrics:** Two products of the late 1970s changed skiwear forever: Gore-Tex and Thinsulate. Gore-Tex was the first of the so-called waterproof/breathable fabrics—materials that not only resisted moisture from snow and rain but also allowed moisture from within (i.e., sweat and condensation) to escape. At the same time, 3M developed Thinsulate—insulating material with far less bulk than down or wool. Several other companies have since come along to develop their versions of waterproof/breathable fabrics and thin insulating materials. But the bottom line is that skiers today have the advantage of clothing that is light, nonbulky, and comfortable, yet still provides warmth and protection against winter's elements.

**Composite poles:** The most recent invention to take the ski world by storm is the "composite" ski pole, made of combinations of graphite, carbon, and kevlar. The earliest composite pole, called Silaflex, was developed in the early 1960s, but it broke too easily. The first commercially viable one, developed by Dave Goode, hit the ski market at the end of the 1980s. Since then, most major pole companies have come out with variations on the theme. Composite poles are far stronger and lighter than their ancestors made of aluminum, steel, and bamboo.

**Cap skis:** Salomon is an innovator among equipment manufacturers; they pioneered the rear-entry boot, for example. In 1990, the former boot-and-binding company hit the market with its first ski, featuring a so-called Monocoque or "cap" structure. The top part of the ski was a single piece, or cap, laid over the base of the ski in a kind of dome configuration. Among the cap-ski advantages—at least those touted by the manufacturers—is that the design transfers extra pressure to the outside of the ski, similar to the way stepping on the middle of a balloon pushes air toward the outside, with the effect of increased edge grip. Just how revolutionary the cap-ski design is remains to be seen, but the march to improve ski equipment still goes on.

## Bests

### Tabby Mannetter
Ski and Snowboard Instructor, Mammoth Mountain Ski School

The spectacular **Night of Lights** Christmas show at Mammoth Mountain's main lodge features laser lights, flare runs, dancing groomers, and snowmobiles, not to mention Santa in his castle amidst a sea of happy children (big and little). If this doesn't get rid of your humbug, nothing can.

A powder day—especially on a snowboard—makes every run my favorite. If you haven't mastered the steep and deep yet, come and see us at the ski school.

A dogsled ride to beautiful **Minaret Vista**—with champagne and dinner at the **Mammoth Mountain Inn**—is very romantic, especially when there's a full moon.

Lunch at **Good Life Cafe.** Don't forget Happy Hour at **Slocum's** restaurant (commonly called "the office") while you wait for the pizza.

### David Mannetter
Instructor/Staff Trainer, Mammoth Mountain Ski School

**Wipe Out,** Chair 23—extended steep pitch—an exhilarating challenge, whatever the snow. Advantage: everyone on the lift can see you. Disadvantage: everyone on the lift can see you.

**Lincoln Mountain,** Chair 22—a mountain playground complete with narrow chutes and steep, tree-covered slopes (with plenty of room to ski in between the pines). Serious advantage: good shelter in stormy weather and challenging skiing where no one can see you.

Satisfy your appetite for Mexican food at **Roberto's Café;** for casual après-ski, try **Slocum's** restaurant, where more than one drink may be hazardous to your driving record. The sushi at **Shogun** is as fresh as you can get this far from the ocean, and the Tuesday and Saturday night karaoke is always entertaining, if not hilarious.

### Kathy Copeland
Manager, Children's Ski Schools, Mammoth Mountain Ski School

The greatest skiing mascot—**Woolly,** a huge, lovable, furry mammoth that skis, hugs kids, and loves to have his picture taken.

Skiing the nooks and crannies of **Chair 14** and stopping for lunch on the sundeck at the little cafe at the bottom.

**Slocum's** is definitely the best après-ski bar—lots of colorful locals and good strong drinks.

Breakfast or lunch at **Anything Goes,** where everything is made from scratch, seasoned with fresh herbs, and tasty.

**Roberto's Café** for an unreal Mexican *comida* and, of course, the mandatory pitchers of beer.

Ride the gondola to the top of 11,000-plus-foot **Mammoth Mountain** for a breathtaking 360-degree panoramic view of the Sierra range.

### Julie Reitman
Manager, Mammoth Mountain Ski School

**Lakefront Restaurant** at **Tamarack Lodge Resort**—Best romantic atmosphere for a quiet dinner for two.

An evening walk along the path around **Horse Shoe** Lake.

Après-ski at **Slocum's**—Best "everybody knows your name" English pub atmosphere.

The view of the ski slopes and the evening alpenglow from the **Dry Creek Lounge** at **Mammoth Mountain Inn.**

### John McGrath
Ski Patrol Supervisor, Mammoth Mountain Ski Area

### Leslie McGrath
Ski Patroller, Mammoth Mountain Ski Area

**Mammoth Mountain Ski Area—Chair 9:** steeps and a deep natural skate park, all on **Dragon's Back.**

Best lunch at the mountain—**Main Lodge Cafe,** for chicken fajitas with extra tortillas.

Christmas offers skiing and the **Night of Lights** fireworks display that's better than Disney's.

**Whiskey Creek**—The rack of lamb is delicious; get an early reservation because it becomes crazy for après-ski in the upstairs bar.

**Hot Creek**—In all seasons, hot volcanic water in a cold stream makes for fun swimming. In the summer, head upstream for catch-and-release fly-fishing at its best.

Opening day of the fishing season (last Saturday of April) at **Crowley Lake**—Fish in the AM and ski the rest of the day.

**Roberto's Café**—Great flour-tortilla chips and yummy shrimp tacos.

One last note—While skiing **Chair 22** or **Chair 9,** go to lunch at the **Hut,** where **Chef Ty** whips up great Filipino concoctions. Have an early lunch and go back up Chair 22 for more radical skiing.

There are dozens of natural hot springs in the Mammoth area, but high snow levels make most of them all but inaccessible. If you crave the chance to get in hot water, though, grab some cross-country skis or rent a snowmobile and head for Hot Creek. It's located about 10 miles from town, behind the Mammoth Lakes Airport, off of US Highway 395. (Look for the sign "Fish Hatchery/Hot Creek" and follow the signs to the springs.) Your reward for the trek is a steaming pool of Mother Nature's purest eau-de-vie. Bathing suits are optional. For more information, call the Mammoth Lakes Visitors Center, 934.2712.

# Aspen Mountain

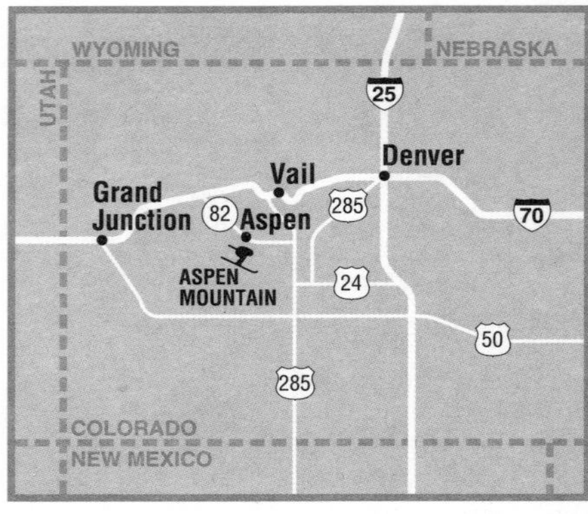


When skiers speak of Aspen, it's easy to tell whether they're referring to the mountain or the community. If the attitude is cool and casual, the topic is the town whose laid-back atmosphere puts everyone at ease. If voices drop to a whisper and beads of sweat appear, you know an alpine flashback is at hand. To approximate the peaks, planes, and ridges that comprise Aspen Mountain in the comfort of your living room, crumple up the Sunday sports section and toss it on the floor. The topography is daunting, with slopes falling sharply off summits laced with advanced and expert terrain. The gentler folds and flats are intermediate territory. It's a strong skier's mountain, no place for novices.

When you face the rock itself, reality comes to the fore. The 12-mile span of summits in the **Roaring Fork Valley** is home to four ski areas—Aspen Mountain, **Snowmass**, **Tiehack**, and **Aspen Highlands**—with a total of more than 274 trails coursing over 4,138 acres of skiable terrain, not all of it, fortunately, as challenging as Aspen proper. The four resorts share an interchangeable lift ticket.

Even if you're not an expert powderhound, you can still see Aspen's slopes up close. Mush with huskies on a sled into the wilderness, where the craggy **Maroon Bells** look close enough to touch. Float in a hot-air balloon over the heads of cross-country skiers. Or rev up a snowmobile for a wild ride through the pines.

The town also accommodates a wide variety of tastes. Chicly clad and coiffed matrons discuss the luxury tax over tea while a flannel-shirted shredder springs for a hot dog at the **Popcorn Wagon.** The streets are lined with stores, many of them architectural artifacts of the Victorian era, selling everything from $10,000 frocks to $10 T-shirts with equal aplomb. Fast-food chains coexist with fancy French restaurants, while basic rooms with shared baths attract budget travelers, and **The Little Nell** and the **Ritz-Carlton** set new standards for pampering their privileged guests. The popular image of Aspen as a private playground for the rich and famous is only half true, as the colorful contrasts found on its streets and slopes attest.

---

**Aspen Skiing Company**
**PO Box 1248**
**Aspen, Colorado 81612**

**Information**................970/925.1220, 800/525.6200

**Reservations**.............970/925.9000, 800/262.7736

**Snow Phone**.....................................970/925.1221

## Fast Facts

*Area code 970 unless otherwise noted.*

**Ski Season** Thanksgiving to Easter

**Location** Aspen Mountain is in Colorado's **White River National Forest,** 204 miles southwest of Denver.

## Getting to Aspen

**By air: Aspen Airport** is six miles from Aspen; **Eagle County Airport,** 75 miles, in the town of **Eagle; Denver International Airport** (DIA), 222 miles. **United Express** offers direct flights from **Chicago** and **Denver** to Aspen during the ski season. **American Airlines** offers nonstop service into **Eagle** from Chicago, **Dallas, Los Angeles, Miami, Minneapolis, New York**, and **Salt Lake City. Aspen Limo** (800/222.2112), **Greyhound Trailways** (945.8501), and **High Mountain Limo** (800/528.8294) provide ground transportation from **Aspen Airport.** Skiers arriving at **Eagle County Airport** must make prior arrangements with **Colorado Mountain Express** (949.4227, 800/525.6363).

**By bus: Greyhound** (800/231.2222) operates buses

from **Grand Junction, Denver,** and **Vail** into **Glenwood Springs,** where a transfer to the **Roaring Fork Transit Agency** (**RAFTA;** 925.8484) buses is available.

**By car:** Most major rental car firms are represented in **Aspen, Denver,** and **Grand Junction.** Four-wheel-drive vehicles and ski racks are available upon request.

**All-weather highways:**

Denver—Interstate 70 West to Highway 82 Southeast

Grand Junction—Interstate 70 East to Highway 82 Southeast

**Driving times from:**

Denver—4 hours (200 miles)

Grand Junction—2.5 hours (130 miles)

## Getting around Aspen

The **Roaring Fork Transit Agency** (**RAFTA;** 925.8484) runs free public buses around Aspen and between **Snowmass** and Aspen until late in the evening. Complimentary shuttle services operate between the four ski areas from 8AM to 4:30PM, stopping at most hotels and lodges.

## FYI

**Area** 631 acres of taxing terrain, draped over three ridges

Beginner—0 percent

Intermediate—35 percent

Advanced—35 percent

Expert—30 percent

**Number of Groomed Runs** Approximately 40

**Longest Run** 3 miles (**Dipsey Doodle** to **North American Spar Gulch** to **Little Nell**)

**Capacity** 10,755 skiers per hour

**Base Elevation** 7,945 feet

**Summit Elevation** 11,212 feet

**Vertical Rise** 3,267 feet

**Average Annual Snowfall** 300 inches

**Snowmaking** 34 percent

**Night Skiing** None

**Lifts** 8 (1 gondola, 1 high-speed quad, 2 regular quads, and 4 double chairs)

| **Lift Passes** | **Full Day** | **Half Day** (starts at noon) |
|---|---|---|
| **Adult** | $49 | $36 |
| **Child** (6 and under) | Free | Free |
| **Child** (7-12) | $27 | $27 |
| **Senior** (65-69) | $33 | $33 |
| **Senior** (70 and over) | Free | Free |

Aspen Mountain, **Snowmass, Tiehack,** and **Aspen Highlands** now share an interchangeable multi-day lift ticket.

**Ski School** Classes can be booked at the ski school desk (925.1227) on the lower level of the gondola building. Full-day, half-day, and private lessons are available.

**Kids' Ski School** There are no ski lessons specifically for children. Alternatives include general beginner classes at the **Aspen Ski School** and children's programs at **Snowmass, Tiehack,** and **Aspen Highlands.**

**Clinics and Special Programs Mountain Masters** is an intensive four-day ski and learning challenge for intermediate and advanced skiers who want to break through to a new skill level. Every day, five hours are spent tackling bumps, racing, and parallel refinement. **Women's Ski Seminar** emphasizes visualization techniques, recognition of fears and strengths, knowledge of equipment specific to women's needs, and interpersonal support. All Aspen resorts offer **Challenge Aspen,** a complimentary program for disabled skiers.

Every Monday at 9:30AM, an **Aspen Mountain Ski School** guide gives a free 1.5-hour mountain tour for skiers who hold a lift ticket. Powder tours are offered on the back side of Aspen Mountain. Strong intermediates using "fat" powder skis should be able to handle this terrain (reached by snowcat).

**Races** NASTAR racing is held Thursdays on **Little Nell.**

**Rentals** A large selection of top-quality equipment and excellent customer service can be found at **Crystal Ski Rentals** (920.1038, 800/992.2979), 555 East Durant Street at the base of Aspen Mountain, open daily 8AM to 9PM. **Pomeroy Sports** at 614 East Durant Street (925.7875) is a great shop for "fat" powder skis, open daily 8AM to 8PM.

**Lockers** Day storage (for boots, shoes, etc.) and overnight lockers are available at the **Sportstalker** beneath the gondola.

**Day Care** A licensed and bonded agency, **Supersitters** (923.6080), requires a three-hour minimum. **Aspen Sprouts** (920.1055), in the **Airport Business Center,** takes up to 12 children, ages 2 to 5, from 8AM to 5PM. Reserve at least two weeks in advance. The **Aspen Chamber of Commerce** (925.1940) also has a list of sitters.

**First Aid** Reach the ski patrol by dialing "0" from designated emergency phones on many trails and near upper and lower lifts. **Aspen Valley Hospital** (925.1220) is located at 200 Castle Creek Road.

Aspen is the site of the most grueling endurance ski race in the world, "Land Rover's 24 Hours of Aspen." Beginning at noon on one day and ending at noon the next, two-man teams, representing eight to 10 nations, ski Aspen Mountain for 24 continuous hours, resting only during the 13-minute gondola rides.

**Parking** There is no parking at the base of the mountain.

**Worth Knowing**

- Every season around Thanksgiving, Aspen holds its annual "Land Rover's 24 Hours of Aspen" race. For this unique event, skiers must ski for a 24-hour period in a downhill tuck (and, boy, does that burn the thighs)—the only rest stops are taken during the gondola rides back up. It's a festive time in Aspen, with former Olympians and World Cup skiers from around the world flying in for the event.

## Rating the Runs

### ■ Intermediate

A four-trail combo, **Dipsey Doodle** to **North American** to **Spar Gulch** to **Little Nell** is a popular three-mile (top to bottom) warm-up run. Ride the gondola (which sometimes opens 15 minutes early) before 9AM and you can really stretch your legs on this medley of trails. Dipsey Doodle curves with the contours, but North American is a bit steeper and more open. It's okay to play the sides on Spar Gulch, but maintain your speed around **Kleenex Corner** (so named because some skiers take this cat track at such velocity that their eyes water). At the top of Little Nell, look for the entrance to the **Compromise,** which was a working mine until the price of silver plummeted.

Though it bears a woman's name, **Ruthie's** is the start of the only **Men's World Cup** downhill race in the US. It's groomed for let-it-all-hang-out skiing. Most people just shoot straight down the slope, but if you're a bump fiend, head for the small mogul field on the left side. The mountain falls away on the other side of the ski area boundary rope which lines this run, allowing a knockout view of the valley below, part of **Aspen Highland's** precipitous **Steeplechase** section, and the snow-clad summits beyond.

### ◆ Advanced

If you want to test your skills on more difficult parts of the downhill, veer onto **Aztec.** A moderately steep run for this mountainside, the lower portion of **Spring Pitch** is a good place to gauge one's black diamond aptitude. Sharp-eyed photographers will find scenic spots at the top of the lower runs where they can snap friends with the town of Aspen, far below, peeking through their ski tips.

Whether it's from pleasure or pain, the moguls rippling around **Bell Mountain** curves will ring your chimes. The **Ridge of Bell** garners the most glory, because this double-diamond spine of the mountain is in full view of the captive audience in the chairlift. Skiers on **Back of Bell No. 1** and **Back of Bell No. 2** navigate open cuts through the pines. On the **Face of Bell,** glades of trees pattern the landscape. If you want to prolong this exhilarating ride, traverse to the right every time the run approaches **Spar Gulch.**

Twist your way through the tiny cirquelike top of **Corkscrew Gully** and funnel into a close channel between the trees. Be careful to hit the moguls right, though, so that the ski patrol doesn't need a corkscrew to pry you out.

### ◆◆ Expert

Good snow conditions on **Keith Glen** last long after storms sweep through because the majority of skiers opt to drop at **Bell** before reaching this slope. Veer off toward the chairlift, and you'll find short, narrow shots through the trees.

Skiers never seem to find their way into **Super Eight Gully,** a short double-diamond run, perhaps because the top is so steep that few moguls form. Once inside, the snow is usually best on the left.

### Snowboarding

Aspen Mountain does not allow snowboarding, but its three sister mountains do. (See "Aspen Highlands," "Snowmass," and "Tiehack" chapters.)

## Mountain Highs and Lows

An intermediate expressway off the mountain, **Spar Gulch** is jammed at the end of the day like rush hour in greater Los Angeles, making it very dangerous. Take a detour to the balmy blue trails on the far side of the mountain and return on the **Magnifico Cutoff** to **Little Nell.**

## At the Resort

*Area code 970 unless otherwise noted.*

✦ **The Sundeck** ★★$$ Plump bratwurst, steaming bowls of pea soup, and a slice of sweet apple or cherry pie will fuel you through a hard day's skiing; and the large fireplace will quickly warm you. With Chef George Mahaffey from **The Little Nell** now in charge of the cuisine, the restaurant has added a gourmet slant to the menu with such offerings as couscous with sun-dried tomatoes, fresh jumbo asparagus with prosciutto, and a variety of unusual chilis and stews. When it comes to the view, there isn't a bad table in the place. On sunny days, the deck is packed with a coterie of fans. ♦ Daily breakfast and lunch. Top of gondola. 925.1220 ext 3338

Aspen Mountain boasts the longest single-stage gondola in the world. The Silver Queen hoists six skiers up 3,267 feet in 13 minutes.

The world's largest silver nugget was discovered in the Molly Gibson Mine in 1894 on Aspen Mountain. Weighing more than 2,000 pounds, it had to be excavated in three parts.

**Restaurants/Clubs:** Red **Hotels:** Blue
**Shops/ Outdoors:** Green **Sights/Culture:** Black

✦ **Bonnie's** ★$$ When a basic burger just won't do, head here for a bowl of white chili bean soup, Caesar salad, or the gourmet pizza of the day. If you're seeking celebrities who love an audience, this is prime paparazzi turf. ♦ Daily breakfast and lunch. Tourtelotte Park. 925.1220 ext 3344

✦ **La Baita** ★★$$ The owners of **Farfalla** (see "Aspen Highlands" chapter) have moved onto the mountain with this second bistro, replacing **Ruthie's.** The place now features innovative Italian fare and treats skiers to gourmet pizza, pasta, and a salad bar in the buffet cafeteria. Those worn out from skiing may enjoy the sit-down service for a more relaxed European-style lunch. This menu features such items as osso buco (tender braised shanks of veal), grilled pheasant with polenta, and a variety of homemade pasta dishes in the dining room that overlooks the resort's World Cup ski course. ♦ Daily breakfast and lunch. Reservations recommended for the sit-down service. Top of Lift 1-A. 920.0728

THE LITTLE NELL

✦ **The Little Nell** $$$$ The town's only AAA Five Diamond property, this hotel's rating is earned in equal parts by its discreet elegance and the superb service. All 92 guest rooms are individually dressed in warm earth tones and feature gas fireplaces, TVs with VCRs, and mini-bar/refrigerator units. Give the ski valet a call in the morning and your equipment will be waiting for you a mere 17 steps from the Silver Queen gondola. You can watch the last run of the day from the steamy vantage point of the patio's Jacuzzi. Other amenities include a heated outdoor pool, spa with exercise and steam rooms, and 24-hour room service. ♦ 675 E Durant Ave (at the base of the mountain). 920.4600, 800/525.6200; fax 920.6328

Within The Little Nell:

**The Bar at The Little Nell** ★$$ The leather-lined walls of this pub, filled with photos of famous racers who honed their skills on the slopes of Aspen Mountain, envelop an ongoing parade of personalities from movie moguls to local ski instructors. ♦ Daily 2PM-closing. 920.4600 ext 6384

**The Restaurant at The Little Nell** ★★★★$$$$ Artfully arranged food is served in a simple yet warm and elegant setting. The oak-trimmed walls, flickering candles on each table, and glimmering wrought-iron chandeliers make this spacious dining room—with floor-to-ceiling windows—a cozy backdrop for the spectacular views of Aspen Mountain. Chef George Mahaffey creates such innovative dishes as sea bass on mashed potatoes spiced with wasabi, and grilled elk steak with sweet potato croquette and a compote of Napa cabbage, wild mushrooms, and sun-dried cherry sauce. ♦ M-Sa breakfast and lunch; Su brunch; daily dinner. Complimentary valet parking. Reservations recommended. 920.6330

**Ajax Tavern** ★★★$$ Formerly **Shlomo's,** this sit-down restaurant is one of the new hot spots in Aspen. The broad-based menu boasts Mediterranean influences, with such specialties as grilled and cedar-planked loin of tuna, garlic shrimp cassoulet, mushroom risotto, vegetable polenta, and a selection of pastas, salads, and sandwiches for lunch. The outdoor terrace remains *the* après-ski hangout of the resort. ♦ Daily breakfast, lunch, and dinner. Reservations recommended. 920.6333

✦ **Ritz-Carlton Aspen** $$$$ This luxury hotel brings tony elegance to town. The 257 rooms and suites in the red-brick building are opulently outfitted with floral fabrics; rich, dark woods; and Italian marble bathrooms. Amenities include 24-hour room service, a restaurant, fitness center, pool, and whirl-pools. For further creature comforts, the **Ritz-Carlton Club** offers private concierge service on the club floor. Après-ski parties with live music are held daily. ♦ 315 E Dean St (at Mill St). 920.3300, 800/241.3333; fax 925.8998

***For more information on the Aspen Mountain area, see "Beyond the Resorts," page 66.***

The Red Onion, Aspen's oldest saloon, celebrates St. Patrick's Day with a tradition all its own. The beer is free until the first customer has to use the facilities.

# What's Hot, What's Not in Ski Gear

There's really no way around it: Any sport that focuses on hurtling down a mountainside in full view of one's peers has more than a hint of exhibitionism to it. So it's not surprising that with the "help" of fiercely competitive ski merchandisers and hard-sell advertising campaigns, skiers have become willing slaves to fashion. It doesn't matter that your rear-entry boots fit like the proverbial glove; they're a year out of style and, ipso facto, so are you. Never has there been a participatory sport in which image has such an overriding emphasis and equipment is so astronomically expensive. To ski is to belong to an exclusive club reserved for those willing to pay (for skis, boots, bindings, poles, goggles, pants, jacket, socks, gloves, hat, sunscreen, ski rack, airfare/ carfare, lift ticket, lessons, lunch, and après-ski libations) to play. So check your credit limit: Here are the membership dues for the upcoming season.

**Bindings:** While Hjalmar Hvam was having his leg repaired by doctors after an unsuccessful cornice leap in 1938, he had an ether-induced vision of a binding that automatically released from the ski under pressure. When the rental-shop owner regained consciousness, he grabbed a pencil and paper and sketched out the design for the modern-day binding. Benefiting from decades of refinement, today's binding —which utilizes such improvements as multidirectional release mechanisms and friction compensation—has all but eliminated below-the-knee injuries that once plagued skiers. Manufacturers' latest binding breakthrough is a control lever that allows you to adjust the ski flex to compensate for snow conditions (softer for powder, stiffer for hard pack), enhancing your performance. Marker's new M1 SC (Selective Control) is easy to use and expensive enough at more than $300 to induce bankruptcy. The binding has garnered favorable reviews, and—of course—looks *really* cool.

**Boots**: Believe it or not, those funky front-entry boots you tossed out in the 1970s are now back in style, but with so many bells and whistles attached that you actually *have* to read the instruction book. The new rage is "custom fitting" (tack on another $ 50 fee to the basic $300 to $500 investment), which tailors the boot to your foot using silicone liners, performance-oriented insoles, and micro-adjustable buckles. So what's the right boot for you? Whatever fits snugly, comfortably, and stands up to your skill level (probably the boots you own now, if you can suffer the humiliation of wearing such antiquated contraptions). Unless you're lucky enough to own a classic pair of Langes (which were the first plastic ski boots, introduced in 1957 by Bob Lange, the maker of Hula Hoops), chances are your boots are outdated, outmoded, and way out of style. Have a nice day.

**Poles**: Okay, so your boots might interest an alpine archaeologist; at least your flashy aluminum poles are still acceptable. Right? Not anymore, thanks to composites. Not only are the new carbon/ graphite pole shafts destined to make all aluminum models obsolete, but even their grips (length-adjustable, multidensity, palm-friendly material), straps (featuring an interlock glove/ grip system), and shapes (contoured for optimum wrist positioning) are revolutionary. So is their cost, somewhere in the neighborhood of $90 to $150. The advantages of composite poles over aluminum are considerable: They're only two-thirds the weight (which equates to swinging 70 fewer pounds for an average day's pole planting) and 7.5 mm thinner, presenting less resistance in powder and absorbing wrist-numbing shocks better. But are they worth the money? They will be in a few years when the price slides a bit, sohold onto your old poles.

**Skis:** The hot skis of the moment are versatile all-terrain models such as the Rossignol 7XK, the Salomon 9000 series, and the K2 GS Race, all of which utilize space-age materials and computer-aided design processes to achieve a combination of the smoothness of a G.S. ski and the short turning radius of a bump ski—a "best of both worlds" recipe. This, along with flashy cosmetic treatments, construction features with mad-scientist names (like VAS X Thermic, Monocoque, Light Inertia System, and Vacuum), and glamorous pro endorsements total up to a $500 to $700 price tag for a ski that may be passé in 12 months. If you plan on spending this much dough, be sure to try out several different pairs of demo skis before you make the investment (often the retailer will credit demo charges toward the ski purchase price). And, don't miss out on the new fatties—wide "powder" skis for demo in most resorts that get big dumps from time to time.

**Skiwear:** As they say on Seventh Avenue, "It's not who you are, it's what you wear." This axiom certainly applies to skiers, the most fashion-conscious of all sports devotees. Although you shouldn't toss out your entire wardrobe—there's a better-than-even chance it will eventually return to vogue—be ready for a barrage of enticing ads encouraging you to spend ungodly amounts of money on the latest labels (listed below). If, however, you don't subscribe to the clothes-make-the-man (or woman) theory, just buy a well-constructed shell—water- and wind-resistant outerwear—and wear layers of warm clothes underneath. You may not turn any heads, but you'll stay warm and dry. In any case, try not to buy skiwear that's better than your skill level; you'll just look silly falling down the mountain in your new $500 ski outfit.

**What's in**—Hard Corps, Spyder, Descente, and Patagonia skiwear, Gordini gloves—all in brighter colors.

**What's out**—Garish one-piece suits, miniskirts, shorts over tight-fitting ski pants, denim, deer-hunter orange, camouflage, or fluorescent colors. And anything fur, especially in Aspen.

**Sunglasses:** The de rigueur eyewear these days is wraparound shades, which comfortably combine the best qualities of sunglasses and goggles. Oakley has leapfrogged the competition and introduced a line of impact-resistant wraparounds dubbed Sub Zeros that are made from pure Plutonite (don't ask). If you don't mind looking like an off-duty arc welder and can afford to part with a bill for these specs, you've got it made.

**Wax:** Ninety-five percent of you don't wax your skis—shame on you. Waxing not only protects the base of the ski from chips and scratches, but a waxed ski is up to 30 percent easier to turn than an unwaxed one, a fact that nullifies the myth that waxed skis pick up too much speed since speed is controlled by turning. Also nullified (thankfully) are the days of ruining your iron to apply a hot wax. The new easy-application ski waxes, fluorinated or fluorocarbon-based, take the drudgery out of the task. Simply spray or wipe them on, trim off the excess, and you're ready to go. Granted, they're not as durable as ironed-on waxes, but for a buck or less per application, who's complaining? Look for Swix's F4 (wipe on), Speed Cote (spray on), and Toko's TF 90 (tube with applicator).

## Bests

### Henry Hornberger
Former director, Aspen Mountain Ski School

Looking up at the spectacular ski runs of Aspen Mountain from the center of town makes you feel as though the town and the mountain are one.

Having a great sit-down lunch in the **Aspen View Room** of **La Baita** restaurant wearing slippers (with ski boots off) and looking out at Aspen and **Red Mountains**.

The sunny side of **Bell Mountain** is the most inviting tree-gladed mogul run I have ever had the pleasure of skiing.

The best way to end a great day's skiing: an invigorating run down **Silver Queen.**

The magnitude of easily accessible skiing when looking from Red Mountain at Aspen Mountain, **Aspen Highlands,** and **Tiehack** is truly inspiring.

### John S. Bennett
Mayor, City of Aspen/Restaurateur, Pour la France! Cafe and Bakery

Stopping for a salmon club sandwich at **The Little Nell** while skiing Aspen Mountain.

A ski weekend in one of the **Tenth Mountain Huts.**

Skiing to the **Pine Creek Cookhouse** for dinner. The cuisine is California with a hint of Budapest, the wines French, and the ski down (guided only by the miner's light worn on your head) infinitely memorable.

Cross-country skiing along the frozen **Roaring Fork River** on the **North Star Nature Preserve**... exhilarating, invigorating, delightful, and free.

Feasting in the heart of the Rockies on perfect yellowtail sashimi at **Takah Sushi.**

A night at the **Sardy House,** Aspen's grande dame of Victorian inns.

Going to **Pour la France!** on Sunday morning for the best cappuccino in Aspen (*of course* I'm biased, but it's true).

### Robert Maynard
President, Aspen Skiing Company

Afternoon tea at **The Little Nell** hotel.

A Powder Tour on the back side of Aspen Mountain.

Fresh tracks on **Green Cabin Run** at **Snowmass** on a powder day.

Burgers at the **Woody Creek Tavern.**

Cross-country skiing to the **Pine Creek Cookhouse.**

Sunday afternoon concerts at the **Aspen Music Festival.**

The only Men's World Cup downhill race in the US, with the unimaginative name of America's Downhill, is held on Aspen Mountain, usually sometime in March.

# Snowmass

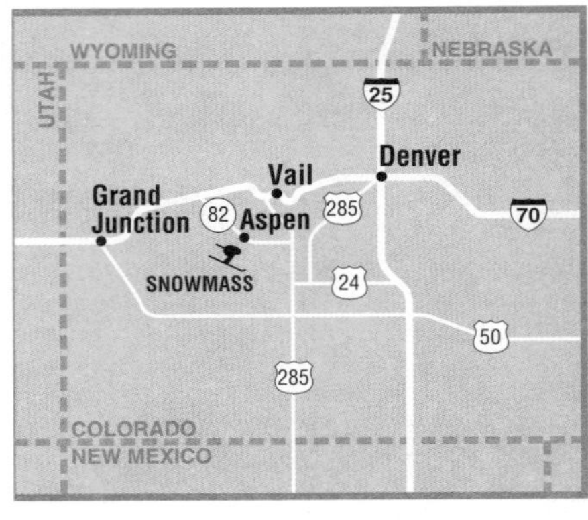


Developed in 1967 as an adjunct to **Aspen Mountain,** Snowmass was designed to attract intermediate skiers intimidated by the steeps of the peaks to the south. Back then, jaded locals jokingly referred to the pedestrian-friendly hamlet at the heart of this massive ski area as "Slowmass." But that label no longer fits. Today, this family-oriented ski town sprawls up and down the mountainside, with lodges, condominium complexes, and a large hotel (all accompanied by a plethora of pools and hot tubs) edging the slopes. More than 20 restaurants, a shopper's paradise of stores, and ample après-ski activities now keep visitors at the resort in the evenings instead of their eloping to Aspen—even though it's only a 12-mile shuttle bus ride away.

But despite its capitulation to consumers, Snowmass has a great deal of character that's remained unchanged. Moms and dads shepherd flocks of mitten-dangling kids to the slopes, skis and poles akimbo. And the down-to-earth **Stew Pot,** with its reliable home cooking, is still one of the town's most popular restaurants.

Most enduring of all is the mountain itself. There's lots of ground to cover for skiers of all abilities, especially intermediates. **Fanny Hill** and **Assay Hill** are the open beginner slopes. **Sam's Knob** has a mix of beginner, intermediate, and advanced runs. It takes two chairlifts and a half-hour to reach the top of **Elk Camp,** but once there, you'll discover some of the longest rolling intermediate runs on the mountain. Snowboarders do their thing on a half-pipe at the base. The mile-wide **Big Burn** brought Snowmass an early reputation as an intermediate's mecca; the slope, with its light sprinkle of trees, still warrants fame. Some of the top easier advanced trails in the region are found in the **Campground** section of the slopes. Experts can hike to several slick-sided and tree-gladed pockets, and can look to the **Cirque** and the **Hanging Valley Wall** (both double-diamond territories) for some real sport.

*Maroon Bells*

M.BLUM

**Aspen Skiing Company**
**PO Box 1248**
**Aspen, Colorado 81612**

**Information**......................................970/925.1220
**Reservations**.............970/923.2010, 800/598.2004
**Snow Phone**......................................970/923.1221

## Fast Facts

*Area code 970 unless otherwise noted.*

**Ski Season** Thanksgiving to early April

**Location** Snowmass is in Colorado's **White River National Forest,** 200 miles southwest of **Denver** and 10 miles west of **Aspen.**

## Getting to Snowmass

See "Getting to Aspen," page 52.

## FYI

**Area** 2,500 acres (72 runs) of tree-lined skiing with an emphasis on long, wide-groomed cruising runs.

Beginner—10 percent

Intermediate—51 percent

Advanced/Expert—39 percent

**Number of Groomed Runs** Approximately 56

**Longest Run** 4.16 miles (**Big Burn** to **Fanny Hill**)

**Capacity** 20,535 skiers per hour

**Base Elevation** 8,223 feet

**Summit Elevation** 12,310 feet

**Vertical Rise** 3,615 feet

**Average Annual Snowfall** 300 inches

**Snowmaking** 2 percent

**Night Skiing** None

**Lifts** 18 (5 high-speed quads, 2 triple chairs, 9 double chairs, and 2 surface lifts)

| **Lift Passes** | **Full Day** | **Half Day** (starts at noon) |
|---|---|---|
| **Adult** | $49 | $36 |
| **Child** (6 and under) | Free | Free |
| **Child** (7-12) | $27 | $27 |
| **Senior** (65-69) | $33 | $33 |
| **Senior** (70 and over) | Free | Free |

**Ski School** The ski school desk (925.1227, hotline 920.0784) is located in the ticket pavilion in the **Snowmass Village Mall.** Full-day, half-day, and private lessons are available. The latter, offered at special rates, are the best bet. Snowboarding lessons start at 9:30AM where the **Fanny Hill** ski slope meets the **Snowmass Village Mall.**

**Kids' Ski School Snow Cubs** is a preschool play/ski program for kids 18 months through 3 years old. For children 4 years old through kindergarten age, **Big Burn Bears** is open daily from 8:30AM to 4:30PM. Advance reservations are strongly recommended. For more information, call 800/525.6200 ext 4570.

**Clinics and Special Programs Mountain Masters** is an intensive four-day challenge for intermediate and advanced skiers; tickets may be purchased at the **Ullrhof Ski School Meeting Place,** located at the top of the Coney Glade chairlift. Snowmass, along with all the Aspen area resorts, offers **Challenge Aspen,** a complimentary program for disabled skiers.

**Races** NASTAR racing is offered at the **Spider Sabich Race Center.**

**Rentals** The first shop at the entrance to **Snowmass Village Mall, Crystal Ski Rentals** (923.4726, 800/992.2979) has the largest selection of top-quality equipment and good prices. **Sidewinder Sports** (923.3708), also on the Mall, rents snowboards. Both shops are open daily from 8AM to 9PM.

**Lockers** Baskets and lockers are available in the **Timbermill.**

**Day Care** A licensed and bonded agency, **Supersitters** (923.6080) requires a three-hour minimum. **Night Hawks** (923.0751) provides evening care for kids. **Aspen Sprouts** (920.1055), in the **Airport Business Center,** takes up to 12 children, ages 2 to 5, from 8AM to 5PM. Reserve at least two weeks in advance. The **Aspen Chamber of Commerce** (925.1940) also has a list of sitters.

**First Aid** Contact the ski patrol by dialing "0" from designated emergency telephones on the mountain or ask for assistance at the top or bottom of any lift. The Snowmass emergency clinic (923.2068) is at the base of **Fanny Hill,** 11 Trauma Lane.

**Parking** Strategically placed signs guide you to the lots in town. Free parking is available at the **Rodeo Lot** with frequent shuttles to and from the lifts. For day parking, use lots alongside the **Snowmass Village Mall** and at the bottom of **Fanny Hill.**

**Worth Knowing**

- **Aspen Mountain,** Snowmass, **Tiehack,** and **Aspen Highlands** now share an interchangeable multi-day lift ticket.

## Rating the Runs

### ● Beginner

A soft-sided slope with a steady pitch to aid easy turning, **Mick's Gully** is a natural for graduates of **Fanny Hill,** Snowmass's primo debutant slope. Views from this long novice run include the audacious **Cirque** and other Snowmass peaks.

### ■ Intermediate

Legend has it that in the 1800s the Ute Indians set this mountainside afire to discourage settlers from moving here during the silver mining boom. No one knows whether the blaze was an act of nature or of man, but the result is one of the Rockies' ultimate intermediate routes. Skiers can explore the mile-wide **Big Burn** all day without repeating a run. It's a good place to start tree skiing, because the pines are spaced far apart.

Prime cruising terrain awaits the few who take the time to reach **Bull Run,** an open slope on **Elk Camp** near the far end of the ski terrain. You take the Elk Camp Chair to get there, which offers the resort's prettiest views of the **Hanging Valley,** the **Maroon Bells,** and **Burnt Mountain.** This is a first-choice run on powder days, or for late-afternoon skiing, when the sun still shines on the slopes.

Only a handful of skiers make an appearance at **Green Cabin,** less hardy souls being put off by the four-minute catwalk from the top of the High Alpine Lift. Consequently, the long ride down is usually an exercise in excellent snow conditions.

### ◆ Advanced

Belying the misconception that Snowmass doesn't have steep terrain, **Hanging Valley** and **Hanging Valley Glades** tempt you to hang onto the trees to control your descent as you drop into the Valley through the glades. For an even quicker trip, check out the 35° to 45° chutes, interspersed with 30- to 100-foot cliffs. The route to this rewarding run is a 10-minute hike from the High Alpine Lift.

### Snowboarding

Snowmass allows snowboarding on the entire mountain, but experts like to hang at **Baby Ruth**—a double-diamond trail that's narrow and gladed with lots of hidden powder. For those with less hot blood in their veins, **Naked Lady** provides a lot of rollers and some ledges to catch air. Cruisers and beginners find **Elk Camp** and **Bull Run** offer great groomed terrain for wider turns. Snowmass also has a half-pipe and a terrain garden designed by world half-pipe champion Jimi Scott.

## Mountain Highs and Lows

Touted as a great beginner slope, **Fanny Hill** is really a broad boulevard that skiers constantly use to get to or from their lodging. Dodging crowds isn't the best way to sharpen your snowplows. Take the ride down **Max Park, Lunchline,** and **Scooper** for more enjoyable debut experiences.

A long cruising black path on the trail map, **Campground** would scarcely rate a blue/black at **Aspen Mountain.** Great as an intermediate's introduction to black diamond runs, this run will disappoint advanced skiers seeking serious challenges.

## At the Resort

*Area code 970 unless otherwise noted.*

✦ **Gwyn's & High Alpine** ★★★$$ Set atop the mountain, this cozy eatery, with the ambience of a French country inn, is three stars above most ski area restaurants. The gourmet kitchen prepares delicious soups, fresh breads, and daily specials for skiers whose tired bodies are ready for a sit-down meal. The poached salmon on a bed of wild rice pilaf is excellent. ♦ Daily breakfast and lunch. Reservations recommended. Top of Alpine Springs Lift. 923.5188

✦ **Dudley's** ★$$ Great views come with the hearty food served at this cozy spot atop **Sam's Knob.** ♦ Daily breakfast and lunch. Reservations accepted for sit-down dining. Top of Sam's Knob. 923.6220

✦ **Up 4 Pizza** $$ For impromptu carbo-loading, head up Chair 4, the Big Burn Lift, for a quick slice of pizza. ♦ Daily lunch. Top of Big Burn Lift. 923.0464

✦ **Ullrhof** ★$$ This classic cafeteria has a wood-burning stove for that extra blast of heat on a cold day. Their New England clam chowder is the envy of the East Coast. ♦ Daily breakfast and lunch. Bottom of Big Burn Lift. 923.5143

✦ **Cafe Suzanne** $$ This is quite an inviting place to go for crepes, soup in a sourdough bowl, and other edibles with a French accent. The cafe's location, way off on the Elk Camp slopes, is often a hungry skier's choice when the rest of the mountain is crowded. ♦ Daily breakfast and lunch. Bottom of Elk Camp Lift. 923.3103

✦ **Krabloonik** ★★★$$$$ It may have a rustic ambience, but the cooking at this tiny log cabin is supremely sophisticated. The menu includes specialties like wild mushroom soup, smoked trout, and pheasant breast with Marsala glaze. Whether you ski in for lunch or drive up for dinner, stop and watch the huskies at play; **Krabloonik Kennels** houses the sled dogs that take visitors into the wilderness. ♦ Daily lunch and dinner. 4250 Divide Rd, alongside the Campground. 923.3953

✦ **Snowmass Village Mall** This tri-level, open-air plaza is home to a variety of shops, the ticket pavilion and ski school desk, and several eateries. ♦ Next to base of Fanny Hill

Within Snowmass Village Mall:

**The Stew Pot** ★★★$ This unpretentious eatery is the perfect meal stop for hungry families. Served with a huge hunk of homemade bread, the old-fashioned beef stew is filled with veggies. Expect a wait unless you're an early bird. ♦ Daily lunch and dinner. 923.2263

**The Tower** ★★★$$$ Doc, the magician/bartender, is still up to his tricks. The big, juicy burgers and onion rings are no illusion, however. Evenings, stick to the specials. ♦ Daily lunch and dinner. 923.4650

**Hite's** ★★$$ Looking for a lively, casual place on the Mall where kids and parents can coexist? This is it. The menu accommodates both haute and hot dog cravings. ♦ Daily dinner. 923.2748

Above Hite's:

**The Rocky Mountain Teddy Bear Factory** The cuddly residents of this store are looking for new homes. ♦ Daily 10AM-5PM. 923.2690

✦ **The Silvertree Hotel** $$$ In an area where family-oriented condos and lodges predominate, this full-service hotel has adult appeal. The 262 rooms and 15 suites, decorated in low-key colors, scale the slopes in a multilevel complex. Inside, you'll find three restaurants, a ski shop, a health club with steam room, two heated pools, whirlpools, and a sauna—all guaranteed to ease your aches. ♦ 100 Elbert La (on the mountain at Fanny Hill Lift). 923.3520, 800/525.9402; fax 923.5494

Within The Silvertree Hotel:

**Cowboys** ★★$$$ Blue jeans and cowboy boots aren't prerequisites for two-stepping to the beat of the country-and-western bands that play here. The cook serves upscale Western chow, such as onion-crusted salmon with roast corn and asiago cheese. ♦ Daily dinner. Bar open until 2AM. Reservations recommended. 923.5249

✦ **Mountain Chalet** $$ This slope-side family-style hotel has 64 utilitarian but comfortable rooms, some with fireplaces. A large outdoor swimming pool and indoor hot tub are a panacea for those who'd rather soak than ski. A rib-sticker breakfast is included in the room rate. ♦ 115 Daly La (on the mountain at Fanny Hill Lift). 923.3900, 800/598.2004; fax 923.3650

✦ **La Boheme** ★★★★$$$$ With descriptors like "simple," "elegant," and "classic," some say that this is the finest French restaurant in the valley. Chef and co-owner Maurice Couturier (who earned his toque in the King of Jordan's kitchen) is credited with the inspired menu, which emphasizes wild game, fresh fish, and organically grown vegetables and meat. Risotto with grilled shrimp, a carpaccio of beef with melon, and crab cakes are among the many exquisite entrées. Enjoy the spectacular views of the Roaring Fork Valley. ♦ Daily dinner. Reservations recommended. In the Gateway Building. 923.6804

Within La Boheme:

✦ **The Brasserie** ★$$$ Spanish tapas and fine wines by the glass go well with the soft jazz played here. Entrées include a shrimp fricassee on angel hair pasta and coq au vin. ♦ Daily lunch and dinner. Reservations recommended. 923.6804

✦ **Laurelwood** $$ This 52-unit establishment has large economical studios close to the slopes with full kitchens and accordion doors you can close to create some privacy in one part of the room. ♦ 640 Carriage Way (on the mountain, 3 blocks above the Snowmass Village Mall). 923.3110, 800/598.2004; fax 923.5314

✦ **The Chamonix** $$$$ Most of the 33 large (two- or three-bedroom) luxury condos in this slope-side community have a bright, contemporary decor and no shortage of great views. ♦ 476 Wood Rd (on the mountain at Wood Run Lift). 923.3232, 800/598.2004; fax 923.5426

✦ **Hotel Wildwood** $$$ Extra special service is the signature of this intimate hotel that sits only a hundred yards from the runs. The 142 rooms and suites have a homey, country motif. The property houses the popular **Pippin's Steak and Lobster** restaurant. Amenities include a continental breakfast and airport shuttle service. ♦ 40 Elbert La (just off Fanny Hill, next to the Snowmass Village Mall). 923.3550, 800/445.1642; fax 923.5192

***For more information on the Snowmass area, see "Beyond the Resorts," page 66.***

## Bests

**William L. Cowan**
Fire Chief, Snowmass Village Fire Department

Après-ski in the **Conservatory Room** of the **Silvertree Hotel.** Slope-side seating in a relaxing atmosphere.

Most resorts have good ethnic restaurants, but Snowmass Village has two of the best. The **Mountain Dragon** has the Dragon Dance and fireworks on Chinese New Year, and **La Piñata** serves creative Mexican seafood dishes.

My favorite ski runs are **Mick's Gulley** and the **Big Burn** on **Snowmass Mountain** for relaxed cruising. This is intermediate terrain with beautiful views and an unmatched vertical descent.

The best powder is found on **Wildcat** off of the **Campground Lift** on Snowmass Mountain.

**Rick Griffin**
Broker/Owner, Snowmass Ranch Realty

**La Boheme**—Best restaurant in the valley.

**Gwyn's & High Alpine**—A gourmet, sit-down restaurant "on the mountain."

**The Wall** on a powder day—Best ski runs.

**St. Benedict's Monastery**—For an unbelievable experience, attend Sunday Mass at this working monastery in old Snowmass.

# Tiehack

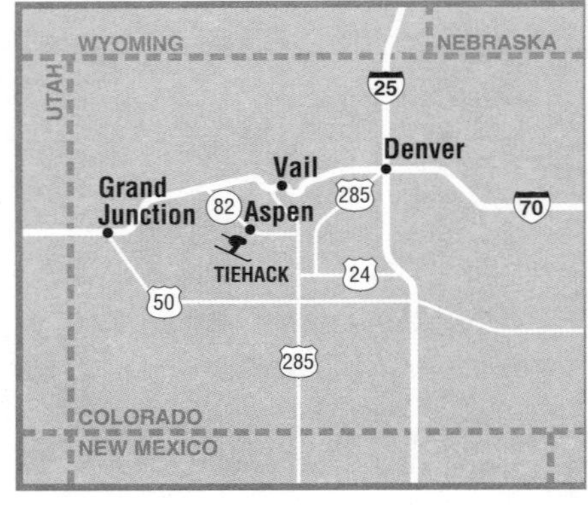


Like a shy sibling, Tiehack (formerly known as **Tiehack/Buttermilk**) has long been overshadowed by her glamorous sister resorts, **Aspen Mountain** and **Snowmass.** So the Aspen Skiing Company decided to promote this third ski area as a teaching venue. Beginners gravitate here because of the abundance of ski school classes, not the least of which is the $129 "Guaranteed Learn to Ski" program. When the lift lines at Snowmass stretch out of the corrals, even intermediates take the shuttle bus to Tiehack. Actually, anyone with skills up to the advanced intermediate stage will enjoy such runs as the **Racer's Edge** on this confidence-building terrain. And when lack of snow grows rocks on the other mountains, underutilized Tiehack inevitably offers better cover.

---

**Aspen Skiing Company**
**PO Box 1248**
**Aspen, Colorado 81612**

**Information**.......................................970/925.1220
**Reservations**....................................800/262.7736
**Snow Phone**.....................................970/925.1221

## Fast Facts

*Area code 970 unless otherwise noted.*

**Ski Season** Thanksgiving to early April

**Location** Tiehack is in the **White River National Forest,** 213 miles from Denver, 2 miles from **Aspen Mountain,** and 12 miles from **Snowmass.**

## Getting to Tiehack

See "Getting to Aspen," page 52.

## FYI

**Area** 410 acres of groomed terrain with 45 trails geared to beginners and intermediates.

Beginner—35 percent

Intermediate—39 percent

Advanced/Expert—26 percent

**Number of Groomed Runs** Approximately 43

**Longest Run** 3 miles (**Tom's Thumb** to **Homestead Road** to **Spruce**)

**Capacity** 6,600 skiers per hour

**Base Elevation** 7,870 feet

**Summit Elevation** 9,900 feet

**Vertical Rise** 2,030 feet

**Average Annual Snowfall** 200 inches

**Snowmaking** 25 percent

**Night Skiing** None

**Lifts** 7 (6 double chairs and 1 platterpull)

| **Lift Passes** | **Full Day** | **Half Day** (starts at noon) |
|---|---|---|
| **Adult** | $49 | $36 |
| **Child** (6 and under) | Free | Free |
| **Child** (7-12) | $27 | $27 |
| **Senior** (65-69) | $33 | $33 |
| **Senior** (70 and over) | Free | Free |

**Ski School** The ski school desk (925.1220, 800/525.6200) is in the base lodge. Half-day and full-day group downhill lessons are available. Private lessons are offered for groups of up to 5 people.

**Kids' Ski School** **Powder Pandas** is for kids ages 3 to 6. Meet at the **Panda House** (925.6336) or in the **Main Restaurant** for beginning to advanced instruction daily 8:30AM to 4PM. Rental equipment is available at the Panda House. **Fort Frog** is an on-mountain learning and video center featuring a fort with look-out towers, old wagons, a jail, a saloon, and a teepee village.

**Clinics and Special Programs** **Learn to Ski** and **Learn to Shred** are three-day, guaranteed clinics (includes lift tickets and lessons). The **Early Bird** program provides 1.5-hour lessons starting at 8:45AM. Snowboard lessons are also available through the **Delaney Adult Snowboard Camps.** Tiehack, along with all the Aspen area resorts, offers **Challenge Aspen,** a complimentary program for disabled skiers.

**Races** There are no designated race courses on Tiehack, but **Eagle Hill** is a great place to practice running gates. Lots of locals lap it, using the short lift.

**Rentals** **Buttermilk Sports** (925.1220 or 800/525.6200 ext 2265), open daily 8:30AM to 5PM, has more than a thousand pairs of skis including the latest deluxe and high-performance models.

Snowboard and snowshoe rentals are also available.

**Day Care** A licensed and bonded agency, **Supersitters** (923.6080) requires a three-hour minimum. **Aspen Sprouts** (920.1055), in the **Airport Business Center,** takes up to 12 children, ages 2 to 5, from 8AM to 5PM. Reserve at least two weeks in advance. The **Aspen Chamber of Commerce** (925.1940) also has a list of sitters.

**First Aid** Summon the ski patrol by dialing "0" from designated emergency phones on many trails and near upper and lower lifts.

**Parking** There is free parking at the base of the mountain.

**Worth Knowing**

- **Aspen Mountain, Snowmass,** Tiehack, and **Aspen Highlands** now share an interchangeable multi-day lift ticket.

## Rating the Runs

### ● Beginner

Even novices can rove all over **Red's Rover** on **West Buttermilk.** Its gentle terrain is an excellent proving ground for progressing from a wedge to a stem christie.

### ■ Intermediate

There are as many fall lines on **Government** as there are bureaucrats in Washington, so you can ski it countless times without getting bored. It's a bit steeper than many of the paths on this teaching mountain, and thus more of a challenge.

### ◆ Advanced

Skiers will keep their skis on edge while on **Racer's Edge,** so named because it's heavily used by up-and-coming Killys on the Aspen Ski Team. The double fall lines and a steep section at the bottom will keep your senses edgy, too. The trail limns the cliffs overlooking **Maroon Creek.**

## Snowboarding

Snowboarders will enjoy the terrain at Tiehack because of its tendency toward natural "kickers" (small jumps and ledges) and a grooming system that provides plenty of wide-open space for carvers as well as for those who just want to cruise. **Timberdoddle Glades** is a favorite for more advanced boarders because of the abundance of powder they find while maneuvering around the nicely spaced trees.

## At the Resort

*Area code 970 unless otherwise noted.*

- **Bumps** ★$$ Thirty-foot ceilings, floor-to-ceiling windows, and a deck with beautiful views of the slopes give this redone base facility a true ski-lodge atmosphere. And the fare is fancy (the same chefs from the new **Ajax Tavern** in Aspen supervise the menu here). Offerings include innovative salads, pastas, brick-oven pizzas, and a variety of daily specials. Also worth sampling are the homemade muffins, fresh baked bread, and delicious made-daily mozzarella. There is a complete selection of wines by the glass and a fresh juice bar. ◆ Daily breakfast and lunch. At the base of the mountain. 925.4027
- **Cliffhouse** $$ Lunch is served with a view of 14,018-foot Pyramid Peak. ◆ Daily lunch. Top of Lifts 2 and 5. 920.4555
- **Cafe West** $$ Homemade soups, sandwiches, and pastries are served in a bistrolike setting. ◆ Daily lunch. Bottom of Lift 3. 925.7858

***For more information on the Tiehack area, see "Beyond the Resorts," page 66.***

# Aspen Highlands

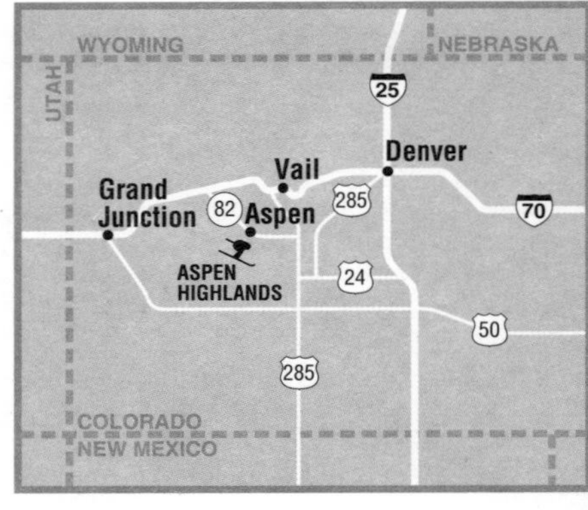


The gradual transfusion of technology has never undermined the charm of Aspen Highlands, but this ski area still has some high-tech aspirations. It has always made a big effort to please skiers rather than worrying too much about fast-pace developments. For instance, the resort stages high-stakes downhill races, where even intermediates can win big, and orchestrates a bit of showmanship—such as ski patrollers jumping off a 54-foot deck—to entertain those more inclined to stay on the sidelines.

Technology with a capital "T" appeared when a Houston developer acquired the resort in 1993 and the purchase triggered a merge with the Aspen Skiing Company. The result has been two additional high-speed lifts (replacing four double chairs) and 45 more acres of expert skiing. And even the purists don't seem to mind getting to the summit twice as fast as before (now the ride's 20 minutes).

The Highlands' terrain is an attraction in its own right, so skiers might even enjoy a half-hour double-chair ride to reach the top: The area boasts the second highest vertical in the US at 3,800 feet. Then, too, the advanced tracks on the mountain rank among the best in ski country. Break out at the top of **Steeplechase** and you're off and running toward the valley floor some 2,000 feet below. The intermediate trails are long and rolling, and beginners have the bottom of the mountain almost all to themselves. They play to an audience of diners at the base restaurant.

Hopefully, the low-key attitude that has always been a staple of the Aspen Highlands will not disappear with the addition of some modern amenities.

---

**Aspen Skiing Company**
**1600 Maroon Creek Road**
**Aspen, Colorado 81611-3352**

**Information**........................................970/925.1220
**Reservations**....................................800/262.7736
**Snow Phone**......................................800/525.6200

## Fast Facts

*Area code 970 unless otherwise noted.*

**Ski Season** Early December to early April

**Location** Aspen Highlands is in the **White River National Forest,** 204 miles from Denver.

### Getting to Aspen Highlands

See "Getting to Aspen," page 52.

## FYI

**Area** 530 acres (81 runs) with approximately 21 miles of terrain including open bowllike skiing and gladed runs.

Beginner—23 percent

Intermediate—48 percent

Advanced—14 percent

Expert—15 percent

**Number of Groomed Runs** Approximately 15

**Longest Run** 3.5 miles (**Broadway** to **Wine Ridge** to **Nugget** to **Park Avenue**)

**Capacity** 10,000 skiers per hour

**Base Elevation** 8,000 feet

**Summit Elevation** 11,800 feet

**Vertical Rise** 3,800 feet

**Average Annual Snowfall** 300 inches

**Snowmaking** 20 percent

**Night Skiing** None

**Lifts** 11 (9/2 high-speed quads, 5 double chairs and 2 surface lifts)

| Lift Passes | Full Day | Half Day (starts at noon) |
|---|---|---|
| **Adult** | $49 | $36 |
| **Child** (6 and under) | Free | Free |
| **Child** (7-12) | $27 | $27 |
| **Senior** (64-69 | $33 | $33 |
| **Senior** (70 and over) | Free | Free |

**Ski School** The ski school desks (925.1220 ext 3020) are in the base lodge and at the **Merry-Go-Round** restaurant. Half-day and full-day group lessons are offered. Private instruction is available for 1.5 hours, half day, and full day.

**Kids' Ski School** Kids ages 3 ½ to 6 can join **Snow Puppy** at the base lodge for lifts, lessons, and lunch. **Kids Camp** is held during holidays, for children ages 6 to 14.

**Clinics and Special Programs** The **First Time Skier Program** offers a three-day class designed to develop top-to-bottom mountain skiing. **Mountain Masters** is a four-day program including video analysis. Other clinics emphasize mogul and powder skiing. Aspen Highlands, along with all the **Aspen** area resorts, offers **Challenge Aspen,** a complimentary program for disabled skiers.

**Races** NASTAR races are held daily from 10:30AM to 2PM on the **Exhibition Run. Rolling Stone Challenge Series Race** is an amateur race program with $10,000 in weekly prizes. **The Killy 500,** run on weekends, is a test for more serious recreational racers.

**Rentals** There's a full-service shop (925.1220 ext 3013) at the base offering standard, demo, and high-performance downhill equipment, as well as snowboards. Standard outfits may be one or two years old, but new gear comes in yearly for the demo and high-performance categories. The shop is open from 8:30AM to 5PM.

**Lockers** Coin-operated lockers are located in the base lodge.

**Day Care** A licensed and bonded agency, **Supersitters** (923.6080) requires a three-hour minimum. **Aspen Sprouts** (920.1055), in the **Airport Business Center,** takes up to 12 children, ages 2 to 5, from 8AM to 5PM. Reserve at least two weeks in advance. The Aspen **Chamber of Commerce** (925.1940) also has a list of sitters.

**First Aid** Call the ski patrol by dialing "0" from designated emergency phones on the mountain, or go to the base of a lift for help.

**Parking** Free parking is available at the base lots.

### Worth Knowing

- **Aspen Mountain, Snowmass, Tiehack,** and Aspen Highlands share an interchangeable multi-day lift ticket.
- There are free mountain tours daily, on request, at **Skier Services** or the ski school.

## Rating the Runs

### ● Beginner

Most of the green runs on this mountain intersect others and create some nasty traffic jams. But only one trail crosses **Red Onion,** increasing the chances of skiing a run in exquisite solitude.

### ■ Intermediate

Don't trumpet too many praises about the great cruising down **Golden Horn,** unless you want the uncrowded, regularly groomed slope to end up playing to a packed house.

With the same pitches as the blue runs under the Cloud 9 Chair, **Grand Prix** and **Pyramid Park** are blissfully out of sight and therefore out of most skiers' minds. Don't race past **Picnic Point** on Pyramid Park; stop and take in the sumptuous view of this sky-high hunk of jagged rock.

### ◆ Advanced

Consider **Alps** to **Le Chamonix** an introduction to some of the black diamond runs on this mountain that rival portions of the Alps. If you're comfortable skiing down these short trails, you may be ready to tackle the next downhill degree.

### ◆◆ Expert

No deception here: You know the terrain is abrupt when the G-forces kick in at **Deception**'s 2,000-foot downhill drop. As you approach the **Maroon Creek Valley,** sneak a peek at the majestic **Maroon Bells.**

Don't be taken in by the terrain at the top of **Kessler's Bowl;** natives refer to this "bowl" as a chute. Just out of eyesight, the ground falls away and you're skiing the longest run on **Steeplechase.**

The private powder stash of **Bob's Glade** is short, but very steep and gladed. Detour here while everyone else heads to the top.

### Snowboarding

This resort beckons snowboarders with arguably the steepest terrain of the **Aspen** area mountains. It offers a large variety of jib runs (a run that has side walls for jumps and tricks) and plenty of cruisers. Advanced intermediate and expert boarders can get a rush on **Steeplechase, Oly Bowl,** and **Moment of Truth** (the name says it all). For glade action, try **Aces of Eight.** Beginners and less daring riders will find a sufficient number of beginner and intermediate terrain on **Grand Prix** and **Pyramid Park.**

## Mountain Highs and Lows

Shown in blue on the trail map, **Upper Meadows** is in the upper reaches for lower intermediates. The trail really rates a blue/black legend because it's usually bumped up.

The great white way of **Broadway** is actually a feeder run to the **Steeplechase** chutes, not a blue to be skied by intermediates for pleasure. Even the ride up is not for the faint of heart: There's a harrowing stretch where the chair brushes close to a cliff while seemingly miles above the ground.

## At the Resort

*Area code 970 unless otherwise noted.*

✦ **Merry-Go-Round** ★$$ Even if you're a fanatic flatlander, the fare at this restaurant is good enough to merit a trip to midmountain. Sample the crabmeat-filled pastry shells. If you're in town on a Friday, head here at noon and take a seat on the deck to watch some of Colorado's best pro freestyle skiers jump and bump down **Scarlett's Run.** ♦ Daily breakfast and lunch. Top of Exhibition 2 Lift. 925.8685

✦ **Schwannie's Base Lodge** Start your day with the hearty breakfast specials, and return to **Schwannie's Bar** in the evening to boogie in your ski boots and sign your name on the wall. Bands usually play on Friday, Saturday, and Sunday. ♦ Base lodge. 925.5622

✦ **Maroon Creek Lodge** $ You won't find mints on your pillow at this ski-in/ski-out lodge, but the friendly staff, reasonable rates, and 12 comfortable apartments easily compensate for lack of turndown service and other hedonistic extras. The Aspen city bus stops at the driveway. ♦ 1498 Maroon Creek Rd. 925.3491; fax 544.3036

✦ **Heatherbed Lodge** $ Contemplating the snow-clad cottonwoods over hot cider from this lodge's snug, fire-lit sunroom is an idyllic end to a day of skiing. Many of the 20 guest rooms feature four-poster beds, antiques, and other country embellishments. ♦ 1679 Maroon Creek Rd (at base of Aspen Highlands). 925.7077, 800/356.6782; fax 925.6120

## Beyond the Resorts

THE GANT

**1 The Gant** $$$ Even though this deluxe condominium complex, with 143 one- to four-bedroom units, is located a mere three blocks from the slopes, its

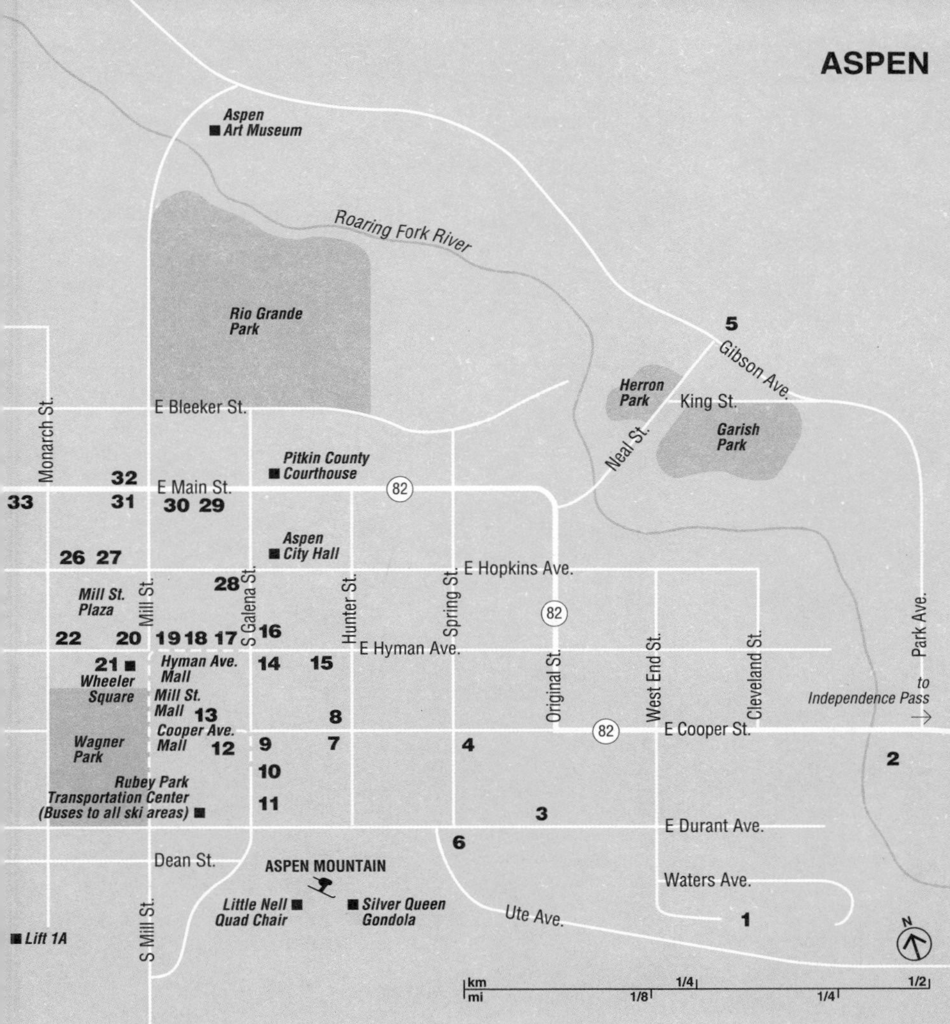


convenient shuttle still saves skiers the trouble of toting their gear back and forth. The premiere suites are worth the few extra dollars. Also included are such hotel-style civilities as a concierge, day and night van service, airport shuttle, and several hot tubs and pools. ♦ 610 West End St (across from Ute Ave). 925.5000, 800/345.1471; fax 925.6891

## Crestahaus Lodge

**2 Crestahaus Lodge** $ Shunning cookie-cutter accommodations, this 30-room European-style lodge gives visitors a choice of ambience. The older rooms charm with oddly angled ceilings, nooks, and crannies, but noise from the living and dining areas can be a problem. The newer rooms, while less architecturally eccentric, have private entrances and are quieter. Guests can gather in front of the fireplaces in the two lounges, or in the Jacuzzi or sauna. Other niceties include a continental breakfast buffet and airport transportation. ♦ 1301 E Cooper St (just before the Park Ave turnoff). 925.7081

**3 The Aspen Club Properties** $$$ This management company handles a mix of moderate to luxurious condos and a few private residences in the Aspen area. Rentals include airport shuttles, and transportation to and use of the prestigious **Aspen Club,** a favorite workout spot for many tennis and ski greats. A concierge service can handle everything from dinner reservations to child care. ♦ 730 E Durant Ave (between West End and Spring Sts). 920.2000, 800/882.2582; fax 920.2020

**4 City Market** Shop around the clock at this fully stocked supermarket. ♦ Daily 24 hours. 711 E Cooper St (at Spring St). 925.2590

**Restaurants/Clubs:** Red **Hotels:** Blue
**Shops/ Outdoors:** Green **Sights/Culture:** Black

**5 Baby's Away** Rent cribs, strollers, high chairs, and other infant equipment from this company. Call to reserve your gear and it will be set up in your room upon arrival. ♦ 931 Gibson Ave (at Neal St). 920.1699

**6 Aspen Club Lodge** $$$ Every time a new owner assumes control of this older property, its 90 rooms are upgraded. As a consequence, little luxuries are in no short supply. The usual heated pool, restaurant, and bar are on the premises. Approximately a month before your arrival, the concierge will call to ask if they can make any advance arrangements for your stay. ♦ 709 E Durant Ave (at Ute Ave). 925.6760, 800/882.2582; fax 925.6778

**7 The Omnibus Gallery** Rare vintage posters advertising such long ago events as the **1935 Monaco Grand Prix** and a **Buffalo Bill Wild West Show** are this gallery's specialty. Artists include Toulouse-Lautrec and Bonnard. ♦ Daily 11AM-10PM. 533 E Cooper St (between Hunter and S Galena Sts). 925.5567

**8 Boogie's Diner** ★★★$ The rock and pop hits on this restaurant's jukebox would be music to Elvis's and Buddy Holly's ears. Classic diner fare, like meat loaf and mashed potatoes or turkey with all the trimmings, is dished up in staggering portions. For dessert, devour a slice of Mom's apple pie. Downstairs you can splurge on trendy clothes, including leather jackets, boots, and belts. ♦ Daily lunch and dinner. 534 E Cooper St (between Hunter and S Galena Sts). 925.6610

**9 Stars** For the hopelessly star-struck, check out the Hollywood memorabilia and rock 'n' roll collectibles for sale at this unique store. ♦ M-W 10:30AM-9PM; Th-Sa 10:30AM-10PM; Su noon-8PM. Closed May, Sept-Nov. 525 E Cooper St (between Hunter and S Galena Sts). 920.2920

**10 Independence Square Hotel** $$ Two blocks from restaurants and shops, this city-center hotel has 28 delightful rooms decorated in Provençal style, although the Murphy beds aren't exactly in keeping with the south of France decor. Take in Aspen's Victorian skyline from the rooftop whirlpool, a sybaritic concession to modernity. There is no restaurant in the hotel. ♦ 404 S Galena St (between E Durant Ave and E Cooper St). 920.2313; fax 925.1233

**11 Double Diamond** ★★$$ The tiny cocktail tables set above the sunken dance floor provide the best view of the reggae or hard rock action. ♦ Daily 9PM-2AM. 450 S Galena St (between E Durant Ave and E Cooper St). 920.6905

**12 Rachael Collection** The hand-blown glass pieces sold here epitomize the delicacy and grace of this fragile medium. Prices range from reasonable to extravagant. ♦ M-Sa 10AM-10PM; Su 10AM-6PM. 433 E Cooper St (between S Galena and Mill Sts). 920.1313

**13 Red Onion** ★$ Aspen's oldest bar is still one of the most popular with locals, despite its ramshackle appearance. The Mexican/American menu offers everything from fajitas and enchilada platters to Philly cheesesteaks and salads. Try the chicken wings smothered in your choice of honey-mustard, teriyaki, or barbecue (in four different degrees of spicy) sauce. The spiked Jell-O shots slide down sweetly, but pack a punch. ♦ Daily lunch and dinner. 420 E Cooper St (between S Galena and Mill Sts). 925.9043

**14 Angelo's** ★★$$$ Although the name has changed, **Ute City Banque** (its former name) is still carved into stone on the walls and the place retains its historic feel. In the 1880s, miners cashed in their claims at this former bank. Today, the bartender deposits your money in the vault behind him, and pays out potables. A mature crowd frequents this restaurant and convivial bar, where the "Western American" menu changes frequently. Typical fare includes chicken pot pie, burgers, elk, and steak. ♦ Daily lunch and dinner. Bar open until 2AM. 501 E Hyman Ave (at S Galena St). 925.4373

**15 Little Annie's Eating House** ★★★$$ This old Western saloon is a great place to drink with friends or enjoy a family meal. The friendly but rushed staff serves such diverse entrées as Chinese chicken and pasta salad and surf 'n' turf late into the evening. ♦ Daily lunch and dinner. 517 E Hyman Ave (between Hunter and S Galena Sts). 925.1098

**16 Hard Rock Cafe** ★★$ The decibel level can be deafening and the tables are jammed together, but crowds keep coming to ogle the rock mementos and chow down on well-priced burgers, barbecue, and salads. Pick up a memorabilia map and start scouting the walls. An elaborately tooled leather-covered Gibson signed by Randy Travis, more than a dozen gold records by bands from Motley Crüe to Journey, and Madonna's bolero and bustier from the "Who's That Girl?" tour are a mere sampling. ♦ Daily lunch and dinner. 210 S Galena St (between E Hyman and E Hopkins Aves). 920.1666

CARNEVALE

**17 Carnevale Ristorante** ★★$$$ The urbane Italian ambience is cutting edge to the core. The menu, though, comes from the countryside: homemade pastas, risottos, and polenta, all lightly sauced. ♦ Daily dinner. Reservations recommended. 430 E Hyman Ave (between S Galena and Mill Sts). 920.4885

**18 Takah Sushi** ★★★$$$ The lively sushi bar is the focus of this intimate, Japanese oasis, where brightly colored murals in yellows, reds, and blues are reflected in mirror-lined walls. Sushi and sashimi prepared in the traditional manner with the freshest of fish keep aficionados of Japanese seafood returning to this 10-table eatery. ♦ Daily dinner. 420 E Hyman Ave (between S Galena and Mill Sts). 925.8688

**19 Curious George** One-of-a-kind sterling buckles and custom-made belts, antique pistols, and a hodgepodge of other offbeat items are purveyed here, ranging in price from inexpensive to out-of-sight. ♦ M-Sa 10AM-9PM; Su 10AM-6PM. 410 E Hyman Ave (between S Galena and Mill Sts). 925.3315

**20 Bentley's at the Wheeler** ★$$ Catch a ball game on TV while you unwind at the bar (a recycled antique English bank counter) or watch the street scene through the tall windows of this historic Victorian building. Pull a pint of light or dark ale, and try out the terrific daily specials: Does a 35¢ roast beef sandwich strike your fancy? ♦ Daily lunch and dinner. Bar open until 2AM. 328 E Hyman Ave (between Mill and Monarch Sts). 920.2240

**21 Eric's Bar** This place is lacking a sign at the door, but since both the owner and the bartender are named Eric, the moniker came naturally. The combination of century-old brick walls, a steel bar, and industrial lighting creates an arty, Soho-type look. At the bar, you'll find 14 beers on tap, and more than 40 single malt scotches. For those seeking edibles, only munchies are available. ♦ Daily 6PM-2AM. 315 E Hyman Ave (between Mill and Monarch Sts). 920.6707

**21 Su Casa** ★★$$ The chef, who hails from north of Mazatlán, prepares a spicy repertoire that includes carnitas, fajitas, and fresh seafood. Mexican tiles lend a south-of-the-border flavor to the decor. ♦ Daily 11:30AM-10:30PM. Bar open until 2AM. 315 E Hyman Ave (between Mill and Monarch Sts). 920.1488

**22 Crystal Palace** ★★★★$$$$ A changing medley of original songs laced with satiric barbs about names in the news entertains the audience at this popular dinner theater. You can choose one of five good, if unremarkable, dinners—including pasta, fish, and chicken dishes—from the preset menu. The staff members play a dual role as waiters and performers in the cabaret show. ♦ Call for show times. 300 E Hyman Ave (at Monarch St). 925.1455

**23 Snow Queen Lodge** $ This hundred-year-old lodge has seven antiques-filled rooms, including two that share a bath. A devoted following of guests return for the homey atmosphere. Owner Norma Dolle has been known to take to the slopes with her guests. ♦ 124 E Cooper St (between Garmisch and Aspen Sts). 925.8455

**24 Little Red Ski Haus** $ Inexpensive lodging in the center of Aspen isn't an impossible dream. This cozy, three-level Victorian has 21 rooms, some with shared bath. There are no phones or TVs to disturb the peace, just comfortable common areas where guests breakfast and chat with Marge Babcock, the personable proprietress who was one of the original Toni Twins (remember the "Does she or doesn't she?" ad slogan?). ♦ 118 E Cooper St (between Garmisch and Aspen Sts). 925.3333; fax 925.4873

**25 Hotel Lenado** $$$ It's more than the heated ski-boot lockers that keeps the clientele faithful to this 19-room establishment. Quarters with carved applewood or four-poster hickory beds, wood-burning stoves, and whirlpool baths do the trick. The two-story lobby is the picture of refined rusticity, with its overstuffed green and red plaid sofas set before a 28-foot fireplace. Wonderful breakfasts feature fresh ground coffee and thick cinnamon French toast or homemade granola. ♦ 200 S Aspen St (at E Hopkins Ave). 925.6246, 800/321.3457; fax 925.3840

**Restaurants/Clubs:** Red  **Hotels:** Blue
**Shops/ Outdoors:** Green  **Sights/Culture:** Black

RENAISSANCE @ THE BAR

**26 Renaissance** ★★★$$$$ The tasteful, contemporary decor provides a simple backdrop for the elegant French food, adding up to one of Aspen's more formal dining experiences. Start with the escargot ravioli with wilted Caesar salad dressing before moving on to the entrée of grilled Hawaiian tuna with rich mashed potatoes and caramelized shallot bordelaise. Oenophiles will appreciate the extensive *carte du vin,* offering selctions from all over the world. ♦ Daily dinner. Reservations recommended. 304 E Hopkins Ave (between Mill and Monarch Sts). 925.2402

Above the Renaissance:

**The R Bar** Chef Charles Dale of the **Renaissance** now owns this "Mountain Mediterranean-style" bar, which has a great view of Aspen Mountain. Basic bar fare, served until 11PM, is accompanied by nightly live music. ♦ Daily 5:30PM-2AM. 925.2403

**27 La Cocina** ★$$ Colorful Mexican handicrafts adorn the walls of this casual cantina. The seafood special (tender shrimp, crab, and whitefish folded in a flour tortilla and topped with melted jack cheese) is tasty indeed. If you're not that hungry, half-orders are cheerfully prepared. ♦ Daily dinner. 308 E Hopkins Ave (between Mill and Monarch Sts). 925.9714

**28 Brand Hotel** $$$$ A pied-à-terre for celebrities, famous financiers, and the money's-no-object crowd. The six commodious suites are individually and exquisitely designed; the **Silver Echo suite,** for example, is a deft blend of antique and contemporary furniture, accented with pre-Columbian pottery, Indian rugs, bright prints, and lush plants. Continental breakfast is brought to your door every morning. Work off the excesses of the night before in the high-tech, high-style health club. Though there's a restaurant in the hotel, guests are also granted temporary membership to the private **Caribou Club,** where on any given night during the winter holidays, you'll find as many famous faces as at Spago's. ♦ 205 E Hopkins St (between S Galena and Mill Sts). 920.1800; fax 920.3602

**29 Farfalla** ★★$$ This contemporary Italian bistro garners vigorous accolades from Aspenites for its excellent value. Entrées extend from pasta and pizza to veal and fish dishes. For openers, share the bruschetta, topped with tomatoes, basil, and garlic. Friendly waiters, contemporary art, and a noise level that's not too overpowering add to the amiable ambience. But the deal doesn't come without a price: During the ski season expect an hour's wait for a table. ♦ Daily lunch and dinner. 415 E Main St (between S Galena and Mill Sts). 925.8222

Pour la France!®

**30 Pour La France! Cafe and Bakery** ★$ When a late-night craving for good cooking hits, head here for some Gallic soul food. Crusty quiche, either the classic Lorraine or Sur la Mer (shrimp, sweet corn, and smoked cheese) are satisfying, as are the turkey pesto or grilled chicken and gruyère sandwiches, served on a baguette. The rich chocolate espresso cheesecake and the fresh fruit tart each merit an indulgence. At breakfast the food is good, but portions tend to be a bit skimpy. ♦ Daily breakfast, lunch, and dinner. 413 E Main St (between S Galena and Mill Sts). 920.1151

**31 Legends of Aspen** A sports bar popular with a young clientele who quaff their choice of more than 40 brands of beer. Basic pub grub composes the menu. ♦ Daily 4PM-2AM. 325 E Main St (between Mill and Monarch Sts). 925.5860

**32 Hotel Jerome** $$$ Originally a deluxe stopover for privileged stagecoach travelers, this hotel is still a classy place for a Western getaway. The 94 rooms and suites are decorated in the Victorian style of the hotel's turn-of-the-century heyday. Despite what the reservation clerks may say, the lodging in the original section of the hotel is more authentic; the rooms in the addition are well-done reproductions. Amenities include two restaurants and the best bathrooms in ski country, with oversize Jacuzzi tubs, two sinks, wonderful lighting, and a large magnifying mirror. ♦ 330 E Main St (between Mill and Monarch Sts). 920.1000, 800/331.7213; fax 925.2784

Within the Hotel Jerome:

**The J Bar** The town's most famous watering hole hasn't changed since the miners celebrated the silver strike here. The pressed tin ceiling, the mahogany back bar, and the simple wood chairs and tables look just the same, only the patrons are more posh. ♦ Daily noon-2AM. 920.1000

**33 Explore Coffeehouse** ★★$$ Aspen's version of an Old World coffeehouse tucked into the upstairs of a brown and white Victorian. Luscious desserts are a caloric complement to the lighter vegetarian dishes, soups, and salads. ♦ Daily breakfast, lunch, and dinner. 211 E Main St (between Monarch and Garmisch Sts). 925.5336

**34 Main Street Bakery & Cafe** ★★$ A local favorite, this small bakery's scones, blueberry muffins, fresh breads, and good coffee make a strong case for continental breakfasts. There is limited table service. ♦ Daily breakfast, lunch, and dinner. 201 E Main St (at Garmisch St). 925.6446

Sardy House

**35 Sardy House** $$$$ The turrets and gables of this historic inn, built with mining riches in 1893, shelter an opulent collection of three guest rooms and five suites outfitted in furnishings appropriate to the Victorian era. The **Carriage House** addition has 11 rooms and a suite, which feature a more updated look. The garret rooms, with their woody warmth, are among the nicest small lodging options in Aspen. Full gourmet breakfasts, with entrées such as brie omelettes or blueberry pancakes, are served on fine china (room service is available). Don't be surprised if you see famous faces in the hall; the professional service and privacy tend to attract prominent guests. ♦ 128 E Main St (between Garmisch and Aspen Sts). 920.2525, 800/321.3457; fax 920.4478

Within the Sardy House:

**Sardy House Restaurant** ★★$$$$ The dining room holds few tables, but on them you'll find culinary classics like Colorado-style

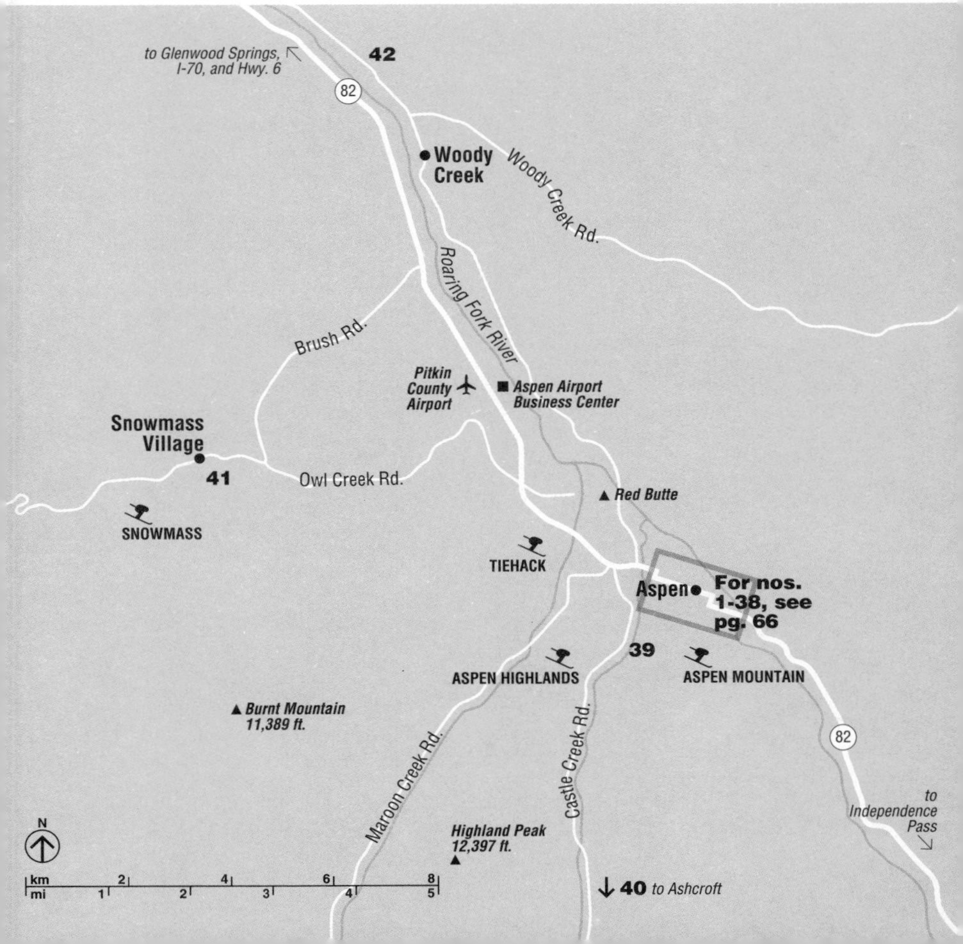

to Glenwood Springs, I-70, and Hwy. 6
42
82
Woody Creek
Woody Creek Rd.
Roaring Fork River
Brush Rd.
Pitkin County Airport
Aspen Airport Business Center
Snowmass Village
41
Owl Creek Rd.
Red Butte
SNOWMASS
TIEHACK
Aspen
For nos. 1-38, see pg. 66
39
ASPEN HIGHLANDS
ASPEN MOUNTAIN
Burnt Mountain 11,389 ft.
82
Maroon Creek Rd.
Castle Creek Rd.
to Independence Pass
Highland Peak 12,397 ft.
N
km 2 4 6 8
mi 1 2 3 4 5
40 to Ashcroft

rack of lamb or grilled Norwegian salmon. Soft candlelight and music enhance the intimate atmosphere. ♦ M-Sa breakfast; Sunday brunch; Daily dinner. Reservations recommended. 920.2525

**36 Hotel Aspen** $$$ This hotel's 45 rooms are unusually large and handsomely decorated in natural pine furniture and old photographs chronicling the town's history. Wet bars, coffeemakers, and mini-refrigerators allow for a modicum of self-sufficiency. Though there's no restaurant in the hotel, a breakfast buffet and après-ski wine and cheese spread are set up in the second-floor lobby, with its eye-catching view of **Ruthie's Run**. The hotel is only a half-block from the shuttle bus stop. ♦ 110 W Main St (between Aspen and First Sts). 925.3441, 800/527.7369; fax 920.1379

**37 Aspen Bed and Breakfast Lodge** $$ A towering, 44-foot river rock fireplace anchors the atrium lobby of this four-story bed-and-breakfast lodge. All 38 guest rooms open onto this space. The upper level rooms have balconies, and others are equipped with Jacuzzi tubs. Breakfast and afternoon hors d'oeuvres are served by the fireplace. A word to the budget-conscious: Lodging of comparable quality located closer to the slopes would cost dearly. ♦ 311 W Main St (between Second and Third Sts). 925.7650, 800/362.7736; fax 925.5744

The 13 sourdoughs who founded the town of Aspen trudged over Independence Pass on snowshoes and spent the rugged winter of 1879 protecting their claims in this silver-rich region. By 1890, 14 trains a day weren't enough to haul the silver out of the valley, and the ore awaiting shipment was stacked in the streets.

**Restaurants/Clubs:** Red
**Shops/ Outdoors:** Green
**Hotels:** Blue
**Sights/Culture:** Black

**38 Boomerang Lodge** $$ An older property in a quiet section of town, this lodge's 34 rooms and apartments have been well maintained and continually renovated. The most recent additions are six luxury rooms, featuring gas fireplaces, marble bathrooms, and wet bars. Amenities include a continental breakfast, pool, and whirlpool. ♦ 500 W Hopkins Ave (at Fourth St). 925.3416; fax 925.3314

**39 Midnight Inn** $$ City folks who dream of finding the archetypal mountain retreat will gravitate to this renovated barn with large windows that frame wide-angle views of the **Steeplechase** section of Aspen Highlands. Formerly a bed-and-breakfast, the inn can now be rented as a four- or six-bedroom house, appointed with antiques, wood-burning stoves, beamed ceilings, skylights, and a hot tub. Four of the rooms have private baths, two share a bath. The inn is on a dirt road, so a four-wheel- or front-wheel-drive vehicle is recommended. ♦ 786 Midnight Mine Rd (off Castle Creek Rd). 925.2349; fax 920.9722

**40 Pine Creek Cookhouse** ★★★$$$ The last half-mile to this log cabin can only be traversed by cross-country skis, snowshoes, or sleigh—but while the location is remote, the gourmet food is *au courant*. The Cookhouse is run by the Ashcroft Ski Touring Company, which has 30 kilometers of trails near the eponymous ghost mining town. ♦ Daily lunch and dinner. Reservations required. 11399 Castle Creek Rd (12 miles south of Hwy 82), Ashcroft. 925.1044

**41 Snowmass Lodge** $$$ A few may find its out-of-the-way location a hindrance (Snowmass is 1.5 miles up the road, and Aspen 15 minutes away), but skiers with a car or those amenable to living on shuttle time will love this luxurious lodge. The exceptional service (a slope-side ski concierge at Snowmass and equipment rentals in the lodge) and spacious guest quarters more than make up for any inconveniences. And the outstanding athletic club, with indoor tennis, racquetball and squash courts, and a host of other fitness facilities, may persuade you to forgo the slopes. The Aspen Skiing Company owns the 76-room lodge and often packages lift tickets with the rooms. Condos (called "villa units") are available, too. ♦ Off Highland Rd (1.5 miles east of Snowmass mountain). 923.5600, 800/525.0710; fax 923.6944

Within Snowmass Lodge:

**Sage** ★★★$$$ A rather eclectic menu is featured at this upscale—but casual—establishment. Although heavy on the seafood side, its menu includes several inventive dishes to appeal to even the most finicky of appetites. The cuisine ranges from Thai noodles with red snapper in a spicy coconut sauce to corn and sage risotto with mushrooms. ♦ Daily breakfast, lunch, and dinner. Reservations recommended. 923.0923

**Sage Bar** The tiny, cozy bar, which stocks more than 24 beers and serves hors d'oeuvres at sunset, has a view of Mount Daly and the Snowmass slopes. ♦ Daily 11AM-midnight. 923.5600

**42 Woody Creek Tavern** ★★$ Gonzo journalist Hunter Thompson made this knotty pine roadside shack famous. But natives in the know come here for the stout buffalo burgers, plump onion rings, baskets of fries, Flying Dog beer, and the chance to shoot some pool with friends. ♦ Daily lunch and dinner. 2 Woody Creek Plaza (7 miles northwest of Aspen). 923.4585

## Bests

### Mike Minarski

Former Marketing Director, Aspen Highlands Skiing Corporation

Skiing **Steeplechase**—five of Aspen's steepest chutes—at the top of Aspen Highlands.

Eating Buffalo wings (the best west of the Mississippi) and drinking draft beer at **Legends of Aspen.** Their slogan: Think globally, drink locally.

Riding the **Aspen Mountain** gondola—Being stuck in a gondola at another resort with five Gucci suits always makes me appreciate good old Aspen Highlands, where your father's profession and the age of your BMW still don't matter.

The **Crystal Palace** dinner theater—a must—is always funny and always sarcastic. Nothing is sacred at the Crystal Palace. The crew consistently puts on a cutting-edge show (waiters and waitresses are also the performers).

A round of golf at Aspen's public course—One of the most scenic anywhere. . . driving at 8,000 feet above sea level can never hurt your game.

Hiking the west or east **Maroon** trails during wildflower season (end of June). Wow!

Skiing **Independence Pass** on the Fourth of July—not for the fainthearted—2,000 feet of corn snow, shorts, sunshine, and fun at the top of the world. Get up early or finish your will before attempting.

### Kiki Cutter

Ski Ambassador, Ritz-Carlton Aspen

The **Ritz-Carlton** is the best hotel in Aspen or any major ski resort for that matter...their Sunday brunch should not be missed.

**The Little Nell** hotel is the hot spot for après-ski.

**The Aspen Club** has the best workout facilities I have seen anywhere. The tennis facilities are used by world-class players such as Martina Navratilova, GiGi Fernandez, and Conchita Martinez.

**La Cocina** is famous for Bert's margaritas and Nick is a most gracious host. They also serve some great Mexican food at a very affordable price.

**La Baita** on the Aspen Mountain has a tiramisù to die for.

**Bonnie's** on Aspen Mountain has incredible food and their chocolate cake fresh on Saturdays is unbelievable.

**Gwyn's** on **Snowmass Mountain** is a very intimate spot for a European-style sit-down lunch serving incredible edibles.

**Spar Gulch** on Aspen Mountain is the best "cruiser run." Always groomed to perfection. The best time to ski Spar is around noon or a little before when the sun is on it.

The top of Tiehack Lift has the most spectacular view anywhere in the world. The vista is an awesome view of the **Maroon Bells,** the most photographed spot in the world.

Best Yukon experience and mushroom soup is **Krabloonik** in **Snowmass.** You can take sleds with actual dogs that compete in the Iditarod and have a great picnic or just go out for a leisurely cruise and come back to enjoy a wonderful lunch at the restaurant.

**Obermeyer** skiwear is also based in Aspen with Klaus Obermeyer at the helm. You can find Klaus doing nonstops daily and yodeling—and he is only 76 years young.

Aspen has some of the best cross-country trails in the country. The **Aspen/Snowmass Nordic System** has over 60 kilometers of trails. There is no charge to use the trails but donations are accepted.

# Keystone

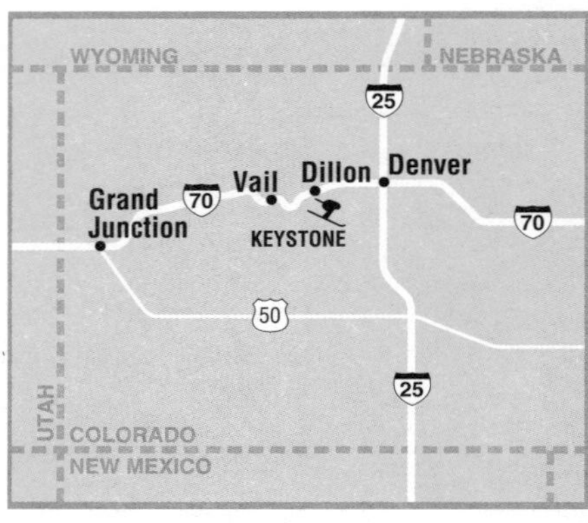


Among Summit County ski resorts (Keystone, **Arapahoe Basin, Copper Mountain**, and **Breckenridge**), Keystone has set a standard, since its inception in 1969, of being not only quick to recognize the needs of skiers, but to respond to them. In fact, the resort has opened two new mountains in the past 11 years. In 1984, the acquisition of **North Peak** added half a dozen high-end intermediate highways and advanced groomed and moguled runs to the territory, scoring points with an increasingly adventuresome clientele. Heeding the hue and cry of its customers once again, Keystone put another notch in its belt in 1991 with the debut of **The Outback.** Twelve deep blue and black trails cut through its trees, designed to test the limits of technique rather than rely on pure power. And last season, a pair of hike-to powder bowls were unveiled on the back side of the slope, blissfully enveloped by wilderness. The original namesake peak is a wooded web of trails that put all ability levels to the test. At night, 13 of its routes are primed for skiing under the lights. The towering trio, with its current total of 89 runs, is accessed by two gondolas and a latticework of lifts.

Down below, life slows to a civilized pace. The village wraps around a picturesque lake with lodging and shops radiating toward the slopes. Perhaps because Keystone's energy is so focused on its ski runs (even after dark), nightlife tends to be comparatively mellow. At the base's **Mountain House** and **Village at River Run**, there are a number of congenial gathering spots for both families and adults, but if you're looking for hard-core carousing, Keystone's après-ski scene might be too quiet for your taste.

Keystone's strong suit is centralized vacation planning. All the details of your stay—lodging, lift tickets, lessons, child care, dining arrangements, and more—are expertly handled by the reservation desk. In addition, the resort offers a variety of special value packages. Such services are definitely time-savers for families and others who have no leisure (or patience) to chart their own ski trip course, and are particularly helpful to first-time visitors.

---

**Keystone Resort**
**PO Box 38**
**Keystone, Colorado 80435**

**Information** .......................................970/468.2316
**Reservations** .............970/468.4242, 800/222.0188
**Snow Phone** .......................................970/468.4111

The 1991-1992 opening of The Outback, Keystone Resort's third peak, was the largest expansion in Colorado ski country of the last decade. The addition of this 256-acre area, with a high-speed quad accessing 17 trails and bowls, increased the resort's ski terrain by more than 40 percent.

## Fast Facts

*Area code 970 unless otherwise noted.*

**Ski Season** Late October to early May

**Location** Keystone is in the heart of the **Colorado Rockies,** 75 miles west of Denver.

## Getting to Keystone

**By air: Denver International Airport (DIA)** is 118 miles east of Keystone. **Eagle County Airport** is 60 miles west of Keystone in the town of **Eagle. American** offers nonstop service to both airports from **Chicago** and **Dallas/Ft. Worth,** and to Eagle from **Miami** and **New York/LaGuardia. Delta** offers direct flights to **DIA** from **Atlanta, Cincinnati, Dallas,** and **Salt Lake City,** and to **Eagle** from **Salt Lake City. United** flies nonstop from Chicago, **Denver, Los Angeles,** all three **New York** metro airports, and once daily between Denver and **Eagle**

**County. Continental, Northwest,** and **TWA** also provide nonstop service to **DIA.** Several airlines service DIA from the West Coast including **America West, Martin Air, Mexicana,** and **Sun Country.**

**By bus:** Several companies run shuttles to the ski resorts, including **Resort Express** (468.7600, 800/334.7433).

**By car:** Winterized cars are available from several major rental car agencies at the airport. From **Denver,** take Interstate 70 West to Exit 205, then go east on US Highway 6.

### All-weather highway:

Denver—Interstate 70 West to Exit 205 (Silverthorne) East to US Highway 6

### Driving time from:

Denver—1.75 hours (75 miles)

## Getting around Keystone

Like all the area's resorts, Keystone has its own shuttle system, and the **Summit Stage** (453.2368) provides free bus service, linking the Keystone, **Arapahoe Basin, Breckenridge,** and **Copper Mountain** ski areas together.

## FYI

KEYSTONE RESORT
COLORADO

**Area** 1,737 acres with 89 trails including bowls, glades, and wide-groomed runs.

Beginner—13 percent

Intermediate—36 percent

Advanced—51 percent

**Number of Groomed Runs** Approximately 30

**Longest Run** 3 miles **(Schoolmarm)**

**Capacity** 26,582 skiers per hour

**Base Elevation** 9,300 feet **(Keystone)**; 10,040 feet **(North Peak)**; 10,460 feet **(The Outback)**

**Summit Elevation** 11,640 feet (Keystone); 11,660 feet (North Peak); 12,200 feet (The Outback)

**Vertical Rise** 2,340 feet (Keystone); 1,620 feet (North Peak); 1,740 feet (The Outback)

**Average Annual Snowfall** 230 inches

**Snowmaking** 49 percent

**Night Skiing** Daily 4PM to 9PM mid-November through April on Keystone Mountain

**Lifts** 19 (2 gondolas, 3 high-speed quads, 1 regular quad, 3 triple chairs, 6 double chairs, and 4 surface lifts)

| **Lift Passes** | **Full Day** | **Half Day** (starts at noon) |
|---|---|---|
| **Adult** | $42 | $35 |
| **Child** (5 and under) | Free | Free |
| **Child** (6-12) | $19 | $17 |
| **Senior** (60-69) | $19 | $19 |
| **Senior** (70 and over) | Free | Free |

The full-day interchangeable lift ticket is good at Keystone, **Arapahoe,** and **Breckenridge.**

**Ski School** Ski school desks (468.4170) are located in the **Village at River Run** and the **Mountain House.** Group and private instructions are available. The **Ladies Day** program, available from 9 February through 30 March, offers four hours of instruction daily from 10:30AM and 3PM to intermediate and advanced skiers. Students are grouped according to ability with a maximum of eight to a group. Meet at the base of Keystone Mountain. Teen programs are offered for youths ages 11 to 16 during the Christmas and spring holidays, and some weekends in January and February.

**Kids' Ski School Mini-Minor's Camp** includes all-day lift, lunch, rental, and lessons for children ages 3 to 4. **Minor's Camp** is a full-day program for kids ages 5 to 12.

**Clinics and Special Programs** The **Mahre Training Centers,** hosted by Olympic medalists and pro-racing champions Phil and Steve Mahre, offer three- and five-day training sessions for all levels. Cost includes lift tickets, six hours of daily coaching, video analysis, an awards party, and social functions. The **Outback Experience** guides advanced skiers—in groups no larger than eight—through glade and bowl skiing on the **North Peak,** the **Outback,** and **Sunny Alp. Three-Day Advanced Skier Workshops** are offered from 6 February through 7 March and focus on skills needed to ski steeps and moguls with a day each spent at North Peak, the Outback, and the bowls at nearby **Arapahoe Basin.** Fee includes videotaping and review, lunches, and social events.

**Races** NASTAR racing is held at the **Packsaddle Race Area** on Keystone Mountain.

**Rentals** Three levels of rental equipment—recreational, sport, and premium—are available in shops located at the base of Keystone Mountain and the **Village at River Run.** All shops are open daily 8AM to 10PM. For information, call 800/253.3715.

**Lockers** Lockers are available at the **Village at River Run** and **Mountain House,** as well as at the summit of Keystone Mountain and in **The Outpost** on **North Peak.** Overnight ski storage is also available.

**Day Care** Reservations are required at the resort's **Children's Center.** The minimum age is 2 months. Ask about the snowplay program, which includes outdoor games and supervised gondola rides.

**First Aid** Treatment is available via the emergency phones around the mountain or by notifying any resort employee. The **Snake River Medical Center** (468.1440) is located at the base of Keystone Mountain near the **Mountain House.**

**Parking** Free parking is available at the outlying areas. Close-in parking is available for a fee at **Keystone Mountain** base and **River Run.**

**Worth Knowing**

- If the slopes haven't given you enough of a workout during the day, join the crowd on **Keystone Lake** for an evening of ice skating. During the summer, ice skating is replaced by nightly lakeside bonfires.

## Rating the Runs

### ● Beginner

You can teach yourself how to ski on **Schoolmarm,** a 3.5-mile long cruise. The gentle pitch continues all the way to the base, so beginners can practice their turns at a constant speed, without resorting to poling.

### ■ Intermediate

Advanced intermediates like to fly down the **Flying Dutchman** on the front face of Keystone. The trail is wide but snakes enough to keep the views ever-changing.

Motivated intermediates shine when setting their sights on **Starfire,** the best of the blue-rated runs on North Peak.

### ◆ Advanced

Respect the trail map's blue/black coloring for **Wildfire**—the only way out is the cat track. Hot intermediate skiers can really burn through the glades and over the bumps on this run.

### ◆◆ Expert

Two gondolas, a chairlift ride, and a 10- to 15-minute hike up the steep pitch above the Outback Express is the arduous path to the **Outback Bowls,** but after that it's all gloriously downhill. The **North Bowl** is a perfect slice of off-piste skiing, especially after a powder storm.

Working **The Grizz** is like skiing through a series of doorways; you're constantly choosing between snowy slots through the forest. This trail is great for repeat runs, because you'll never take it the same way twice. It's tree skiing at its tightest, and the undergrowth has been cleared out.

### Snowboarding

Snowboarding is prohibited on all three peaks.

## Mountain Highs and Lows

On busy days when the better skiers are using **Schoolmarm** as a high-speed boulevard to the base camp, beginners will wish this green run had a crossing guard.

The only intermediate exit off the back side of Keystone is **Mozart,** and this blue route isn't always a rhapsody. Because of its typical blanket of natural and not-so-natural snow, skiing is as unpredictable as Amadeus's arias. Many opt to hop the Outpost Gondola to **North Peak** and descend on **Prospector.**

## At the Resort

*Resort facilities can be reached by calling the dining and activities numbers (970/468.4130 or 800/451.5930) unless otherwise noted.*

- ✦ **Village at River Run** Located at the base of the Skyway Gondola, this new development replaces River Run Plaza. Reminiscent of an old-West mining town, the still-growing base area is home to a variety of shops, boutiques, restaurants, and cafes, as well as such services as ski rental shops and ticket kiosks. ♦ At the base of Skyway Gondola
- ✦ **The Inn** $$$ The 103 rooms and suites at this hostelry are the best deal for moderate lodging at the base of the slopes. The suites have loft bedrooms, kitchenettes, and balconies. ♦ Near Mountain House. 468.4242; fax 468.4343
- ✦ **Chateau d'Mont** $$$$ Romantics love the luxuries this complex has to offer. All of its 20 two- and three-bedroom condos are appointed with fresh flowers and thirsty terry robes; each unit has a glass-enclosed porch with a large hot tub and a stone fireplace in the living room; kitchens are stocked with coffee, juice, and other basic provisions. Guests request housekeeping services by appointment. Continental breakfast and an afternoon cocktail party are hosted in the concierge suite. ♦ Near Mountain House. 468.4242, 800/222.0188; fax 468.4343
- ✦ **The Outpost** The best food on the mountain comes from the kitchens of this immense log cabin perched on the side of North Peak. ♦ North Peak

  Within The Outpost:

  **Alpenglow Stube** ★★★★$$$$ This commodious restaurant still has a cozy feel thanks to its friendly Bavarian decor. Colorado cuisine is the theme of the six-course dinners, combining fowl, fish, and game with sumptuous sauces. No problem with parking: Diners ride two gondolas to reach this North Peak restaurant. ♦ Daily lunch and dinner; Su brunch. Reservations required

  **Der Fondue Chessel** ★★★$$$ Say cheese! Fondue and raclette are the specialties of the **Timber Ridge Room,** with an alpine-influenced interior. A lederhosen-clad accordionist entertains the many families

dunking their dinner. ♦ M-Sa dinner. Reservations recommended.

✦ **Mountain House** Centrally located between the **Village at River Run** and the lake, this lodge is best used for skier services. There are a few shops and eateries, but most people come here for the ski school, rental and repair shops, and ticket windows. ♦ At the base of Argentine, Peru Express, and Packsaddle chairs

✦ **Gassy's** This is the après-ski spot of choice if you end the day near the **Mountain House.** Tired skiers congregate at this comfortable bar on cold afternoons, warming up with spirited coffee drinks and telling tales about the day's best run. ♦ Daily lunch and dinner. In Mountain House

✦ **Ernie's Deli** ★$$ A stalwart source for eating on the run, this **Mountain House** deli tosses fresh salads and builds deli sandwiches to order. ♦ Daily lunch. In Mountain House

✦ **Keystone Lodge** $$$ Even sticklers for service will be impressed by the first-rate staff and concierge at this cushy lodge, whose 152 spacious rooms overlook pretty, little Keystone Lake. Enjoy an après-ski cocktail poolside before dining in the lakeside restaurant or spending a relaxing evening before the fire in the lounge. ♦ On Hwy 6. 468.4242, 800/222.0188; fax 468.4343

Within Keystone Lodge:

**Garden Room & Steakhouse** ★★$$$$ Big appetites meet their match in the **Bighorn Room.** Slabs of slow-roasted prime rib are served in eight-ounce to one-pound portions. The marinated veal chop with fresh herbs and forest mushrooms is also a winner, as is the Rocky Mountain trout with roast-corn chili relish. All entrées come with side dishes, soup, and salad, so it's impossible to leave hungry. A children's menu is available. ♦ Daily dinner. No reservations

---

The country's highest gourmet restaurant is the aptly named Outpost, located in Keystone Resort at the top of North Peak (elevation 11,444 feet).

---

With 13 floodlit trails covering 205 acres (more than 42 percent of its runs), Keystone Mountain operates the nation's largest night skiing facility.

✦ **Nonnino's** ★★$$ Watch the skaters gliding by on Keystone Lake while enjoying a taste of northern Italy at this family-style restaurant. Special dishes include *pappardelle carbonara* (broad, flat noodles with a garlic, pancetta, parmesan, and cream sauce) and *cioppino* (a seafood stew in a tomato broth over linguine). ♦ Daily dinner. No reservations. West end of Keystone Lake

✦ **MonteZuma's Rock 'n' Roll Saloon** A boisterous crowd fills this cavernous bar, where denizens play pool, dance to loud music, and otherwise amuse themselves. Local favorite Breckenridge Brew and other regional beers are poured. ♦ 7:30PM-2AM. West end of Keystone Lake. 468.2316

✦ **Ida Belle's Bar and Grille** ★$$ Those in the know say the key to the Southwestern-style burgers and burritos at this old miner's namesake is Elwood's Hot Sauce. Drinks served in Mason jars add to the casual ambience. ♦ Daily lunch and dinner. North end of Keystone Lake

IDA BELLE'S BAR & GRILLE

✦ **Lakeshore** $$$ These 38 studio to two-bedroom condominiums are among the newer residences in Keystone Village. The larger units have spacious loftlike living areas. All are privately owned, so expect a personal touch in furnishings. The ground floor is devoted to small shops. ♦ East end of Keystone Lake. 800/222.0188; fax 468.4343

✦ **Lenawee** $$$ If you can't stand cramped quarters, reserve one of these 25 condos, with their soaring cathedral ceilings and lakefront sundecks. The amenities of the Village are sjust a five-minute walk away. ♦ East end of Keystone Lake. 800/222.0188; fax 468.4343

✦ **Keystone Ranch** ★★★★$$$$ Dinner at this graciously restored 1930s homestead is a leisurely, eveninglong affair. The prix-fixe menu spotlights sophisticated, contemporary Western dishes such as almond-encrusted bass with smoked salmon ravioli. Dessert and drinks are served in the living room—if you're lucky, you might see elk grazing in the meadow outside. ♦ Daily dinner. Reservations required. Keystone Golf Course.

***For more information on the Keystone area, see "Beyond the Resorts," page 87.***

---

# Arapahoe Basin

A purist's peak, Arapahoe Basin is a holdover from the good old days of skiing—pre-plastic boots and carbon poles. The smallest of Summit County's four resort areas (**Keystone**—its sister property—**Copper Mountain**, and **Breckenridge** round out the quartet), A-Basin has been a favorite destination for skiers from **Colorado's Front Range** since the mid-1940s. When it was purchased by Keystone in 1978, the new owners listened to the pleas of old-time powderhounds and took a light hand when it came to renovations. They smoothed out the green and blue trails leading to the Basin's 13,050-foot summit, making it easier for intermediate skiers on Keystone's slopes to enjoy up-close views of the procession of 14,000-foot peaks that form the **Continental Divide.** But they didn't tamper with the precipitous **Palivacinni**, a collection of bumpy, black-as-night paths with names like **Bear Trap** and **Rock Garden.**

Also left in their original state were A-Basin's elemental facilities, consisting of a modest base lodge and a midmountain warming hut, just a few miles from **Keystone Village.** The warming hut is especially popular on sunny, late-spring days when swimsuit-clad skiers break out the beach chairs and gather 'round the flaming barbecue to toast the end of Arapahoe's long season.

**Arapahoe Basin Ski Area**
**PO Box 38**
**Keystone, Colorado 80435**

**Information**......970/468.2316

**Reservations**......970/468.4242, 800/222.0188

**Snow Phone**......970/468.4111

## Fast Facts

*Area code 970 unless otherwise noted.*

**Ski Season** Mid-November through early June

**Location** Arapahoe Basin is in the **Arapahoe National Forest,** 75 miles west of **Denver** and a few miles from **Keystone.**

### Getting to Arapahoe Basin

**By air: Denver International Airport (DIA)** is 112 miles east of Arapahoe Basin. **Eagle County Airport** is 66 miles west of A-Basin in the town of **Eagle. American** offers nonstop service to both airports from **Chicago** and **Dallas/Ft. Worth,** and to **Eagle** from **Miami** and **New York/LaGuardia. Delta** offers direct flights to **DIA** from **Atlanta, Cincinnati, Dallas,** and **Salt Lake City**, and to **Eagle** from **Salt Lake City. United** flies nonstop from Chicago, **Denver, Los Angeles,** all three **New York** metro airports, and once daily between Denver and **Eagle County. Continental, Northwest,** and **TWA** also provide nonstop service to **DIA.** Several airlines service DIA from the West Coast including **America West, Martin Air, Mexicana,** and **Sun Country.**

**By bus:** Several companies run shuttles to the ski resorts, including **Resort Express** (468.7600, 800/334.7433).

**By car:** Winterized cars are available from several major rental car agencies at the airport. From **Denver,** take Interstate to Exit 205, then go east on US Highway 6.

**All-weather highway:**

Denver—Interstate 70 West to Exit 205 (Silverthorne) East to US Highway 6

**Driving time from:**

Denver—1.75 hours (75 miles)

### Getting around Arapahoe Basin

**Summit Stage** (453.2368) provides free bus service for the **Keystone,** Arapahoe Basin, **Breckenridge,** and **Copper Mountain** ski areas. Shuttles between Keystone and Arapahoe run approximately every 20 minutes.

## FYI

**Area** 490 acres of above tree-line skiing with 61 trails.

Beginner—10 percent

Intermediate—50 percent

Advanced—20 percent

Expert—20 percent

**Number of Groomed Runs** Approximately 10

**Longest Run** 1.5 miles (**Dercum's Dash** to **Wrangle**)

**Capacity** 6,066 skiers per hour

**Base Elevation** 10,800 feet

**Summit Elevation** 13,050 feet

**Vertical Rise** 2,250 feet

**Average Annual Snowfall** 360 inches

**Snowmaking** None

**Night Skiing** None

**Lifts** 5 (1 triple chair and 4 double chairs)

| **Lift Passes** | **Full Day** | **Half Day** (starts at 12:30PM) |
|---|---|---|
| **Adult** | $37 | $28 |
| **Child** (5 and under) | Free | Free |
| **Child** (6-12) | $19 | $17 |
| **Senior** (60-69) | $19 | $17 |
| **Senior** (70 and over) | Free | Free |

The full-day interchangeable lift ticket is good at **Keystone,** Arapahoe, and **Breckenridge.**

**Ski School** The ski school desk (800/222.0188) is located in the base lodge. Alpine and snowboard group and private lessons are available.

**Kids' Ski School** The ski school offers half-day and full-day group lessons for children ages 3 to 12. Lessons include lift ticket and rentals, plus a hot meal with full-day instruction.

**Clinics and Special Programs** Many of the clinics offered by the ski school utilize the mountains at **Keystone** and Arapahoe Basin, including race camps and ski weeks. The **Mahre Training Centers,** hosted by Olympic medalists and pro-racing champions Phil and Steve Mahre, are three- and five-day training sessions with coaching and après-ski activities.

**Races** There are no race courses on Arapahoe Basin. All racing programs are handled through **Keystone.**

**Rentals** Recreational, sport, and premium equipment is available at the base of Arapahoe Basin. The shop is open daily 8AM to 5PM.

**Lockers** Lockers can be found at the base of Arapahoe Basin.

**Day Care** The **Children's Center** (800/255.3715) is located at the base of the mountain. To attend, kids must be at least 18 months old. Reservations are required.

**First Aid** Go to the ski patrol stations for first aid. The **Snake River Medical Center** (468.1440) is located at the base of **Keystone Mountain.**

**Parking** Free parking is available at the base of Arapahoe Basin.

**Worth Knowing**

- A couple of miles up the road from Arapahoe lies a portion of the **Continental Divide,** where many adventurers and backcountry-types try the route down when the snow is good.

## Rating the Runs

### ● Beginner

You'll get great views from the top of **Wrangler,** which starts in open territory just above timberline. As the trail descends, it tapers into an easy tree-lined path.

### ■ Intermediate

Every trip down the constantly changing runs of **Lenawee Face** and **Norway Face** will improve your skiing skills. Features usually reflect the recent weather: soft and forgiving after a snowstorm, hard and sometimes slick on cold days. Norway is the easier of the two; Lenawee is steeper, its pitch unpredictable. Neither is suitable for lower intermediates.

### ◆ Advanced/◆◆ Expert

Anyone with acrophobia will feel faint peering over the edge of **Palivacinni,** but that rarely deters good skiers who thrive on challenges. Jump over the lip or ski down the ridge line and enter on a more gentle angle. Winds often puff powder to the middle of this narrow bowl, with its rim so steep that bumps rarely build at the very top. But descending, you'll find mogul heaven. If Pali isn't steep enough, enter the virtually vertical **First Alley** or **Second Alley** farther down the ridge.

### Snowboarding

The location of the resort, mostly above tree line, provides great terrain for carvers and those who need the extra space to master that toe turn. West wall runs such as **Norway Face** get bumped up and are not groomed, so they offer the best terrain for experts. Runs on the east wall such as **East Gully** offer steep, smooth pitches where boarders can take a different line every time.

## Mountain Highs and Lows

Modestly rated black diamond, **Hidden Chute** and **Aerobic Alley,** the slim, nearly vertical trails hacked between trees, would earn double–black–diamond status at any other resort.

## At the Resort

*Resort facilities can be reached by calling 970/468.0718.*

- ✦ **Alpenglow Cafeteria** $$ Arapahoe's culinary philosophy belongs to the "real skiers don't eat quiche" school, made plain in this cafeteria offering basic breakfasts (eggs, pancakes) and lunches (soups, burgers). ♦ Daily breakfast and lunch. At the base lodge
- ✦ **Alpine Hut Barbecue** ★$$ In the winter, this is a serviceable spot for a quick bite. But the Hut really comes to life when the sun shines in the spring. Work on your tan while watching the boarders and snowbunnies around the outdoor barbecue area. ♦ Daily lunch. Top of Exhibition Lift

***For more information on the Arapahoe Basin area, see "Beyond the Resorts," page 87.***

# Copper Mountain

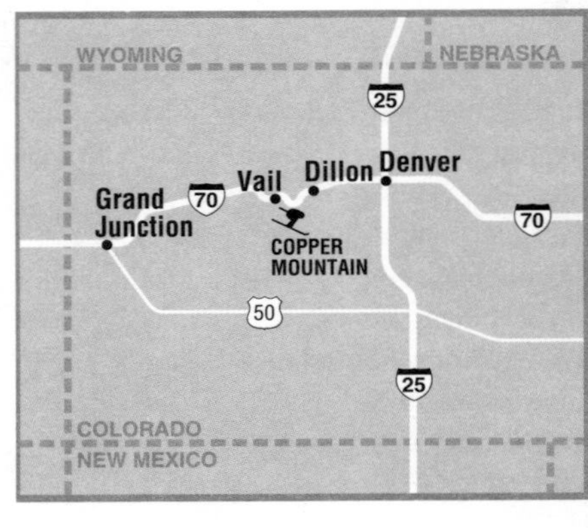


Although the snow-covered crests and timbered flanks of **Copper Peak** and **Union Peak** have a certain rugged beauty, the lure of Copper Mountain isn't limited to its looks. From a skier's point of view, its real appeal lies in the intelligently designed system of trails and lifts. Thanks to the layout of Copper's 19 chairs, more than 28,000 skiers per hour can schuss down the 52-plus miles of runs.

The terrain is divided into more-or-less distinct zones, each dedicated to a different skill level. Novices reign over the western edge of the skiable slopes, where three lifts serve the mostly green-rated runs that cover nearly the entire height of the peak. Here beginners are free to polish their skills without worrying about intrusions by experienced skiers racing to the base. The central part of the mountain is covered with blues for intermediates. Advanced and expert skiers challenge a complex of steep, often mogul-ridden runs at the eastern end of the slopes. Even more adventurous skiers can try guided snowcat tours to **Copper Bowl** which has 700 acres of open bowl and glade skiing.

One of Summit County's four major ski resorts (along with **Breckenridge**, **Keystone**, and **Arapahoe Basin**), Copper Mountain projects a casual atmosphere conducive to good, clean family fun. The resort's considered balance of individual comforts extends to the village, which has all the necessary ski vacation amenities: good restaurants, lively bars, hotel rooms, condos, and the ubiquitous hot tubs. If you'd like a taste of a genuine Western town, however, **Dillon** and **Frisco**, although a bit touristy, are just down the road.

**Copper Mountain Resort**
**PO Box 3001**
**Copper Mountain, Colorado 80443**

**Information**........................................970/968.2882
**Reservations**......................................800/458.8386
**Snow Phone**.......................................970/968.2100
..............................from metro Denver 970/893.1400

## Fast Facts

*Area code 970 unless otherwise noted.*

**Ski Season** Mid-November through mid- to late-April

**Location** Copper Mountain is in Colorado's **Arapahoe National Forest,** 75 miles west of Denver off I-70.

## Getting to Copper Mountain

**By air: Denver International Airport (DIA)** is 127 miles west of Copper Mountain. **Eagle County Airport** is 50 miles west of Copper in the town of **Eagle. American** offers nonstop service to both airports from **Chicago** and **Dallas/Ft. Worth,** and to **Eagle** from **Miami** and **New York/LaGuardia. Delta** offers direct flights to **DIA** from **Atlanta, Cincinnati, Dallas,** and **Salt Lake City,** and to **Eagle** from **Salt Lake City. United** flies nonstop from Chicago, **Denver, Los Angeles,** all three **New York** metro airports, and once daily between Denver and **Eagle County. Continental, Northwest,** and **TWA** also provide nonstop service to **DIA.** Several airlines service DIA from the West Coast including **America West, Martin Air, Mexicana,** and **Sun Country.**

**By bus:** Several companies run shuttles to the ski resort, including **Resort Express** (468.7600, 800/334.7433).

**By car:** Winterized cars are available from several major rental car agencies at the airport. From **Denver,** take Interstate 70 West to Exit 205, then go east on US Highway 6.

### All-weather highway:

Denver—Interstate 70 West to Exit 205 (Silverthorne) East to US Highway 6

### Driving time from:

Denver—1.75 hours (75 miles)

## Getting around Copper Mountain

Like all the area's resorts, Copper Mountain has its own shuttle system, and the **Summit Stage** (453.2368) provides free bus service, linking the **Keystone, Arapahoe Basin, Breckenridge,** and Copper Mountain ski areas together.

## FYI

**Area** 1,360 acres; 700 acres of **Copper Bowl** via snowcat tours.

Beginner—22 percent

Intermediate—27 percent

Advanced—35 percent

Expert—16 percent

**Number of Groomed Runs** Approximately 18

**Longest Run** 2.8 miles **(Easy Road)**

**Capacity** 28,250 skiers per hour

**Base Elevation** 9,712 feet

**Summit Elevation** 12,313 feet

**Vertical Rise** 2,601 feet

**Average Annual Snowfall** 255 inches

**Snowmaking** 20 percent

**Night Skiing** None

**Lifts** 19 (3 high-speed quads, 6 triple chairs, 6 double chairs, and 4 surface lifts)

| **Lift Passes** | **Full Day** | **Half Day** (starts at 8:30AM or 12:30PM) |
|---|---|---|
| **Adult** | $39 | $29 |
| **Child** (5 and under) | Free | Free |
| **Child** (6-12) | $18 | $14 |
| **Senior** (60-69) | $27 | $27 |
| **Senior** (70 and over) | Free | Free |

**Ski School** Ski school desks (968.2318 ext 6330) are in the **Center**, the **Union Creek Learning Center**, and in **Solitude Station.** Alpine, nordic, and snowboard group and private lessons are available.

**Kids' Ski School** The **Children's Ski School** (968.2318 ext 6346) offers lessons (including rental and lunch) for children ages 4 through 12, grouping students by age and ability. Group lessons come in the form of **Copper Choppers** for the older kids and **Scooters** for the younger students. There are also 1.5-hour private lessons customized for the specific interests of the student or parents.

**Clinics and Special Programs** The ski school offers **Diamond Cutter** workshops, women's seminars, early season ski seminars, and other special programs. Advanced and expert skiers can take guided snowcat tours into **Copper Bowl,** which should be lift accessible for the 1995-96 season. For information on the disabled skier program, call 453.6422.

**Races** NASTAR and coin-operated self-timer race courses are on **Loverly.**

**Rentals** Rental shops are located in the **Center** building and at **Union Creek.** Downhill and cross-country skis, boots, poles, and snowboard rentals are available. The shops are open Monday through Friday from 8AM to 5PM, and Saturday and Sunday from 7:30AM to 5:30PM. Reserve high-performance equipment in advance.

**Lockers** Daily and overnight ski check services are at the bases of the American Flyer and G Lifts. Small baskets are located on the ground floor of the **Center.**

**Day Care** The aroma of fresh-baked cookies wafting from the **Belly Button Bakery** will lure children into the nursery. **Belly Button Babies** (2 months to 2 years old) and Belly Button Bakery (2 to 4 years old) are in the **Mountain Plaza.** Make reservations when booking lodging.

**First Aid** Ski patrol stations are located at the top of the B1, E, and Timberline Express Lifts. The main ski patrol center is in **Copper Commons.** The **Copper Mountain Resort Medical Center** (968.2330) is in **Bridge End.**

**Parking** Early risers can nab a place in a free lot close to the lifts. Late arrivals will have to park in an outlying lot and take a shuttle to the base area. Two pay lots, at **Mountain Plaza Circle** and behind the **Copper Commons,** are close to the slopes.

**Worth Knowing**

- Copper Mountain is home to the only North American **Club Med** winter facility. Like the warm-weather resort program, this **Club Med** locale is a good choice for the single skier.

## Rating the Runs

### ● Beginner

You'll be talking to yourself about the splendors of nature if you ski **Soliloquy** when the sun is shining on its fluffy, fresh powder. Heading downhill, keep an eye peeled for **Roundabout,** which tenders a scenic ride along the ski area's edge. A short steep stretch at the top of Soliloquy starts you rolling, but farther along it flattens out, which helps keep your skiing under control.

### ■ Intermediate

Steer toward **Andy's Encore** when you're ready to practice upper intermediate skills like edging and negotiating a few moguls. This trail varies in pitch, and includes some short steeps, a few bumps, and smooth terrain for swooping GS turns. A double fall line kicks in just past the split to **Oh No,** so you can ski the trail a bit differently if you do a repeat run.

Andy's next-door neighbor, **Collage,** is another winner. The trail is a bit narrower, but fewer people paste the path's sections together for a top-to-bottom trip, making it less crowded. Head here when ready to test your stamina on a long, nonstop run.

### ◆ Advanced/◆◆ Expert

There's no backing out once you've hurtled over the edge of the steep headwall called **Drainpipe,** but keep going (it's hard to stop) until you reach a short lip. Then you'll have to choose between a tight patch of trees where the powder lingers, or **Sawtooth,** whose bumps can be as jagged as its name implies.

Weak-kneed skiers should stay away from **Spaulding Bowl** and its groups of mean chutes. Winds build the cornice guarding **Patrol Chute** up to 10 feet. Aggressive skiers might be tempted to angle into the bowl via **Murphy's.** The bowl feeds into **Cross Cut,** a runout with moguls formed by experts carving their way back to the Resolution Bowl Chair.

### Snowboarding

Although the snowboard park here was recently closed, there is still plenty of terrain to enjoy. To get started, you may want to enroll in the new one- and two-day snowboard camps which offer both freestyle and carving instruction. The ski school has separate camps for adults and children. Wide trails such as **Loverly, Roundabout,** and **Carefree** provide room to master the basics. For tricksters and boarders who want to catch some air, **Christmas Tree Glade** offers a series of natural obstacles (thanks to forest fires over the years). Advanced boarders head to **Union Bowl** and **Spaulding Bowl** for a great combination of steepness and wide-open space.

## Mountain Highs and Lows

At the lower part of **Loverly,** the pitch suddenly steepens and nervous novices start traversing back and forth across the slope, creating hazards for other skiers. Complicating matters, the mix of natural and artificial snow can be fickle, making some folks tighten up on the trail even more.

Wimpy **Coppertone** looks entertaining from the top, but this green run peters out, forcing some skiers to resort to poling. The fall line is also askew, resulting in uneven footing.

The sides of black-diamond **Union Bowl** are sharp, but the bottom curves are much too tame.

## At the Resort

*Resort facilities can be reached by calling the resort's main number (970/968.2882) unless otherwise noted.*

✦ **Solitude Station** ★$$ On powder days, have continental breakfast at this midmountain eatery before grabbing first tracks. At lunch, the cafeteria dispenses deli sandwiches, stuffed potatoes, and other similarly satisfying fare. ♦ Daily breakfast and lunch. Top of American Eagle Lift. ext 6520

✦ **Flyers** $ This snack shack is perfect for warming up with hot chocolate. ♦ Daily breakfast and lunch. Top of American Flyer Lift. ext 6534

✦ **The Woods at Copper Creek and the Legends** $$$$ Small groups and large families will appreciate the breathing room at these town homes. With up to four bedrooms, they're the most spacious living quarters at Copper. The 26 residences rim the golf course and are only a short shuttle-bus ride from the lifts. ♦ East side of the village. 800/458.8386; fax 968.2733

✦ **The Clubhouse** $$ On balmy afternoons, a casual crowd convenes on the patio over burgers and beer to compare notes about the slopes. ♦ Daily breakfast and lunch. Base of B Lift. ext 6514

✦ **Farley's Prime Chop House** ★★$$ Copper's oldest (1973) steak house has switched to Mexican fare but has retained its English atmosphere (captain's chairs, a billiards table, and woody decor). ♦ Daily lunch and dinner. Base of B Lift. 968.2577

✦ **Double Diamond Bar & Grill** ★★$$ Artist Bev Doolittle's portraits of Native Americans line the rough-hewn walls of this casual, always-bustling restaurant. Drawn by the sandwiches-to-steak menu and reasonable prices, families descend at the dinner hour. Party animals move in later. ♦ Daily breakfast, lunch, and dinner. Base of B Lift. 968.2880

Four bowls at Copper rise above the timberline: Hallelujah, Spaulding, Union, and Resolution.

✦ **O'Shea's** ★★★$$ Park your skis on the patio and step into this popular haunt for the hungry. The breakfast buffet is unbeatable, and later in the day, the succulent ribs sustain heartier appetites, while the chicken salad is just right for light eaters. Children eat for free with every adult entrée ordered. Live music entertains Thursday through Sunday nights. ♦ Daily breakfast, lunch, and dinner. Base of American Eagle Lift. ext 6504

✦ **The Commons** ★★★$ With a wall of windows overlooking the ends of some well-used runs, this cafeteria-style restaurant is a fine place to hone your après-ski people watching skills. **Kokomo's** bar is open daily until around 11PM. ♦ Daily breakfast and lunch. Base of American Flyer Lift. ext 6591

✦ **The Pub** Ales in three-foot-tall glasses and single malt scotches are savored at the hand carved bar in this bastion of British reserve. ♦ Daily 11AM-11PM. Copper Commons, lower level. ext 6584

✦ **Mountain Plaza** $$$ In the heart of the village, this hotel houses 60 two-bedroom units, including individually owned condos. The AAA Four Diamond award ensures a comfortable stay. ♦ 209 Ten Mile Circle. 800/458.8386; fax 968.2733

Within Mountain Plaza:

Pesce FRESCO

FRESH-FISH
and Pasta too!

**Pesce Fresco** ★$$$ Fresh fish, cooked plain or fancy, is served in sprightly surroundings. If you're looking for more carbohydrates than the spicy Cajun trout or rosemary salmon offer, try the pesto pizza. Jazz bands play Wednesday through Sunday nights. ♦ Daily breakfast, lunch, and dinner. 968.2318 ext 6505

✦ **Copper Mountain Athletic Club** Take a break from the slopes and book a racquetball or tennis court at this top-notch full-service athletic facility. A weight room and swimming pool are among the club's other facilities. ♦ M-F 6AM-10PM; Sa-Su 8AM-10PM. Center of village, on Copper Rd. ext 6380

Within the Copper Mountain Athletic Club:

**Rackets** ★★★$$$$ Befitting its location, this health-conscious restaurant boasts the most complete salad bar in the region. A spectacular mountain view accompanies the fare, which includes wild game posole stew; Southwestern shrimp tempura; and chargrilled lamb with roasted garlic, wild mushrooms, and balsamic vinegar sauce. ♦ Daily dinner. Reservations recommended. ext 6386

✦ **Club Med** $$$$ Smallish rooms don't seem to bother guests at this, one of only two US outposts of **Club Med** (the other is in Florida). This facility has 118 rooms altogether and an all-inclusive package covers lodging, meals, lifts, instruction, and après-ski activities, parties, and entertainment. Ski lessons are provided by the club's own ski instructors, who work with the same group all week. The children's programs and ski school will make your kids beg to leave you. ♦ 50 Beeler Pl (1 block from the American Flyer Lift). 800/CLUBMED

✦ **Telemark Lodge** $$$ Skiers who want condo comforts without the attendant prices will like this 80-room lodge with deluxe studios and one-bedroom units featuring jetted bathtubs. Ask for a unit with a fireplace, too. Guests meet and mingle in the lobby, where a wine and cheese board stands by the great stone hearth. Some good restaurants and shops are just a short walk away. ♦ On Copper Rd, west end of the village. 800/458.8386 ext 6896; fax 968.2733

✦ **Union Creek** ★★$$ The reputation of their six-foot deli sandwiches (sold by the inch) is as long as the weekend lift lines. Pack some up for a picnic or grab a table on the deck. ♦ Daily breakfast and lunch. West end of village, at the base of H and K Lifts. ext 6532

***For more information on the Copper Mountain area, see "Beyond the Resorts," page 87.***

Copper Mountain has sister ski resorts in Bariloche, Argentina; Ishiuchi Maruyama, Japan; Whakapapa, New Zealand; and Muju, Korea.

**Restaurants/Clubs:** Red | **Hotels:** Blue
**Shops/ Outdoors:** Green | **Sights/Culture:** Black

# Breckenridge

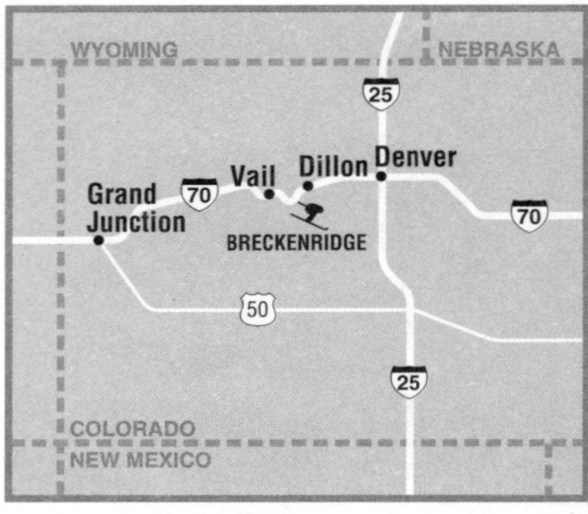


The oldest continuously occupied town on Colorado's Western front, Breckenridge was settled in 1859 by a party of prospectors who discovered gold in the **Blue River.** As the glittering veins faded away, the town itself began to edge toward obsolescence. But when the fledgling ski industry started lacing its slopes with lifts in the early 1960s, the town took its first steps back from the brink. By the 1980s, Breck hit its stride with the region's first high-speed quad chairlift and an emphasis on innovative, high-quality children's programs. The success of the skiing enterprise caught on in town, where entrepreneurs opened shops in restored Victorian houses and inspired chefs converted burro barns into gourmet restaurants. Breckenridge's celebrated **Main Street** sets it apart from Summit County's three other ski areas (**Keystone, Arapahoe Basin,** and **Copper Mountain**). The street retains all the color of its frontier origins while nixing the contemporary contrivances that too often pollute tourist destinations.

Rising high above the restored rooftops of town, 16 lifts zip up three summits, pragmatically named **Peak 8, Peak 9,** and **Peak 10.** They're home to a sundry collection of narrow bump runs, steep-sided bowls above the timberline, well-groomed intermediate cruisers, and lots of beginner slopes. Since the lift system is an often confusing amalgam of high-speed quads situated to compensate for the shortcomings of the older chairs, skiers can maximize these mountains by studying the trail map before heading uphill.

Peak 8 has something for everyone, but the layout is vexing and most runs are short. Much of the mountain's vertical rise is measured within the **Horseshoe** and **Imperial** bowls, expert territory high above the ski trails. Peak 9 is less frustrating for the middling skier, as it's loaded with intermediate and beginner courses. The runs down Peak 10 are a balance of open blue blazes and black-diamond trails, and are frequently filled with moguls. The latest jewel in the Breckenridge crown is **Peak 7.** Accessible only by hiking over from Peak 8, it offers experts pristine pitches in an untamed area.

---

**Breckenridge Ski Corporation**
**PO Box 1058**
**Breckenridge, Colorado 80204**

**Information**........................................970/453.5000
**Reservations**....................................800/221.1091
..................................................fax 970/453.7302
**Snow Phone**.....................................970/453.6118

## Fast Facts

*Area code 970 unless otherwise noted.*

**Ski Season** Mid-November through early May

**Location** Breckenridge is in Colorado's **Arapahoe National Forest,** 85 miles west of Denver.

## Getting to Breckenridge

**By air: Denver International Airport (DIA)** is 118 miles east of Breckenridge. **Eagle County Airport** is 60 miles west of Breckenridge in the town of **Eagle. American** offers nonstop service to both airports from **Chicago** and **Dallas/Ft. Worth,** and to **Eagle** from **Miami** and **New York/LaGuardia. Delta** offers direct flights to **DIA** from **Atlanta, Cincinnati, Dallas,** and **Salt Lake City,** and to **Eagle** from **Salt Lake City. United** flies nonstop to DIA from Chicago, **Denver, Los Angeles,** all three **New York** metro airports, and once daily between Denver and **Eagle County. Continental, Northwest,** and **TWA** also provide nonstop service to DIA. Several airlines service the West Coast including **America West, Martin Air, Mexicana,** and **Sun Country.**

**By bus:** Several companies run shuttles to the ski resort, including **Resort Express** (468.7600, 800/334.7433).

**By car:** Winterized cars are available from several major rental car agencies at the airport. From **Denver,** take Interstate 70 West to Exit 205, then go east on US Highway 6.

**All-weather highway:**

Denver—Interstate 70 West to Exit 205 (Silverthorne) East to US Highway 6

**Driving time from:**

Denver—1.75 hours (75 miles)

## Getting around Breckenridge

From town, you can take a shuttle (453.2251) to the three bases of the mountain and between lodges; within town, there is a free trolley. The **Summit Stage** (453.2368) is a free shuttle bus serving all Summit County ski areas, as well as **Dillon, Frisco,** and **Silverthorne.**

## FYI

**Area** 1,915 acres with 126 runs and bowl skiing off **Peaks 8, 9,** and **10.**

Beginner—15 percent

Intermediate—27 percent

Advanced—58 percent

**Number of Groomed Runs** Approximately 70

**Longest Run** 3.5 miles **(Four O'Clock)**

**Capacity** 24,430 skiers per hour

**Base Elevation** 9,950 feet

**Summit Elevation** 12,998 feet

**Vertical Rise** 3,398 feet

**Average Annual Snowfall** 255 inches

**Snowmaking** 18 percent

**Night Skiing** None

**Lifts** 17 (4 high-speed quads, 1 triple chair, 8 double chairs, and 4 surface lifts)

| **Lift Passes** | **Full Day** | **Half Day** (starts at noon) |
|---|---|---|
| **Adult** | $42 | $33 |
| **Child** (5 and under) | Free | Free |
| **Child** (6-12) | $19 | $17 |
| **Senior** (60-69) | $19 | $19 |
| **Senior** (70 and over) | Free | Free |

The full-day interchangeable lift ticket is good at **Keystone, Arapahoe,** and Breckenridge.

**Ski School** Offices are located at the **Peak 8** (ext 7510) and **Peak 9 Village** (ext 7350) base areas. Group half-day and full-day lessons, and discounted one-hour private lessons are available.

**Kids' Ski School Junior Ski School** is designed for kids ages 4 and 5. There's also a special half-day program for three-year-olds. Children ages 6 to 12 start their ski school lessons at the **Fanta-Ski Kingdom** at **Peaks 8 and 9. The Kinderhut Children's Ski School** at the base of Peak 9 transports little ones to the top of the teaching area via the Magic Carpet Lift. Advance reservations are required; call 800/541.8779. **The Kids' Castle,** at the base of Peak 8, offers one-stop shopping for rentals, lessons, lift tickets, and snacks.

**Clinics and Special Programs** Breckenridge conducts early season ski clinics, women's ski seminars, advanced skiing clinics, and racing clinics. Ask about the **Clinic du Jour,** designed to meet daily ski conditions. Programs are available for physically and developmentally disabled skiers (453.6422). Free guided mountain tours can be arranged.

**Races** NASTAR races are held on **Country Boy** and **Freeway** from 11AM to 3:30PM, and the two self-timer race courses are open daily on the same trails.

**Rentals** Ski and snowboard equipment rentals are available at a number of private ski shops at each of the base areas. Most shops are open daily 8AM to 8PM.

**Lockers** Coin-operated lockers are located at the base of **Peaks 8** and **9.**

**Day Care The Breckenridge Children's Centers** are located at the bases of **Peak 8** and **Peak 9.** The Peak 8 center accepts children 2 months to 1 year old. The Peak 9 center cares for children ages 3 to 5. Special combination childcare/ski programs are available for kids ages 2 to 5. Make reservations in advance.

**First Aid** Contact the ski patrol via emergency telephones on the mountain or ask any ski area employee for assistance. The **Mountain Medical Center of Breckenridge** (453.7600) is located at 130 Ski Hill Road.

**Parking** There is free parking nearby and shuttles available from parking lots to base lifts.

**Worth Knowing**

- The Breckenridge **Ski Free/Stay Free** promotion traditionally runs through January and early February. Participants receive a free night of lodging and day of skiing when paying for four or more nights' lodging and three or more days of lifts.

## Rating the Runs

### ● Beginner

Unlike some green trails that are so narrow novices must concentrate on skiing around each other as well as downhill, **Silverthorne** is wide enough so lots of beginners can share the slope with safety. Snow guns are triggered whenever the flakes fail to appear, so the ground cover here is always adequate, if not excellent.

Beginners don't like surprises, and they shouldn't find any on **Trygve's** and **Dyersville,** two well-groomed, wide slopes with even fall lines. The routes share their own lift at the base of **Peak 8,** sheltered from better skiers schussing down the upper slopes.

### ■ Intermediate

Stake your claim on **Claimjumper,** a gold mine of a run rimming the side of **Peak 8.** The nuggets include lightly gladed snowfields and views of the rugged wilderness of the **Ten Mile Range.** The trail ends near the foot of the Colorado Quad so you can restake your claim to this trail quickly.

A superhighway heading straight down the face of **Peak 10, Centennial** descends from 11,600 feet to about 9,000 feet. It's canted for intermediate cruising, without any distracting turns or bends.

### ◆ Advanced

The chilly ride up the T-bar to **Horseshoe Bowl** is offset by the panoramic vista of **Keystone Mountain** and **Ten Mile Range.** Your path down this double-diamond terrain depends on your derring-do; the cirque's pitches start at 32°. When the wind blows out of the north, it scours snow off neighboring **Peak 7** and sweeps it into this scoop.

A hellishly twisty, narrow, chutelike run, **Devil's Crotch** quickly separates serious shredders from the wannabes.

### Snowboarding

Snowboarders may use all trails and bowls, as well as the **Gold King Trail Snowboard Park,** which features a half-pipe and a terrain garden.

## Mountain Highs and Lows

Many advanced skiers are drawn to the double diamond **Mach 1, Tiger,** and **Southern Cross** because of their long-time reputations as proving grounds for the pros. But the runs, though steep and moguled, are too short to fulfill their promise. Adding to the disappointment, there's often a long wait for the aging Chair 4.

## At the Resort

*Resort facilities can be reached by calling the resort's main number (970/453.5000) unless otherwise noted.*

✦ **Bergenhof** $$ Sizzling bratwursts attract hungry skiers at lunchtime and after the lifts close. The lounge is an après-ski hot spot. ♦ Daily breakfast and lunch. Base of Peak 8.

✦ **Vista House** ★★★$$ The best of Breckenridge's on-mountain restaurants has homemade pizza that's sure to please, full bar service, and a great view of the surrounding peaks and the town of Breckenridge. Within the **Vista** is **Piz Otto's**, offering an Italian lunch buffet. ♦ Daily breakfast and lunch. Top of Colorado SuperChair.

**Restaurants/Clubs:** Red **Hotels:** Blue
**Shops/ 🌳 Outdoors:** Green **Sights/Culture:** Black

✦ **Peak 9 Restaurant** $$ An array of hot and cold sandwiches and daily specials constitutes the simple but substantial fare served here. ♦ Daily breakfast and lunch. Top of Mercury SuperChair.

✦ **Falcon's Aerie** ★$$ Weather permitting, this high-flying restaurant fires up the brazier to supplement the snacks, soups, and sandwiches on the menu. ♦ 9AM-4PM. Top of Peak 10.

✦ **Gold Strike Saloon** ★$$ Locals prefer the relative peace of this pub to the upstairs **Maggie's.** ♦ Daily lunch and dinner. Base of Quicksilver.

✦ **Maggie's Restaurant** $$ Après-ski aficionados gather at this cafeteria to do what they do best: boast and toast. ♦ Daily breakfast, lunch, and dinner. Above the Gold Strike Saloon

✦ **The Village at Breckenridge** If you're the first on the slopes and the last to leave après-ski festivities, you'll appreciate the location of this complex. Some 350 guest rooms (most of them in condominiums with up to three bedrooms) fill four mid-rise buildings that are centered around a small group of shops and restaurants. The facility has two indoor/outdoor pools, a health club, and 12 (yes, 12) hot tubs. The quality of the condominiums can delight or disappoint. ♦ 535 South Park Ave (at the base of Peak 9). 453.2000, 800/800.7829; fax 453.1878

Within The Village at Breckenridge:

**Hotel Breckenridge** $$$ Situated in a quieter area away from the mall, this hotel has 30 particularly comfortable deluxe studios. All of the rooms have been refurbished in the last two years and come with queen-size beds, full kitchens, separate sitting areas, and private balconies. Guests enjoy privileges at The Village pools, health club, and hot tubs. ♦ 453.2000, 800/800.7829

**Breckenridge Cattle Company** ★★★ $$$ The masculine ambience of this steak house—all done up in oak, brass, and glass—complements the beefy menu. The Miner's Stew, chocked with meat and vegetables, is served in a hollow sourdough loaf. ♦ Daily dinner. Reservations recommended. 453.2000

✦ **Beaver Run Resort** $$$$ Nothing has been overlooked at this sprawling slope-side property. The complex has two heated pools, seven hot tubs, an indoor miniature golf course, grocery/deli, video store, ski shop, and family-style and fine dining restaurants, not to mention its own nightclub. Skiers will happily find Peak 9's Mercury Chair right at the door. The 520 units include hotel rooms, studios, and one- to four-bedroom condos. Some of the latter are luxurious, but many of the older ones could stand some refurbishing.

♦ 620 Village Rd (on the mountain at Mercury Chair). 453.6000, 800/525.2253; fax 453.4284

Within Beaver Run Resort:

**Tiffany's** A fast-rapping deejay spins hits by the glow of faux Tiffany lamps at this prime singles' rendezvous. ♦ Daily 11AM-2AM. 453.8754

✦ **Breckenridge Hilton** $$$ A change of purpose proved fortunate for guests at this Hilton; the rooms owe their above-average dimensions to the building's condominium origins. All rooms are outfitted with coffee-makers, refrigerators, and wet bars. Other amenities include a small indoor pool, exercise room, restaurant, and lounge. Children of all ages stay free in their parents' room. ♦ 550 Village Rd (at the base of Peak 9). 453.4500, 800/321.8444; fax 453.0212

## Beyond the Resorts

**1 Ski Tip Lodge** $$ Set on a wooded mountainside a few miles from **Keystone**'s slopes, this lodge recalls the classic style favored during the sport's by-gone days. Completing the old-time aura are the 19 antiques-filled guest rooms, authentically lacking phones or TVs. Some share a bath. Rough plaster walls, a stone hearth replete with roaring fire, and timbered ceiling round out the alpine ambience. ♦ From Hwy 6 heading towards Arapahoe Basin, turn right on Keystone Rd, then left on Montezuma Rd. Look for the sign. 468.4130, 800/222.0188; fax 468.4343

Within Ski Tip Lodge:

**Ski Tip Lodge Restaurant** ★★★★$$$ Quaint and cozy, the restaurant extends the alpine theme with its dark timber beams, thick wood tables, and huge stone fireplace. Reminiscent of its roots as a wooden-ski maker, all door handles are made from original ski tips. Fixed-price meals feature American cuisine accompanied by fine wines. A perennial favorite with visitors, priority seating is given to lodge guests, so the remaining tables are booked far in advance. There are two seatings for the elaborate four-course dinner. The menu changes nightly but always includes poultry, fish, and beef or game selections; two favorites are the loin of lamb with potatoes and the roast split duckling in a berry glaze. ♦ M-Sa breakfast, lunch, and dinner; Su brunch and dinner. Reservations required. 468.4130

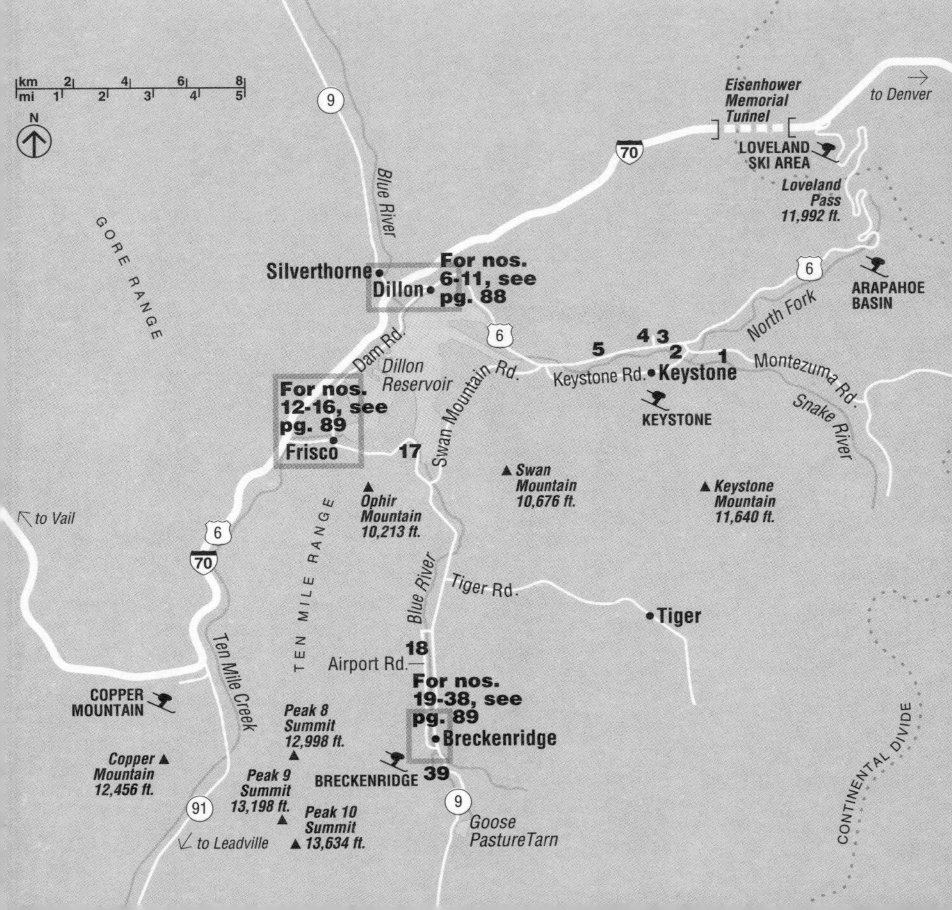

**2 Snake River Saloon** ★★★$$$ Behind this ramshackle facade lurks an accomplished kitchen, popular with discerning locals. A rustic atmosphere is enhanced with white linen tablecloths, a circular copper bar, and red-brick fireplace. Arrive for sunset to view the rays streaming through the spectacular stained-glass window; plenty of plate glass windows line the other walls. The eclectic menu includes dry-aged Kansas City sirloin, Cajun smoked chicken, and Alaskan king crab. Live music in the lounge attracts a toe-tapping crowd. ♦ Daily dinner. Hwy 6, about a mile east of Keystone Lodge. 468.2788

**3 Bandito's** ★★$ At Happy Hour, bartenders ladle out frozen margaritas and scorpions from steel vats to the boisterous crowd. Mexican food is also served. ♦ Daily lunch and dinner. Hwy 6 (in Mountain View Plaza), Keystone. 468.0404

**4 Sts. John** $$$ These spacious studios and one- to three-bedroom condos, all with fireplaces, also come with multiple mountain views: **Keystone,** the Continental Divide, and a fraction of the Gore Range are framed by large windows. On the shuttle bus route, the 60-unit complex has a Jacuzzi and underground parking. ♦ Sts. John Rd (at Hwy 6). 800/222.0188; fax 468.4343

**5 Keystone Grocery** While convenient for skiers staying at the resort, serious shoppers will find the stock limited and items generally more expensive than at the **City Market** (see page 89). ♦ Daily 7AM-7PM. 21799 Hwy 6 (near Keystone Rd). 468.1102

**6 Lake Dillon Resort Association** This office runs **Summit County Central Reservations,** a rental service for a wide range of lodging in the vicinity. ♦ 121 Dillon Mall, Suite No. 102 (across from Snow Bank), Dillon. 800/365.6365

**7 Spinnaker at Lake Dillon** $$$ Request one of the units overlooking Lake Dillon. An excellent value, each of these 30 posh condos has a washer/dryer, fireplace, and patio or balcony. Sheltered parking, a hot tub, sauna, and indoor pool are other niceties. ♦ 317 La Bonte St (between Buffalo St and Lake Dillon Dr), Dillon. 468.8001; fax 262.5786

**8 Arapahoe Cafe and Pub** ★★★$$ The Guacabacachezzaburgah (which includes what the name implies) is a major mouthful, and not just to those hooked on phonics. This historic log cabin's time-worn **Pub Down Under** and the candle-lit tables upstairs share the same home-style menu. ♦ Daily breakfast, lunch, and dinner. 626 Lake Dillon Dr (at La Bonte St), Dillon. 468.0873

**9 Sunshine Cafe** ★★$$ Moderately priced, healthy food is the bill of fare at this pleasant, nonsmoking cafe. Choose from three kinds of hearty chili at lunchtime. Dinner often features such seafood specials as Cajun catfish. ♦ Daily breakfast, lunch, and dinner. Summit Place Shopping Center, off I-70, Silverthorne. 468.6663

BLUE MOON

**9 Blue Moon Baking Company** ★★★$ At breakfast, the irresistible aroma of freshly ground coffee and baked goods sweetens the air of this small space. Such creative lunch dishes as red pepper linguine with shrimp and scallops are equally appealing. ♦ Daily breakfast and lunch. Summit Place Shopping Center, off I-70, Silverthorne. 468.1472

**9 Nick-N-Willy's Take-N-Bake Pizza** ★★$ Unusual pizza combinations are the order of the day here. The Rio Grande, layered with chilis, refried beans, and salsa, is delicious, and the vegetarian Earthbone's Delight is unsurpassed. You can buy pizza by the slice to eat on the premises, but you have to take whole pies home to bake. ♦ Daily lunch and dinner. Summit Place Shopping Center, off I-70, Silverthorne. 262.1111

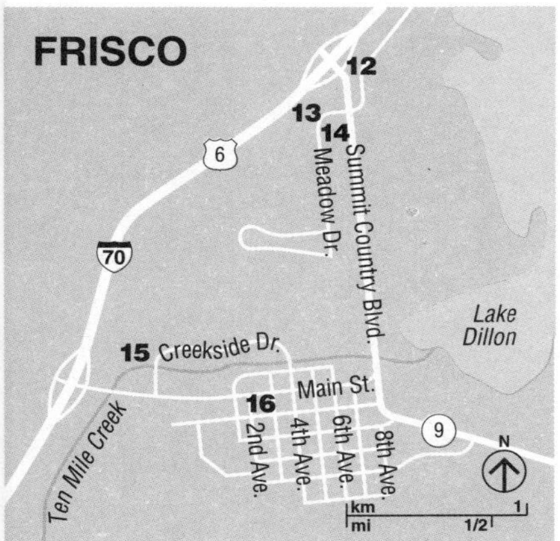


**9 City Market** This large, full-service grocery store is open around-the-clock. ♦ Daily 24 hours. Summit Place Shopping Center, off I-70, Silverthorne. 468.2363

**10 Silverthorne Factory Stores** More than 50 discount outlets for manufacturers of shoes, clothing, luggage, and sporting goods are clustered at this mall, with prices guaranteed to turn browsers into buyers. Among the names you'll recognize are **Anne Klein, American Tourister, Capezio, Bass Shoes, Gitano, Leather Loft,** and **Nike.** ♦ M-Sa 9AM-9PM; Su 10AM-6PM. 145 Stephens Way, off I-70 Exit 205, Silverthorne. 468.9440

**11 Old Dillon Inn** ★★★$$ Natives and newcomers alike are so attached to this weathered restaurant that a pre-dinner wait at the bar is almost assured. As popular as the terrific Mexican food is the country-and-western music and dancing on weekends. ♦ Daily dinner. 311 Blue River Pkwy (near Silver La), Silverthorne. 468.2791

**12 Holiday Inn** $$ Romantics book the honeymoon suite for its private hot tub, but all vacationers will love the hotel's central location, convenient to all four of the county's resorts. The 216 rooms allow a choice of king- or queen-size beds. Kids are kept busy when off the slopes in the Holidrome's indoor pool, Jacuzzi, and sauna. A restaurant serving basic American and Mexican fare—including surf and turf, burgers, and nachos—satisfies hungry skiers after a day on the slopes. ♦ I-70 Exit 203 (just off the exit), Frisco. 800/782.7669; fax 668.0718

**13 Best Western Lake Dillon Lodge** $$ Families will appreciate the extra space in some of the larger rooms, which feature three double beds. The 127-unit hotel has an informal dining room, cocktail lounge, small indoor swimming pool, and hot tub. ♦ I-70 Exit 203 (just off the exit), Frisco. 800/727.0607; fax 668.0571

**14 Safeway** Stock up the larder at any hour in this supermarket. ♦ Daily 24 hours. 1008 Summit Country Blvd (near Meadow Dr), Frisco. 668.5144

**15 Cross Creek** $$$ If high quality and low prices mean more to you than a location at the base of the lifts, book a condo at this resort. Most of the 25 two- and three-bedroom units are outfitted in oak trim and cabinetry, with river rock fireplaces, whirlpool tubs, and attached garages. Some two-level homes have private balconies overlooking **Ten Mile Creek.** Basic workout amenities (including a pool and sauna) are found at the clubhouse. ♦ 223 Creekside Dr (near Main St), Frisco. 668.5175, 800/365.6365; fax 668.3479

**16 Twilight Inn** $$ A wood-burning stove warms the air and the ambience at this easy-going bed-and-breakfast inn, where guests chill their own wine in the kitchen refrigerator and trade slope secrets in the ski-tuning room or hot tub. Eight rooms have private baths, and four bunk-bed rooms on the third floor share bathrooms. Owners Jane Harrington and Rich Ahlquist, a former ski instructor who has lived in Summit County for 30 years, are fonts of insider knowledge. Dogs are allowed. The neighboring **Daily Planet Bookstore** is handy for visitors who crave *The New York Times.* ♦ 308 Main St (between Third and Second Aves), Frisco. 668.5009, 800/262.1002; fax 668.0561

**17 Summit Adventure Park** Younger and older thrill-seekers can bounce and skitter their way downhill on inner tubes at this amusement area. The park also offers more passive activities, such as snowmobile tours, sleigh rides, and dogsled treks. ♦ Daily 8AM-4PM. Hwy 9, 4 miles east of Frisco. 453.0353, 800/253.0723

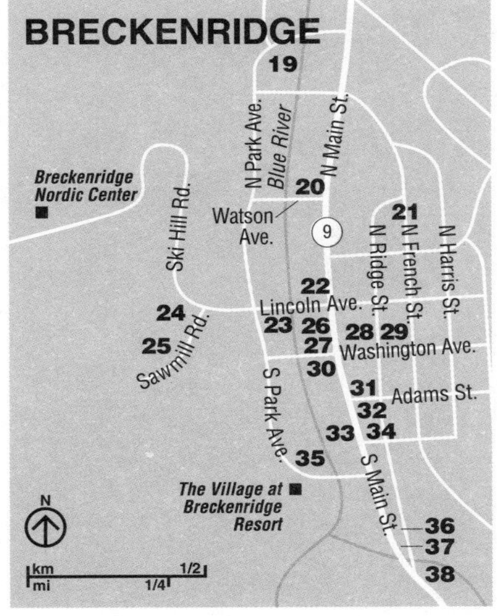

**18 Breckenridge Recreational Center** Ready to reverse your downhill slide and *climb* mountains? Put on your spikes and start scaling the indoor rock wall, while your kids expend their energy zipping down the giant water slide. The center has a weight room, aerobics classes, and much more. Childcare is available. ♦ M-F 6AM-10PM; Sa-Su 8AM-10PM. 880 Airport Rd (off Hwy 9). 453.1734

**19 City Market** This large grocery store is located at the north end of town. ♦ Daily 6AM-midnight. Closed Christmas Day. 400 N Park Ave (near N French St), Breckenridge. 453.0818

**20 Williams House B&B** $$$ Furnishings from the days when gold fever raged fill this cozy 1885 home. The four bedrooms, each with a bath, are snug little chambers. Hearty breakfasts and afternoon snacks are served in the parlor. ♦ 303 N Main St (near Watson Ave), Breckenridge. 453.2975

**20 The Near Gnu** Check the great deals on the racks at this second-hand shop before investing in a new winter wardrobe. Most of the clothing is in very good to excellent condition. ♦ Daily 9:30AM-5PM. 301 N Main St (at Watson Ave), Breckenridge. 453.6026

**21 The Brown Hotel and Restaurant** $$$ "The Brown" started life as a private home, and dining here still has an intimate, personal quality. Regional and continental fare is served fireside or in small dining rooms in this 1860s Victorian restaurant. ♦ Daily dinner. 208 N Ridge St (near N French St), Breckenridge. 453.0084

**22 The Gold Pan Saloon** ★★$ Opened in 1881, this tavern is still going strong, making it the oldest continuously operating bar west of the Mississippi. Skiers show up for plate-filling apple and spice pancakes in the morning and Baldy Mountain burritos at lunch. At night, barflies buzz around the pool table. ♦ Daily breakfast and lunch. 103 N Main St (near Lincoln Ave), Breckenridge. 453.5499

**23 River Mountain Lodge** $$$ The prime location of this lodge combined with current renovations, including the addition of east and west wings, make this an ideal choice. Some of the 90-plus studios and one-bedroom units have fireplaces. Guests vie for the cushy leather chairs around the copper fireplace in the bar. ♦ 100 S Park Ave (across the street from the Four O'Clock run), Breckenridge. 453.4711, 800/553.4456 (in Colorado), 800/325.2342 (in the US); fax 453.1763

**24 Breckenridge Park Meadows Lodge** $ Folks putting budget before beauty will appreciate this 30-room lodge of studios and one-bedroom units with accompanying kitchenettes. Each one-bedroom unit features either a sofa bed or a trundle bed in the living room. You can ski to within a few hundred yards of the lodge on the Four O'Clock run, but you'll have to rely on a shuttle to reach the base lifts. ♦ 110 Sawmill Rd (at Ski Hill Rd), Breckenridge. 453.2414, 800/344.7669; fax 453.8301

**25 Wildwood Suites** $$$ Although you can ski into the Four O'Clock run and the hubbub of Main Street is just two blocks away, the 20 river-view suites have a secluded feeling, their tranquillity enhanced by the natural wood and soft hues of the interiors. To maintain this mood, opt for an upstairs unit—unless you don't mind the clump of ski boots overhead. The hot tub is set down by the river under tall pines. Continental breakfast is included in the tariff at this 36-suite establishment. There is no restaurant on the premises. ♦ 120 Sawmill Rd (off Ski Hill Rd), Breckenridge. 453.0232, 800/866.0300; fax 453.7325

Breckenridge hosts two summer symphony groups: the National Repertory Orchestra and the Breckenridge Music Institute.

**Restaurants/Clubs:** Red **Hotels:** Blue
**Shops/ Outdoors:** Green **Sights/Culture:** Black

**26 Eric's Underworld** Bands literally rock this brick-walled basement club, where dancers are eerily framed by a nocturnal cityscape mural. Across the courtyard, **Downstairs at Eric's** (★$$) purveys pizza and beer. ♦ Daily 9PM-2AM. 109 S Main St (between Washington and Lincoln Aves), Breckenridge. 453.8559

**27 Pierre's Restaurant** ★★★$$$$ Patrons are faced with a pleasant choice between two dining areas: a greenhouse room overlooking the picturesque Breckenridge skyline or a more intimate, formal setting with fresh flowers gracing the tables. Some rave about Pierre's French and American nouvelle cuisine; others are less enthusiastic. Try the open ravioli with shrimp and scallops in a pesto sauce or loin of veal sautéed with diced tomatoes and fresh basil. ♦ Daily dinner. Reservations recommended. 111 S Main St (between Washington and Lincoln Aves), Breckenridge. 453.0989

**28 Shamus O'Toole's Roadhouse Saloon** Locals claim the best time to come here is when Shamus himself is in attendance. Play darts, shoot some pool, or just belly up to the bar and let the owner—who built this historic-looking saloon 20 years ago—charm you with tales of his Irish ancestors. The kitchen serves up burgers, sandwiches, and light pub grub. If you're in Breckenridge during St. Patrick's Day, don't miss the pub crawl, which starts and ends here. ♦ Daily 11AM-2AM. 115 S Ridge St (between Washington and Lincoln Aves), Breckenridge. 453.2004

**29 Hearthstone Inn** ★★★$$$ The former home of **Andrea's Pleasure Palace,** this popular restaurant now pleases the palates of a more refined clientele. An intimate, Victorian atmosphere is created with white lace curtains, walls of maroon and gold, and flickering candlelight. The eager waiters may suggest the jalapeño-wrapped shrimp stuffed with cream cheese (have a cool brew at the ready if you accept). Other inventive specialties include the lamb tenderloin rolled in roasted garlic and fresh rosemary and a sinfully rich Snickers bar pie. ♦ Daily dinner. Reservations recommended. 130 S Ridge St (between Washington and Lincoln Aves), Breckenridge. 453.1148

**30 Breckenridge Activity Center** The helpful staff can book a plethora of pursuits, from sleigh rides and heli-skiing to gambling excursions to **Central City,** which is about 1.5 hours by bus from Breckenridge. Central City is one of three places in the state where gambling is legal (the others are Black Hawk and Cripple Creek). ♦ Daily 9AM-5PM. 201 S Main St (at Washington Ave), Breckenridge. 453.5579

**31 Poirrier's Cajun Café** ★★★$$ Short on ambience but long on authentic Cajun and Creole dishes, this cafe regularly wins a "Taste of Breckenridge" award. ♦ Daily lunch and dinner. 224 S Main St (between Adams St and Washington Ave), Breckenridge. 453.1877

**32 Kinkopf Gallery** This gallery has an intriguing display of fine art and crafts, with one-of-a-kind furnishings, jewelry, sculpture, and more made by talented Western and Midwestern designers. ♦ Daily 10AM-6PM. 320 S Main St (between S Park Ave and Adams St), Breckenridge. 453.9095

**33 Flying Colors Too** The creators of these hand-sewn kites and flags are indisputably young at heart. A zoological spectrum soars overhead, where angelfish kites keep company with parrots and unicorns. One banner depicts a technicolor trout leaping to grab a lure; another shows a multihued hummingbird feeding from a flower. Kite classes can help keep your purchase flying high in the sky. ♦ Daily 9AM-7:30PM. 311 S Main St (between S Park Ave and Adams St), Breckenridge. 453.1644

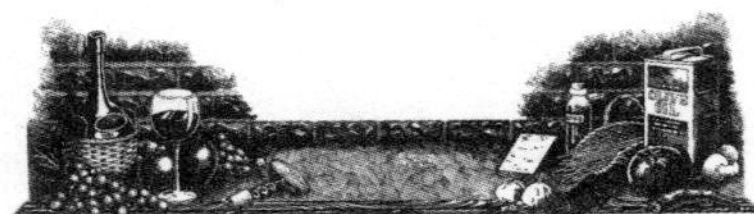

34 **Pasta Jay's** ★★★★$$ Robust pastas, pizzas, and Italian specialties attract a loyal following to this family-friendly restaurant. Expect to wait for a table, but the shops on Main Street provide an interesting diversion until you're seated. Loaded with toppings, the Roman Orgy pizza encourages eating to excess. ♦ Daily lunch and dinner. 326 S Main St (between S Park Ave and Adams St), Breckenridge. 453.5800

35 **JohSha's** Long Happy Hours and $1.50 pints, plus a changing list of drink specials, lure shoulder-to-shoulder crowds who dance to cutting-edge bands such as Zulu Spear and Savoy Truffle. **Nacho Taco,** the bar's restaurant, serves lunch and dinner daily, with a menu that features American cuisine (plus nachos, of course). ♦ Daily noon-2AM. 500 S Park Ave (near Village Rd), Breckenridge. 453.4146

36 **Blue Moose Restaurant** ★★★★$ At first glance, the peeling Formica tables and nonchalant clientele may not be a harbinger of culinary accomplishment, but this eatery turns out some of the tastiest healthy food in town. *Yakisoba* (fresh vegetables and soba noodles in Indonesian peanut sauce) and chicken breasts marinated in tequila and lime juice are but two items from the eclectic menu. ♦ Daily breakfast, lunch, and dinner. 540 S Main St (near S Ridge St), Breckenridge. 453.4859

37 **Breckenridge Brewery & Pub** ★★★$$ This bi-level brewpub produces ales and lagers that appeal to hip hopsters with sophisticated tastes. Fermenting tanks of sweet amber Avalanche and rich Oatmeal Stout give a chic industrial overtone to the scene. ♦ Daily lunch and dinner. 610 S Main St (near S Ridge St), Breckenridge. 453.1550

Breckenridge Mountain Lodge

38 **Breckenridge Mountain Lodge** $ Legions of Europeans stay here, enthralled by the frontier atmosphere (lodgepole pine construction, antler chandeliers in the firelit lobby, hunting trophies on the wall). Too bad the 71 guest rooms are a dreary testament to modern times. Extras include a bar, restaurant, pool, and hot tubs. ♦ 600 S Ridge St (at S Main St), Breckenridge. 453.2333, 800/525.2224; fax 453.5426

39 **Allaire Timbers Inn** $$$$ This stunning log-and-stone cabin (pictured above) has 10 uniquely styled guest rooms; two luxury suites feature cathedral ceilings, river rock fireplaces, and Jacuzzi tubs. Though there's no restaurant in the hotel, a two-story great room serves as the inn's social focal point, where breakfast and après-ski snacks are laid out. While close to downtown, the lodge is situated so most windows are filled with tall pines and mountain views. Children 12 years and under are not allowed. ♦ 9511 Hwy 9 (first right after Boreas Pass Rd). 453.7530, 800/624.4904; fax 453.8699

Summit County is in the upper reaches of the Rockies, and altitude sickness affects many visitors. Symptoms may include headaches, dizziness, fatigue, dryness of mouth, and shortness of breath. You can alleviate the symptoms by limiting physical activity the first few days of your visit, drinking plenty of water, and limiting alcohol and caffeine consumption. If symptoms persist or become severe, consult a doctor.

**Restaurants/Clubs:** Red **Hotels:** Blue
**Shops/ Outdoors:** Green **Sights/Culture:** Black

## Bests

### Max and Edna Dercum

Co-owners, Ski Tip Ranch/Retired ski instructors

**The High Country**—a beautiful mixture of sage-covered hills, aspen groves, lodgepole pine and spruce forests, rolling tundra, and snow-filled glaciated cirques. Careful observers may spot wildlife such as fox, coyote, puma, bobcat, black bear, pine marten, weasel, badger, porcupine, mule deer, elk, or even a moose.

**Schoolmarm** trail, at 3.25 miles, is one of the country's best for learning.

### Rachel Flood

Public Relations Coordinator, Breckenridge Ski Area

In Summit County:

Après-ski at the **Hearthstone Inn** for the 50¢ jalapeño-stuffed shrimp and drink specials.

Music by Jim Salestrom at **Breck's Lounge** in the Breckenridge Hilton.

Music by Mo Dixon at **Tiffany's** in the **Beaver Run Resort.**

Favorite night spots—**Downstairs at Eric's, Shamus O'Toole's Roadhouse Saloon,** and **JohSha's.**

My favorite place to ski, especially on a powder day, is anywhere off the T-bar on **Peak 8,** usually **Horseshoe Bowl** or the **North Bowl.**

The **Breckenridge Brewery,** a favorite local hangout, brews its own "real beer." It's great anytime, especially after a 5K- or 10K-road race.

Historical snowmobile tour in the mountains.

Mountain biking anywhere.

### Scott Rawles

Professional Skier/Coach, Team Breckenridge

The **Mach I** on a spring day, with slushy moguls flying in your face from the top of the run to the bottom—a little slice of heaven.

**Ullr Fest World Cup Freestyle** celebrates the God of Snow and the best skiers in the world. The **Ullr Parade** must be seen to be believed, from political comment to some of the coldest skiing anywhere.

**Shamus O'Toole's St. Patrick's Day** pub crawl through numerous Breckenridge watering holes. Green beer, green attire, green scene.

The **Palivacinni** ski run at **Arapahoe Basin**—1,300 vertical feet of thumping, bumping, bone-rattling skiing. "Spacin' at the Basin" is where it's at.

**Loveland Pass**—Skiing on top of the world and into the great wide open. Bring your dog.

### C.J. Mueller

Speed Skier/Member of the 1992 Olympic Team

In Summit County:

Summit County skiing—Nothing else matters; skiing is why we're here.

Skiing with lifts (and great snow) from October through June. Then hiking to remote snowfields in July, August, and September.

Skiing in blizzard conditions (bring a good hat and double-lens goggles).

Driving from Frisco to Breckenridge on a moonlit night in spring, looking at the peaks.

Best skiing? **Peak 10** in the fall; **Peak 8** in the winter; **Arapahoe Basin** in late spring; **Copper Mountain** in early spring.

Hiking to the top of **Peak 8** (12,988 feet high), looking at the view, then making a hundred turns down the **Imperial** run.

Wherever I ski, I particularly enjoy being on the first chairlift of the day to see the mountain when it's not covered with skiers.

Lunch at the Peak 9 Restaurant; they serve great pastries.

Dinner at **Poirrier's Cajun Café** or the **Hearthstone Inn.**

Getting wild at night at **JohSha's** or **Eric's Underworld.**

Hanging out anytime at **Shamus O'Toole's Roadhouse Saloon,** especially when Shamus is there.

# Beaver Creek

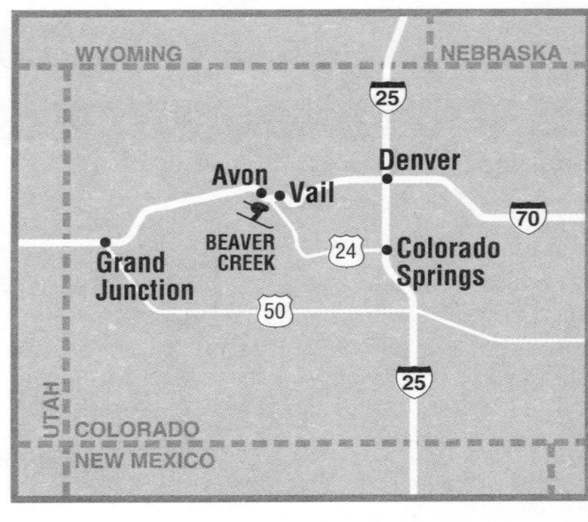


Don't let Beaver Creek's multimillion-dollar homes and air of exclusivity fool you: The slopes are decidedly democratic. Anchoring the western end of the **Vail Valley**, this resort is blessed with terrain that will please novices and experts alike, thanks in part to a little high-tech help. The runs were completely mapped out on a computer before a single tree was felled, resulting in trails that follow the natural fall lines with a maximum width of 200 yards, minimizing the effect on deer and elk migrations. (A first at the time, in 1980, the method has since been widely adopted by other ski resorts.) Liberated from their customary base-level lot, beginners can head straight to the summit, where they learn on a playground surrounded by the pinnacles of the **Gore** and **New York** ranges. Blue runs flow around islands of trees in ecologically sensitive arrangements; on **Grouse Mountain**, Beaver Creek's second peak, the black paths give new meaning to "upper crust"; and, in appropriately lofty fashion, nordic trails wend their way around the top of the resort, bestowing cross-country skiers with rare, far-reaching views.

Away from the powder, Beaver Creek's restaurants and clubs have a more formal feel than those in the surrounding area, and après-ski preferences run to polished piano lounges rather than sawdust-strewn saloons. Accommodations include luxury resorts and cabins decked out in southwestern style, but budget-friendly motels and condos can be found beyond the "high-rent" district.

**Beaver Creek Resort**
**PO Box 915**
**Avon, Colorado 81620**

**Information**........................................970/949.5750
**Reservations**......................................800/622.3131
**Snow Phone**........................................970/476.4888

## Fast Facts

*Area code 970 unless otherwise noted.*

**Ski Season** Mid-November to mid-April

**Location** Beaver Creek is 10 miles west of **Vail** and 110 miles west of **Denver.**

### Getting to Beaver Creek

See "Getting to Vail," page 98.

### Getting around Beaver Creek

**Dial-A-Ride** (949.1938) is a free, on-demand shuttle for guests of the Beaver Creek Resort. **Avon Beaver Creek Transit** (949.6121) provides bus service between **Vail** and Beaver Creek.

## FYI

**Area** 1,125 acres with 61 marked runs.

Beginner—18 percent

Intermediate—39 percent

Advanced—22 percent

Expert—21 percent

**Number of Groomed Runs** Approximately 16

**Longest Run** 2.75 miles **(Centennial)**

**Capacity** 17,228 skiers per hour

**Base Elevation** 8,100 feet

**Summit Elevation** 11,440 feet

**Vertical Rise** 3,340 feet

**Average Annual Snowfall** 330 inches

**Snowmaking** 37 percent

**Night Skiing** None

**Lifts** 10 (3 quads and 7 double chairs)

| **Lift Passes** | **Full Day** | **Half Day** (starts at noon) |
|---|---|---|
| **Adult** | $46 | $39 |
| **Child** (12 and under) | $33 | $28 |
| **Senior** (65-69) | $37 | $36 |
| **Senior** (70 and over) | Free | Free |

Lift passes may be used both at Beaver Creek and **Vail.**

**Ski School** The **Vail and Beaver Creek Ski School** (476.3239) runs the operations at both ski areas. In Beaver Creek, the ski school is located at **Village Hall** in the base area and at the midmountain **Spruce Saddle** lodge. The teaching system is the same nine-level program found at Vail. Levels 1 to 4 are introductory, 5 to 7 are intermediate, and 8 to 9 promote advanced skills. The ski school offers all-day and half-day alpine lessons, private lessons, and many special programs.

**Kids' Ski School Children's Skiing Center** (845.5464) is located at the **Village Hall,** and it opens daily at 8AM. At this ski area, kids learn skills as they chase outlaws through **Tombstone Territory,** a specially created adventure zone on the mountain. (Children even have their own "Adventure Zone" trail map.) **Mogul Mice,** for children ages 4 to 6 who can't yet stop on their skis, includes lessons and lunch. **Super Stars** is for youngsters in the same age group who can ski around the mountain. Teen guides lead groups scheduled during peak weeks, when **Bump and Bash** and **Freestyle** camps are scheduled. Après-ski teen activities include picnics, snowshoeing, and broomball.

**Clinics and Special Programs Building Blocks Workshops** are designed to improve basic ski skills. Technique seminars help master style, bumps, and terrain conditions. **Technique Weeks for Women** is a program taught by and for women. Super Guides uses a coaching approach for expert skiers. A program for disabled skiers is also available.

**Races** Both NASTAR and pay-to-race programs are held on Bear Trap.

**Rentals** New equipment is purchased yearly at **Beaver Creek Sports** (949.2310), and standard equipment is usually new to one year old. Hours are 8AM to 8PM daily and reservations are suggested.

**Lockers** Coin-operated lockers (quarters or tokens) are located at the base in the Village Hall. The Ski Corral at the base of the Centennial Lift offers overnight ski storage.

**Day Care Small World** (845.5325), for nonskiers, is located creekside below the **Activities Desk** on **Beaver Creek Mall.** Open from 8AM to 4:30PM, Small World accepts children ages 2 months through 6 years. Reservations are required.

Tuesday's "Kid's Night Out Goes Western" is a dinner theater for children in kindergarten through sixth grade. "Kid's Night Out Goes Hollywood" is a pizza and movie evening for 10- to 14-year-olds, scheduled frequently during Christmas and spring vacations. Beaver Creek shares a series of children-only and family evening entertainment with Vail.

**Worth Knowing**

- Free "Meet the Mountain" tours are offered on Monday and Wednesday beginning at **Spruce Saddle.**
- The **Premier Passport** is designed for skiers who want to ski Beaver Creek, **Vail,** and the four **Aspen** properties, and can stay for two weeks or longer. This joint pass includes a one-way ground transfer among the six resorts and offers a minimum 10- out of 12-day lift ticket and a maximum 18- out of 21-day lift ticket.

**First Aid** To reach the ski patrol, dial 6111 from any mountain phone. The **Beaver Creek Village Medical Center** (949.0800) is located in **Strawberry Park,** 1280 Village Road, on the third floor.

**Parking** Free parking lots are located at the entrance to Beaver Creek resort, just off Interstate 70's Avon exit. A free shuttle takes skiers to the base of the lifts. Paid parking is available under the **Village Hall.**

## Rating the Runs

### ● Beginner

At most ski areas, beginners are herded together at the base and progress uphill only as they become more proficient. But at Beaver Creek, they own a section of the summit and its jaw-dropping views of the **Gore Range, Vail Mountain,** and the **Flat Tops Wilderness. Sheephorn** narrows and winds through groves of spruce, with gentle drop-offs adding some texture to the trail. The start for the **World Alpine Championship** is on this course.

A top-to-bottom run promising novices sweeping vistas, **Flat Tops** is followed by a variety of diversions on **Cinch,** the long, easy catwalk that slaloms across steeper slopes.

### ■ Intermediate

Named after the flowers that bloom on this slope in the spring, **Larkspur** is a natural east-facing bowl. Wide swaths of bumps alternate with groomed sections, allowing skiers of varying abilities to share the same chairlift, but head downhill on individually challenging terrain.

A flight down **Raven Ridge** gives advanced intermediates a bird's-eye preview of what to expect on the steeper slopes on **Grouse Mountain.** The run, which begins near the summit, widens as it follows a natural fall line. Primarily an advanced and expert area, Grouse Mountain is accessed via a high-speed lift that you rarely have to wait for.

Slated to be the site of the men's downhill competition when Colorado was a contender to host the **1976 Winter Olympic Games, Centennial** was ultimately nixed by voters. But this run's pitch still promotes ever-faster cruising down its flawless fall line. Try the bottom blue half of the run first; then, if you're comfortable—and feeling gutsy—add the upper portion with its black-diamond cant.

### ◆ Advanced

The **Rose Bowl** trio of **Ripsaw, Spider,** and **Web** can be either sharp-edged or silky smooth, depending upon the size and shape of the moguls.

Soar with the best over the **Birds of Prey** runs. You might go airborne off of **Golden Eagle**'s monster moguls when the path is in its prime.

### ◆◆ Expert

On one of the steepest faces at the resort, **Screech Owl** falls off the top of **Grouse Mountain** at several access points and nestles into a narrow valley. Swooping between the walls, skiers must choose their strategy quickly: tree-weaving or bump-bashing.

Gliding through **Goshawk Glade** is a high for truly expert skiers on the hunt for untracked powder days after a storm. The trees are tight up top, but the chutes widen—albeit only a tad—lower down. When the glade is open, the entrance is reached via a short traverse near the top of Chair 8.

### Snowboarding

Home of the **Brian Delaney Snowboard School**—named after the US and Australian snowboarding champion—Beaver Creek attracts a great number of snowboarders. The gentle, wide-open terrain make the mountain a natural for beginners.

## Mountain Highs and Lows

Though rated intermediate, **Stone Creek Meadows** is so gentle that lots of kiddie and beginner classes ski it.

The fall line of **Red Tail** is true blue, but some of the pitches have an uncanny resemblance to those on the black **Birds of Prey** runs. If there were a blue-black category here, this trail would set the standard.

Too many skiers try to fly down the moguled face of **Peregrine,** a tough advanced/expert trail. If you want to soar without an overhead audience (it's under a lift), and on less battered slopes, take to the runs on either side.

## At the Resort

*Area code 970 unless otherwise noted.*

✦ **Beano's Cabin** ★★★★$$$$ At lunchtime, this upscale eatery is open only to members of the elite Beaver Creek Club; however, in the evening its six-course fixed-price dinner can be enjoyed by anyone. The cuisine is gourmet American, and diners have the choice of pasta, fresh fish, meat, and vegetarian entrées. The starlit snowcat ride to the top of Beaver Creek is just the start of a special evening. Ask the host to tell you the fascinating history of mountain man Beano and his original 1919 homestead, the ruins of which are nearby. ♦ Daily dinner. Reservations required. Top of Beaver Creek Mountain. 949.9090

✦ **McCoy's Bar and Restaurant** $$ Grab a quick full breakfast or bomb down for lunch at this efficient cafeteria. Stop by after the lifts close if you enjoy acoustic music and sing-alongs. ♦ Daily breakfast and lunch. Base of Beaver Creek. 845.7808

✦ **Spruce Saddle** This huge, contemporary lodge offers midmountain views and decent fare at the **Spruce Saddle Cafeteria.** ♦ Daily breakfast and lunch. Top of Centennial Express. 949.5740

Within Spruce Saddle:

**Rafters** ★★$$$ A la Italy, the entrées at this ristorante come with a bracing glass of grappa, port, or cognac—great if you're ready to let the chairlift carry you back downhill. The Sunday Champagne brunch is always a sellout. ♦ M-Sa lunch; Sunday brunch. Reservations recommended. 845.5528

✦ **Red Tail Camp** $$ A good stop for a quick bite any day, this base camp is also great for barbecue when it's warm outside. Try the bratwurst or buffalo burgers, too. The terrace is sited for maximum sun exposure, making it a real party spot in the spring. ♦ Daily lunch. Base of Lifts 9, 10, and 11. 949.5750

✦ **Trappers Cabin** $$$$ The ultimate indulgence may be a stay at this three-bedroom log cabin perched on a secluded mountainside. Guests can ski in or take a chairlift to a snowcat taxi. On arrival, an open bar and exotic hors d'oeuvres (rattlesnake strips, anyone?) are waiting by the fire. Dinner depends upon your whims, but could include elk steaks with bourbon mushroom sauce or baby pheasant stuffed with herbs and white wine. Take binoculars when you soak in the outdoor hot tub to view the elk and deer grazing nearby and the Flat Tops Wilderness and Castle Peak in the distance. The cabinkeeper/chef heads downhill for the night, leaving guests to amuse themselves with the player piano and a bevy of board games, and returns in the morning to prepare breakfast. ♦ Reservations required. Near the top of the Strawberry Park Lift. 845.7900

✦ **Hyatt Regency Beaver Creek** $$$$ Although this Hyatt has 300 rooms, it has the warmth of a cozy inn, from the country French decor to the personal attention guests receive. The executive rooms feature seating areas and fireplaces, but what sets this hotel apart are the trend-setting programs designed for guests. **Rock Hyatt** entertains the teenage set, and for youngsters, **Camp Hyatt** goes far beyond ordinary day care. Kids go on scavenger hunts, bake cookies, do kiddie aerobics, and in the evening enjoy s'mores and stories by the fire. Packages tailored toward single adults and solo parents are also available. A pair of fine restaurants, a deli, and—a most civilized touch—a library round out the amenities. Ask about spa treatments and skiing with a pro. ♦ 136 E Thomas Pl (off Offerson Rd). 949.1234, 800/233.1234; fax 949.4164

Within the Hyatt Regency Beaver Creek:

**Crooked Hearth Tavern** ★★$$ Thirsty skiers can select from more than 60 domestic and imported beers at this convivial restaurant and watering hole, which does indeed have a curiously crooked hearth. At noon, you can bask under heat lamps at the terrace tables before or after the meal. Come dinner, sit down to a steak dinner cooked the way you like it. ♦ Daily lunch and dinner. Reservations recommended. 949.1234

**Double Diamond Deli** ★$ The lighter fare served here—pasta salads, sandwiches, and such—won't weigh you down on the slopes. ♦ Daily breakfast, lunch, and dinner. 949.1234

✦ **The Pines Lodge** $$$ Comfy, oversize couches greet guests as they enter the lobby of this 60-room lodge nestled away from the heart of Beaver Creek in a more private location atop the valley. It's the small touches that count, like twice-daily maid service, morning coffee, complimentary newspapers, and afternoon tea. All the guest rooms are spacious and tastefully decorated with antiquelike pine pieces and bright floral curtains billowing over big, open windows. The on-premises **Grouse Mountain Grill** offers an elegant atmosphere and exotic dishes like free-range fowl and game and nightly fresh fish selections such as Chilean sea bass. ♦ 141 Scott Hill Rd (off Village Rd). 845.7900; fax 845.7809

✦ **The Charter** $$$ Doors with leaded glass windows and lots of natural woods lend a Tudor touch to the 156 luxurious one- to five-bedroom condos at this comfortable complex. Daily maid service and a 24-hour valet free visitors from vacation household chores. A fitness center and swimming pool complete the perks. ♦ 120 Offerson Rd (off Village Rd). 800/525.6660; fax 949.6709

✦ **Beaver Creek Lodge** $$$ If cramped quarters stunt your style, check into the 73 units at this all-suites hotel. The snug living rooms have a fireplace and a queen-size sofa bed, and are separated from the bedroom by a door; the kitchenettes come with a microwave and coffeemaker. Two televisions and a VCR should keep the kids occupied (those 12 and younger stay free with their parents) when they're not charging down the nearby slopes. Other amenities include a baby-sitting service, indoor/outdoor pool, restaurant, and ski shop. The lodge also has 16 condos to let. ♦ 26 Avondale La (off Village Rd). 800/732.6777; fax 845.8242

***For more information on the Beaver Creek area, see "Beyond the Resorts," page 102.***

*Beaver Creek Lodge*

# Vail

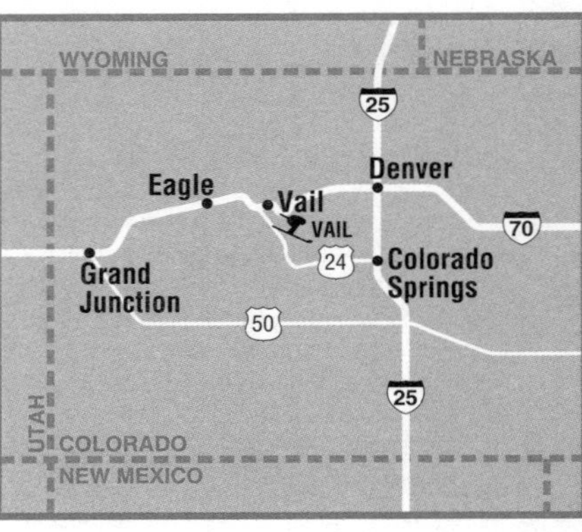


Resplendent in its white robes, Vail is unquestionably Rocky Mountain royalty. The resort's skiable area spans seven miles and contains an astonishing variety of terrain within its folds. The Vista Bahn Lift, with its bubble-top lid shielding the chic in inclement weather, rises over a mountain face webbed with advanced runs, top-to-bottom blue trails, and novice slopes. And Vail's celebrated **Back Bowls**, which sprawl across the mountain's south side, boast enough acreage to swallow several lesser ski areas.

Vail and its sister resort, **Beaver Creek** (both are owned and operated by Vail Associates), merit special mention for their children's programs, which combine the playful and the practical with Disneylike adroitness. In ski school, kids join forces with costumed characters to solve the riddle of the Dragon's Treasure. Schussing through storybook adventure environments—sliding down a sluice and poling past an ore car filled with glittering fool's gold in a pretend mine—they hone their skiing skills. Vail even publishes a kids-only trail map. The adventures continue at night with special children's programs.

Off the slopes, the cosmopolitan kingdom of **Vail Village** is a stylish shopping district—an archrival of **Aspen**—with dozens of trendy boutiques and au courant art galleries, many charging princely sums for their goods. More than one hundred restaurants keep even the terminally hip table-hopping until the wee hours.

---

**Vail Associates**
**PO Box 7**
**Vail, Colorado 81658**

**Information**........................................970/476.5601
**Reservations**....................................800/525.2257
**Snow Phone**.................................970/476.4888/9

## Fast Facts

*Area code 970 unless otherwise noted.*

**Ski Season** Mid-November to mid-April

**Location** Vail sits on the western side of Colorado's **Gore Range** of the **Rocky Mountains,** 100 miles west of **Denver.**

### Getting to Vail

**By air: Denver International Airport (DIA)** is 128 miles east of Vail. **Eagle County Airport** is 35 miles west of Vail in the town of **Eagle. American** offers nonstop service to both airports from **Chicago** and **Dallas/Ft. Worth,** and to **Eagle** from **Miami** and **New York/LaGuardia. Delta** offers direct flights to **DIA** from **Atlanta, Cincinnati, Dallas,** and **Salt Lake City,** and to **Eagle** from **Salt Lake City. United** flies nonstop from Chicago, **Denver, Los Angeles,** all three **New York** metro airports, and once daily between Denver and **Eagle County. Continental, Northwest,** and **TWA** also provide nonstop service to **DIA.** Several airlines service DIA from the West Coast including **America West, Martin Air, Mexicana,** and **Sun Country.**

**By bus:** Airport-to-Vail shuttle services include **Colorado Mountain Express** (949.4227 or 800/525.6363), and **Vans to Vail** (476.4467 or 800/222.2112).

**By car:** Winterized cars are available from several major rental car agencies at **Denver International Airport.** From **Denver,** take Interstate 70 West and choose one of three Vail exits.

**All-weather highway:**

Denver—Interstate 70 West

**Driving time from:**

Denver—1.5-2 hours (100 miles)

### Getting around Vail

The resort's villages are pedestrian oriented. Linking the three base areas is Vail's extensive shuttle bus system, headquartered in the **Vail Transportation Center.** Free buses run from early morning to late at night.

## FYI

**Area** 4,014 acres with 121 trails, including three large bowl areas (almost a third of the mountain)—some of it suited to intermediates.

Beginner—32 percent front, 0 percent back

Intermediate—36 percent front, 36 percent back

Advanced—25 percent front, 36 percent back

Expert—7 percent front, 28 percent back

**Number of Groomed Runs** Approximately 20

**Longest Run** 4.5 miles (**Flapjack** to **Riva Ridge**)

**Capacity** 41,855 skiers per hour

**Base Elevation** 8,200 feet

**Summit Elevation** 11,450 feet

**Vertical Rise** 3,250 feet

**Average Annual Snowfall** 335 inches

**Snowmaking** 11 percent

**Night Skiing** None

**Lifts** 25 (1 high-speed quad with bubble top, 7 high-speed quads, 2 quads, 1 gondola, 3 triple chairs, 6 double chairs, and 5 surface lifts)

| **Lift Passes** | **Full Day** | **Half Day** (starts at noon) |
|---|---|---|
| **Adult** | $46 | $39 |
| **Child** (12 and under) | $33 | $28 |
| **Senior** (65 to 69) | $37 | $36 |
| **Senior** (70 and over) | Free | Free |

Lift passes may be used at both Vail and **Beaver Creek.** The **Premier Passport** is designed for skiers who want to explore **Beaver Creek,** Vail, and the four **Aspen** properties, and can stay for two weeks or longer. This joint pass includes a one-way ground transfer among the six resorts and offers a minimum 10- out of 12-day lift ticket and a maximum 18- out of 21-day lift ticket.

**Ski School** The **Vail and Beaver Creek Ski School** (476.3239) oversees operations at both ski areas. At Vail, the ski school offices are located at **Golden Peak,** the base of the **Vista Bahn,** and at **Lionshead.** On-mountain ski school services are available at **Two Elk, Mid-Vail,** and **Eagle's Nest.** The teaching system encompasses nine skill levels: 1 to 4 are introductory, 5 to 7 are intermediate, and 8 to 9 promote advanced skills. The ski school offers all-day and half-day alpine and snowboard lessons, private lessons, and many special programs. Ask about Vail's customized instruction for groups of up to five people.

**Kids' Ski School Children's Skiing Centers** (479.5044) are located at **Lionshead** and **Golden Peak. Mogul Mice,** which is for children ages 4 to 6 who can't yet stop on their skis, includes lesson and lunch. **Super Stars** is for youngsters in the same age group who can ski around the mountain. Willing, potty-trained three-year-olds may attend **Mini Mice.** Teen guides lead groups scheduled during peak weeks, when **Bump and Bash** and **Freestyle** camps are scheduled. Après-ski teen activities include picnics, snowshoeing, and broomball.

**Clinics and Special Programs Building Blocks Workshops** are designed to improve the basics. **Pepi's Wedel Weeks** are early-season, multi-day clinics designed to tune up both body and skiing. **Super Guides** is for expert skiers who like to move fast and receive coaching. A program for disabled skiers is also available.

**Races** NASTAR races are held on **Race Track** daily 12:30PM to 2PM. The self-timed pay-to-race course on **Swingsville** is open daily 10AM to 3PM.

**Rentals** Skiers may rent standard, high-performance, and demo downhill and snowboard equipment at several shops in Vail. **Vail Associates** (daily 8AM-6PM; 479.2050) has rental shops at **Lionshead** and **Golden Peak** that offer recreational and high-performance equipment. **Christy Sports** (M-F 8AM-7PM, Sa-Su 8AM-9PM; 476.2244) is located near the **Vista Bahn.** Most rental shops offer free overnight storage, and prices are generally competitive. Reservations are recommended.

**Lockers** Lockers take tokens or quarters and are located at the base near the **Vista Bahn.**

**Day Care The Small World Play School** (479.2044), for nonskiers, is located in the **Children's Skiing Center** at **Golden Peak.** Open 8AM to 4:30PM, Small World accepts children ages 2 months through 6 years. Toddlers and preschoolers have snowplay. Reservations are required.

Vail has a series of kids-only and family evening entertainment. Thursday's "Kid's Night Out Goes Western" is a dinner theater for kindergarten-age kids through sixth graders. "Kid's Night Out Goes Hollywood" is a pizza and movie evening for 10- to 14-year-olds, scheduled frequently during Christmas and spring vacations. Sport Goofy, the "Disney Ambassador of Skiing, Fun, Fitness, and Health" (whew!) shows up at "Family Night Out" on Tuesday night.

**First Aid** You can reach ski patrol by dialing 1111 from any mountain phone or asking attendants at the base or top of the lifts. The **Vail Valley Medical Center** (476.2451) is located at 181 W Meadow Drive.

**Parking** Pay parking garages are located in the center of **Vail Village** and in the **Lionshead** parking structure. When these are full, drivers are directed to outlying lots and commute to the slopes on shuttle buses; both the lots and the buses are free.

**Worth Knowing**

- The **Mountain Plus** ticket is an economical multi-day ticket for Vail, **Beaver Creek,** and **Arrowhead** that may also be used for snowmobiling at **Piney River Ranch,** cross-country skiing, and discounts on ski and snowboard rentals and lessons.

## Rating the Runs

### ● Beginner

You'll never go astray on **Lost Boy,** because the wide ridge trail tenders views stretching from the **Holy Cross Wilderness** to the **Sawatch Range,** making it easy to keep your bearings. The Boy winds its way around the rim of **Game Creek Bowl,** providing a fine vantage point from which to choose your next challenge from among the trails below.

When beginners are set loose on the well-groomed run **Born Free,** they experience the sense of liberty better skiers enjoy. The trail conveniently starts and ends near the Lionshead gondola, which means that skiers can clock a maximum number of runs without wasting time.

Novices can knead the slopes of **Sourdough** endlessly, practicing turns and stops on its smooth surface. **Flap Jack** is an even longer course; ski down from **Camp 1** to the base of Chair 11, which you can ride to the top of the adjacent summit for another run. (When the names of these green trails make your stomach growl, head up the Sourdough Lift to **Two Elk,** the most popular lunch spot on the mountain.)

### ■ Intermediate

Vail's legendary **Back Bowls** are within the grasp of intermediates who venture into the **Poppyfields.** Unlike Dorothy, who fell asleep in a poppyfield on her way to Oz, you won't be caught napping on this run down **China Bowl,** as it's surrounded by serious steeps being navigated by experienced skiers.

The consummate intermediate cruiser, **Avanti** is almost always impeccably groomed. This trail has a progression of "whoopty-woos," gentle drop-offs caused by natural dips in the mountainside, creating a roller coaster effect. It's easy to ride uphill for more, via the Avanti Express.

Tucked away between two popular runs off Vail's Mountaintop Express, **Powerline** is a secret hideaway skiers in the know head to when the mountain is crowded. The wide path cut through trees is easy going when recently groomed, but can confound even advanced intermediates when it's been scuffed into bumps.

### ◆ Advanced

During the Gold Rush, railroad workers who laid tracks were dubbed **Gandy Dancers,** a name inspired by the unwieldy tool they used. Sometimes this steep pitch is a milky way of bumps; at others, it's a real high-speed demon—making skiers long for a ride on a passing freight train.

The eight **Back Bowls** cover so much terrain—encompassing 2,734 acres—that skiers can't overcrowd their slopes even on the busiest days (although the same can't always be said for Chair 5). Just keep cruising around the rims until you find a line that tempts you, then take the plunge.

When **Riva Ridge** is groomed, you'll race downhill with the speed and style of a Kentucky Derby-winning steed, but when it's moguled, prepare for a wild ride. The trail was christened after the spot in Italy's Apennines mountain range where nearly 1,000 members of the 10th Mountain Division perished during World War II.

### ◆◆ Expert

Enjoy a private waltz through the woods on **Riva's Glade,** dancing on paths carved and bumped between tight trees.

### Snowboarding

Allowed over the entire mountain, boarders may prefer the challenge of the snowboard parks, including the largest half-pipe in the US. Located off Chair 6, the parks offer freestyle riders everything from gaps and tabletops to whales and waves. For those who crave wide, sweeping GS turns, the **Back Bowls** are the place to go. Carvers prefer such runs as **Forever, Apres Vous,** and **Yonder.** For an out-of-the-way place where boarders can meander through the trees, try **Powerline** off of the Mountaintop Express Chair. Snowboard clinics include a half-pipe workshop and **Jam Sessions** for better riders.

## Mountain Highs and Lows

On the trail map, intermediate **Eagle's Nest Ridge** looks like a nice nonstop cruise, but it's barely slanted enough to allow skiers to glide from Chair 3 onto several other runs. Keep your speed up or you'll have to tuck and pole to move along this trail.

If you're a novice from the Midwest, be forewarned: Sections of the beginner-rated **Ramshorn** are as steep and intimidating as an intermediate track in your neck of the woods.

Don't get suckered into **Tourist Trap** when it's icy. Skiers flying down **Riva Ridge** get caught before they realize that this section is too slick for comfort. Escape by detouring along **Skid Road** to **Compromise** and you'll wind up back on the blue portion of Riva Ridge.

## At the Resort

*Area code 970 unless otherwise noted.*

✦ **Two Elk** ★★★$$$ The tariff may be steep for a mountaintop cafeteria and the place is usually crowded, but folks flock to this massive stone and timber lodge for two good reasons: the outstanding food and unparalleled views of the Gore range. Take a trip to the potato bar for quick carbohydrates, or stoke up for the afternoon with a rich, chewy brownie and a cup of cappuccino. ♦ Daily breakfast and lunch. Top of China Bowl. 479.4560

✦ **Mid-Vail** This midmountain center has a cafeteria and delis on several levels. ♦ Top of Vista Bahn.

Within Mid-Vail:

**The Cook Shack** $$ Despite its name, this snack shack does provide table service and is pleasant enough for a leisurely lunch, but you won't rave about the victuals. ♦ Daily lunch. Reservations recommended. 476.2030

✦ **Golden Peak** $$ Grab a fast cafeteria breakfast or the basic burgers, sandwiches, and salads at lunch. ♦ Daily breakfast and lunch. Base of Golden Peak. 479.2032

✦ **Wildwood Shelter** ★$$ This small, unprepossessing snack spot slow cooks home-smoked meats in tasty barbecue sauce. ♦ Daily lunch. Top of Chair 3. 476.5601

✦ **Wok 'N' Roll Express** $$ Logically located in China Bowl, this ski-by pagoda cooks up fried rice and *yakitori* (Chinese chicken). ♦ Daily lunch. Base of Orient Express. 476.5601

✦ **Wine Stube** ★$$$ You'll find a tantalizingly eclectic menu at this intimate restaurant, with a view of the action on Eagle's Nest. ♦ Daily lunch. Reservations recommended. Top of Lionshead gondola. 479.2034

✦ **Bobsled** Hold on to your hat when you careen around the 3,500-foot track on this recreational bobsled. The dizzying ride delivers a modified version of the speed and thrills Olympians experience. ♦ Daily noon-3:30PM. Lion's Way. 476.9090

✦ **Manor Vail** $$$ These 215 rental residences reflect the tastes of the various owners. What they have in common is that all are nicely sized and have rustic rock fireplaces. You'll find a selection of one- to three-bedroom condominiums and "lodge rooms" (lock-off rooms adjoining the condos) to let. Sublimely situated at the base of Golden Peak, these units allow skiers to just walk out their doors to the lifts. Other on-site extras include a restaurant, ski shop, heated outdoor pool, hot tub, and sauna. ♦ 595 E Vail Valley Dr (Base of Golden Peak). 800/525.9165; fax 476.4982

✦ **The Lodge at Vail** $$$$ Personal service has earned this hostelry its sparkling share of stars and diamonds, and the Vista Bahn awaits just a few steps away. Most of the 60 rooms and 40 suites are redolent with Old World charm. Modern luxuries are a mainstay (the bathroom towel warmers take the nip out of chilly mornings), but occasionally the hotel's standard slips. The quality of some of the guest quarters may not warrant what you are being charged; it pays to check out your room before you check in. The complete fitness facilities, though, are flawless. ♦ 174 E Gore Creek Dr (across from the Vista Bahn). 476.5011, 800/331.5634; fax 476.7425

Within The Lodge at Vail:

**Wildflower Inn** ★★★$$$ Accolades abound for this elegant, flower-bedecked restaurant and its innovative menu. Thai-spiced lobster and grilled squab on a bed of grits exemplify the chef's creativity. ♦ Daily dinner. Reservations recommended. 476.5011

**Mickey's Bar** Mickey Poage's nightly ramble over the ivories is a Vail tradition at this mellow lounge, where conversations aren't drowned out in an après-ski din. ♦ Daily 6PM-1AM. 476.5011

✦ **Golden Peak House** $ Its seven tiny studios and five condos range from run-down to run of the mill, but guests here are more concerned with beating the lines at the Vista Bahn, which is right next door. Visitors have access to the **Christiania's** pool and Jacuzzi. ♦ 356 E Hanson Ranch Rd, top of Bridge St. 476.5641

Within Golden Peak House:

**Los Amigos** ★★$ The après-ski siesta on the deck of this casual restaurant has been a fixture at Vail since the early 1970s. Inside, the kitchen dishes up burritos, *chiles rellenos,* and other Mexican fast food. A children's menu is available. ♦ Daily lunch and dinner. 476.5847

✦ **The Westin Resort Vail** $$$$ A resort in its own right, this hotel pampers its patrons in 322 attractive rooms, a cafe, and a restaurant. If you crave living space with character, ask for a dormer room. Having to take a short shuttle trip to town may be a letdown for those eager to cut first tracks on the slopes, but at day's end, skiers take the **West-Ho** trail back to the hotel where a bellman dispenses hot cider as your skis are checked. Hotel guests may use the neighboring deluxe **Cascade Health Club,** with full spa, exercise equipment, and squash courts, at a reduced rate. ♦ 1300 W Haven Dr (1 mile north of Vail Village). 800/228.3000; fax 479.7020

✦ **Kenny's Double Diamond** This ski shop near the gondola was expanded a few years ago to handle the hordes demanding Kenny's expertise in all things alpine. Equipment adjustments, sales, and repairs are done here. ♦ Daily 11AM-10PM. Base of Lionshead. 476.5500

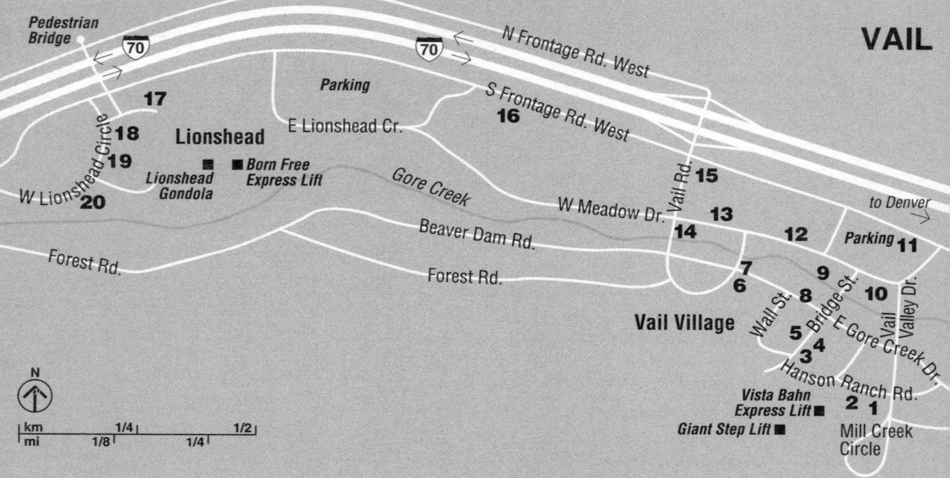


✦ **Bart & Yeti's** ★$$ The back country cuisine—tangy smoked ribs, steaks, and hearty sandwiches—is as authentic as the ambience in this genuine log cabin. ♦ Daily lunch and dinner. No reservations. 551 E Lionshead Circle (just north of the Lionshead gondola). 476.2754

✦ **Montauk Seafood Grill** ★★$$$ Pair a cold platter of oysters with a spicy Bloody Mary at this East Coast outpost. The fresh fish nets positive reviews, as do the steaks, chops, and pastas. ♦ Daily dinner. 549 E Lionshead Circle (just north of the Lionshead gondola). 476.2601

## Beyond the Resorts

**1 Tivoli Lodge** $$ This family-owned enterprise, a holdover from Vail's early days, has a classic ski-lodge ambience: Deep leather sofas flank the fireplace in the common room where skiers gather under a beamed ceiling for continental breakfast and après-ski. The 49 guest rooms are simply decorated; those facing the street are on the small side compared to rooms with mountain views. ♦ 386 E Hanson Ranch Rd (between Vail Village and Golden Peak). 476.5615, 800/451.4756; fax 474.6601

**2 Christiania at Vail** $$$ Skiers return year after year to this upscale, 22-room lodge, which preserves the Bavarian decor so in vogue when Vail opened. Such alpine accents as hand-carved dressers, headboards, and chairs have a timeless appeal. A mere four minutes from many restaurants and the Vista Bahn, the hotel also has a Jacuzzi, sauna, and outdoor heated pool. Seven privately owned condos are also for rent. ♦ 356 E Hanson Ranch Rd (across from the Vista Bahn). 476.5641

**3 The Red Lion** ★★★$$ A tried and true après-ski venue, this lively tavern is a piece of Vail's history. The bustle of Bridge Street can be observed through the bar's windows, but most eyes are glued to the 14 TVs tuned to various sporting events. The kitchen is competent, doling out hefty sandwich plates that keep drinkers from going hungry. Adding to the revelry is live music on some nights. ♦ Daily 11AM-closing. 304 Bridge St (at Wall St). 476.7676

**4 The Daily Grind** ★★$ Neighborhood java junkies arrive early to read the morning paper and catch up on the latest gossip while perched on high stools in this tiny coffee bar. Open your eyes with a hot cup of the blend-of-the-day and try an oversize cranberry or blueberry muffin for a soul-satisfying breakfast or snack. The made-to-order sandwiches are tasty, too. ♦ Daily breakfast, lunch, and dinner. 228 Bridge St (between E Hanson Ridge Rd and E Gore Creek Dr). 476.5856

**5 Plaza Lodge** $$$ Vacationers who want to share living space and cut costs should investigate five- and seven-bedroom condos smack in the center of the village. The proprietors of this seven-unit lodge have invested both time and money into this attractive, small property, where most of the units are not on the rental market. The seven-bedroom space (granted, one bedroom is barely larger than a walk-in closet) spans two floors, with a kitchen on each level and a private hot tub on the roof; and the five-bedroom unit has a spacious living room. Guests can use the lodge's Jacuzzi. ♦ 291 Bridge St (between E Hanson Ridge Rd and E Gore Creek Dr). 476.4550

**6 The Squash Blossom** Traditional and contemporary pottery and jewelry by Native Americans fill this gallerylike shop, its shelves animated by bright colors and graphic geometrical patterns. Historic photographs, old weavings, and other artifacts may also be found. Artisans include Maria Martinez, Joseph Lonewolf, Ray Tracey, and Edward Curtis. ♦ Daily 10AM-9PM. 198 E Gore Creek Dr (in the Lodge Promenade Shops). 476.3129

**7 Sweet Basil** ★★★★$$$$ The creative American menu changes with the seasons, and the restaurant's faithful following keeps pace with every delicious update. Colorful, contemporary paintings contrast well with accents of granite, slate, and cherry wood in this lively American bistro. Ask for a table in the back and enjoy a great view of Gore Creek. The food is a visual feast as well: Golden saffron angel hair pasta is tossed in a seafood cream sauce flecked with chives, and barley spinach risotto and eggplant fries are a colorful, offbeat addition to the rack of lamb. Don't let the sophisticated fare deter you—the setting is strictly casual. ♦ Daily lunch and dinner. Reservations recommended. 193 E Gore Creek Dr (across from the Lodge Promenade Shops). 476.0125

**7 Blu's** ★★★$$ When the weather is lousy and an enjoyable lunch would brighten your day, lock up your skis at the base and walk on over to this chase-the-blues-away bistro, where there's bound to be a friendly crowd ready to commiserate with you. The "Kick Ass California Chicken Relleno" and a frosty mug of beer are a surefire way to improve your mood. Reservations are not accepted, so expect a wait at dinnertime on busy nights. ♦ Daily breakfast, lunch, and dinner. 193 E Gore Creek Dr (across from the Lodge Promenade Shops). 476.3113

**8 Pepi's Restaurant and Bar** ★★$$$$ The dimly lit dining room oozes old-fashioned European elegance, with solicitous waiters serving continental fare spiced with a German accent. Game dishes, swimming in rich sauces, are succulent, but dieters beware. The bar attracts an exuberant après-ski crowd, and patrons vie for space on the prime people watching deck on sunny afternoons. ♦ Daily lunch and dinner. 231 E Gore Creek Dr (at Bridge St). 476.5626

**9 Pazzo's Pizzeria** ★★$ By the slice or by the pie, order pizza with the usual toppings or experiment with fresh tomatoes and basil, shrimp, feta cheese, or chopped garlic. An equally inventive variety of pasta dishes and calzones are offered for eating in the casual restaurant or to go. ♦ Daily lunch and dinner. 122 E Meadow Dr (at Bridge St). 476.9026

**9 Gotthelf's Gallery** Artist Dale Chihuly tops this gallery's roster of glass crafters, who create delicate, decorative, and functional works. Impulse buyers will find it difficult to resist the collection of perfume bottles and jewelry. Given the fragile environment, parents with kids might want to confine themselves to window shopping. ♦ M, Su 10AM-7PM; Tu-Sa 10AM-9PM. 122 E Meadow Dr (at Bridge St). 476.1777

**10 Vail Athletic Club Hotel** $$$ Energetic types can work off steam by scaling the climbing wall, playing racquetball, pumping iron, or swimming laps at the deluxe fitness club in the basement of this hotel, then retreat to one of its 38 elegant rooms to recover. More sedentary guests can wrap up the ski day with a massage and a steam or Jacuzzi bath. ♦ Club: Daily 6:30AM-8:30PM. 52 E Meadow Dr (at Valley Dr). 476.0700, 800/822.4754; fax 476.6451

Within the Vail Athletic Club Hotel:

**Terra Bistro** ★★★$$$ This spirited cafe is a big hit with fashionable foodies. Chef Cynthia Walt has a talent for orchestrating seemingly dissonant ingredients into superb dishes. Lobster rolls with avocado, tomato, and herb aioli; grilled chicken breast with apple wheatberry stuffing; and marinated pork chops with pineapple salsa and sweet potato samosas earn the kitchen a standing ovation. No smoking is allowed in the restaurant. ♦ Daily dinner. Reservations recommended. 476.6836

**11 Colorado Ski Heritage Museum** The museum depicts the hundred-year history of skiing in the Centennial State, from the days when Norwegian miners taught townsfolk how to make cross-county skis, through the saga of the 10th Mountain Division, to the Shredi Masters of today's slopes. Faded photographs of skiers lashed to rope tows, warped wooden skis with bear trap bindings, and other memorabilia are convincing testimony to how technologically advanced the sport has become. ♦ Tu-Su 10AM-5PM. 231 S Frontage Rd East, third floor (in the Transportation Center). 476.1876

**12 Hubcap Brewery and Kitchen** ★★★$ You might think you've stepped into a garage with gourmet ambitions: Hubcaps from old cars hang on the shiny stainless steel walls of the town's sole microbrewery, where more than basic burgers (which, incidentally, tip the scales at a half-pound) are on the menu. "Incoming Spuds" is a colossal potato baked to fluffy perfection and piled high with toppings tailored to your taste; and shrimp wontons are also worth a try. The five-ounce samples of draft beers, such as Vail Pale Ale or Beaver Tail Brown Ale, are popular with the enthusiastic evening crowd. ♦ Daily lunch and dinner. Crossroads Shopping Center, 143 E Meadow Dr (at Willow Bridge Rd). 476.5757

**12 This Wicked West** Dressing down in style is the forte of this resortwear shop, where the racks are filled with creative casual clothing for adults and children, much of it in denim duded up with studs and other novelty trimmings. The boutique has a second location in the **Lionshead Gondola Building.** ♦ Daily 11AM-7PM. Crossroads Shopping Center, 143 E Meadow Dr (at Willow Bridge Rd). 476.7900

**13 Alpenrose Restaurant and Tea Room** ★★$$$ Napoleons, tortes, and fruity strudels tempt from the bakery case just inside the front door, proof that the European owner/chef's culinary lineage is sweetly intact. Balcony seating provides some theatrical privacy for espresso-sipping skiers. The tearoom is often packed during the afternoon, but takes on a more sedate air at dinnertime when a classical guitarist sets a more soothing tone. The restaurant has four intimate dining areas and a menu featuring Swiss and Austrian cuisine; specialties of the house include osso buco and saltimbocca. ♦ Daily lunch and dinner. Village Inn Plaza, 100 E Meadow Dr (between Willow Bridge and Vail Rds). 476.3194

**13 Claggett/Rey** Dave McGary's intricately beaded bronze sculptures are showcased here, along with works by other American artists of a traditional bent. Ask for a copy of the **Vail Valley Gallery Association**'s guide to the artistic venues of the village, which display a range of expressions from aboriginal art to European masters. ♦ M-Th 9AM-6PM; F 9AM-7PM; Sa 9AM-9PM. Village Inn Plaza, 100 E Meadow Dr (between Willow Bridge and Vail Rds). 476.9350, 800/252.4438

**14 Sonnenalp Resort of Vail** $$$ The Faessler family, owners of the Sonnenalp Resort in Bavaria since 1919, have imported their gemütlichkeit to the states. The Vail branch is a compound of three separate lodges: the **Austria Haus** (33 rooms, 4 suites), the **Swiss Haus** (57 rooms, 2 suites), and the **Bavaria Haus,** which has been remodeled into 88 luxurious suites with gas log fireplaces and sitting areas. Other chambers have brick and barnwood walls, beds covered with cozy down comforters, high-backed armchairs, and handcrafted pine furniture (the armoires are so massive that they had to be assembled inside the rooms). Florian, the Bavarian patron saint of fire, guards the hearth at Austria House, where guests gather après-ski to nibble on linzertorte and other traditional sweets. Such caring touches as a supply of sunblocking lip balm in the bathrooms, complimentary overnight ski check at the slopes, daytime boot storage, and instant service with a smile, spoil visitors. The house charge card you receive at check-in makes it more than convenient to indulge at the full-service spa and restaurant in the **Swiss Chalet** (see below), and at **Ludwig's** and the **Bully Pub** in the Bavaria Haus. A full buffet breakfast comes with the rooms, and includes fresh juice, fruit, breads, and cereals, plus eggs, pancakes, and waffles made to order. ♦ 20 Vail Rd (at E Meadow Dr). 476.5656, 800/654.8312; fax 476.1639

Within the Sonnenalp Resort of Vail:

**Swiss Chalet Restaurant** ★$$$ The fine—albeit pricey—Swiss cuisine includes warming fondues and raclette, served with style by a friendly staff. Recommended are the Wiener schnitzel and the pfeffersteak, a tender filet topped with four-peppercorn whiskey cream sauce. ♦ Daily dinner. Reservations recommended. 476.5656

**15 Vail Gateway Plaza** This mélange of eateries and pricey stores is an only-in-Vail experience. The **Battle Mountain Trading Post** purveys accessories with cowboy collectibles and Native American artifacts accenting their collection of antler chandeliers and furniture. The walls of the **Gateway Gallery** are lined with paintings by Robert Katona and other contemporary Western artists of note. Those seeking a singular Stetson should head to **Miller Stockman** to peruse the Westernwear. Over at the **Twisted Pine,** outrageous (and expensive) fur and leather apparel is available. The handcrafted holiday ornaments and decorations at the **Christmas Store** will add seasonal spirit to cabins and condos alike. And if this all leaves you famished, you'll find refreshment at **Michael's American Bistro** (476.5353), **Siamese Orchid** (476.9417), or **Gambetta's Pizza and Pane** (476.7550). ♦ M-Sa 10AM-9PM; Su 10AM-5PM. 12 S Frontage Rd (at Vail Rd). 476.6824

Within the Vail Gateway Plaza:

**Palmos Cappuccino & Spirits** ★★$$ At this European-style coffeehouse and bar, the delicious pastries threaten doom for waist-watchers. Après-ski and into the night, the quaint wicker chairs in this small space are continually occupied. ♦ Daily 3PM-2AM. 476.0646

**16 Evergreen Lodge** $$ The 128 comfortable but nothing-special rooms are slightly larger than others in this price range. The hotel has a lobby bar with fireplace, a casual restaurant, indoor Jacuzzi, and a rather frenetic nightclub. It's a long hike from the lifts, but skiers saving their energy for the slopes hop on the shuttle bus. ♦ 250 S Frontage Rd West (near E Lionshead Circle). 476.7810, 800/284.8245; fax 476.4504

**17 The Lifthouse Condominiums** $ These lodgings are a steal for solo travelers or cost-conscious couples who want to be in the center of the village activity and minutes from the mountain. Although "condominium" connotes multiple bedrooms, the 45 units are all studios. The living room, with fireplace, and kitchen area are set off from the bed by a partial wall, actually an oak cabinet with substantial shelving and drawer space. ♦ 555 E Lionshead Circle (near the Pedestrian Bridge). 476.2340, 800/654.0635; fax 476.9303

**18 D.J. McCadams** ★★$$ Join the hungry crowd at the counter and tables in this diner for enormous omelettes, crepes, and blintzes. The fruit smoothies are a decadent way to get your dose of vitamin C. The place is packed at breakfast, but worth the wait. ♦ Tu-Su breakfast, lunch, and dinner. W Lionshead Circle (in Concert Hall Plaza). 476.2336

---

A sample of some of the questions novice skiers have asked a Vail instructor and an Alta information desk attendant:

- Where do you put the moguls in the summer?
- How do I get down if the lifts close?
- Does it matter which end of the ski goes in front?
- At what altitude do deer turn into elk?
- Does the mountain weigh more with snow on it?
- Does the altitude change here during the summer?
- Where do you store the manmade snow?
- Can I get a refund if it snows?
- Do these boots go on over my shoes?

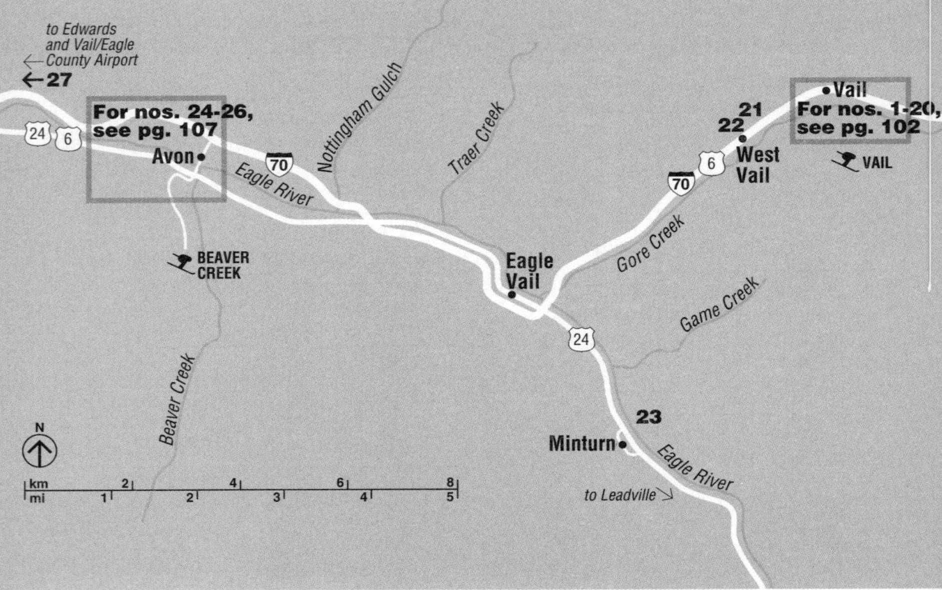


**18** **Boot Lab** There's a science to fitting and fixing ski boots, and the wizards here know all the tricks of the trade. The place is always busy, so plan accordingly. ♦ Daily 8AM-6PM. 616 W Lionshead Circle (in Concert Hall Plaza). 476.5009

**19** **Montaneros** $$$ Striking mountain vistas greet visitors from the 42 one- to three-bedroom condos, each with comfortable furnishings, paneled walls, and oversize living room with fireplace. Some of the upper units have high ceilings and lofts. Soothe your slope-stressed muscles in the outdoor pool or the Jacuzzi. ♦ 641 W Lionshead Circle (across from the Lionshead gondola). 800/237.0643

**20** **Marriott Vail Mountain Resort** $$ Formerly owned by Radisson, this 350-unit hotel maintains its checkbook-friendly room rates to entice vacationers to its prime location—just a short stroll from both the gondola and the eateries and shops at Lionshead. If you're looking for slightly more luxurious surroundings than the standard rooms offer, with their coffeemakers and compact refrigerators, the hotel does have several cushy suites featuring fireplaces. And should cramped quarters be a major concern, inquire about condo lodging—also at surprisingly low prices for a resort of this caliber. All the expected perks—nightclub, restaurants, health club (no charge to guests), pool, sauna, and Jacuzzi—are on-site. ♦ 715 W Lionshead Circle (across from the Lionshead gondola). 476.4444, 800/648.0720; fax 476.1647

**Restaurants/Clubs:** Red　**Hotels:** Blue
**Shops/ Outdoors:** Green　**Sights/Culture:** Black

**21** **Imperial Fez** ★★★★$$$ Emily Post would never approve: Diners at this Moroccan restaurant delve into their plates fingers first. The manners maven might also object to lounging about on pillows while eating, another custom encouraged at this exotic eatery. Owner Rafih has bridged the gender gap by having belly dancers of both sexes entertain nightly. ♦ Daily dinner. Reservations recommended. 1000 Lionsridge Loop (1.5 miles west of Vail), West Vail. 476.1948

**22** **Safeway** Stock up on supplies at this full-service supermarket. ♦ Daily 24 hours. 2131 N Frontage Rd (1.5 miles west of Vail), West Vail. 476.3561

**23** **The Saloon** ★★★$$ Autographed photos of some now-faded stars pepper the walls, a graphic reminder of how long this country tavern has been a favorite with visitors to the Vail Valley. There's no decor to speak of, but diners don't seem to mind at all, concentrating on the good times and good food. Most of the entrées are classic Mexican, but dishes like "quail and enchilada" surprise with their flair. You'll need a car to get here; some skiers share a cab. ♦ Daily dinner. 146 S Main St (6 miles east of Vail), Minturn. 827.5954

**24** **Comfort Inn** $ Plain but comfortable rooms, a pool and Jacuzzi, free continental breakfast, and rock-bottom prices combine to make this 147-unit motel a most serviceable place to stay. Located in Avon, it's within walking distance of restaurants and lounges. ♦ 161 W Beaver Creek Blvd (I-70 to Exit 167), Avon. 800/221.2222; fax 949.7762

**25** **Beaver Creek West Condominiums** $$ If you want to save bucks by lodging away from the high-rent districts, consider this 174-unit complex with relatively spacious living areas, wood-burning fireplaces, and private balconies. ♦ 360 Benchmark Rd (at W Beaver Creek Blvd), Avon. 949.4840, 800/222.4840; fax 949.4391

**26 Falcon Point** $ Some of these 55 condos have lake views, and all are modestly priced. Avon's low-key restaurants are within walking distance. Pleasure perks include a sauna, Jacuzzi, and indoor/outdoor pool. ♦ 340 Benchmark Rd (at W Beaver Creek Blvd), Avon. 949.4416

**27 Lodge at Cordillera** $$$$ A gated entrance opens onto Cordillera and its 3,100 sylvan acres overlooking Vail Valley. The 28 rooms and suites are decorated in an elegantly rustic style, all subtly coordinated to the smallest detail. Aperitifs are served in the antiques-filled living room to the classical strains of the Steinway baby grand. The luxury spa is on par with ski country's finest facilities, with hydrotherapy and massage a favorite après-ski treatment. Yoga and aerobics classes are held in the mirrored exercise room. Day packages might include a sauna session or a workout in the pool. The lodge has its own network of cross-country trails and provides skiers with complimentary chauffeur service to Beaver Creek (20 minutes) or Vail (25 minutes). ♦ 2205 Cordillera Way (7 miles west of Beaver Creek), Edwards. 926.2200, 800/548.2721; fax 926.2486

Within the Lodge at Cordillera:

**Restaurant Picasso** ★★★★$$$$ Some consider the culinary arts practiced at this fine restaurant to be edible equivalents to the Picasso drawings that adorn the walls. The modern French cuisine emphasizes light entrées created from the freshest ingredients on the market, so the menu changes nightly. Elk carpaccio, quail in a phyllo nest, and raspberry mousse presented in a chocolate cup please even the most sophisticated palates. A la carte and fixed-price dinners are offered. ♦ Daily lunch and dinner. Reservations recommended. 926.2200, 800/548.2721 (outside Colorado)

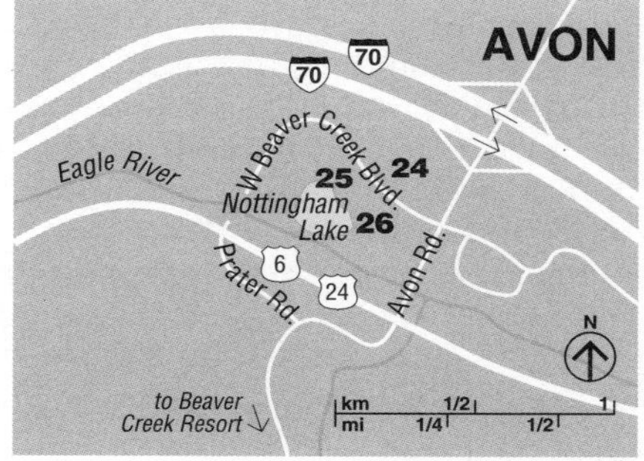

# Crested Butte

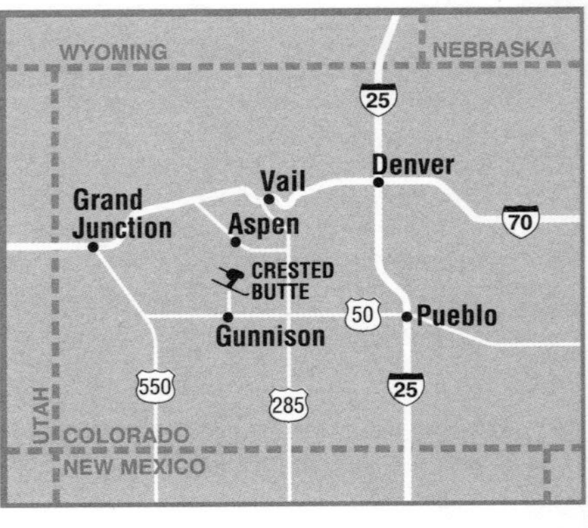


One quick glimpse around the laid-back town of Crested Butte makes it clear that this little village could care less about glitz. Cowboy boots are still more common than those furry après-ski numbers, and residents want to keep it that way. Visit during the annual spring Flauschink Festival and you'll find yourself in small town USA, with the locals (and visiting friends) parading down Main Street on horseback and children smiling and waving from floats. The festival is just a symbol of the town's determination to hang on to its image as a small hamlet where folks still get mail addressed to general delivery and smile at visitors spontaneously.

This resort really has two faces: the relatively new slopeside village of **Mount Crested Butte** and the historic Western mining town of Crested Butte, three miles down the road. The ski slopes lace the flanks of the mountain, which is crowned with a jagged plume of rock that gives the area its name. A small complex of lodges, condos, and hotels at the base of the lifts is popular with skiers who want to roll out of bed and catch the first ride uphill. But those looking for more nightlife may want to opt for Crested Butte. Although small, it has a large number of good restaurants. You can cruise the whole town in 15-minutes, and a shuttle-bus system takes skiers to and from the slopes.

Crested Butte was incorporated in 1880 as a supply stopover for the miners heading to camps and boomtowns up in the **Elk Mountains.** After the silver industry collapsed, coal became king for almost a century. Then, in the late 1950s, the tourism boom began. Today many of the town's shops, lodges, and restaurants are in the original historic buildings from the mining days. (Check out the two-story outhouse still standing behind the **Masonic Hall.**)

Crested Butte's slopes are a good choice for groups of skiers with widely varying levels of expertise. The gentle front side of the mountain has some long runs for novices; plenty of blue terrain surrounds several of the lifts, so you can always find a run in the sun (if it's shining); and the mountain also boasts some of the steepest avalanche-controlled slopes in North America on the **Extreme Limits.** This terrain is so steep the resort hosts the **US Extreme Skiing Championships,** an annual competition that tests the style and sheer survival skills of daredevil competitors on terrain once considered beyond the pale.

Heaven for the value-oriented skier, the resort has a "Ski Free" season from late November through mid-December. Just walk up to the window for a free "no-strings-attached" lift ticket. If you want to spend the night, book one of the discount lodging deals. Economy packages combining lifts, lodging, and ski lessons are offered the rest of the year as well. Outstanding clinics include the Women's Ski Adventures, led by a female extreme skier, and the Extreme Clinics, taught by two sets of extreme-skiing brothers. Everything from airfare and lodging to child care, lessons, and rentals can be booked through the central reservations toll-free telephone number.

Other outdoor activities at Crested Butte include snowmobiling and dogsledding, horse-drawn sleigh and hot-air-balloon rides. The nordic center has cross-country ski lessons; trail maps for the extensive, groomed nordic track system; and guides ready to take you on a backcountry tour.

**Crested Butte**
**PO Box A**
**Mount Crested Butte, Colorado 81225**

**Information**........................................970/349.2333
**Reservations**......................................800/544.8448
**Snow Phone**........................................970/349.2323

## Fast Facts

*Area code 970 unless otherwise noted.*

**Ski Season** Mid-November through beginning of April

**Location** Crested Butte is in southwest **Colorado,** 230 miles from **Denver.**

### Getting to Crested Butte

**By air: Gunnison County Airport** is 31 miles from the ski area. Both **Continental Express** and **United Express** fly in from **Denver** year-round. During ski season, nonstop jet service is offered from **Atlanta, Chicago, Dallas/Ft. Worth,** and **Houston.** Shuttle service is available from the airport to the resort.

**By car:** The ski area is about 40 minutes from **Gunnison,** where winterized cars are available from several major rental agencies. From **Denver,** take Highway 285 and Highway 50 to Gunnison, then Highway 135 to Crested Butte.

## FYI

**Area** 1,162 acres, plus 550 acres of **Extreme Limits**

Beginner—13 percent

Intermediate—30 percent

Advanced—57 percent

**Number of Groomed Runs** Approximately 85

**Longest Run** 1.6 miles (**Treasury** to the bottom of the East River Lift)

**Capacity** 16,802 skiers per hour

**Base Elevation** 9,375 feet

**Summit Elevation** 12,162 feet

**Vertical Rise** 2,775 feet lift-served; 3,062 feet to the peak

**Average Annual Snowfall** 260 inches

**Snowmaking** 85 percent

**Night Skiing** None

**Lifts** 13 (2 high-speed quads, 3 triple chairs, 4 double chairs, and 4 surface lifts)

| **Lift Passes** | **Full Day** | **Half Day** (starts at 12:30PM) |
|---|---|---|
| **Adult** | $42 | $31 |
| **Child** (12 and under with paying adult) | Pays age for ticket | |
| **Senior** (65-69) | $21 | $16 |
| **Senior** (70 and over) | Free | Free |

Crested Butte's "Ski Free" season is late November through mid-December.

**Ski School** The **Ski School** desk (349.2252 or 800/544.8448 ext 2252) is in the **Gothic Cafeteria.** Group half-day and full-day, and private lessons are available.

**Kids' Ski School** The **Children's Ski Center** (349.9262), in the **Whetstone Building,** offers a variety of ski programs and ski rentals. **Tag-A-Long Lessons** are available for parents who want to be actively involved in their child's instruction.

**Clinics and Special Programs** Crested Butte runs a variety of innovative programs, including **Women's Ski Adventures** (for all skill levels), hosted by veteran **US Ski Team** members and extreme skier Kim Reichhelm; and the **Extreme Team** ski clinics run by the Egan and DesLauriers brothers. Also available are **Bump and Powder Workshops, North Face/Double Diamond Workshops,** two-hour NASTAR race clinics, and three- to five-day advanced skiing clinics. The **Physically Challenged Ski Program** (349.2296), located in the **Treasury Center** at the base, offers lessons and adaptive equipment as well as après-ski activities, including snowmobiling and nordic skiing.

**Races** NASTAR races are offered daily at 1PM, on **Smith Hill** and **Canaan.** The cost is $5 for the first three runs and $1 for each additional run.

**Rentals** The **Crested Butte Rental Shop** (daily 8AM-5PM; 349.2240) carries alpine, cross-country, and telemark equipment, snowboards, and snowrunners. Other rental shops at the base of the ski area have similar equipment, including high-performance and demo equipment, at competitive prices. The **Alpineer** (daily 9AM-7PM; 349.5210) in town rents backcountry and telemark gear.

**Lockers** Coin-operated lockers are located in the **Gothic Cafeteria,** the **Crested Butte Rental Shop, Elfin Sports,** and the **Treasury Center.** Locking ski racks are located at the base.

**Day Care** The **Children's Ski Center** (349.9262), in the **Whetstone Building,** offers day-care programs and provides a list of baby-sitters.

**First Aid** Call the ski patrol for assistance at on-slope emergency phones (ext 2236). Two clinics are located at the base: **Gunnison Valley Family Physicians** (349.2980) in the **Axtel Building;** and the **Crested Butte Medical Clinic** (349.6651), 611 Gothic Road.

---

In the late 1800s, Butch Cassidy, the Sundance Kid, and their Hole in the Wall Gang hid inside the rocky valley walls of Cement Creek, a few miles south of Crested Butte. A local tale claims that, while drinking a beer at Kochevar's Saloon and Gaming Hall (still here today), Cassidy saw a posse on Main Street. He dashed for the door, forgetting his pistol, and never returned.

---

The double-diamond black acreage that Crested Butte calls its Extreme Limits boasts lower "Powder Rock Glade," the only sustained 50° inbounds

**Parking** Pay parking is available at the base area. You can park free by the shuttle-bus stop in the town of Crested Butte and take the shuttle.

**Worth Knowing**

- Not far from Crested Butte is **Irwin Lodge,** a rustic ranch-style inn surrounded by wilderness. Miles of cross-country touring trails as well as snowcat skiing for powder seekers make a vacation—or just a day trip—worthwhile.

## Rating the Runs

### ● Beginner

The short, open runs off the Painter Boy Lift are a good place to practice the basics. Though the runs off the Gold Link Lift are rated intermediate, they provide the perfect in-between terrain for beginners who want to start challenging blue runs.

### ■ Intermediate

Wide and situated in the sun, **Paradise Bowl** funnels into several cruising runs with enough terrain variation to hold the interest of all levels of intermediate skiers.

Out of sight of the lifts, thus less traveled, **Upper** and **Lower Treasury** are full of rolls, with a few steeper pitches to keep the adrenaline pumping.

A suitable transitional run for intermediate skiers who want to sample steeper slopes, **Upper Keystone** is long enough to get you into the swing of skiing steeper terrain without having to venture onto a black run.

When groomed, **International**—an open, black-rated slope leading to intermediate terrain—is your next step after Upper Keystone toward the advanced slopes.

### ◆ Advanced

The two parallel runs down the front side of the mountain, **Twister** and **Crystal,** provide a good introduction to skiing bumps. Both runs are angled so that skiers create moderate-size bumps.

Skiers must maneuver through trees on **Horseshoe Springs,** but there's still some room to breathe.

### ◆◆ Expert

Nestled in the upper reaches of Crested Butte are the daredevil runs known as the **Extreme Limits.** This is backcountry-style skiing—inbounds. Ride the North Face Lift up, and then start in the main bowl on the **North Face.** After the first run down, you'll know if you're ready to move on to the narrow, bumped trails that weave through woods, past cliffs, into gladed areas, and down chutes. Take a free guided tour before tackling the **Headwall,** and even then study your route down carefully because of the rock outcroppings that mar the slope's face. The drops are guaranteed to provoke acrophobia even if you don't head into the chutes.

On **Upper Peel** and **Peel,** with their slim tracks tucked in the trees, your only choice is to play the bumps created by other skiers—there's no room to do anything else.

### Snowboarding

A recently opened terrain park featuring log slides, quarter-pipes, gaps, and machine-made moguls provides something for all boarders. The park is located midmountain off the Keystone and Silver Queen Lifts. Outside of the park, **Forest Queen** and **Treasury** off the Paradise Lift and **North Star,** off the Silver Queen Lift, provide terrain for everyone from intermediate carvers to advanced freestylers. For extreme terrain, thrill seekers can take a shot at **Upper Peel, Hot Rocks**, or **Forest,** located down from the Silver Queen Lift, or dive into one of the bowls off of the North Face Lift.

## Mountain Highs and Lows

At the base of **Paradise Bowl,** skiers are presented with several choices, including **Canaan**. Locals call this one the "turkey trench"—because timid skiers tend to cluster at the top of the run, then slide their way downhill instead of skiing. Most days, it's icy and speckled with fallen bodies. Better alternatives: **Forest Queen** and **Ruby Chief** (a tad steeper than Forest Queen).

Unless you're a beginner, veer in any direction but onto **Houston.** Beginners may like the length (unless they tire easily), but better skiers will find it flat and boring.

## At the Resort

*Area code 970 unless otherwise noted.*

- **The Nordic Inn** $$ After a few evenings of relaxing fireside chats with the owners of this cozy, 29-room inn, skiers find themselves returning again and again to sample its hospitality, including a hearthside continental breakfast, hot tub, Jacuzzi, and sundeck for warm days. ◆ On Emmons Loop, within walking distance of the lifts. 349.5542, 800/542.7669; fax 349.6487
- **Crested Mountain Village** $$$$ Some of the 58 slope-side condos are gorgeous, others are borderline, so question closely before booking. Many have fireplaces, and all have kitchens, daily maid service, and access to hot tubs, a swimming pool, and saunas. ◆ Slope-side in the Penthouse, Crested Mountain, Crested Mountain North, Butte, and Crested Butte Lodge buildings. 349.4600, 800/544.8448; fax 349.2397
- **Wong's Chinese Restaurant** ★$$ Tasty, inexpensive food and good service are dished up at this Asian oasis. Lunch is an especially

good buy. House specialties include Szechuan- and Mandarin-style dishes (no MSG). ♦ Daily lunch and dinner. Reservations recommended. In the Crested Butte Lodge at the base. 349.4399

✦ **Swiss Chalet Bierstube and Restaurant** ★★★$$ You won't want to check your cholesterol level after dining on the house specialties: raclette and fondue. But you might want to quench that ski-induced thirst with Oktoberfest beer on tap while unwinding on the deck on a sunny day. ♦ Daily dinner. Après-ski from 3:30PM. Reservations recommended. 621 Gothic Rd, across the street from the ski area base. 349.5917

✦ **The Rafters** $$ This barn-size room offers the hottest après-ski action at the base of the slopes. Live entertainment, laughter, and rock music reign until 2AM. ♦ Daily lunch and dinner. Après-ski Happy Hour until closing. Atop the Gothic Building. 349.2298

✦ **Artichoke** ★★★$$ Start with the house specialty—lemon artichoke ale soup—before moving on to hefty burgers or chicken fajita salads at this popular slope-side restaurant. Stop in for a microbrewery beer after skiing. ♦ Daily lunch and dinner. At the Treasury Center. 349.6688

✦ **Rocky Mountain Chocolate Factory** Chocoholics will be in heaven amidst the truffles and fudge—all worth the pricey tariff to the chocolate-addicted. ♦ Daily 10AM-9PM. At the Treasury Center. 349.0933. Also at: 314 Elk Ave. 349.1059

✦ **Mt. Crested Butte Grocery & Deli** This small grocery store has a deli counter and sells limited groceries, sundry items, and liquor. ♦ Daily 8AM-9PM. At the ski area base, in the Emmons Building. 349.6394

✦ **Grande Butte Hotel** $$$$ The 262 comfortable rooms at this full-service hotel at the base of the lifts have whirlpool baths and wet bars. Ask about the corner "family" suites with a private bedroom and two bathrooms. Amenities include two restaurants, two lounges, a small indoor pool, a hot tub, a gameroom, and laundry facilities. ♦ 500 Gothic Rd (near Silver Queen Lift). 349.4000, 800/544.8448; fax 349.6487

Within the Grand Butte Hotel:

**Giovanni's Grande Cafe** ★$$$ Guests sit on plush chairs surrounded by imported Italian marble while feasting on Northern Italian cuisine at this upscale-looking restaurant. Despite the decor, casual après-ski clothing is the dress of choice. ♦ Daily dinner. 349.4999

✦ **Gateway** $$$ One of the resort's best values, this 10-unit complex features condos with kitchens, living areas, and fireplaces; underground parking; a sauna; and an outdoor hot tub. ♦ Near Peachtree Lift. 349.2390, 800/821.3718; fax 349.7621

✦ **San Moritz** $$ The two- to four-bedroom ski-in/ski-out condos have rock fireplaces; some have lofts. Each building has a hot tub and sauna. The popular private shuttle ferries skiers to the lifts or downtown in the evening. ♦ 18 Hunter Hill Rd (near Peachtree Lift). 349.5150, 800/443.7459; fax 349.7750

✦ **Timberline** $ While some of these condos are wearing around the edges, all are well kept and come with fireplaces. This complex is a real bargain, offering an outdoor hot tub, free shuttle service to the lifts at the base, and excellent service overall. ♦ 300 yards from the T-bar slope. 349.9831, 800/451.5669

## Beyond the Resort

**1 The Elk Mountain Lodge** $ Built in 1919 by the Colorado Fuel and Iron Company, this 16-room lodge was originally used as an employee housing facility. In 1952, the lodge was converted to a hotel which now hosts skiers who spend the night in compact rooms and congregate by day or evening in the attractive common area. Perks include a complimentary continental breakfast and indoor hot tub. ♦ 129 Gothic Ave (between Second and First Sts). 349.7533, 800/374.6521; fax 349.5114

**2 Last Resort Bed and Breakfast** $$ For a relaxing, home-away-from-home feeling, try one of this charming inn's six spacious antiques-filled bedrooms. A Jacuzzi, steam room, library, and solarium by the creek complete the ambience. ♦ 213 Third St (between Maroon and Gothic Aves). 349.0445, 800/349.0444

**3 Kochevar's Saloon and Gaming Hall** ★$$ This authentic remnant of the wild West was built with hand-hewn logs in 1896. Today locals and visitors mix it up playing pool, darts, and shuffleboard or rocking to the sound of live entertainers. The kitchen serves blue-plate specials, sandwiches, and entrées from around the world. ♦ Daily dinner. 127 Elk Ave (between Second and First Sts). 349.6745

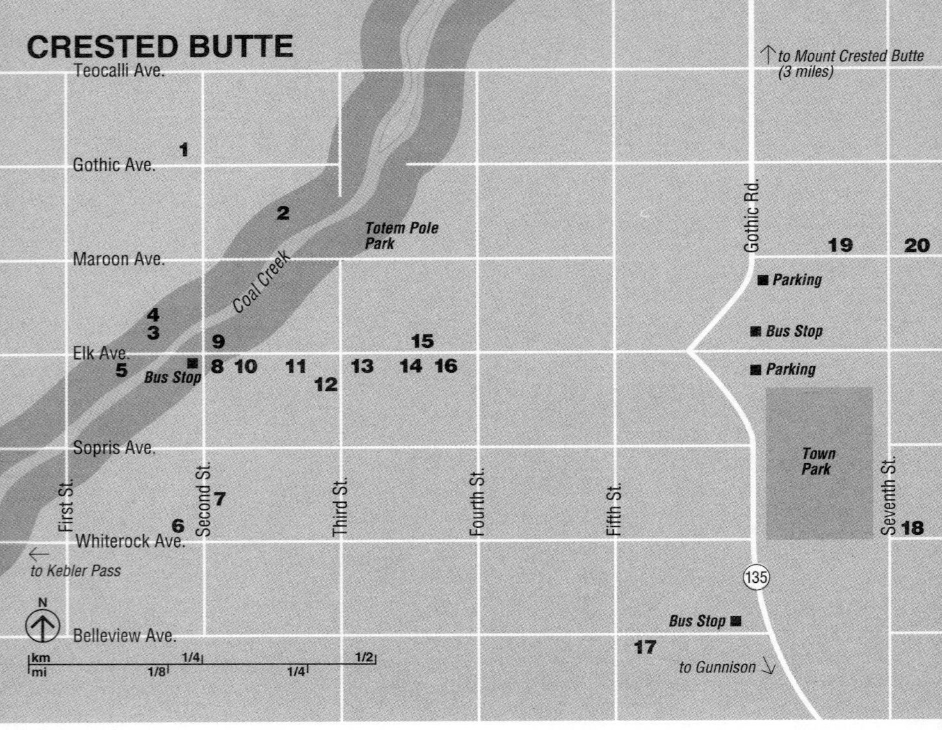


**4 Soupçon** ★★★★$$$ The log cabin exterior doesn't hint at the innovative French cuisine served on the rustic tables inside. A frequently changing menu features such selections as elk with lingonberries, fresh salmon, oysters, and mouthwatering desserts. ♦ Daily dinner. 127 Elk Ave, in the alley just off Second St behind the Forest Queen. 349.6168

**5 Penelope's** ★★★$$$ In this noisy and popular restaurant, guests dine either in rooms complementing the style of this century-old house or in the airy, plant-filled greenhouse. Cuisine ranges from Colorado rack of lamb and fresh seafood to grilled buffalo, pasta, and vegetarian specialties. ♦ Daily dinner; Sunday brunch. Bar opens at 5PM. 120 Elk Ave (between Second and First Sts). 349.5178

**5 Powerhouse Bar Y Grill** ★$$ Watch out for the killer margaritas served in this remodeled warehouse/barn. Choose between a long list of Mexican beers and 25 types of tequila before chowing down on Tex-Mex food, mesquite-grilled steaks, seafood, and other fare. ♦ Daily dinner. Happy Hour 5PM-6PM. 130 Elk Ave (between Second and First Sts). 349.5494

Dr. Bill Calder, a University of Arizona ornithologist who spends summers studying hummingbirds in Gothic (just north of Crested Butte), netted a banded warbler on a remote volcano in southern Mexico. It turned out to have been banded in Gothic by the director of the Rocky Mountain Biological Laboratory two years earlier.

**6 Slogar's** ★★★★$$ Even such old standbys as mashed potatoes are whipped up with extra flair and flavor at this family-style restaurant which often seats large parties. Formerly a hangout for miners, the place has been restored to resemble an 1800s dining establishment, complete with antiques and stained glass windows. Homemade dishes include skillet (nongreasy) fried chicken and steak with tomato chutney and creamed corn on the side. ♦ Daily dinner. Second St (at Whiterock Ave). 349.5765

**7 Crested Butte Club** $$$ Seven charming Victorian rooms are hidden away on the upper floor of a building that also houses an elegant pub anc a popular athletic club. The rooms feature many special touches, including fireplaces, queen-size waveless waterbeds, and clawfoot tubs. Guests enjoy after-hour privileges in the health club, a complimentary breakfast, and Happy Hour. ♦ 512 Second St (between Whiterock and Sopris Aves). 349.6655

**8 Something for Everyone** An eclectic collection of clothing for men and women, jewelry, accessories, and items for kids are sold here. ♦ M-Sa 9:30AM-7:30PM; Su noon-5PM. 202 Elk Ave (at Second St). 349.6852

**9 Le Bosquet** ★★★$$$ Slip into this romantic bistro for an evening of sipping wine and dining on classic French cuisine. Locals have long favored this restaurant for such selections as elk medaillons in Cabernet sauce and home-smoked trout. ♦ Daily lunch and dinner. Reservations recommended. Second St (at Elk Ave). 349.5808

**10** **Bacchanale** $$ Families will feel comfortable in this Northern Italian restaurant with a children's menu. ♦ Daily dinner. 208 Elk Ave (between Third and Second Sts). 349.5257

**11** **Wooden Nickel** ★★$$ The old West lives at this wood saloon, which is usually packed until the wee hours. The menu roams from shrimp and steamed clams to burgers and prime rib. ♦ Daily dinner. Two Happy Hours (3PM-5PM and 10:30PM-midnight). 222 Elk Ave (between Third and Second Sts). 349.6350

**11** **Stefanic's General Store** Stop at this authentic old-fashioned general store for anything from staples to sundries. There's also a deli/lunch counter and soda fountain. ♦ Daily 8AM-9PM. 228 Elk Ave (between Third and Second Sts). 349.5477

**12** **Gourmet Noodle** ★★$$ Elk cannelloni? Come prepared to sample some odd-sounding but great-tasting homemade pasta combinations. ♦ Daily dinner. Reservations recommended. 411 Third St (at Elk Ave). 349.7401

**13** **Bakery Cafe** ★★$ Locals keep the ovens busy baking delicious muffins and other homemade goodies. Coffees, casseroles, soups, pizza, salad bar, and espresso are also on the menu. ♦ Daily breakfast, lunch, and dinner. Third St (at Elk Ave). 349.7280

Above the Bakery Cafe:

**Pfisters Handwork** Your search for intriguing cards, jewelry, pottery, and other handcrafted novelties ends here. ♦ Daily 9AM-9PM. 349.6731

**12** **Goodman Gallery** This tiny gallery features Southwestern, wildlife, and natural artwork. ♦ Daily 10AM-8PM. Third St (at Elk Ave, in the Bakery Building). 349.5470

**14** **Mountain Moppets** You'll find mountains of children's clothing, outerwear, books, and small gift items here. ♦ Daily 10AM-8PM. 318 Elk Ave (in the Butte Plaza Mall). 349.7508

**15** **Cookworks** Gourmet kitchen equipment, foodstuffs, and coffee beans fill this shop, which also has a coffee bar. ♦ M-Sa 9AM-8PM; Su noon-5PM. 321 Elk Ave (between Fourth and Third Sts). 349.7398

**16** **Tradition** Here's a fun place for picking up those items—throws, candles, Christmas ornaments, and games—that you never buy at home. ♦ Daily 10AM-9PM. 326 Elk Ave (between Fourth and Third Sts). 349.6379

**16** **Donita's Cantina** ★★$$ This is the place for huge servings of traditional Mexican fare along with dishes like vegetarian spinach-and-tofu enchilada. Be prepared to wait, with margaritas, on busy evenings. ♦ Daily dinner. Bar opens at 4PM. 330 Elk Ave (between Fourth and Third Sts). 349.6674

**17** **McDell's Market** Stock up on staples at this local grocery store. ♦ 500 Belleview Ave (between Gothic Rd and Fifth St). 349.6492

**18** **Claimjumper Bed and Breakfast** $$ This log home could be a time capsule for the 20th century. The six "themed" guest rooms feature oddball items and memorabilia like Mickey Mantle's **Yankees** jersey, a 1950s Shell gas pump, and the town's only stoplight. Private and shared baths are available. ♦ 704 Whiterock Ave (at Seventh St). 349.6471

**19** **Cristiana Guesthaus** $$ Amenities at this informal, 21-room European-style lodge include breakfast served fireside in a pleasant lounge, an outdoor hot tub, and a sauna. No smoking permitted. ♦ 621 Maroon Ave (between Seventh St and Gothic Rd). 349.5326, 800/824.7899; fax 349.1962

**20** **Elizabeth Anne Bed and Breakfast** $$ The friendly proprietors serve a country breakfast at this four-room bed-and-breakfast filled with Queen Anne furniture, antiques, and Victorian touches. No smoking permitted. ♦ 703 Maroon Ave (at Seventh St). 349.0147

## Bests

### Allen Beck
Retired Physician/Writer

**Keystone run**—Great when it's smooth and flat.

The **Artichoke** and **Paradise** decks on "deck days."

The roast duck at **Soupçon** restaurant.

Barstool-hugging at **Kochevar's Saloon.**

A danish at the **Bakery Cafe;** anything from street vendors.

Ski talk on the **Mountain Express** buses.

### Laura Wilson
Public Relations Coordinator, Crested Butte Mountain Resort

Sitting at **Paradise** deck on a sunny day, drinking a glass of wine (on my day off, of course).

Watching the **US Extreme Skiing Championships...**

Chicken salad sandwiches at the **Bakery Cafe.**

Moonlight cross-country skiing.

Romantic dinners at **Giovanni's Grand Cafe.**

Margaritas at **Donita's Cantina.**

# Purgatory

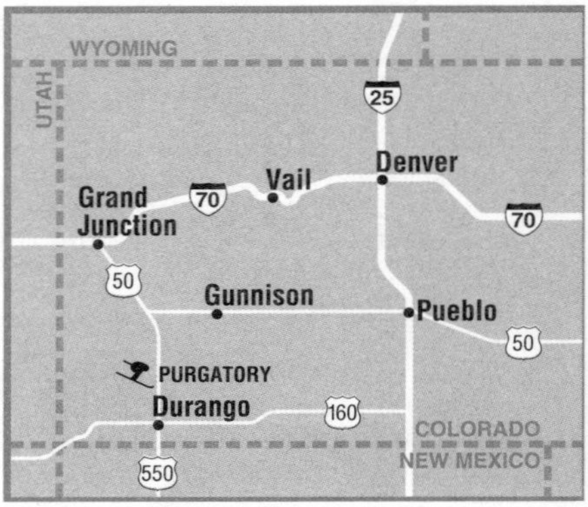

WYOMING
UTAH
25
Denver
Vail
Grand Junction
70
70
50
Gunnison
Pueblo
50
PURGATORY
Durango
160
COLORADO
NEW MEXICO
550

Wearing your "No! I'm not a Movie Star" button promises instant entrée to the "in" crowd at this southwestern Colorado ski resort, where last spring's big event was "Noncelebrity Week."

Only Purgatory would make a middle-aged guy in a shapeless orange ski jacket the star of its ad campaign. Call it anti-glitzy or pro-Joe and Jane Blow, this resort—a combination of 19th-century mining town and built-for-skiing village—blatantly courts the common skier, spouse, and their 2.5 kids.

Soon after buckle boots were invented, the residents of Durango—a century-old gateway for ranchers, fur traders, and prospectors seeking glittering ore in the **San Juan Mountains**—decided to prospect for "white gold" wintertime tourists. Twenty-five miles north, a ski area called Purgatory had opened in 1965 and was gaining fame for runs slanted just right for "ballroom skiing." The two areas combined their resources to create a gigantic resort with the slogan "Purgatory-Durango, 25 miles wide!" Thirty years later, the resort's name became Purgatory once again.

Today honky-tonk music still drifts from Durango's saloons, where miners once paid for drinks with gold dust, and the mountainsides above town are scattered with mining ruins. But the atmosphere in the tiny village anchoring the ski slopes is strictly contemporary.

Purgatory has nine chairlifts that traverse a series of glacier-carved steps on the mountainside that form roller coaster fall lines. But this 2,029 vertical-foot mountain (with 70 runs) offers far more than you can survey from the chairlifts. A motherlode of entertaining skiing awaits out of sight, on the less trafficked slopes and in glades.

Novices start at **Columbine Station,** a green-rated area below the ski village that faster skiers rarely enter. Once they gain some confidence with stops and turns, beginners move on to rolling runs, where widely spaced islands of aspen and pine let skiers parallel the experience of skiing through the woods.

Kids call the **Adventure Park** in the slow-skiing **Family Zone** "the fun place." This special trail has an obstacle course and other terrain designed to improve children's skiing skills while they play. Simple signs on the trees tell the colorful history of the **Four Corners** (where **Colorado, Arizona, Utah,** and **New Mexico** meet).

The smoothly groomed intermediate trails, which cover nearly 50 percent of the mountain, draw fans from Texas, Oklahoma, Nebraska, and California. (Although the accents of the skiers during last season's holiday weeks suggest that word is spreading east of the Mississippi.)

The **Legends,** a jumble of slopes and glades, contains the majority of the steep black trails. **Bottom's Chute, Elliot's,** and **Coyote's Chute** are "bad" enough to earn the respect of 19-year-olds from nearby **Fort Lewis College** who don't know the meaning of terror and seem to have rubber knees.

Although the resort affects a laid-back style, Purgatory works hard to keep skiers returning. A binding mechanic roves the mountain assisting skiers with problems, so they won't have to wend their way downhill (sometimes without skis) to get their gear fixed. Nets encircle trash cans under the chairlifts, encouraging riders to practice freehand tosses. (The web snares the shots that don't make the basket).

Purgatory caters to the cheap streak in all of us, rich and famous or not. With the exception of Christmas week and spring break, children 12 years and younger ski free if they are with a paying adult. On-mountain child care is available for children as young as two months, and some lodges let kids sleep free in their parents' room.

Lodging for folks who like to head uphill with the ski patrol is a limited commodity. There are a few options at the base, and several condo complexes on the highway near the resort. But lots of skiers opt to stay in Durango, where the après-ski hours are livelier. The historic downtown sector has a variety of galleries, T-shirt stores, and more than 20 "outlet" stores selling all kinds of duds at a discount. **Fort Lewis College** sits on a hillside above the downtown sector, so the town has an abundance of inexpensive food—burgers, Mexican food, pizza, and pasta. Not to worry, though—a few gourmet restaurants thrive here as well.

The ski area is surrounded by fascinating places to visit. Colorado's southwestern corner, a geographically unique zone where mountains, mesas, and canyons collide, has been inhabited by Native American Indian tribes for many centuries. The lone mesa housing **Mesa Verde,** designated a world cultural site by the United Nations because of the **Anasazi cliff dwellings,** is about an hour's drive from Durango. (Anasazi, the Navajo word for "ancient ones," describes the populace that lived here from approximately AD 1 to 1276—covering four archaeological periods.) Why these "ancient ones" abandoned their dwellings is something that experts are still debating. The excavated archaeological sites trace the evolution of the "ancient ones" from pit dwellings to the "apartment houses"—multicelled stone shelters built in caves halfway up sheer sandstone cliffs. Only part of the park is open in the winter, but you can also learn about the region's history indoors at the **Anasazi Cultural Center** near **Cortez.** Galleries in Durango and Cortez, a gateway to the southwestern desert, display art, pottery, and jewelry created by residents of the Indian reservations that are spread over much of the Four Corners region.

For a front-row seat to some of the region's most spectacular scenery, catch the steam-driven, narrow-gauge train that once hauled gold-rich ore from the **Silverton** mines 3,000 feet above Durango. All summer, and from Thanksgiving to New Year's Day, it chugs through a rugged wilderness that can't be reached by car.

**Purgatory Ski Resort**
**1 Skier Place**
**Durango, Colorado 81301**

**Information**........970/247.9000
**Reservations**........800/525.0892
**Snow Phone**........970/247.9000

## Fast Facts

*Area code 970 unless otherwise noted.*

**Ski Season** Thanksgiving through early April

**Location** Purgatory is in the **Four Corners** region of **Colorado** in the southwestern corner of the state, 348 miles from **Denver.**

### Getting to Purgatory

**By air: Durango-LaPlata County Airport** is 42 miles from the base. **Continental Express** and **United Express** offer daily flights from **Denver, Mesa Airlines** has daily flights from **Albuquerque** and **Phoenix,** and **America West** has daily flights from Phoenix. **Durango Transportation** (259.4818) offers regular shuttle service to and from the airport. Several hotels, including the **Purgatory Village Hotel** at the ski area base, run airport shuttles for guests.

**By car: Avis, Budget,** and **Hertz** rental cars can be picked up at the airport. Head north 21 miles on US 550. Durango is 348 miles from **Denver** via Interstate 25, US 160, and US 550.

### Getting around Purgatory

**Durango Lift** (259.LIFT) provides bus service between Durango and Purgatory. **Durango Transportation** (259.4818) runs vans between the two villages; groups of up to 14 people can charter a van/driver. Skiers who want freedom of movement are wiser renting a car.

## FYI

**PURGATORY RESORT**
DURANGO COLORADO

**Area** 690 acres with 75 runs featuring varied terrain, including glades.

Beginner—23 percent

Intermediate—51 percent

Advanced/Expert—26 percent

**Number of Groomed Runs** 60

**Longest Run** 2 miles **(BD&M Expressway)**

**Capacity** 12,700 skiers per hour

**Base Elevation** 8,793 feet

**Summit Elevation** 10,822 feet

**Vertical Rise** 2,029 feet

**Average Annual Snowfall** 250 inches

**Snowmaking** 22 percent

**Night Skiing** None

**Lifts** 9 (4 triple chairs and 5 double chairs)

| **Lift Passes** | **Full Day** | **Half Day** (starts at 12:30PM) |
|---|---|---|
| **Adult** | $37 | $27 |
| **Child** (12 and under) | Free* | Free* |
| **Senior** (62-69) | $19 | $14 |
| **Senior** (70 and over) | Free | Free |

*Children 12 and under receive one free pass per paid parent ticket, except during Christmas week and Spring Break when full- and half-day passes are $19 and $14, respectively.

**Ski School** The freestanding office (247.9000 ext 5145) is located in the plaza at the base of the slopes. Half-day and all-day group lessons are offered.

**Kids' Ski School** Children ski free when they are participating in **Children's Ski School.** Kids 3 to 12 years old are placed in ability groups—the **Junior Demons, Ski Demons,** or **Demons Elite**—for half-day or all-day lessons that include lunch. (Also see "Day Care," below).

**Clinics and Special Programs Dante's Workshops** are concentrated two-hour clinics for advanced skiers and for intermediates who can make parallel turns. Highlighting how to ski the conditions of the day, these classes are often small, so you may get valuable individual attention. Three-day women's workshops are for advanced and intermediate skiers (the women's workshops are taught by women), and **SnoMasters Classic** is a weeklong clinic for skiers 55 years and older. The "Start 'Em Off Right" program for first-time skiers, 12 years old and up, includes a free half-day beginner lesson with the purchase of a lift ticket; or two free half-day lessons on consecutive days with the purchase of a two-day or multi-day lift ticket. Half-day clinics are also available for telemark and snowboarding. **Purgatory Adaptive Sports Association** (259.3074) offers an award-winning program for disabled skiers, including adaptive equipment and full-day private lessons. Advance reservations are requested.

**Races** A NASTAR course is located on **Pitchfork** and costs $4 for one run, $5 for two runs, and $6 for four runs.

**Rentals** Recreational and sport alpine equipment can be rented at **Purgatory Sports** (247.9000 ext 5112), on the second floor of the **Purgatory Village Center.** Alpine, demo, and telemark equipment is available at the **Expert Edge** (ext 5102) in the **Village Mall,** across from the ski school. Snowboards may be rented at **San Juan Snowboards** (ext 5197), on the second floor of **Purgatory Village Center.** All shops are open daily from 8AM to 5PM.

**Lockers** Coin-operated lockers (quarters only) are located at several places, including the ski rental shop, both on-mountain restaurants, and the ground level of the **Purgatory Village Center.**

**Day Care** Take younger children, 2 months to 4 years old, to **Kids Central** (247.9000 ext 5438) across from the **Teddy Bear Camp** on the second floor of the **Purgatory Village Center**. The youngest kids (under 2 months old) will be sent to **Teddy Bear Camp** (8:30AM-4:30PM). Cub Care is for youngsters 2 months to 3 years old. **Polar Bears,** a program focusing on a mixture of skiing and other fun activities, is for 3- to 4-year-olds. **Grizzly Bears,** for children approximately 4 years old to kindergarten, is a daylong session designed to teach skiing but there is still some time devoted to games and storytelling. **Kodiak Clan**, whose primary focus is on skiing, is for children 5 years old and up. **Shred Bears** is for kids who want to snowboard. Children's rental equipment is available on site. Reservations are required.

**First Aid** The medical clinic (247.9000 ext 3042) is located in the plaza, next to the ski school building. This clinic is a branch of **Mercy Medical Center** (247.4311), 375 E Park Avenue.

**Parking** Free parking is available at the base.

**Worth Knowing**

- Free one-hour guided skiing tours of Purgatory's backside are given from the top of Lift 6.

## Rating the Runs

### ● Beginner

Some skiers swear it's their sacred duty to worship skiing on **Divinity,** a gentle beginner trail that puts you in tune with nature while skirting around islands of trees. The wide spaces between the pines leave plenty of room for learners to turn, while relishing the feeling of skiing through the woods.

Buddhists say it is a state of perfection, one you may just reach as you wind down **Nirvana**'s long trail through the trees. The pitches are gentle, and the trail is wide. If your ski group is a mix of beginners and intermediates, the more advanced skiers can tackle **Boogie, Peace,** or **Snag** and regroup at the bottom.

## ■ Intermediate

Boredom and **Boogie** don't mix. The trail curves, swoops, and changes angles, so skiers never know exactly what's next. Because this run is off Chair 3, the longest, slowest lift on the mountain, many skiers don't venture here. Their loss! The better skiers boogie off and on little paths that snake through the trees, dancing their way downhill.

The ski area's first mountain manager, Chet, didn't always think in a straightforward manner, according to locals, and you shouldn't either when heading down his namesake run, **Chet's.** The roller coaster fall line here prompted some Texans tangoing down the slope to label Purgatory the number one resort for "ballroom" skiing. The edges can be a bit rough, and the trail is slightly off camber, so maximize your entertainment by playing the edges. Chet and its next-door neighbor, **Sally,** sing the best "blues" on this mountain.

## ◆ Advanced

You can imitate the bull elk that **Bull Run** takes its name from, crashing downhill through the bumps, or you can take a finer approach to navigating the terrain. The upper half—a single black-diamond designation—is a mere warm-up for what's to come. The ungroomed lower half simply gets steeper and steeper as the bumps get bigger and bigger. One consolation: there's no lift overhead, so other skiers can't rate your performance.

Like Dante's River Styx which encircled the underworld, Purgatory's **Styx** can seem like an endless flow of knee-bruising bumps. Two fall lines ensure a different ride every time you travel the "river." When it's been groomed, this rim run becomes a high-speed cruiser. You can't jump into Styx involuntarily; it's only open to those seeking it off Chair 6.

## Snowboarding

Boarders should feel right at home seeing some of their own kind here in a patroller uniforms. The snowboard park—complete with log slides, banked turns, snow ramps and gaps as well as a wide-open carving area—is located on **Limbo** (a snowboarders-only area). Away from the park on the backside of the mountain, **Demon** offers lots of banks, bumps, and kickers for jumps, making it a popular hangout for free riders. **Dead Spike** (the widest trail on the mountain) and **Paradise** provide plenty of space for great GS turns; each time it's possible to take a different line down the mountain.

# Mountain Highs and Lows

Locals designate The **BD&M Expressway** "Boring, Dull, and Monotonous," although the formal name is **Boudreaux, Dirty, and Major.** It's a barely tilted catwalk, so don't ski it unless you're trying to get from Lift 8 to the base. On powder days, you'll need poles for one section. Why is it colored blue on the map? Management doesn't want beginners here because there are no easy trails off the top of this run.

Ray Duncan, founder of Purgatory, used to survey his domain from what is now called **Ray's Ridge.** The stony, snow-clad **San Juan Mountains** are in clear view at the top, but you'll have to risk taking your eyes off the heavy-duty bumps. The black-diamond rating is accurate except when the moguls are mowed down. When gossip spreads about Ray's "haircut," the locals show up to ski this sweet blue/black cruiser, where they can zip down a steep headwall before the run mellows out. The narrow trail begins on the ridge before sinking into the trees, but there are bail-out cat tracks that lead to easier terrain.

# At the Resort

*Resort facilities can be reached by calling the central information number (970/247.9000) unless otherwise noted.*

✦ **Farquahrts** $ At lunchtime, this shingled barn of a building is packed with skiers lined up at the counter for pizza and the sort of hamburgers that taste best when you're really hungry. Pick up your food and find a space at one of the tables on the three levels. When the sun's out, head for the second-floor deck that faces the ski mountain. After the lifts close, you can spot characters of all sorts, from dolled-up Texas debutantes to mangy-haired snow-cat drivers. The bartender, Toby, is a former All-American swimmer, who is distinguished by his loss to Mark Spitz in the Olympic trials. ◆ Daily lunch and dinner. 1 Skier Pl (at the base)

✦ **Sterling's** $ This upscale-looking cafeteria has downscale prices. Morning choices range from cold cereal to breakfast burritos. Best bets for lunch are the daily specials, such as the roast beef or chicken breast sandwiches. Light snacks are served in the afternoon. ◆ Daily breakfast and lunch. Bar open until 8PM. Purgatory Resort Village Center

✦ **Heaven Eleven Market and Deli** For breakfast on the run, race through and grab a cinnamon roll or an Egg McMillie (a McMuffin clone) to munch on the lift. This quick-stop has groceries, crisp roasted chickens, soups, chili, and other dishes you can take to your condo for an at-home dinner. ◆ Daily 7:30AM-7:30PM. Kendall Building (at the base)

✦ **Dante's** ★$$ Take the lift to reach this cafeteria, located in the mountain lodge near the top of Chair 5. It's divided into sections where you can get soup and salad, Mexican dishes, and the usual burgers and sandwiches. ◆ Daily lunch. Near the top of Chair 5

Within Dante's:

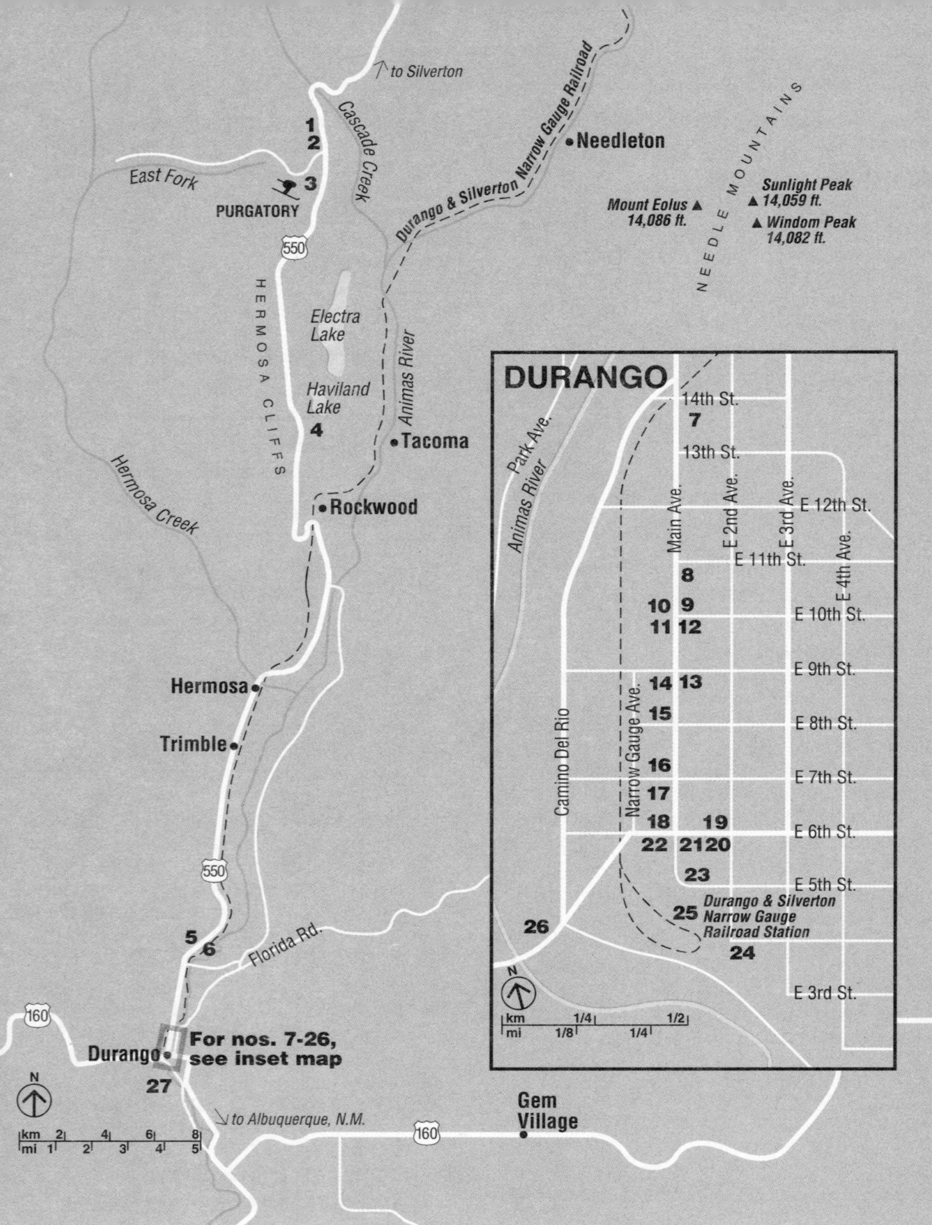


✦ **Dante's Den** ★★★$$ Treat yourself to a leisurely meal at this sit-down restaurant. The fillet of beef with crabmeat and boursin cheese is outstanding, and the grilled salmon with Granny Smith apples in a roquefort Port sauce is equally tempting. If you intend to resume serious skiing, choose the fresh fruit sorbet for dessert. Otherwise, throw calories out the window and order the chocolate raspberry decadence. This torte, with its layer of raspberry sauce, is the reason they invented stretch clothing. ♦ Daily lunch. Reservations recommended

✦ **Powderhouse** ★$$ Perched at the top of Chair 2, the best choices at this restaurant are the chicken breast or beef brisket sandwiches from the outdoor barbecue line. ♦ Daily lunch. Top of Chair 2

✦ **Purgatory Village Hotel** $$$$ Rooftop hot tubs, an outdoor pool, and decent soundproofing between the 126 units make this slope-side ski resort property extremely attractive. Most of the units have wood-burning fireplaces, steam showers, whirlpool baths, well-equipped kitchens, and washers and dryers. The majority of shops and restaurants at the base are either inside the hotel buildings, which wrap around several lifts, or a short walk away. ♦ Bottom of Lift 4. 385.2100, 800/693.0175; fax 382.2248

## Beyond the Resort

**1 Cascade Village** $$$ Jacuzzi tubs and wood-mantled fireplaces make for warm lodgings at these individually owned and decorated studios, condos, and town homes. Some of the 125 units have balconies overlooking the Needles Mountain Range. Try to get a second-floor unit, since these have higher ceilings and a more open feeling. The **Forester** town homes have spacious upper-floor bedrooms with two-person Jacuzzis. A general store, ski shop with rentals, large indoor pool, outdoor hot tub, and excellent restaurant are also within the complex. ♦ 50827 Hwy 550 (just north of the entrance to Purgatory Ski Resort). 259.3500, 800/525.0896; fax 259.3500 ext 239

Within Cascade Village:

**Cafe Cascade** ★★★★$$$ Though the decor is nothing fancy, the food is delicious. The menu, which changes nightly, includes wild game—such as boar, buffalo, and antelope—and saltwater fish dressed in imaginative sauces. ♦ Reservations recommended. Daily dinner. 259.3500 ext 256

**2 Sow's Ear** ★★★ $$$ The climbing wall around the pub gives new meaning to the term "barfly." Definitely not a pig in a poke, this rustic tavern has so much wood that you'll swear you're inside a sauna. A big elk head lords over the fireplace, where the slightly zany owners and staff serve the best steaks in the resort. Start with the usually spicy meatballs du jour, then proceed to the steak, which can take the form of a dainty eight-ounce charbroiled (or blackened) fillet, or a gargantuan 18-ounce Hodgeebaba rib eye smothered with sautéed onions and mushrooms. The Half a Daffy is a duck properly crisped on the outside and served with a piquant Grand Marnier sauce. They have a special children's menu. ♦ Daily dinner. Reservations recommended on busy weekends. 49617 Hwy 550 (at the entrance to Purgatory Ski Resort). 247.3527

**3 Silver Pick** $$ These wood-framed condominiums with fireplaces and private decks are a good deal, and they're less than a mile from the resort entrance. Relax in the outdoor hot tub while the kids check out the gameroom. There are 36 condominiums. ♦ 48475 Hwy 550 (near the entrance to Purgatory Ski Resort). 259.6600 (in Colorado), 800/221.PICK (elsewhere in the US)

**4 Tamarron** $$$ Rustic looking, but with elegant amenities, this lodge offers guests a choice of two restaurants and 125 spacious rooms in the main building as well as a choice of condominiums, and three-bedroom town homes, all wrapped around a golf course and tall pines. Shuttle service is provided to the ski area, and guests who stay on-site can play broomball, skate on the pond, or use the health club's indoor/outdoor pool, saunas, whirlpool, or indoor hot tub with terrific views. ♦ 40292 Hwy 550 (18 miles north of Durango center). 259.2000, 800/678.1000; fax 259.0745

**5 Days Inn Durango** $ Definitely your conventional Days Inn motel rooms, but not your typical property, the recently renovated 94-room establishment offers perks including an indoor Olympic pool, two giant Jacuzzis, and men's and women's saunas. The motel has a restaurant and lounge, and in the evening a shuttle to downtown stops here. Ask about ski packages and AAA and other group discounts. ♦ 1700 Animas View Dr (off Hwy 550, 3 miles north of Durango center), Durango. 259.1430, 800/325.2525; fax 259.5741

**6 Iron Horse Inn** $ The 140 bi-level rooms are among the best values in the region. Let the kids sleep on the bed (or sofa bed) before the fireplace downstairs, while you get your z's in the upstairs loft. Other attractions are the indoor pool, large Jacuzzi, saunas, Ping-Pong tables, restaurant, and a friendly, helpful staff. Ski and car rentals available. ♦ 5800 N Main Ave (off Hwy 550, 3 miles north of Durango center). 259.1010, 800/748.2990; fax 385.4791

Within the Iron Horse Inn:

**Buckskin Charlie's** ★★★$$$ Locals would prefer that tourists not discover this restaurant, a hunting lodge takeoff complete with fireplace and mounted animal heads. Chuck Norton, one of Durango's favorite chefs, serves imaginative cuisine such as duck and artichoke gumbo, elk tenderloin medaillons with mushroom sauce, and buffalo burgers. Black Angus beef, pasta, and seafood are also on the menu. ♦ Daily breakfast and dinner. 5800 N Main Ave. 259.1010

**7 Manufacturer's Marketplace** Seven outlet stores, including **Bugle Boy Outlet, Socks Galore & More, Van Heusen,** and **Levi's Outlet by Most,** are tucked into this shopping center. You'll find lots of real deals, but don't forget to check for flaws. ♦ Most stores open M-Sa 10AM-9PM; Su 11AM-6PM. Main Ave (at 14th St)

**8 Carver's Bakery and Brew Pub** ★★★$ This is *the* place for breakfast in Durango—and a few beers at the lively microbrewery pub in the evenings. Go early (before 8:45AM on weekends) or you'll have to wait for the mouth-watering blueberry pancakes and freshly brewed coffee. Skiers swing by for muffins or bagels from the pastry case along with huge cups of rich java. For a maximum "power breakfast," order the breakfast burrito packed with eggs, black beans, and spiced sausage. Egg Beaters are available for the health-conscious. At night, brewski-loving skiers crowd the wood tables to sample the four or more beers made on the premises: Honey Pilsner, Iron Horse Stout, Amber Ale, and a specialty beer of the season. Try the sampler tray, featuring every beer on tap. Chicken stew in a hollowed out round of bread, salads, and charbroiled and deli sandwiches are on the lunch and dinner menus. ♦ Daily breakfast and lunch; M-Sa dinner. Pub open M-Sa until 10PM. 1022 Main Ave (at E 11th St). 259.2545

Olde Tymer's Cafe

**9 Olde Tymer's Cafe** ★★★$ A fancy ski sweater or chic ensemble marks you as a tourist in this former Wall Drug Store turned restaurant, where locals dress down for the good—and generous—nightly specials. Monday is burger night, when $3.95 buys a huge greasy burger with fries, and a $1.50 gets you a draft beer. Friday is taco night, and most folks migrate toward the cheap margaritas. Saturday night's fajita plate easily feeds two average eaters. ♦ Daily lunch and dinner. 1000 Main Ave (at E 10th St). 259.2990

**10 Jarvis Suite Hotel** $$ This little-advertised treasure is hidden on a side street in the heart of downtown Durango. The outside of this historic building—originally Durango's first burlesque theater—is unimpressive, but inside are 22 comfortable suites, all with full kitchens, some with lofts and high ceilings. Even the studio suites are larger than most hotel rooms downtown. ♦ 125 W 10th St (at Main Ave). 259.6190, 800/824.1024; fax 259.6190

**11 Durango Diner** Owners Gary Broad and Bart Rabkin have been entertaining (and feeding) locals for 15 years. They're known for their super spuds, *chiles rellenos,* and green chili burgers. Don't leave without a T-shirt. ♦ Daily breakfast and lunch. 957 Main Ave (at W 10th St). 247.9889

**12 Maria's Bookshop** Books and novels about the Southwest, including works by Tony Hillerman and Louis L'Amour, are the specialty of this shop. The shop also carries topographical maps and Navajo rugs. ♦ M-Sa 10AM-5:30PM. 960 Main Ave (between E Ninth and E 10th Sts). 247.1438

**13 The Red Snapper** ★★★★$$$$ Exotic fish swim in the huge saltwater aquariums surrounded by tables and the staff wears colorful Hawaiian shirts at this restaurant voted number one in town by the *Durango Herald*'s readers. Easterners make the oyster bar their first stop. Fresh seafood heads the bill, but tender prime rib and steaks are offered, too. The salad bar has more than 40 items, including homemade dressings and fresh breads. Low-calorie fish entrées leave room to indulge in the Death By Chocolate. ♦ Daily dinner. Reservations recommended for large parties. 114 E Ninth St (at Main Ave). 259.3417

**14 Toh-Atin Gallery** An exceptional selection of hand-crafted jewelry and pottery fills the display cases, and museum-quality rugs adorn the walls of this gallery. Serious collectors around the country are familiar with Toh-Atin, run by a family that has been trading with the region's Native American tribes for four generations. But be aware that some collectors believe the prices for certain pieces are higher than you might find at galleries located away from a tourist area. ♦ M-Th, Sa 9AM-6PM; F 9AM-9PM. 145 W Ninth St (at Main Ave). 247.8277

**15 Smelter's Coalroom** Take a look at the Southwestern women's clothing and Sara Campbell designs in this tiny shop tucked in a century-old building. The stock rotates, so some days the store is a gold mine and other days it's a waste of time. ♦ M-Sa 10AM-6PM. 801½ Main Ave (at W Eighth St, below London Fog). 259.3470

**15 Durangler's** Just step over the black Labrador and you can chat with the guys tying flies if the shop isn't busy. An excellent selection of trout flies, fly rods, and other fishing gear can be found here, and guided fly-fishing trips on the gold-medal San Juan River, 65 miles away, are offered during the winter. ♦ M-Sa 7:30AM-5PM. 801½ Main Ave (at W Eighth St). 385.4081

**16 Farquahrts Bar** ★★$$ The downtown counterpart to the **Farquahrts** at Purgatory attracts an eclectic crowd: Aging hippies hang out with college students, and yuppies dance with "puppies" (Professionally Underpaid People Into Extreme Sports), a local phenomenon. Great pizza is dished up in a dining room that looks like a funky garage, with license plates and old tin signs on the wood walls. Thursday nights are smoke-free, and on weekends the place jumps with folks who love live rock 'n' roll and bluegrass. ♦ M-Sa 11PM-2AM; Su 11AM-midnight. 725 Main Ave (at W Seventh St). 247.5442

**17 Strater Hotel** $$ The wild West tarries in the meticulously restored interior of this 93-room hostelry. Louis L'Amour often checked into the room over the saloon to write his Western tales (which sold in the millions) because the music filtering through the floorboards inspired him. Guests are surrounded by Victoriana, from walnut beds with high, carved headboards to plush velvet love seats and brocade-covered chairs. The antiques are framed by classy touches, such as hand-stenciled wallpaper and electrified, brass gas-jet-style chandeliers. ♦ 699 Main Ave (between W Sixth and W Seventh Sts). 247.4431, 800/227.4431 (in Colorado), 800/247.4431 (in the US); fax 259.2208

Within the Strater Hotel:

**Diamond Belle Saloon** ★★★$$ The tinkling of a ragtime piano floats past the swinging doors, enticing skiers to come inside and step back in time. Hostesses are costumed circa the late 1880s, and the bartender sports a garter on his sleeve in this wild West remake, with its fussy wallpaper, paintings of nude women, and an orgy of red velvet hangings and trim. Don't miss it! ♦ Daily 11AM to closing

**18 Francisco's** ★ $$ The Mexican fare tends to be mild, but you can request that they turn up the heat. Choices extend north of the border to include steak, seafood, and chicken. The decor has a Southwestern feel, with leather booths, tile tabletops, and kiva fireplaces. ♦ Daily dinner. 619 Main Ave (at W Sixth St). 247.4098

**18 The Solid Muldoon Publishing Company** You won't find books being printed, just a youngish crowd bellied up to the bar. Old skis, a kayak, a sink, old 45s, dolls, and a broken tricycle contribute to the oddball decor. A lucky spin of the "Wheel of Fortune" may earn you discounts, such as dollar shots or a 25¢ beer for anyone with a hole in his or her shirt. There are pinball games and four lanes for darts if chatting isn't enough. ♦ M-Sa 3PM-1AM; Su 3PM-midnight. 117 W Sixth St (at Main Ave). 247.9151

Ski runs on the front side of Purgatory's mountain (i.e., Styx, Catharsis, Hades, Paradise, Limbo, Demon, Salvation, Pitchfork) got their names from Dante's epic poem *The Divine Comedy*.

The Needles, a 13,000-foot wall of mountains that can be seen from Purgatory's slopes, are some of the oldest stone in the Rockies. The gray granite is a Precambrian sea bed that was laid down two billion years before the invention of skis, and was upthrust to near vertical by volcanic action when the Rockies began forming on a warm afternoon about 65 million years ago.

**Restaurants/Clubs:** Red **Hotels:** Blue
**Shops/ Outdoors:** Green **Sights/Culture:** Black

**19** **Ore House** ★★ $$$ Handwoven Indian blankets, rusty coffee pots, tobacco cans, and other artifacts of the Old Southwest ornament the walls in this popular steak (and fish and lobster) house. One wall has a whimsical mural of Durango, circa 1890, with "townsfolk" like John Wayne, the Lone Ranger, and Tonto walking the street while a "lady of the evening" perches on a windowsill of the Strater Hotel. ♦ Daily dinner. 147 E Sixth St (between E Second and Main Aves). 247.5707

**19** **Sundance Saloon** Just listen for the country-and-western music at the corner of Sixth Street and East Second Avenue and follow it into this saloon, where cowboys, cowgirls, and city slickers kick up their heels. Western clothes and cowboy hats aren't required, but leave those colorful ski sweaters and penny loafers in your hotel room. Don't be shocked if a guy in a black hat asks your permission, "sir," to dance with "the lovely lady." ♦ M-Sa 7PM-2AM. 601 E Second Ave (at E Sixth St). 247.8821

**20** **Pronto Pizza and Pasta** ★★★$ Fort Lewis College students, locals, and skiers on a budget crowd into this plain spot for the weekend pizza and pasta buffet nights. (Wanna-be diners wait patiently in a crowd by the door.) The buffet's delicious thin-crust pizza is covered with homemade sauce, lots of cheese, and a variety of toppings. Fettuccine, linguine, and other pasta is made on the premises. Pizza, pasta dishes, and sandwiches can also be ordered from the menu. Beer and wine are available. ♦ Daily dinner. 160 E Sixth St (at E Second Ave). 247.1510

**21** **O'Farrell Hat Co.** Former president Ronald Reagan ordered custom-made O'Farrell cowboy hats for his cabinet members, but an "off-the-rack" Stetson will require fewer gold nuggets. Even so, expect to pay for quality. ♦ M-Sa 8:30AM-6PM. 598 Main Ave (at E Sixth St). 259.2517

Purgatory derives its name from a small creek that runs down the front face of the mountain. Purgatory Creek eventually flows into El Rio de Las Animas Perdidas, the River of Lost Souls. According to legend, it was named by Spanish explorers after a horseman fell into the river and drowned. His body was swept away without benefit of last rites or a proper burial.

**22** **General Palmer Hotel** $$ Four-poster beds with hand-crocheted canopies, pewter bed frames, fringed lamp shades, and other French Victorian niceties are teamed with modernized bathrooms and various amenities to ensure this 39-room hotel's AAA four-diamond rating. Public areas include an airy solarium where guests can enjoy the continental breakfast. The hotel is affiliated with the **Palace Grill Restaurant** right next door. The two Queen Murphy suites are slightly larger rooms with queen-size Murphy beds, wet bars, and refrigerators. ♦ 567 Main Ave (at W Sixth St). 247.4747, 800/523.3358; fax 247.1332

**23** **Izod/Gant** Savings of 30 to 50 percent off the retail prices on men's shirts, pants, sweaters, and belts aren't uncommon at this discount outlet. But the real closeout deals offer quality shirts for as little as $10 to $15. Izod/Gant is just one of several outlets on this side of Main Avenue between Fifth and Sixth and on those two side streets. Look for **Polo, Sequel Outdoor Clothing** (activewear manufactured in Durango), **Benetton, Sergio Tacchini** (ski jackets), **Just A Second** (fleece activewear), and **Bula** (colorful sports accessories). ♦ M-Sa 10AM-7PM; Su noon-6PM. 558 Main Ave (at E Fifth St). 247.1119

During the past 22 years, Purgatory temperatures were at or above statewide resort averages 91 percent of the time, and nine degrees above average 25 percent of the time. One-third of the time, Purgatory had the mildest reading of all Colorado resorts.

Durango helped to warm up the 1994 Winter Olympics in Lillehammer, Norway. Bula, a Durango-based company, was the official headwear sponsor of the US Ski Team. Bula was formed by two local boys, US Ski Team racers who went to the Fiji Islands for a vacation. They took their Bula out of "bula bula," the Fiji equivalent of "howdy."

Famous Western author Louis L'Amour penned many of his novels while staying in the rooms above the Strater Hotel's Diamond Belle Saloon. He wrote about his cowboys to the clinking of glasses and the tinkling of ragtime piano seeping through the floorboards.

**Restaurants/Clubs:** Red **Hotels:** Blue
**Shops/ Outdoors:** Green **Sights/Culture:** Black

**24 Gazpacho** ★$$ The menu disclaimer "Not responsible for too hot chile" sets the tone at this northern New Mexican cantina. Other specialties include guacamole salad, frijoles, enchiladas, chalupas, tamales, and delicious puffy sopaipillas. Find a spot in the bar and work on the margaritas while waiting for a table. This place is also great for parties. ♦ M-Sa lunch and dinner. 431 E Second Ave (at E Fourth St). 259.9494

**25 Durango & Silverton Narrow Gauge Railroad** From Thanksgiving to New Year's Day (except Christmas Eve and Christmas Day) and all summer long, a narrow gauge train, driven by an antique locomotive, chugs through rugged wilderness that can't be reached via automobile up to the Cascade Wye. Visitors have an hour to explore the canyon and eat lunch before re-boarding for the return trip. Long a popular summer excursion, the train is rapidly becoming a favorite day trip for wintertime visitors as well, so reserve seats when you reserve lodging. The train leaves at 10AM and returns around 3PM. There is a concession car, but you can pick up a better brown bag lunch at **Mr. Rosewater's Delicatessen,** 552 Main Avenue, near the train depot. ♦ Reservations recommended. 479 Main Ave (between E Fourth and E Fifth Sts). 247.2733

RED LION INN

**26 Red Lion Inn** $$$ If you want standardized, comfortable hotel rooms—what you might find in the mid-price range in a city—this is the right choice. Two blocks from the train depot, the 159-room inn has a restaurant, indoor pool, sauna, spa, exercise room, and free airport shuttle. ♦ 501 Camino Del Rio (2 blocks west of the train depot). 259.6580, 800/547.8010; fax 259.4398

**27 Durango Area Chamber Resort Association** Visit the information center, south of town, to collect information, leaflets, and brochures about restaurants, attractions, and activities in the city and surrounding countryside. ♦ M-F 8AM-5PM. 111 S Camino Del Rio (three-quarters of a mile south of Durango center). 247.0312

## Bests

**Mary Riddell**
Student, Egnar Middle School

My favorite places to ski are Mammoth Mountain in California and Purgatory.

I like the Purgatory ski area because it is like the Old West—The Durango area has Indian ruins about 30 miles away called **Mesa Verde.**

**Beth Warren**
Writer/Fund-raiser/Social Activist, KSUT Four Corners Public Radio

**Carver's Bakery and Brew Pub**—Breakfast to start your day and home-brewed beer to end your day.

**Farquahrts Bar**—Best après-ski fun on the mountain.

**Christopher Wing**
Bartender/Waiter/Busser/Manager, Sow's Ear Restaurant

For a view of Durango from the rim, drive up to **Fort Lewis College** at night. Take someone special.

Hike or ski to **Spud Lake** up **Old Lime Creek Road**—Quiet, beautiful, and close by.

**Durango Diner** T-shirt; their spuds ain't bad, either.

A hat from **O'Farrell Hat Co.**

Saturday after Thanksgiving bonfire at **Sow's Ear**—Big fire, cheap beer.

Elk wintering in the pastures of the **Hermosa Valley,** halfway between town and the resort.

Lift No. 4, because it's slow; Lift No. 3, ditto.

**Styx**—Trail just long enough you probably won't see anybody else.

Skiing, skating, or tubing at night on **Chapman Hill**—Skiing like it used to be—cheap, cold, and damn fun.

**Robert L. Beers**
Retired Businessman/Active Ski Instructor

Teaching a beginning, intermediate, or advanced student is an extremely rewarding experience. Instruction over the years has not been without its humor and fun. I remember the young man with a really pained expression (until we changed his boots to the right feet); the young lady who fell and came clear out of her boots, which turned out to belong to a very large male; and the lady who reluctantly took lessons at the insistence of her experienced skier spouse and in three days could leave him behind on the mountain.

My favorite runs: **Legends, Dead Spike,** and **Limbo.**

**Jack Turner**
Resort Worker, Purgatory Resort/Fifth-generation native of Durango

My favorite place to have a beer is **Carver's Bakery and Brew Pub** with the "Brew Brothers," Jim and Bill Carver. We are all kayaking buddies (they get invited on a lot of river trips because they always bring a couple of kegs of Carver's Stout).

The best hash browns and fried eggs in town are served at the **Durango Diner** by the owner, Bart. They grate hash browns right onto the grill and cook them in butter—one whole, big potato per order. Lots of locals eat here.

Places mentioned above are low-budget, serve big helpings, and are run by nice locals.

# Steamboat

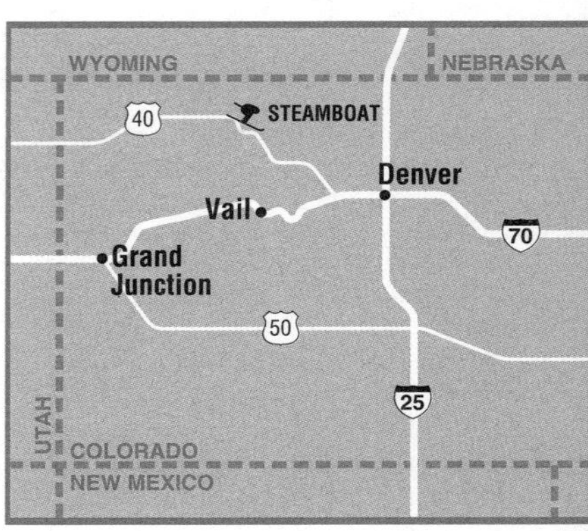


Take one: Horsemen thundering through snowdrifts piled before an aging barn. Take two: High-speed quad chairs with pull-down bubble tops zipping up a mountainside. These mixed images featured in Steamboat's ads accurately depict a resort that fuses two worlds: a contemporary ski village and the old Western town of **Steamboat Springs**, where ranchers stride along in cowboy boots and Stetsons.

**Mount Werner** is the focal point of this modern ski resort. Twenty-one lifts, including the eight-passenger Silver Bullet gondola and two high-speed quads, glide over terrain spread across its four peaks, and cruising trails await skiers of every skill level. Never-evers and parents eager to take a toddler uphill for a run or two can report to the free **Preview** beginner's lift. Novices will find a niche at the base of the mountain, several green trails higher up on **Thunderhead Peak**, and an easy patch of terrain near **Rendezvous Peak** that locals jokingly call "Wally World." Intermediates roam from peak to peak, exploring a wealth of wide-open slopes and glades. Advanced skiers can look forward to lots of moguled runs (though limited extreme steeps) and some of the best tree skiing in the West. **Storm Peak** attracts experienced skiers eager to test their skills on its open upper face and lower moguled runs, and the tree skiing in the **Closet** is memorable. Snowboarders delight in the ever-popular **Dude Ranch.** And if you want to make the first tracks in virgin powderfields, hitch a ride high into the backcountry with **Steamboat Powder Cats** (879.5188).

The town of Steamboat Springs, founded in 1876, wears its history on weathered wood and brick buildings. Shuttle buses move skiers between town and the resort area, which together have more than 60 restaurants and bars for après-ski, plus a variety of shopping and entertainment destinations. The most popular place in Steamboat Springs after a day on the slopes is the rec center, where skiers warm their aching bones in generously sized pools fed by hot mineral springs.

Besides skiing, many other activities lure vacationers to Steamboat in the wintertime, including bobsledding at **Howelson Hill**, hot-air ballooning over the ski slopes, cross-country touring through the woods, and snowmobiling to natural hot springs.

**Steamboat Ski & Resort**
**2305 Mount Werner Circle**
**Steamboat Springs, Colorado 80487-9012**

**Information**....................970/879.6111
....................fax 970/879.7844
**Reservations**....................800/922.2722
**Snow Phone**....................970/879.7300

## Fast Facts

*Area code 970 unless otherwise noted.*

**Ski Season** Late November through mid-April

**Location** Steamboat is in **Colorado**'s **Routt National Forest**, 157 miles from **Denver.**

## Getting to Steamboat

**By air: Steamboat Springs Airport** is five miles from Steamboat. At press time, this airport receives only charter flights, but expects to be handling some commercial airlines by winter 1995. **Yampa Valley Regional,** 22 miles away in **Hayden,** is currently the nearest commercial airport. During ski season, **American** offers nonstop flights from **Chicago, Dallas/Ft. Worth,** and **Newark. Continental** offers nonstop flights from **Cleveland** and **Houston. Northwest** flies nonstop from **Minneapolis/St. Paul,** and **United** flies nonstop from Chicago, **Los Angeles,** and **San Francisco. Continental Connection** and **United Express** fly between **Denver** and the **Yampa Valley Regional Airport.** Shuttle service is available from the airports to the resort.

**By bus:** **Greyhound** (303/293.6555) buses depart daily from downtown **Denver. Panorama**'s (800/922.2722) *Steamboat Express* buses depart twice daily from **Denver International Airport.**

**By car:** Winterized cars are available at both airports from **Avis, Budget, Hertz,** and **National.** Take US 40 east from these airports. From **Denver,** take Interstate 70 west to the Silverthorne exit and go north on Highway 9 to Kremmling, then west on US 40. From **Grand Junction,** take Interstate 70 east to Rifle, go north on Highway 13 to Craig, then take US 40 east.

**Driving times from:**

Denver—3 hours (157 miles)

Grand Junction—3.5 hours (182 miles)

## Getting around Steamboat

**Steamboat Springs Transit** (879.3717) runs shuttles from the town to the ski area. Taxi service is available from **Alpine Taxi** (879.2800).

## FYI

**Area** 2,500 permitted acres with 108 trails spread over four mountain peaks

Beginner—15 percent

Intermediate—54 percent

Advanced/Expert—31 percent

**Number of Groomed Runs** Approximately 81

**Longest Run** 3 miles **(Why Not)**

**Capacity** 30,541 skiers per hour

**Base Elevation** 6,900 feet

**Summit Elevation** 10,568 feet

**Vertical Rise** 3,668 feet

**Average Annual Snowfall** 325 inches

**Snowmaking** 36 percent

**Night Skiing** None

**Lifts** 21 (1 8-passenger gondola, 2 high-speed quads, 1 regular quad, 6 triple chairs, 7 double chairs, 1 ski school chair and 3 surface lifts)

| **Lift Passes** | **Full Day** | **Half Day** (starts at 12:15PM) |
|---|---|---|
| **Adult** | $42 | $37 |
| **Child** (12 and under) | $25 | $25 |
| **Senior** (65-69) | $25 | $25 |
| **Senior** (70 and over) | Free | Free |

**Ski School** Located near the base of the gondola, the ski school (879.6111 ext 531) offers a variety of group and private lessons. It's best to make reservations in advance.

**Kids' Ski School** Classes are for first graders through 15-year-olds. The **Kids' Rough Rider's Week** includes five all-day lessons, an on-mountain barbecue, four lunches, a NASTAR race, and more. During peak season, a teen program is also offered.

**Clinics and Special Programs** **Smell the Roses, Women's Seminars,** and the **Black Diamond Adventure** are among the clinics at Steamboat. Other choices include telemark, style, bump, and powder clinics. A program for disabled skiers offers private lessons and adaptive equipment. The **Steamboat Ski Weeks,** including five all-day lessons, a NASTAR race, video analysis, and more, are a good buy for both adults and children. The beginners' "guarantee" assures you a free repeat of your first class if you can't ski from the top of the Preview Chair in a safe and controlled manner. The **Billy Kidd Center for Performance Skiing** offers a variety of bump, racing, and "challenge" camps for all ages.

**Races** Recreational NASTAR races are held daily at the **Bashor Race Arena** from 10:30AM to 12:30PM. The **NASTAR Training Center** offers practice runs on the race course from 9:30AM to 3:30PM.

**Rentals** Several ski shops have rentals, and pricing is generally competitive. At participating shops, one child under 12 can rent gear for free with each parent who has a five-day rental (restrictions apply). **Steamboat Ski Rentals and Storage** (daily 8AM-9PM; 879.6111 ext 345) offers rental packages with the latest equipment for recreational, sport, and high-performance skiing. **Breeze Ski Rentals** (daily 8AM-7PM; 800/525.0314) has similar packages and a free junior rental program.

**Lockers** Coin-operated lockers are located on the ground level of the lower **Silver Bullet Terminal** and at **Thunderhead. Steamboat Ski Rentals and Storage** charges for overnight storage if you didn't rent skis at their shop.

**Day Care** The **Kids' Vacation Center** (879.6111 ext 469), open from 8AM to 5PM, includes programs for kids 6 months to 12 years old. Activities for various age groups include ski games, on-snow exploration, and ski lessons. **Kids' Adventure Club at Night** is an indoor camp-style event open from 6PM to 10:30PM. Adventure nights for kids ages 8 to 12 include sledding and trips to the hot springs.

**First Aid** Ski patrol may be reached by emergency phones scattered around the mountain and at the on-mountain restaurants. For medical care, call 911 or the **Routt Memorial Hospital** (879.1322) at 80 Park Avenue.

**Parking** Free parking is available in four separate lots around the ski village. A free shuttle transports skiers from the lots to the transportation center and to the gondola. Pay parking is available in the **Gondola Square** lot next to the transportation center off Mount Werner Circle.

**Worth Knowing**

- Steamboat's **Kids Ski Free** program enables children 12 years and under to ski free with parents purchasing a five-day or more lift ticket on a one-child to one-parent basis, while staying in a participating property for a minimum of five nights.

## Rating the Runs

### ● Beginner

This great white way of **Broadway** presents beautiful views from the picnic area and it tends to be the least crowded green run on this part of the mountain, since so many beginners hang around nearby **Elk Head.**

Kids hoot and holler as they steam through **Giggle Gulch,** one of the longer, and often less crowded, green trails on the lower mountain. Young children (and kids at heart) take the paths through the trees on the Gulch—a good choice for a warm-up run.

Swing into a series of broad turns as you cruise down less traveled **Swinger,** the smart skier's shortcut on the lower mountain.

### ■ Intermediate

The intermediate **Buddy's Run** was named after Buddy Werner, one of Steamboat Spring's first Olympic ski racers, who was killed in an avalanche on a Swiss mountainside in 1964. Race down Buddy's Run or play the terrain variations.

Crowd-free **Flintlock** strikes a spark of enthusiasm in families skiing on **Sunshine Peak.** Most skiers stay on runs that can be seen from the lift, but don't be gun-shy about shooting toward Flintlock just because it's out of sight.

Wide enough for big rounded turns, **Vagabond** rambles downhill allowing you to amble along like a footloose traveler and take in the views of the **Sleeping Giant,** the **Mount Zirkel Wilderness Area,** and the miniature town far below.

### ◆ Advanced

Truly fickle **Flying Z** has a fall line that sags two ways, and a knobby covering on the upper ridge for extra spice. The trees are spread out in this meadowlike run, which offers superb views of the valley and town.

Up-close and personal views of tree trunks await those who enter the **Twilight** zone, a challenging glade with plenty of terrain changes and bumps between the trees.

Word is that **West Side** promises a comfortable after-lunch run, especially if you've dined at **Ragnar's.** Steep and always groomed, locals rate West Side as the best black-colored cruiser on the mountain.

### ◆◆ Expert

Start your serious tree skiing on **Shadows,** where some of the trees are far enough apart that they cast shadows on the snow. But if you're afraid of Shadows, you won't want to hide in the **Closet.**

Finding room to move on Closet challenges even the experts, as the trees are crammed together as tightly as clothes in a crowded closet. A 10-foot-wide, semiopen swatch slashes across one section of the constantly changing terrain, offering a slightly easier way out.

### Snowboarding

The **Dude Ranch** features quarter-pipes, rail slides, gaps, and other obstacles, providing snowboarders the freedom to perform jumps and tricks amid a steady flow of spectators. Due to this park's popularity, it was expanded during the 1994-95 season, and the ski school has increased the number of snowboarding instructors. Riders are also allowed on the rest of the mountain.

## Mountain Highs and Lows

When deciding whether to try **Why Not,** the key word is "Not." This beginner's trail is too narrow for shaky beginners and too crowded for comfort.

On the trail map, green-colored **Duster** looks great, but you'll be dusting the slopes with your poles just to keep moving.

The resort's best-known cruising trail, **Heavenly Daze** has perfect pitch—a slope so ideal that too many skiers cruise its wide face. At day's end, this blue run is over-trafficked with exiting skiers. But early risers will find it great for a first-run leg burner.

Skidding beginners on intermediate **High Noon** create numerous push piles, and the slope in between them often gets slick, making a showdown—like the one in the Western flick *High Noon*—a distinct possibility.

The views from the advanced-rated **Upper Valley View** are terrific, but too many skiers make the surface so slick you can't stop to enjoy the scenery.

## At the Resort

*Area code 970 unless otherwise noted.*

✦ **Thunderhead** Three of the restaurants at this facility deliver distinct dining experiences. ♦ The top of the Silver Buffet gondola. 879.6111 ext 465

Within Thunderhead:

**B.K. Corral** ★$$ This cafeteria sells burgers, snacks, and sandwiches, but the pizza bar is your best bet. During peak weeks, head up the gondola for breakfast here. You'll be skiing the best of the mountain while late risers are still waiting for a chairlift. At night there's all-you-can-eat Western barbecue. Lively country-and-western bands and swing dancing come with the meal. ♦ Daily breakfast, lunch, and dinner. Dinner reservations recommended. Third level. 879.6111 ext 465

Billy Kidd, Steamboat's Director of Skiing, won an Olympic medal in 1964 and soon after became the first American male to be named skiing's World Champion. He went pro and won the World Pro Championship two weeks later, making him the first to win both championships in a single year.

**Stoker Bar & Restaurant** $$ If you're in a hurry, this is the place to stop for quick tableside service. The dining room isn't fancy, but the fare includes big sandwiches, soups, and a muffin of the day. ♦ Daily lunch. First level. 879.6111 ext 465

**Hazie's** ★★★★$$$$ This bi-level restaurant, which is named after the mother of Olympic-great Buddy Werner, serves continental cuisine in an elegant setting. The west wall—made entirely of glass—provides an awesome, panoramic view of the Yampa Valley (seating in the loft offers an even better view). For lunch, try fine baked brie amandine, smoked Muscovy duck breast salad, and other specialties. Four-course dinners feature such selections as venison loin chanterelles, chateaubriand béarnaise, and fillet of salmon with roasted bell-pepper sauce. ♦ Daily lunch and dinner. Reservations required for dinner. First floor. 879.6111 ext 465

✦ **Rendezvous Saddle** Park your skis at this on-mountain lodge halfway down the **High Noon** trail. The **Rendezvous Cafeteria** echoes the one at Thunderhead—pizza, burgers, snacks, and sandwiches served at lunchtime. The outdoor barbecue is packed on nice spring days. Grab a seat on "the beach"— the deck where everyone sunbathes. ♦ Halfway down the High Noon trail. 879.6111 ext 465

Within Rendezvous Saddle:

**Ragnar's** ★★★★$$$$ This intimate Scandinavian restaurant, with its alpine, wooden beam decor, is an exceptional place to dine—especially when the weather turns blustery. Sit at a rustic table and admire the antique wooden skis and pictures of the early days in Steamboat Springs adorning the walls. Start with the smorgasbord platter: an assortment of herring, dried lamb, and other delicacies. The *Fyldt Pannekaker* (baked crepes filled with crab and shrimp, and topped with a white wine, mushroom, and cream sauce) will warm you up for an afternoon of serious skiing. More conventional choices include mesquite-grilled fresh Norwegian salmon and pasta of the day. The dinner package includes a gondola ride to **Thunderhead,** as well as a sleigh ride to **Rendezvous Saddle.** ♦ Daily lunch and dinner. Reservations recommended for lunch and required for dinner. First level. 879.6111 ext 465

✦ **Express-Oh!** ★$ Before heading uphill on a cold day, get stoked with a cup of espresso or hot chocolate and a flaky pastry at this coffee bar in the lower Silver Bullet terminal. ♦ Daily 8AM-5PM. In the Lower Gondola Bldg, Gondola Sq. 879.6111 ext 465

✦ **Steamboat Activities Center** Stop here to book such nonskiing activities as snowmobiling, 4x4 rides to **Strawberry Park Hot Springs,** and hot-air ballooning. ♦ Daily 8AM-8PM. Gondola Sq (next to Gondola General Store). 879.2062

✦ **Thunderhead Lodge** $$$ Though this complex (not to be confused with the **Thunderhead** on page 126) is not new, its location on the edge of the slopes, just off Gondola Square at the base of the mountain, and value make it a standout. The 56 lodge and hotel rooms are nicer than many in the area. ♦ In Ski Time Sq (100 yards from Gondola Sq). 800/525.5502; fax 879.1297

Within Thunderhead Lodge:

**The Conservatory** Piano music mingles with happy chatter in the intimate Conservatory, where guests relax on couches with cocktails in front of the stone fireplace. ♦ Daily après-ski hour through closing. 879.9000

✦ **Torian Plum** $$$$ These 40 condos with oak trim and brass fixtures, whirlpool baths, gas fireplaces, and balconies are among the best places to stay slope-side. The concierge and staff are ready to help, and a courtesy van shuttles guests around town. The ski-in/ski-out complex also has a sauna, outdoor pool, and hot tubs. ♦ 1855 Ski Time Square Dr (near the Silver Bullet gondola). 800/228.2458; fax 879.8060

✦ **Barton's of Steamboat** Fine handcrafted pottery, paintings, and handwoven rugs by Native American Indians are sold in this slope-side shop. ♦ Daily 10AM-9PM. Torian Plum Plaza (near the Silver Bullet gondola). 879.6777

✦ **Sheraton Steamboat Resort Hotel and Conference Center** $$$$ Lodging here means plunking yourself down right in busy **Gondola Square.** Each of the 267 rooms and suites has its own private balcony and, in late 1994, were totally refurbished and decorated in a contemporary Western/Alpine theme. All are comfortable with light oak furniture and jewel tones of green, blue, and copper, but on snowy days you may hear the snowplows long before you're ready to wake up. Children 17 and under stay free (up to two in a parent's room). Other pluses include two restaurants, two lounges, a heated outdoor pool, hot tubs, and good service. ♦ 2200 Village Inn Court (in Gondola Sq). 879.2220, 800/848.8877 in Colorado, 800/325.3535 in the US; fax 879.2220

✦ **Avalanche Ranch** Rack your skis outside the door and browse through an interesting selection of handmade jewelry, Southwestern leather goods, sweaters, and gifts to take home. ♦ Daily 10AM-9PM. 2305 Mount Werner Circle (in Gondola Sq). 879.4392

✦ **Inferno** ★$$ Expect to find a twenty-something crowd in this dark, smoky room with lots of noise. Burgers and sandwiches are the main fare. ♦ Cover for bands. Daily lunch and dinner. 2305 Mount Werner Circle (in Gondola Sq). 879.5111

✦ **Ptarmigan Inn** $$$ Set at the base of the mountain near the gondola, this 78-room inn has a great location, but many of the rooms are small and the decor varies. Amenities include in-room refrigerators, an outdoor heated pool, a hot tub, a restaurant, and a lounge. ♦ 2304 Après Ski Way (on the mountain, behind the Gondola Building). 800/538.7519; fax 879.2302

✦ **Dulany** $$$ Attractive Western-style interiors with lots of native wood and ceramic tile highlight these 25 ski-in/ski-out condos. Private balconies, gas fireplaces, Jennair grills, and other niceties are standard, along with a complimentary bottle of wine. ♦ 2286 Après Ski Way (on the mountain, behind the Gondola Building). 879.6000, 800/525.5502; fax 879.2353

✦ **Chateau Chamonix** $$$ These 27 deluxe ski-in/ski-out condos have Jacuzzi tubs and brick fireplaces, and some rooms feature large windows that frame beautiful views. An outdoor pool and Jacuzzi are also on site. ♦ 2340 Après Ski Way (on the mountain, behind the Gondola Building). 800/833.9877; fax 879.9321

✦ **Bear Claw** $$$$ Guests often rave about the lodgings in these privately owned, independently furnished condos. Many of the 66 units have open dining areas that flow into living rooms with fireplaces and decor that is rustic but upscale. Within the complex are an outdoor heated pool, whirlpool, and sauna. The first run of the day is right outside your door. ♦ 2420 Ski Trail La (near the top of the Southface Lift). 800/BEARCLAW; fax 897.8396

## Beyond the Resort

**1** **The Ranch at Steamboat** $$ Gaze down at the slopes from one of these 60 comfortable units with fireplaces and a bathroom for each bedroom. Some units boast cathedral ceilings and walls of windows for great views. It's a good choice for value-conscious skiers, with amenities including an outdoor pool, indoor and outdoor hot tubs, shuttle service to the base and restaurants, and door-to-door shuttle service in the evening. ♦ 1 Ranch Rd (from Natches Wy). 879.3000, 800/525.2002; fax 879.5409

**2** **Storm Meadows Club Resort** $$ Natural wood interiors and fireplaces framed with brick decorate many of the more than 200 condos and town homes located just 200 yards from the slopes. Access ski trails wind down to the gondola area, and the complex has a free shuttle leaving every half-hour to **Ski Time Square** and **Gondola Square.** Guests can use the resort's private athletic club. Some rooms are terrific while others are just fair, so be careful when you make arrangements. ♦ 33250 Storm Meadow Dr (off Burgess Creek Rd). 879.5555, 800/248.7547; fax 879.5057

**3** **Mattie Silks** ★★★★$$$$ Named after one of the town's more famous madams, this restaurant is elegant in a bordello sort of fashion. Ornate, gilded mirrors and crystal chandeliers combine well with burgundy velvet window curtains and red silk billowing from the ceiling for a rich, hedonistic atmosphere. Mattie Silks still pampers her clients, but nowadays with delicious food from an eclectic menu that travels the globe. Lemon-pepper veal, Jamaican jerked chicken or elk, and fresh grilled Atlantic salmon are a few favorite selections. ♦ Daily dinner. Reservations recommended. Ski Time Sq (at Clubhouse Dr). 879.2441

**3** **Dos Amigos** ★★$$ Free chips and salsa, wicked margaritas, Mexican decor, and lots of off-duty ski patrollers can be found here. This cantina is usually packed from the time the lifts close until late. ♦ Daily dinner; bar menu

2:30PM-midnight. Ski Time Sq (at Clubhouse Dr). 879.4270

3 **Heavenly Daze Brewery** ★$$ Watch your head! A ski-lift chair, kayak, windsurfer, and other sporting toys hang from the ceiling of Steamboat's first brewpub. Lodgepole pine frames several levels, where skiers come to refuel and celebrate après-ski hours. Try the beer sausage rolled in honey and spiced peanuts. ♦ Cover for bands. Reservations recommended. Daily lunch and dinner. Ski Time Sq (at Clubhouse Dr). 879.8080

3 **Tugboat Saloon & Eatery** ★$$ Noise and smoke set the mood at this saloon, popular since the resort's earliest days. Good omelettes are followed by soups, salads, burgers, and Mexican fare later in the day. This is one of the best stops for food and close-to-the-slopes partying. ♦ Cover for bands after 9PM. Daily breakfast, lunch, and dinner. Ski Time Sq (at Clubhouse Dr). 879.7070

4 **La Montaña** ★★★★$$$ Yes, it's Mexican, but the ambience is refreshingly atypical. Colorful photos of Southwestern landscapes—taken by owner Tom Garrett—tastefully adorn the walls. Locals swear this top-rater has the best Tex-Mex in town, along with other Southwestern fare like Navajo fry bread, red chile pasta, and braided sausage, a specialty made with elk, lamb, and chorizo sausages. The casual atmosphere is great for families and groups. ♦ Daily dinner. Reservations recommended. 2500 Village Dr (at Après Ski Way). 879.5800

5 **Lodge at Steamboat** $$ Price and location make this lodge a first choice for families. It's just a stone's throw from the gondola, restaurants, and shops, and features 120 units with floor-to-ceiling windows, some overlooking a stream. The lodge's heated outdoor pool and two outdoor hot tubs overflow with guests in the late afternoon. ♦ 2700 Village Dr (at Après Ski Way). 879.8000, 800/525.5502; fax 879.2353

6 **Trappeurs Crossing** $$ Pleasant surroundings, an attentive staff, and reasonable prices mark these 26 condos. Two blocks from the gondola, the complex has a ski shuttle, evening grocery shuttle, indoor/outdoor pool, and two hot tubs. ♦ 2900 Village Dr (at Medicine Springs Rd). 879.8811, 800/228.2458; fax 879.8485

7 **Waterford Townhomes** $$$ These 28 roomy and comfortable town homes have attractive timber interiors and fireplaces set in brick. Amenities include a hot tub and sauna. Complimentary shuttle service to the base of the mountain is available. ♦ 2025 Walton Creek Rd (near Columbine Dr). 879.7000, 800/525.5502; fax 879.7263

8 **Shadow Run** $ Located on the bus route, this complex offers 81 clean and inexpensive condos. However, the condition of the units is inconsistent; so ask for one that's been more recently renovated. Relax your weary bones in one of the indoor or outdoor hot tubs. ♦ 2900 Whistler Rd (at Walton Creek Rd). 879.6686, 800/525.2622; fax 525.2622

9 **Inn at Steamboat B&B** $$ This is the only bed-and-breakfast-style inn near the slopes. The owners, who live on the premises, truly go the extra yard for guests, making reservations for dinner and activities, and shuttling them the half-mile to the base. The shuttle service also provides transportation to other locations during evening hours. Although the decor is a bit dated, the breakfast is hearty and hot, and the 32-room property is well managed. ♦ 3070 Columbine Dr (off Walton Creek Rd). 879.2600, 800/872.2601

10 **Alpine Meadows Townhomes** $ These 24 small town homes are the best inexpensive accommodations at Steamboat. Each unit has a wood-burning stove, and all share a big outdoor Jacuzzi. The two-level units have passage doors that let you party with your friends. ♦ 2145 Resort Dr (at Whistler Rd). 800/525.2622; fax 525.2622

THE CHART HOUSE

11 **Chart House** ★★$$$ In the West, Chart House restaurants and ski resorts seem to come in pairs. Expect such seafood as fresh salmon, swordfish, and shrimp teriyaki, as well as steaks and prime rib served in casual surroundings. ♦ Daily dinner. 2165 Pine Grove Rd (at Mt. Werner Rd). 879.6976

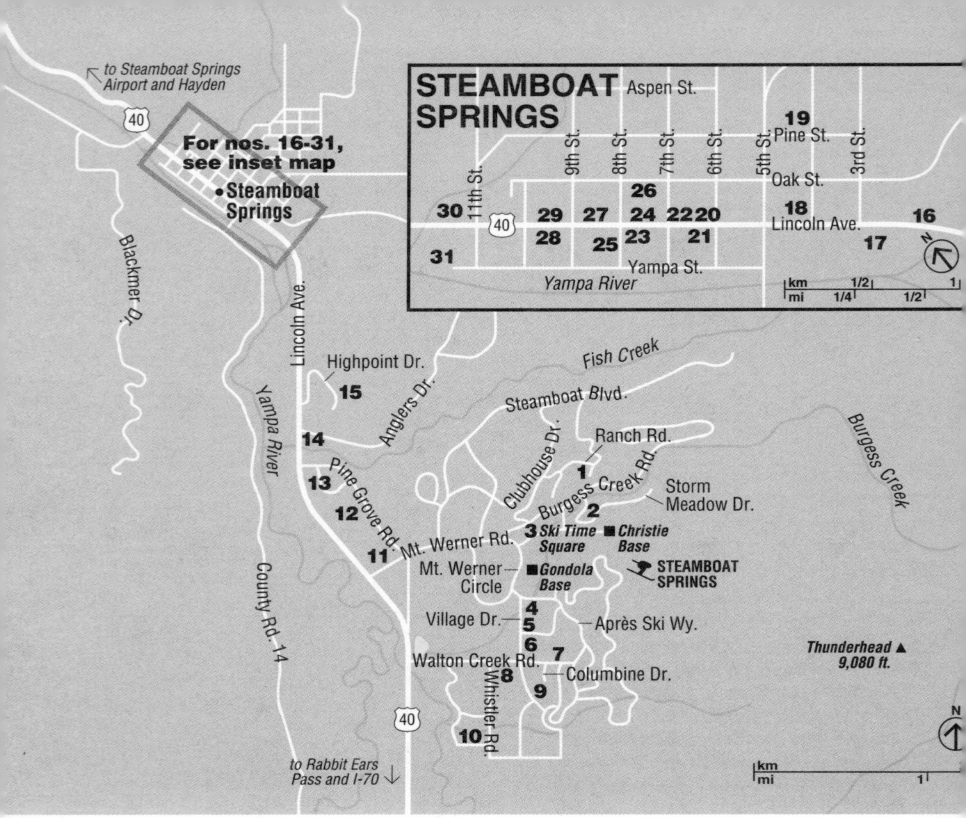

to Steamboat Springs Airport and Hayden
40
For nos. 16-31, see inset map
•Steamboat Springs
Blackmer Dr.
Lincoln Ave.
Yampa River
Highpoint Dr.
15
Anglers Dr.
14
Pine Grove Rd.
13
12
11
Mt. Werner Rd.
Fish Creek
Steamboat Blvd.
Clubhouse Dr.
Ranch Rd.
1
Burgess Creek Rd.
Burgess Creek
Storm Meadow Dr.
2
3 Ski Time Square
Christie Base
Mt. Werner Circle
Gondola Base
STEAMBOAT SPRINGS
4
Village Dr.
5
Après Ski Wy.
6
7
Walton Creek Rd.
8
Columbine Dr.
9
Whistler Rd.
10
County Rd. 14
40
Thunderhead ▲ 9,080 ft.
to Rabbit Ears Pass and I-70
km mi 1

STEAMBOAT SPRINGS
Aspen St.
19 Pine St.
11th St. 9th St. 8th St. 7th St. 6th St. 5th St. 3rd St.
Oak St.
26
30 40 29 27 24 22 20
18 Lincoln Ave. 16
28 25 23 21 17
31
Yampa St.
Yampa River
km 1/2 1
mi 1/4 1/2

**12 City Market** To enjoy a home-cooked meal in your condo or stock up on the basics, visit this large local supermarket. ♦ Daily 24 hours. 1825 Pine Grove Rd (in Central Park Plaza). 879.3290

**13 Ore House at the Pine Grove** ★★$$$$ Visitors love the casual, Western-style ambience at this restaurant, which serves elk, buffalo, and other game dishes in a picturesque barn. A children's menu is available. ♦ Daily dinner. Pine Grove Rd (at Hwy 40). 879.1190

**14 Safeway** Condo guests pack their fridges with goods from this full-service supermarket. ♦ Daily 24 hours. 37500 Hwy 40 (at Anglers Dr, between town and mountain). 879.3766

**15 Overlook Lodge** $$ Perched atop a crest with great views of both town and mountain, this 177-room lodge is continually renovating its guest rooms and suites. Rates include a breakfast buffet and use of the indoor pool, hot tub, and gameroom. ♦ 1000 Highpoint Dr (off Hwy 40). 879.2900, 800/752.5666; fax 879.7641

**16 Steamboat Springs Health and Recreation** Steamboat's hot mineral spring-fed pools are the town's most popular après-ski activity. The rec center has an Olympic-size swimming pool with a water slide, and four soaking pools that fill up as the chairlifts close down. ♦ Daily morning through mid-evening, but hours vary. 136 Lincoln Ave (just before Third St). 879.1828

**17 Rabbit Ears Motel** $ If you can overlook the garish pink bunny sign you're in for a great budget buy. This 65-room motel has rooms overlooking the river and units with refrigerators or coffeemakers. ♦ 201 Lincoln Ave (at Third St). 879.1150, 800/828.7702; fax 870.0483

**18 Alpiner Lodge** $ The 178 rooms in this Bavarian-style lodge are small, but its downtown location and free shuttle to slope-side sister property, the **Ptarmigan Inn**, make it a great value. Guests can store their skis overnight at the inn. ♦ 424 Lincoln Ave (between Fourth and Fifth Sts). 879.1430, 800/538.7519

**19 Steamboat Bed & Breakfast** $ Antique furniture and hardwood floors make the seven guest rooms in this lovely old house a charming place to stay. For a small fee, friends can join you for breakfast. ♦ 442 Pine St (between Fourth and Fifth Sts). 879.5724

**20 Old Town Pub** Locals frequent this pub to catch up on the latest gossip while seated around the mahogany bar or playing darts in the back. Old-timers know how to pound pinball machines, but there are video games, too. Live bands make the place rock on some weekends. ♦ Cover for bands. Daily 11AM-midnight. 600 Lincoln Ave (at Sixth St). 879.2101

**21 Winona's** ★$ It may just be basic American deli fare, but generous portions of soup and salads and big sandwiches stuffed with such offbeat combinations as chicken salad with grapes, served with a side of tabbouleh or carrot salad, keep the regulars coming back. ♦ Tu-Su breakfast and lunch. 617 Lincoln Ave (at Sixth St). 879.2483

**22 Go-Fer Foods** This downtown market and convenience store makes it easy to "go-fer" whatever you need. ♦ Daily 6AM-midnight. 644 Lincoln Ave (at Seventh St). 879.6723

**23 Harbor Hotel** $$ Located in the heart of downtown, this restored landmark has 62 compact yet comfortable rooms furnished with English antiques. The soundproofing between the rooms isn't the greatest, so bring earplugs if you're a light sleeper. Complimentary continental breakfast is served in the English pub-style lounge. The hotel has two hot tubs and a sauna, and guests receive a pass for unlimited use on the bus line to the mountain. ♦ 703 Lincoln Ave (between Seventh and Eighth Sts). 879.1522, 800/334.1012 (in Colorado), 800/543.8888 (in the US); fax 879.1737

**24 Canton Chinese Restaurant** ★★★$$ If you're craving Chinese, the fine Cantonese, Mandarin, and Szechuan dishes here should satisfy. The double soup order makes a good starter. ♦ Daily lunch and dinner. 720 Lincoln Ave (between Seventh and Eighth Sts). 879.4480

**25 Antares** ★★★$$$ Housed in a grand old bank building, this new restaurant, run by the former chef of **L'Apogée,** specializes in nouvelle American cuisine. Walls of stone and an old-time pressed tin ceiling contrast well with the warm interior. An emphasis is placed on light and healthy foods, featuring such specialties as grilled whole fish of the day with pineapple pommery fondue, and Maine lobster in a mushroom-lobster cream on chili pepper linguine. ♦ Daily dinner. 57½ Eighth St (between Yampa St and Lincoln Ave). 879.9939

**26 Cugino's** ★$ Locals love Cugino's for its tasty and inexpensive sandwiches, stromboli, pizza, and pasta. ♦ Daily lunch and dinner. 825 Oak St (between Seventh and Eighth Sts). 879.5805

**27 Allen's** Forget your ski pants? Stop where those in the know shop for some of the town's most affordable skiwear. ♦ Daily 10AM-9PM. 828 Lincoln Ave (between Eighth and Ninth Sts). 879.0351

**27 FM Light** Real ranchers and cowboys have been buying Western gear and cowboy boots here for years. Now it's your turn. ♦ Daily 10AM-9PM. 830 Lincoln Ave (between Eighth and Ninth Sts). 879.1822

**28 Steamboat Art Company** This shop has a nice selection of Southwestern art, jewelry, gifts, and collectibles. ♦ M-Sa 9AM-10PM; Su 10AM-9PM. 903 Lincoln Ave (between Ninth and 10th Sts). 879.3383

**28 L'Apogée** ★★★★$$$$ Fans of this first-class French restaurant include *Bon Appétit* and *Gourmet* magazines. Linen-clad tables and candlelight set the stage for excellent service and a fine menu that changes every three months. Some traditional hits include baked North Atlantic salmon rubbed with ginger and crushed pepper, served over pickled ginger cream and fried leeks; and veal scallopini sautéed with forest mushrooms, served with a fresh rock shrimp stuffing. Ask the sommelier to help you choose from among the more than 500 wines. ♦ Daily dinner. Reservations recommended. 911 Lincoln Ave (between Ninth and 10th Sts). 879.1980

**28 Harwigs Grill & Bar** ★★★$$$ **L'Apogée**'s more casual sister restaurant serves delicious international cuisine, ranging from a "Down Under" lamb burger to Black Forest Chasseur (mixed game stew). Dinner conversation is backed by the mellow sounds of jazz. Wine connoisseurs can select from more than 40 wines by the glass. ♦ Daily dinner. Reservations recommended. 911 Lincoln Ave (between Ninth and 10th Sts). 879.1980

29 **Steamboat Smokehouse** ★★$$ Toss the shells from your free peanuts on the floor at this tavern, where the beer arrives in big frosty mugs. The pungent hickory s-l-o-w-smoked ribs, turkey, or brisket are best bets. There's a separate menu for kids. Bands play some nights. ♦ No cover. Daily lunch and dinner. 912 Lincoln Ave (between Ninth and 10th Sts). 879.5570

Giovanni's Ristorante

30 **Giovanni's Ristorante** ★★★$$$ Red-checkered cloths deck the tables in this cozy restaurant that serves excellent veal and other Italian dishes. Try the fillet Antonio, a tenderloin stuffed with prosciutto ham and fontina and herb garlic cheeses, then covered with Madeira mushroom sauce. Be sure to leave room to overdose on the tiramisù. ♦ Daily dinner. Reservations recommended. 127 11th St (at Lincoln Ave). 879.4141

30 **Old West Steak House** ★★$$$ You'll find 22-ounce T-bones, elk steak, Australian lobster tail, and Alaskan king crab legs on the menu at this rustic steak house. Ask for the children's menu. ♦ Daily dinner. Reservations recommended. 1104 Lincoln Ave (at 11th St). 879.1441

30 **Riggio's** ★★★$$$ The atmosphere is upscale chic, with white tablecloths and an open layout. Popular with locals who like Italian food with flair, this ristorante serves the classics as well as a few creative dishes, such as stir-fry Italiano (fresh vegetables sautéed in olive oil with herbs and tossed with pasta pesto). ♦ Daily dinner. Reservations recommended. 1106 Lincoln Ave (at 11th St). 879.9010

31 **Double Z Bar and Bar-B-Q** ★★★$ Two hands are required to hold the well-stuffed and thoroughly delicious barbecue beef sandwiches, served with a basket of house-made fries, at this local dive with stone walls and simple wood tables and chairs. ♦ Daily dinner. 1124 Yampa St (at 12th St). 879.0849

## Bests

**Jim Meyers**
Salesperson, Ski Haus sports shop

Best backcountry powder skiing—**Hahns Peak.**

Best ski run—**Twilight**, in fresh powder.

Best Italian restaurant—**Cugino's.**

Best and friendliest restaurant—**Old West Steak House.**

Best cross-country ski trail—**Hogan Park** to Mount Werner.

Best mountain-bike and hiking trail—**Silver Creek No. 1106,** up or down.

Best road—**Highway 131** south from Steamboat Springs to Vail.

**Vernon Sumner**
Rancher/Lifetime Resident of Steamboat Springs

**Old Town**—a look into the history of skiing.

Silver Bullet gondola—Ride up in the daytime or evening and dine at the restaurant at the top.

**Howelson Hill**—One of the best-known ski-jumping complexes in the nation.

**Rabbit Ears Pass**—View of Yampa Valley from the west side is one of the best.

**Steamboat Springs Health and Recreation**—swimming pools on East Highway 40 in Old Town.

### Charles "Chuck" O'Connell

Manager, SportStalker specialty ski shop

I moved to Steamboat for the same reason everyone else did and still does. . . the skiing. Steamboat is particularly famous for its champagne powder and tree skiing, but that's not all. You'll find long bump runs, perfectly groomed cruisers, and steep chutes if you're willing to hike. Here are some of my favorites:

**Sundown** lift line...specifically the skiers' left side, which has a fantastic ever-steepening pitch.

**Closet/Shadows**...The Closet being the area of pine trees, and the Shadows the aspens as you go farther left.

**Storm Peak face to Rainbow** is a never-ending run of perfect "corduroy" accessed by the Storm Peak Express chair.

**Heavenly Daze,** the run right under the gondola, seems about as wide as a football field. There's nothing like cruising under the gondola in the early morning when there's not another soul around.

For après-ski, my wife, Trish, and I have a few favorite spots: The **Heavenly Daze Brewery and Grill,** the **Double Z Bar-B-Q** for the best barbecue and french fries in town, and the **Steamboat Smokehouse.**

One of my favorite restaurants: **La Montaña,** for Mexican/Southwest food (and the margaritas are pretty good, too).

Special events throughout the season include the **Cowboy Downhill** and the **Cardboard Classic.** One of my all-time favorites is the **St. Patrick's Day Chute Bump Off,** a head-to-head mogul contest in the Avalanche Chutes. You have to see it to believe it.

### Stacey Kramer

Public Relations/Film Board Manager, Steamboat Springs Chamber Resort Association

Backcountry skiing on the pass—For the solitude and the view.

The bobsled run at **Howelson Hill.**

Skiing the **Toutes**—Always good powder.

**La Montaña**—Great margaritas and fabulous food.

**Mattie Silks**—For dessert and after-dinner drinks.

**Riggio's**—Excellent service complements excellent food.

**Harwigs Grill & Bar**—Nice bar.

**Double Z Bar-B-Q**—Good ribs.

I'm keeping my favorite ski run(s) to myself.

# Telluride

Gone are the days when dusty miners descended from the mountains around Telluride to brawl in the town's bars and bordellos, and Butch Cassidy practiced fast getaways on Main Street before robbing his first bank. Today, the town once nicknamed "City of Gold" is home base for the country's hottest ski scene, and the list of the rich and famous snatching up property is beginning to rival **Aspen**'s.

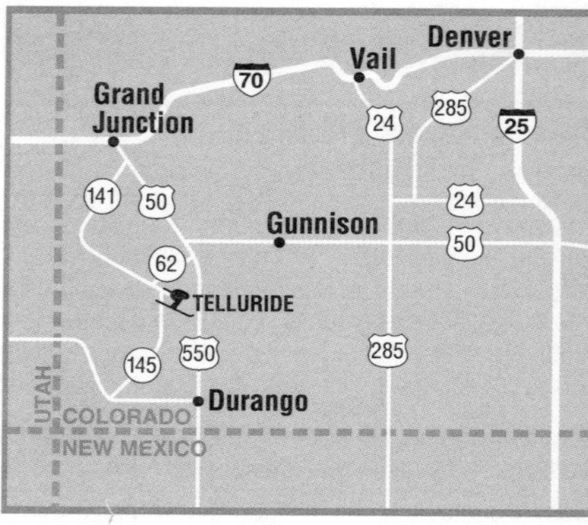


All this commotion can be blamed on the challenging ski slopes, which are so varied that the trail map has six ratings. Experts rank the steeps among the "Ten Toughest" in the US (some say this explains why the mountain attracts more male than female skiers, creating an après-ski social atmosphere that defies national statistics). But beginners are raving about the resort as well, thanks to **Sunshine Peak,** a secluded paradise off the beaten track with lengthy runs reached by the longest high-speed quad chair in the country. In the last few years, vast areas of the mountain have been specially groomed for intermediates, and a network of smooth midlevel runs now winds around **Gorrono Basin.** Telluride's gift to adventure skiers is the **Ultimate** terrain, 400 acres of expert glades and above-timberline skiing located a 10- to 15-minute hike along the ridge just beyond the lift-serviced summit.

Visitors have their choice of overnight locales. Though condo creep is gradually surrounding the Victorian charm of the town of Telluride (designated a National Historic District), it still retains much of its 19th-century identity, and it's the place to stay if you're looking for lots of nightlife. The fast-growing **Mountain Village** (which is accessible via lift during the day and by shuttle bus day and night) offers more luxurious accommodations. At press time a new gondola, linking the town, ski slopes, and Mountain Village was being built. Construction was expected to be completed for the 1995-96 season.

But skiing only tells part of the story at Telluride. During warm-weather months, the lone road into town is jammed with carloads of people flocking to the jazz, rock, blues, and film festivals; and a Winter Festival Series wraps "ski free" packages around such events as the Folk, Country, and Bluegrass Celebration weekends. The resort also runs a half-price skiing promotion for guests staying in neighboring towns, an excellent alternative for vacationers who want to tour other parts of colorful southwestern Colorado as well.

Ice climbing, cross-country skiing along the **San Miguel River,** snowmobiling to ghost towns in the **San Juan Mountain Range**, and heli-skiing are just a few of the options available beyond conventional downhill skiing. **Telluride Central Reservations** will answer questions about and arrange reservations for lodging and various activities.

---

**Telluride Ski and Golf Company**
**565 Mountain Village Boulevard**
**PO Box 11155**
**Telluride, Colorado 81435**

**Information**........................................970/728.3856
......................................................fax 970/728.6364
**Reservations**......................................800/525.3455
**Snow Phone**.......................................970/728.3614

Butch Cassidy readied himself for his first bank robbery by practicing fast getaways on horseback down Telluride's main street. The first bank he held up was the San Miguel Valley Bank on Telluride's very own Main Street, on 24 June 1889.

## Fast Facts

*Area code 970 unless otherwise noted.*

**Ski Season** Late November to mid-April

**Location** Telluride is in **Colorado's Uncompahgre National Forest,** 65 miles south of **Montrose,** 125 miles northeast of **Durango,** 127 miles southeast of **Grand Junction,** and 325 miles southwest of **Denver.**

## Getting to Telluride

**By air: Telluride Regional Airport** is five miles and **Montrose County Airport** is 65 miles from the resort. **America West** flies from **Phoenix** and **Mesa; GP Express** (the **Continental** connection) and **United Express** fly from **Denver** to both airports. **Continental** also flies from **Houston** to **Montrose. United** flys nonstop from **Chicago** and **Los Angeles** to Montrose on Saturdays.

Telluride boasts the highest commercial airport in the country, located on a mesa top at 9,800 feet. Planes land at **Montrose** when the weather is inclement for flying, and buses offer transportation to the resort. Several major carriers also service **Grand Junction** and **Durango** (see "Purgatory" chapter). The **Telluride Transit Company** (728.6000, 800/800.6228) shuttles skiers to and from all four airports, where rental cars are also available.

**By bus: Trailways** (242.6012) buses go to **Montrose. Telluride Transit** (728.6000, 800/800.6228) provides service from nearby towns and airports. Reservations are required.

**By car: Budget** and **Hertz** rent winterized cars at both airports. From **Telluride Regional,** take Highway 145 south; from **Montrose County,** take Highway 50 south to Highway 550, then Highway 62 to Highway 145. Telluride is a 330-mile drive from **Denver** through the mountains via Interstate 70 to Highway 50; from there follow the above directions from Montrose County.

## Getting around Telluride

**San Miguel Transit** (728.5700) provides shuttle service throughout the area. Taxis are available from **Skip's Taxi and Shuttle Service** (728.6667).

## FYI

**Area** 1,050 acres with 62 trails

Beginner—21 percent

Intermediate—47 percent

Advanced/Expert—32 percent

**Number of Groomed Runs** Approximately 20

**Longest Run** 2.85 miles **(See Forever)**

**Capacity** 10,000 skiers per hour

**Base Elevation** 8,725 feet

**Summit Elevation** 11,890 feet (lift-serviced); 12,247 feet (hike to summit)

**Vertical Rise** 3,165 feet

**Average Annual Snowfall** 300 inches

**Snowmaking** 45 percent

**Night Skiing** None

**Lifts** 10 (1 high-speed quad, 2 triple chairs, 6 double chairs, and 1 poma)

| **Lift Passes** | **Full Day** | **Half Day** (starts at 9AM or noon) |
|---|---|---|
| **Adult** | $43 | $34 |
| **Child** (5 and under) | Free | Free |
| **Child** (6-12) | $24 | $19 |
| **Senior** (65-69) | $24 | $19 |
| **Senior** (70 and over) | Free | Free |

Purchase a **Telluride Card** and pay only $20-$33 per day of skiing, depending on the time of usage.

**Ski School** Ski school offices (728.4424) are located at 565 Mountain Village Boulevard in the **Mountain Village** base facility, at the bottom of Lifts 3 and 4. Full-day and half-day lessons as well as private alpine and snowboard lessons are offered.

**Kids' Ski School** Children's programs include **Snowstars** for ages 3 to 5 and **Telstars** for ages 6 to 12. Reservations are recommended. Lift ticket prices are reduced for children participating in ski school.

**Clinics and Special Programs** Pace-setter clinics are held Wednesdays through Sundays at 10:50AM, including two runs on the NASTAR course. Three- and five-day race camps are offered once a month throughout the ski season. The ski school offers three-day clinics called "The Telluride Experience," which include video analysis. Powder, racing, bumps, and telemark clinics are also given. Telluride's ski school director, Annie Vareille Savath, has been a leader in developing **Women's Ski Weeks,** and the resort runs both three- and five-day clinics throughout the ski season. The **Telluride Adaptive Skier Program** for disabled skiers provides private lessons and some adaptive equipment.

**Races** NASTAR races are held Wednesdays through Sundays at 1PM on **Competition.** A pay-to-race course is located next to Competition, with runs daily from 10AM to 3PM.

**Rentals** Between two ski shop chains, with stores at several locations, skiers will find plenty of quality rental equipment and clothing. Hours are daily from 8AM to 5PM. **Telluride Sports** (800/828.SKIS) rental shops have five locations, including stores adjacent to the lift-ticket offices at the **Oak Street, Coonskin,** and **Mountain Village** base facilities. All locations rent regular, demo, and high-performance alpine and snowboard equipment. Renters get free tune-ups and overnight storage. **Paragon Sports** (728.4525) has four locations, including shops at the gondola base and near the Coonskin and Oak Street Lifts. This shop offers cheap (but good) tune-ups and guarantees low-price rentals.

**Lockers** A cluster of lockers is located at the **Mountain Village** base. Storage baskets can be rented at the **Coonskin** base facility, and overnight ski storage is available at **Telluride Sports** (728.4039) and **Olympic Sports** (800/828.SKIS) rental shops.

**Day Care** Children 2 months to 3 years old can stay in the **Village Nursery** (728.6727 or 800/544.0507), located in the **Mountain Village.** Space is limited, so reservations are required. Hours are daily 8AM to 5PM.

**First Aid** Ski patrol can be contacted through the attendants at the top or bottom of any lift. **Telluride Medical Center** (728.3848) is located at 500 W Pacific Avenue.

**Parking** Free parking is available at the base.

**Worth Knowing**

- On **Recycle Days,** bring six empty Coca-Cola cans (with a coupon found on specially marked 12-packs) and receive $12 off any single, day lift ticket.
- Free one-hour mountain tours, including a history of this historic mining region, leave daily at 10AM from the top of the Coonskin Lift.
- From 23 November to 16 December and 1 to 9 April, **Ski Free at Telluride** allows guests to receive free lift tickets at **The Peaks at Telluride** hotel and spa when they book reservations through **Telluride Resort Accommodations.** Discounted lodging rates are also offered.

## Rating the Runs

### ● Beginner

The long beginner trail **Double Cabin** cuts a wide swath on **Sunshine Peak,** where the runs are too easy for advanced skiers and intermediates, ensuring a more relaxed downhill trip for novices.

You'll cross over and under bridges when you veer off Double Cabin onto **Bridges,** another open, gently curving green trail leading to the base of Sunshine Peak.

### ■ Intermediate

Don't expect a lot of traffic on **Peak-A-Boo**—only insiders know that the combination of small bumps and groomed terrain on this trail is irresistible.

Okay, maybe the name isn't completely accurate, but on **See Forever** you can see as far as Utah's **La Sal Mountains**—127 miles away—on a clear day, but that's still quite a view. See Forever is Telluride's longest run, starting at 11,890 feet above sea level.

### ◆ Advanced

Taking **The Plunge** used to be a terrifying experience, but the fear factor has changed since it was double designated, and now most of it is ballroom skiing down a steep, smooth-shaven face. Just for memories—and bump doggies—a small swatch of the original Plunge's precipitous bumps plummets downward along one side of the slope.

### ◆◆ Expert

Egotists love to strut their stuff on **Kant-Mak-M,** a steep chunk of mountainside running right down the lift line. Head elsewhere if you're not a top-level bump skier ready to perform.

In the spring, you could bury Hyundais under the bumps on **Zulu Queen,** a squiggly, narrow mogul trail. It feels like an East Coast run, but with Rocky Mountain snow.

Another steep mogul chute reminiscent of Eastern trails but covered with light Western snow, **Allais Alley** is electrifying enough to make New Englanders think about moving west.

### Snowboarding

Telluride's layout, with terrain difficulty shifting from beginner to expert as you traverse west to east, enables boarders to select the best runs for their skill level. The wide and often empty runs (such as **Double Chin** and **Galloping Goose**) under the Sunshine Express (Lift 10) create an ideal place for snowboarders to learn the basics. For more challenging terrain, **East Drain** and **West Drain** are popular because they have natural half-pipes and places to catch plenty of air. On powder days, most boarders head to **Gold Hill** for its steep chutes and knolls.

## Mountain Highs and Lows

Advanced intermediates are often seduced by the easy entrance to **Bushwacker.** But make no mistake, this is a steep cruising run that will burn more time and calories (from sheer nervous energy) than you may have bargained for. . . unless you're truly an advanced skier.

Technically, **Telluride Trail** is the easiest way down the mountain to the town of Telluride, but expect a few zingers at the end of the day. The front face of the mountain gets the sun in the morning and often hardens to an icy texture by late afternoon. Skiers of all skill levels—many tired and on the edge of control—bunch up on this egress route. If you fit that description, get smart and download on Chair 7.

## At the Resort

*Area code 970 unless otherwise noted.*

- ✦ **Gorrono Ranch Restaurant and Saloon** ★★$$ Lots of hearty soups and thick chilis are sold in this cafeteria. Mexican food lovers should try the moderately hot pork green chili. ♦ Daily breakfast and lunch. Midmountain in Gorrono Basin. 728.7567
- ✦ **Giuseppe's** ★★$$ You won't find too many ski areas with an Italian restaurant at the top of the lifts. Best bets are the fat meatball sandwiches, mini-pizzas, and shoe-size baked potatoes with a choice of trimmings. ♦ Daily lunch. At the top of Lift 9. 728.7503

✦ **Mountain Village Market** This convenience market is located in the **Blue Mesa** building, along with a liquor store and the post office. ♦ Daily 9AM-7PM. Center of Mountain Village, at the base of Lift 1. 728.9758

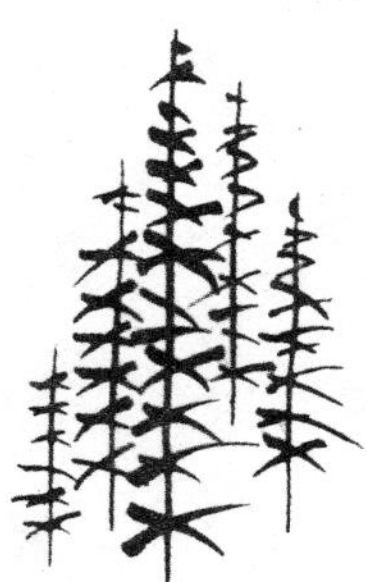


✦ **The Peaks at Telluride** $$$$ Muted colors and earth tones both outside and in keep the focus where it belongs: on the magnificent scenery. This hotel's big windows frame ski trails and mountains—among them the 14,000-foot peaks of the Wilson Range. Even the smallest of the 171 guest rooms are a comfortable size, and their large bathrooms are complete with marble vanities and separate bathtubs and showers. The corner one-bedroom suites are the most attractive. There's also a full service spa and athletic facility (see below). ♦ In the Mountain Village at the base of Lift 1. 728.6800, 800/789.2220; fax 728.6567

Within The Peaks at Telluride:

**The Spa at the Peaks** Guests at **The Peaks** can get their fill of pampering at this 42,000-square-foot facility—one of the largest in the US. Skiers can treat themselves to the **Peaks Bath** (a sensual aromatherapy bath, coupled with champagne and chocolates, and soothing music) or try the **Miner's Bath** (a therapeutic mineral salt bath followed by a sports therapy massage). Altogether, there are 44 individual treatment rooms which offer guests over 30 different programs including skin-care treatments, hydrotherapy spa sessions, sports enhancements, and spirit of life activities. ♦ Daily 7AM-6PM. 800/SPAKIVA

**KidSpa** This day-care center is open to any child, even if the parent is not staying at the hotel. Some locals bring their children here to play indoors and outdoors (in a yard) and to use the pool, basketball court, and other spa facilities. The youngsters also go on ice-skating, sledding, and other supervised outings. Children ages 3 to 16 are accepted, but few children older than 12 show up. Groups are divided according to age. ♦ 800/SPAKIVA

**Legends at Telluride** ★★★★$$$$ With dark wood accents and framed photographs of the surrounding countryside adorning the walls, this 130-seat restaurant is decorated Southwestern style. The outdoor sundeck offers the best views of Mountain Village and the surrounding mountains. In keeping with the health-conscious nature of the environment, the kitchen offers a Peak Performance menu with an emphasis on low-fat fare, including a list of calorie and fat gram content. For those with heartier appetites, the Ranchlands menu offers such traditional fare as crusted chicken, steaks, pasta, and daily specials as well as a variety of appetizers and salads. ♦ Daily breakfast, lunch, and dinner. 800/SPAKIVA

✦ **Peregrine Log Home** $$$$ The ultimate in luxury, this five-bedroom log home is more than 5,000 square feet, decorated in French Country style with cathedral ceilings. It's loaded with such amenities as two stone-framed fireplaces, an indoor Jacuzzi, wraparound deck overlooking the ski trails, and ski-in/ski-out access. ♦ 531 Russell Dr (bottom of Lift 10). 728.6727, 800/544.0507; fax 728.4633

✦ **Aspen Ridge Townhomes** $$$$ Only 12 of these luxurious town homes are in the rental pool, but many of the available units feature waveless waterbeds. The large three-bedroom units boast indoor Jacuzzis overlooking the slopes. ♦ Off the main road in Mountain Village. 728.7100, 800/525.3455; fax 728.6265

✦ **Cactus Cafe** ★★$$ Blue-corn nachos, sizzlin' green-chili-and-chicken soup, and crawfish enchiladas con queso are among the dishes skiers sample at this slope-side cafe. Artwork from the Southwest adorns the walls. ♦ Daily lunch. The Mountain Village Resort, in Mountain Village. 728.6310

✦ **Evangeline's** ★★★$$$ Chef/owner Charles Moore cooks southern Louisiana-style fare influenced by his culinary training in France. Lunch is à la carte, but Moore serves a prix-fixe dinner every evening. This intimate place has a few whimsical touches, like one-of-a-kind oddball salt-and-pepper shakers.

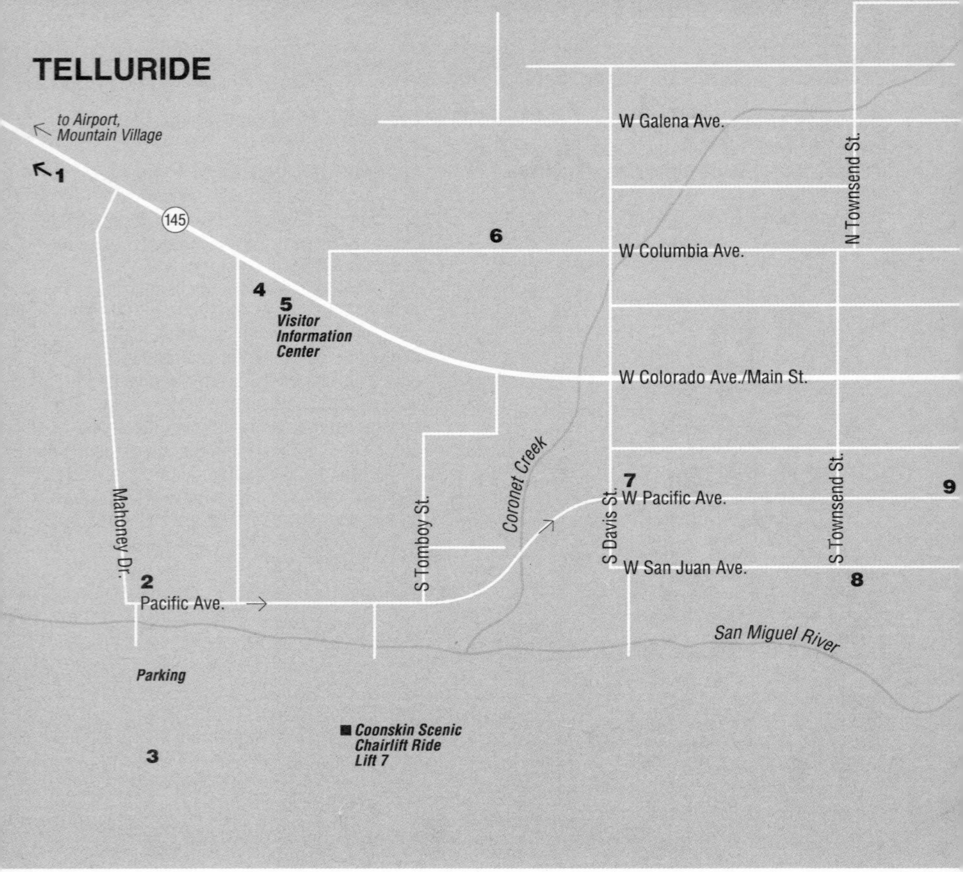

## TELLURIDE



♦ Daily lunch and dinner. Reservations recommended. In the Westermere building in Mountain Village. 728.9717

## Beyond the Resort

**1 Skyline Guest Ranch** $$$ Owned and run by the Farney family, this is a sweet spot to try if you're looking for a more rustic holiday. The 10 lodge rooms—each named after the mountain peak it faces—are small, but cozy, with knotty pine walls, log beds, and fluffy down comforters. Just as homey are the six housekeeping cabins, which vary in size from two- to eight-person capacity. Amenities include full breakfast, shuttle service to and from the ski area, and spectacular views of the San Juan Mountains and surrounding lakes. Many guests come here for the cross-country skiing and the horseback riding; others simply want to relax and enjoy the back-to-nature setting. For ranch guests only, the lodge kitchen serves a hearty American menu, specializing in fish and pasta dishes. ♦ 7214 Highway 145, 3 miles south of Mountain Village. 728.3757; fax 728.6728

**2 Lulu City** $$$$ Solariums with spas, fireplaces, and steam cabinets are among the luxuries to be found in many of the 31 condominiums here. The complex has a hot tub and swimming pool. ♦ Mahoney Dr (at Pacific Ave). 728.6621, 800/525.3455; fax 728.3356

**3 Etta Place/Etta Place Too** $$$ Jacuzzi tubs and gas fireplaces (a ban prevents building new wood-burning fireplaces in Telluride) make Etta's 30 spacious condos popular. ♦ Base of the Coonskin Lift at the end of Mahoney Dr. 728.6621, 800/525.3455; fax 728.3356

**4 Rose's Supermarket** This full-service market stocks everything from staples to gourmet items, and fresh fish arrives twice weekly. You can dine sumptuously in your condo after a stroll through the deli section. ♦ Daily 8AM-9PM. 700 W Colorado Ave (between W Columbia Ave and Mahoney Dr). 728.3124

**5 Visitor Information Center** Telluride's **Central Reservations** office is located here. Skiers may collect information about and book a variety of activities, including cross-

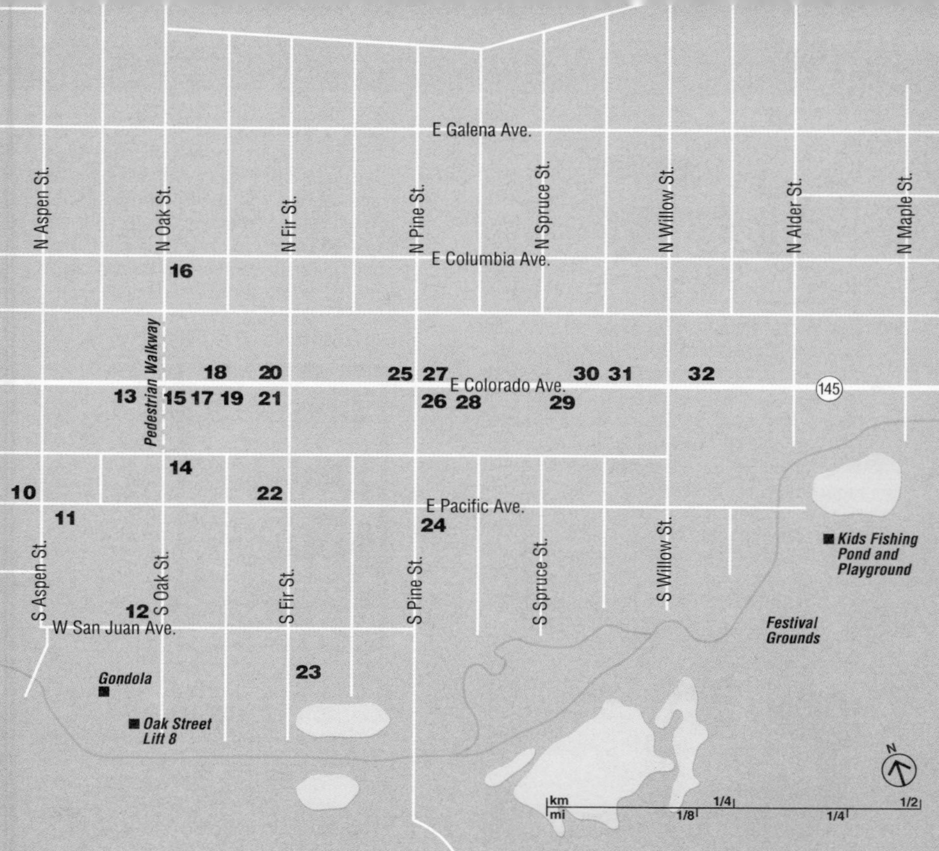


country skiing, sleigh rides, climbing, and snowmobiling. ♦ 666 W Colorado Ave (between W Columbia Ave and Mahoney Dr). 728.3041, 800/525.3455

**6 Tomboy Inn** $$ These 48 motel rooms are well worn, but a few come with kitchenettes. ♦ 619 W Columbia Ave (between S Davis St and W Colorado Ave). 728.6160, 800/538.7754; fax 728.3716

**7 Leimgruber's Bierstube & Restaurant** ★★$$ The decor is decidedly unfancy, but no one cares: This bierstube holds the record for pouring the most Paulaner beer in the US. Wiener schnitzel, sauerbraten, and other classic German dishes complement the drinking. Don't leave without tasting the apple strudel. ♦ Daily dinner. Reservations recommended. 537 W Pacific Ave (at S Davis St). 728.4663

**8 San Juan Brewing Company** ★$$ Trains stopped arriving at this former **Rio Grande Southern Depot** when the mining boom went bust. The Brewing Company opened its restaurant and pub here on the depot's hundredth anniversary. A massive etched-mahogany and stained-glass bar and a glass-enclosed atrium are highlights of the interior. The menu features the freshest and most interesting items the chefs can buy. A typical week might include chicken with seasonal vegetables, fresh tuna, barbecued baby back ribs, and chimichangas. ♦ Daily lunch and dinner. 300 S Townsend St (at W San Juan Ave). 728.0100

**9 Campagna** ★★★★$$$$ Memorable country food from Italy's Tuscany region is prepared by owner Vincent Esposito, who grew up cooking in his father's restaurant in New York. The entrées change nightly, but always incorporate creative uses of fresh herbs on homemade pasta, grilled or roasted poultry and meat, and fresh fish. Esposito's wife, Joline, oversees the dining areas in this small Victorian house turned restaurant, which also has a lengthy wine list. ♦ Daily dinner. Reservations recommended. 435 W Pacific Ave (between S Aspen and S Townsend Sts). 728.6190

---

The hot tub in the basement of the Sheridan Opera House was the place for parties, gossip, and politics in the 1960s.

---

A lucky trash hunter once walked away with a large-screen color TV in perfect condition from Telluride's "Free Box," a traditional source of useful and useless items free for the taking.

**10** **The Victorian Inn** $$ This brightly painted inn is dressed in colors befitting that era, but the building is circa mid-1970s. Only some of the 27 rooms have private baths, but within the last few years all have been furnished with new beds, bedspreads, and refrigerators. Other amenities include a Jacuzzi and complimentary continental breakfast, but there's no communal sitting area. ♦ 401 W Pacific Ave (between S Aspen and S Townsend Sts). 728.6601, 800/525.3455; fax 728.6621

**11** **The San Sophia** $$$ Handmade quilts on brass beds in the 16 guest rooms, stained-glass windows and original artwork on the walls, boot dryers, and a Jacuzzi are just some of the niceties at this hostelry. The observatory, a nook in a tower atop the inn, is a wonderful place to visit with friends or to read a book. The hotel is a block from Main Street and near several restaurants. ♦ 330 W Pacific Ave (at S Aspen St). 728.3001, 800/537.4781; fax 728.6226

**12** **221 South Oak** ★★★$$$ Chatting with friends and sipping a glass of wine while relaxing on a comfy sofa in this bistro is a nice way to ease into a meal. The menu offers a variety of fixed-price meals created with the best ingredients the chef can find at the market that day. The grilled vegetable baguette sandwich makes a nice lunch. ♦ Daily lunch and dinner. 221 S Oak St (steps away from the Oak Street Lift). 728.9507

**13** **Eddie's** ★$ Twelve beers on tap and a constantly hissing espresso machine are star attractions at this eatery. Good bets on the menu are New York-style pizza, large Cobb or Caesar salads with homemade dressings, pasta, and charbroiled steak. Don't miss the Sunday brunch, with omelettes, pancakes, and waffles. ♦ Daily lunch and dinner; Su brunch. 300 W Colorado Ave (between S Oak and S Aspen Sts). 728.6108

**14** **The Dahl House Condos** $$ The tiny rooms in these five condos are arranged in unusual configurations on either two or three levels, and some have spiral staircases. Despite the generous size of the accommodations, the rates for these units are among the cheapest in town. ♦ 122 S Oak St (three blocks from the bottom of Lift 8). 728.4158, 800/525.3455

**15** **Sunshine Pharmacy** Sunglasses, sweatshirts, cards, hats, prescriptions, and the sundries you forgot to toss in your suitcase are all available here. ♦ Daily 9AM-9PM. 236 W Colorado Ave (at S Oak St). 728.3601

**16** **Oak Street Inn** $ Once a youth hostel, this inn still offers the most basic of accommodations in 24 rooms; only a few have private baths. The building dates from the turn of the century, when it was a church. ♦ 134 N Oak St (at W Columbia Ave). 728.3383, 800/525.3455; fax 728.6621

The PowderHouse
RESTAURANT AND BAR

**17** **The Powder House** ★★★$$$ The decor is casual, the lighting dim, and the cuisine gourmet in this restaurant owned by Golden Glove title winner Tony Clinco (former head chef for the Radisson Corporation) and his wife, Cindy. Innovative nightly specials have included pheasant sausage pasta. Duck, seafood, and more conventional pastas are on the menu, too. ♦ Daily dinner. Reservations recommended. 226 W Colorado Ave (between S Fir and S Oak Sts), downstairs. 728.3622

**Restaurants/Clubs:** Red **Hotels:** Blue
**Shops/ Outdoors:** Green **Sights/Culture:** Black

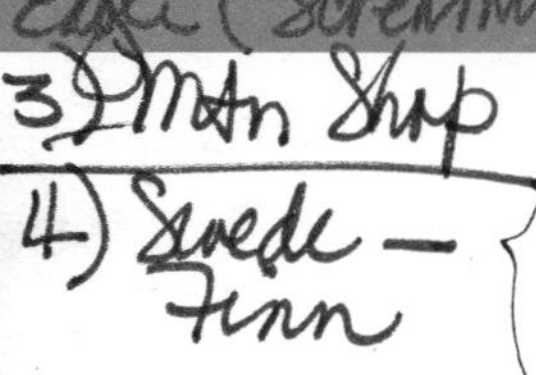

**18** **New Sheridan Hotel** $$ Some of the finest accommodations between Denver and San Francisco could be found at this hotel in the 1890s. Recent renovations have restored the 27-room historic inn to its luxurious heyday. Consulting with local old-timers and historical archives, the hotel has managed to capture the 1890s style for which it was once famous. The antiques-filled **William Jennings Bryan Suite** is one of five charming suites that are part of an addition to the original 1891 site. A restaurant was scheduled to open at press time. ♦ 231 W Colorado Ave (between N Fir and N Oak Sts). 728.4351, 800/200.1891; fax 728.5024

Within the New Sheridan Hotel:

**New Sheridan Bar** The oldest bar in town has a pressed tin ceiling and a mirror behind the long wood bar, dating from the days when gunslingers wanted to see who was entering the room behind them. ♦ Daily 3PM-2AM. 728.4351

**Telluride Heli-Trax** For a day of heli-skiing, contact this helicopter service for a ride into the San Juans. The company organizes daily flights on a "space available" basis. Make reservations at least 48 hours in advance, but prepare for last-minute changes: A final decision on flying is always made the morning of the scheduled day. ♦ 728.4904

**19** **Between the Covers** ★$ Don't feel like skiing today? Hide out here with a book, a cappuccino, and a pastry. Shakes are available for the kids. ♦ Daily 9AM-midnight. 224 W Colorado Ave (across from The New Sheridan). 728.4505

**20** **Deli Downstairs** ★★$ Look for the green awning for homemade soups, sandwiches, and vegetarian and Mexican dishes. The Nutburger (nuts and veggies served on a bun with any or all of the trimmings) will win kudos from vegetarians. Call in your order and you shouldn't have to wait long to eat once you arrive at the restaurant. ♦ Daily lunch and dinner. 217 W Colorado Ave (at N Fir St). 728.4004

---

Telluride's first public library was housed in the old jail just off Main Street, and was initially run in 1974 with the help of citizens who were working off "dog fines" for their pets' misbehaviors.

---

**21** **Canyon Sam's** A "Telluride" logo is silkscreened or embroidered onto every piece of the "mountain formal" (clean shirt and jeans) clothing carried in this store. ♦ Daily 9AM-9PM. 204 W Colorado Ave (at S Fir St). 728.3418

**22** **The Village Market** This full-service market is right in the center of town. ♦ Daily 7:30AM-9:30PM. 157 S Fir St (at W Pacific Ave). 728.4566

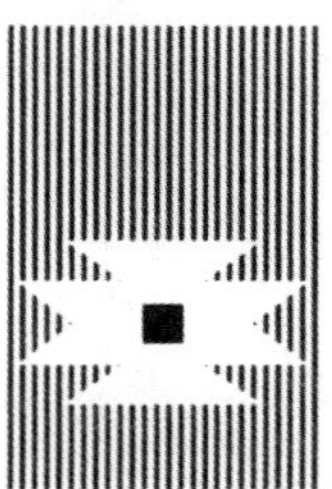

THE ICE HOUSE

**23** **The Ice House** $$$ This luxurious Southwestern-style guest house is filled with furniture crafted specifically for the property. Guests can sit in the library around the fireplace, loosen kinked ski muscles with an in-house massage, or order from **La Marmotte** restaurant next door. All 42 rooms and suites have comforters on the beds and six-foot tubs in the bathrooms. Twelve condominiums, a steam room, Jaccuzzi, and indoor/outdoor swimming pool have been added to the complex. Continental breakfasts are complimentary and there's now a Happy Hour after skiing. ♦ 310 S Fir St (2 blocks from the Oak Street Lift). 728.6300, 800/544.3436

**24** **Falline** $ Skiers on a budget stay in these condos for the price and the proximity to the Oak Street Lift. The eight available units are somewhat dated, but they all have kitchens with microwaves and coffeemakers, and there's a Jacuzzi in an inner courtyard. ♦ Southeast corner of E Pacific Ave and S Pine St. 728.6621, 800/525.3455; fax 728.6265

---

From the early mining days through Prohibition, as many as 26 "soda parlours" and "female boardinghouses" fronted thriving bordellos in Telluride. The Silverbell was the last to close down, shutting its doors in 1959.

---

**25 Floradora** ★★$$ No one by the name of Floradora ever presided over this eating and drinking establishment. Owned and operated by Howie and Lois Stern (who started as dishwasher and waitress 16 years ago), this restaurant brings in a family crowd, who fill the wood booths to dine on Southwestern dishes, steaks, charbroiled burgers, and goodies from a salad bar stocked with everything from chopped chicken livers to soup. ♦ Daily lunch and dinner. 103 W Colorado Ave (at N Pine St). 728.3888

**26 Last Dollar Saloon** The aging look of this former miner's supply store and garage translates as rustic, casual, and just the stop for skiers who like to play pool or throw darts. This saloon packs them in when the town is full. ♦ Daily 3PM-2AM. 100 E Colorado Ave (at S Pine St). 728.4800

**27 Telluride Trappings & Toggery** Don't expect New York chic at this shop, but clothes that are the essence of relaxed Western style, i.e. cowboy boots and Stetsons. ♦ Daily 9AM-9PM. 109 E Colorado Ave (at N Pine St). 728.3338

**28 Sofio's Mexican Cafe** ★★★$$ Huevos rancheros, waffles and pancakes made from scratch, seafood Benedict, fresh-squeezed orange juice, and freshly ground coffees make this a very popular breakfast spot. The dinnertime menu includes four varieties of fajitas, *chiles rellenos,* and other Mexican dishes with a side of fresh salsa, plus Mexican beers, of course. ♦ Daily breakfast and dinner. 110 E Colorado Ave (near S Pine St). 728.4882

**29 Fly Me To The Moon Saloon** Dancers get extra rhythm from this saloon's spring-loaded floor, which *SKI* magazine once voted "the best in the West." This is the place to be when bands are jamming, or just to hang out and play pool, foosball, or video games. The Moon has a nonsmoking section. ♦ Cover varies. Daily 5PM-2AM. 132 E Colorado Ave (near S Spruce St). 728.MOON

**30 At Home in Telluride** Homegrown foods, handmade Telluride mugs, home furnishings, and gift baskets filled with gourmet goodies are among the items for sale. ♦ Daily 10AM-9PM. 137 E Colorado Ave (near N Spruce St, under the purple awnings). 728.6865

**31 Hell Bent Leather & Silver** A treasure trove of silver jewelry inset with turquoise and other stones, as well as hand-tooled belts, leather clothing, and arts and crafts made by Native Americans are some of the finds in this shop. ♦ Daily 10AM-9PM. 209 E Colorado Ave (near N Willow St). 728.6246

**32 Dakota Home Furnishings** Among the offerings are an attractive collection of country antiques, including pine tables and cabinets, and decorative accessories like pinecone candleholders. ♦ M-Sa 10AM-8PM. 317 E Colorado Ave (off N Willow St). 728.4204

Town Marshall Jim Clark maintained law and order during the rowdy mining days, but his off-duty occupation was robbing stagecoaches while in disguise. He was mysteriously murdered shortly after the town fathers learned about his escapades.

## Bests

### Steve West

Manager, New Sheriden Hotel

Après-ski every afternoon at **Leimgruber's Bierstube.** This Bavarian restaurant is packed every afternoon, with Paulaner beer on tap, and an occasional "oompah-pah" band.

Lunch on the sundeck at **The Peaks at Telluride** resort. The outdoor seating area of the **Legends** restaurant cannot be beat, with fantastic Southwestern-style food, incomparable views of the 14,000-foot **Wilson Mountain Ranges,** and live music some days. The helicopter landing pad below the deck adds a little excitement to the meal.

**Telluride Historical Museum**—More than one hundred years ago Telluride was a prominent mining community, and this museum offers a delightful look into its past. Find out about Telluride being the first city in the world to have alternating current electricity.

**"Glider Bob"** offers an incredible glider ride above the **Rockies** in his motorless sailplane.

Backcountry skiing with **San Juan Hut Systems.**

Snowmobile with **Telluride Outside;** you'll go to a ghost town and see the forest like you've never seen it before.

Hike up **Aspen Street** and follow **Coronet Creek** about one-quarter mile to an incredible waterfall. It is frozen completely and goes up a red stone cliff about one hundred feet. You can actually walk all the way around this ice waterfall. Be sure to wear boots.

Read the *Daily Planet* newspaper every morning.

And don't leave without having a beer in the **New Sheridan Bar.**

### Erin Hess

Director/Advertising, Telluride Ski and Golf Company

I feel very fortunate living in this beautiful canyon—just a walk through our town would make anyone understand why.

Lunch at **Giuseppe's** is a must for the spectacular views and the food.

**Leimgruber's** is a great German bierstube and a big après-ski place.

**Campagna**—for old-style Northern Italian cuisine in a quaint old Victorian home.

The **San Miguel County Museum** has an amazing collection of photographs and artifacts that reconstruct Telluride's colorful mining past.

Definitely see a movie in the old **Sheridan Opera House.**

# Sun Valley

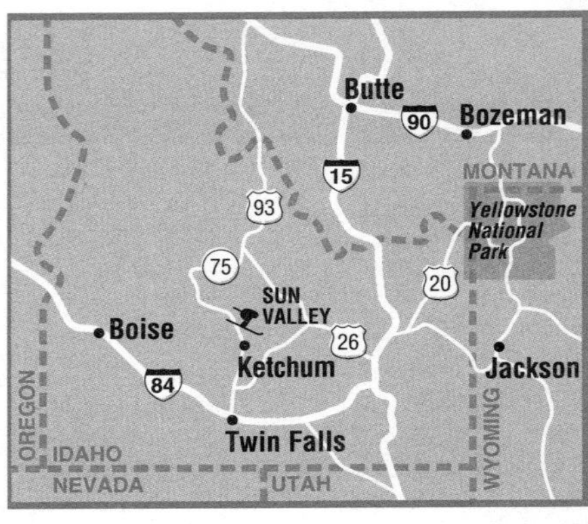


When Averell Harriman, head of **Union Pacific Railroad,** decided to promote vacation travel on **U.P.'s** northern line, he was convinced that America's rich and recognizable would ride his trains to distant, untracked slopes. The year was 1935, a time when most people—even movie stars—perceived skiing as both dangerous and romantic. Undaunted, Harriman commissioned Count Felix Schaffgotsch of Austria to search for bright sun, windless days, and big mountains, a perfect combination he found in the three-street Idaho mining town of **Ketchum.**

Deep snowbanks, gilded shop signs, a clock tower, opera house, horse-drawn sleighs, ice rinks, and—just as Harriman predicted—celebrities characterize Sun Valley, a mile up **Trail Creek** from the century-old Ketchum. In the 1930s and 1940s, Ketchum/Sun Valley became the resort of choice for Claudette Colbert, Ingrid Bergman, Gary Cooper, Clark Gable, and Ernest Hemingway. Paying tribute to that early tradition, contemporary stars such as Clint Eastwood, Bruce Willis, and Arnold Schwarzenegger have been known to pound a few of the ski runs here, particularly **Limelight** and **Warm Springs.** The resort core resembles a Tyrolean village—an image amplified by the numerous Austrian instructors at **Sun Valley Ski School**—with a diverse array of restaurants, boutiques, and upscale accommodations designed to appeal to a well-heeled clientele.

But the main reason skiers (movie stars and regular folk alike) come to Sun Valley is to tackle **Bald Mountain,** a world-class peak surrounded by snow-covered hillsides, or to master the snowplow on gentle **Dollar Mountain.** "Baldy" is known as a skier's mountain—big, varied, and challenging; discounting the rare traverse between runs, it has no natural rest areas. Nationally ranked runs such as Warm Springs and Limelight drop relentlessly toward the Challenger Quad, a detachable chairlift that rises an incredible 3,400 feet in 11 minutes.

After a day of Baldy's high-speed quads and thigh-punishing steeps, skiers are usually only too willing to pull on their cowboy boots and bolo ties and saunter on down to Ketchum's saloon-style restaurants and bars for a hot meal and a cold beer (or a glass of white wine, as today's crowds seem to prefer), followed by a little star-gazing. Who knows? You could overhear "The Terminator" wax poetic on life, love, and the surrounding peaks; it's only part of a traditional winter vacation in Sun Valley.

---

**Sun Valley Ski Area**
**Sun Valley Company**
**Sun Valley, Idaho 83353**

**Information**........................................208/622.4111

**Reservations**......................................800/786.8259

**Road Conditions**......................(local) 208/886.2266

..........................................(statewide) 208/336.6600

**Avalanche and Weather**....................208/622.8027

**Snow Phone**.......................................800/635.4150

## Fast Facts

*Area code 208 unless otherwise noted.*

**Ski Season** Thanksgiving through late April

**Location** Sun Valley is 85 miles north of **Twin Falls** on Highway 75; 160 miles northeast of **Boise** on Interstate 84 (to Highway 20 and then Highway 75).

## Getting to Sun Valley

**By air: Friedman Airport,** 11 miles south of Ketchum/Sun Valley, is serviced daily by **Horizon Air** (800/547.9308) and **Sky West** (800/453.9417).

**By bus:** During winter, **Sun Valley Stages** (733.3921) offers transportation from **Boise** to **Friedman Airport** and to **Sun Valley Lodge.**

**By car:** Several major car rental agencies offer winterized cars at **Boise** and **Friedman Airports.**

### Driving times from:

Boise—2.5 hours (160 miles)

Twin Falls—1.5 hours (85 miles)

## Getting around Sun Valley

**Ketchum Area Rapid Transit** (**KART;** 726.7140) offers free bus service between downtown **Ketchum, Sun Valley,** and the **Warm Springs** and **River Run** lift areas. For taxi service, call 726.9351. A horse-drawn carriage, which you'll find parked outside **Pioneer Saloon,** operates in downtown Ketchum during winter.

## FYI

Sun Valley

**Area** 1,275 acres featuring 75 groomed runs, open-bowl skiing, and glades.

Beginner—38 percent

Intermediate—45 percent

Advanced/Expert—17 percent

**Number of Groomed Runs** Bald Mountain—65; Dollar Mountain—13

**Longest Run** 3 miles (Bald Mountain's summit to the base of **Warm Springs Lodge**)

**Capacity** 28,180 skiers per hour

**Base Elevation** 5,800 feet

**Vertical Rise** Bald Mountain—3,400 feet; Dollar Mountain—628 feet

**Average Annual Snowfall** 220 inches

**Snowmaking** 73 percent

**Night Skiing** None

**Lifts** 17 (7 quads, 5 triple chairs, 5 double chairs)

| **Lift Passes** | **Full Day** | **Half Day** (starts at 1PM) |
|---|---|---|
| **Adult** | $47 | $33 |
| **Child** (12 and under) | $26 | $18 |
| **Senior** (65 and over) | $27 | $20 |

**Ski School** The main office (622.2248) is in the **Sports Center** on **Sun Valley Mall,** with a second desk at **Warm Springs Lodge,** a third in **Lookout Restaurant** at Bald Mountain's summit, and a fourth in **Dollar Cabin.** Lessons range from hourly private lessons to three-hour group clinics.

**Kids' Ski School Tiny Tracks** is a one-hour introductory class for ages 3 to 4. Four-hour lessons are offered to 5- to 12-year-olds, separated into beginners/low-intermediates (Dollar Mountain) and intermediate/expert (Bald Mountain). Lift tickets and equipment are not included.

**Clinics and Special Programs Sun Valley Ski School** offers private instruction on powder, moguls, and racing techniques, and clinics for master racers and snowboarders. **Women's Clinics,** including a seminar on equipment and skier video analysis, are offered for two, three, and five days. One- to five-day racing clinics are held for groups of no more than eight persons.

**Races** NASTAR races are held Tuesdays, Thursdays, and Fridays at 12PM. At press time, the NASTAR course was located at **Warm Springs** on Bald Mountain, but we suggest verifying the current location with the ski school. The cost is $6 for three runs and $1 for each additional run.

**Rentals Sturtevants** (726.4501; daily 8:30AM-7PM), on Lloyd Drive in the **Warm Springs Base Area** and also off Highway 75 in downtown **Ketchum,** offers a performance package that includes upper-end boots, skis, and poles; equipment for children and adults; demos; and snowboards. **Paul Kenny's Ski and Sports** (726.7474; daily 8:30AM-5:30PM), also on **Lloyd Drive,** carries brand-new equipment for children and adults, including snowboards. **Formula Sports** (726.3194; daily 8AM-7PM), off Highway 75 in downtown **Ketchum,** rents top-end giant slalom and slalom equipment, as well as snowboards and children's gear. All three shops require a credit-card imprint to rent.

**Lockers** Coin-operated lockers are located at **Warm Springs Lodge, Lookout Restaurant** on Bald Mountain's summit, and at **Paul Kenny's Ski and Sports,** where ski storage/lockers are also available, at the base of **Warm Springs.**

**Day Care Sun Valley Resort Play School** (622.2288) on **Sun Valley Mall** (next to the post office) accepts infants to 6-year-olds and offers a **Pre-Ski Program** that buses children to Dollar Mountain where they ski with instructors from 1:30PM to 3:30PM. Full-day and half-day activities include ice-skating, sledding, and arts and crafts.

**First Aid Wood River Medical Center** (622.3322), adjacent to **Sun Valley Mall,** has an excellent orthopedic clinic, an emergency room, and full surgical facilities, plus a staff of doctors involved with family care. The **Sun Valley Ski Patrol** (622.2380) provides on-mountain first aid.

TV celebrity Adam West (a.k.a. Batman) has devised a whole new concept to the unlisted telephone number. When you look up "West, Adam" in the Sun Valley area phone book, you'll find instructions to see "Wayne, Bruce (Millionaire)." Turn to Wayne, Bruce, and it says, "Please consult 'Crimefighters' in the Yellow Pages." Do that and you'll find, "Batman. See White Pages." Just when you think you've unmasked the caped crusader's number, you plow through the White Pages only to read, "Batman. See West, Adam."

**Parking** Free parking is available on the street at **Warm Springs Base,** as well as at the **KART** stop on **Warm Springs Road** (near the Presbyterian Church) and at **River Run.**

**Worth Knowing**

- Purchase a ticket before 1 December for only $23 and it can be used until 22 December. Most locals buy them up in droves, as there's no limit.
- After much research, developers decided to build the **Sun Valley Lodge** on the area containing the most cow dung. Cows hang out in the sunniest spots, after all. And soon thereafter, such celebrities as Doris Day, Ginger Rogers, and Jacqueline Kennedy-Onassis also made it their hot spot.

## Rating the Runs

### ● Beginner

Surrounded by spectacular views, gentle rolling **Half Dollar** (Dollar Mountain), with its perfect pitch and flawless grooming, has schooled generations of beginners in the mysteries of bent knees, quiet hands, and gliding wedge turns.

Between the gentle grade, perfect grooming, and fire-breathing quad lift, "never ever" beginners can boast they skied Baldy—even if it is on **Lower River Run** (Bald Mountain)—with never ever breaking out of a wedge.

### ■ Intermediate

Serviced by an 11-minute ride on the Challenger Quad chairlift and consistently rated among North America's Top 10 runs, **Warm Springs** (Bald Mountain) drops 3,400 vertical feet in the same unrelenting pitch. In one nonstop thigh-smoking run from top to bottom, skiers are alternately parboiled by this trail's face, jerked about midway by the bumps, then born again during a broad drop to **Warm Springs Lodge.**

Accessed off **Lower College** run and blessed by Baldy's massive York snowmaking, **Graduate** (Bald Mountain) offers an advanced degree in perfect bumps and cold, consistent snow. Here skiers can bail out left to **Flying Squirrel,** right to **River Run,** or ride the fall line deep into **Frenchman's Gulch** and the Gulch Lift.

Sun Valley has always been difficult to reach, but Leif Odmark, a Swedish ski instructor, set the record for tenacity. Captivated by the movie *Sun Valley Serenade,* which showcased the area's superb snow and sparsely populated valley, and stranded by a major snowstorm in Shoshone, Odmark skied (nordic style) 50 miles over the drifted inroads. One look at the snowbound Wood River Valley and he never left (in fact, he still lives here).

### ◆ Advanced

Once known as a stage run where alpine actors projected their brilliant lines to a cheering audience in the chairs above, **Limelight** (Bald Mountain) has benefited from widening, snowmaking, and the removal of the Limelight Double chairlift, which once divided the run and tended to force skiers up against the trees. When deep snow blankets Sun Valley, Limelight's perfect fall line, steep grade, and moderate moguls are paradise found.

Skiers searching for flawless fall lines need look no further. Hidden beneath **Upper College, Plaza** (Bald Mountain) is one of Baldy's lesser-skied runs. Though moguls form here, they are a perfect testament to this run's steep pitch and deep, consistent snow.

### ◆◆ Expert

Big bumps, a sheer pitch, changeable snow, and spectacular views of **Pioneer Mountains' Devils Bedstead** formation—**Upper River Run** (Bald Mountain) offers all this *and* is serviced by the Christmas Detachable Quad. What more could a skier who takes pride in blazing feet, massive thighs, and unshakable courage ask for? Intermediates should leave this run's changing lines and radical drops to experts who are as comfortable in the air as on snow.

The bold and beautiful hoping to catch the eye of the burgers-and-brew crowd at **Lookout Restaurant** dive off the cornice into **Lookout Bowl** (Bald Mountain) and its sun-softened south face. Between this bowl's endless moguls and 2,000 vertical feet, mere mortals might be advised to "Watch out!"—only the best skiers take this run nonstop.

### Snowboarding

With the exception of **Seattle Ridge,** the entire mountain is open to snowboarders. Most hard-plate riders head to **Mid River Run** or **Grey Hawk,** because the terrain at these areas provides the best opportunity for powder and wide-open, long runs for GS turns. Freestyle boarders have fun cruising through the trees at **Warm Spring. Picabo Street,** a new run named after the Olympic silver medalist, and **Frenchman's** are usually bumped up offering opportunities for plenty of "air" maneuvers.

## Mountain Highs and Lows

Grooming a blue fall line won't necessarily change it to green. Leave that alchemy to mountain managers searching for more beginner terrain. By the time Ketchum grade-schoolers graduate to **New Bowl** and **Old Bowl** (Dollar Mountain), they've traded their snowplow for a solid parallel. Rate these runs a sky blue.

Why **Mayday Bowl** (Bald Mountain) rates a robin's egg blue while **Lookout Bowl** gets an expert black remains a mystery; both bowls share the same exposure, pitch, changing snow, and massive moguls. Give the ungroomed Mayday a midnight black rating, then follow the ridge down to **Sigi's Bowl** for true blue.

This may be one of Baldy's best-loved north-facing groomed runs, but dressing **International** (Bald Mountain) in black diamonds is like putting on an evening gown for a barn dance. Curving gently to the right through old-growth firs, with small bumps on top and an off-camber fall line below, this run deserves a midnight blue.

Squeezed into the woods on the skier's right of **Seattle Ridge**'s green-rated **Gretchen's Gold,** the **Fire Trail** (Bald Mountain) tempts the unwary with a mild blue upper section that quickly funnels into a gutter filled with massive moguls and old-growth firs. Rated a single black diamond now, this deceiver deserves a diamond and a half.

## At the Resort

*Area code 208 unless otherwise noted.*

✦ **Sun Valley Lodge** $$$ Fronted by a snow sculpture of a smiling sun, this lodge dominates the resort core. During the summer of 1936, **Union Pacific Railroad** workers formed the structure's concrete exterior using Douglas fir. As the brown-colored cement cured, it cast the rough grain of the wood, giving the lodge its rustic appearance. Part marketing ploy, part nostalgic archive, hundreds of old black-and-white photographs documenting Hollywood at play fill the lodge's long hallways. (To entice the stars to this remote corner of Idaho, **Union Pacific** provided them with rooms, meals, and entertainment.) Note the shotguns, golf clubs, fly rods, horses, champagne glasses, and other toys brandished in the pictures. Some of the photos show starlets sunning beside the outdoor heated pool. In a quieter time, Ernest Hemingway settled in the lodge to work on *For Whom The Bell Tolls,* and Gary Cooper, Jane Russell, Clark Gable, and Ingrid Bergman danced in the **Duchin Room Lounge.**Today, the lodge offers 138 rooms, all redecorated in French country château, reflected in the hand-carved French Richelieu furniture and French-print–adorned coverlets, dusters, and throw pillows. The west-facing rooms enjoy panoramas that encompass Bald Mountain, while east-facing rooms look toward Trail Creek Ridge. Amenities include a ski room, sauna, beauty salon, and bowling in the basement, plus a concierge and bell and room service. ♦ Sun Valley Rd. 622.4111, 800/786.8259; fax 622.2030

Within Sun Valley Lodge:

**The Lodge Dining Room** ★★★$$ Opened in 1936, the "LDR" recalls an era when the nation traveled on rails and the word "service" wasn't always followed by "station." The waiters, decked out in black jackets and white gloves, could have been lifted intact from the photos that line the lodge's hallways. Hollywood's most luminous stars have dined, danced, and, in one well-documented case, brawled (over Claudette Colbert) in this dining room. The cuisine is continental. ♦ Tu-Su dinner; Sunday brunch. 622.2150

**Gretchen's** ★★$$ Named after local celebrity Gretchen Fraser, who in 1948 became the first American to win Olympic ski medals, this airy cafe overlooks the nearby ice rink. Paintings of Gretchen when she won the gold and the silver serve as decor, along with watercolors by local artists. Try one of the special salads. ♦ Daily breakfast, lunch, and dinner. 622.2144

**Duchi Room Lounge** Movie stars have danced, schmoozed, and made headlines over cocktails in this lounge for almost 60 years. Known locally as the "Doo Dah Room," this elegant bar attracts an older crowd, reared on the Big Band sound. The Joe Foss Trio entertains six nights a week. ♦ Daily 11AM-2AM. 622.2145

✦ **Sun Valley Skating Rink** The 179- by 89-foot, outdoor ice rink is open to the public all winter long; the indoor rink is also open to all, when not reserved for hockey games or figure-skating events. (You can rent skates here for a couple of dollars if you forgot to bring your own.) In summer, ice shows feature such Olympic talents as Katarina Witt, Brian Boitano, and Kristi Yamaguchi. ♦ Fee. Daily 10AM-10PM. Outside Sun Valley Lodge's main lobby. 622.2194

✦ **Wildflower Condominiums** $$$ Surrounded by spruce trees and aspens, these condominiums offer a choice of one- to three-bedroom units with fireplaces, vaulted ceilings, hot tubs, and access to all **Sun Valley Lodge** amenities. ♦ Next to Sun Valley Lodge. 622.4111, 800/786.8258; fax 622.2030

✦ **Sun Valley Sports Center** Purchase your ski tickets, check out the posted snow conditions, and find out the answers to all your questions about sports in Sun Valley. To the right of the sports desk, sleigh rides can be booked for dinner at **Trail Creek Cabin.** You'll also find the main office for the **Sun Valley Ski School** (622.2247), one of the oldest ski schools in the US. ♦ Sun Valley Mall. 622.2231

One story has it that Ketchum was born as a mining town in 1880 when local prospector Daniel Scribner's dog chased a rabbit down a badger hole. While digging for the rabbit, the dog unearthed a trace of silver and the rush was on. Named after Scribner's daughter, the resulting Minnie Moore Mine produced more than $15 million in silver and lead ore.

**Restaurants/Clubs:** Red | **Hotels:** Blue
**Shops/ Outdoors:** Green | **Sights/Culture:** Black

✦ **Pete Lane's Sports** In 1936, when Pete Lane heard that an Austrian count was in town asking a lot of questions about the local weather, he cautioned other Ketchum store owners to refuse to cash the "foreigner's" checks—or so local legend has it. Little did Lane realize what a major impact Felix Schaffgotsch would have on his hometown. Residents and tourists alike, however, are welcome at **Pete Lane's Sports** (now owned by **Sun Valley Company**), which offers a full range of ski rentals. ♦ Daily 8AM-9PM. Across from Sun Valley Sports Center. 622.2276

✦ **Konditorei** ★$ Modeled after an Austrian *konditorei,* this corner restaurant specializes in coffees, desserts, sandwiches, and chicken crepes. ♦ Daily breakfast, lunch, and dinner. Sun Valley Mall. 622.2235

✦ **Sun Valley Delicatessen** ★$ Make this your one-stop shop for deli sandwiches, baked muffins and breads, soup and salad, pretzels, beer, liquor, and wine. ♦ Daily 9AM-10PM. Sun Valley Mall. 622.2060

✦ **Sun Valley Drugstore** This full pharmacy also carries magazines, makeup, sunblock, and film. ♦ Daily 9AM-9PM. Sun Valley Mall. 622.2083

✦ **Kitzbühel Collection** Despite the allusion to lederhosen and dirndls, the Kitzbühel's Geiger clothing line specializes in boiled-wool jackets and dresses. ♦ Daily 10AM-6PM. Next to Sun Valley Drugstore. 622.2227

✦ **Sun Valley Gift Shop** Owned by **Sun Valley Company,** this gift shop carries artwork, ski pins, and other collectibles. If the service seems a bit sketchy, blame it on the fact that the help would rather be skiing then selling. ♦ Daily 9AM-9PM. Sun Valley Mall. 622.2206

Above Sun Valley Gift Shop:

✦ **Sun Valley Travel** When deep powder blankets Baldy the night before skiers are scheduled to leave, many call the agents here to rebook their flights. ♦ M-F 8:30AM-5PM. 622.4451, 800/231.4451

✦ **Brass Ranch** Named after the 4,300-acre ranch on which **Union Pacific** president Averell Harriman built his resort, this boutique specializes in upscale sportswear (labels include Bogner and Skea), ski suits, and after-ski boots. Accessories by Ralph Lauren and local jeweler Christina Healy can be found in the display cases. ♦ Daily 9:30AM-9PM. Sun Valley Mall. 622.2021

✦ **Ex Libris** When it snows, fair-weather skiers jam this well-stocked bookstore, which features an extensive selection of Ernest Hemingway titles and books on Idaho. ♦ Daily 10AM-10PM. Sun Valley Mall. 622.8174

✦ **Sun Valley Opera House** Accented by massive truss beams and hanging chandeliers, this opera house shows *Sun Valley Serenade* every afternoon at 5PM. Starring Sonja Henie and John Payne, this classic movie put Sun Valley on the map. Contemporary movies also run nightly at 7PM and 9:15PM, and local plays and concerts appear on a regular basis. ♦ Showtimes: daily 5PM, 7PM, 9:15PM. Behind Sun Valley Sports Center. 622.2244

✦ **Ram Bar and Restaurant** ★$$ Located beneath a golden ram's head, the most intimate of Sun Valley's restaurants serves fresh pastas and grilled steaks and chops. ♦ Daily dinner. Across from Sun Valley Pond. 622.2223

✦ **Sun Valley Inn** $$ It may have been designed from set sketches for the 1936 film *I Met Him in Paris,* but this 120-room inn lacks such amenities as a concierge and beauty salon (and thus is slightly less expensive than **Sun Valley Lodge**). It does, however, offer a heated outdoor pool, plus a cafeteria, sauna, and weight room. ♦ Opposite end of Sun Valley Mall from Sun Valley Lodge. 622.4111, 800/786.8259; fax 622.2030

✦ **Moritz Community Hospital** Accident-prone skiers can take comfort in the fact that this hospital includes one of the nation's finest orthopedic fracture clinics. ♦ Daily 24-hour emergency service. Southeast end of the Sun Valley core. 622.3323

✦ **Sun Valley Nordic Center** With 25 miles of groomed nordic tracks, this ski center has consigned wood, mohair, and fishscale skis to the garage rafters. The operative word here is "skate," an efficient pole/skate/glide technique that turns nordic skiing into a Zen exercise. Managed by Hans Muehlegger, the center offers rentals, lessons, and most of all—spectacular skiing, with trails ranging in difficulty from first-time beginner to advanced racer. ♦ Fee. Daily 9AM-3:30PM. 622.2250

✦ **Sun Valley Heli-Ski Guides** Weather and snow conditions permitting, you can ski five runs of 2,000 to 3,000 vertical feet on some of the Rockies' best helicopter terrain. A rare adventure is the helicopter-in/helicopter-out two-night yurt trip with a stay in Devils Bedstead, a mountain formation composed of four peaks. The yurt, a conical Mongolian tent, offers a warm, dry refuge and unforgettable views of the Pioneer Mountains. ♦ Sun Valley Gun Club (one-half mile east of Sun Valley Lodge). 622.3108

✦ **Trail Creek Cabin** ★★$$ Half the fun of eating here is the sleigh ride in, during which you can study the Idaho night and the steam rising off the draft horses while snuggled beneath heavy woolen blankets. Once inside the log cabin, you'll feel as if you've stepped back in time. Virtually all of Sun Valley's celebrities once partied here; black-and-white photos capture Ernest Hemingway and Gary Cooper toasting each other in the early morning hours. The fresh-baked bread, lamb, steaks, ribs, and trout are generally good, but on busy nights the food may have cooled by the time it gets to your table. ♦ Daily lunch and dinner. Trail Creek Rd (1.5 miles east of Sun Valley Lodge). 622.2319

## Beyond the Resort

**1 Ketchum Korral Motor Lodge** $$ Ernest Hemingway lived in one of the 17 log cabins here for a short while after moving to Ketchum. Today the decor is rustic Western, with cedar-paneled rooms and rock fireplaces, plus kitchen facilities and a hot tub and spa. The Korral is on the **KART** bus line and a short walk to downtown Ketchum's bars and restaurants. ♦ 310 S Main St/Hwy 75, just south of town. 726.3510

**2 River Street Inn** $$ This nine-room inn, located on a quiet residential street within easy walking distance of downtown Ketchum, offers excellent breakfasts and Japanese soaking tubs. ♦ 100 River St West (between First and Washington Aves). 726.3611; fax 726.2439

**3 The Tyrolean** $$ With 58 rooms, this lodge offers a hot tub, continental breakfast, laundry facilities, and a gameroom without compromising its quiet atmosphere. It's accessible by the **KART** bus line. ♦ 260 Cottonwood St (near Third Ave). 726.5336; fax 726.5757

**4 Williams** The new owners of this grocery store, formerly called **Perrons,** have changed its name and fixed up the place. As a result, locals have returned and are impressed not only with the excellent deli but the friendly staff, wide selection of food, and lower prices. ♦ Daily 8AM-9PM. 100 S Main St (between First and Second Sts). 726.3771

**5 Sawtooth Club** ★$$ The name may spin an image of flying chips, green lumber, and sweaty loggers, but the reality cuts more toward a meat market heavy on docksiders, pleated pants, pin-striped shirts, and cashmere sweaters. White wine is the drink of choice, typically sipped by languid couples utterly bored with it all. Hamburgers and other dishes are also served. ♦ Daily dinner. 231 S Main St (between Second St and Sun Valley Rd). 726.5233

**6 The Casino Club** In years past this club had a reputation for being down and dirty. A low-ball poker game usually could be found in the back, and rusted rolling-block rifles, steel traps, dusty coyote mounts, and beer signs covered the walls. A serious remodel, however, drove many of the old charismatic alcoholics who used to hang out here out the back door. In recent years they've been replaced by tanned ski bums sipping white wine and discussing moguls, deep powder, and the long-range forecast. ♦ Daily 10:30AM-2AM. 200 S Main St (between Second St and Sun Valley Rd). 726.9901

**7 Whiskey Jacques Bar** By keeping the original log walls and Crosby Demoss paintings above the bar, this historic watering hole has somehow managed to preserve Ketchum's colorful past and still stay in business. The locals who jam in here on Friday and Saturday nights hardly pretend to have discovered a culinary paradise (though the Whiskey does serve Ricco's pizza); they come to drink, press the flesh, and dance to country, reggae, and rock 'n' roll music. ♦ Cover varies. Daily 4PM-2AM. 206 S Main St (between Second St and Sun Valley Rd). 726 5297

**8 Pioneer Saloon** ★★★$ This is a Ketchum keystone that has anchored local nightlife for more than four decades. If you don't like mounted elk, deer, and buffalo heads or

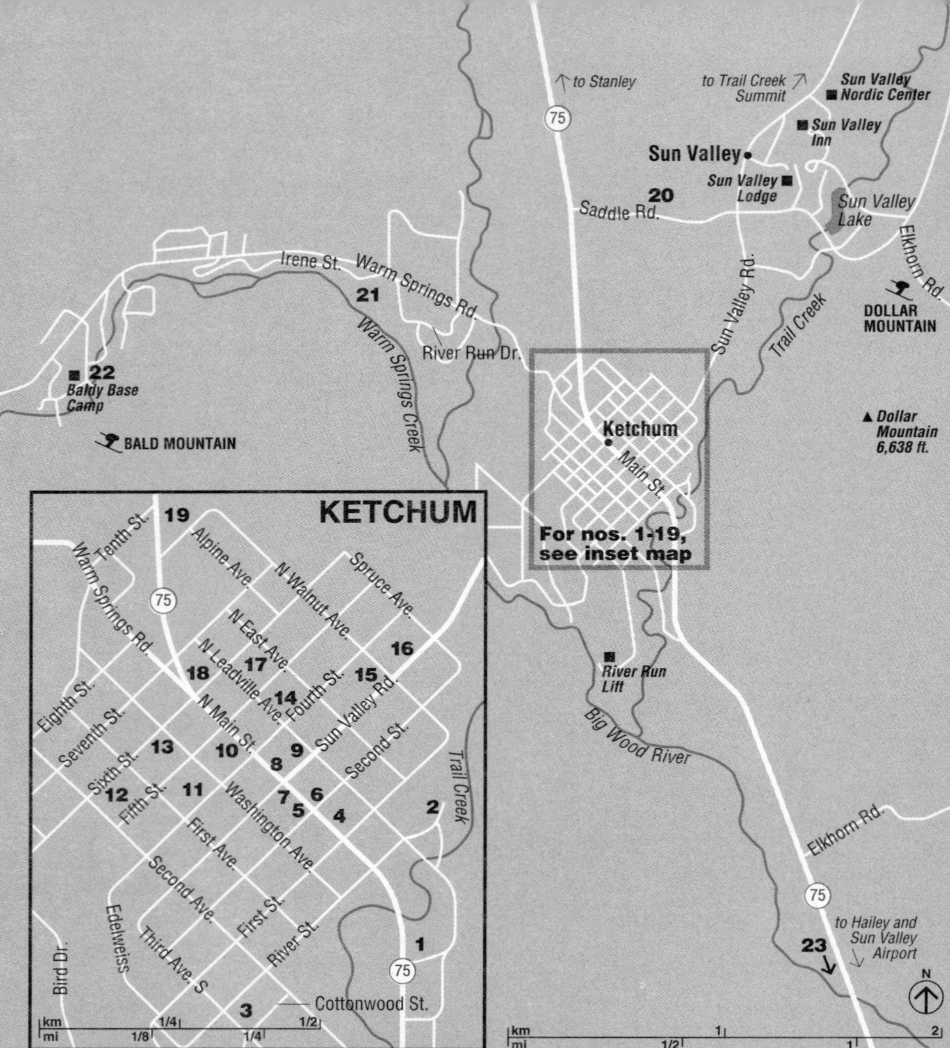


cowboy and hunting artifacts, best steer clear of the Pio. The Kansas City corn-fed beef and fresh seafood attract a loyal following, but meat lovers should order the 32-ounce Pioneer prime rib. Before or after dinner, belly up to the bar to hang out with Ketchum's resident Hollyood stars. But be forewarned: Even when pressed, owner Duffy Witmer refuses to betray the rich, famous, or recognizable who frequent his establishment. ♦ Daily dinner. 308 N Main St (between Sun Valley Rd and Fourth St). 726.3139

**9 Louie's Pizza** ★$ Ski bum Louie Mallane borrowed $150 and started "throwing" pizzas in the kitchen of **Nedder's Bar** in 1965; two years later he moved into Ketchum's first church, a building he still occupies. Today Louie serves veal, pasta, and seafood, in addition to a wide range of pizzas. ♦ Daily lunch and dinner. 331 Leadville Ave North (at Sun Valley Rd). 726.7775

**10 Ketchum/Sun Valley Chamber of Commerce** A wealth of brochures, guides, and historical walking-tour maps for Ketchum can be found at the local COC, a busy office that also serves as a booking agency for lodging, recreation, and Avis car rentals. ♦ Daily 9AM-5PM. 410 N Main St (at Fourth St). 726.3423, 800/634.3347; fax 726.4533

**11 Desperadoes** ★★$ Owner Jim Funk prides himself on his chimichangas, *chiles rellenos,* and *carne asada* burritos. ♦ M-Sa lunch and dinner. 211 Fourth St (between First and Washington Aves). 726.3068

**12 Peter's** ★★$$ Owner/chef Peter Weisz and his wife, Stacy, have earned a reputation for fine Austrian specialties and Northern Italian cuisine. Try the Wiener schnitzel or Viennese lamb shanks for dinner. ♦ M-F lunch; daily dinner. 180 Sixth St (at Second Ave). 726.9515

**13 Bob Dogs Pizza** ★★$ Bob "Dog" Parks sold skis before inventing his famous recipe for Sun Valley-style pizza, a pie that's based on an herb crust and topped with both familiar and exotic combinations. Takeout is also available. ♦ Daily lunch and dinner. 200 Sixth St (at Washington Ave). 726.2358

**14 Atkinsons Market** Founded in 1956 and rebuilt after fire burned it to the ground in 1983, this is Ketchum's primary supermarket. The service, fresh produce, deli, baked goods, gourmet foods, and wine section in this family-run (third-generation) business are as good as you'll find in any major city. ♦ Daily 7:30AM-9PM. Giacobbi Sq (Fourth St, between Leadville and East Aves). 726.5668

**14 Chateau Drugs** Locals depend on this "drug" store for stereo equipment, vacuums, birthday cards, fishing rods, pots and pans, jewelry, fertilizer, licenses, and much more. ♦ Daily 8AM-9PM. Giacobbi Sq (Fourth St, between Leadville and East Aves). 726.5696

**14 Silverado Western Wear** The Western-wear carried here is in keeping with Ketchum's roots. ♦ M-Sa 10AM-6PM; Su 11AM-5PM. Giacobbi Sq (Fourth St, between Leadville and East Aves). 726.9019

**15 Michel's Christiania Restaurant** ★★$$ The owners of the former **Chez Michel** took over the **Christiania Restaurant** in 1993, introducing its well-known menu of wild-game entrees. Start off with the escargots in basil and pesto, and move on to one of the specialty dishes featuring New Zealand venison, or pheasant, quail, and partridge purchased from game farms. With just a day's notice, chef/owner Michel Rudigoz will whip up any duck, venison, pheasant, or trout customers bring in (he's a hunter himself). A bit of trivia: French-born Rudigoz coached the **US Women's Ski Team** from 1978 to 1984, retiring after the Sarajevo Olympics. The dining room also features dancing and live entertainment on Saturdays. ♦ Daily dinner. Reservations recommended. 303 Walnut Ave (at Sun Valley Rd). 726.3032

Within Michel's Christiania Restaurant:

**15 The Olympic Bar** ★★$$ Set on an upper level overlooking the dining room, the bar is decorated with Olympic memorabilia from over the years. Sun Valley's racing heritage is displayed in the action shots of such stars as Tamara McKinney, Suzi Patterson, and Alberto Tomba. And the resort's newest star—Olympic silver medalist Picabo Street—has given the spot a pair of her skis for display. The bar serves lighter fare than the restaurant. ♦ Daily 4:45PM-midnight. 726.3032

**16 Best Western Christiania** $$ With 38 rooms, cable TV, kitchen facilities, and senior discounts, this motel-style establishment is an easy walk to downtown Ketchum. ♦ 651 Sun Valley Rd (between Walnut and Spruce Aves). 726.3351; fax 726.3055

**17 Panda** ★$ Ketchum's feeble tribute to San Francisco's Chinatown serves decent, though unremarkable, Chinese fare. The decor runs to a few Chinese characters and fans hanging on the walls. All is not lost, however, for the fortune-cookie notes are perpetually optimistic, the General's Chicken is good, and Panda *does* offer a change of pace from the pizzas and steaks that typically fuel skiers. ♦ M-F lunch; daily dinner. 515 N East Ave (between Fifth and Sixth Sts). 726.3591

**18 The Clarion Hotel** $$ Beer and wine receptions in the lobby welcome guests to this 58-room hotel, conveniently located within walking distance of downtown (though it's also on the **KART** bus route and has an airport shuttle). The spacious rooms come with log furniture, balconies, fireplaces, hot tubs, and unobstructed views of Mount Baldy. Complimentary cooked-to-order breakfast. ♦ 600 N Main St (at Sixth St). 726.5900; fax 726.3761

**19 The Knob Hill Inn** $$$ Set on the north end of Ketchum's downtown, Joe Koenig's elegant inn combines Western hospitality and European service. The 24 rooms, which feature wet bars and marble bathrooms, face Bald Mountain and the Boulders, and guests have access to indoor and outdoor pools, plus a sauna, Jacuzzi, exercise room, airport shuttle, restaurant, and a *konditorei* serving espressos and pastries. ♦ 960 N Main St. 726.8010; fax 726.2712

---

If Bald Mountain has a weakness, it's the lack of a dependable storm track. History records that December of 1936 marked Sun Valley's grand opening *and* the fourth month of zero precipitation. Following some tough snowless winters, Sun Valley invested $16 million in York computerized snowmaking. With 16 miles of pipe servicing 454 computer-controlled snowguns, the system is the largest in the world and covers nearly 73 percent (600 acres) of Baldy's skiable terrain. It subsequently turned the drought-plagued winter of 1991-92 into an unqualified success.

Within The Knob Hill Inn:

**Restaurant Felix** ★★★$$ This small, intimate restaurant—run by chef Felix Gonzales and his wife, Karla—features Mediterranean cuisine with a Spanish accent. The arched ceilings, peach walls, and light wood trim provide a simple background for the impressive works displayed by local artists. A plethora of windows also provide great views of Mother Nature's artwork—the Boulders. Felix is best known for his lamb and paella dishes. Try the lamb shanks, braised with rioja wine or the *paella à la Valenciana* (chicken, chorizos, calamari, shellfish in a saffron rice). ♦ Daily dinner. Reservations recommended. 726.1166

**20 Idaho Country Inn** $$ This inn has only 10 rooms, all of which play up a specific theme. For instance, you can stay in the Anglers Room or the Rodeo Room. Other amenities include two fireplaces, a sitting room and library, outdoor hot tub, and superb views. A full gourmet breakfast is complimentary. The **KART** bus stops at the bottom of the street. ♦ 134 Latigo La (off Saddle Rd). 726.1019; fax 726.5718

**21 Warm Springs Ranch Restaurant** ★$ Overlooking the **Warm Springs Golf Course** and fronted by a trout pond filled with lunkers any fly-fisher would be proud to catch and release, this restaurant is known for its sheepherder potatoes and fresh-baked scones (crumble them into the pond and you will produce a feeding frenzy). ♦ Daily dinner. Reservations recommended. 1801 Warm Springs Rd (between River Run Dr and Irene St). 726.2609

**22 Baldy Base Club** ★★$ A local après-ski hangout, the Base Club serves health-oriented entrées that don't sacrifice good taste. The various pasta dishes on the menu include Mediterranean prawns, chicken fettuccine, and *camagna* (a combination of sun-dried tomatoes and roasted peppers). ♦ Daily lunch and dinner. 106 Lloyd Dr (at Warm Springs Base). 726.3838

It was no coincidence that Hollywood movie stars showed up for Sun Valley's grand opening in 1936. Publicist Steve Hannagan underwrote their rooms, meals, and bar tabs, as well as their transportation. Small investment, big return.

Union Pacific President Averell Harriman paid $4,300 for the 3,500 acres on which Sun Valley resort is now located, a princely sum by Great Depression standards. Today that amount would be less than two percent of what a very, very small lot costs in Sun Valley.

**Restaurants/Clubs:** Red   **Hotels:** Blue
**Shops/ Outdoors:** Green   **Sights/Culture:** Black

**22 Warm Springs Resort and Property Management** $$$$ If staying next to the ski lifts is a priority, these condominiums are the perfect choice. Amenities include a heated pool, saunas, and hot tubs. ♦ Lloyd Dr (at Warm Springs Base). 726.8274; fax 726.8376

**23 Sun Valley Soaring** Weather permitting, this glider operator offers rides over Bald Mountain and the surrounding backcountry. The gliders take off from **Friedman Airport** in Hailey. ♦ Hwy 75, 11 miles south of Ketchum. 788.3054

## Bests

### Ned Hamlin

Architect/Planner

Yielding to the wayward moose while nordic skating up **Trail Creek,** only minutes from Sun Valley's core. As far as the moose is concerned, you're out of your element.

Standing at the top of the Mayday Lift, smug in your ability to assess the weather anywhere in Idaho. Catching Mike Murphy's après-ski show at the **Ram Bar.**

Watching the action at **Sun Valley Company**'s kids' ski program on **Dollar Mountain.**

Bundling up for the Friday night Sun Valley Gallery Association gallery walks.

Feeling exhilarated (as well as being reminded of your age) while standing breathless at the bottom of **Warm Springs** run after a nonstopper.

Being startled by the gentle whoosh of the glider passing overhead while sunning on the **Lookout Restaurant** deck. No wasted words here: Bold letters on the bottom of the starboard wing announce "RIDES."

Finishing the 30K **Boulder Mountain Tour** cross-country ski race.

Enjoying a beer, casual talk, and chicken wings at the **Pioneer Saloon.**

Halfway up the Christmas triple lift, I never tire of pointing out (to anyone who will listen) the deepest, darkest blue sky they'll ever see. It occupies its own niche in the color spectrum; we call it "Sun Valley Blue."

### Gretchen Fraser

First American to win Olympic ski medals, gold and silver, 1948, in Switzerland

The best ski mountain in the world—**Bald Mountain.**

Favorite dining adventure—A wintry sleigh ride to **Trail Creek Cabin.**

Après-ski activity—Gliding across the miles of cross-country trails at the **Sun Valley Nordic Center** and competing in the **Reidy Memorial Cross Country** ski race.

Cross-country ski picnics along **Trail Creek,** packing

a thermos full of mushroom soup made from morels we picked last summer.

Favorite ski lift—Lookout Express high-speed quad, the chairlift that services my ski run—**Gretchen's Gold.**

Favorite SV adventure—**Helicopter skiing** around **Sun Valley, Balcom Ridge,** and **Durrance Mountain.**

### Susan Stanek Winget

Real Estate Broker/Partner, Winget Fulton Daniels McCoy and Associates

**Woodriver** trail system—Miles of running, nordic skating, and biking trails through the woods and up the hills, adjacent to the city limits of Ketchum.

**Atkinsons Market**—The place to meet all your gourmet grocery needs, and more important, a place for the locals to meet their friends and to gauge the influx of tourists. This is our way of staying in touch.

**Sun Valley Ice Rink**—Includes summer evening ice shows presenting world-famous skaters. Sturtevants also utilizes the indoor rink for winter ice hockey for kids from four to 18. Silver medalist Linda Fratiani can be seen regularly on the rink and may be persuaded to give your children figure-skating lessons.

**Warm Springs Lodge** for gourmet lunches.

**Ski Education Foundation**—Encompasses nordic, alpine, and boarding lessons for the local children. Instructors are the best.

**Art galleries**—Very united, diverse, and numerous, they join together the first Friday of every month to offer a gallery walk that includes wine and food.

### John Wells

Owner, Warm Springs Resort

**Greyhawk Run**—Year in, year out, the place to make high-speed GS turns all the way to the bottom for a beer or three.

**Pioneer Saloon** has the best burgers, best steak, and best people watching.

**Sawtooth Club.**

**Fox Creek Trail**—Best short trail run (under seven miles), good (not killer) vertical, and great scenery.

**Griffon Butte Loop**—Best mountain-bike ride close to town.

**Wood River**—Best trout fishing in town.

**Bald Mountain Trail,** which starts at the River Run access, is the best way up the mountain on foot.

**Boulder Tour Ski Trail**—30 kilometers of cross-country ski trail that's maintained almost all winter—is the best place to run the dog in the winter (you ski, the dog runs).

# Big Sky

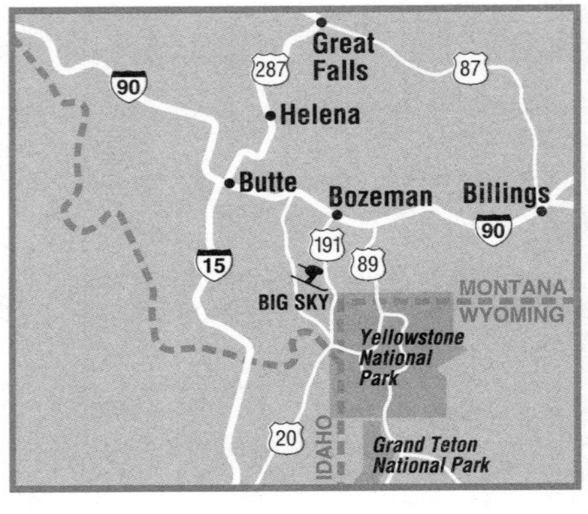


A fundamental contradiction underlies Big Sky's vitality. Although it's the resort hub of southwestern Montana and the region's indisputable magnet for skiers, all of its empty spaces bring one question to mind: "Where is everybody?" The underpopulated ski slopes presided over by storm-scoured **Lone Peak** characterize the intrinsic appeal of southwestern Montana. Skiers who appreciate a wilderness minimally scathed by human meddling are fans of Big Sky. But they want their creature comforts, too.

The loudest sound at night here is the wind in the trees; moose sometimes wander across the ski trails. Yet rusticity blends well with the trappings of civilization. You can choose French, Italian, Mexican, or American cuisine for dinner and do your morning stretches to the accompaniment of CNN on TV. But anything that even hints at glitz is frowned on, especially by those who come here to take refuge from **Aspen** or **Vail.**

The **Mountain Village** is unlikely to win any architectural awards, due in part to its piecemeal development in the 25 years since newscaster Chet Huntley and others bought the land and developed it. The seven-story, modern **Shoshone Condominium Lodge** looms unbecomingly over the forests, and the **Mountain Mall**, the resort's hub, has the ambience of an airplane hangar. That said, however, the village functions well as a reasonably tight, interconnected cluster, and the buildings have none of the hokey Tyrolean gingerbread of other US resorts.

Big Sky's ski area has matured in recent years. It once had a reputation for unchallenging skiing: smooth going for novices and inexperienced intermediates, but so gentle as to put experts to sleep. But Big Sky has always had small, hidden pockets of exceptional expert skiing—runs barely publicized because they were barely skied—until the Challenger Chair opened a few seasons ago, giving skiers access to 1,750 vertical feet of expert runs. As a result, Big Sky can now legitimately call itself a well-rounded ski area, with long, gradual beginner slopes, open bowls for intermediate and advanced skiers, plus steep chutes and faces for experts. Somewhat misleading, however, is Big Sky's 3,030-foot vertical drop. The ski area's configuration (on two separate mountains) makes it impossible to connect the highest and lowest points in a single run. A typical run is more likely to cover between 1,500 and 1,800 vertical feet.

These days the big (but certainly not new) issue at Big Sky is the conflict between natural beauty and economic viability. One reason so few skiers vacation at the resort is that there are relatively few accommodations to house them. The area has approximately 3,670 beds to accommodate an estimated hourly lift capacity of 13,360 skiers. (This is how Big Sky maintains its hard-earned "no lift lines" reputation.) Hoteliers would like to increase their guest capacity, while other ambitious speculators have bought land anticipating new development. How all these plans will wash out in coming years remains to be seen. For the time being, though, Big Sky manages—perhaps better than any other ski resort in the West—to find a workable balance between recreational comforts and the allure of a mountain wilderness.

**Big Sky Ski & Summer Resort**
**PO Box 160001**
**Big Sky, Montana 59716**

**Information**....................................406/995.5000
**Reservations**....................................800/548.4486
**Snow Phone**....................................406/995.5900

## Fast Facts

*Area code 406 unless otherwise noted.*

**Ski Season** Late November to early April

**Location** Big Sky is in southwestern **Montana,** about 50 miles south of **Bozeman.**

## Getting to Big Sky

**By air: Bozeman Airport** is 48 miles north of Big Sky. **Delta, Frontier, Horizon Air,** and **Northwest** airlines offer service to and from **Bozeman. City Taxi** (586-2341) and **Karst Stages** (586-8567) provide transportation from the airport to Big Sky.

**By bus:** There is no regularly scheduled long-distance bus service to Big Sky. However, **Greyhound** (800/231.2222) goes to and from **Bozeman.**

**By car: Budget, Hertz, National,** and **Thrifty** rent winterized cars at the airport; several local car rental agencies at nonairport locations offer more moderately priced rentals. From **Bozeman,** take Route 84 west to Route 191. Follow Route 191 south for 34 miles to the Big Sky access road.

## FYI

**Area** 2,200 acres, with about 68 miles of marked trails

Beginner—14 percent

Intermediate—46 percent

Advanced—40 percent

**Number of Groomed Runs** Approximately 50, groomed on a rotating basis

**Longest Run** 3 miles (**The Bowl** plus **Mr. K**)

**Capacity** 13,360 skiers per hour

**Base Elevation** 6,970 feet

**Summit Elevation** 10,000 feet

**Vertical Rise** 3,030 feet

**Average Annual Snowfall** 400 inches

**Snowmaking** 20 percent

**Night Skiing** F, Sa 4PM-9PM

**Lifts** 12 (2 gondolas, 2 high-speed quads, 1 fixed-grip quad, 2 triple chairs, 2 double chairs, and 3 surface tows)

| **Lift Passes** | **Full Day** | **Half Day** (starts at 12:30PM) |
|---|---|---|
| **Adult** | $38 | $34 |
| **Child** (10 and under with paying adult) | Free | Free |
| **Senior** (70 and over) | $19 | $17 |

**Ski School** The ski school office (995.5743) is located at the ticket sales building, between the **Mountain Mall** and **Shoshone Lodge.** Half-day and multi-day group lessons are very reasonably priced compared with lesson prices at other major Western resorts. One of the ski school's best bargains is a full-day private lesson if three skiers share the cost. Also affordable are learn-to-ski packages, which include lift tickets (limited to certain lifts), equipment rentals, and lessons.

**Kids' Ski School Children's Ski Day Camp** offers half-day and full-day lessons for children ages 6 to 14.

**Clinics and Special Programs** The **Race Clinic** requires a minimum of three students and is held daily 2PM-4PM, meeting at the NASTAR Knob (separate from the NASTAR course). **Rent an Instructor** requires a minimum of three participants and includes a mountain tour of varied terrain, depending on skill level, 2PM-4PM. The ski school also offers two-hour clinics for honing techniques in powder, moguls, and snowboarding.

**Races** The NASTAR course runs daily starting at 1PM on **NASTAR Knob.** It costs $5 for the first run and $2 for each additional run.

**Rentals** Equipment rental is available at **Lone Mountain Sports** (daily 8:30AM-6PM; 995.4471) on the lower level of **Arrowhead Mall** and **Big Sky Sports** (daily 8:30AM-5:30PM; 995-5840) on the ground level of the **Mountain Mall** at the base of the slopes.

**Lockers** Coin-operated lockers are located on the upper level of **Arrowhead Mall.**

**Day Care** The **Big Sky Playcare Center** (995.2828) is located on the lower level of the **Mountain Mall.** The center is open daily from 8:30AM to 4:30PM, and provides care for children of all ages but requires advance notice for infants under 18 months. Montana law requires immunization certificates to accompany children.

**First Aid** The ski patrol office is stationed on the lower level of the **Mountain Mall.**

**Parking** There is free overnight parking for all guests staying at the **Mountain Village.** A free day-skier lot is located between the **Huntley Lodge** and **Beaverhead Condominiums.** A smaller pay lot is more conveniently located near the **Mountain** and **Arrowhead Malls.**

**Worth Knowing**

- Big Sky's frequent-skier card offers $9 discounts off daily passes.
- Children 10 and under ski free, with a limit of two kids per paying adult.

Ted Turner, the king of CNN, has a ranch just north of Big Sky. Covering more than 120,000 acres, it is one of the largest ranches in Montana.

## Rating the Runs

### ● Beginner

A wide run beneath the Southern Comfort Lift, **El Dorado** covers more than a mile in 1,250 vertical feet. It's virtually impossible to get into trouble here; any skier who might lose confidence on the two stretches where the grade increases slightly can simply traverse the width until the pitch eases off again.

Although the slope is no more threatening than other beginner trails, **Southern Comfort** takes a long, narrow curve from top to bottom. Those who appreciate woodsy solitude like skiing this trail. It is not simply one of Big Sky's best novice trails; it's one of Big Sky's best trails, period.

### ■ Intermediate

One of the most popular runs off Ramcharger Quad, **Ambush** cuts underneath the lift and has a couple of steep pitches that might worry nonaggressive intermediates. **Elk Park Meadows,** a long, steady, groomed descent that catches the morning sun, does not return skiers to the bottom of the Ramcharger Quad where it begins. Take the Mad Wolf Quad back to the summit.

Appropriately named given the rocky ridges and face of **Lone Peak** that rise above you, **The Bowl** is cause for celebration on sunny days. But in snowy, socked-in weather, forget it. Sky and slope merge into one color; all definition is lost and so is most of the fun. Note that on any day this run can have big bumps; in that case, **Never Sweat** and **Upper Morning Star,** which wind over and around a moraine, are good groomed alternatives.

### ◆ Advanced

Mogul maniacs are drawn to **Mad Wolf,** the conspicuous, wide, steep slope on the left as you drive up to Big Sky. Moguls develop in **The Bowl,** as mentioned above, but Mad Wolf is considerably longer.

Advanced skiers uninterested in bumps can take the long traverse across The Bowl from the top of the Lone Peak Chair to **South Wall.** The pitch here is steeper and more consistent than in the main bowl, and with few skiers willing to cross over this far, moguls rarely form. Also, this run's northerly exposure protects the snow from the sun, so it's fresher here.

### ◆◆ Expert

Many local expert skiers (who are partial to **Bridger Bowl,** just north of **Bozeman**) were skeptical that Big Sky could conjure up legitimate expert skiing by putting in the Challenger Chair. If they're still uncertain, they should stand at the top of the chutes leading into **Big Rock Tongue,** a seriously steep slice of terrain accessed by Challenger. Although not extraordinarily long, steepness and variety make up for distance. Wide, sheer **Little Tree,** where it's possible to scoot right or left to find lesser-skied slots and chutes among trees and rocks, is a popular, topnotch run.

### Snowboarding

Big Sky has no snowboard park, but boarders will find plenty of variety in the terrain, as well as a half-pipe on **Lone Mountain.** Carvers like the wide openness of **Elk Park Ridge** or **The Bowl** for cruising and fat GS turns. Free riders head to **Ambush,** a steep, challenging run that's often bumped up. For a real thrill, follow the skiers to **Big Rock Tongue**—but beware of the trees and rocks.

## Mountain Highs and Lows

Although considered advanced intermediate, **The Bowl**'s true rating can vary considerably according to snow and weather conditions. On clear days in fresh snow, it's a piece of cake—a real intermediate run on which you can always bail out by traversing. But when the weather turns stormy and white-out conditions prevail, moguls become invisible, driving home the fact that this is steeper than your average intermediate run. Under such conditions, The Bowl can sharpen its teeth as expert terrain.

A main thoroughfare from the gondolas, **Crazy Horse** is rated as intermediate, but it doesn't ski like one. The rating, presumably, comes from two or three short pitches that are indeed in the intermediate range. But because these pitches aren't sustained—the trail flattens out before you've even noticed the steeper going—Crazy Horse ought to be labeled a beginner run, not necessarily for first-timers, but for almost anyone else.

## At the Resort

*Area code 406 unless otherwise noted.*

✦ **Shoshone Condominium Lodge** $$$$
Seven stories high, Big Sky's most prominent structure would be attractive in an urban setting, but it's overwhelming here. Still, the lodge's handsome interior features blond wood and stone—the predominant decorating statement around Big Sky. The most noticeable fixture is the life-size bear sculpture located in the lobby, the main rendezvous point at Big Sky. ("Meet me at the bear.") The concierge desk is one of the best places to make recreational and travel arrangements for shuttle-bus rides, daily lift tickets, snowmobiling in Yellowstone, and so on. Condo units sleep between four and six, and

the 94 rooms are the resort's classiest and most expensive. ♦ First big building to the right as you drive into the village. 995.5800, 800/548.4486; fax 995.5001

Within the Shoshone Condominium Lodge:

**The Lone Spur** Western clothing and leather items (including boots) are sought after here by urban cowboys. This is dress-up clothing more likely to be worn two-stepping than riding on the range. ♦ Daily 10AM-6PM. 995.5844

**Alpenglow Massage and Spa** Services include facials, mud baths, and herbal body wraps, as well as massages. ♦ Daily 9AM-9PM. 995.4663

✦ **Huntley Lodge** $$$ Previously plain and dated, this property's 204 motel-style rooms were undergoing renovations at press time. They lack kitchens, but if you plan to eat out, they're perfectly serviceable and considerably more affordable than Shoshone accommodations. The Huntley and the Shoshone are connected by an indoor passageway. ♦ Next to the Shoshone Lodge. 995.5000, 800/548.4486; fax 995.5001

Within Huntley Lodge:

**Huntley Lodge Dining Room** ★★$$$ A large, airy dining room that serves both Huntley and Shoshone guests, the restaurant's huge windows provide a broad view of the ski slopes. An enormous morning buffet, with just about every imaginable breakfast item and then some, makes for one of the best meals at Big Sky, although the early rush (especially when there is a conference group around) can overtax the young, well-meaning staff. Dinner is usually a much more relaxed affair, helped in that regard by an excellent wine list. ♦ M-Sa breakfast; daily dinner; Su brunch. Reservations recommended for dinner. 995.5000

**Chet's Bar** The entertainment at this watering hole, despite occasional live bands, doesn't garner it much of a reputation as a hot spot. The 30-and-unders tend to look for action elsewhere. ♦ Daily 4PM-2AM. 995.5784

---

Southwestern Montana is bear country, one of the prime habitats for grizzlies in the lower 48 states. Sightings have increased considerably in recent years in the Absaroka and Madison ranges and in the Yellowstone watershed. An active effort to replenish grizzly populations has been aided by the mild winters of the late 1980s and early 1990s, which rangers say have raised the survival rate of bear cubs.

---

Big Sky has been a favorite stop for ski-movie makers and has also made it into the big time. It was a location for the 1991 feature film *True Colors,* starring John Cusack and James Spader.

✦ **Mountain Mall** Big Sky's top shopping and dining complex has convenience on its side, but don't expect any surprises. ♦ 24 hours daily. At the base of the mountain. 862.6255

Within the Mountain Mall:

**Serendipity's** This coffee-and-sweets spot prepares such simple-carbohydrate excesses as mud pies and milk shakes. ♦ Daily 8AM-10PM. 995.2439

**Crystal Images** Photographers from this shop are out on the mountain during the day taking pictures of random skiers; the day's photos are put on display in the late afternoon or early evening. There's no obligation to buy, but if they catch you in perfect form, you'll be tempted. ♦ Daily 9AM-6PM. 995.2426

**Big Sky Sports** This is a good place to pick up new accessories. Replace your worn or outmoded hats, gloves, and goggles here, but don't expect any bargains on skiwear. ♦ Daily 8:30AM-5:30PM. 995.5840

**One Track Snowboard Shop** A mecca for riders, this shop stocks the kind of clothing with attitude that snowboarders wear to differentiate themselves from mundane skier types. ♦ 995.5845

**General Store** A limited selection of groceries, including milk, soft drinks, beer, dry goods, frozen foods, and some fresh fruits and vegetables are available here, but for stocking up, Bozeman is the place for food shopping. ♦ 995.4376

**Village Drug** High prices are harsh punishment for leaving pharmacy or cosmetic items at home, but the only real alternative to this drugstore is an hour drive to Bozeman. ♦ Daily 8:30AM-5PM. 995.4649

**Levinsky's** ★$ Families who want a quick meal and can't be bothered with table etiquette stop here for pizza and hot sandwiches. If the brightly lit, picnic-table setting isn't to your taste, opt for takeout and await your order downstairs in **The Caboose,** a pub reached via a steep stairway with a mine-shaft feel to it. Levinsky's also offers free delivery within the mountain village. ♦ Daily lunch and dinner. 995.4646

**The Whiskey Jack** ★★$$$ This restaurant and bar does reasonably well at playing multiple roles—as a lunch stop, après-ski hangout, restaurant, and live-entertainment spot. Safe bets on the menu are steak and chicken, usually well prepared. The late-afternoon crush and live bands on weekends can be either fun or intrusive, depending on your mood. On sunny days, skiers mingle and lunch on the big front deck. ♦ Daily lunch and dinner. 995.5777

**M.R. Hummer's** ★★$$ A more intimate, pub-style alternative to the bustling scene at **The Whiskey Jack, Hummer's** grills menu staples such as steaks and seafood. Good mesquite chicken and king crab's legs are also noteworthy. ♦ Daily lunch and dinner. 995.4543

✦ **Arrowhead Mall** Significantly smaller than the **Mountain Mall** and less suited to strolling and browsing, this complex has a couple of businesses worth patronizing. ♦ 24 hours daily. At the base of the mountain. 995.9607

Within Arrowhead Mall:

**Lone Mountain Sports** This sports gear shop is a good place to rent equipment or get your skis tuned. But with its small selection and immodest prices, *buy* equipment or clothing only if you're in a bind. ♦ Daily. 995.4471

**Twin Panda** ★★★$$$ As you walk in, you'll notice this doesn't look like your typical paper-lantern–clad Asian restaurant. A square bar in the center of the room, light wood trim, and clean lines make this an attractive, modern-looking place to dine. The menu is extensive, but the shrimp with cashew nuts or the house special, *General Tsao's chicken* (chicken chunks deep-fried and sautéed with vegetables in hot sauce) are both worth a try. They offer take-out service, too. ♦ Chinese ♦ Daily dinner. 995.2425

**Scissorbill's** ★$$ While billed as a bar and grill, this place is more suitable for relaxing over a drink. You'll find a good selection of wines by the glass and, on some nights, live entertainment. ♦ Daily dinner. 995.4933

✦ **Arrowhead Condominiums** $$$$ An out-of-control skier who fails to make the last left turn on Silver Knife or Tippy's Tumble could wind up in the living room of one of these 23 true ski-in/ski-out units. The wood-sided chalets are Big Sky's most attractive architectural statement. Inside, the three-bedroom units compete with Shoshone units for the title of Most Luxurious in Big Sky. They are also among the resort's priciest. ♦ At the base of the mountain, to the far left as you face the mountain. 800/548.4486; fax 995.5001

---

1993 marked the 10th anniversary of an act of Congress that established the Lee Metcalf Wilderness, which encompasses much of the Madison Range surrounding Big Sky. The act prohibits road construction and timber harvesting in these 260,000 acres, which explains why the Big Sky access road (built before 1983) is the only paved road to penetrate wilderness land.

---

Skiing is not just a winter sport at Big Sky. Following a season of heavy snow, locals have been known to scramble to the Lone Peak summit to ski the slush as a way of celebrating the Fourth of July.

✦ **Stillwater Condominiums** $$ Smaller and more economical than either the **Arrowhead** or **Shoshone** units, these condos (studios, one bedrooms, and two bedrooms) are best for families and groups on a budget who want to be close to the slopes. The apartments have kitchenettes but lack fancy options such as Jacuzzis. Approximately 40 of the 64 units are available for rental. ♦ Across the parking lot from the Mountain Mall. 800/548.4486; fax 995.5001

✦ **Beaverhead Condominiums** $$$$ This complex of 40 town houses offers, like **Arrowhead,** ski-in/ski-out convenience. Set off by itself on the far side of the trail network, however, the buildings are just far enough from the Mountain Village center that the 5- to 10-minute walk can be unpleasant in bad weather. The two- and three-bedroom units are gussied up and spacious. The three-bedroom units with lofts can comfortably sleep 10. ♦ On your left as you first drive into the village on the main road. 800/548.4486; fax 995.5001

✦ **Big Horn Condominiums** $$$$ Each of these 48 luxury three-bedroom condominiums is decked out Western style in shades of hunter green and/or deep red, with redwood ceilings, natural wood floors, and a pine fireplace. Amenities include private Jacuzzi, kitchen, washer/dryer, and great views. These ski-in ski-out condos are located at the base of the Bear Back Lift. ♦ Take the first left as you drive into the village. 800/548.4486; fax 995.5001

✦ **Lake Condominiums** $$$ These condos are so named because—surprise—they are along the lakeshore. That location has greater value for summer visitors; for skiers, it means being a quarter mile from the base. However, this otherwise ordinary complex has a couple of things going for it. Each two-bedroom unit has a washer/dryer, and there is a heated outdoor pool, the only one at Big Sky. Because this is a time-share facility, there is limited availability. ♦ Take the first right as you drive into the village. 800/548.4486; fax 995.5001

✦ **Skycrest Condominiums** $$$ Anyone who doesn't mind (or actually would prefer) to stay at a distance from the central village area should consider one of these 20 condos, set a half mile away. This is the only complex that offers four-bedroom units (as well as two- and three-bedroom units). The furnishings are tasteful, and you can climb out of your rental car in a heated indoor parking garage. ♦ One-quarter mile past the entrance to the village, on your right. 800/548.4486; fax 995.5001

## Beyond the Resort

**1 Lone Mountain Ranch Restaurant** ★★★★$$$$ The atmosphere is rural chic, the food fresh and first-rate, and the surroundings salubrious (smoking is prohibited in the dining room and no offensive additives are used in the food). The emphas is is on light ingredients, but any restaurant that serves salmon wrapped in puff pastry gives more than a passing nod to dietary indulgence. The restaurant, part of the **Lone Mountain Ranch** cross-country ski resort, caters to those who like a little Western corniness with their dinner, in the form of evening sleigh rides to a log cabin where meals are cooked on a hundred-year-old stove. Don't be surprised—or embarrassed—if a sing-along is the postprandial activity. ♦ Daily breakfast, lunch, and dinner. Reservations recommended for dinner and required for the sleigh ride. 4 miles east of Mountain Village off the Big Sky access road. 995.4644

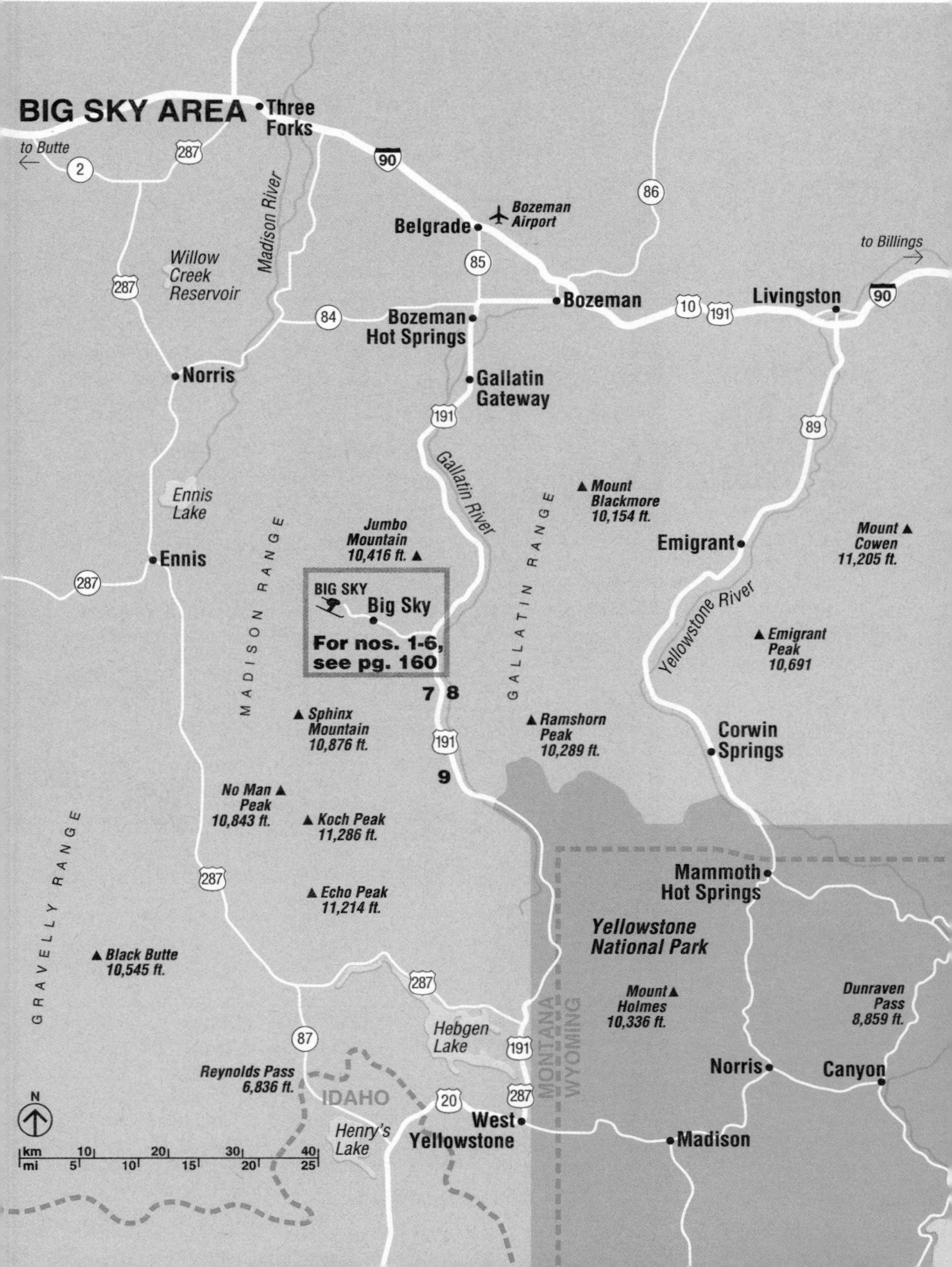

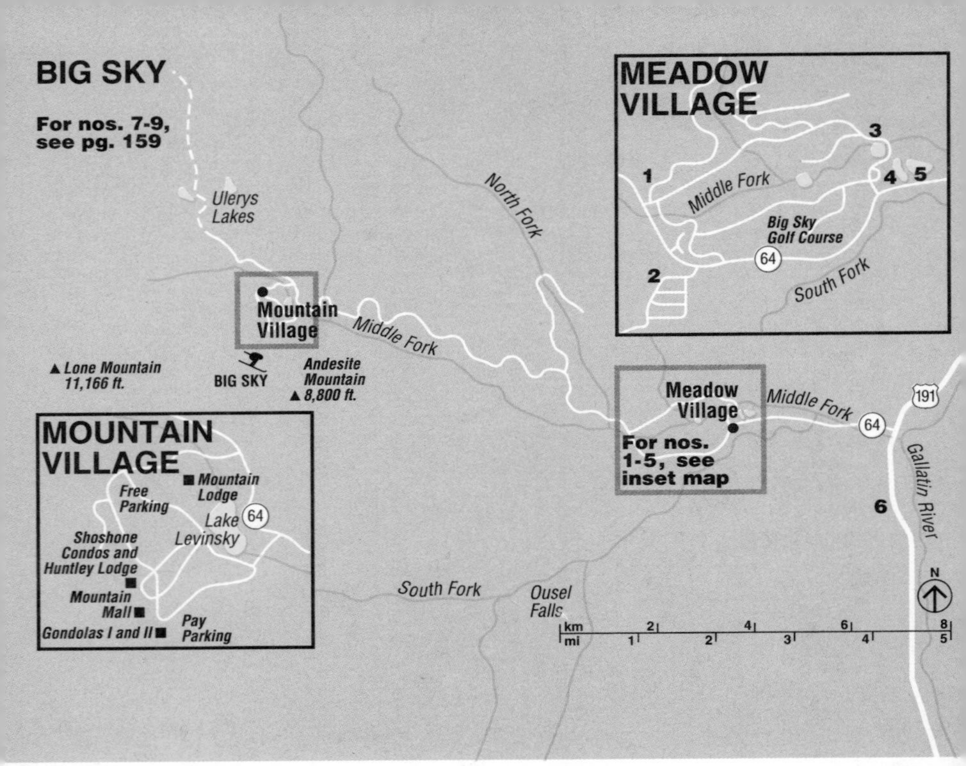

# BIG SKY

For nos. 7-9, see pg. 159

Ulerys Lakes
North Fork
Mountain Village
Middle Fork
Lone Mountain 11,166 ft.
BIG SKY
Andesite Mountain 8,800 ft.
Meadow Village
For nos. 1-5, see inset map
Middle Fork
64
191
Gallatin River
6
South Fork
Ousel Falls
km 2 4 6 8
mi 1 2 3 4 5
N

## MEADOW VILLAGE

1
2
3
4 5
Middle Fork
Big Sky Golf Course
64
South Fork

## MOUNTAIN VILLAGE

Mountain Lodge
Free Parking
Lake Levinsky
64
Shoshone Condos and Huntley Lodge
Mountain Mall
Gondolas I and II
Pay Parking

**2 Blue Moon Bakery** ★★$ Purchase warm breads and pastries for a quick breakfast here or get a few sandwiches to take up to the mountain. ♦ M-S 7AM-6PM. West Fork Mall in the Meadow Village. 995.2305

**3 Golden Eagle Lodge** $$ Skiers seeking economical, hotel-style lodging will find this hostelry satisfactory. It offers 17 simple, clean rooms as well as some suites, a restaurant and bar, and shuttle bus service to the ski area, although at this location, it's best to have your own wheels. ♦ Meadow Village, a quarter-mile from the entrance. 995.4800; fax 995.2447

Within Golden Eagle Lodge:

**Rocco's** ★$$ When you've been guzzling après-ski beers long and late and suddenly need a meal, this eatery fills the bill. Palatable Mexican and Italian food at fair prices make this place the **Meadow Village**'s quick-fix headquarters. Live music and margaritas come with the deal. ♦ Daily breakfast, lunch, and dinner. 995.4200

**4 First Place** ★★★$$$ If you're trying to impress a date, this is where to do it. After all, this restaurant sets itself apart from other Big Sky eating establishments by advertising "tablecloth dining." Beef takes a backseat to seafood on the French-influenced menu. ♦ Daily dinner. Reservations recommended. Meadow Center in the Meadow Village. 995.4244

**5 Edelweiss** ★★$$$$ Most restaurants at Big Sky mix and match cuisines to please a variety of palates. Edelweiss doesn't. Its German/Austrian meals are a dieter's minefield. Schnitzel, bratwurst, rich sauces, and imported beer replenish calories lost during a day's skiing. ♦ Daily lunch and dinner. Reservations recommended. Montana Building in the Meadow Village. 995.4665

**6 Buck's T-4 Lodge** $$ Picture the familiar decor of Best Western lodging with a few rustic touches. That's Buck's—not swanky, and not located at an especially beautiful spot considering the scenic possibilities of this part of the world. But it's a comfortable and moderately priced 75-room motel, with a good restaurant to compensate for the lack of a view. ♦ Rte 191, 1 mile south of the Big Sky entrance. 995.4111, 800/822.4484; fax 995.2191

Within Buck's T-4 Lodge:

**Buck's T-4 Restaurant** ★★$$$ This roadhouse competes with the **Corral Bar & Cafe** as the number one choice in these parts. Buck's is slightly more upscale and expensive, but its log walls and stone chimney still create the casual atmosphere you'd expect in a

Montana roadhouse. Steaks, fish, and game are the principal fare, although some richly prepared specials are more suggestive of southern France than southern Montana. If you drink past your limit, Buck's has a shuttle bus running to and from Big Sky. ♦ Daily breakfast, lunch, and dinner. Reservations recommended. 995.4111

**7 Corral Motel** $ If all you want is a room with a bed, bathroom, and TV, you could do a lot worse than this eight-room motel. Book well in advance since low rates and size make availability somewhat scarce. ♦ 42895 Gallatin Rd, 5 miles south of the Big Sky entrance on Rte 191. 995.4249

Within the Corral Motel:

**Corral Bar & Cafe** ★$$ Come to check out the local color. This is the sort of place where the antlered heads of dead animals adorn the walls. Montana is beef country and this cafe represents it well, with steaks and sloppy burgers headlining the menu. Local bands sometimes play here. ♦ Daily breakfast, lunch, and dinner. 995.4249

**8 Rainbow Ranch Lodge** $$ Despite the ranch/lodge name confusion, the **Rainbow** is something between a hotel and bed-and-breakfast. Each of the 12 rooms has a private bath, but you're treated like a guest of the family. Breakfast is included in the room rate. ♦ Rte 191, 5 miles south of the Big Sky entrance. 995.4132

**9 320 Ranch** $$$ Unlike places such as **Lone Mountain Ranch,** the 320 makes an effort to sustain a working-ranch atmosphere, even if tourism rather than ranching is the main business these days. Guests can stay in one of 52 low-slung log cabins, a few of which have kitchenettes. Sleigh rides and snowmobiling provide alternatives when you don't feel like skiing. ♦ 205 Buffalo Horn Creek, Gallatin Gateway, 12 miles south of the Big Sky entrance, off Rte 191. 995.4283, 800/243.0320; fax 995.4694

Within 320 Ranch:

**320 Ranch Restaurant** ★★$$$ This relaxed, unpretentious place caters to families and strives to generate a Western atmosphere. The menu features steaks, pan-fried chicken, and Rocky Mountain oysters (if you have to ask what they are, you don't want them), a wide selection of native game ranging from elk to buffalo, and nightly pasta and seafood specials. ♦ Daily breakfast, lunch, and dinner. Reservations recommended. 995.4283 ext 113

**Half Moon Saloon** Locals come here to drink a few beers, shoot pool, play a hand on a video-poker machine, and talk. While the joint is normally low-key, every once in a while a self-appointed pianist steps from the bar to perform, the upshot of which is as likely to be musical mayhem as musical entertainment. Food is now served at this saloon and includes burgers, chicken, and steak. ♦ Daily lunch and dinner. Bar open until 2AM. Rte 191, 3 miles south of the Big Sky entrance. 995.4533

## Bests

**Tom Anderson**
Lawyer/Professional Ski Patrol, Big Sky

Big Sky means no lift lines, no crowded slopes, no worries about collisions, and no hassles with hordes of other skiers. It also means incredibly light powder snow (lighter than Utah's); a higher annual snowfall than most everywhere in Colorado; a family resort with easy runs that you can have all to yourself; and some of the best, most challenging, lift-accessed extreme skiing on the North American continent.

I love working on the Big Sky Challenger Lift; at 10,000 feet above sea level, it's like being on top of the world, and sure beats sitting in a law office listening to grumpy people with legal problems.

---

Spanish Peaks, the prominent cluster of mountains immediately to the north of Big Sky, reputedly was named after a group of Spanish trappers in the area who were set upon by Crow Indians in 1836.

---

If you hear someone refer to the Poop Chute, it's a run from the bottom of the Mad Wolf Chair that leads toward the Meadow Village. The trail was cut not to please skiers but to install a sewer line.

M. BLUM

# Taos Ski Valley

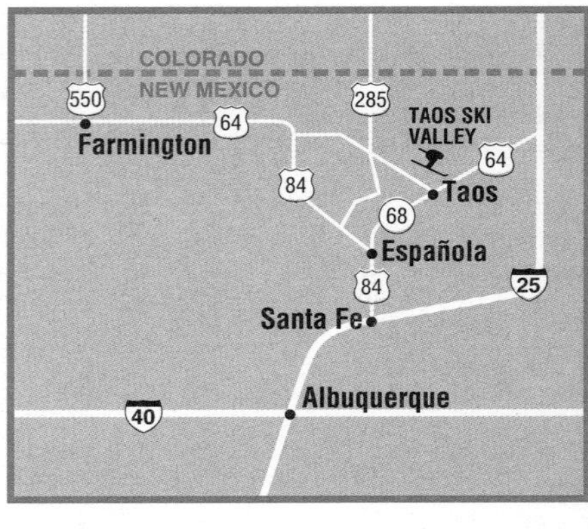


The mystical, tenderly beautiful, and haunting character of northern New Mexico pervades the craggy peaks of the southernmost range of the Rockies, which wrap their arms around Taos Ski Valley. Here, in the **Sangre de Cristo** (Spanish for "Blood of Christ") **Mountains,** one feels transported to another realm. There is something of a magical aura that is impossible to define.

Taos Ski Valley (TSV) exists within its own world, blending the cultures of its European founders and the region's Hispanic and Pueblo Indian residents. Cut off from the surrounding high desert terrain and tucked within the folds of the **Hondo Valley**, the ski village seems unusually wedded to its environment.

Serious skiers flock to Taos from around the world, drawn to the multicultural ambience and the old-fashioned emphasis given to skiing rather than creature comforts or flash. Many return again and again for the incredibly light and prodigious snowfall (more than 25 feet a year) and the challenging skiing found amid the highest peaks in the state.

Yet, in its rustic fashion, this is also a place that makes first-time skiers and families feel at home—where a hotel owner, bartender, day-care provider, or ski instructor will remember you from the year before. And, while the ski lifts no longer shut down for lunch, the pace does seem a little slow, perhaps colored by New Mexico's *mañana* attitude. Or maybe it's the warm sunshine that bathes these mountains in light day after day that has taken the hard edge off life and mellowed those who live, work, and visit here.

One of the nation's oldest ski areas, TSV was founded in 1955 by the late Ernie Blake, his wife, Rhoda, their children, and a handful of associates. It's still family owned and operated, and the focus—unlike that of many modern resorts—remains on skiing. The ski school, which emphasizes not merely how to ski but how to ski better, has often been named as the nation's best. Getting in touch with the environment is the paramount principle of Taos, whose founders believed mountains had something to teach us (they also had a ball pioneering deep powder skiing).

Taos lays claim to some of the nation's most radical skiing terrain. Indeed, more than half of the runs are rated expert or beyond. But because of its vast size, Taos also has many intermediate slopes, though some people would eagerly tack black diamonds on runs Taos downplays with blue squares. Even when regularly groomed, as are all their beginner and intermediate slopes, these runs can offer a substantial challenge.

Only 20 miles away is the funky, captivating, and thoroughly unique town of Taos, which was founded in the 17th century by Spanish settlers near the ancient—and still thriving—**Taos Pueblo.** Many people ski during the day and spend the night in town. If you're staying at TSV, you should seriously consider venturing into Taos to peruse the galleries and have a meal at one of the wonderful restaurants. You might, however, find it hard to tear yourself away from the skiing. Oh well, you can always return in the summer.

**Taos Ski Valley**
**Taos, New Mexico 87525**

**Information**....................................505/776.2291
**Reservations**....................................800/776.1111
**Road Conditions**..............................505/827.5594
**Snow Phone (24 hours)**....................505/776.2916
**Chamber of Commerce**....................800/732.8267

## Fast Facts

*Area code 505 unless otherwise noted.*

**Ski Season** Late November through Easter.

**Location** Taos Ski Valley is in the **Hondo Valley** of the **Sangre de Cristo Mountains** in north-central **New Mexico,** 20 miles from the town of **Taos,** which is 70 miles north of **Santa Fe** and 130 miles north of **Albuquerque.**

## Getting to Taos

**By air: Albuquerque International Airport (ABQ)** is served by **America West, American, Continental, Delta, Mesa, Ross, Southwest, TWA, United,** and **USAir.**

**By bus:** Bus service is available to Taos Ski Valley and the town of **Taos** from **Albuquerque** and **Santa Fe** via **Faust's Transportation** (758.3410), **Pride of Taos** (758.8430), **Shuttlejack** (800/452.2665), and **TNM&O Bus Lines** (758.3410). Faust's also runs shuttles all day long between various Taos hotels/motels and the ski valley.

**By car:** Winterized rental cars are available from **Advantage, Avis, Budget, Dollar, Hertz,** and **National** at **Albuquerque International.** Take I-25 north to **Santa Fe** and exit at St. Francis Drive onto US 84/285. Continue through **Española** on US 84/285 to NM 68. Drive north through **Taos** to the blinking light and NM 150, which dead-ends at the ski valley.

**By train:** The closest **Amtrak** (800/USA.RAIL, 988.4511) train depot is in **Lamy,** near **Santa Fe.**

## FYI

**Area** 1,100 acres with 72 lift-served runs

Beginner—24 percent

Intermediate—25 percent

Advanced/Expert—51 percent

**Number of Groomed Runs** 35

**Longest Run** 5.5 miles **(Rubezahl)**

**Capacity** 14,000 skiers per hour

**Base Elevation** 9,207 feet

**Summit Elevation** 11,819 feet

**Vertical Rise** 2,612 feet (lift-served)

**Average Annual Snowfall** 306 inches

**Snowmaking** 65 percent

**Night Skiing** None

**Lifts** 11 (3 quad chairs, 1 triple chair, 6 double chairs, and 1 surface lift)

| **Lift Passes** | **Full Day** | **Half Day** (starts at 12:30PM) |
|---|---|---|
| **Adult** | $37 | $24 |
| (low season)* | $23 | $20 |
| **Child** (12 and under) | $22 | $16 |
| (low season)* | $13 | $11 |
| **Senior** (65-69) | $15 | $15 |
| **Senior** (70 and over) | Free | Free |

*Low seasons are from 24 November through 18 December and 27 March through 9 April.

Lift tickets can be purchased at the windows next to the skier shuttle depot. Additional discounts for multi-day tickets (including a new two-day ticket—$70/adult, $40/child) and for groups of 25 people or more are available.

**Ski School** The ski school office (776.2291) is located next to the base rental shop. Private and group lessons are available for beginner through expert skiers. A program for first-time skiers includes lift tickets. There are also multi-day and single-day courses in moguls, powder, and steeps.

**Kids' Ski School** Daylong programs offered through **The Kinderkafig,** Taos's new children's center, include **Junior Elite I** for potty-trained 3- to 5-year-olds, featuring morning and afternoon ski sessions and lunch. The **Junior Elite II** program is designed for ages 6 through 12, with a two-hour morning lesson, lunch, and an afternoon ski session. Both programs include lift tickets.

**Clinics and Special Programs** Taos's renowned **Ski Better Week** for intermediate and advanced skiers is a five- or six-day program, run Sunday through Friday, including lift tickets, video analysis, and NASTAR race. The **Super Ski Week** is for advanced skiers only and offers afternoon instruction and après-ski seminars, with an emphasis on gate racing and advanced techniques. Similar to **Super Ski Week** but structured to suit the needs of skiers over 50, **Masters Ski Week** also includes social functions.

**Races** A coin-operated dual racecourse is located under Lift No. 7 (open daily 10AM-3PM; fee is $1). NASTAR races are held from 10AM to 2:30PM Wednesdays through Fridays, and some Saturdays. Two runs cost $5.

**Rentals** The **TSV Rental and Repair Shop** (776.2291 ext 1265), located in the base complex next to the ticket window, has plenty of standard equipment as well as a limited number of demo models. The shop is open daily from 8AM to 5:30PM, and free overnight storage is available. There are no cross-country ski or snowboard rentals. A driver's license and a cash or credit card deposit is required. Several private ski shops near the base complex specialize in high-performance skis and boots.

**Lockers** Coin-operated lockers are located on the lowest level of the **Resort Center** complex. For oversize items, see **Bag Lady Baskets** on the lower level of the Taos Ski Valley base complex. The daily fee includes multiple re-entry. The **Ski Shack** at the base of Lift No. 1 and many rental shops provide overnight ski storage.

**Day Care** Reservations are recommended (776.2291). **Bebekare,** for infants 6 weeks to 1 year old, features separate rooms for napping and play. Hourly, half-day, and full-day programs are available. **Kinderkare** is a half- or full-day program (with lunch) for 1- to 2-year-olds. All programs, as well as a cafeteria, rental shop, and sportswear shop just for kids, are housed in Taos's new children's center, **The Kinderkafig.**

**First Aid** The TSV ski patrol headquarters and first aid station (776.2291) is located at the base of the mountain next to the skier shuttle depot. Hours are daily 9AM-4PM. The **Mogul Medical Clinic** (776.8421), located above the **Hotel Edelweiss,** is a private practice and first-aid station specializing in family and ski medicine. It's open daily 9AM-4:30PM. **Holy Cross Hospital** (758.8883) is in the town of **Taos** at 630 Paseo del Pueblo Sur.

**Parking** There is a free parking lot at the base served by a shuttle, and reserved parking for on-mountain accommodations.

**Worth Knowing**

- Special rates are available for novice skiers if they stick to certain lifts.
- Lift tickets are only $23 during **Super Saver Days** (24 November-18 December and 27 March-9 April).3

## Rating the Runs

### ● Beginner

For the views alone, **Bambi,** which begins at the very top of the lift-accessed skiing, should not be missed. Other than **Strawberry Hill,** Bambi is the easiest run for beginners on the mountain and, because of its altitude, normally has very good snow. The run can be skied from Lifts No. 2 and No. 6. Continue on down **Whitefeather** to get back to the base.

Try **Honeysuckle** to **Lower Totemoff** if you want to ski into the "back basin" of Taos—the vast **Kachina Bowl,** noted for its prodigious snowfall, dense spruce and fir forests, and solitude. Facing mostly east, the Bowl gets good morning sunshine, making it a pleasure to ski before noon. To return to the base, take Chair No. 7 and the chair named 7th Heaven back to the top and ski Bambi and Whitefeather or continue on down the **Winkelried** and **Rubezahl** runs.

If you're a raw beginner, it's advisable to start literally at the bottom of the mountain and work your way up. Strawberry Hill will help you get your ski legs, acclimatize you to the altitude, and give you a feel for the snow conditions.

Once you're feeling confident, head up Chairs No. 1 or No. 5 and follow the trail signs to Whitefeather, whose roller coaster terrain, small bowls, and forest-lined trails provide a wonderful variety of skiing experiences. The trail ends, regrettably, with a long catwalk. At some point, much of the upper mountain terrain funnels into this catwalk, which gets crowded with skiers.

### ■ Intermediate

One of the two intermediate runs on the older, front side of the mountain, **Porcupine** is still one of the best in its class in the entire area. A few short pitches will challenge you, but consider them a lesson in confidence building. During lean snow periods, however, the run can get icy.

Intermediates will appreciate **Skalako** to **Midway** in **Kachina Basin.** The top of the basin often has the greatest snow accumulation within the entire lift-served portion of the ski area. Views up Kachina Peak are unforgettable.

The series of linked runs called **West Basin to Lower Stauffenberg to Don't Tell** gives you a lengthy route down the mountain with a fairly consistent pitch throughout—great for getting into a nice rhythm. It's wide and, at points, lined with banked sides. Let your momentum carry you up the banks, then swoop back down. The spectacular West Basin Bowl is ringed above by avalanche chutes and rock outcroppings.

### ◆ Advanced

The run that made Taos's reputation, thrasher **Al's Run** begins with a sustained steep pitch, pummels you with a long series of flatter runs and small drops, then finishes with another cranked pitch—all under two chairlifts. And it's loaded with great skiers who make it look easy. If you call yourself an advanced skier, you haven't skied Taos until you've conquered Al's.

Getting to **Hunziker Bowl** requires a short sidestep up a knoll, but the reward is well worth the work. The bowl has great snow and awesome views and will flatter your skiing. It's a dished slope that isn't as daunting as Taos's other black diamond runs (a good intermediate skier can handle it). The next two sections, **High Noon** and **El Funko,** are more difficult. Stay to your far right when you reach the flat below Hunziker and traverse to the next little bowl, High Noon. Again, stay to your right and cut into El Funko. This is an unusual route down to Chair No. 4, along the edge of the ski area's boundary.

Not many people try **Lorelei,** which is surprising, considering its beauty, isolation, and quality skiing. The top part is quite steep, with scattered pines. Especially fine on fresh powder, Lorelei can be rough going after a thaw and freeze cycle.

Unlike Al's, which runs almost straight down the fall line, **Spencer's Bowl to Snakedance to Showdown** snakes across the mountain face, giving you two fall lines to contend with, plus big moguls and rocks that appear early in the season.

The exhilarating run of **Stauffenberg Chute** is one of a handful of avalanche chutes accessed via the gnarly **High Traverse,** which may be the only double black diamond traverse in the country, with some serious exposure above cliffs. The chutes get heavy snow and drift snow and, because of the altitude and northern orientation, consistently some of the best snow on the mountain. Stauffenberg opens narrowly between rock outcroppings, then widens into a huge V above the West Basin.

### ◆◆ Expert

For the ultimate "in-bounds" out-of-this-world skiing, treeless **Kachina Peak** sits at the end of **Highline Ridge** like a monolith beckoning to adventurous skiers. It takes an hour or more to hike to the summit at 12,481 feet. From there, down a route called **Main Street,** are more than a thousand vertical feet of moderately steep powder skiing into **Kachina Basin.** The steely nerved can cut into the top of **Hunziker Bowl.**

One of the mighty runs off of the infamous ridge, **Niños Heroes** provides some of the continent's best "in-bounds" extreme skiing terrain. You have to hike about 200 vertical feet up from the top of Chairs No. 2 or No. 6 to reach the ridge, which is composed of Highline Ridge (to the left looking uphill) and **West Basin Ridge** (to the right). Niños Heroes is off Highline—a few minutes' walk past the juncture of the two subridges. It's consistently steep but also very wide, with plenty of room for recovery if you lose it. Most exciting moment? Probably the 5- to 12-foot drop over the cornice to begin the run.

Snaking through narrow openings and pockets in the forest, **Sir Arnold Lunn** is a powderhound's dream. Because this run faces east, you'll want to ski it before the sun comes out, though shade can hide some powder long after you'd think it would be gone.

A beautiful little bowl at the top, **Tresckow** starts off with some sweet turns in deep powder, then a vague meandering through thick forest along the ridge itself, followed by a hard left and a drop through an avalanche chute. During dry spells, this is often home to some of the last powder on the mountain. Someone who knows the mountain is a friend indeed on this run.

One of the steepest shots of the entire ski area, **Upper Stauffenberg Chute**, if skied with élan, will make you a minor god.

A run so obscure that many skiers don't even know it's there when skiing by its top off **Lorelei, Werner Chute** will cause you to lock up in fear if you don't get physical with this very narrow slash through cliffs and massive trees. It dumps out onto **Longhorn,** where you'll find more powder stashes along the edges and then a series of tough mogul fields.

### Snowboarding

Not permitted at this resort.

> Novel snowmaking techniques were supposedly employed in Taos Ski Valley. During rare droughts, Ernie Blake would visit the Indians of Taos Pueblo and request a snow dance.

## Mountain Highs and Lows

Because Taos Mountain is so challenging, you'll find that ratings at most other US ski areas seem to pale in comparison. A black diamond elsewhere might be an upper-level blue square at Taos, while Taos's diamonds and black diamonds could be doubles at other resorts. Take this into account when judging your abilities and a run's rated level of difficulty.

Although it is rated as an expert run, good intermediates shouldn't have any problem tackling **Hunziker Bowl.**

The two runs of **Corner Chute** and **Niños Heroes** are accessed from **Highline Ridge,** which has many dangerous trails. Resort management rated them as extremely difficult to keep novices out of the area. However, they are not very steep, and in good snow conditions are appropriate for beginning experts.

## At the Resort

*Area code 505 unless otherwise noted.*

✦ **Hotel St. Bernard** $$$$ The heart and soul of Taos Ski Valley can be found within these thick stone walls. Named after the patron saint of skiers, this hostelry reflects the European roots of the ski valley's early founders. Owner Jean Mayer, a former member of the French National Ski Team and chief of the US Army ski patrol in Garmisch, Germany, has been a central figure in Taos's success, both with this lodge and as director of the renowned ski school for more than 30 years. He opened this hotel with eight rooms and a restaurant in 1959. Except for room upgrades over the years, it has remained essentially unchanged. Guest rooms aren't luxurious, but everything else is outstanding; firelight dances off the golden, wooden interior; sounds of music and animated conversation emanate from the bar; and the delectable aroma of dinner being prepared wafts from the kitchen. This is the "highest" lodging in the core of the ski village, and you can ski right up to the front door. Another perk is the commodious teakwood hot tub. Rooms are available only through the "Ski Better Week" plan, which consists of daily ski lessons, six nights' lodging, all meals, and special children's activities (including early supervised dinner). The food is superb: energy-packed breakfasts, elaborate lunches, and seven-course dinners featuring continental, nouvelle American, and Southwestern fare. There's limited public dining on a space-available basis. ♦ Base of the lift. 776.2251

Within Hotel St. Bernard:

**The Rathskeller** ★$ Gourmet sandwiches, red chilies, fresh soups, cookies, and other snacks can be savored in the bar of the **St. Bernard.** The slope-side location can't be beat. When it's sunny, head upstairs to the open-air deck for a great view of the mountain and a decent grilled chicken filet sandwich or a burger. This pub is also the ski valley's center for après-ski entertainment. ♦ Daily lunch. Bar daily 11AM-11PM. 776.2251

THE INN AT SNAKEDANCE

✦ **The Inn at Snakedance** $$$$ The oldest structure in the ski valley, this former hunting lodge constructed in 1946 of massive hewn logs is a local treasure. In the summer of 1993, the 60-unit lodge underwent a complete renovation, expansion, and name change (from **Hondo Lodge**), while maintaining its character and improving the facilities. The expansion provided for suites, a spa offering sauna and massage, a library, fireside dining, and a glass-walled bar. This inn also has easy accessibility—a fact you'll appreciate after skiing the mountain all day. Like many of the leading ski valley lodges, this one operates on the "Ski Better Week" plan, which includes lift tickets, lessons, meals, and lodging, but you can also bed down here for shorter stays with or without the plan's usual accoutrements. ♦ Just below Hotel St. Bernard. 800/322.9815; fax 776.1410

Within The Inn at Snakedance:

**The Hondo Restaurant** ★$$ Located in the historic portion of the inn, this nostalgic wood-paneled and hewn-log assemblage proclaims its mountain roots. The restaurant features contemporary American and Southwestern specialties, and—a rarity in the ski valley—fresh seafood. It also hosts wine-theme dinners. ♦ Daily breakfast, lunch, and dinner. 776.2277

**Hondo Bar** One of the valley's hidden bars, this intimate space features a great view of the mountain and such light eats as baked brie with a red-chili pesto, calamari, nachos, sandwiches, and burgers. Live entertainment is occasionally offered après-ski and in the evening. ♦ Daily noon-closing. 776.2277

**Bumps** A godsend to those staying in condos, this store carries all the essentials (in case you forgot to buy them in Taos): light grocery items, liquor, tobacco, snacks, newspapers, and small gifts. Some video rentals are also available. ♦ M-Sa 8AM-9PM; Su 8AM-7PM. Lobby level. 776.1621

✦ **The Resort Center** Within this massive three-story structure at the center of the ski area's base complex, you'll find a variety of places to eat and drink, a handful of shops, rest rooms, pay phones, storage lockers, a deli, and other facilities. ♦ No phone

Within The Resort Center:

**Twining Provisions** This is the complement to **Bumps** for valley residents and condo renters, offering a complete line of deli foodstuffs and gourmet items, soups, soft drinks, and shakes—to be eaten here or taken out. ♦ Daily 8AM-6PM. Lowest level. 776.8602

**Chocolate Extreme** Chocolate lovers will find a full assortment of chocolate and other sweet treats. ♦ M-Sa 1PM-6PM. Lowest level. 776.2291

**Quast Gallery** Traditional sculpture and paintings by about 22 artists, mostly local, are for sale. You'll find works from such artists as wildlife woodcarver J. Tester Armstrong, desert skyscape painter Marilyn Yanke, and oil portraitist Miles Mathis. ♦ Daily 10AM-5PM. Lowest level. 776.1004

**Cold Smoke Photography** You'll see photographers from this shop on the mountain taking pictures of skiers. At the end of the day, stop here to buy a picture of yourself. They also offer custom photography and take group shots. ♦ Daily 8:30AM-9:30AM, noon-1PM, 3PM-5PM. Lowest level. 776.8567

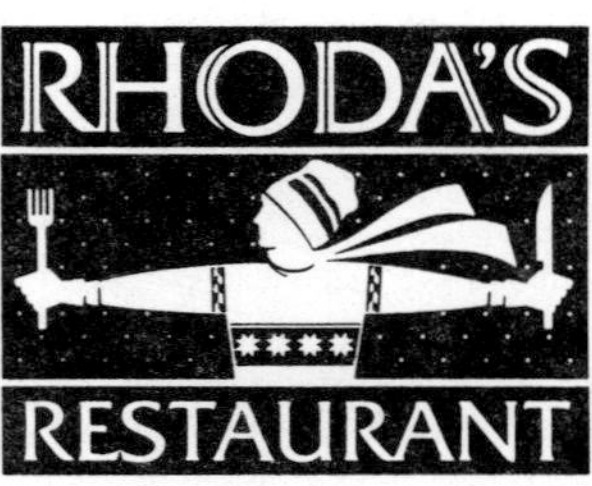


**Rhoda's Restaurant** ★$$ This relatively new addition to the valley dining scene is named after Rhoda Blake, the wife of Taos Ski Valley founder Ernie Blake. It features Southwestern specialties and wild game brochettes, from buffalo to alligator. For lunch, try the turkey verde sandwich. There's a good but limited wine list. ♦ Daily lunch and dinner. Upper level. 776.2005

Taos Ski Valley typically receives the second or third greatest annual snowfall of any major Rocky Mountain ski area.

**Martini Tree Bar** In the spring, the deck facing **Al's Run** is a fine place to catch some rays and watch the skiing action. Also, head here for après-ski entertainment Thursday through Sunday from 4PM to 6PM. ♦ M-Sa 10:30AM to closing; Su noon-midnight. Upper level. 776.2291

✦ **Taos Ski Valley Complex** To the left of **The Resort Center** as you look down the mountain, this complex houses a number of Taos Ski Valley shops and facilities, including the rental shop, repair shop, ticket windows, ski and boot shops, and clothing and accessories stores. ♦ No phone

Within Taos Ski Valley Complex:

**TSV Rental and Repair Shop** (See "Rentals," page 163.)

**Box Canyon** Site of the **US Post Office,** this small store also has fax machines, message center services, and overnight film developing, plus books, newspapers, cards, gifts, and games. If you hate lugging your skis to and from airports (and who doesn't?), they will ship them home for you. ♦ M-Sa 8AM-5PM. Lower level. 776.1256

**Andean Softwear** Owner Andrea Heckman haunts South American markets in search of the beautiful textiles she sells here. The incredibly soft alpaca sweaters—dyed in an array of vibrant colors—are handmade by Andean artisans, as are the rugs, pillows, wall hangings, and ethnic crafts. Most unusual are her handmade après-ski boots. ♦ Daily 10AM-9PM. Lower level. 776.2508

**TSV Sportswear** This is the place to buy caps, hats, pins, and other memorabilia carrying the official Taos Ski Valley logo. The well-stocked shop also offers a wide selection of ski clothing—from socks to powder suits. For those not wishing to sink a small fortune into skiwear, they rent bibs, parkas, and other high-end items. ♦ Daily 8AM-9PM. Upper level. 776.2291

**Taos Ski & Boot** High-performance ski equipment and accessories, including top-of-the-line sunglasses, are sold in this shop, which also carries high-performance demo rentals. If you end up buying something, they'll deduct the rental price from the sales price. ♦ Daily 8AM-9PM. Upper level. 776.2291

✦ **Hotel Edelweiss** $$$$ This historic hotel is one of Taos's oldest operations and it was recently renovated by its new owners—the Wooldridge family. The Edelweiss still exudes that same sense of refinement and moderation for which it's always been known. People don't shout here; they converse. The 16 rooms are fairly large by valley standards, each with a view overlooking the ski slopes. For relaxing after a day on the mountain, there's a large Jacuzzi and a cedar sauna set among plants in a glass-enclosed room. The hotel operates on the "Ski Better Week" plan, which includes daily ski lessons, lift tickets, and all meals. Another bonus: They offer ski-in/ski-out access, so you don't have to walk to the slopes. ♦ Located between the skier shuttle depot and the beginner slopes. 776.2301; fax 776.2533

Within Hotel Edelweiss:

**La Croissantery** ★★$$ In the morning, large windows overlooking the slopes fill the room with New Mexico's energizing sunshine as you dig into the European-style buffet of yogurt, fruits, pastries, granola, and hot cereals. At lunch, homemade bread, soups, sandwiches, and some hot entrées are provided—weather permitting—on an outside deck. ♦ Daily breakfast, lunch, and dinner. Dinner reservations are occasionally available. 776.2301

**Looney Tunes** Since 1976, owners Danny and Dana Brienza have been providing locals and visitors with as fine a ski tune-up as you can find anywhere in the world. These people know how to take your ordinary, banged-up ski and turn it into a machine perfectly matched to your ability and preferences. In addition, they offer excellent custom boot modifications and boot fitting. They also carry a select line of new skis, boots, and accessories, as well as high-performance demo rentals. The Brienzas are two of the best skiers in the valley. ♦ Daily 8AM-8PM. 776.8839

✦ **Tim's Stray Dog Cantina** ★★$ Looking for a taste of New Mexico's famed local cuisine? Amble over to Tim's for some favorful chili concoctions. For breakfast, load up on one of his huge omelettes or the blue corn/blueberry pancakes; for lunch, try a green-chili burrito or tortilla soup; and for dinner, you can't go wrong with the red-chili enchilada or pan-fried trout. Probably the best margaritas in the valley are served here. ♦ Daily breakfast, lunch, and dinner. Cottam's Alpine Village, just below the skier shuttle depot. 766.2894

The legend of the late Ernie Blake, founder of the Taos Ski Valley, grows larger as time passes. Blake, son of a Swiss mother and German father, immigrated to the US in 1938. Apparently he had an attraction to dynamite and would keep it under his bed to pack into cigar boxes and use as avalanche bombs. Ernie was also a master of public relations. He used to write letters to magazines extolling Taos's sterling virtues and have friends in distant cities and countries mail them for him.

✦ **The Boot Doctor** As well as being a tremendous skier and oft-published writer on boot technology, Bob Gleason has been operating this shop since 1987. If you have a problem with how your boots fit, he can solve it. Or, if you're ready to throw your old torture devices into the garbage and get a new pair, Bob is the man to see. His shop carries a nice selection of high-performance skis and a wide array of high-tech ski clothing and accessories. ♦ Daily 8AM-7PM. Cottam's Alpine Village. 776.2489

✦ **Alpine Village Condominiums** $$$ Set beside the rushing waters of the Hondo Stream amid aspens and blue spruce, these seven modern yet casual condo units offer flexible arrangements to suit parties ranging from two to 10 people (and it's just a few minutes' walk from the lifts). Most units have fully equipped kitchenettes, and all have telephones, TVs, ski lockers, and daily maid service. ♦ Cottam's Alpine Village. 800/322.8267; fax 776.8542

✦ **Cottam's Ski Shop** The Cottam family is synonymous with the development of skiing in Taos and is a major player in local ski business. John and Barbara Cottam run two stores in town, one on the road to the ski valley and this one, which offers some of the lowest rental and service prices in the area, as well as a selection of high-performance skis, overnight tuning, and other services. ♦ Cottam's Alpine Village. 776.8540

✦ **Thunderbird Lodge** $$$ One of the valley's "old guard," this 30-unit lodge may not look impressive or have spacious rooms, but it shines with friendly service, a high-spirited atmosphere, and excellent food. Resident-owners Elizabeth and Tom Brownell and their staff make guests feel at home. Amenities include men's and women's saunas, a coed whirlpool, a massage room, recreation room, and supervised dinner for children. The lodge operates on the "Ski Better Week" plan, which includes all meals, daily ski lessons, and lift tickets. The famed Saturday night buffet is open to the public on a space-available basis. ♦ 150 yards behind and below Lift No. 1. 800/776.2279; fax 776.2238

Within Thunderbird Lodge:

**Twining Tavern** Named after the ski valley's original mining boomtown, this bar, with its rustic stone fireplace, is just the spot to warm those chilled bones. The staff prides itself on being able to mix any drink known to humanity—see if you can stump them. Live music is offered nightly, from country-and-western acts to great jazz. Every January, this tavern hosts the **Jazz Legends** series, with performances by the likes of Ralph Sutton, Ray Brown, Herb Ellis, and Warren Vache. The series is open to the public, but lodge guests get first shot at tickets. ♦ Daily noon to closing. 776.2280

✦ **Dolomite** ★$ Tasty pizza by the slice, savory pesto dishes, and other fare is served in this simple restaurant. ♦ Daily breakfast, lunch, and dinner. Across the road from the Thunderbird Lodge. 776.8153

✦ **Le Ski Mastery** Alain Veth, former World Cup ski technician and ex-member of the French National Ski Team, offers top-notch ski tuning. His shop also rents new top-of-the-line skis. ♦ Daily 8AM-6PM. Across from the Thunderbird Lodge. 776.1403

✦ **Terry Sports** This shop specializes in rental packages for kids and adults ranging from beginner to expert. It also provides ski tuning and offers free overnight ski storage. ♦ Daily 8AM-6PM. Two valley locations: next to the ticket windows and between the Thunderbird Lodge and Sierra del Sol. 776.8292

✦ **Sierra del Sol** $$$ This group of 30 condominiums offers easy access to the lifts, spacious layouts, fireplaces, fully equipped kitchens, cable TV, on-site parking, and balconies overlooking the Hondo Stream. They aren't luxurious but are comfortable and pleasant, with lots of light. Within the complex (pictured above) are two indoor hot tubs and saunas. ♦ Below the resort complex, across the bridge. 800/523.3954; fax 776.2347

✦ **Twining Condominiums** $$$ Just a few minutes walk from the lifts, these 20 comfortably furnished studio units for two guests each feature a full kitchen, TV, and phone. Guests share a hot tub and sauna. ♦ Next to Sierra del Sol. 800/828.2472; fax 776.9243

✦ **St. Bernard Condominiums** $$$$ Though this modern complex of cast concrete and glass was considered a monstrosity when built, time has taken some of the edge off its urban look and boosted its approval rating. Because of its height and distance from the slopes, the 12-unit complex provides some of the best views of the mountain in the valley. Guests have the option of taking meals at a sister institution, the **Hotel St. Bernard,** as part of the "Ski Better Week" plan, or of opting for lodging only. Units are available for nightly stays on a space-available basis only. ♦ On the south-facing side of the valley, behind and above the Thunderbird Lodge. 776.8506

✦ **Chalet Montesano** $$$

If you're looking for a homey atmosphere and plenty of quiet isolation, this is the place. The seven-room chalet is set off by itself in the forest yet is only some 300 yards from the lifts. Various accommodations—from apartments for two to a large suite, even use of the entire chalet—can be arranged. All rooms have phones, a TV, and fireplace, and there's an on-site lap pool—a real rarity in the region—and spa. Children under 14 are not allowed. ♦ Behind Twining Condominiums. 776.8226; fax 776.8760 ext 110

✦ **Innsbruck Lodge** $$$ The lodge is owned and operated by Franz and Teresa Voller, who were born and raised in Austria. Their heritage is reflected in the decor and atmosphere of the inn and its condominium units. Amenities include a lounge, whirlpool, and gameroom. Lodging is available by the night, with or without meals, or through the "Ski Better Week" plan—which includes all meals, daily ski lessons, and lift tickets. Accommodations include six rooms and five condos. The location allows you to ski to and from the slopes but also requires a hefty walk to reach the village center. ♦ Far right side of the beginner area (looking uphill). 800/243.5253

✦ **Phoenix Restaurant** $ One of two restaurants located on the mountain itself, this one serves simple food such as burgers, soups and stews, sandwiches, salads, and a wide variety of snack foods like yogurt. Wash it all down with beer, wine, bottled water, or soft drinks. While it's nothing special, the wholesome fare will recharge and refresh you. On warm days, they fire up the outside grill on the spacious deck. ♦ Daily lunch. At the base of Lift No. 4 in Kachina Bowl. 776.2291

The first Spanish mission church in Taos was founded in 1598. Taos is one of the oldest European-influenced towns in the US.

✦ **Whistlestop Cafe** $ The other on-mountain restaurant, this small place features pizza, sandwiches, and snack foods (but no liquor). Brown baggers can sit inside or at the outdoor picnic tables. ♦ Daily lunch. At the base of Lift No. 6 on the "frontside." 776.2291

## Beyond the Resort

**1 Salsa de Salto** $$$$ Originally built as the home of Dadou Mayer (brother of Jean Mayer, owner of the **Hotel St. Bernard,** see above), this inn is filled with personal touches. The eight bedrooms are furnished with finely crafted local furniture, and down comforters on the king-size beds seem to swallow you up on a cold winter night. The master suite has its own fireplace and private entrance. Daily maid service, delicious breakfasts, afternoon hors d'oeuvres, a heated pool, and a hot tub are among the perks. Located in the foothills of the mountains with great views, this hostelry basks in the sun long after the ski valley has plunged into deep shadow. ♦ Just off NM 150 on the north side of Arroyo Seco. 776.2422

**2 The Abominable Snowmansion** $ Other than a friend's sofa, this is about the cheapest place to sleep in Taos. It's a no-frills, 60-bed skiers' hostel, but the price—including full breakfast—is right and it's located in the sleepy village of Arroyo Seco. No smoking permitted. ♦ On NM 150 halfway between Taos and the ski valley, Arroyo Seco. 776.8298; fax 776.2107

**3 Casa Cordova** ★★★★ $$$$

When you want first-class food, service, and ambience, by all means dine here—one of the best restaurants in New Mexico. It has survived for more than 35 years in this remote location. Begin dinner with a drink in the sedate and dimly lit bar. The dining rooms are small and intimate, and one is lit by an aromatic piñon fireplace. Exquisite cuisine ranges from steak *au poivre* and veal piccata to lamb chops or pork loin with jalapeño sauce. ♦ M-Sa dinner (cocktails 4:30PM). Off NM 150, about 8 miles north of Taos just south of Arroyo Seco (look for the sign). 776.2500

Chile
CONNECTION

**4 Chile Connection** ★★$$$ Skiers converge here for dinner before hitting the road. Its forte (surprise) is New Mexican chili dishes: *rellenos* (whole green chilies stuffed with cheese, dipped in batter, and fried), enchiladas, and *chimichangas* (flour tortillas filled with various items then deep-fried). Other favorites are the *fajitas* and the buffalo steaks. The restaurant is known for its vast selection of cognacs (one of the largest in the country), home-brewed beer, and tasty margaritas. Owner Judith Vick suggests you request Hornitos tequila in your margaritas. ♦ Daily dinner. One mile north of the blinking light on NM 150. 776.8787

**5 Quail Ridge Inn** $$$ This 110-unit complex is a nice blend of New Mexican Pueblo-style architecture and modern comforts, offering a 20-meter heated pool, indoor tennis courts, saunas, hot tubs, a coin-operated laundry, satellite TV, fireplaces, phones, and daily maid service. Accommodations range from decent standard hotel rooms for two to two- and three-bedroom casitas. Children under 18 stay for free. A Mediterranean-style restaurant, **Renegade Cafe**, and a bar are on the premises. ♦ About 1 mile north of the blinking light on NM 150. 776.2211, 800/624.4448; fax 776.2949

There's a story behind the name of every run at Taos. Lorelei is the blond German siren who sits on a tall rock in the Rhine River combing her hair in the sun and singing songs that lure fishermen to their deaths in the whirlpools. Stauffenberg honors the German general who almost succeeded in assassinating Hitler with a bomb in 1944. Maxie's is named for the late Maxie Anderson, a New Mexico ski pioneer and hot-air balloonist who made the first Atlantic balloon crossing. Whitefeather refers to the English custom of giving a white feather to gentlemen who didn't volunteer for the Boer War (i.e., cowards).

**6 Taos Pueblo** If you do just one thing when you're in Taos besides ski, visit the oldest continuously occupied apartment dwelling in the US. Built of mud and straw, the pueblo's two huge multistoried brown structures (the tallest section is five stories high) rise from the plain. Wooden ladders lead from one level to the next, and doorways are visible on every level. With its soft mud curves, this pueblo was the forerunner of the architecture that is symbolic of the entire region, and it exists in much the same form as it did in 1540, when members of the expedition led by Spanish explorer Francisco Vásquez de Coronado found it during their search for the Seven Cities of Cibola—the legendary cities of gold. If the explorers arrived at sunset, they must have thought this was one of them. (The Indian pueblos may have given rise to the legend.)

An Indian community existed at Taos more than 500 years before Columbus came to the New World. The people, though primarily peaceful, were the most rebellious of all the pueblos and led the revolt that drove the Spanish from the region in 1680. Even when the southern pueblos were subjugated by Don Diego de Vargas in 1692, Taos Pueblo continued to rebel for another five years. A century later, when the Taos Valley was under repeated attacks by Plains Indians, many of the Spanish settlers took refuge in the pueblo. Today, about 1,500 Taos Indians (who speak the native Tiwa language) reside here. A certain exhilaration is sparked by the age and primitive beauty of the structures. But a kind of bitterness hangs heavily in the air because the pueblo derives much of its income from tourism. Visitors are charged for parking and charged again if they photograph, sketch, or paint the pueblo; if you photograph individuals, you are expected to ask permission and to tip them. Some ground-floor apartments house small shops selling jewelry, other crafts, and bread. These are a proud, independent people, and pueblo residents do not wholly welcome the intrusion of tourism. A visit to the pueblo is still a memorable experience. ♦ Admission. Daily approximately 8AM-5PM. Taos Pueblo road, off Paseo del Pueblo Norte, 2 miles north of Taos. 758.9593

Within Taos Pueblo:

**Taos Indian Horse Ranch** The ranch offers limited horseback riding in the winter, but when the snow is too deep, they hitch up horse-drawn sleighs for a jingly prance over the fields and back roads of Taos Pueblo. ♦ 758.3212, 800/659.3210

**7 El Pueblo Cafe** ★★$ Some funky-looking restaurants are great and others are horrendous. Happily, this cafe falls into the former class. Service is fast, the prices are modest, and the food is wonderful. Sample *fajitas,* tacos, or a New Mexican staple—*posole* (a rich stew of hominylike puffed corn, shredded bits of pork, spices, and broth topped with a splash of spicy green or red chili). Local lore has it that *posole* is the best-known cure for a cold or a hangover. For the timid, the kitchen also serves steaks, chicken, and other such fare. ♦ Daily breakfast, lunch, and dinner. 625 Paseo del Pueblo Norte (at Camino de las Placitas). 758.2053

**8 Kachina Lodge** $$ This classic upscale 118-room motel has been a fixture in Taos since 1961. The sleeping quarters are of your standard motel variety, but all the public spaces are decorated in Southwestern Indian imagery—including a substantial collection of kachina dolls. (These miniature replicas of Pueblo Indian deities are predominantly worshiped today by the Hopi of Arizona.) Within the lodge are the **Kiva Coffee Shop, Hopi Dining Room, Zuni Lounge** (a bit of a dive), and **Kachina Cabaret.** The cabaret is one of the few "hot spots," so to speak, of Taos nightlife. Over the years it's presented the likes of Jerry Jeff Walker, Freddy Fender, and John Prine. ♦ 413 Paseo del Pueblo Norte (north of Civic Plaza Dr). 758.2275, 800/522.4462; fax 758.9207

**9 Reel Cowboys** "Cowboy culture gone high camp" is a good way to describe this shop, where you can pick up an inexpensive memento of the wild West. Movie icons such as Dale Evans, the Lone Ranger, and Roy Rogers live again on T-shirts, pocketknife handles, comic books, coffee mugs, and so forth.

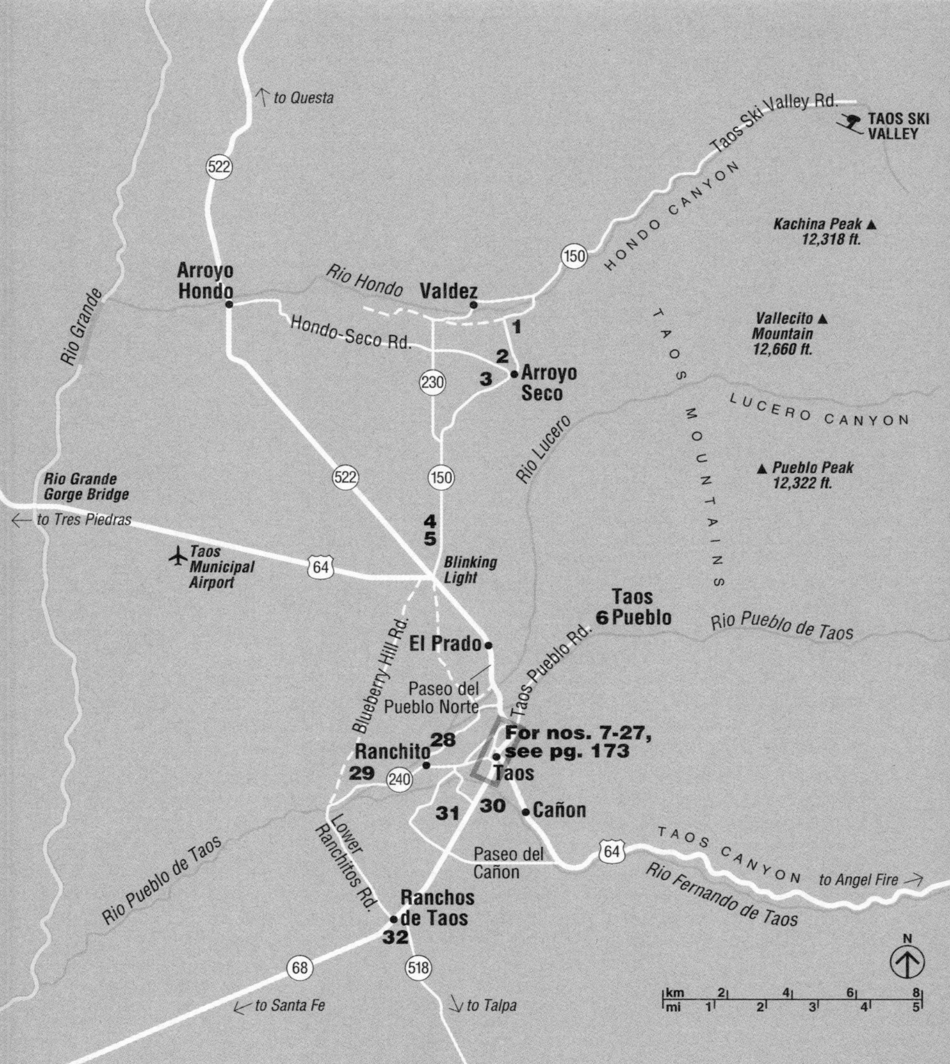

♦ Daily 10AM-5PM. 101 Bent St (between Paseo del Pueblo Norte and Camino de las Placitas). 758.8005

**10 Merlin's Garden** This offbeat, faintly old hippie/New Age place is primarily a bookstore, with subject headings such as "angels," "channeled," "death & rebirth," and "crystals/gems." But it also carries a diverse selection of other items, including seldom-seen cassette tapes by the likes of Navajo flutist Carlos Nakai, incense, candles, feather jewelry, herbal and essential oils, and cards. ♦ M-Sa 10AM-5PM; Su 11AM-5PM. 127 Bent St (between Paseo del Pueblo Norte and Camino de las Placitas). 758.0985

**11 Tapas de Taos Café** ★★$ A bright, colorful decor inspired by the Mexican "Day of the Dead" festival adorns the interior of this 300-year-old adobe. Spanish music, carved wooden skulls and other artifacts from Oaxaca, tiny dining rooms, and unusual food make you feel you've left the US. *Tapas* (appetizers) include *queso fundido* (baked cheese with smoked chilies topped with sautéed mushrooms and scallions) and fried calamari. But many other items compete for attention: fire-roasted corn on the cob with green-chili butter, chili with shredded beef over black beans, flan, and *liquados* (ice blended with fresh fruits). ♦ Daily lunch and dinner. 136 Bent St (between Paseo del Pueblo Norte and Camino de las Placitas). 758.9670

**12 Southwestern Arts** Both historic and contemporary Navajo weavings—from classic "Chief's Blankets" to "Eye Dazzlers" and modern, folksy pictorials—are carried in this small shop. Also of note are a selection of contemporary Santa Clara Pueblo and Acoma Pueblo pottery, old silver and turquoise jewelry, crosses made of straw overlay on wood, and lovely black-and-white photographs by owner/artist Dick Spas. ♦ M-Sa noon-6PM. 124 Bent St (between Paseo del Pueblo Norte and Camino de las Placitas). 758.8418

**13 Bent Street Deli** ★★★$ Original and tempting first-rate fare is served at this centrally located deli. If you don't want your food to go, you can sit indoors or on a heated patio. The Reuben, chock-full of lean corned beef, may be the best this side of New York City, and the Taos (sliced turkey, fresh green chili, bacon, and guacamole rolled in a flour tortilla) is excellent. You also can have the kitchen create a custom sandwich. ♦ M-Sa 8AM-9PM. 120 Bent St (between Paseo del Pueblo Norte and Camino de las Placitas). 758.5787

**14 Taos Community Auditorium (TCA)** For a small town, Taos has a surprisingly robust performing arts community to complement its visual arts scene. TCA, run by the **Taos Art Association,** is home to plays, poetry readings, dance performances, classical music concerts, film screenings, and other interesting happenings year-round. ♦ Admission. 133 Paseo del Pueblo Norte (behind the Stables Art Center). 758.2052

**15 Taos Inn** $$$ A National Historic Landmark, this is considered the town's premier hotel. It is composed of several now-united houses—some date from the 1600s—which were built around a small plaza. Today's rustic lobby grew out of that plaza, combining wood furniture, adobe archways, and walls adorned with rugs and artwork. The 40 guest rooms have the same Southwestern motif, with Indian-style wood-burning fireplaces; cable TV brings guests into the late 20th century. Since becoming an inn in 1939, it has served as a focal point for Taos's social, cultural, and intellectual life. The **Adobe Bar** (ext 146), a popular hangout for local artists, writers, and other bohemian types, frequently presents "Meet the Artist" lectures/ exhibitions. ♦ 125 Paseo del Pueblo Norte (at Bent St). 758.2233, 800/826.7466

Within Taos Inn:

**Doc Martin's** ★★$$$ The former home of Dr. Paul T. Martin (for decades the only physician in the county) from the 1890s to the early 1940s, today it's one of the city's best-known restaurants. Friendly service and excellent food are the hallmarks of this romantic dining spot. Nightly specials compete with regular entrées like roasted pheasant, grilled lamb loin, or pasta penne with mushrooms, eggplant, bell peppers, and onions topped with a hearty tomato sauce. Or make an outstanding meal out of a variety of unusual appetizers, such as smoked duck quesadillas or New Mexico polenta. The extensive wine list has been repeatedly honored by *The Wine Spectator* (the wines are also available for purchase in the inn's wine shop, **The Wine Cellar**). ♦ Daily breakfast, lunch, and dinner. 758.1977

**16 Brooks Indian Shop** Look here for a good selection of stellar Indian arts and crafts. Fine pieces by Julian Lovato stand out in the jewelry case. Black, lustrous pottery made by the grandchildren of renowned potter Maria Martinez is another highlight. Also featured are intricately hand-painted, black-on-white Acoma Pueblo pots by Geraldine Sandia and Jemez Pueblo redware by Lucy Lewis. ♦ M-Sa 10AM-5PM. 108G Kit Carson Rd (near Paseo del Pueblo Sur). 758.9073

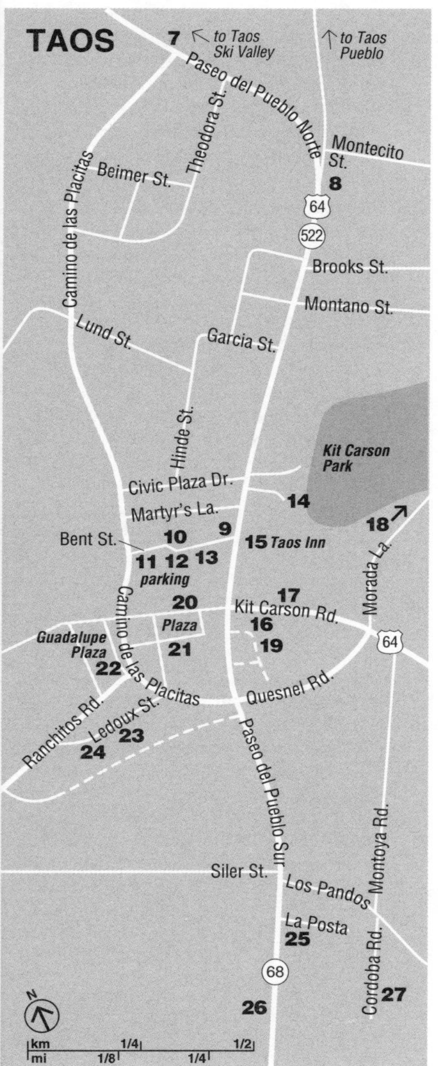


**17 Kit Carson Home** No name blankets the region more than that of this famous frontiersman, scout, trailblazer, and soldier. The home that he lived in during his years in Taos is now a museum, and the street it sits on bears his name, as does the park in which he is buried and the immense **Carson National Forest,** which surrounds Taos. A native of Kentucky, Carson ran off at age 17 with a group of fur traders and trappers headed for Santa Fe. Making Taos his operational base, he bought this 12-room adobe in 1843, and it remained his home until his death in 1868. Three of the rooms are furnished much the way they would have been in his lifetime. ♦ Admission. Daily 8AM-6PM in summer; daily 9AM-5PM in winter. 113 E Kit Carson Rd (between Dragoon La and Paseo del Pueblo Norte). 758.0505

Lumina

**18 Lumina Gallery** Owner Felicia Ferguson describes this enterprise as Taos's most elegant gallery, and she's correct. Located inside the former home of famed Taos artist Victor Higgins, this gallery features platinum and color photographs by Ferguson's husband, Chuck Henningsen, monoprints by Bill Gersh, Indian pottery, and Hispanic religious art. ♦ Daily 10:30AM-5:30PM. 239 Morada La (north of Kit Carson Rd). 758.7282

**19 Eske's** Some of the best handcrafted beer anywhere is made by brewmaster Steve Eskeback and his wife, Wanda, right in the basement of their pub. Typically, they have about six brews on tap out of a stable of 22 or so. Most are English-style ales but without the typical bite of commercial brands. Perhaps the most popular is the zesty "Taos Green Chile," but if you're burned out on chili, ask for the "Seco Stout." Sandwiches, salads, and other pub fare is served. Try the vegetarian burrito. There's often live music in this nonsmoking establishment. ♦ M-Th 4:30PM-10:30PM; F-Su noon- 10:30PM. 106 Des George's La (a block southeast of Kit Carson Rd and the main drag). 758.1517

**20 New Directions Gallery** One of the few galleries in Taos with a good selection of contemporary—often abstract—art, this place displays art by the likes of Larry Bell (with works on paper unlike anything you've ever seen), sculptor Ted Egri, and painter Gloria Corbet. ♦ Daily 10AM-5PM. 107B North Plaza (between Paseo del Pueblo Norte and Camino de las Placitas). 758.2771

**21 Taos Mountain Outfitters, Inc.** If you want to rent equipment for "alternative" modes of winter downhill transportation, including cross-country skis, telemark skis, or even snowshoes, this is about the only place in the area that can help you. The shop also carries a large selection of winter clothing and expedition materials. ♦ Daily 9:30AM-6PM. 114 South Plaza (between Paseo del Pueblo Norte and Camino de las Placitas). 758.9292

**22 Main Street Bakery** ★★$ Filled with the heavenly smell of fresh bread and pastries baking away, this unassuming place makes an excellent spot for breakfast. Try the homemade granola, *huevos* (fried eggs) with salsa on a corn tortilla, *migas* (scrambled eggs with tortilla chips), or delicious French toast made from date nut and orange bread. Sandwiches, soups, and daily lunch specials round out the menu. ♦ Daily breakfast and lunch. Guadalupe Plaza (just west of the plaza off Camino de las Placitas). 758.9610

**23 Blumenschein House** From 1919 to 1960, this house belonged to Ernest Blumenschein, a pivotal artist and co-founder of the Taos art colony. Furnished as it was during his residence, the large, 200-year-old adobe contains works by the artist, as well as those by Mary Greene Blumenschein and Helen Blumenschein, his wife and daughter—two overlooked but talented creators. ♦ Admission. Daily 9AM-5PM. 222 Ledoux St (between Camino de las Placitas and Ranchitos Rd). 758.0505

**24 Harwood Foundation** Those interested in Taos's history as a world-renowned arts center should visit this museum operated by the **University of New Mexico.** It's the second-oldest museum in the state, dating back to 1923, and contains some 550 paintings, drawings, prints, photographs, and sculpture by early Taos artists such as Oscar Berninghaus, Nicolai Fechin, Victor Higgins, and Andrew Dasburg, as well as some contemporary artists. ♦ Admission. M-F noon-5PM; Sa 10AM-4PM. 238 Ledoux St (between Camino de las Placitas and Ranchitos Rd). 758.3250

**25 Lambert's** ★★★★$$$ When Taos residents are asked to name the best dining spot in town, they almost always answer **Lambert's.** Opened in 1989 by Zeke Lambert, formerly the head chef at the **Taos Inn,** this restaurant is set in a remodeled Victorian house with no frills—just plain white walls in several dining rooms. Some tables offer a view of Taos Mountain. The food is wonderful—the menu changes according to what's available fresh from the market—and can be ordered in full or petite sizes. Try the swordfish or the tenderloin of pork in chipotle sauce. Combined with an appetizer, the very reasonably priced smaller portions should satisfy. An appetizer of minced grilled quail with Oriental pasta salad is a treasure. Leave room for one of the superlative desserts, maybe bread pudding in a rum sauce. The service is casually impeccable without ever being obtrusive. Good California wines are served, and some are surprisingly inexpensive. ♦ M-F, Su lunch and dinner; Sa dinner. Reservations recommended. 309 Paseo del Pueblo Sur (south of La Posta). 758.1009

**26 Amigos Natural Grocery and Deli** It seems like almost everybody in Taos is trying to reach the next level of consciousness, or at least recover from last week's disaster, and that means healthy eating. This is the place to buy natural foods. Organic fruit and vegetables, meats, dairy products, juices, coffee beans, and loads of take-out stuff—from tabbouleh to spicy tofu sandwiches—are offered. You can also chow down at the lunch counter. ♦ M-Sa 9AM-7PM; Su 11AM-5PM. 326 Paseo del Pueblo Sur (south of La Posta). 758.8493

**27 Casa de las Chimeneas** $$$ This luxury bed-and-breakfast has garnered substantial media coverage since Susan Vernon started welcoming guests in 1988. A rare tranquillity and graciousness are found within the seven-foot-thick adobe walls. Common areas, brightened by skylights and French doors, feature exceptional regional art, tiled hearths, and exposed *vigas* (ceiling beams). Each of the four rooms has cable TV, a telephone, mini-refrigerator, bathroom, private entrance off the terrace, and one or more kiva fireplaces. There's also a group hot tub. Smoking is not allowed. Each morning, a different entrée is featured at breakfast. ♦ 405 Cordoba Rd (south of Los Pandos). 758.4777; fax 758.4822

Taos Country Inn
at
Rancho Rio Pueblo

**28 Taos Country Inn** $$$ Set in the beautiful and sedate Rio Pueblo Valley, with tremendous views across pastures of sacred **Taos Mountain** (considered one of Earth's power points), this bed-and-breakfast inn provides a pleasurable stay. The atmosphere is very New Mexican, with Saltillo tile floors, *nichos* (sculptured recesses) in the adobe walls, Southwestern textiles, carved wood cabinets and shelving, and local art. All nine rooms are suites, each with a TV and phone. Especially enchanting is the **Deveaux Room,** with windows on three sides, a sitting room, and a fireplace. Owner/manager Yolanda Deveaux is of the old Taos Deveaux family. The "muy simpático" staff serves a huge breakfast. ♦ Several miles west of the plaza, off Ranchitos Rd. 758.4900; fax 758.0331

**29** **Martinez Hacienda** One of the few standing examples of an 18th-century Spanish hacienda in the nation, this classic colonial structure provides insight into what life must have been like in frontier New Mexico. The exterior is windowless to protect against raids by the Apache and Comanche Indians. ♦ Admission. Daily 9AM-5PM. State Road 240 (Ranchitos Rd), 2 miles southwest of Taos. 758.1000

**30** **Sun God Lodge** $$ Built in the early 1950s, this 55-room motel has one of the best classic neon signs you'll ever see. Thankfully, the rooms aren't quite as old, having been completely remodeled a few years ago. The Mexican-made furniture, sculpted walls dividing the bedrooms and bathrooms, and other touches make this a surprisingly nice place to stay. Though there's no restaurant on the premises, there are many located just a short walk or drive away. ♦ 919 Paseo del Pueblo Sur, 1.5 miles south of the Plaza. 758.3162, 800/821.2437; fax 758.1875

**31** **Sagebrush Inn** $$$ This is another of the town's classic inns that has epitomized the flavor of Taos—from the ambience to the architecture—since its opening in 1929. The vast wooden lobby capped with exposed *vigas* (ceiling beams) and scattered with leather easy chairs is decked with Indian and Hispanic art and artifacts and a large fireplace. To one side of the lobby is a sizable dance floor, where country-and-western bands perform nightly (one of the few night spots in town). All 80 bedrooms are nicely decorated with Southwestern furniture and art. Especially alluring for art buffs is the Georgia O'Keeffe Room, named after the famous artist who resided there for several summers. Accommodations include a free breakfast at the **Sagebrush Restaurant**. ♦ 1508 Paseo del Pueblo Sur, 2.5 miles south of Taos. 758.2254; 758.5077

**32** **Ranchos de Taos Church** Perhaps the most photographed and painted church in the nation, **San Francisco de Asis Church** has become an icon for American artists. One visit and you'll understand why it has been the object of so much fascination. The design is organic and sculptural—especially its "backside" with large adobe buttresses designed to keep the walls from slumping. Built in 1815, it is still actively used. ♦ Daily 9AM-4:30PM; Mass Sa 7PM, Su 7AM, 9AM, and 11:30AM. St. Francis Plaza, Ranchos de Taos, 4 miles south of Taos (at the blinking light). 758.2754

## Bests

### Dana Brienza
Ski Model/President, Looney Tunes

**Taos Ski Valley** has the feel of an old Alpine resort. Part of the experience is the **Taos Ridge,** a short hike to breathtaking views and challenging trails. I recommend **Juarez** for the first trip because it's a wide, easy-to-find, classic slope that leads back to the chairlift.

My favorite breakfast is eggs Benedict, the Sunday morning special at **La Croissantery** in the **Hotel Edelweiss.** Next door, **Tim's Stray Dog Cantina** serves good food—and lots of it—at a low price. Blueberry cornmeal pancakes are a popular breakfast choice. The **Snakedance Inn** features a great salad bar and perfectly cooked steaks.

The ski week at the ski school is a definite recommendation. It's an excellent way to learn the terrain as well as the local history.

The town of Taos is full of historic adobes and art galleries to browse through. **The Fechin House, Weaving/Southwest,** and the **Ranchos de Taos Church** are a few I like. A real treat is the **Deer Dance** or the **Pow-Wow** at **Taos Pueblo**. At sunset, drive about eight miles south of town to the **Rio Grande Gorge** overlook. It's even better at sunrise.

### Ken Gallard
Photographer

The **West Basin** area has many runs that go straight down: **Fabian, Oster, Pollux, Pipeline, High Somewhere, Silver Tree, Meatball,** and more.

New Mexican food and the ambience at **Tim's Stray Dog Cantina.**

Western swing dancing at the **Sagebrush Inn.**

**Taos Pueblo** and its people—The uniqueness that is **Taos** is largely attributable to the Native Americans who have kept this a very special place.

The art galleries on **Kit Carson Road** and **Bent Street**—A museum-level experience.

**The Taos Community Auditorium**—For movies, drama, dance, and music from troupes around the world.

### Marcia Ready
Physical Therapist, Taos Physical Therapy

**Eske's**—Microbrewery in a home-style setting.

**Chair 6**—Do laps on this chairlift and you'll find the locals and steep runs.

**Kachina Peak**—The overall experience of the hike, the view, and the run will make your visit to Taos unique.

**Two Bucks Cornice** (a.k.a. **Kitchen Wall**)—Best air in Taos.

**Tim's Stray Dog Cantina**—Green-chili cheeseburgers, videos, and music. Close to the lifts for après-ski.

---

The first major lift in Taos—a poma surface tow built by an all-Indian crew from Taos Pueblo—crawled up Al's Run in 1957. It used to sweep lightweight skiers off their feet at the steepest sections.

---

Al's Run was named after Dr. Al Rosen, who, owing to a heart condition, skied Taos wearing a face mask hooked to oxygen bottles carried in a backpack.

# Mount Bachelor

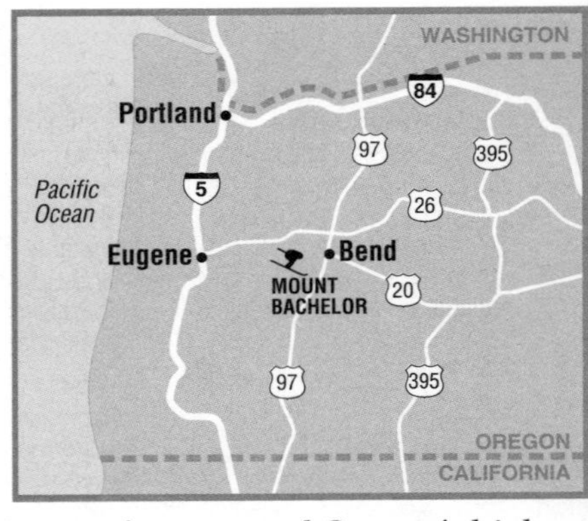


Unlike other Western ranges, the **Cascade Mountains** don't fall into a neat picket fence of pinnacles crossing the horizon. Instead, this assortment of extinct or dormant volcanoes, cinder cones, and solid volcanic plugs is strewn helter-skelter on the landscape.

One of the most majestic massifs is **Mount Bachelor** (formerly known as **Bachelor Butte**), a 9,065-foot cone that juts up from central Oregon's high desert region. While it may not be the tallest Cascade peak in the state (**Mount Hood** stands at 11,245 feet), it is certainly the biggest draw for skiers, attracting about 600,000 annually. Alpiners can head off in any direction from Bachelor's summit, tackling groomed runs or some superb virgin powder. The mountain lies far enough east that its snow is drier than the heavy moisture-laden "Cascade crud" that's typical in this area. Conditions aren't always perfect—the claim of 300 sunny days a year is wildly optimistic—but there's certainly enough bluebird weather between snowfalls to open up some impressive views. Looking south, you can spot California's **Mount Shasta**, while **Mounts Jefferson** and **Hood**, in Oregon, and Washington's **Mount Adams** poke up in the north. Even folks who never leave the base parking lots can get an eyeful of nearby **Broken Top Crater** and the **Three Sisters** peaks.

Bachelor's groomed slopes are an intermediate skier's fantasy. Almost every run is within an intermediate's ability, and if you like to cruise, this is the mountain for it. The double-diamond crowd might be somewhat less enthusiastic, citing a shortage of expert slopes. Still, there are enough steeps here to keep most daredevils happy, and high-speed quad lifts give proven skiers plenty of time on the better runs. At the same time, Bachelor's low-angle, wide-open trails put grins (not grimaces) on every novice's face. One warning, though, applies to all: Watch out for snowboarders—they know no bounds at Bachelor.

After a dismal attempt to market Bachelor as the "Aspen of the West," the resort has returned to touting what it does best: catering to families. The atmosphere is low-key and glitz-free. You don't fall out of bed into the lift lines at Bachelor because there's no lodging at the resort, but the town of **Bend**, just 22 miles to the east, is well endowed with hotels, restaurants, and plenty of shops. Plus, even in winter, Bend tends to remain snow-free, so you can get in your daily jog on its streets before hitting the slopes.

Bend is still going through the usual pains of having been discovered by city escapees. There are plenty of chichi restaurants here, where the clientele sports day-glo outfits and clingy après-ski ensembles. But Bend hasn't completely lost its friendly small-town flavor. Be advised that a fur coat and its attendant pretensions are best left at home. And please forget the faux cowboy hat with the partridge feathers splattered across its crown. A few people affect Western dress in Bend, but this ain't no cow town. If you see a rancher here, he probably raises llamas.

**Mount Bachelor Ski Area**
**PO Box 1031**
**Bend, Oregon 97709**

**Information**....................................503/382.2442
**Reservations**............503/382.2442, 800/829.2442
**24-Hour Snow Phone/Ski Report**.......503/382.7888
**24-Hour Road Conditions**.................403/976.7277

## Fast Facts

*Area code 503 unless otherwise noted.*

**Ski Season** Mid-November through the end of June

**Location** Mount Bachelor is 22 miles west of **Bend,** near the geographic center of **Oregon.**

### Getting to Mount Bachelor

**By air: Roberts Field,** located in the town of **Redmond,** 15 miles north of **Bend,** is served by **Horizon Air** (from **Portland**) and **United Express** (from Portland and **San Francisco**). Regular shuttles leave from this airport, bound for Bend and nearby resorts. Private planes may land at the smaller **Bend Airport** (388.0019), five miles east of town. Runways are lighted and paved, and full air services are available. **CAC Transportation** (382.1687), **Independent Taxi/Shuttle** (593.5244 or 800/227.5244), and **Owl Taxi** (382.3311) provide taxi service for both airports.

**By bus: Greyhound Bus Lines** (382.2151 or 800/231.2222) serves **Bend** once a day from **Portland, San Francisco,** and **Seattle.**

**By car:** Winterized rental cars are available from **Budget, Hertz,** and **National** at **Roberts Field.** Take US Highway 97 to **Bend** and then head west along Century Drive to Mount Bachelor.

**All-weather highways:**

Portland—US Highway 26 East to US Highway 97 South

Seattle—Interstate 5 South to Vancouver, Washington, then follow Interstate 205 South to US Highway 26, and at Madras, take US Highway 97 South

Greater San Francisco—Interstate 5 North to Weed, then US Highway 97 North

**Driving times from:**

Portland—3 hours (160 miles)

Seattle—4.75 hours (260 miles)

Greater San Francisco—8.25 hours (450 miles)

**By train: Amtrak**'s (800/USA.RAIL) *California Zephyr,* southbound from **Seattle** to **Los Angeles,** stops every evening in the town of **Chemult,** 60 miles south of **Bend.** The northbound train from LA passes through Chemult once each morning. **Independent Taxi/Shuttle** (593.5244 or 800/227.5244) serves Chemult station from **Sunriver.**

### Getting around Mount Bachelor

All the major resort and hotel properties in **Bend** operate their own shuttle services to the mountain. Mount Bachelor Resort also has a shuttle service that runs every day linking stops along Bend's Century Drive.

## FYI

**Area** 3,228 acres; runs cutting through evergreen stands dominate the mountain's lower third, while the top two-thirds are open terrain

Beginner—15 percent

Intermediate—35 percent

Advanced—25 percent

Expert—25 percent

**Number of Groomed Runs** 60, covering about half of Bachelor's skiable acreage

**Longest Run** 2.2 miles (**Healy Heights** to Interstate 5)

**Capacity** 21,000 skiers per hour

**Base Elevation** 5,800 feet

**Summit Elevation** 9,065 feet

**Vertical Rise** 3,100 feet

**Average Annual Snowfall** 325 inches

**Snowmaking** None

**Night Skiing** None

**Lifts** 12 (5 high-speed quads, 1 high-speed triple, 3 triple chairs, 1 double chair, and 2 surface lifts)

| **Lift Passes** | **Full Day** | **Half Day** (starts at noon) |
|---|---|---|
| **Adult** | $33 | $28 |
| **Child** (6 and under) | Free | Free |
| **Child** (7-12) | $18 | $13.50 |
| **Senior** (55 and over) | $19 | $16 |

**Ski School** Offices (382.2442 or 800/829.2442) are located in **West Village Lodge, Sunrise Lodge,** and **Pine Marten Lodge.** Group and private lessons (for individuals or groups of no more than four people) are available. Lessons range from one hour to multi-day packages.

**Kids' Ski School** A special one-hour introductory skiing program is offered daily to 3-year-olds, but older children participate in more traditional lessons. Half-day and full-day programs are broken down by age group (4 to 6; 7 to 12) and include lift tickets and lesson, with rentals available at an additional cost. Full-day instruction also includes lunch. Under the **First Time Beginner Program,** new skiers, ages 7 to 12, get a 3.5-hour lesson, including lift tickets and rentals.

**Clinics and Special Programs** Mount Bachelor one of only three ski areas in the US, and the only one on the West Coast, to offer the "Perfect Turn" instruction program. There are seven levels of "Perfect Turn" instruction, all of which emphasize the skier's strengths, rather than focus on weaknesses. **Thanksgiving Race Camp,** a three-day workout available during the holiday weekend, covers slalom, giant slalom, and free-skiing techniques. A video analysis of your performance is included. **Christmas Race Camp** follows the same format, at the same price, and is available midweek, between Christmas and New Year's Day. **Mount Bachelor Snowboard Camps** are held in late March or early April, depending on snow conditions. Camp sessions are six days long and include lodging, meals, lift tickets, and coaching.

**Races** NASTAR races are held four times a week, starting from the Yellow Chair at the **West Village** base area. On Wednesday, Friday, and Saturday, they begin at 1PM; on Sunday, at 10:30AM. **Pacesetter** clinics are held 90 minutes before each day's race.

**Rentals** Rental shops at **West Village Lodge** (382.2607 ext 2121) and **Sunrise Lodge** (ext 2251) offer three packages of skis, boots, and poles, broken into three ability levels. There's also a high-performance ski-and-boot demo program, and snowboard and telemark ski rentals. Fifty percent of the rental inventory is replaced annually, and since the skis have been well maintained, they are great bargains. Multi-day rentals are available and a driver's license is required as a guarantee. Both shops are open Monday through Friday, 8AM to 5PM, and Saturday and Sunday, 7:30AM to 5PM.

**Lockers** Coin-operated lockers are located in **West Village Lodge** and at **Sunrise, Pine Marten,** and **Blue Lodges.** Season passholders have larger lockers (with room for four pairs of skis) in a private changing and storage area at the West Village base. Long-term guests can arrange for day use of these lockers, depending on availability. Outdoor ski and basket storage is at the ski corrals in the West Village base area and at Sunrise Lodge. Locked ski storage is available just outside of **Pine Marten Lodge.**

**Day Care** Full-day and half-day programs are offered at **West Village Lodge** and **Sunrise Lodge** and can handle 126 children a day, ages six weeks and up.

**First Aid** There are first-aid stations (382.2442) in all four of Bachelor's lodges. On the slopes, medical attention is administered by the resort's professional staff and members of the National Ski Patrol. **St. Charles Medical Center** operates a weekend **Mountain Medical Clinic** at the **West Village** base area. Minor injuries can be treated on site, but skiers suffering major injuries are stabilized for the 26-mile trip to St. Charles's main facility (382.4231) in **Bend,** at 2005 NE Neff Road.

There are three types of volcanoes: extinct, dormant, and active. Extinct volcanoes are dead, done, flamed out. Dormant volcanoes still have some life in them and could, like Washington's Mount St. Helens, come alive and start spewing ash or pouring lava at any time. "Active" describes the state St. Helens was in when it came back to

**Parking** Free parking is available at the **Sunrise** and **West Village Lodges** and at the base of the Skyliner Lift.

**Worth Knowing**

- If you're not sure how much skiing you want to do on any particular day, or the weather looks iffy, try the **Pay-Per-Run** ticket. This electronic ticketing system functions just like it sounds and is valid for up to three years from the date of purchase.
- Under the "Share Lift" program, 10,000 tickets are sold for $20 each during the last weekend in January, and the proceeds go to a local charity.

## Rating the Runs

### ● Beginner

The name **Marshmallow** says it all. This gently sloping, wide-open run (reached from the Sunrise Express Chair) is so sweet that even raw beginners won't quake in their boots, and advanced beginners will feel like Olympians.

### ■ Intermediate

No worries, mate, **Down Under**—a wide path with a consistent pitch—looks much harder than it really is. So pluck up your courage and *go.* Later, over a tinny of beer and some chips, you can brag to the blokes about your excellent form. Reach Down Under via—what else?—the Outback Express Chair.

### ◆ Advanced

The top two-thirds of Mount Bachelor is so barren, with so few natural boundaries, that many runs never earn official designations. But you can find them easily enough, thanks to the Summit Express Chair (board at midmountain). Ungroomed bowl routes on the mountain's west side are long and varied, a proper test of your skiing skills. The pitch varies from steep to moderate and when you get into the trees lower down, the challenge increases.

### ◆◆ Expert

There is scarier-looking terrain at Bachelor (consider the **Pinnacles**), but when it comes to challenge, the evergreen-studded slopes between **Boomerang** and **Down Under** are an expert's playground of the steep and deep. Take the Outback Express up. Note that when the snow elsewhere on the mountain is mediocre, it's still terrific on the west side. See ya at the bottom!

## Snowboarding

The park located off the Skyline Chair near **Pat's Way** has quarter-pipes, whales, tabletops, and ramps. When they're not in the park, riders flock to **Down Under** and **Ed's Garden** located in the "Outback" for wide runs, bumps, and tree skiing. Mount Bachelor has snowboarders on its patrol team and benches at the top and bottom of all lifts, specifically for boarders.

## Mountain Highs and Lows

If the off-camber, hard-to-reach run called **LeeWay** is designed to help beginners grow accustomed to skiing, then Bob Dylan is ready to sing the tenor lead in *Il Trovatore*.

The problem with **Thunderbird** isn't that the trail is over- or underrated for beginners, but that it's too crowded and uneven, and better skiers use it as a speedway.

How flat does an intermediate run have to be before it qualifies as terminally boring? As flat as **DSQ,** where even a few rolls can't break the monotony.

The only challenge on **Old Skyliner** is staying awake long enough to reach a lift to get to some *real* intermediate skiing.

You say you met this guy who looked like Pierce Brosnan in ski togs, and he told you that **Tippytoe** was scary? So you skied it, only to realize that Tippytoe is neither that steep nor that intimidating to deserve its black-diamond rating. Lesson? Never accept expert-run recommendations from anybody who may be preserving his looks.

Yes, **Boomerang,** a double-black, starts with some steepness, but most of it can be tackled on autopilot.

## At the Resort

*Resort facilities can be reached by calling the central information number (503/382.2442) unless otherwise noted.*

✦ **Skier Development Center** Make arrangements at this kiosk for the "Perfect Turn" instruction program. ♦ M-F 9AM-4PM; Sa-Su 8AM-4PM. Next to the West Village Lodge, second floor

✦ **Guest Services** Ticket windows line one side of this building. Inside are public lockers, the locker room for season passholders, large bathrooms, and a Will Call booth. ♦ M-F 9AM-4PM; Sa-Su 8AM-4PM. Middle of the West Village parking lot

✦ **Bachelor Ski & Sports** Alpine rentals are handled upstairs, in a facility with easy egress to the slopes. Downstairs are ski and snowboard shops, both spacious and well stocked. The former is rather staid, while the snowboard outlet is much hipper and flashier. A repair shop is also on the premises. ♦ M-F 9AM-4PM; Sa-Su 8AM-4PM. Next to West Village Lodge

✦ **West Village Lodge** This V-shaped structure is one of the original buildings at Bachelor. The ground floor contains a day care area and a common room with vending machines for skiers who are desperate to renew their sugar supply. An information booth, espresso stand, and convenient automatic bank teller machines are found on the second story. Upstairs at the **Cold Smoke Photography** booth, you can schedule individual or group portraits on the slopes (prints are developed overnight). The remainder of the top floor is a serviceable cafeteria, where you can order low-fat dishes, as well as the three major food groups: burgers, fries, and hot dogs. ♦ M-F 9AM-4PM; Sa-Su 8AM-4PM. Southeast corner of the West Village parking lot

Within West Village Lodge:

**Castle Keep Restaurant and Lounge**
★$$ It's only appropriate that this subterranean lounge should be dark and dingy. You'll feel somewhat less like a mole as you ascend to the upper levels or out to the decks. The rib-sticking menu has broadened to include fruit and veggie plates and a Sunday brunch with a full complement of natural whole-grain cereals. ♦ M-Sa breakfast and lunch; daily dinner; Sunday brunch

✦ **Pine Marten Lodge** This midmountain lodge makes extensive use of glass, so that visitors can enjoy the stunning perspectives of the Cascade Mountains from 7,700 feet. Architects have maximized the views with two exterior glass elevators—even though the building is only two stories tall. The lower level contains a ski shop, espresso bar, bathrooms, and a **Skier Development Center** booth. A cafeteria (serving uncharacteristically healthy cuisine) and a restaurant are upstairs. ♦ M-F 9AM-3:45PM; Sa-Su 8AM-3:45PM. Accessible off the Pine Marten Express Quad Chair

Within Pine Marten Lodge:

**Skier's Palate/South Sister Restaurant**
★★$$$ Cordoned off from the main cafeteria, this small eatery is *miles away* with respect to ambience; white cloths and china adorn the tables. Meals aren't meant to be inhaled, but to be savored. Try the Dungeness crab and bay shrimp sandwich or the grilled pistachio oysters. The margaritas routinely receive raves, as does the superb view of **South Sister** peak. ♦ Daily lunch. Reservations recommended. Second floor

✦ **Blue Lodge** This place was once integral to Bachelor's lodge plan, but over the years its role has been so diminished that you wonder whether the "Blue" in its moniker refers to its color or its attitude. Just a few basic services remain—rental and retail ski shops, bathrooms, lockers—ideal for skiers who tread the nearby intermediate and beginner runs. A cafeteria dishes up daily Italian specialties, as well as burgers, hot dogs, and soups. ♦ Sa-Su, holidays 8AM-4PM. Bottom of Skyliner Express Chair

Scandinavian loggers brought skiing to central Oregon in the late 1800s. Their skis, hand-hewn from local pine trees, were 10 to 12 feet long and best suited for going straight downhill.

✦ **Sunrise Lodge** There are three rules of operation here: function, function, and function. This lodge serves the northeastern slopes of Mount Bachelor, including the summit runs. Ticket windows are found to the left of the main entrance, and there are lockers and a cafeteria just beyond. The lower level houses rest rooms, a child care facility, and a ski rental, retail, and repair shop. ♦ M-F 9AM-4PM; Sa-Su 8AM-4PM. Bottom of Sunrise Express Chair

Within Sunrise Lodge:

**Sunrise Lounge** Come to this small but open and airy bar to study the mountain's northeast slopes. While you plot your next assault on the slopes, order a plate of fajitas or a burrito. ♦ M-F 11AM-4PM; Sa-Su 10AM-4PM. Upper floor

**Oregon Trail of Dreams Training Camp** Sleds pulled by 12-dog teams slide through the Deschutes National Forest, close to Mount Bachelor. Unlike other operations in the area, these are real racing dogs in training, and when trail conditions are just right, the sleds practically fly. This is a fantastic way to get into the backcountry. ♦ Tu-Su 9AM-5PM. Reservations required

## Beyond the Resort

1 **The Inn of the Seventh Mountain** $$$ This 300-room inn enjoys quiet surroundings and all the amenities necessary for an extended stay. The après-ski opportunities are abundant, from ice skating to horse-drawn sleigh rides, clover-shaped hot tubs, and swimming pools. Guest rooms are comfortable and contemporary, and most contain a fireplace and cooking facilities. Three restaurants (including one deli), a general store, and a ski shop can also be found on the property. Regular shuttle service runs to Mount Bachelor. ♦ 18575 SW Century Dr, 16 miles from Mount Bachelor, Bend. 382.8711, 800/452.6810; fax 382.3517

1 **Best Western Entrada Lodge** $$ A "lodge"? Sorry, this is a motel, pure and simple. But it's off the road (three miles west of Bend) and backed by woods, so the charm factor surpasses that of most accommodations of this ilk. All 79 rooms feature storage lockers for ski gear. There's also a heated outdoor pool for guests, and the hearty skier breakfast is enough to keep you going all day. ♦ 19221 SW Century Dr, 16 miles from Mount Bachelor, Bend. 382.4080, 800/528.1234; fax 382.4080

2 **Mount Bachelor Village** $$$ Don't be misled: This condominium development has nothing whatsoever to do with the ski area. It is commendable, however, for its location—set back from the road, with superb vistas of the Cascades and the Deschutes River. All 100 units come with kitchens and balconies, and some include hot tubs. A heated pool, tennis courts, and meandering walking trails along the river are available to all guests. ♦ 19717 Mount Bachelor Dr, 20 miles from Mount Bachelor, Bend. 389.5900, 800/452.9846; fax 388.7820

3 **Bend Alpine Hostel** $ Bend has needed a place like this for years: clean, fiscally feasible lodging for skiers more concerned with the great outdoors than indoor amenities. Opened in early 1993, the 42-bed Hostel has separate men's and women's dorms, and rooms for couples and families. A shared kitchen is available, as well as laundry facilities and a comfortable common room. Shuttle buses to Mount Bachelor leave from a stop five minutes away. ♦ 19 SW Century Dr (at Simpson Ave), Bend. 389.3813, 800/299.3813

4 **WestSide Bakery and Cafe** ★$ Enter here, all ye beautiful people. This is the place to be seen en route to the mountain. The fare is wholesome, whether you choose a full plate of huevos rancheros or blueberry flapjacks, or settle simply for baked goods washed down with good coffee. Sandwiches are built with thick slices of homemade bread. Expect crowds on weekends and holidays; most people will be wearing shades. ♦ Daily breakfast, lunch, and dinner. 1005 NW Galveston Ave (between NW Columbia and NW Federal Sts), Bend. 382.3426

5 **Lara House Bed and Breakfast** $$ A bed-and-breakfast inn of the highest order, this is a rambling 1910 residence in Bend's oldest neighborhood. The six guest rooms, scattered over three floors, are comfortable, and out-of-towners assemble around a large oak table each morning for a most filling repast. A large stone fireplace in the main room attracts cold hands and feet in the winter. Downtown is a five-minute walk away. ♦ 640 NW Congress St (at NW Louisiana Ave), Bend. 388.4064

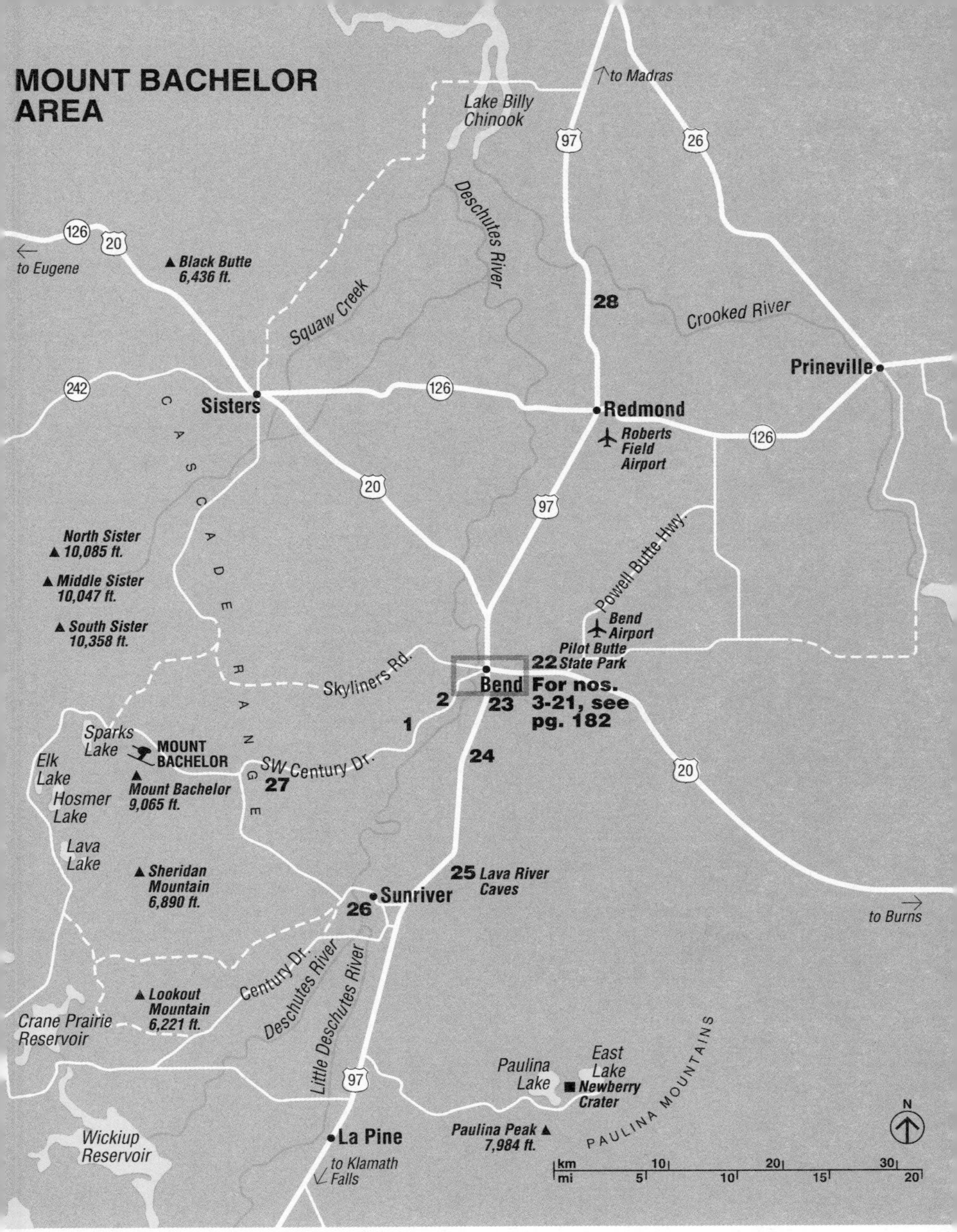

# MOUNT BACHELOR AREA

to Madras
Lake Billy Chinook
97
26
Deschutes River
126
20
to Eugene
Black Butte 6,436 ft.
Squaw Creek
28
Crooked River
Prineville
242
Sisters
126
Redmond
Roberts Field Airport
126
CASCADE RANGE
20
97
Powell Butte Hwy.
North Sister 10,085 ft.
Middle Sister 10,047 ft.
South Sister 10,358 ft.
Bend Airport
Pilot Butte
22 State Park
Skyliners Rd.
Bend
2
23
For nos. 3-21, see pg. 182
1
Sparks Lake
MOUNT BACHELOR
Elk Lake
SW Century Dr.
24
20
Mount Bachelor 9,065 ft.
27
Hosmer Lake
Lava Lake
Sheridan Mountain 6,890 ft.
25 Lava River Caves
Sunriver
26
to Burns
Century Dr.
Deschutes River
Little Deschutes River
Lookout Mountain 6,221 ft.
Crane Prairie Reservoir
Paulina Lake
East Lake
Newberry Crater
PAULINA MOUNTAINS
97
N
Wickiup Reservoir
La Pine
Paulina Peak 7,984 ft.
to Klamath Falls
km 10 20 30
mi 5 10 15 20

**6 Deschutes Historical Center** Pioneer artifacts and the history of central Oregon are the focus of the exhibits at this downtown museum. ♦ W-Sa 1PM-4:30PM. 129 NW Idaho Ave (between NW Bond and NW Wall Sts), Bend. 389.1813

**7 Cafe Sante** ★★$ Health foods are the order of the day, from real granola and floppy whole-wheat pancakes for breakfast to crunchy salads for lunch. The atmosphere is relaxed, with more locals than tourists finding their way here. ♦ Daily breakfast and lunch. 718 NW Franklin Ave (at NW Brooks St), Bend. 383.3530

**7 Baja Norte** ★★$ This restaurant is a godsend: an inexpensive, festive Mexican joint with window seating for congenial people watchers. The burritos are *muy buenos*. ♦ Daily lunch and dinner. NW Franklin Ave (at NW Wall St), Bend. 385.0611

**8 D&D Club** ★$ The "D Club," as it's often called, is a necessary stop on the locals' tour of Bend. Meals are of the lumberjack variety—the kind generally associated with places named "Ma's"—and the breakfasts are no exception. ♦ Daily breakfast, lunch, and dinner. 927 NW Bond St (at NW Minnesota Ave), Bend. 382.4592

**9 Columbia Outfitters** Columbia Sportswear is America's numero uno ski line, and this outlet store for the Portland-based company is a must-stop for visiting skiers. The selection of Columbia goods is broad and well priced, and the shop magnanimously carries other outerwear and accessory lines. ♦ M-Sa 10AM-6PM; Su 11AM-5PM. 939 NW Bond St (between NW Minnesota and NW Oregon Aves), Bend. 389.8993

**9 Café Paradiso** This cafe caters to the Bend intelligentsia with a decorative mix of funk and kitsch and consumable staples that run to fine beers, wine, coffees, and pastries. Look for an endless chess game in one corner, a group arguing politics around one of the large tables, and someone stretched out on a couch reading a book. Live music is offered on some weekends. ♦ Cover (when there's music). M-Th 8AM-11PM; F 8AM-midnight; Sa 10AM-midnight; Su 3PM-9PM. 945 NW Bond St (between NW Minnesota and NW Oregon Aves), Bend. 385.5931

**9 Stuft Pizza** ★$ Located in one of Bend's oldest buildings, this is the quintessential family restaurant. Pizzas are named after movie stars. The Basil Rathbone, for instance, features sun-dried tomatoes and pesto. Takeout is available. ♦ Daily lunch and dinner. 125 NW Oregon Ave (between NW Bond and NW Wall Sts). 382.4022

**10 Rosette** ★★★$$$ If you're homesick for a chic, intimate, well-lighted bistro, more upscale than down-home, with white linen tablecloths and relaxed ambience, here is central Oregon's version of same. The Northwest cuisine includes such delectables as rack of lamb with a Port, cherry, and morel glaze, and sautéed salmon in a sauce of pink peppercorn, Pinot Noir, and crème fraîche. And there's an excellent wine list to complement. ♦ Daily lunch and dinner. Reservations recommended. 150 NW Oregon Ave (between NW Bond and NW Wall Sts), Bend. 383.2780

**11 Goodys** How did this soda fountain survive this far into the late 20th century? Who cares, just be happy it has. Shakes, sundaes, and cones of rich ice cream and frozen yogurt, as well as candies are sold here. Those with a sweet tooth and families with children should make this an after-dinner destination. ♦ M-Th

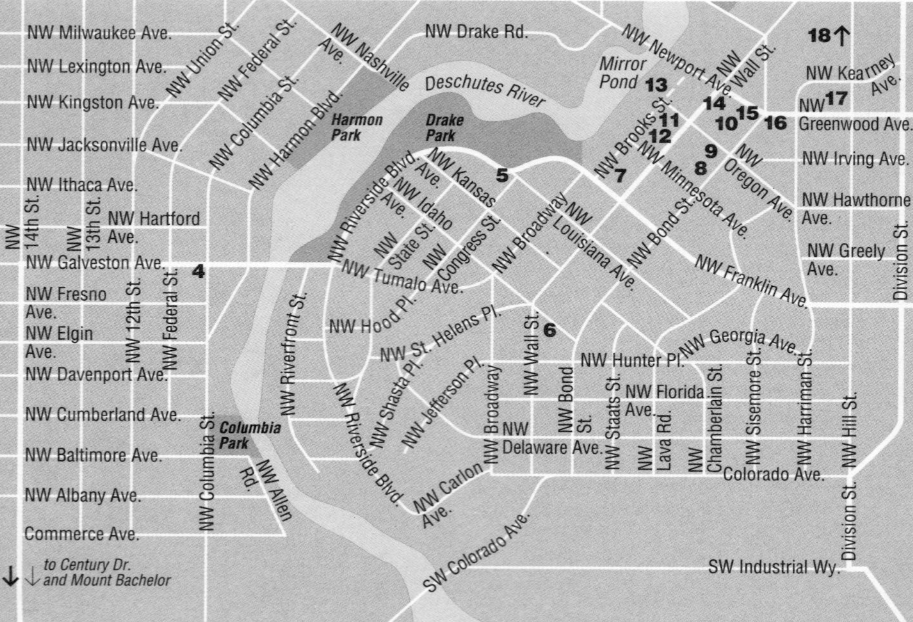

10AM-9PM; F-Sa 10AM-10PM; Su noon-8PM. 957 NW Wall St (at NW Oregon Ave). 389.5185

**12 Hudson's Grill** ★★$ Bend's best burgers and malts are served amidst a campy decor straight out of the 1950s. ♦ Daily lunch and dinner. 917 NW Wall St (between NW Minnesota and NW Oregon Aves), Bend. 385.7098

**13 Pine Tavern Restaurant** ★★$$ The late chef James Beard, a champion of classic American cooking, would have loved this place. It's an Oregon institution, half a century old, set amidst ancient pines and overlooking Mirror Pond. (Request a window table in the main dining room.) Gourmands looking for gargantuan portions might be a bit disappointed by the servings here, but diners searching for a pleasant atmosphere and well-prepared standards will go away happy. Prime rib is the prime draw, but steak and lamb together with pasta and seafood round out the menu. Local businesspeople eddy up in the small bar after work. ♦ Daily lunch and dinner. Reservations recommended. 967 NW Brooks St (foot of NW Oregon Ave, at Mirror Pond), Bend. 382.5581

**14 Sports Vision** Welcome to the most happening young people's store in town, with cutting-edge fashions and hard-to-find sunglasses. Owner and retail soothsayer Roberta Turley is well respected for her ability to forecast coming trends. ♦ M-Sa 10AM-6PM; Su 11AM-4PM. 1000 NW Wall St (between NW Oregon and NW Greenwood Aves), Bend. 388.1972

**15 McKenzie's Bar and Grill** ★★$$ Over the years and under several names, this restaurant has reliably purveyed middle-of-the-road meals, with an emphasis on steaks, fish, local game, and chicken. Keeping up with the health-conscious, McKenzie's salad bar is now renowned. Those in the market for a bar of a more sociable sort will find the après-ski scene lively indeed. ♦ Daily lunch and dinner. Reservations recommended. 1033 NW Bond St (at NW Greenwood Ave), Bend. 388.9099

**16 Yoko's Japanese Restaurant** ★★★$$ Some people praise the fare as the equal of what's found in San Francisco's Japantown. Aside from the sushi, try the chicken teriyaki and the tempura dishes. ♦ Daily lunch and dinner. Reservations recommended. 1028 NW Bond St (at NW Greenwood Ave), Bend. 382.2999

**16 Deschutes Brewery and Public House** ★$ Nowadays, it's near-impossible to visit a Northwest town of any size and not find a locally brewed beer. This brewery turns out some outstanding ales (try the Cascade Golden Ale), a fine, rich Black Butte Porter, and a memorable Bachelor Bitter; seasonal specialties are also on tap. Food is of the bourgeois brewpub type—say, lamb-vegetable soup and black bean chili. If the management banned snowboarders and anyone under 25 years of age, there wouldn't be a soul here most nights. ♦ Daily lunch and dinner. 1044 NW Bond St (at NW Greenwood Ave), Bend. 382.9242

**17 Community Theater of the Cascades** This small but exceptionally fine theater company is often blessed with performances by actors with big-city stage experience. Housed in a converted auto garage, the theater boasts a year-round schedule of dramas, comedies, and musicals. ♦ Call for schedules and showtimes. 148 NW Greenwood Ave (near NW Hill St), Bend. 389.0803

**17 Cafe News** You know that a town has become a happenin' place when it can support a club for new music, hip-hop, and reggae. This is the main after-dark venue for the young and hip. Tables get moved out of the way when dancing begins. ♦ Cover. F-Sa 9PM-2AM. 118 NW Greenwood Ave (near NW Hill St), Bend. 388.8330

**18 Bend Riverside Motel II** $$ There's nothing fancy about the 92 rooms here—some are even a bit worn—but this motel, right on the banks of the Deschutes River, is ideally located—a 10-minute walk from downtown. Try to get one of the few older, single-story units closest to the river, which are larger and peaceful. ♦ 1565 NW Hill St (adjacent to Pioneer Park), Bend. 388.4000, 800/228.4019; fax 388.4000

**19 The Riverhouse** $$ If you prefer comfort and familiarity to surprises, this 220-room inn offers standardized decor in natural surroundings. The Deschutes River bisects the property, and the wooded countryside nearby is full of walking options. No need to go elsewhere for meals and entertainment: Dine at the inn's fine continental restaurant and go dancing at the **Fireside Lounge** on weekends. If you can't dance country, no need to worry, free lessons are offered on Sunday evenings. Live music is offered nightly. ♦ 3075 N Hwy 97 (at Mount Washington Dr), Bend. 389.3111; fax 389.0870

---

The Last Chance run at Mount Bachelor was named by former mountain manager Cliff Blann, who said that beyond that point, skiers would not be able to find their way back to the lodge. Today, of course, there's skiing well beyond this run that has now changed it's name to LeeWay.

---

LE BISTRO

**19 Le Bistro** ★★★$$$ Upscale restaurants come and go in Bend, but this very French bistro has remained a constant. Though housed in what once served as a church, this restaurant manages to overcome the respectful austerity of its facade. Owner/chef Axel Hoch's sublime sauces garnish first-rate food, from duck breast with plum sauce and braised lamb shanks to seafood Wellington and chateaubriand. The wine list is remarkable for a Bend restaurant. Desserts (including a seductive Grand Marnier truffle) are homemade. Lighter eaters may prefer appetizers in the lounge. ♦ Daily dinner. Reservations recommended. 1203 NE Third St (between NE Greenwood and NE Revere Aves), Bend. 389.7274

**20 Mexicali Rose** ★★$$ The Cal/Mex cuisine served here is not as hot or as spicy as the usual south-of-the-border fare, but still extremely palatable and plentiful. Mexicali's bar is a popular hangout for locals. ♦ Daily dinner. 301 NE Franklin (at NE Third St), Bend. 389.0149

**21 Willie D's** New management claims they've mellowed this former disco enough for you to bring the kids—if you want to. If you still long for strobe-light dancing, come on Tuesday night dressed in your best 1970s outfit. Wednesday is karaoke night; Thursday is comedy; and Friday and Saturday are reserved for live country or blues bands. Free country dance lessons are offered on Sunday night. ♦ Cover on weekends. Daily 4:30PM-1AM. 197 NE Third St (near NE Burnside Ave), Bend. 382.2687

**22 Pilot Butte State Park** A twisting road leads to the top of this old volcanic cinder cone; the view over Bend and the snowcapped Cascades is unsurpassed. ♦ Daily 8AM-6PM. NE Greenwood Ave (between NE 12th St and McCartney Dr), Bend. No phone

**23 Chan's** ★★★$$ Without question, this is the best bang-for-your-buck eatery in Bend. Szechuan, Hunan, and Cantonese cookery all conspire to delight diners with servings so big that leftovers inevitably travel home with you. ♦ Daily lunch and dinner. Reservations recommended. 1005 SE Third St (across from Bend Cinemas), Bend. 389.1725

**24 High Desert Museum** Only now, long after the death of the wild West, are Americans beginning to appreciate what this part of the country was like before freeways crisscrossed the land. This museum is a memory jogger for our collective conscience. In this repository (founded in 1974) of natural and manmade history, you can learn about "a day in the life of the high desert," complete with a cave simulation, sweat lodge nestled up to a faux river bank, fur trader's camp, and working saddlery. Early paintings by Charles M. Russell and black-and-white photos by Seattle's Edward Curtis share wall space. Outside the museum are 20 acres of nature trails, where gawkers can take in cavorting river otters and porcupines, as well as a re-created settler's cabin. The museum's **Doris Swayze Bounds Collection,** believed to be one of the nation's largest holdings of American art and artifacts, includes items associated with Chief Joseph and Crazy Horse, leather clothing, beadwork, horse regalia, and porcupine quillworks. This museum is an absolute must for all, especially families. ♦ Admission. Daily 9AM-5PM. 59800 S Hwy 97 (5 miles south of Bend). 382.4754

**25** **Lava River Caves** Okay, it's not Carlsbad Caverns, but these cavities in the earth still earn oohs and aahs from vacationing spelunkers. Descending a mile-long lava tube, you'll feel rather like the intrepid explorers in Jules Verne's *Journey to the Center of the Earth.* Bring a jacket along, for despite legends of fire at the planet's core, it's *cold* down there. A visitors' center provides a panorama over central Oregon's volcanic landscape and plenty of interesting historical displays. ♦ Mid-March through end of October. 12 miles south of Bend, off US Hwy 97. 593.2421

**26** **Sunriver Resort** $$$$ This is central Oregon's most complete resort-cum-small town. Lodging varies from small condo units to privately owned houses, and it takes both hands and two feet to tick off all the amenities available. There are 145 condos and 211 guest rooms in total. Suffice it to say the setting is magnificent, the restaurants satisfying, and plenty of activities are available for children. In summer, guests use the property's golf courses and hiking trails, but in winter, you'll have to settle for indoor racquetball courts and flesh-filled hot tubs. Shucks. Shuttle buses take skiers to the mountain, 18 miles away. ♦ 15 miles south of Bend, off US Hwy 97, Sunriver, Oregon. 593.1221, 800/547.3922; fax 593.5458

**27** **Fantastic Recreation and Rentals** In the market for guided or unguided snowmobile tours through the **Deschutes National Forest?** This is your opportunity. The **Fantastic** folks schedule two- and four-hour excursions through the forest, with longer ones available by prior arrangement. ♦ Daily 9AM-4PM. Reservations required. Tours leave from Wanoga Sno Park, S Century Dr, 13 miles from downtown, Bend. 389.5640

**28** **Smith Rock State Park** For years, Smith Rock was a quiet place, admired for its wonderfully colored volcanic rock cliffs, looming over the Crooked River. But since the international rock-climbing community discovered the park, it's now renowned for having some of the most difficult sport-climbing routes in the world, which attract legions of rock jocks. Hikers and mountain bikers can also find what they're looking for—quiet, wooded trails. ♦ Daily 8AM-6PM. 9241 NE Crooked River, 22 miles north of Bend, Terrebonne. 548.7501

## Bests

### Stuart Craig
Ski instructor, Mount Bachelor

In Mount Bachelor:

Catching sight of the deer and elk herds that winter on the **Inn of the Seventh Mountain Golf Course.**

Cruising at speed on **Coffee** or **West Boundary;** cruising at speed, with air time, on **Cliffhanger.**

Morning run on the **Cinder Cone,** then admiring your tracks on the ride up the Pine Marten Chair.

Powder hunting in the **Western Bowls.**

Bump jumping under Red Chair, or the challenge of the massively ungroomed on **Grotto,** right next door.

Views of the **Three Sisters, Broken Top,** even **Mount Shasta** to the south from the summit.

Skiing the vast backside.

A romantic ride up Rainbow Chair, you and a special friend. Added bonus: The terrain around Rainbow is all of the cruising variety, usually deserted, and typically holds the last of the untracked powder.

High-flying adventure on the nordic trails: Skating down **Devecka's Dive** to **Oli's Alley** and on to **Rich's Range;** everything an adrenaline/endorphin junkie could want: Mach 5 descents over twisty trails, serious air time, long uphills, and the solitude alpine skiers can only dream about.

In Bend:

**Deschutes Brewery,** for a cask-conditioned Obsidian Stout.

A malt at **Goodys** or **Hudson's Grill.**

**Stuft Pizza,** for an Italian sausage, black olive, green pepper, sun-dried tomato, and pepperoni pizza; the leftovers make a superb pre-ski breakfast.

A trip to **Smith Rock State Park** in Terrebonne is like traveling into a Western movie.

### Tom DeWolf
Owner, Westside Video & Comics/Film Critic, KTVZ/City Commissioner

**Cafe Sante**—Delicious vegetarian fare.

**Skyliner**—Head out of town toward Tumalo Falls and cross-country ski where all the "real people" go.

**Cougar Hot Springs**—It's actually 90 miles west, toward Eugene, but there's no better place on earth to soak in the hot springs, looking up through the pines into a beautiful night sky, with snowflakes falling on your face.

# Deer Valley

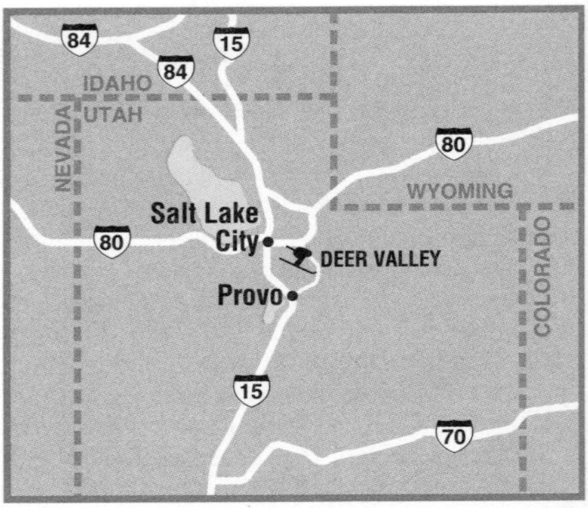

When Deer Valley opened in 1980, it was on the premise that some skiers wouldn't mind spending a few extra dollars to avoid muddy parking lots, long lift lines, and rubbery slope-side food. The concept has certainly paid off. Today, Deer Valley, the most expensive of Utah's resorts, has garnered glowing accolades in nearly every skiing, travel, and food magazine.

Arriving at Deer Valley, visitors are greeted by ski valets who not only unload your equipment but keep an eye on it while you park. The on-mountain restaurants raise the standard of ski cuisine to a pinnacle; some say they're the best of any US resort. Ticket sales are limited to ensure short (or even nonexistent) lift lines. And the mountains' maintenance is—in a word—immaculate.

Only one mile away from the **Park City** ski resort in the **Wasatch Mountains,** Deer Valley is made up of three mountains—**Bald, Flagstaff,** and **Bald Eagle.** The terrain is suitable primarily for beginners and intermediates, so hard-core mogul mashers and black-diamond skiers might find the slopes a bit tame. But for skiers who enjoy caressing baby-bottom smooth runs, Deer Valley is the place to be.

**Deer Valley**
**PO Box 3149**
**Park City, Utah 84060**

**Information**........................................801/649.1000

**Reservations** ............801/649.1000, 800/424.DEER

**Snow Phone** ........................................801/649.2000

**Road Conditions**................................801/946.6000

## Fast Facts

*Area code 801 unless otherwise noted.*

**Ski Season** Early December to early April

**Location** Situated on the eastern slope of the **Wasatch Mountains,** Deer Valley is 35 miles from **Salt Lake City.**

### Getting to Deer Valley

**By air:** The nearest airport is **Salt Lake International Airport**; it's a 40-minute drive to Deer Valley. **Delta** offers the most frequent service to **Salt Lake City,** with 44 nonstop flights daily. **American** offers daily nonstops from **Chicago** and **Dallas/Ft. Worth. America West** flies nonstop daily from **Phoenix** and **Las Vegas.** Other carriers include **Continental, Northwest, Sky West, Southwest, TWA, United,** and **Vanguard.** When you touch down, you can take one of many regularly scheduled shuttle buses to the resort: **All Resort Express** (649.3999, 800/457.9457); **Lewis Brothers Stages** (1/359.8347, 800/826.5844); **Park City Transportation** (649.8567, 800/637.3803); **Summit Transportation** (649.3292, 800/388.5289); **Super Express Shuttle Service** (1/250.4600, 800/321.5554). Taxi service is also available.

**By bus: Greyhound** (800/231.2222) makes daily stops in **Salt Lake City.** The station is located at South Temple and 200 West, across from the Salt Palace. The shuttle companies listed above service the bus station.

**By car:** Winterized rental cars are available at the airport from **Alamo, Avis, Budget, Dollar, Hertz,** and **National.** From **Salt Lake City** follow Interstate 80 East to State Road 224. Turn south and drive six miles to the base area. Deer Valley is one mile away; follow signs to the resort.

**By train: Amtrak** (800/USA.RAIL) stops daily at the **Rio Grande Depot** in downtown **Salt Lake City.** Transportation to the resort may be arranged with one of the companies listed above.

### Getting around Deer Valley

**Park City Transit** (645.5129) offers free shuttle service linking stops between **Park City** and Deer Valley resorts. Buses run every 20 minutes from 6AM-1AM.

## FYI

**Area** 1,100 acres with 67 runs

Beginner—15 percent

Intermediate—50 percent

Advanced—35 percent

**Number of Groomed Runs** 30

**Longest Run** 2.2 miles **(Sunset/Ontario)**

**Capacity** 22,800 skiers per hour

**Base Elevation** 7,200 feet

**Summit Elevation** 9,400 feet

**Vertical Rise** 2,200 feet

**Average Annual Snowfall** 300 inches

**Snowmaking** 22 percent

**Night Skiing** None

**Lifts** 13 (2 high-speed quads, 9 triple chairs, and 2 double chairs)

| Lift Passes | Full Day | Half Day (starts at 1PM) |
|---|---|---|
| **Adult** | $47 | $34 |
| **Child** (12 and under) | $26 | $19 |
| **Senior** (65 and over) | $32 | $22 |

**Ski School** The office (649.1000) is located at **Snow Park Lodge.** Group lessons run daily from 11AM to 4PM. Private lessons, lasting from one hour to all day, are available for one or two people.

**Kids' Ski School** Children ages 6 to 12 can sign up for a fully supervised daylong program (10AM to 4PM); lunch included.

**Clinics and Special Programs Teen Equipe** is a workshop teaching advanced techniques for 13- to 18-year-olds. **The Black Diamond Workshop** is for adult skiers who want to improve their skills on a variety of challenging terrains.

**Races The Medalist Challenge** takes place on the **Race Course** run above the **Silver Lake Lodge.** It's open Monday, Wednesday, Friday, and Saturday, 10AM to 1PM. Serious downhillers should check out the course on Friday, when the pacesetter is none other than Stein Eriksen, Olympic gold medalist and Deer Valley's Director of Skiing. On the remaining days of the week, a self-timed dual slalom is in operation.

**Rentals The Deer Valley Rental Shop** (649.1000 or 800/424.3337) is located on the bottom level of **Snow Park Lodge.** Open daily 8AM to 5PM, it offers junior, standard, sport, high-performance, and premium packages. Ski tune-ups are performed by certified technicians.

**Lockers** Daytime or overnight ski storage is complimentary at the outdoor ski corrals next to the **Snow Park** and **Silver Lake Lodges.** Basket checks for other gear are located inside the lodges on the lower levels.

**Day Care** Indoor day care for children, ages 2 months to 12 years, is available in **Snow Park Lodge** from 8:30AM to 4:30PM.

**First Aid** Full service medical stations, open daily 9AM to 5PM, are located in **Snow Park Lodge** (645.6618) and in the **Royal Plaza Building** (645.6900) next to **Silver Lake Lodge.** The nearest hospital is the **Park City Family Health and Emergency Center** (649.7640) at 1665 Bonanza Drive.

**Parking** There is free parking at the base. **Park City** operates a free municipal shuttle connecting all hotels to the base; these run approximately every 20 minutes.

**Worth Knowing**

- Those who need a break from alpine skiing have their choice of helicopter tours, mountaineering, sleigh riding, snowcat riding, and snowmobiling.
- Deer Valley earns its reputation for pampering its guests. It may have just about the best on-mountain lunch cuisine in the country. Small extras like tissues at the lifts—and even chocolate goodies at some—go a long way.

## Rating the Runs

### ● Beginner

Flat but cruiseable nonetheless, **Success** gives beginners the opportunity to ride Carpenter Express, one of the area's high-speed quads. The pitch lets you really feel the breeze in your face without losing control. There's some great scenery, too.

For recent masters of the snowplow, **Wide West** is a great place to gain basic experience.

### ■ Intermediate

Although crowded at times, **Birdseye** is a broad route that allows for incredibly smooth turning. The fall line is nearly perfect and the grooming impeccable.

Feeding off Carpenter Express, **Solid Muldoon** offers a quick and cool cruise to the bottom. Narrow on top, the path widens out as it nears the base, allowing for some nice sweeping turns.

### ◆ Advanced

Yes, Deer Valley does have bumps, and the best are on **Rattler,** the black beauty that skirts below the lower end of the Wasatch Lift.

An expansive glade of aspen between **Reward** and **Tycoon, Triangle Trees** (on **Bald Mountain**) is where the locals head after storms clear. Not really a run, the terrain is steep and ungroomed, the powder glorious, and the trees spaced just right.

### Snowboarding

There is no snowboarding permitted at Deer Valley. Head to the **Park West Resort,** the only mountain in the **Parley's Canyon** area to welcome snowboarders. Boasting two half-pipes, the resort also offers 2,200 vertical feet, seven double chairlifts, 850 acres, and snowmaking capabilities.

## Mountain Highs and Lows

It may be that **Big Stick** is occasionally left to grow moguls, or it could be that the patchwork of shade and sun gives an unpredictable texture to the snow, but for some reason this run requires a bit more stamina and turning ability than other intermediate trails. Try it if you feel strong, but check on the snow conditions first.

Not really steeper than nearby **Success, Dew Drop** would be a simple slide if it were not for one steep pitch. Ski it anyway; it's a fun run.

## At the Resort

✦ **Olive Barrel** ★★★★$$$ It's hard to believe that pizza can taste this good, or this pricey. Designed to look like a small Italian market (and they do sell culinary items for your own Italian kitchen), this intimate place takes the concept far beyond gobs of bland mozzarella and boring canned tomato sauce. How does a brie cheese, spinach, and Italian sausage combo sound? ♦ Daily lunch and dinner. Reservations recommended. Silver Lake Lodge at Deer Valley. 647.7777

✦ **McHenry's Grill** ★★★$$ If you don't feel like traying it, come here for a good, casual meal with table service. Generous portions of above-average lodge fare like grilled sandwiches, chili, soups, and salad are available for lunch while the evening menu offers light fare as well as more substantial pastas, grilled specialties, and seafood. An après-ski menu with a variety of creative appetizers and specialty beers attracts skiers from 2:30PM to 5:30PM. ♦ Daily lunch and dinner. Silver Lake Lodge at Deer Valley. 645.6724

✦ **Mariposa's** ★★★★$$$ This upscale dining room offers guests a rustic but elegant atmosphere and serves unusual continental fare. Specialties include sautéed tiger prawns with a shrimp tamale and roasted corn sauce or charbroiled fillet of beef wrapped in maple-peppered bacon with horseradish béarnaise sauce. For those with more traditional tastes, try the grilled pork tenderloin with cranberry chutney, rack of lamb with crisp potatoes, or roasted chicken with spinach and shiitake mushrooms. ♦ Daily dinner. Silver Lake Lodge at Deer Valley. 645.6715

✦ **Stein Eriksen Lodge** $$$$ Ski out after spending the night in this exquisite 126-room lodge and you'll think you're heading for the Alps. From the big stone fireplaces to the artful arrangements of dried flowers, the place radiates European charm. You'll definitely spend big bucks to stay here, so lie back and savor how the watchful but unobtrusive staff anticipates and attends to your every whim. ♦ 7700 Stein Way (the Silver Lake Village at Deer Valley). 649.3700, 800/453.1302; fax 649.5825

Within Stein Eriksen Lodge:

**Glitretind** ★★★★$$$$ This award-winning restaurant is considered to be the crème de la crème of Deer Valley eateries. An appetizer is a must—try potato lasagna or a grilled vegetable tart. Entrées include such tantalizing creations as peppered tuna, Peking duck, and New Zealand red deer. Arrive early for their daily breakfast and lunch skiers' buffet to beat the in-the-know crowd. ♦ Daily breakfast, lunch, and dinner. Reservations recommended. 645.6455

***For more information on the Deer Valley area, see "Beyond the Resorts," page 192.***

**Restaurants/Clubs:** Red | **Hotels:** Blue
**Shops/ Outdoors:** Green | **Sights/Culture:** Black

## Bests

### Bradley A. Olch
Mayor of Park City

Skiing at **Deer Valley**—high-speed, nonstop runs down **Stein's Way** and **Reward.**

Lunch at **Deer Valley**—The best food of any ski resort in the world.

Skiing at the **Park City Ski Area**—Bottomless powder in **Jupiter Bowl.**

Best restaurants—**Riverhorse Cafe** and **Mariposa's.**

Best restaurant for families—**McHenry's Grill.**

Best restaurant for locals—**Nacho Mama's.**

Best new sport in Park City—Ski jumping at the new **Winter Sports Park** (lessons are available).

### Stein Eriksen
Director of Skiing, Deer Valley Resort

Dining at the quaint and rustic **Mariposa's.**

Staying at the lodge offering European elegance that just happens to bear my name, the **Stein Eriksen Lodge.**

An evening stroll on Park City's historic **Main Street,** home to a number of galleries, boutiques, and restaurants.

Evening sleigh rides or a morning hot-air balloon excursion for a beautiful view of the **Wasatch Mountains.**

Relaxing at **McHenry's Beach** on a warm spring afternoon.

### Charlie Lansche
PR/Communications Director at Park City

The historic Victorian neighborhoods near **Main Street,** where it feels like you've stepped back one hundred years in time.

Blue tacos and Mexican beers with friends at **Nacho Mama's** in **Prospector Square.**

Sunny afternoon lunches with the boys at the historic **Mid-Mountain Lodge** deck—relaxing alpine tranquillity, good food, and one of the largest outdoor decks in Utah can be found at this former miner's boardinghouse.

The 15-minute hike from the top of the Jupiter Chairlift to **Jupiter Peak.** You'll be rewarded with a spectacular view of the **Wasatch** and **Uinta Mountains.** I usually ski **Hourglass Chute** or the fickle **Twilight Zone** off the peak and always experience that "life is wonderful" feeling when I look back up at my tracks in **Puma Bowl.**

Long, fast cruises down **Keno, Legal Tender,** or **Wizard**—the billiard table–smooth runs accessed from the Sultan Chair at Deer Valley. This is the place to carve big turns on Deer Valley's famous "ego" snow.

Relaxing in the afternoon sun at **McHenry's Beach,** where you're likely to see as many famous faces as friends. The food inside the **Silver Lake Lodge** or **McHenry's Grill** rivals the best restaurants in town.

Listening to joyous shouts and screams emanating from the trees and secret powder caches in **Jupiter Bowl** on the first run of an epic powder day.

Après-ski entertainment, beer swilling, and people watching at **Steeps** in the **Gondola Building.**

Blueberry sourdough pancakes, exotic coffees, and interesting people at the **Morning Ray Cafe & Bakery.**

The dogs that gather in front of the **Alamo Saloon** on **Main Street** are a Park City institution and an integral part of ski town culture.

The Motherlode triple chair is a scenic ride—and there's never a lift line, even on the busiest holidays. You'll find good bumps on **Ford Country** and groomed cruising on **Sunnyside.**

# Park City

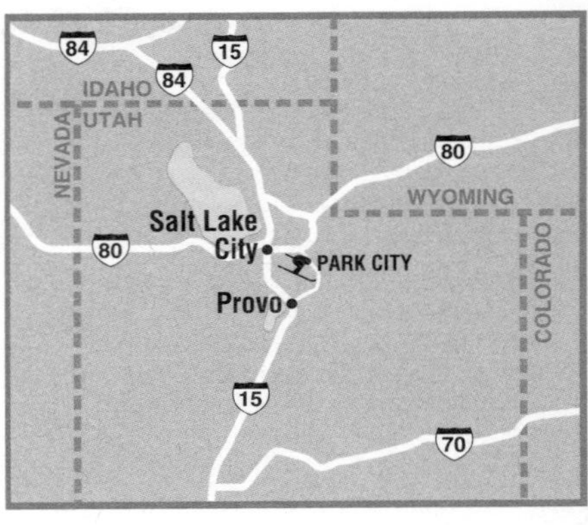


The fact that Park City is **Utah's** only real ski town might give some ski enthusiasts who equate quality with ritzy après-ski recreational opportunities cause for concern. Yes, Park City is sprouting clusters of new town houses behind its gossamer white veils of trails with head-spinning regularity. And the resort has several other strong selling points to silence even the harshest of critics. Perhaps the most persuasive is its logistics. Located just 40 minutes from the **Salt Lake International Airport**, it's the most conveniently located ski destination in the country. Another appeal is the fact that Park City, unlike other so-called ski towns, is the real thing: a year-round, fully outfitted town with a mind-boggling array of restaurant and hotel choices. Toss in its flamboyant past, and Park City comes up with character to spare.

In the late 1800s, Park City was abuzz with all of the commotion of a prosperous silver mining town. Dozens of saloons lined Main Street and there was a thriving red-light district. A pair of train depots welcomed throngs of newcomers intent on striking it rich. Although the surrounding mountains no longer resound with the din of picks and shovels, today you can still discover the Park City that once was by visiting its fascinating, preserved Main Street district.

But Park City's Old West flavor aside, it is the skiing that attracts so many winter visitors to the back side of the **Wasatch Mountains.**

Utah's largest ski resort, Park City Ski Area boasts an incredible variety of terrain serviced by a very efficient lift system. Every level of skier will feel at home here. Beginners aren't relegated to poling around the base area; they can quickly chalk up miles on one of 14 easy-to-navigate runs. Nearly half of the area's 89 trails are intermediate in difficulty. Some are mogul runs, but most are regularly groomed for some truly wonderful cruising. This is not to say, however, that expert skiers should look elsewhere for thrills. In fact, Park City has some 650 acres of challenging turf in the bowls that shroud **Jupiter Peak.** Wide open and ungroomed, they are the stuff of which a powderhound's dreams are made.

As you hurtle down the hills at Park City, you may want to check out your slope mates. Chances are they could be Olympic contenders: The **US Ski Team** moved its headquarters here from Colorado in 1974. Take your cue about Park City from this elite group: They *know* where to ski.

---

**Park City Ski Area**
**PO Box 39**
**Park City, Utah 84060**

**Information**........................................801/649.8111

**Park City Chamber of Commerce/Visitors Bureau**
..................................801/649.6100, 800/453.1360

**Snow Phone** ......................................801/647.5335

**Road Conditions**................................801/946.6000

## Fast Facts

*Area code 801 unless otherwise noted.*

**Ski Season** Mid-November to mid-April.

**Location** Situated on the eastern slope of the **Wasatch Mountains,** Park City Ski Area is 27 miles from **Salt Lake City.**

## Getting to Park City

**By air:** The nearest airport is **Salt Lake International Airport,** a 35-minute drive from Park City. **Delta** offers the most frequent service to **Salt Lake City,** with 44 nonstop flights daily. **American** offers daily nonstops from **Chicago** and **Dallas/Ft. Worth. America West** flies nonstop daily from **Phoenix** and **Las Vegas.** Other carriers include **Continental, Northwest, Sky West, Southwest, TWA, United,** and **Vanguard.** When you touch down, you can take one of many regularly scheduled shuttle buses to the resort: **All Resort**

**Express** (649.3999, 800/457.9457); **Lewis Brothers Stages** (1/359.8347, 800/826.5844); **Park City Transportation** (649.8567, 800/637.3803); **Summit Transportation** (649.3292, 800/388.5289); **Super Express Shuttle Service** (1/250.4600, 800/321.5554). Taxi service is also available.

**By bus: Greyhound** (800/231.2222) makes daily stops in **Salt Lake City.** The station is located at South Temple and 200 West, across from the Salt Palace. The shuttle companies listed above service the bus station as well.

**By car:** Winterized rental cars are available at the airport from **Alamo, Avis, Budget, Dollar, Hertz,** or **National.** From **Salt Lake City** follow Interstate 80 East to State Road 224. Turn south and drive six miles to the base area.

**By train: Amtrak** (800/USA.RAIL) stops daily at the **Rio Grande Depot** in downtown **Salt Lake City.** Transportation to the resort may be arranged with one of the aforementioned shuttle companies.

## Getting around Park City

**Park City Transit** (645.5129) offers free shuttle service linking stops between Park City and **Deer Valley** resorts. Buses run every 20 minutes.

## FYI

Park City Ski Area

**Area** 2,200 acres with 89 runs

Beginner—16 percent

Intermediate—45 percent

Advanced—39 percent

**Number of Groomed Runs** 58

**Longest Run** 3.5 miles (Following the Gondola, take **Claimjumper** to **Bonanza,** then **Sidewinder** to the base.)

**Capacity** 23,000 skiers per hour

**Base Elevation** 6,900 feet

**Summit Elevation** 10,000 feet

**Vertical Rise** 3,100 feet

**Average Annual Snowfall** 350 inches

**Snowmaking** 18 percent

**Night Skiing** Daily 4PM-10PM, from Christmas through March

**Lifts** 14 (1 gondola, 2 high-speed quads, 1 quad, 6 triple chairs, 4 double chairs)

| **Lift Passes** | **Full Day** | **Half Day** (starts at 1PM) |
|---|---|---|
| **Adult** | $45 | $32 |
| **Child** (12 and under) | $20 | $15 |
| **Senior** (65-69) | $22 | $22 |
| **Senior** (70 and over) | Free | Free |

**Ski School** Two offices (800/227.2SKI) are located at **Ski Area Plaza,** and at the top of the Prospector high-speed quad and the Gondola. Choose from either a half-day (two-hour session) or an all-day group lesson (two four-hour sessions). Private lessons are also available.

**Kids' Ski School** Full-day, half-day, group, and private lessons are offered through **Kinderschule** (649.8111) to children ages 3 to 6. A lift ticket is included for all students. Reservations are suggested for these high-demand classes.

**Clinics and Special Programs** The **Mountain Experience Class** is a four-hour lesson that takes high-intermediate and expert skiers into the high bowls, glades, and less-visited runs. **Ski Week** is a Monday to Wednesday clinic offering advanced lessons in a fun-filled group setting, including an après-ski party, video critique, three-day lift tickets, and a race day. The **Women's Ski Challenge** is hosted by former **US Ski Team** racer Kristi Terziaj (1994 National Slalom Champion). Park City has also developed a nationally recognized ski program for the disabled. Private lessons are provided and various race events take place throughout the season.

**Races** A NASTAR course, open Wednesday through Saturday (10AM to 2PM), is offered on **Lost Prospector.** For a small fee, racers can also whiz down **Clementine** in the daily **Park City Challenge,** a timed run on a dual course.

**Rentals** There are 10 rental shops at the **Park City Resort Center,** open daily 8AM to 6PM and until 10PM for night skiing. All offer recreation, performance, and demo grade packages. Most provide free overnight storage for their customers. **Breeze Ski Rentals** (649.2736); **Cole Sport Ltd.** (649.4600, 800/345.2983); **Destination Sports** (649.8092, 800/247.6197); **Gart Brothers** (649.2002, 800/284.4754); **Jakes** (649.0355); **Jans** (649.2500, 800/745.1020); **Kindersport** (junior equipment only; 649.5463) **Park City Sport** (645.7777, 800/523.3922); **Ski Connection** (649.8430); and **Ski-n-See** (649.9690).

**Lockers** Coin-operated lockers are located in the **Gondola Building.**

**Day Care** Although no child care is available at the resort itself, youngsters ages 3 to 6 may be enrolled in the **Kinderschule** program, open daily 8:30AM to 4:30PM. This half- or all-day program includes ski lessons, lunch, and plenty of skilled supervision. Children should be out of diapers and have their own ski equipment. A number of off-slope day-care facilities are available. **Baby's Away** (645.8823) will pick up and deliver children to and from facilities. The **Professional Sitters' Service** (649.0946) offers in-room care.

> Proof that Park City is the country's most accessible ski town are the nearly 500 commercial airline pilots who call it home. Their idea of a commute is driving to Salt Lake International Airport and catching a plane to the hub city of their respective employers.

**First Aid** Mountain clinics are located at either end of the **Gondola.** The one at the bottom is full service. Call the main switchboard at 649.8111. The **Park City Health and Emergency Center** (649.7640) is located at 1665 Bonanza Drive.

**Parking** There is free parking at the base. The city provides a free bus shuttle from every hotel and property. It runs approximately every 15 minutes.

**Worth Knowing**

- At Thanksgiving, Park City hosts the annual America's Opening, which marks the start of the World Cup season. It's not unusual to see World Cup starts like Alberto Tomba or Tommy Moe parading around town and tearing up the slopes.

## Rating the Runs

### ● Beginner

Actually three runs (**Claimjumper, Bonanza,** and **Sidewinder**) in one, the **Easiest Way Down** long-distance haul will give novices the thrill of skiing the Gondola from top to bottom. It is also recommended for intermediates eager to rack up some vertical footage.

With the help of an instructor, first-timers will find their ski legs in no time on **Three Kings,** a short and gentle run.

### ■ Intermediate

With just the right fall line, and groomed to perfection, **Hidden Splendor** is a real confidence builder for intermediates. Ride the Prospector high-speed quad to get in several quick runs before advancing to tougher slopes.

When it's not too crowded **Pay Day** is a joy. Arcing to the right of the chairlift of the same name, this broad, sweeping blue trail offers great cruising right into the base area. It's also the longest nighttime run in the Rockies.

### ◆ Advanced

To find powder paths that are unsurpassed, head for the Jupiter Lift and **Jupiter Bowl** first thing after a storm. When it comes to playing it steep, this run has it all: chutes, evergreen glades, and wide-open faces.

The bumps on **Thaynes** will give your knees a good knocking. The moguls are nicely sized, and the trail is served by its own chairlift—a boon for anyone who abhors skiing catwalks.

### Snowboarding

No snowboarding is permitted at the Park City Ski Area. Head to the **Park West Resort,** the only mountain in the **Parley's Canyon** area to welcome snowboarders. Boasting two half-pipes, the resort also offers 2,200 vertical feet, seven double chairlifts, 850 acres, and snowmaking capabilities.

## Mountain Highs and Lows

A short pitch directly above the **Gondola Angle Station, Silver Queen** is much easier than the trail map indicates. Regularly groomed and not quite as steep as the average black-diamond run, it's where intermediates go to pretend they're Jean-Claude Killy.

## At the Resort

*Area code 801 unless otherwise noted.*

✦ **Shadow Ridge** $$$ Located near the foot of the lifts, this condo/hotel offers some of the most convenient and commodious rooms in town. Each of the 50 condominium units—perfect for families—includes one or two spacious bedrooms, an even larger living area, a kitchen, a wood-burning fireplace, and two or three baths. ♦ 50 Shadow Ridge Rd (off Empire St). 649.4300, 800/451.3031; fax 649.5951

✦ **Baja Cantina** ★★ $$ Home cooking—Mexican style—is what this fun base-of-the-mountain restaurant is all about. The Baja Fiesta combination plate is really a deal: The prescient staff presents it with a large doggie bag. ♦ Daily lunch and dinner. Base of Park City Ski Area. 649.2252

✦ **Mid-Mountain Lodge** ★★$ In the 19th century this day lodge served as sleeping quarters for silver miners. Painstakingly relocated and renovated (including adding an 11,000-square-foot outdoor deck), it now serves cafeteria lunches that are tastier than the typical on-mountain fare. ♦ Daily lunch. Base of the Pioneer Chairlift. 649.3044

## Beyond the Resorts

1 **Wasatch Brew Pub** ★$ Don't be surprised if friends back home ask you to bring back a six-pack of the Wasatch Ale or Slickrock Lager from this pub, Utah's first modern-day brewery. ♦ Daily lunch and dinner. 250 Main St (at Daly Ave). 649.0900

**Restaurants/Clubs:** Red **Hotels:** Blue
**Shops/ Outdoors:** Green **Sights/Culture:** Black

**2 El Cheepo Southwestern Grill** ★★$ Yes, it is easy on the budget. Start out with the wings or Bar BQ Bones, then move on to a chicken dish. The atmosphere is casual, and kids are welcome. ♦ Daily lunch and dinner. 255 Main St (between Second and Third Sts). 649.0883

**3 Morning Ray Cafe & Bakery/Evening Star Dining** ★★$ Actually two restaurants in one, the **Morning Ray** serves breakfast and lunch, while the **Evening Star** is strictly for dinner. Leave enough wake-up time for the *huevos rancheros* or the organic buttermilk pancakes. Lunch is mostly sandwiches, while dinner is a mix of veggie dishes. ♦ Daily breakfast, lunch, and dinner. 268 Main St (between Daly Ave and Forth St). 649.5686

**4 The Eating Establishment** ★★$$ Although this is primarily a barbecue and steak place, the roasted peppers and cilantro used generously throughout the menu give it a southwestern accent. Try the Texas meat loaf prepared with *chorizo.* ♦ Daily breakfast, lunch, and dinner. 317 Main St (between Daly Ave and Forth St). 649.8284

**5 The Egyptian Theatre** This 1926 Main Street landmark is modeled after Warner's Egyptian Theatre in Pasadena, California. Built to replace the **Dewey Theatre,** which collapsed under heavy snow, it is home to **Park City Performances.** Check the schedule for Broadway musicals and comedy shows. Even if you don't take in a play, be sure to marvel at the ornate facade. ♦ 328 Main St (off Forth St). 649.9371

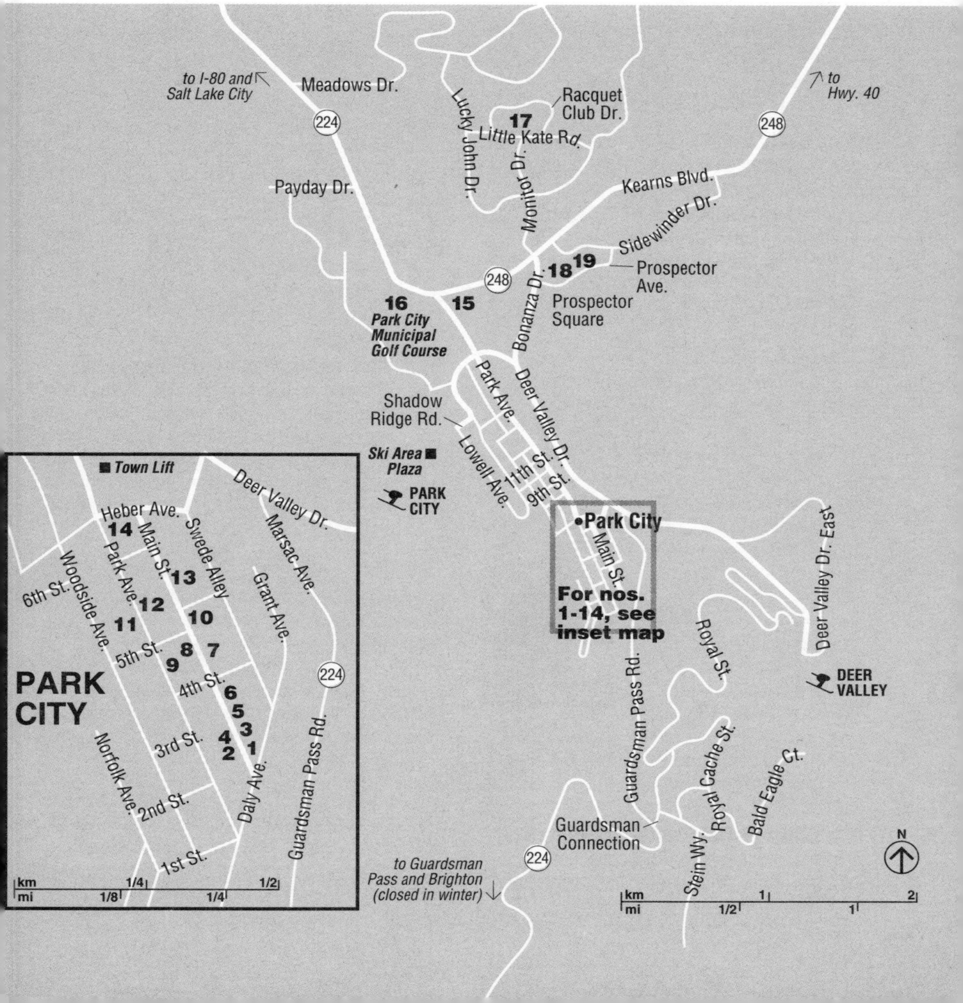

**6 Barking Frog Grill** ★★★$$$ With fare that's as fun as its name, this restaurant is a must for mildly intrepid diners. Venison, prickly pear cactus, and tomatillos are just a few of the exotic ingredients in their interpretive dishes. ♦ Daily dinner. Reservations recommended. 368 Main St (off Fourth St). 649.6222

**7 Cafe Terigo** ★★★$$ In this relaxed cafe setting, decorated with original artwork, choose from a variety of pasta and seafood dishes. The shellfish is as fresh as you'll find in landlocked Utah. The bakery up front supplies homemade cakes and pies, so leave room for dessert. ♦ M-Sa lunch; daily dinner. 424 Main St (between Fourth and Fifth Sts). 645.9555

**8 The Club** Hopping with action every night of the week, this private club (the $5 membership fee is good for two weeks) provides a taste of nightlife Park City-style. ♦ Daily 11:30AM-2AM. 449 Main St (at Fifth St). 649.6693

**9 Blue Church Lodge & Townhouses** $$ Not your typical bed-and-breakfast, this 1897 historic church (converted into seven condos) now ministers to powder worshipers. Four more units are in the town house across the street; guests at either facility can use the church's gameroom and hot tub. Continental breakfast is included. ♦ 424 Park Ave (between Fourth and Fifth Sts). 649.8009, 800/626.5467; fax 649.0686

**10 Park City Visitor Center/Museum** This information center sports a collection of historic memorabilia. In the basement, down a flight of creaky stairs, is the old town jail. ♦ M-Sa 10AM-7PM; Su noon-6PM. 528 Main St (in the Old City Hall). 649.6104

**10 Riverhorse Cafe** ★★★$$$ The pressed tin ceilings set a period tone in this elegant restaurant, housed in a historic building. There is an eclectic mix of seafood, meats, and pasta on the menu, as well as some tasty regional recipes. ♦ Daily dinner. 540 Main St (in the Old City Hall), upper level. 649.3536

**11 Washington School Inn** $$$ Built in 1889, this large cut-stone structure was Park City's first permanent schoolhouse. Its once-cavernous rooms have been converted into cozy overnight accommodations—12 rooms and three suites. A sauna and Jacuzzi are appropriately located in the school's old coal bin down in the basement. ♦ 543 Park Ave (off Fifth St). 649.3800, 800/824.1672; fax 649.3802

**12 Norwegian School of Nature Life** Offering ski touring with a twist, this school emphasizes living an "unselfish and simple life in nature." In addition to cross-country ski lessons, the school can arrange overnight cabin and snow cave trips for the more adventurous. ♦ 544 Park Ave (off Fifth St). 649.5322

Although today's Park City is regarded as a liberal bastion in an otherwise conservative state, the town's reputation took root in the 19th century. With 27 saloons along Main Street and a busy red-light district, it earned the shameful sobriquet "Sin City." One wordly wise newspaper editor went so far as to label it the "Hong Kong of Utah." Horrors.

**Restaurants/Clubs:** Red **Hotels:** Blue
**Shops/ Outdoors:** Green **Sights/Culture:** Black

**13 Ichiban Sushi** ★★★ $$$ The town's sole sushi bar is further distinguished as having the only female sushi chef in the country. If sushi isn't your cup of soy sauce, there's a lot more on the menu to choose from: Try one of the tempura, teriyaki, or sukiyaki dishes. They're all good. ♦ Daily dinner. Reservations recommended. 586 Main St (between Fifth and Sixth Sts). 649.2865

**14 Kimball Art Center** A notable art center in the Rocky Mountain region, this remodeled 1929 garage features the works of Utah artists in its two galleries. ♦ M-Sa 10AM-6PM; Su noon-6PM. 638 Park Ave (at Heber Ave). 649.8882

**15 Albertson's Food Center** This is the best place for condo-renters to stock up on groceries. The store features fresh produce, a complete butcher counter, and a pharmacy. ♦ Daily 24 hours. 1800 Park Ave (at Kearns Blvd). 649.6134

**16 Adolph's** ★★★$$$ For fine dining, this restaurant receives high marks with its combination of German and American food. The prices are definitely upscale, but the atmosphere doesn't require dressing-up. If you're in the mood for chateaubriand for two or fondue, this is the place. Enjoy a nightcap in the piano bar. ♦ Daily dinner. Reservations recommended. The Park City Municipal Golf Course (off Park Ave and Kearns Blvd). 649.7177

**17 Park City Sleigh Company** ★★★$$ After a brisk evening sleigh ride through Park City's outlying fields, you'll come down-home. An old-fashioned barn is the setting for what is best described as chuck wagon food: barbecued ribs or chicken, baked beans, corn on the cob—you get the idea. A little night music (with a country beat) is provided.

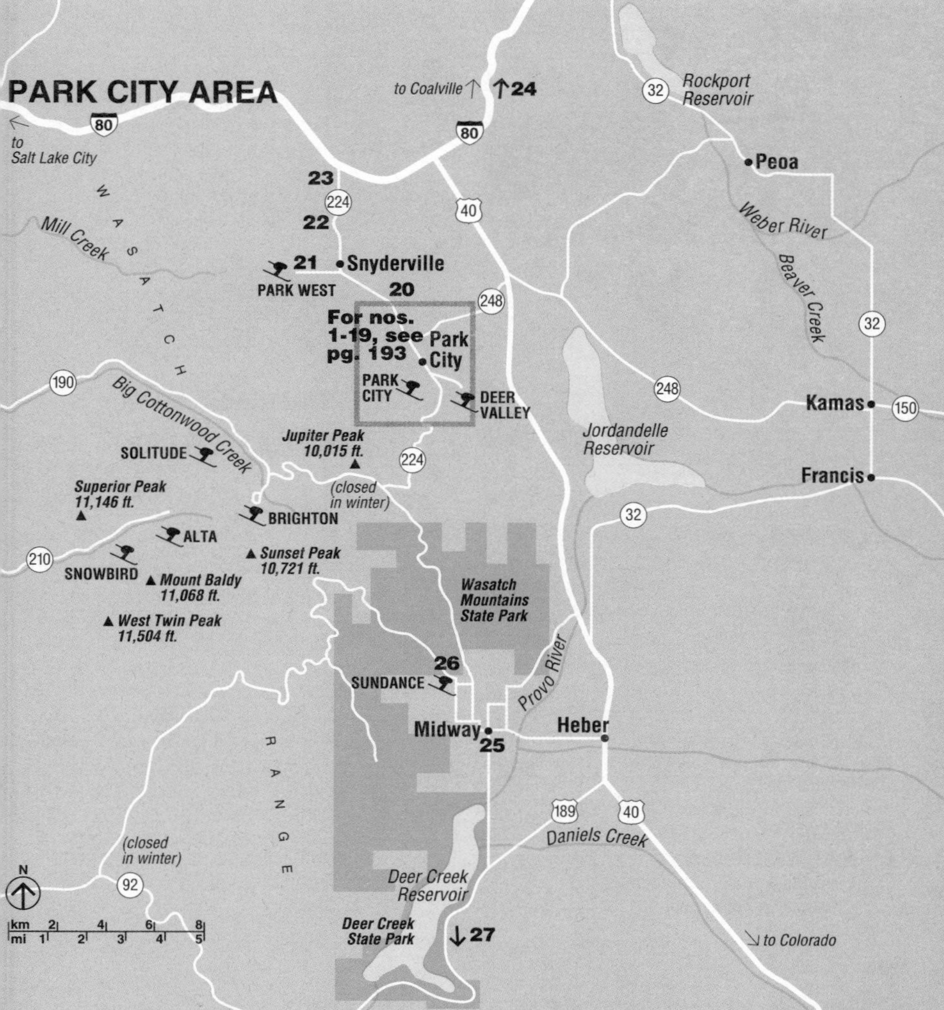

♦ Daily dinner at 6:15PM and 8:30PM. 1200 Little Kate Rd (off Monitor Dr). 649.3359, 800/523.0666

**18** **Nacho Mama's** ★★$ This fun, crowded eating joint is popular with locals as well as visiting skiers. On busy nights, expect a 30-minute wait for standard Mexican fare and some Southwestern dishes. ♦ Daily dinner. 1821 Sidewinder Dr (at Prospector Square). 645.8226

**19** **Olympia Park Hotel** $$ This hotel features 205 great rooms with a nifty array of amenities, including a skiers' breakfast, après-ski beverages, a sack lunch for the slopes, and room service. An inviting indoor pool and two popular restaurants—**Worthington's Eatery & Pub** and **Mr. G's Ristorante Italiano**—are on site. ♦ 1895 Sidewinder Dr (in Prospector Square). 649.2900, 800/SKI.EASY; fax 649.4852

**20** **Snowed Inn** $$$ On the outskirts of Park City, this 10-room bed and breakfast is a charming Victorian re-creation. European antiques and accents make it an intimate spot to nestle in for a long winter's night. ♦ 3770 North Hwy 224 (just before Park West ski area). 649.5713, 800/545.7669; fax 645.7672

Within the Snowed Inn:

**Snowed Inn Restaurant** ★★$$$ Replete with a European staff, this restaurant offers an authentic cross-cultural dining experience. ♦ Daily breakfast, lunch, and dinner. 647.3311

**Snowed Inn Sleigh Company** For an amorous après-ski adventure, hop aboard a sleigh for a twilight ride, topped off with a filling dinner of prime rib or mesquite broiled chicken. Daytime rides are also available. ♦ Daily sleigh rides only; Tu, Th, F, Sa dinner and sleigh ride. Reservations required. 649.5713

**21** **Park West Resort** Although this resort has gone through some ownership changes, it remains a popular destination for Salt Lakers on a budget. It is the only mountain in the Parley's Canyon area to welcome snowboarders, boasting two half-pipes. In addition, the resort logs some 2,200 vertical feet, seven double chairlifts, 850 acres, and snowmaking capabilities. ♦ 4000 Park West Dr (off Hwy 224), 3 miles north of Park City. 649.5400

Within the Park West Resort:

**Trail's End Cantina** ★★$$ This casa cooks up south-of-the-border dishes at easy-to-handle prices. Après-ski nachos and margaritas are especially popular. ♦ Daily lunch and dinner. Base of the ski area. 649.5400

**Saddle & Spur** ★★$$$ Bring some hungry carnivorous friends along to do justice to "Grandma Buck's Downhome Style" banquet dinners: ham, pot roast, and short ribs. ♦ Daily dinner. Base of the ski area. 649.5400

**22** **Winter Sports Park** At press time, the government was building this state-of-the-art complex north of Park City to be ready for the **2002 Winter Olympics.** The nordic and freestyle jump facilities are already in use. ♦ In Bear Hollow, 3.5 miles north of Park City. 649.5447

**23** **Best Western Landmark** $ This out-by-the-highway hotel has 106 rooms and is quite comfortable with such amenities as an indoor pool, spa, and exercise area. ♦ 6560 N Landmark Dr (at Hwy 80). 649.7300, 800/548.8824; fax 649.1760

**23** **PowderWood Resort** $$$ Situated six miles from Park City Ski Area, this 52-unit deluxe condo property makes up in perks what it lacks in proximity to the slopes. Included are a free shuttle bus, après-ski parties, an outdoor whirlpool, a large heated swimming pool, a complete recreation center, covered parking, and a sledding hill. ♦ 6975 North 2200 West (near Hwy 80). 649.2032, 800/223.7829; fax 649.8619

**24** **Danish Viking Lodge** $ Midway between Park City and the **Sundance Ski Resort,** this 34-room motel offers budget-minded skiers some of the best prices in the area. Amenities include an indoor spa area, in-room refrigerators, and a coin laundry. ♦ 989 S Main St (off Hwy 40), Heber. 654.2202, 800/544.4066

25 **Homestead** $$ Set on a hundred-year-old farm adjacent to **Wasatch Mountains State Park,** this is easily one of the finest country resorts in the West; its 117 stellar accommodations are four-diamond all the way. In addition to an indoor lap pool, spa, sauna, and nightly sleigh rides, Homestead also features snowmobile tours and hot-air ballooning. ♦ 700 N Homestead Dr (next to Wasatch Mountains State Park), Midway. 654.1102, 800/327.7220; fax 654.5087

Within Homestead:

**Homestead Restaurant** ★★★★$$$ Dinner at this fine establishment merits the 20-minute drive from Park City. Entrées include rack of lamb, veal chops, crab cakes with shrimp sauté, and breast of duck. Don't miss the delectable desserts. ♦ Daily breakfast, lunch, and dinner. Reservations required. 700 N Homestead Dr, Midway. 654.1102, 800/327.7220

25 **Inn On The Creek** $$$ This eight-room bed-and-breakfast offers very comfortable accommodations in Midway, located 20 minutes from Park City. A full homemade breakfast will stoke you up for the slopes. ♦ 375 Rainbow Ln (off 350 W St), Midway. 654.0892; fax 654.5871

26 **Sundance Ski Area** With a vertical rise of 2,150 feet and a network of 41 trails running over Mount Timpanogoes, this cozy resort offers enough skiing terrain to make stopping worthwhile. What makes it a standout, though, is that the founder and guiding light, Robert Redford, goes to great lengths to cultivate a community emphasizing recreation, the arts, and environmental interests. There's almost always something culturally exciting happening here. ♦ 10 miles east of Provo in the North Fork Provo Canyon. 225.4107

Within the Sundance Ski Area:

**Sundance Accommodations** $$$ Guests may rent either a condominium cottage tucked among the spruces, or a mountain home. The atmosphere is one of rustic elegance: handmade furniture, stone fireplaces, and other fixtures designed to harmonize with nature. There are 90 condos and eight homes available. ♦ 225.4107; fax 649.3581

**The Tree Room** ★★★$$$ Luxurious but low-key, this restaurant serves a variety of poultry, steak, and seafood specialties, including fresh Utah trout. Native American art pieces and Western memorabilia from Robert Redford's private collection give the room a personal, eclectic ambience. ♦ Daily dinner. Reservations recommended. Next to General Store. 225.4107

**The Grill Room** ★★★$$ For a more casual dining experience at Sundance, this eatery features lighter, American bistro entrées. ♦ Daily breakfast, lunch, and dinner. Next to General Store. 225.4107

26 **High Country Tours** This snowmobiling tour service travels to the top of **Guardsman Pass** to explore some of Utah's most scenic mountainland. Bundle up for the moonlight dinner rides. ♦ Guardsman Pass Rd near Silver Lake Village. 645.7533, 645.8350

# Alta

As any serious skier worth his or her weight in bindings can tell you, Alta features the kind of terrain ski legends are fashioned from. To wit, the notorious chutes that rise precipitously above the base area. Sporting such menacing names as **Wildcat Face, Rock Gully, Stone Crusher,** and **Alf's High Rustler,** they're intended for nerves-of-steel experts gunning for new powder challenges. Once primed, skiers can continue up the mountain and get revved up by the steep and deep in the open bowl territories of **Mount Baldy, Greeley Bowl,** and **Devil's Castle.**

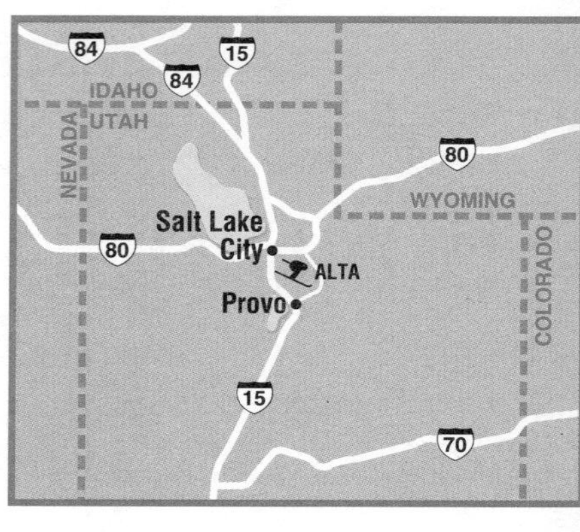


Alta's unpretentious attitude about skiing has always been its hallmark. Look no farther than its full name to understand why: Alta Ski Lifts Company. The word "resort" isn't even mentioned. This is not to say you won't find comfortable rustic lodges here and restaurants that earn good reviews. You will. But Alta, America's second-oldest ski area, is firmly dedicated to the premise that skiing is simply the art of getting down the mountain.

Once bare to the bones, Alta's lift system took a giant step forward in 1991 with the addition of two triple chairs. A bit short on creature comforts, the area compensates with pleasurable prices. Whereas many ski resorts charge upwards of $40 for lift tickets, Alta squeaks by at $25. If a no-frills, egalitarian concept of skiing is what you're after, that philosophy is still going strong at Alta.

**Alta Ski Lifts Company**
**PO Box 8007**
**Alta, Utah 84092-8007**

**Information**........................................801/742.3333

**Reservations**......................................801/942.0404

**Snow Phone**.......................................801/572.3939

## Fast Facts

*Area code 801 unless otherwise noted.*

**Ski Season** Mid-November to late April

**Location** Alta is located 25 miles southeast of **Salt Lake City** in **Little Cottonwood Canyon.**

### Getting to Alta

**By air:** The nearest airport is **Salt Lake International Airport,** about an hour away. **Delta** offers the most frequent service to **Salt Lake City,** with 44 nonstop flights daily. **American** offers daily nonstops from **Chicago** and **Dallas/Ft. Worth. America West** flies nonstop daily from **Phoenix** and **Las Vegas.** Other carriers include **Continental, Northwest, Sky West, Southwest, TWA, United, Continental,** and **Vanguard.** Ground transfers may be obtained from **Canyon Transportation** (800/453.3000), which runs several vans daily. Taxi service is also available.

**By bus: Greyhound** (800/231.2222) makes several stops daily at the **Salt Lake City** bus station, located at South Temple and 200 West. Taxis and **Utah Transit Authority** (**UTA;** BUS.INFO) buses are available to take you to the resort.

**By car:** Winterized rental cars are available at the airport from **Alamo, Avis, Budget, Dollar, Hertz,** or **National.** From **Salt Lake City** drive south on Wasatch Boulevard to the mouth of **Little Cottonwood Canyon.** Then follow Highway 210 for seven miles until you reach Alta.

**By train: Amtrak** (800/USA.RAIL) makes daily stops at the **Rio Grande Depot** in downtown **Salt Lake City.** To get to the resort, take either a taxi or a **UTA** bus (see above), which makes regular trips from several downtown locations to **Little Cottonwood.**

### Getting around Alta

The **UTA** (see above), Salt Lake Valley's public transportation system, offers bus service linking **Salt Lake City,** major hotels, and **Snowbird** and Alta ski resorts.

## FYI

**Area** 2,200 acres with 39 runs

Beginner—25 percent

Intermediate—40 percent

Advanced—35 percent

ALTA

**Number of Groomed Runs** Depends on current snow conditions; Alta is staunch about providing groomed runs from top to bottom.

**Longest Run** 3.5 miles (**Gunsight Pass** through **Albion Basin** to base area—no particular runs)

**Capacity** 9,100 skiers per hour

**Base Elevation** 8,550 feet

**Summit Elevation** 10,550 feet

**Vertical Rise** 2,100 feet

**Average Annual Snowfall** 500 inches

**Snowmaking** None

**Night Skiing** None

**Lifts** 12 (2 triple chairs, 6 double chairs, and 4 surface tows)

| **Lift Passes** | **Full Day** | **Half Day** (starts at 9:15AM or 1PM) |
|---|---|---|
| **All** | $25 | $19 |
| **Beginners** (**Albion Basin** lifts only) | $18 | $13 |

**Ski School** The three offices of the **Alf Engen Ski School** (742.2600) are located at **Wildcat, Watson Shelter,** and **Albion** (near the lower Albion Parking Lot at the base of the Albion and Sunnyside Lifts). Two-hour group lessons address nine skill levels, from first-time skiers to experts out to refine their technique. One-hour, two-hour, half-day, and all-day private lessons are also offered.

**Kids' Ski School** Full-day and two-hour lessons are available for ages 4 to 12, all ability levels. Register 30 minutes prior to lesson.

**Clinics and Special Programs** A series of 2.5-hour group sessions are offered for the top four skill-level skiers. Sign up for **Skill Builders; Bumps, Bumps, Bumps; Conditions Du Jour;** and **Diamond Challenge.** Workshops meet near the base of Germania Lift.

**Races** Gate skiing takes place at the **Sunnyside Arena** at the top of the Sunnyside Lift. The first run is $5, unlimited usage is $7.

**Rentals** Equipment offered by Alta's four rental shops range from sport to demo quality. Sources include: **Alta Sports** (742.3110; daily 8:30AM-5:30PM), **Deep Powder House** (742.2400; daily 8:15AM-6PM), **Goldminer's Daughter** (742.2300; daily 8:30AM-5:30PM), and **Ski Rack** (742.3000; daily 7AM-5PM).

**Lockers** Coin-operated ski storage lockers are located at the **Wildcat Ticket Office** and at the **Albion Day Lodge.**

Although little evidence remains today, Alta was once a busy mining camp. During the late 1800s, the year-round population topped 1,000, rising in the summer to 8,000 inhabitants.

Having started up its first lift on 15 January 1939, Alta is the second-oldest ski area in the nation (Sun Valley predates it by three years). Alta's original lift was pieced together using parts of an old ore tram. The $2.50 ticket price generated complaints that the sport was strictly for the well-to-do.

**Day Care** The **Alta Children's Center** (742.3042), a state-licensed facility open daily 8:30AM to 5PM, is located on the top level of the **Albion Ticket Building.** Infants and children up to 12 years old are welcome. Reservations are requested.

**First Aid** Alta has a first-aid station at the base of the Wildcat Lift. The nearest hospital is **Alta View** (576.2600), 9660 South 1300 East in Sandy.

**Parking** There is free parking at the base.

**Worth Knowing**

- If you play your cards right, you might just get "snowed in" at Alta. When it snows too much in Little Cottonwood Canyon, the danger of avalanches requires closing down the roads. Translation: You don't have to share all that great powder with those skiers stranded in town! Of course, that also means you should keep an eye on the weather forecast.

## Rating the Runs

### ● Beginner

Beginners can really hone their skills on **Crooked Mile,** a vast, picturesque run on the **Albion Basin** side of the mountain. The Albion Lift is the ticket to racking up a cool 850 vertical feet with each downhill sweep.

True to its name, **Sweet 'n Easy** glides gently among forest-rimmed parks. The skiing is a cinch, and the surrounding scenery as good as any available to black-diamond bombers.

### ■ Intermediate

Running parallel to Sugarloaf Lift, **Devil's Elbow** offers more than 1,300 vertical feet of groomed powder heaven. Both the fall line and pitch vary enough to make it tricky.

Swooping down from the top of Supreme Lift, **Big Dipper**—a wonderful cruiser—drops among glades of well-spaced trees. A detour into nearby **Sleepy Hollow** lets intermediates dabble in expert powder terrain.

### ◆ Expert

With Alta's many outstanding black-diamond runs to choose from, it's difficult to name the best. Certainly **Alf's High Rustler**—heroically steep and unforgiving in length—would be on every list.

Worth the traverse, the **East Greeley** area is one of Alta's many wide open bowls—a powderhound's delight.

### Snowboarding

No snowboarding permitted on entire mountain.

## Mountain Highs and Lows

Not only is the drop somewhat steeper than the norm, intermediate **Race Course Saddle** can only be reached from expert runs.

## At the Resort

*Area code 801 unless otherwise noted.*

✦ **Snowpine Lodge** $$$ As homey as a ski lodge gets, this family-run hotel is Alta's oldest and smallest—capacity 48. But the overnight options are plentiful: everything from dorm-style bunk beds to private rooms. Spend quality lounge-time in front of toasty fireplaces, or soak those ski-weary bones in the outdoor hot tub or indoor sauna. Breakfast and a four-course dinner are included in the rate. ♦ Near the upper end of Alta. 742.2000

✦ **Rustler Lodge** $$$$ This is the place if you want the best of both worlds: a rustic mountain inn atmosphere with spiffy accommodations and a gourmet restaurant. Though smaller, more affordable rooms are available, the mainstay are 40 deluxe rooms—the most of any property at Alta. Don't miss a dip in the heated outdoor pool. The dining experience here is one of the prettiest—three sides of the room have a glass-enclosed view of the mountains. The menu changes daily, and the bread and pastries are baked on site. Meals are included in the tariff. Rustler operates a free shuttle service to Snowbird. ♦ Near the upper end of Alta. 742.2200, 800/451.5223; fax 742.3832

✦ **Alta Lodge** $$$$ Owned by the mayor of Alta and run by his children, this 57-room lodge has been welcoming return guests for more than 50 years. Many regulars insist on staying in one of the original rooms built in 1939, but the lodge has more deluxe accommodations as well. New wrinkles include afternoon tea, Sunday dinner buffet, and children's dinner hour and program of activities that give parents a chance to soak in the Jacuzzi while the kids are kept busy. Rate includes meals. ♦ Across from the Alta Town Offices in Alta. 742.3500, 800/707.ALTA; fax 742.3500

✦ **Shallow Shaft Restaurant** ★★★$$ Head here when pizza cravings hit. Or try the Utah lamb chops or the New York steak broiled with prawns. ♦ Daily dinner. Reservations recommended. Next to the Alta Town Offices. 742.2177

**Restaurants/Clubs:** Red **Hotels:** Blue
**Shops/ Outdoors:** Green **Sights/Culture:** Black

✦ **Goldminer's Daughter Lodge** $$ This friendly, informal 94-room property features ski-to-the-door convenience, plus an equipment rental and retail shop. A large outdoor patio is the place to socialize while you catch some rays. Hot tubs, game and exercise rooms, and a cocktail lounge also add to after-hours fun. Buffet breakfast and dinner (by reservation only) are included in the reasonable rates. ♦ Base of the Collins and Wildcat Lifts. 742.2300, 800/453.4573

✦ **Watson Cafe** ★★$ Conveniently located in the thick of Alta's intermediate and advanced runs, this restaurant offers basic lunches at bargain prices. After a morning of skiing, you can recharge with a fresh burger, bratwurst with sauerkraut, or seafood chowder. ♦ Daily lunch. Near the base of Germania Lift. 742.3037

✦ **Alta Peruvian Lodge** $$$ This mid-range lodge offers a total of 104 rooms in a variety of accommodations—from a dormitory to a two-bedroom suite—most of which are pleasantly affordable. Rates include breakfast, lunch (order it bagged for eating slope-side), dinner, and a lift ticket. Extras include a club (read: bar), ski-rental shop, nightly movies, and Alta's largest outdoor pool—heated, of course. ♦ Lower end of Alta. 742.3000, 800/453.8488; fax 742.3007

Within the Alta Peruvian Lodge:

**Albion Grill** ★★$ Come to this cafeteria-style restaurant for a hearty breakfast and lunch, as well as for all those snacks in between. The menu satisfies every appetite. ♦ Daily breakfast and lunch. At the base of the Albion Chair. 742.2500

**Chic's Place** ★★★★$$$$ For those seeking a unique, gourmet dining experience on the slopes, this is the place. Rustic elegance defines the decor, with white linen tablecloths, fresh flowers, and captain's chairs, as well as a fireplace by which skiers can don slippers and relax after a big day on the slopes. Popular with the locals, this restaurant is known for its pasta, seafood, daily specials, and great views. ♦ Daily breakfast and lunch. Located midmountain at the base of the Germania Lift and above Watson Shelter. 742.3037

**Alpenglow** ★★★$ Recently rebuilt (during the summer of 1994), this cafeteria features great views and the best french fries in town. ♦ Daily breakfast and lunch. At the base of Sugarloaf Lift. 742.2424

✦ **Blackjack Condominium Lodge** $$$ Blackjack's location on **Peruvian Ridge**, which separates Alta and Snowbird, makes it possible for you to ski to either base area from the door. Amenities at this 10-condo establishment include in-room fireplaces, full kitchens, a sauna, game and exercise rooms, laundry facilities, and more. Choose from a studio that sleeps two comfortably and one-bedroom units that accommodate four. ♦ Bypass Rd (between Alta and Snowbird). 742.3200, 800/343.0347; fax 742.4902

***For more information on the Alta area, see "Beyond the Resorts," page 205.***

## Bests

**Connie Marshall**

Marketing Director, Alta Ski Lifts Company

The **So Long** ski run offers the solitude and beauty that represents Alta, especially after a powder storm.

Favorite on-the-hill lunch spot—**Chic's Place,** with white tablecloths and deck seating. Trade your ski boots for a pair of slippers, relax by the fire, then order a glass of wine and a tasteful entrée.

Just how salty is the Great Salt Lake? While the saline concentration fluctuates, it has peaked at 27 percent—eight times saltier than the ocean. No fish live in the soup, although tiny brine shrimp thrive there.

In the realm of collegiate skiing, the team to beat year after year is the University of Utah. Having developed what is often considered the best ski program in the nation, the Salt Lake City–based racers were the national champions eight times in the last 17 years (1978-1995)—more times than any other single university. With Utah's main rivals hailing from Vermont, the finals competition is often referred to as "the Beast vs. the East."

# Snowbird

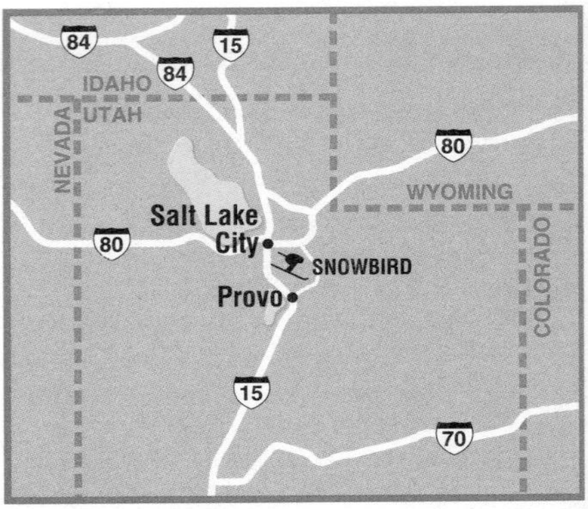

Rarely is nature so accommodating to skiing as it is at Utah's Snowbird Resort. Here, in the scenic **Little Cottonwood Canyon,** fall prodigious amounts of what Utah's license plates rightfully call the "Greatest Snow on Earth." But all of the champagne powder (more than 500 inches a year on average) wouldn't amount to a bunny hill if the terrain weren't equally ideal for skiing.

Snowbird is blessed with an overflow of natural glades, chutes, and face, and is crisscrossed with heart-stopping advanced and expert runs. Adrenaline junkies can dive into the **Peruvian Cirque** (where angular headwalls will rattle your equilibrium) or free-fall into the upper reaches of **Gad Valley** yawning to the west. **Great Scott, Silver Fox, Gad Chutes,** and **Barry Barry Steep** have all rightfully earned double black-diamond status. Snowbird's incredible moguls are not to be missed either. The ride is pure poetry for those who master them. Meanwhile, beginners and intermediates can head for runs with names like **Lower Big Emma** and **Bassackwards.**

A high-tech highlight of the resort is the 125-passenger Snowbird Aerial Tram, which whisks skiers nearly 3,000 vertical feet to the summit of **Hidden Peak** in eight easy minutes, giving them access to the entire mountain, a feat few ski areas can match.

Only a mile down the road from **Alta,** Snowbird is definitely the richer relation. When night falls, the base area swings into action. Upscale hotels, restaurants, and nightclubs contribute to a world-class operation that rivals such posh resorts as Gstaad, St. Moritz, and Aspen. **Salt Lake City,** just 25 miles away, is another lodging option, with the added bonus of being home to some of the area's finest restaurants. Whether on or off the mountain, Snowbird spares no expense in providing a complete ski experience.

**Snowbird Ski & Summer Resort**
**Snowbird, Utah 84092-9000**

**Information**........801/742.2222
**Reservations**........800/453.3000
**Snow Phone**........801/742.2222 ext 4285

## Fast Facts

*Area code 801 unless otherwise noted.*

**Ski Season** Mid-November to early May

**Location** Snowbird is located 25 miles southeast of **Salt Lake City** in **Little Cottonwood Canyon.**

## Getting to Snowbird

**By air: Salt Lake International Airport** is about an hour from Snowbird. **Delta** offers the most frequent service to **Salt Lake City,** with 44 non-stop flights daily. **American** offers daily nonstops from **Chicago** and **Dallas/Ft. Worth. America West** flies nonstop daily from **Las Vegas** and **Phoenix.** Other carriers include **Continental, Northwest, Sky West, Southwest, TWA, United,** and **Vanguard.** Ground transfers may be obtained from **Canyon Transportation** (800/453.3000), which runs vans several times a day. Taxi service is also available.

**By bus: Greyhound** (800/231.2222) buses make several daily stops at the **Salt Lake City** bus station, located at 160 West South Temple Street. Taxis and **Utah Transit Authority** (**UTA;** BUS.INFO) buses are available to take you to the resort.

**By car:** Winterized rental cars are available at the airport from **Alamo, Avis, Budget, Dollar, Hertz,** or **National.** From **Salt Lake City** drive south on Wasatch Boulevard to the mouth of **Little Cottonwood Canyon.** Then follow Highway 210 for six miles until you reach Snowbird.

**Driving time from:**

Salt Lake City—35 minutes (25 miles)

**By train: Amtrak** (800/USA.RAIL) makes daily stops at the **Rio Grande Depot** in downtown **Salt Lake City.** To get to the resort, take a taxi or **UTA** bus (see above), which makes regular trips from several downtown locations to **Little Cottonwood.**

## Getting around Snowbird

**BASS** (**Bird Area Shuttle Service;** 742.2222 ext 4037) runs free shuttles on an as-needed basis from the main center to the main and **Gad Valley** parking areas, and to all resort lodges. **UTA** (see above), **Salt Lake Valley**'s public transportation system, offers bus service linking **Salt Lake City,** major hotels, and Snowbird and **Alta** ski resorts.

## FYI

**Area** 2,000 acres with 47 runs

Beginner—20 percent

Intermediate—35 percent

Expert—45 percent

**Number of Groomed Runs** 25

**Longest Run** 2.5 miles (**Chip's Run** and **Rothman Way**)

**Capacity** 9,200 skiers per hour

**Base Elevation** 7,900 feet

**Summit Elevation** 11,000 feet

**Vertical Rise** 3,100 feet

**Average Annual Snowfall** 500 inches

**Snowmaking** None

**Night Skiing** None

**Lifts** 8 (a 125-passenger aerial tram and 7 double chairs)

| **Lift Passes** | **Full Day** | **Half Day** (starts at 9AM or 12:30PM) |
|---|---|---|
| **Adult** | $33 | $27 |
| with tram | $40 | $33 |
| **Child** (12 and under) | $21 | $18 |
| with tram | $26 | $21 |
| **Senior** (62-69) | $21 | $18 |
| with tram | $26 | $21 |
| **Senior** (70 and over) | Free | Free |

**Beginners Only** The Chickadee Lift pass is $10

**Ski School** The **Snowbird Ski School** (742.2222 ext 5170) has three offices: on level 1 of the **Cliff Lodge** and on levels 2 and 3 of the **Snowbird Center. Adult Super Classes** provide half-day and full-day instruction for all skill levels. Private lessons, for all ages and skill levels, are also available.

**Kids' Ski School** Child/Teen Super Classes, for ages 5 to 15, are half-day and full-day programs, including lunch. The **Chickadees** program, for beginners age 3 to 4, pairs two children with an instructor for a 1.5-hour session. This popular class requires reservations.

**Clinics and Special Programs** Accelerated half-day clinics for intermediate skiers include the **Style Workshop** and **Bumps & Diamonds Workshop.** Upper-level skiers can enroll in the **Race Workshop.** A special **Powder Plus** program teaches you to ski the steep and deep with wide-bodied skis. For advanced skiers in the 50 and over set, there is the **Silverwings** class. Experts can enroll in a Mountain Experience session, which offers a full day of skiing on challenging, steep terrain. Four-day **Women's Seminars** are taught by top female instructors, with sessions scheduled for 12-15 December, 16-19 February, and 13-16 March.

**Races** NASTAR races take place on the **Big Emma** or **Lower Wilbere Ridge,** and a coin-operated race course is on Lower Wilbere as well. Contact Snowbird's **Race Department** (742.2222 ext 4180) for specific dates, times, and prices.

**Rentals** Packages at Snowbird's three ski rental shops include basic, sport, and deluxe equipment. Base area shops include **Cliff Lodge Ski Rental** (742.2222 ext 5800) on level 1 of the **Cliff Lodge,** and **Breeze Ski Rentals** (ext 4198) and the **SportStalker** (ext 4192) on level 3 of the **Snowbird Center.** The ski rental shops are open daily 8AM to 6PM. **Powder Tools** (daily 8AM-8PM; ext 4187), on level 3 of the **Snowbird Center,** is a complete snowboard shop with snowboard rentals.

**Lockers** Ski storage is available on levels 1 and 3 of the **Snowbird Center.** An attendant is on hand from 8:30AM to 5PM.

**Day Care Camp Snowbird** (742.2222 ext 5026), a state-licensed facility, is open 8AM to 5PM and located on level 1 of the **Cliff Lodge.** Special half-day and all-day programs are offered for tots ages 6 months to 3 years, and for children 3 to 12 years old. A 14-day advance reservation is required for children, and a 30-day advance registration is required for infants. Baby-sitting services for infants are also available.

**First Aid** A full-service first-aid clinic (742.2222 ext 4195) is located on level 1 of the **Snowbird Center.** The nearest hospital is **Alta View** (576.2600) at 9660 S 1300 E Street in Sandy.

**Parking** There is free parking at the base.

**Worth Knowing**

- Helicopter skiing in the **Wasatch Mountains** is available through **Wasatch Powderbird Guides** (742.2800). Prices start at $75 for a one-lift tour and climb to $420 for all day. Their office is located on level B of the **Cliff Lodge.**

## Rating the Runs

### ● Beginner

A gentle descent from the midway unloading station on the Mid Gad Lift, **West Second South** offers a fun way down. And, since it's not linked to other runs, it's relatively free of faster-paced intermediate and expert skiers.

Accessed by both the midway station on the Mid Gad Lift and the Wilbere Lift, **Lower Big Emma** is a wide-open cruiser for beginners ready for a little speed.

### ■ Intermediate

After descending into **Peruvian Gulch** via a narrow catwalk, **Chip's Run** opens up into several beautiful valleys. Some variations are possible along the bottom third of the run, including a couple of short expert pitches. Where else can intermediates tally up 3,000 vertical feet in one day?

Dropping the length of the **Gad Valley, Bassackwards** greets a variety of glades and drop-offs along the way. Regularly groomed, with only a few slow spots, this run is ideal for long-distance cruising.

### ◆◆ Expert

A popular mogul run, **Gadzooks** drops off of the Gad 2 Lift. Although short, it's intense—your legs will be screaming for relief in no time.

Among the many double black-diamond runs accessed from the top of the tram, **Great Scott** is legendary for its incredibly steep pitch. Snowbird regulars insist: "If you aren't scared, then you aren't skiing it right."

### Snowboarding

Snowbird, with its steeps, open bowls, and 500 inches of annual snowfall provides a natural playground for boarders. Although there's restricted riding off the Gad 2 chairlift, boarders have the freedom to go off piste. The resort features a snowboard patrol and top schooling from such professionals as Jane Mauser, a member of the PSIA National Snowboarding Team.

## Mountain Highs and Lows

First-time skiers may find **Lower Big Emma** a treat, but a steep pitch makes **Upper Big Emma** definitely intermediate territory. If your turning and stopping still need work, off-load at the midway station of the Mid Gad Lift and save the upper end for another time.

## At the Resort

*Area code 801 unless otherwise noted.*

✦ **Cliff Lodge** $$$ First-time visitors are sometimes surprised by the utilitarian look of this 532-room lodge. But it doesn't take long to see that form follows function. The building blends in well with the surrounding canyon scenery, and inside the lodge is like an entire ski village under one roof: two outdoor pools, an elaborate spa facility, five restaurants, and ski and sundry shops, plus comfortable rooms and valet parking. If you plan to wine and dine at Snowbird restaurants, be sure to join the **Club at Snowbird** upon check-in. ♦ Little Cottonwood Canyon, 25 miles southeast of Salt Lake City. 742.2222 ext 5000, 800/453.3000; fax 742.3300

Within the Cliff Lodge:

**Aerie** ★★★$$$ The atmosphere here is, well, airy. Located on the top floor of the **Cliff Lodge,** this elegant restaurant has obvious Asian influences: the free-standing silk screens, black marble, and garden of greenery. Its seafood—including such must-try entrées as poached filet of Norwegian salmon and Southwestern crab cakes—deserves high marks. All windows face the slopes, so the down-canyon views are spectacular. Make reservations, especially for sunset dining. ♦ Daily breakfast and dinner. Reservations recommended. Top floor. 742.2222 ext 5500

**Junction Keyhole** ★★★$$ Try the fajitas or burritos for dinner, or make a meal out of such après-ski appetizers as stuffed jalapeños and macho nachos. ♦ Daily breakfast, lunch, and dinner. Level A. 742.2222 ext 5100

✦ **The Forklift** ★★$$ Combining ski-in convenience with sit-down service, this eatery offers no-fuss dining on the cheap. Standard fare is served for breakfast and lunch, while dinner is more exotic, with chicken stir-fry and other international selections. ♦ Daily breakfast, lunch, and dinner. Level 3 of the Snowbird Center. 742.2222 ext 4100

✦ **SportStalker** This sporting-goods chain stocks a great selection of skis, boots, bindings, clothing, and accessories. Rentals are also available. ♦ Daily 8AM-8PM. Level 3 of the Snowbird Center. 742.2222 ext 4192

✦ **Rocky Mountain Chocolate Factory** Send mouth-watering chocolates to the folks back home. ♦ M-Th, Su 8:30AM-9PM; F-Sa 8:30AM-10PM. Level 2 of the Snowbird Center. 742.2222 ext 4277

✦ **Wine & Liquor Store** The selection of 120 varieties of wine will even please connoisseurs. ♦ M-Th 3:30PM-10PM; F-Sa noon-10PM. Level 2 of the Snowbird Center. 742.2222 ext 4075

✦ **General Gritts** Jam-packed with a variety of groceries, this store has snack items, canned goods, and soft drinks. Stop by the deli counter for hoagies to go. ♦ Daily 8AM-10PM. Level 1 of the Snowbird Center. 742.2222 ext 4035

✦ **The Lodge at Snowbird** $$$ Comfortable and low-key, this 136-unit condominium property features studios, one-bedrooms, and one-bedroom units with a loft. All have balconies and ski storage. Amenities include safety deposit boxes, a laundry room, gameroom, steam room, whirlpool, and outdoor pool. ♦ Adjacent to the Snowbird Center. 742.2222 ext 3000, 800/453.3000; fax 742.3300

Describing himself as "super curious" and "super enthusiastic," Snowbird co-founder and owner Dick Bass has racked up some impressive accomplishments since opening the resort in 1971. Not only is he the first person to have reached the highest summit on every continent, but he was also the oldest person to ever scale Mount Everest when he made his ascent. He was 55 at the time.

**Restaurants/Clubs:** Red **Hotels:** Blue
**Shops/ Outdoors:** Green **Sights/Culture:** Black

Within The Lodge at Snowbird:

**Lodge Club** ★★★$$$ Set in a glass atrium, this comfortable, cozy restaurant offers great views of the mountain and nearby pine forest. Candlelight, fresh flowers (year-round), and tones of plum and gray combine for a romantic setting. Tempting entrées such as grilled breast of duck on fettuccine distinguish the innovative cuisine. The kitchen conveniently grows its own fresh herbs right here all year long. If you're in the mood for lighter fare, try the bistro menu in the bar, where it's also great to relax in front of a fireplace. ♦ Daily dinner. Reservations recommended. Pool level of the Lodge at Snowbird. 742.2222 ext 3042

✦ **Iron Blosam Lodge** $$$ These popular time-share condos are similar in price to the Lodge at Snowbird, with the added bonus of a health spa and masseuse. However, availability is limited because of the nature of the time-share structure. ♦ West of the Snowbird Center. 742.2222 ext 1000, 800/453.3000; fax 742.3300

Within the Iron Blosam Lodge:

**Wildflower Ristorante & Lounge** ★★★$$$ Welcome to the Mediterranean! If you're ready to escape the ubiquitous Western theme, the aged bottles of Chianti, clusters of grapes, and colored bottles of oil and vinegar decorating this place may help. Try the cioppino or any of the pasta, veal, or seafood dishes at this Italian restaurant. The lounge is known for stocking beers from around the world. ♦ Daily dinner. Reservations recommended. Level 3. 742.2222 ext 1042

## Beyond the Resorts

*La Caille*

1 **La Caille at Quail Run** ★★★★$$$$ Easily the area's finest—and most expensive—dining spot, this replica of a French château is situated in the midst of a 22-acre preserve, complete with gardens and duck ponds. Begin with escargots, then try the superb wilted spinach salad before moving on to impeccable entrées. The staff is dressed in period costume and the decor is ornate. ♦ Daily dinner; Sunday brunch. Reservations required. 9565 Wasatch Blvd (near intersection with 9400 S St), Sandy. 942.1751

2 **Frontier Pies Restaurant & Bakery** ★★★$ Generous portions of home-style cooking—including incredible pies—are served at this restaurant/bakery. ♦ Daily breakfast, lunch, and dinner. 905 E 9400 S St (at 700 E St), Sandy. 561.7467

3 **Hampton Inn** $ Conveniently located by the interstate, this 131-room hotel has a pool and laundry facilities. There are quite a few

restaurants within walking distance. ♦ 10690 S 160 W St (at Hwy 15), Sandy. 571.0800

4 **Dean's Hungry i** ★★★$$ Try the seafood Santorini or the *souvlaki* and you'll wonder why you don't eat Greek cuisine more often. ♦ Daily lunch and dinner. 1440 Foothill Blvd (at 900 S St), Salt Lake City. 582.8600

5 **Trolley Square** Look for the landmark water tower to find this mall built in an old trolley-car barn. A wide array of shops, boutiques, and restaurants can be found here. The atmosphere is quaint and cute in a touristy sort of way. ♦ M-F 10AM-9PM; Sa noon-5PM. 600 S St (at 700 E St), Salt Lake City. 521.9877

6 **Deseret Inn** $ Cheap and basic, this is the kind of place students pack 12 to a room on a college ski trip. The 86-room spot is not far from downtown restaurants and nightclubs. ♦ 50 W 500 S St (at Main St), Salt Lake City. 532.2900; fax 532.2900

6 **Little America Hotel & Towers** $$ The premier property of this Rocky Mountain chain offers 850 rooms and suites, with a restaurant and coffee shop, a pool, fitness facilities, and free airport pick-up service. As with most major Salt Lake hotels, you can catch a **UTA** bus to the slopes for only $4. ♦ 500 S Main St (at W 500 S St), Salt Lake City. 363.6781; fax 596.5911

7 **Market Street Grill** ★★★★$$$ Strong word-of-mouth advertising and great food keep this charming restaurant packed with happy diners. Perhaps it's because of the atmosphere: Ceramic tile floors, blonde wood booths, chalkboard menus, and long-aproned servers bring you back (as intended) to a classic 1920s grill. Or, more likely, it's due to the fresh seafood flown in daily from around the world. For lunch—which is a better deal than the rather pricey steak and seafood dinners—try grilled crab cakes with red pepper hollandaise or linguine with rock shrimp and pesto cream sauce. ♦ Daily breakfast, lunch, and dinner. Reservations recommended. 48 Market St (between Main and W Temple Sts), Salt Lake City. 322.4668

8 **Squatter's Pub Brewery** ★★★$ Order a house favorite such as the Squatterburger, chicken stir-fry, or bratwurst platter, along with one of the many ales brewed in the upper floors of the building. ♦ Daily lunch and dinner. 147 W Broadway (a block south of the Salt Palace), Salt Lake City. 363.BREW

9 **Peery Hotel** $$ This hostelry offers 77 comfortable beds in a historic downtown building. Walk to the nearby restaurants, or try the **Peery Pub & Cafe,** as locals do. ♦ 110 W 300 S St (at West Temple St), Salt Lake City. 521.4300; fax 575.5014

9 **Zephyr** One of Salt Lake's more popular nightclubs, this spot hops seven nights a week with popular local bands and nationally recognized acts. ♦ 301 S West Temple St (at 300 S St), Salt Lake City. 355.5646

9 **Red Lion Hotel** $$ Centrally located in downtown Salt Lake, this Red Lion has 503 comfortable rooms and all-inclusive amenities. ♦ 255 S West Temple St (between 300 S St and W Pierpont Ave), Salt Lake City. 328.2000; fax 532.1953

10 **Cafe Pierpont** ★★★$ Metal floors and tabletops contribute to the cafe's noisy, fun-filled atmosphere. The prices are right, and young children eat free. Try any of the taco, enchilada, or burrito plates at this Mexican restaurant. ♦ Daily lunch and dinner. 122 W Pierpont Ave (at 200 W St), Salt Lake City. 364.1222

11 **Rio Grande Cafe** ★★$ This former hole-in-the-wall is now spruced up, but the good Mexican food and the charm remain. ♦ M-Sa lunch; daily dinner. 270 S Rio Grande St (inside the Rio Grande Train Depot), Salt Lake City. 364.3302

12 **Chart House** ★★★$$$ Located in the 1870 **Devereaux Mansion** at the Triad Center, this link in the Chart House chain specializes in seafood and beef entrées. Just eating inside the refurbished English mansion is a treat. ♦ Daily dinner. Reservations recommended. 334 W South Temple St (one block west of the Salt Palace), Salt Lake City. 596.0990

13 **Temple Square** In part the reason for Salt Lake City's existence, Temple Square is the center of the Mormon faith. Stroll the grounds and visit the **Mormon Tabernacle, Assembly Hall,** and two visitor centers. The temple itself is open only to Mormons. ♦ 50 W North Temple St (bounded by Main and West Temple Sts, and South and North Temple Sts), Salt Lake City. 240.2534

---

Utah's drinking laws are somewhat Byzantine. At most restaurants it is possible to order wine or cocktails with your meal. Nightclub visitors, however, must first buy a $5 membership card, which is good for two weeks.

---

Imagine combining Alta, Snowbird, Solitude, Brighton, and Park City into one gigantic ski area. That is, in essence, what Ski Utah Interconnect does. By using strategically located backcountry routes, it's possible to ski all five resorts in a single day. Tours are led by Forest Service-permitted guides and, because some hiking is required, skiers should be in good physical shape.

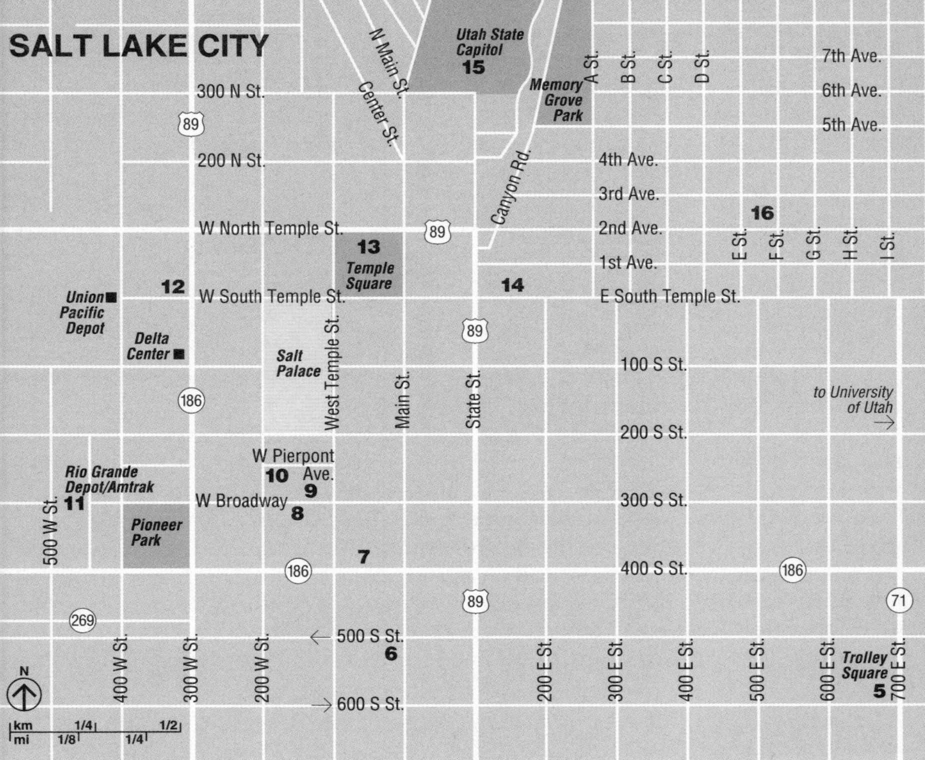


NINOS

**14 Ninos** ★★★$$$ Located 24 stories up, on the roof garden of the historic **University Club Building** in downtown Salt Lake, this glass-enclosed ristorante offers a panoramic view of the entire city. Brass railings and comfortable, overstuffed chairs simply add richness to the fine dining. Start with a Caesar or wilted spinach salad, prepared tableside; and proceed to one of the innovative pasta dishes—try the healthy garden vegetable pasta. If you can save room, finish with one of the housemade desserts—bananas Foster, anyone?—they're worth every calorie. ♦ M-Sa dinner. Reservations recommended. 136 E South Temple St (between 200 E and State Sts), Salt Lake City. 359.0506

**15 Utah State Capitol** Fashioned after the nation's capitol, this impressive granite structure was completed in 1915 after the state hit a windfall in inheritance taxes. The front steps command an expansive view of the Salt Lake Valley. Inside, Depression-era paintings depict the state's history. ♦ 350 N State St (on Capitol Hill), Salt Lake City. 538.3000

**16 The Avenues** $ For skiers on a budget, this hostel offers cheap accommodations in a historic Salt Lake neighborhood. It's clean and comfortable and within walking distance of downtown. ♦ 107 F St (between Second and Third Aves), Salt Lake City. 359.3855

**17 Brigham Street Inn** $$ Located along early Salt Lake City's most fashionable avenue (formerly known as Brigham Street), this historic bed-and-breakfast has eight distinctly different rooms and a suite. The turn-of-the-century three-story mansion was lovingly restored by the family that now runs the inn. ♦ 1135 E South Temple St (near the University of Utah), Salt Lake City. 364.4461; fax 521.3201

## Bests

**Kristen Ulmer**
Pro Athlete

Discovering new and exciting lines to ski.

Shredding with the snowboarders.

Skiing bumps under the Peruvian Chair and hearing people whoop when you ski hot.

Tucking **Hoopi's Crotch** and going close to 60 mph.

**Chic Morton**
Retired General Manager/President, Alta Ski Lifts Company

Après-ski—sunset against **Mount Superior,** with alpenglow covering Alta's alpine scenery.

The powder runs under **Devil's Castle** after a fresh overnight snowfall.

Cross-country skiing in the **Albion Basin** beneath a full moon.

Corn snow on Mount Superior at 8AM in April.

# Jackson Hole

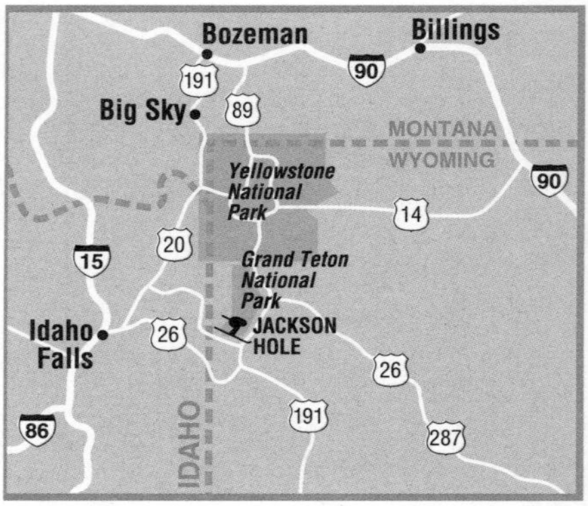

Just the mention of Jackson Hole can inspire joy, terror, or both in a skier's heart. True, this resort dramatically set in the rocky steepness of the **Grand Tetons** lays down ski tracks where ordinary mortals wouldn't dare to tread. But Jackson's fearsome reputation obscures the fact that it also has some of the best intermediate skiing in the country.

Jackson Hole's geographical stats are as awe-inspiring as the breathtaking scenery. The mountain's vertical rise of 4,139 feet is the largest of any US ski area, and its face is marked by a free-form layout of open bowls, steep chutes, and sheer cliffs. A creative spirit goes a long way when skiing such terrain. Though it has plenty of straightforward, groomed slopes, the best way for advanced skiers to make the most of the mountain is to find the most interesting lines with the best snow—rather than sticking to marked trails—and go for it. While Jackson may not be known for coddling beginners, runs such as **Eagle's Rest** and **Teewinot** are acceptable for novices. Intermediates can play all day on **Gros Ventre**, which is one of the better cruising runs in the US.

Winter is really the off-season around Jackson Hole. Vacationing families who came to visit the Grand Tetons and **Yellowstone National Park** are gone, and the town of **Jackson,** which in summer is transformed into something out of a Western cartoon, regains its dignity. Located 12 miles from the ski area, the town is the place to stay if you're interested in après-ski activities. Thanks in part to the strength of summer business, winter prices for food and lodging are reasonable.

**Jackson Hole**
**PO Box 290**
**Teton Village, Wyoming 83001**

**Information** .................... 307/733.2292

**Reservations** ....... 307/733.4005, 800/443.6931

**Jackson Hole Visitors Council** ..... 800/782.0011

**Snow Phone** .................... 307/733.2291

## Fast Facts

*Area code 307 unless otherwise noted.*

**Ski Season** Early December through early April

**Location** The Jackson Hole Ski Resort is 12 miles northwest of **Jackson, Wyoming. Salt Lake City,** about 275 miles southwest of Jackson, is the closest major metropolitan area.

### Getting to Jackson Hole

**By air: Jackson Hole Airport** is eight miles north of **Jackson. American** (800/433.7300) has direct service from **Chicago** and **Dallas/Ft. Worth. Continental** (800/525.0280) offers connecting flights to Jackson through **Salt Lake City. Delta** (800/221.1212) has connecting flights from **Denver. A-1 Taxi** (733.5809) and **Tumbleweed Taxi** (733.0808) provide transportation to and from the airport. Many inns and hotels in the area operate free airport shuttles.

**By car:** Winterized rental cars are available at the airport from **Avis, Budget, Hertz,** or **National.** Take Highway 22 West for four miles to Highway 390 North. After six miles, you'll see signs to **Teton Village** on your left.

**All-weather highways:**

Salt Lake City—Interstate 15 North to Highway 89

Denver—Interstate 25 North to Interstate 80 West to Highway 191 North

**Driving times from:**

Salt Lake City—6 hours (275 miles)

Denver—10 hours (500 miles)

### Getting around Jackson Hole

**Southern Teton Area Rapid Transit** (**START;** 733.4521) buses run daily between the ski area and the town of **Jackson.** Several rental car agencies have facilities in Jackson.

The Tetons and the Gros Ventre mountains were named by French trappers: teton for "breast," and gros ventre for "big belly."

## FYI

**Area** 2,500 acres of skiing with several bowls and lots of glades.

Beginner—10 percent

Intermediate—40 percent

Advanced-Expert—50 percent

**Number of Groomed Runs** 62

**Longest Run** 4.5 miles (a combination of runs from the **Rendezvous** summit)

**Capacity** 8,642 skiers per hour

**Base Elevation** 6,311 feet

**Summit Elevation** 10,450 feet

**Vertical Rise** 4,139 feet

**Average Annual Snowfall** 400 inches

**Snowmaking** 3 percent

**Night Skiing** None

**Lifts** 10 (1 aerial tram, 2 quad chairs, 1 triple chair, 4 double chairs, and 2 surface lifts)

| **Lift Passes** | **Full Day** | **Half Day** (starts at 12:30PM) |
|---|---|---|
| **Adult** | $40 | $31 |
| with tram | $44 | $34 |
| **Child** (14 and under) | $20 | $16 |
| with tram | $23 | $18 |
| **Senior** (65 and over) | $20 | $16 |
| with tram | $23 | $18 |

**Ski School** The main office of the **Jackson Hole Ski School** (739.2663) is located in the **Ski School Chalet** (halfway between the tram building and the Teewinot Chair). Half-day (two hours) and full-day (four hours) group lessons can be combined with a rental package. One-hour, half-day, and full-day private lessons are available, ranging from a two-hour morning session for one student to a full-day session (six hours) for a group of up to six students.

**Kids' Ski School** The **Cowboy Kids Ranch** (739.2691) offers the **Rough Riders** day program, a combination of child care and instruction for children ages 3 to 5. Tots new to skiing can enroll in the full-day program with child care; those who know the basics can enroll in group lessons. **SKIwee** is Jackson Hole's program for children ages 6 to 13, providing two-hour and full-day group lessons, and three- to five-day full packages.

**Clinics and Special Programs Mountain Experience** is a daily program for advanced or expert skiers that lets you test out powder, steep, and isolated runs. The length of the session will vary from three to four hours depending on the size of the group. The **Snow King Clinic** provides a guide service for skiers interested in exploring some of the area's more challenging, less frequented terrain. Programs geared to teenagers and the physically challenged, special clinics for moguls and steeps, and a snowboard program are offered.

**Races** NASTAR racing is held Tuesday, Thursday, and Sunday at 1PM on **Easy Does It**, under the Casper Lift. The ski school also organizes a pre-Christmas race camp for adults and one for children during Christmas and spring school breaks.

**Rentals** Equipment rentals, including snowboards, are available at **Jackson Hole Sports** (739.2687), located near the Teewinot Chair base, open daily 8AM to 5:30PM.

**Lockers** Coin-operated lockers are located in the upper level of the **Mountain Mall** building, next to the **Tram** building.

**Day Care** Half-day and full-day programs are offered at the **Kids Ranch** (739.2691). **Tenderfoots** is for tots 2 to 18 months old, and **Wranglers** is for ages 19 months to 5 years. Reservations are required.

**First Aid** The main ski-patrol office (739.2650) is located in the lower level of the **Tram** building.

**Parking** Free parking is available at the **Teton Village** base area.

**Worth Knowing**

- For skiers who want to check out the other side of the **Tetons**, a round-trip bus (fare includes lift ticket) leaves daily from Jackson Hole to **Grand Targhee Ski Resort,** on the eastern slope of the Tetons. It's a good alternative when snow conditions at Jackson are iffy; Grand Targhee, on average, gets about 15 feet more snow a year than does Jackson. For information, call 800/827.4433.
- The new **Jackson Hole Ski Three** book consists of five lift vouchers which can be used at Jackson Hole, Grand Targhee, or **Snow King** and includes full-day lift and aerial tram pass.

## Rating the Runs

### ● Beginner

Though **Eagle's Rest** and **Teewinot** don't cater strictly to beginners, there *is* some suitable terrain here for absolute first-timers and young children. These two main thoroughfares are wide, flat, and short (Teewinot, the longer of the two, is just over a half-mile long).

Wide, groomed, and relatively easy skiing can be had in **Casper Bowl,** but the easiest route down, the long **South Traverse,** can be tricky for debutants.

## ■ Intermediate

Jackson's glory begins to reveal itself in **Casper Bowl** at the intermediate level. **Easy Does It,** Casper's main thoroughfare, lives up to its name, although at less than a mile long, it's over much too quickly. Casper Bowl's vertical rise is just over a thousand vertical feet, but why spend all day skiing runs this short at a ski area that out-verticals any other in the US?

Despite the quality of the terrain on **Après Vous Mountain,** surprisingly few skiers are drawn here. **Werner** and **Moran** are two terrific, long cruisers, with a couple of pitches that are steeper (but not unmanageably so) than anything on Easy Does It. This mountain is also a good place for intermediates to get into the exploring spirit, with plenty of widely spaced trees to poke around in. The only drawback is its southerly exposure; when the weather warms up, the snow turns soggy fast.

Known by locals as "GV," **Gros Ventre** is one of the country's best long cruising runs; it's more than two miles long and covers close to 3,000 vertical feet from the top of the Thunder Chair to the base area. The first half of the trail runs through wide-open **Rendezvous Bowl;** then it cuts a wide swath through the trees before flattening out near the end. Local skiers try to catch the GV early, when it's still freshly groomed, and ski it top-to-bottom, nonstop, making big-radius turns at breakneck speed.

An alternative to GV's second half, **Sundance Gully** offers fast, big-radius turns, with the added thrill of banking off the sides of the gully.

## ◆ Advanced/◆◆ Expert

Depending on the line you choose, **Rendezvous Bowl** can be a challenge or a pushover. The ski patrol sets up stakes to outline the easiest route, consisting of long traverses back and forth. A more direct route usually means an encounter with big moguls, which tend to be less severe the farther you venture from the tram. At the bottom of the bowl, choose whether to ski trails from the Upper Sublette quad or the Thunder double chair.

A better choice than the Thunder Chair after a fresh snowfall, Upper Sublette provides access to two large bowls, **Cheyenne Bowl** and **Laramie Bowl.** Laramie also attracts a mogul-skiing crowd if it isn't a day for powder skiing. The main groomed run in Laramie is **Rendezvous Trail,** inaccurately marked expert—at least for part of its course—on the trail map.

When Rendezvous Trail is too crowded, check out the groomed skiing at the Thunder Chair, with **Grand** on the southerly side of the ridge and **Gros Ventre** on the north. **Thunder** used to be Jackson Hole's major mogul run, but now that it's groomed from time to time, the moguls rarely get big. Its northern exposure translates into good snow when conditions elsewhere are iffy.

Skiers who favor soft moguls will like **St. Johns,** tucked away on the far side of **Après Vous Mountain.** Under the softening effects of the sun, these moguls tend to be more forgiving and less steep than in places like **Laramie Bowl.**

Only a resort accustomed to the world's best skiers would mark **Corbet's Couloir** as a trail on its map. Once into the couloir, the skiing, though extremely steep, can be very good, since the snow is protected from sun and wind. The problem is *getting* in. Sometimes you can rappel in by rope; otherwise, it's a leap and a prayer over a cornice and rocks. If you miss that first turn, the best you can hope for is that your long, fast slide to the bottom won't result in injury. Corbet's attracts more skiers who *look* over the edge than actually ski over it.

Expert skiing at Jackson Hole is more a matter of connecting runs than selecting them. If you're seeking fresh, sun-shielded snow, begin in the trees along the left side of Rendezvous Bowl, cut over to the Thunder Chair to ski north-facing **Tower Three Chute,** an unmercifully narrow and steep sliver, and wind up in a cup on the mountainside that locals have dubbed **Toilet Bowl** (so-called because of the few steep lines that flush into it). An alternate route from Rendezvous Bowl is to cut across to **Cirque,** with a southerly exposure that can result in soft snow, or to traverse beneath Corbet's to **Ten Sleep Bowl,** with a more northerly turn and usually drier snow.

## Snowboarding

Boarders head to **Dick's Ditch** off the Thunder Chair for the natural half-pipe. More radical riders like to try tricks on the **Paintbrush** and **Toilet Bowl** trails for the abundance of natural obstacles including high, round walls, rock outcroppings, and lots of jumps. At the bottom, they can easily traverse over to Dick's Ditch for more fun. The **Rendezvous Bowl** and **Gros Ventre** area offer excellent high-speed cruising for experts, while intermediate boarders like to cruise **Moran's Face** on **Après Vous Mountain** because of its nice, wide-open tree runs. Nearby is an artificial half-pipe.

---

Grand Teton National Park was first established in 1929 as a 96,000-acre preserve that covered only the mountains themselves. In 1943 President Franklin Roosevelt designated another 180,000 acres, including a large chunk of the valley floor, as Grand Teton National Monument. It was a move that irked local ranchers not keen on the federal government claiming land in their territory. In 1949 the Rockefeller family donated another 33,000 acres, and in 1950 the entire land package was brought together as a national park by an act of Congress.

---

Jackson Hole shortchanges itself by officially claiming 2,500 skiable acres. In fact, there is so much terrain that the resort can afford to close off several hundred acres called The Hobacks to be held in reserve for fresh powder days. When the snow is fresh and deep, this area is one of the great powder-skiing caches in America.

## Mountain Highs and Lows

Jackson Hole's lower bowls and ridges—**Lower Sublette Ridge** to **North Colter Ridge**—often look tempting from the tram. But more often than not, the snow is uneven crust or sludge and not much fun to ski.

## At the Resort

*Area code 307 unless otherwise noted.*

✦ **Teton Village Condominiums** $$$ If you want to stay close to the slopes, 14 separate condo/chalet clusters can be found on the periphery of Teton Village. Price, size, amenities, and relative luxury vary considerably from one condo to the next, but expect to pay a little extra for this kind of convenience. ♦ Teton Village. 733.4610, 800/443.6840; fax 733.3183

✦ **The Alpenhof** $$$$ The theme here is Austrian-Bavarian. Designed after an Alpine chalet, this 42-unit luxury hotel has rooms with hand-carved Bavarian furniture, down comforters, and sunny balconies (though not much of a view). Amenities include a good restaurant, and a hot tub, pool, and sauna. ♦ North of Teton Village parking lot. 733.3242; fax 739.1516

Within the Alpenhof:

**Alpenhof Dining Room** ★★★$$$ The casually elegant atmosphere is a bit staid for laid-back Teton Village. Still, an abundance of plants, one whole wall of glass looking out on the tramway, and sections of river rock along the other walls make this a warm and inviting place to dine. The food is excellent, with beef, veal, game, and seafood served in an unabashedly rich style. Desserts are a highlight, with pastries, tortes, and such treats as bananas Foster, flambéed at the table. Those who find this room too fancy can retreat upstairs to the informal **Dietrich's Bar & Bistro** and its outdoor deck. ♦ Daily breakfast, lunch, and dinner. Dinner reservations recommended. 733.3462

✦ **Jack Dennis Sports** This ski shop sells and rents equipment, but clothing (skiwear and beyond) is its strong suit. ♦ Next to the Alpenhof. 733.3270

✦ **Sojourner Inn** $$$ With one hundred rooms, this is the largest hotel in Teton Village. What started as a fairly compact lodge has grown into a rambling hotel through progressive additions. As a result, rooms vary in size and modern amenities. The hotel has a pool, sauna, and hot tub. ♦ Next to the Alpenhof. 733.3657, 800/445.4655; fax 733.9543

Within the Sojourner Inn:

**Fondue Pot** ★★$$$ Fondue in various guises, including cheese, chocolate, beef, and seafood, is served in a romantic fireside setting, making this the best place in Teton Village to take a date. ♦ Daily dinner. Reservations recommended. 733.3657

**Rendezvous Lounge** **Mangy Moose** is the first après-ski stop in Teton Village, but the Rendezvous is a reliable back-up, especially for those seeking a less hectic scene. Ski movies on a big-screen TV and free hors d'oeuvres are the highlights. ♦ M-Sa 11:30AM-midnight; Su 11:30AM-10PM. 733.3657

**Village Steakhouse** ★$$$ The main objective here is to feed **Sojourner Inn** guests, which translates into decent if not spectacular food served in a decent if not spectacular setting. A steak house by name only, the restaurant also prepares chicken and seafood entrées. ♦ Daily breakfast, lunch, and dinner. 733.3657

✦ **Village Center Inn** $$ Located right in the heart of Teton Village, this 15-unit condo hotel has studios to two-bedroom units. The accommodations are no-frills, but you can't beat the price or location close to the lifts. ♦ Next to the Tram building. 733.3155, 800/735.8342; fax 733.3183

✦ **Nick Wilson's Cowboy Cafe** ★$ This quick-stop spot is the place for donuts and coffee in the morning, burgers and fries midday, and pitchers of beer on the sundeck later. ♦ Daily breakfast, lunch, and après-ski. In the Tram building. 733.6657

✦ **Wilderness Sports** In addition to offering clothing, equipment, and rentals, this sports store likes to tout its boot-fitting service. ♦ Daily 8AM-9PM. In the Mountainside Mall. 733.4297

✦ **Mangy Moose** ★★$$ Teton Village's immensely popular après-ski hangout serves such inexpensive fill-'er-up fare as beef, chicken, and pasta. The scene is especially boisterous when live bands play. ♦ Daily dinner. In the Mangy Moose building. 733.4913

Within the Mangy Moose building:

**The Rocky Mountain Oyster** ★★$ Grab a slice of pizza, one of the daily sandwich specials, or a fresh muffin. ♦ Daily breakfast, lunch, and dinner. 733.5525

✦ **Crystal Springs Inn** $$ This inn has basic motel-style accommodations at a fair price, plus a refrigerator in each of the 15 rooms. ♦ South of the Tram building. 733.4423; fax 733.3183

✦ **Teton Village Sports** This full-service shop is probably the best in the Village for ski tuning and equipment repairs. ♦ Daily 8AM-9PM. In the Crystal Springs building. 733.2181

**Restaurants/Clubs:** Red **Hotels:** Blue
**Shops/ Outdoors:** Green **Sights/Culture:** Black

Within Teton Village Sports:

**High Mountain Helicopter Skiing** If you would rather not wait for the tram, these pilots will whisk you to the top of the slopes in record time. Daily helicopter skiing trips in the mountains surrounding Jackson (though not in the national parks) are offered. ♦ Daily 8AM-9PM. 733.3274

✦ **Inn at Jackson Hole** $$$$ This inn vies with the **Alpenhof** for the title of fanciest hotel in Teton Village, though it offers more flexibility, with kitchenettes, lofts, and fireplaces in some of its 83 rooms. It may be part of the Best Western chain, but the Inn's distinctive character can be seen in such touches as tables in the lobby made from tree trunks. ♦ South of the Tram building. 733.2311, 800/842.7666; fax 733.0844

Within the Inn at Jackson Hole:

**Jenny Leigh's Dining Room** ★★$$$ Game—elk, boar, buffalo—headlines the menu here, though other continental dishes are also available. In keeping with the hunting spirit, animal heads are mounted on the walls. ♦ Daily breakfast and dinner. Dinner reservations recommended. 733.7102

✦ **The Range** ★★★$$$ This intimate restaurant makes a genuine effort to serve regionally produced food, with such items as local beef and free-range chicken on the prix-fixe menu. ♦ Tu-Su dinner. Reservations recommended. 733.5481

✦ **Teton Village Market** Newspapers, snacks, soft drinks, and a few grocery items can be picked up at this convenience store. ♦ Daily 7AM-9PM. At the Teton Village Chevron station. 733.2747

✦ **Hostel** $ Young, budget-conscious skiers will appreciate the inexpensive, no-frills accommodations. If you cram four into a room, it's possible to pare per-night lodging costs to under $15 per person. ♦ South of Teton Village parking lot. 733.2311

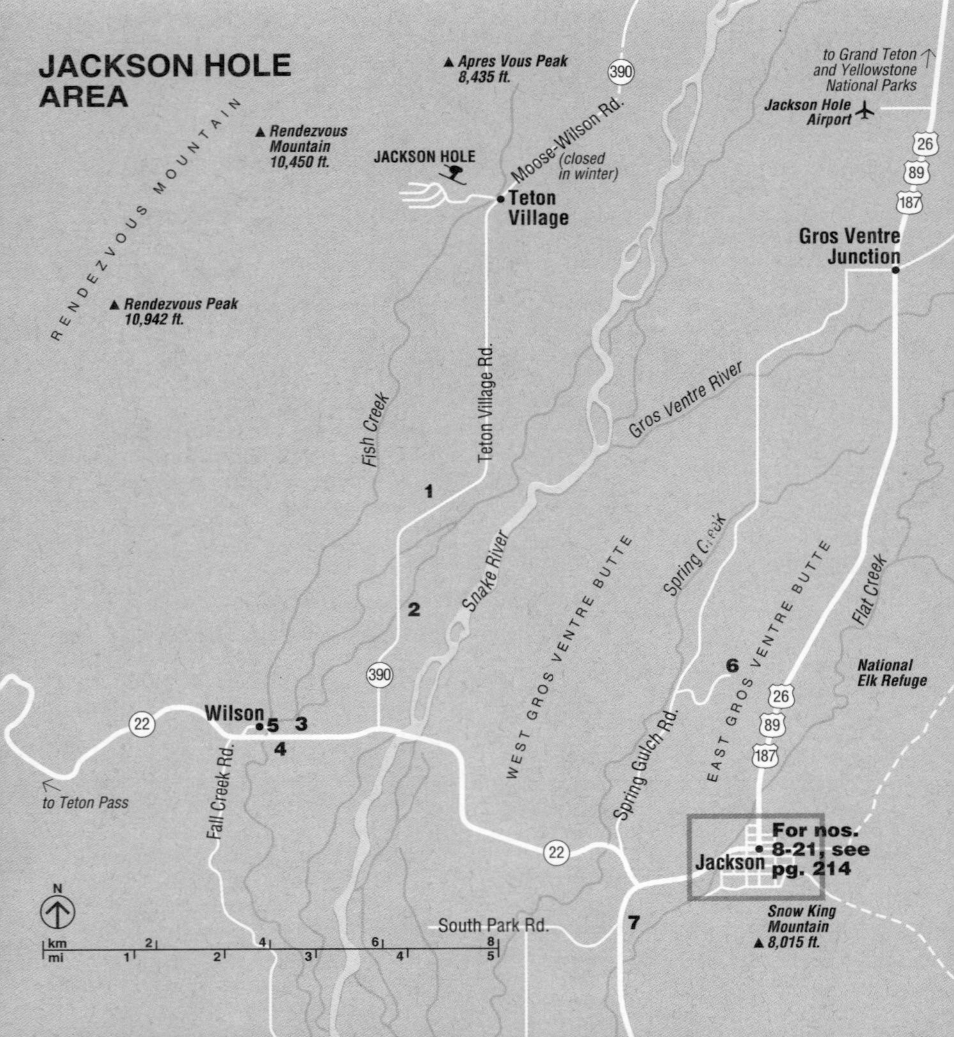

## Beyond the Resort

**1 Jackson Hole Racquet Club** $$$ Fitness junkies who can't satisfy their fix with a day of skiing can burn more energy at the fitness center, indoor running track, indoor tennis courts, and racquetball courts. The posh accommodations are in studio to four-bedroom condos and a few houses, and all 120 units feature kitchens and fireplaces. ♦ 4 miles south of Teton Village. 733.3990, 800/443.8616; fax 733.5551

Within the Jackson Hole Racquet Club:

**Stiegler's Restaurant** ★★★$$$ Austrian lace curtains, flowered linen tablecloths, and the stucco and wooden beams make this a charming eatery. The spirit of Tyrolian gemütlichkeit is enhanced by the two large stone fireplaces, set back-to-back, which separate the copper bar from the dining room. Schnitzels, game in rich sauces, and other Austrian dishes are the specialty here. ♦ Tu-Su lunch and dinner. Dinner reservations recommended. 733.1071

**2 Vista Grande** ★★$$ Mexican restaurant basics—adobe walls, tile floors, chips and salsa, big burritos, enchilada and chimichanga plates, and moderate prices—make this casa the most popular place in the village for south-of-the-border fare. ♦ Daily dinner. No reservations. Teton Village Rd, 5 miles south of Teton Village. 733.6964

**3 Nora's Fish Creek Inn** ★★$$ This log-cabin roadhouse attracts both skiers and ranch hands who arrive in pick-up trucks. Breakfast is the big meal; arrive before 8AM to share pancakes and coffee with local working folk; later to eat with the skiing crowd. Standard American fare—fish, steaks, pasta—makes this a good family place for dinner. ♦ Daily breakfast, lunch, and dinner. Hwy 22, a mile west of the Teton Village Rd, Wilson. 733.8288

**4 Stagecoach Bar** Sunday night is the big night at this bar in Wilson, where the country-and-western Stagecoach Band has played every Sunday for 25 years. On other nights, shoot pool or the breeze with a local crowd. ♦ Hwy 22, a mile west of the Teton Village Rd, Wilson. 733.4407

**5 Teton Tree House** $$ Rustic yet elegant, this is the best bed-and-breakfast establishment in the area. The four-story building has exposed-beam interiors and rooms with private baths; some of the six rooms have good views of the valley. The owners have years of experience guiding many trips, from river excursions to backcountry ski tours. ♦ Hwy 22, 2 miles west of the Teton Village Rd, Wilson. 733.3233; fax 733.3233

SPRING CREEK RESORT

**6 Spring Creek Resort** $$$$ One of the best condominium complexes in the area, this resort is all rough-hewn wood on the outside, modern and nicely furnished inside. The 118 units are away from it all atop a butte between Teton Village and Jackson, with commanding views of the Tetons. It is isolated, however: Jackson is a 10-minute drive on a steep road that can be slick when it snows. ♦ 2 miles from the Spring Gulch Rd turn-off from Hwy 22, a mile west of the Hwy 187 intersection. 733.8833; fax 733.1524

Within Spring Creek Resort:

**The Granary** ★★★$$$$ Ask locals to name the restaurant they'd pick for a special occasion, and this elegant place is the likely choice. The relaxing Western decor is luxuriously offset by white linen tablecloths and silver settings. Whether you're in the lounge on the upper level or the dining room on the lower level, you may have to catch your breath as you look out the walls of 16-foot windows at the awesome Grand Tetons. The menu leans toward innovative meat dishes—such as medaillons of elk—with a nod to lighter fish and vegetable entrées as well. Sleigh rides offered at the resort are topped off with dinner here. ♦ Daily lunch and dinner. Dinner reservations recommended. 733.8833

**7 Days Inn** $$ On the southwest periphery of town are a couple of modern, ultrafamiliar chain motels. This 90-room "inn" may be your best choice. ♦ Off Hwy 89, a half-mile south of Hwy 22. 733.9010, 800/325.2525; fax 733.0044

**8 Bubba's Bar-B-Que** ★★$ This is the kind of place where you don't just eat; you chow down and lick your fingers. Barbecued chicken and spare ribs are best bets. Bring your own booze, as there's no liquor license. ♦ Daily breakfast, lunch, and dinner. No reservations. 515 W Broadway (at Pearl St). 733.2288

**9 Rusty Parrot Lodge** $$$$ Hand-crafted furniture, beds with big down comforters, and fireplaces (in some of the 32 guest rooms) give this lodge a comfy country feel. Breakfast is taken in the Gathering Room. This is the best high-end place to stay in town. ♦ 175 Jackson St (at Gill Ave). 733.2000, 800/458.2004; fax 733.5566

**10 Blue Lion** ★★★$$$ You'll feel like you're visiting friends when you step into this small, comfortable house on a Jackson side street for dinner. The linen-covered oak tables are topped with vases of dried wildflowers and the

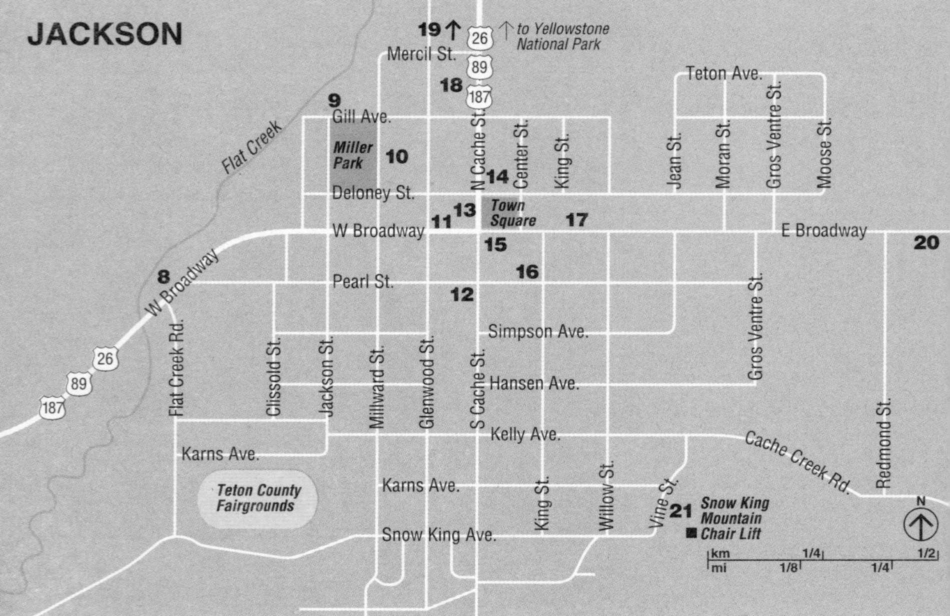


light walls are adorned with black and white photographs as well as pastel watercolors of the surrounding countryside. Adding to the coziness is a wood-burning stove used to heat the place. The imaginative menu features a unique continental-style selection with such dishes as rack of lamb, elk, seafood and homemade pasta. ♦ Daily dinner. Reservations recommended. 160 Millward St (between Deloney St and Gill Ave). 733.3912

**11 Wort Hotel** $$$ This Jackson institution has been providing lodging for more than 50 years. At one time it housed an illegal gambling operation that was winked at by public officials. The large staircase in the main lobby conveys the spirit of the hotel's roots, although all 60 rooms have been refurbished and have a nice mix of old-hotel style and modern amenities. ♦ 50 Glenwood St (at W Broadway). 733.2190, 800/322.2727; fax 733.2067

Within the Wort Hotel:

**JJ's Silver Dollar Bar & Grill** Mosey on up to the bar to see the more than 2,000 silver dollars imbedded in it. This bar is the third stop in Jackson's nightlife triangle, after the **Million Dollar Cowboy Bar** and **The Rancher** (see below for both). There's usually live music and dancing. ♦ M-Sa 11AM-2AM; Su 11AM-10PM. 733.2190

**Freebird Alaskan Adventures** Choose from a half-day or full-day dog-sledding trip. Either ride on a sled or drive your own. ♦ Meets at JJ's Silver Dollar Bar & Grill. 733.7388

Depending on the harshness of the winter, about 8,000 head of elk collect in the National Elk Refuge each year. That number represents at least half of the total herd in the Jackson area.

**12 Antler Motel** $$ This is one of the largest (100 guest rooms) moderately priced motels in Jackson. Some rooms have fireplaces. ♦ 43 Pearl St (between Cache and Glenwood Sts). 733.2535, 800/522.2406; fax 733.4158

**13 Cadillac Grille** ★★★$$$ Santa Monica meets Jackson at this hip eatery. The sleek interior, with colored neon lighting and Deco trim, seems more appropriate for a beachside bistro. But the decor complements the nouvelle California cuisine, heavy on seafood and fruit garnishes. The surprise is that it all works. ♦ Daily lunch and dinner. Dinner reservations recommended. On Town Square (between W Broadway and Deloney St). 733.3279

**13 Million Dollar Cowboy Bar** This bar is Jackson's Empire State Building: A landmark that every visitor should visit at least once. Despite such unabashed schlock as saddle seats at the bar, it still ropes 'em in, with many patrons trying to dress and behave like the real McCoys, especially when two-stepping on the dance floor. The place is big, loud, and crowded late into the night. ♦ M-W noon-midnight; Th-Sa noon-2AM; Su noon-10PM. On Town Square (between W Broadway and Deloney St). 733.2207

**14 The Bunnery** ★★$ Stop by for fresh breakfast pastries and breads. ♦ Daily breakfast and lunch. Hole-in-the-Wall Mall, 130 N Cache St. 733.5474

**15 The Rancher** True party animals spend a few hours at the **Cowboy** or the **Silver Dollar** (see above for both), then close out the night here. That's night one; the next night, they reverse the sequence. ♦ M-Sa 10AM-2AM; Su noon-10PM. 20 E Broadway (south side of Town Square). 733.3886

Sweetwater Restaurant

**16 Sweetwater Restaurant** ★★$$ Log-cabin walls, well-worn floors, and a flannel-shirt-and-jeans dress code give this place a warm, homey feel. Soups, sandwiches, and salads for lunch are where the restaurant's kitchen shines. ♦ Daily lunch and dinner. Dinner reservations recommended. King and Pearl Sts. 733.3553

**17 Jedediah's House of Sourdough** ★★$ This log cabin in a grove of pines is a prime breakfast stop for pancakes—including, of course, sourdough pancakes. ♦ Daily breakfast, lunch, and dinner. Dinner reservations recommended. 135 E Broadway (one block east of Town Square). 733.5671

**18 The Bunkhouse** $ Lodging at this 30-room joint is dormitory-style, but it's clean, cheap, and includes a communal kitchen, hot tub, and laundry facilities. ♦ 215 N Cache St (between Gill Ave and Mercil St). 733.3668; fax 733.3957

**19 National Elk Refuge** The largest elk herd in North America spends its winters in this refuge north of town, created more than 80 years ago to keep elk from raiding food supplies intended for ranchers' livestock. Naturalists lead sleigh rides to get up close and personal with the elk—one of the Jackson area's quintessential photo opportunities. ♦ Sleigh rides leave approximately every 20 minutes between 10AM and 4PM. Hwy 89, 2 miles north of Jackson. 733.0277

**19 Flagg Ranch** Though a number of ranches in the area offer snowmobile rentals and tours, this one comes out ahead because of its location. **Yellowstone National Park** is to the immediate north; **Grand Teton National Park** is to the south. Guided and unguided tours are available. ♦ 2 miles south of entrance to Yellowstone National Park on Hwy 89. 543.2861, 800/443.2311

**20 Lame Duck Restaurant** ★★$$$ Chinese food in cowboy country? Yes, and it's quite good, if somewhat short of the high standards found in big-city Chinese restaurants. The enormous menu even includes a few Japanese items. ♦ Daily lunch and dinner. Reservations accepted for large parties. 680 E Broadway (just east of Redmond St). 733.4311

**21 Snow King Resort** $$$ Skiing—including night skiing—right out the back door is the highlight of this 250-unit condominium resort with a cool glass-and-wood exterior that seems almost New Age. ♦ 400 Snow King Ave (off Vine St). 733.5200, 800/522.5464; fax 733.4084

## Bests

### Pepi Stiegler

Director of Skiing, Jackson Hole Ski Corporation/Olympic Medalist in 1960 and 1964

Favorite ski runs: **The Hobacks** for powder. The **Gros Ventre** for cruising. The **Out-of-Bounds** for spring corn snow. (A tip: The last one on the aerial tram is the first one off—and the first to make tracks in fresh powder.)

Favorite dining: Horsefeathers at **The Rocky Mountain Oyster.** *Leberknoedel* and gemütlichkeit at **Stiegler's Restaurant** (my brother's place).

Other favorites: Cross-country tours into **Grand Teton National Park. Yellowstone National Park** in winter—**Old Faithful,** frosty buffalo, crystal-clear blue skies, and no crowds. **Brooks Lake Lodge**—accessible by cross-country ski, dogsled, or snowmobile (10 miles round trip). A hearty lunch is your reward.

### Wade McKoy

Photographer/Journalist/Publisher, Focus Productions

First tracks in **Rendezvous Bowl—"The Bowl"** at the Jackson Hole ski resort contains more turns than most people can make without stopping, a moderately steep pitch with a view, and gobs of elbow room. One run there in untracked snow can make you smile for a year.

**Big storms**—In Wyoming, it sometimes snows for weeks on end. The flakes pile up so deep that you walk *up* out of the indoors. You can ski fresh powder every day, and it is never the same. The wind (or lack of it), the temperatures, and the amount of snow combine to make each ski experience different from the day before.

**Après-ski**—In Europe, where skiing began, they ski a little and eat and drink a lot. Here, we do a lot of both.

**Spring ski mountaineering**—I don't know where else in the world you can drive to the base of a 6,000-foot vertical ski run, climb it in the middle of the night, and then, while most mortals are punching a time clock, ski the 40° pitch of corn snow back to your car. A big American breakfast tastes mighty good after that. Ahhh, springtime in the Tetons.

In 1970, long before "extreme" skiing was in vogue, Bill Briggs climbed and skied down the Grand Teton. A few years later, Briggs and his partner, Boomer McClure, skied an even more daring descent from the summit of neighboring Mount Owen. Shortly thereafter, McClure died trying to become the first person to ski the Matterhorn. Today Briggs is the director of the ski school at the Snow King Resort.

# Ten Up-and-Coming Ski Areas

**Alyeska Resort**
**PO Box 249**
**Girdwood, Alaska 99587**
**Information** ..............................907/754.1111

Twice Alyeska has stopped short of hitting the big time in the ski world. When it was acquired by Seibu, Japan's giant resort empire, developers dreamed of attracting thousands of Asian visitors—but when the oil boom ended and the economy faltered, airlines canceled their direct flights from Japan. And a few years back, it made a bid for the Winter Olympics but lost out.

But if the third time's the charm, Alyeska's future looks bright. The 307-room **Alyeska Prince Hotel** is a luxury retreat complete with restaurants, indoor swimming pool, health club, and a 60-passenger tram to the summit.

No question about it, the mountain's scale merits such extensive facilities. Six chairlifts assail its 2,500 feet of vertical, culminating in spectacular **Glacier Bowl**, where the sons of sourdoughs follow high traverses to fields of powder. For intrepid intermediates, there's a heart-stopping ridge run called **Mitey-Mite**, which has a sheer drop-off to the bottom of the world. The top of the mountain is above the tree line, but midway down the white slopes funnel into forested areas.

Skiing Alyeska brings you face to face with the wonders of nature. There are weird little climatic quirks called "sun dogs"—small whirlwinds of suspended ice particles that glisten in the sunlight just above the slopes. Inspiring views of **Cook Inlet**, its silver ice floes shifting with the tides, will distract even the most dedicated downhiller. And with the lowest base elevation of any major American ski resort (a scant 250 feet above sea level, and topping out at 2,750), you never have to worry about getting winded from lack of oxygen.

Alyeska itself also offers some condos and an excellent restaurant, but most visitors stay in **Anchorage**, with its urban array of hotels and motels, and catch "The Lift"—a bus that leaves five days a week from three Burger King locations—to the slopes. ♦ Adult lift ticket: $29 full day, $24 after 1PM. Nearest major airport: Anchorage, 40 miles.

**Bear Valley Ski Area**
**PO Box 5038**
**Bear Valley, California 95223**
**Information** ..............................209/753.2301

People who like their mountains pure are passionate about Bear Valley, which, high above the fabled Gold Rush town of **Angels Camp,** is truly the resort that time forgot. Still nurturing an aura of antiquity (none of those newfangled, high-speed quad chairs here), the resort boasts the most authentic rustic ski lodge in California. Deliciously worn around the edges, the **Lodge at Bear Valley** is an architectural classic, with vaulted beamed ceilings, a giant stone fireplace, and a double-height great room.

Beyond the **Bear Valley Village** and up the road a few miles (by the free shuttle bus), you'll find the ski area. An unusual feature about this place is that the day lodge and your arrival point are actually at midmountain. There's a naturally occurring division of ability levels at Bear Valley. Beginners rule the terrain in front of the lodge; intermediates have the run of the back side, known as **Bear West,** with its sylvan, forested glades; and advanced and expert skiers can tackle the open slopes and moguled trails in **Grizzly Bowl** below the lodge. A network of nine chairlifts and two surface lifts services the area's 1,280 skiable acres, which contain 60 trails spread over 1,900 vertical feet.

A few creature comforts keep visitors happy—a general store, deli, ski shop, and several restaurants. On weekends, live entertainment is often booked. ♦ Adult lift ticket: $28 full day, $20 after 12:30PM. Nearest major airport: Stockton, 104 miles.

**Big Mountain**
**PO Box 1400**
**Whitefish, Montana 59937**
**Information** ..............................406/862.3511

The infectious, wild West spirit of **Whitefish,** Montana, attracts a crowd from both sides of the border, luring Canadian cowboys as well as serious skiers to its saloons and slaloms. Eight miles north of town the aptly named Big Mountain looms over the plains. Seven chairlifts cover 4,040 acres of slopes. The mountain, with its vertical drop of 2,400 feet, boasts long intermediate cruisers, as well as a beginner's run of 2.5 miles. Mostly, this place impresses you with a lot of terrain above the tree line on the front face, matched with glade skiing on the back side.

There's a small village and limited lodging near the base of Big Mountain (try the **Kandahar Lodge**), but the real party animals head to town, where a full range of accommodations is available. The proximity to **Glacier National Park** offers the opportunity to take an inspiring side trip. ♦ Adult lift ticket: US $35/CAN $40 full day, US$28/CAN $32 after 1PM. Nearest major airport: Kalispell, 19 miles.

**Grand Targhee**
**PO Box SKI**
**Alta, Wyoming 83422**
**Information** ............................800/TARGHEE

The annual snowfall at Grand Targhee—a whopping 500 inches—puts it in a class with some of the country's higher-profile ski resorts. But the character of this **Grand Teton** peak differs from that of the hot spots. If you'd rather ski than be seen, Targhee might be your kind of place.

Three chairlifts deposit skiers on 1,500 acres of some of the West's best open bowls, ridges, and glades. An additional 1,500 acres for powder skiing are accessible by snowcats. Since the resort is perched at 8,000 feet, almost every trail begins and ends above the tree line. The longest of the 62 groomed runs is 2.75 miles, and the vertical drop is 2,200 feet. Nightly dustings of dry snow leave a fluffy, forgiving surface in the morning—the best time to hit the slopes. When there's a clear, deep blue sky, with the hoarfrost on the trees creating bizarre ice sculptures, skiing here is otherworldly.

The base area, decidedly down to earth, sets a no-frills tone for après-ski, along the lines of burgers and beers at the **Trap Bar**. A trio of overnight lodges stands adjacent to the lifts, along with a condominium complex that's great for families and groups. If watching the purple alpenglow bathe the spires of the Tetons is too tranquil for your tastes, you can head for raucous **Jackson Hole,** 75 minutes away, but fair warning: Driving the steep and hazardous pass at night is apt to jangle the steadiest nerves. ♦ Adult lift ticket: $30 full day, $20 half day (after 9:30AM or 12:30PM). Nearest major airport: Idaho Falls, Idaho, 87 miles.

**Mount Hood Meadows**
**PO Box 470**
**Mount Hood, Oregon 97041**
**Information** ............................503/337.2222

Despite Mount Hood's tendency to throw sudden, stormy tantrums in any given season, ski-savvy Portlanders have been cruising its slopes for years. Two resorts cling to its flanks: historic **Timberline,** which is known primarily for its summer glacier skiing, and Mount Hood Meadows, the larger and more diverse of the pair. Citing impressive statistics—2,777 feet of vertical drop, 2,150 skiable acres, 82 trails, and 9 chairlifts—it's clear the Meadows can hold its own against any place in the West.

Long intermediate runs, typified by the three-mile **North Canyon** trail, are bountiful here. For powder pigs, there's **Heather Canyon** above the tree line, and snowboarders can wallow in plenty of radical ravines. Gulch, a new quad lift, has opened up 10 additional runs, most of them of moderate difficulty, while neophytes and small fry aren't forgotten, with lots of benign territory set aside for their use. And three evenings every week (Thursday through Saturday), night owls can hit the well-lighted runs.

Most of the skiers at Mount Hood Meadows are day-trippers (or weekend warriors) who head back home at day's end. For overnight stays in the area, check out **Government Camp** (10 miles away) or **Welches** (22 miles away). Shredders of a different sort might want to bed down in the town of **Hood River,** which is the self-proclaimed windsurfing capital of the world.

♦ Adult lift ticket: $32 full day, $27 after 12PM, $37 full day and night. Nearest major airport: Portland, 67 miles.

**Santa Fe Ski Area**
**1210 Luisa, Suite 10**
**Santa Fe, New Mexico 87501**
**Information** ............................505/983.9155

The more popular **Taos Ski Valley** may get all the thunder in the world with advanced skiers, but it's Santa Fe that seems to get all the powder. Nestled at the 12,000-foot mark of New Mexico's **Sangre de Cristo Range** at the southern end of the **Rockies** (making this one of the highest slopes in the country), the Santa Fe area is a skier's nirvana.

The snow is as dry as the high desert sands below and puffs into cold smoke when your skis slice through it. Eight lifts tap into terrain that challenges powder-hounds of every ability, and you'd better keep your legs limber, especially if you intend to tackle the contours of **Big Tesuque Bowl**. If you're not quite that daring, there's plenty of glade skiing in sheltered valleys for intermediates and beginners, with runs up to three miles long.

What really makes a vacation here so exceptional are the sophisticated pleasures of New Mexico's capital city. Museums, art galleries, and historical sites appeal to skiers seeking cultural diversions, while a splendid array of specialty stores and boutiques

satisfy the most serious shoppers. And as far as restaurants are concerned. . . well, you'll have to work awfully hard to find a disappointing meal here. The best area to stay in is around the **Plaza,** where amenities are just a stroll away. Lodgings in this storied district tend to be upscale, pueblo-style hotels, dominated by **La Fonda** on the Plaza, and charming inns, such as the **Hotel St. Francis**, which is listed on the National Register of Historic Places. ♦ Adult lift ticket: $35 full day, $24 half day (after 9AM or 12:30PM). Nearest major airport: Albuquerque, 65 miles.

**Schweitzer Mountain Resort**
**PO Box 815**
**Sandpoint, Idaho 83864**
**Information** ..............................208/263.9555

One of the sleepers of the ski world, Schweitzer (locals say "Sweitzer"), Idaho, is getting the secret out quickly. The formerly bone-jarring, five-mile access road to the mountain is now paved, and an ambitious expansion plan for the resort, particularly the base area, is well underway.

When storms sweep across western Canada, the **Selkirk Mountains** get their share of the dump, and Schweitzer's slopes are beneficiaries. The half-dozen chairlifts, strategically laid out along the crest, service 47 cut runs snaking over 2,350 skiable acres. The mountain's vast bowls are natural powder-catchers that afford stunning views of **Sandpoint** resort and **Lake Pend Oreille** below. Some of the best intermediate trails in the West—stretching up to 2.7 miles—take skiers through spectacular and unusual trees on the quiet, intimate back basin.

The 82-room **Green Gables Lodge** is the nucleus of an emerging village settlement, which presently consists of the base facilities and a smattering of condos. Many visitors choose to stay in Sandpoint (an easy 11-mile drive) or at the **Coeur d'Alene Resort,** 90 minutes to the south, for three or four days, and ski Schweitzer and **Silver Mountain** (see below), 35 miles down the road. ♦ Adult lift ticket: $32 full day, $25 after 12:30PM. Nearest major airport: Spokane, Washington, 75 miles.

**Sierra-at-Tahoe**
**1111 Sierra-at-Tahoe Road**
**Twin Bridges, California 95735**
**Information** ..............................916/659.7453

This unpretentious area near **South Lake Tahoe** started life as the **Sierra Ski Ranch,** a mom-and-pop ski camp that just kept getting bigger. Now under new management, it's a full-service ski resort with 10 chairlifts, including three high-speed quads and lots of wide, fall-line terrain that is reminiscent of Colorado.

Sierra-at-Tahoe may be the most underrated ski resort in California. Spread-eagled across three mountainsides, it's nevertheless sheltered from high winds, a boon during inclement weather. It has the region's longest beginner run, **Sugar-n-Spice,** a cool 3.5 miles. For intermediates, the routes served by the Cougar Chair are fast, wide, well-groomed trails that undulate through heavy forest. The **Backside,** with its mounds and gullies, is a funhouse ride, and just above the base area mogul-mashers can find a bevy of challenging bumps.

The preferred hangout for lunch is the **Grand View Grill & Lake View Deck,** which affords postcard views of **Lake Tahoe** and the surrounding Sierra peaks. Sierra-at-Tahoe has no overnight lodging and no village, but with the bright lights of South Lake Tahoe and **Stateline** flickering only 12 miles away, this poses no problem. ♦ Adult lift ticket: $37 full day, $25 after 12:30PM. Nearest major airport: Reno, Nevada, 72 miles.

**Silver Mountain**
**Kellogg, Idaho 83837**
**Information** ..............................208/783.1111

The story of Silver Mountain is that of a born-again boomtown. When the mineral mines of **Kellogg** dried up, the residents joined forces with some visionary developers (including the Hagadone Hospitality Company, owners of the neighboring **Coeur d'Alene Resort**) to create the country's first large-scale ski area in nearly a decade. Just four years old, the resort now prospers from the 320 inches of white gold that annually cover the slopes.

Silver Mountain's single-stage gondola is the largest in the world; it carries skiers from an almost snowless base of 2,300 feet up to the main lodge at 5,700 feet. The 19-minute ride dips into a small canyon before scaling the mountain. The gondola, along with six chairlifts, covers two peaks and 50 trails.

Although Kellogg's modest inns are cozy and comfortable, many visitors opt to stay at the posh Coeur d'Alene Resort, 35 miles away, taking advantage of its off-season rates and ski packages. To hit Silver's slopes, guests simply hop on one of the regular shuttle buses. ♦ Adult lift ticket: $31 full day, $23 after 12:30PM. Nearest major airport: Spokane, Washington, 70 miles.

**Winter Park**
**PO Box 36**
**Winter Park, Colorado 80482**
**Information** ..............................303/726.5514

Half the fun of going to Winter Park is taking the West's last bona fide ski train, which pulls out of **Denver**'s old **Union Station,** chugs up and over the **Continental Divide,** and arrives, about two hours later, right next to the lifts. From there, it's all uphill again. And what a hill! Twenty chairlifts spread like spider webs across three mountain faces, the highest of which peaks at 12,060 feet. After 55 years of operation, this venerable resort chalks up more than a million skier visits a season.

The area has 120 designated trails and is divided into the **Winter Park, Mary Jane,** and **Vasquez Ridge** sections. Beginner territory covers nearly half of the front side, intermediates claim most of Vasquez, and experts can romp till they drop at Mary Jane. Runs extend up to 4.5 miles in length, and the terrain ranges from friendly to formidable. On the friendly side are a 20-acre **Learn to Ski Park** with its own lifts and low-cost lessons and equipment rentals for special-needs skiers at the **National Sports Center for the Disabled,** the most comprehensive program of its kind in the world.

Winter Park's eight facilities serve tasty meals—it's a strong soul indeed who can pass up **Mama Mia's** pizza at the **Snoasis Midmountain Restaurant.** Around the base area cluster five overnight lodges, most of them condominiums, with the Iron Horse Resort rated one of the best. In the town of Winter Park, motels, bed-and-breakfasts, and inns, plus some 30 restaurants and 19 bars, offer ample lodging and dining options. But don't expect the shoppers' bonanzas of Vail or Aspen. ♦ Adult lift ticket: $40 full day, $26 half day (after 9AM or 12PM). Nearest major airport: Denver, 67 miles. A special weekend ski train, the **Winter Park/Rio Grande Railroad,** operates between Denver and the resort. **Amtrak** (800/USA.RAIL) offers daily service from **Chicago** and the West Coast.

# Index

## C

## D

## N



## O

## P



## Q



## R

## T

## U



## V



## W

## Y



## Z



## Restaurants

Only restaurants with star ratings are listed below. All restaurants are listed alphabetically in the main (preceding) index. Always call in advance to ensure a restaurant has not closed, changed its hours, or booked its tables for a private party. The restaurant price ratings are based on the average cost of an entrée for one person, excluding tax and tip.

★★★★ An Extraordinary Experience
★★★ Excellent
★★ Very Good
★ Good

$$$$ Big Bucks
$$$ Expensive
$$ Reasonable
$ The Price Is Right

### ★★★★



### ★★★

## Hotels

The hotels listed below are grouped according to their price ratings; they are also listed in the main index. The hotel price ratings reflect the base price of a standard room for two people for one night during the peak season.

$$$$ Big Bucks
$$$ Expensive
$$ Reasonable
$ The Price Is Right

### $$$$

$$



$

## Features



## Bests